THE PAST AND FUTURE OF EU LAW

This book revisits, in a new light, some of the classic cases which constitute the foundations of the EU legal order and is timed to celebrate the 50th anniversary of the Rome Treaty establishing a European Economic Community. Its broader purpose, however, is to discuss the future of the EU legal order by examining, from a variety of different perspectives, the most important judgments of the ECJ which established the foundations of the EU legal order. The tone is neither necessarily celebratory nor critical, but relies on the viewpoint of the distinguished line-up of contributors—drawn from among former and current members of the Court (the view from within), scholars from other disciplines or lawyers from other legal orders (the view from outside), and two different generations of EU legal scholars (the classics revisit the classics and a view from the future). Each of these groups will provide a different perspective on the same set of selected judgments. In each short essay, questions such as 'What would have EU law been without this judgment of the Court?'; 'What factors might have influenced it?'; 'Did the judgment create expectations which were not fully fulfilled?' and so on, are posed and answered. The result is a profound, wide-ranging and fresh examination of the 'founding cases' of EU law.

The Past and Future of EU Law

The Classics of EU Law Revisited on the 50th Anniversary of the Rome Treaty

Edited by

Miguel Poiares Maduro

and

Loïc Azoulai

·HART·
PUBLISHING

OXFORD AND PORTLAND, OREGON
2010

Published in North America (US and Canada) by
Hart Publishing
c/o International Specialized Book Services
920 NE 58th Avenue, Suite 300
Portland, OR 97213–3786
USA
Tel: +1 503 287 3093 or toll-free: (1) 800 944 6190
Fax: +1 503 280 8832
E-mail: orders@isbs.com
Website: http://www.isbs.com

Hart Publishing Ltd, 16C Worcester Place, Oxford, OX1 2JW
Telephone: +44 (0)1865 517530 Fax: +44 (0)1865 510710
E-mail: mail@hartpub.co.uk
Website: http://www.hartpub.co.uk

British Library Cataloguing in Publication Data
Data Available

ISBN: 978-1-84113-712-4

Typeset by Columns Design Ltd, Reading
Printed and bound in Great Britain by
TJ International Ltd, Padstow, Cornwall

MIX
Paper from
responsible sources
FSC® C013056

Contents

List of Contributors

Alberto Alemanno is Associate Professor of Law at HEC Paris and a former Référendaire at the European Court of Justice.

Julio Baquero Cruz is a Member of the Legal Service of the European Commission

Roger van den Bergh is Professor of Law and Economics at the Law Faculty of the Erasmus University Rotterdam.

Nicolas Bernard is a Senior Lecturer at Queen Mary University.

Andrea Biondi is Professor of European Union Law and Co-Director, Centre of European Law, King's College London.

Brun-Otto Bryde is Judge of the German Federal Constitutional Court, 1st Senate, and Professor of Public Law and Political Science at the Justus-Liebig University, Giessen.

Damian Chalmers is Professor of European Union Law at the London School of Economics.

Carlos Closa Montero is CSIC Senior Research Fellow and a former Deputy Director at the Centre for Political and Constitutional Studies (CEPC), Madrid.

Paul Craig is Professor of Law at St John's College, Oxford.

Pedro Cruz Villalón is former President of the Spanish Constitutional Court and Professor of Constitutional Law at the Autonomous University of Madrid.

José Narciso da Cunha Rodrigues is Judge at the Court of Justice and former Attorney General of Portugal.

David Edward is a former Judge at the European Court of Justice and Professor Emeritus of the University of Edinburgh.

Piet Eeckhout is Professor of Law and Director of the Centre of European Law at King's College London.

Nial Fennelly is a Judge of the Supreme Court of Ireland and a former Advocate General at the European Court of Justice.

Daniel Halberstam is the Eric Stein Collegiate Professor of Law and Director of the European Legal Studies Program at the University of Michigan. He also holds a position as Professor of Law in the European Legal Studies Department at the College of Europe, Bruges.

Christophe Hillion is Professor of European Institutional Law, Law Faculty Leiden.

Herwig Hofmann is Director of the Centre of European Law at the Faculty of Law, Economics and Finance of the University of Luxembourg.

Marko Ilešič is Judge at the European Court of Justice and former Professor of Civil, Commercial and Private International Law and Dean of the Faculty of Law at the University of Ljubljana.

Francis Jacobs KCMG, QC, is a former Advocate General at the European Court of Justice and Professor of Law at King's College London.

Jean-Paul Jacqué is Honorary Director General of the Council of the European Union and Professor at the University of Strasbourg.

Zdenek Kühn is Judge at the Supreme Administrative Court of the Czech Republic and Associate Professor at the Charles University Law School in Prague.

Mattias Kumm is Professor of Law at the New York University School of Law.

Síofra O'Leary is Référendaire at the European Court of Justice and Lecturer at the College of Europe, Bruges.

Koen Lenaerts is Judge at the European Court of Justice and Professor European Law, Institute for European Law, Catholic University Leuven.

Petros Mavroidis is Edwin B Parker Professor of Foreign and Comparative Law at Columbia Law School, New York and a Professor of Law at the University of Neuchâtel.

Franz Mayer is Professor of Law at the University of Bielefeld and Senior Fellow at the Walter Hallstein-Institute for European Constitutional Law, Humboldt Universität Berlin.

Agustín José Menéndez is permanent research professor at the Law School of the University of León (Spain) and senior RECON researcher at ARENA, Centre for European Studies, University of Oslo.

Paolo Mengozzi is Advocate General at the European Court of Justice and former Professor of European Union Law at the Faculty of Law of the University of Bologna.

Kalypso Nicolaïdis is Professor of International Relations and Director of the European Studies Centre, St Antony's College, University of Oxford.

Ingolf Pernice is the Dean for International Relations of the Humboldt-University Law Faculty as well as founder and managing director of the Walter Hallstein-Institut for European Constitutional Law at Humboldt University, Berlin.

Pierre Pescatore is a former Judge of the ECJ.

Robert Post is Dean and Sol and Lillian Goldman Professor of Law at Yale Law School.

Morten Rasmussen is Assistant Professor at the Centre for Modern European Studies, University of Copenhagen.

Donald Regan is the William W Bishop Jr Collegiate Professor of Law and a Professor of Philosophy at the University of Michigan.

Allan Rosas is Judge at the European Court of Justice and former Armfelt Professor of Law at the ÅboAkademi University and former Deputy Director-General of the Legal Service of the European Commission.

Damaso Ruiz-Jarabo Colomer is Advocate General at the European Court of Justice.

Daniel Sarmiento is Référendaire at the European Court of Justice and Assistant Professor at the Law School of the Complutense University of Madrid.

Eleanor Sharpston is Advocate General at the European Court of Justice and Fellow of King's College, Cambridge.

Jo Shaw holds the Salvesen Chair of European Institutions and is Dean of Research in the College of Humanities and Social Science, University of Edinburgh.

Denys Simon is Professor of Law at the University of Réunion.

Alec Stone Sweet is Leitner Professor of International Law, Politics and International Studies, Yale Law School.

Christiaan Timmermans is Judge at the European Court of Justice.

Takis Tridimas is Sir John Lubbock Professor of Banking Law at the Centre for Commercial Law Studies, Queen Mary, University of London.

Stefaan Van den Bogaert is Professor of European law at Leiden University.

Neil Walker holds the Regius Chair of Public Law and the Law of Nature and Nations at the University of Edinburgh.

Horatia Muir Watt is Professor of Private International and Comparative Law at the University of Paris I (Panthéon-Sorbonne).

Stephen Weatherill is the Jacques Delors Professor of European Community Law and serves as Associate Director of the Centre for the Advanced Study of European and Comparative Law, University of Oxford.

Bruno de Witte is Professor of Law at the European University Institute, Florence.

Introduction
The Past and Future of EU Law

MIGUEL POIARES MADURO AND LOIC AZOULAI

Lawyers anthropomorphise courts. They do so because the reconstruction of the case law for the purposes of a coherent legal argument is more effectively done by narrating it as driven by a single rationality. Yet, courts have a composite rationality. The jurisprudential reason arises out of a multitude of reasons provided in different cases and the sometimes conflicting, sometimes convergent, reasons of different judges. A court's jurisprudence cannot be immediately ascertained by looking at individual cases. It is also the product of a broader community of actors than courts themselves. It is woven by judges interacting with lawyers and legal scholars, all acting in a particular social context. The importance of a particular judgment can only be properly assessed by seeing its solution and its reasons repeated in subsequent cases. It is this repetition in different contexts that consolidates a particular legal reasoning and transforms judicial adjudication into legal interpretation. But a particular judgment can also acquire a particular importance only at a later stage when the full effects of its underlying reasoning are brought to life by a subsequent judgment, the reaction of the legal community or the practice of the political institutions. And a new jurisprudence may emerge out of the need to reconcile apparently irreconcilable cases. A narrative of the case law born outside the court may also make its way into the case law of a court by the intellectual persuasion of judges arising from the work of lawyers and legal scholars.

The 'classic' judgments in the jurisprudence of a Court are those that survive the passing of time but also those which, even when their concrete legal answer has become obsolete or has even been overturned, have lived on through their multiple effects in other areas of the law. They are judgments of systemic impact, embodying a broader normative lesson about the legal order in which that Court operates. To identify them we must look not only at the particular judgment itself but also at how it has been interpreted and developed by the Court in other cases. We also need to look at the attention paid to it by lawyers, legal scholars and other social actors. The law is also a function of how the judicial decisions are interpreted and challenged by the broader legal and social communities in which a court operates.

These were the criteria we used to identify the 'classics' of the case law of the European Court of Justice. The starting point is simple: we have invited commentators from a diversity of view points and asked each of them the same questions: What would have EU law been without this judgment of the Court? What factors might have influenced it? Did the judgment create expectations which were not entirely fulfilled? Are the potential legal developments arising from these judgments and their legal reasoning fully explored or can they still open new paths for the case law of the Court of Justice and EU law? Did they create some legal path dependences and are they justified? To what extent is the *acquis* embodied in these cases effectively consolidated?

We specifically asked the authors not to co-operate or divide tasks among them. We did so because we expect one of the added values of the book to be what we can learn by comparing different narratives on the same cases, particularly when they are linked to different viewpoints as we explain below. We wish to provide multiple viewpoints or, perhaps better, a 'multiple' intelligence or kaleidoscopic view of the case law. Another added value arises from the time distance which separates us from most of these cases. This allowed us to measure the lasting effects of such cases and to contextualise them in the light of a much larger body of case law and other legal developments (including how the case law interacted with the constitutional and legislative processes, at the Community and national levels). Curiously, this distance in time also favours a perspective into the future. First, it helps identify persisting inconsistencies in the EU legal order and how the principles developed in those cases may not yet be fully implemented or tested in the entire legal order (legal coherence requires more than consistency among identical cases). Second, by 'forcing' scholars to revisit old cases it creates an additional incentive to scratch beneath the surface. As the reader will see, throughout this book, largely ignored passages of certain cases may gain a new-found importance with time while classic passages are, with time, reconstructed and reconsidered. All this allowed our authors to also suggest new legal developments on the basis of the most classic of cases. Overall, going back to the classics and doing it from such a diverse array of perspectives offers us the best glimpse at the future of EU law. To paraphrase TS Eliot, we have travelled throughout time just to be back to the cases where we started to know them for the first time.

For such an ambitious endeavour we needed a very good and diverse group of contributors. For each set of selected judgments, four authors drawn from different backgrounds were invited to comment: former and current members of the Court (the view from within); some of the best among the more established names of EU legal scholarship (the classics revisit the classics); a selection of some of the most brilliant minds among the new generation of EU legal scholars (the view from the future); and scholars from other legal and social disciplines or lawyers from other legal orders whom we asked to take a perspective from outside EU law (the view from the outside). Together they provide the 'ideal interpreter'. But what is such an 'ideal interpreter'?

He or she must depart from the facts. All judgments have elements that are unique to themselves. The need to provide justice in the case at hand requires courts to attend to particular facts. When stating the law in a case courts merge what is specific to that case with what is general on the rules to be applied. Therefore, when interpreting past decisions lawyers must engage themselves in the task of distinguishing what is specific to the case from what is a statement of the law. This task, which may initially seem conceptually clear, is much less so once one realises that rules only acquire meaning in their application and, as a consequence, the facts and consequences of the cases in which rules are applied actually shape the meaning of those rules. He or she must also contextualise. To a certain extent, lawyers should approach a legal rule in the same way that architects approach a new building: they must identify the *genius loci* (the spirit of the place, the context) in which they will be intervening. A rule only makes sense in its context, the context of the legal system to which it belongs but also the economic, political and social context in which it was adopted and in which it is going to be applied. Its meaning only becomes clear once the text and its ambiguities are contrasted, compared, reconciled with its context. The economic, social and political context are necessary to understand how the rule was adopted and compare its intended effects with the effects that its different possible interpretations may generate in the present context. The coherence and integrity of the legal order also assumes and requires fitting and, if necessary, reconciling individual decisions and individual rules into the broader legal context of the legal order to which those rules and decisions belong. This requires assessing the systemic impact of different interpretations and to dogmatically organise them, abstracting from the specific to identify what is common, what is general and what appears in tension. In this light, apart from being a legal architect the lawyer must also be a narrator. He or she must put forward an interpretation of the legal rule that appears a natural development of past jurisprudence; a credible new chapter of the narrative of the legal order. Even when it innovates, a new interpretation must be consistent and coherent with the conception of the legal order that emerges from the body of past decisions, as in a story where a sudden twist may initially surprise us but, on second thought, appear as a foreseeable development of the previous episodes and the characters' traits. Further, the interpreter must also be an historian. He must identify continuity and change in the case law. Finally, however, there is no good interpreter deprived of imagination and creativity. Not to depart from the reality of the law but to see this reality with different eyes. Creativity is at the core of giving meaning to what exists by seeing beyond the others. Someone who can uncover a general principle in what looks like a very particular case. Someone who can imagine new ways in which a rule can preserve its meaning by actually adapting to its changing context. Someone who can discover something new in what is old and relate what seems unrelated. In sum, someone who can provide a new interpretation without changing the law. It is in this way that the process of interpretation breathes new life into the legal order without undermining the conditions of its legitimacy.

This book has the contribution of many great legal interpreters but, most of all, it wants to make of the reader the ideal interpreter. It does so by providing the reader with a variety of viewpoints and different narratives on a set of cases that, in our view, embody the identity of the Community legal order and of the jurisprudence of the European Court of Justice. We can divide them into three categories, according to the character and nature of their impact on the Community legal order. Some cases belong to more than one such category and that only highlights how different developments of the case law can actually be seen as instrumental to a broader and coherent (albeit contestable) conception of the Community legal order. Together they provide a good representation of the development of the Community legal order in the case law of the Court of Justice.

First, we have the cases that established and guarantee the authority of the Community legal order. The well-known judgments of the Court in *Van Gend en Loos*, *Costa v ENEL*, *Simmenthal* and *Internationale Handelsgesellschaft* guaranteed the effective incorporation of Community rules in the national legal orders and, by affirming a principle of supremacy, granted them the status of higher law. They created, as a consequence, the basis for a legal order of a federal type. These cases are also famous for their proclamation of the autonomy of the Community legal order and the direct relationship it establishes with individuals. In so doing the Court distinguished the Community legal order from both national and international legal orders and vested upon individuals rights emerging directly from the Community legal order that it itself had to guarantee and protect. It is in the light of this conception of the Community legal order as a Community of rights that the development of a system of guarantees and of a general principle of effectiveness in the application of EC law has to be understood. *Francovich* is perhaps the most representative case of these developments and their link to the protection of the rights of individuals under EC law.

Second, it is possible to identify cases that legitimise the authority acquired by Community legal order by embodying it with a system of values similar to those of national constitutional orders. This is the case of the protection of fundamental rights (*Internationale Handelsgesellschaft*, *Nold*, *Wachauf* and *ERT*) and the affirmation of the Community legal order as a Community based on the rule of law (*Les Verts v Parliament*). But the legitimacy of the Community legal order is also dependent on the values that are particular to that legal order. Such values are inextricably linked to the creation of the internal market (*Dassonville* and *Cassis deDijon*) but also to the introduction of elements of social justice into that market (*Defrenne*, *Bosman* and the citizenship cases of *Martinez Sala* and *Baumbast*). In all these cases, the Court is occupied with the definition of the system of values of the Community legal order and with the balance between the different political, economic and social dimensions of European integration.

Finally, we have cases where the Court defined the borders of Community law and the scope of application of its rules, and regulated the potential conflicts between Community and national powers. In *ERTA* and *Open Skies* the Court defined the scope of the Community's external competences and its relationship with national competences but, at the same time, also with the internal competences of the Community. In *CILFIT* and *Foto-Frost*, the Court regulated the judicial architecture of the Communities and its decentralised application by national courts. In the free movement cases, the Court was engaged in the separation of powers between the Community and the Member States and between public intervention and market freedom. In all these cases, the Court defined both the extent and the nature of the normative authority of the European Communities and, in doing so, became involved in the construction of a new political and legal community.

This book also helps in answering the why. What makes a case a leading case? Particularly, what made possible these judgments and the importance they acquired? Context and institutional variables seem to matter. Economic context and the problems with the Community political process may help explain the role of the Court's case law in the development of the internal market. At other times, the Court seems, instead, to follow up on the initiative of the political process and take it to its full (if sometimes) unexpected consequences (as in the case of European citizenship). In these cases, the Court appears as an agent of integration, defending the interests of the European majority against the interests of individual Member States. It plays the role of a supranational constitutional court involved in defining and supporting the conditions necessary for a new political community. At other times, however, the Court acts as a limit to Community power such as when it expanded the scope and grounds for judicial review of Community acts. In these instances, the Court is, instead, acting in a counter-majoritarian way. It plays a role more similar to that of domestic constitutional courts when constraining political power.

It is difficult to anticipate the legal importance of a case. Sometimes, the Court establishes an important legal principle in a seemingly unimportant case (such as in *Wachauf* or *Martinez Sala*). At other times it is the ingenuity of the parties or of national judges that puts before the Court an ambitious legal construction that the Court endorses. But, most of all, the importance of a case is determined as much by the judgment as it is by the follow-up to that judgment in the broader political, social and legal communities. The law is as much a product of judicial interpretation as it is of the reactions to that interpretation by the political process and other relevant actors. It is the internalisation of the legal solution embodied in a particular judicial decision in the institutional practices of the relevant actors that determines the real success of that legal solution. At the same time, other actors or the legal academic world may sometimes derive conclusions from a judicial decision that the Court has not fully articulated or even thought about (one of the contributions to this book highlights how the Commission 'took control' of the *Cassis de Dijon* narrative to develop its own legislative programme). These conclusions may actually shape social practices 'as the law' and it is not uncommon for them to come to be endorsed by the Court at a subsequent opportunity. Equally, however, it may happen that a leading case may already exist and be ignored until a later judicial decision makes clear its legal and/or social consequences (another contributor asks if *Martinez Sala* was not simply a natural consequence of *Gravier*).

All this highlights how the impact and meaning of a particular judgment is as much a product of the Court's work as it is a product of a larger epistemic and discursive European legal community. The Court's greatest success may have been the role its jurisprudence played in the development of this legal epistemic and discursive community. One of main the reasons for this success can be found in the tendency of the Court, in all these leading cases, to not simply decide a case but articulate the law. Most of the judgments commented in this book are remarkable by the way in which, through language, the details of a case are abstracted into general and broad principles. Think of the statements in *Dassonville* that 'all trading rules enacted by Member States which are capable of hindering, directly or indirectly, actually or potentially, intra-Community trade are to be considered as measures having an effect equivalent to quantitative restrictions' or in *Grzelczyk* that 'Union citizenship is destined to be the fundamental status of nationals of the Member States, enabling those who find themselves in the same situation to enjoy the same treatment in law irrespective of their nationality, subject to such exceptions as are expressly provided for'. The Court has not been afraid to clearly state principles, instead of hiding them behind the particular legal solution of the case. This certainly opened the Court up to criticism but, at the same time, created a large space for argumentation and debate which was instrumental in the development of that legal and epistemic community. It also provided guidance to national courts in future cases, something of indisputable importance in a decentralised legal order such as the EU. Furthermore, such form of what some would call judicial maximilism offers a yardstick from which to assess the Court's coherent development of the legal order. On the other hand, broad judicial decisions may not only be charged of judicial activism but also risk not fully anticipating all legal problems, making the Court too path-dependent and ultimately exposing it to contradictions and reversals. This may explain why some have noted some alternation between judicial maximilism and judicial minimalism in the Court's case law.

What is clear is that the nature of the legal reasoning of the Court and its judicial role has changed over time and will continue to do so. The Court, as any institution, is and ought to be responsive to its social and institutional context. This does not mean, however, that the variations in the forms and degrees of judicial review are a product of empirical pressures or subjective preferences. They can, instead, be fitted into a particular normative theory of judicial adjudication; one that conceives of legal interpretation as a process bounded by rules but also recognises that rules only acquire meaning in their context of application. This requires a more contextual form of legal reasoning and greater awareness of the institutional choices involved in judicial deliberation. Once one recognises that law changes even when the legal texts remain unchanged then one should expect (and, sometimes, welcome) variations in the case law of courts. The role of the Court of Justice is bound to change not only to reflect changes in the legal rules but also changes in their context of application and in the institutional alternatives to the Court in the development of EU law (including the political process and national courts).

It is in this light that one can envision the future of the European Court of Justice and its role in shaping EU law. There are some known and unknown variables that may affect the future role of the Court. First, it is now clear that the Court is operating under much stricter public scrutiny. Eric Stein famously described the context in which the Court developed its 'constitutional framework for a federal-type structure in Europe' as that of a Court 'tucked away in the fairyland Duchy of Luxembourg and blessed, until recently, with the benign neglect by the powers that be and the mass media'. This is no longer true. The Court's initial audience of specialised Community lawyers now includes lawyers from many disciplines which were initially foreign to Community law. Their reaction to Community law and to its impact on their legal subjects is often framed by the terms of reference of their original discipline. This often entails a new criticism of the Court's jurisprudence which not only challenges particular legal solutions but some of the established paradigms of Community law. At the same time, the social, political and economic impact of Community law, and that of the Court's decisions, has led to an increased mediatism and public scrutiny of the role of the Court. Some famous recent decisions were read by both legal and non-legal audiences. As a consequence, the Court is increasingly subject to both academic and non-academic scrutiny and criticism. Independently of the correctness of such criticisms this is a reality which the Court will have to learn to live with. Courts usually cannot answer to such criticisms in the public arena but they can adapt their judicial language so as to be responsive to such public debates without letting themselves be guided by them.

Furthermore, the institutional role played by the Court in the process of European integration is bound to acquire additional relevance in the current context of constitutional and economic crises. The constitutional crisis generated by the failed ratification of the Constitutional Treaty and the difficult ratifcation of the Lisbon Treaty may entail a challenge to the constitutional characterisation of the Union. For some, this requires scaling back such constitutional ambitions and, if necessary, even questioning parts of the constitutional acquis developed in the case law of the European Court of Justice. Others, instead, will claim that the failure of the Constitutional Treaty was not only partial (limited to some Member States) but mostly due to the limited constitutional ambition of the Treaty. As a consequence, the lesson to be learned ought to be that one needs to be even more constitutionally ambitious and protective of the current constitutional *acquis*. In this context, they will stress the importance of the Court remaining faithful to the fundamentals of European integration protecting it from the risks of protectionism and other forms of state selfish and populist behaviour likely to occur in a general context of economic and social crisis. Some will even argue that, as in the past, the Court should lead the way in further constitutionalising the Union as only such a path will be able to solve its crisis of legitimacy and give it the tools to help address the current economic and social crisis.

At the same time, contexts of crises tend to hinder the decision-making capability of the political process and lead to legislative agreements reflective of deeply contested and compromised solutions, de facto deferring to courts the definition of the practical meaning of such rules. This means that the Court is likely to be confronted with two opposing forces: on the one hand, the constitutional uncertainty and the likely increased political deadlock of the Union will increasingly put the Court at the centre of highly political and socially sensitive issues; on the other hand, this same context will tend to increase the contestability of judicial decisions and rigidify their legal outcomes (because the political process is less capable of overcoming them). It is in these troubled waters that the Court will have to navigate, aware of its institutional context, while faithful to its normative role as a court of law.

The Court itself has changed. The number of its members has almost doubled in size as a consequence of recent enlargements and one must not ignore the impact this may have in the deliberative process of the Court. The increased number of judges (and, possibly in the near future, of Advocate Generals) allows the Court to increase its judicial output but, at the same time, brings with it new challenges: the relative weight of institutional memory decreases and collegiality tends also to be reduced. In a Court without dissenting opinions (leaving aside that Advocate Generals' opinions may sometimes, de facto, have that role), collegiality is particularly important both to facilitate deliberation and to guarantee a clear articulation of the legal reasoning supporting a particular judicial decision. The Court will have to make an important effort to balance the quantity and quality of its judicial output.

Finally, current and foreseeable changes in EU law and EU institutions may also require the Court to fine tune its judicial role. First, there is a growing importance of fundamental rights litigation in the case law of the Court and this will only tend to grow as a consequence of a threefold development: increased EU legislation expanding the scope of an EU fundamental rights policy (such as the legislation regarding non-discrimination adopted under Article 13 EC); increased visibility of EU fundamental rights due to the Charter of Fundamental Rights; increased EU legislation with the potential to enter into conflict with fundamental rights (such as in the domain of justice and internal affairs). This will further constitutionalise the Court and will probably require it to progressively articulate a theory of fundamental rights review. Second, and particularly if the Treaty of Lisbon enters into force, EU competences will be extended as well as majoritarian decision making. This will require the Court to increasingly control how and when the Union exercises its competences. Also in this respect, the Court will have to further develop its constitutional facets. While the competences of the Union were relatively limited and controllable by the states through unanimous decision making, it made sense for the Court to concentrate its judicial scrutiny on the risks of state evasions from the broader collective interests of the Union (which, using traditional constitutional jargon, we could qualify as a majoritarian judicial approach). However, the increased scope of EU powers and its majoritarian character will increasingly plead for the Court to also develop a more traditional counter-majoritarian approach in reviewing the actions of the EU political process.

It is in this context that the present book and its revisitation of classic EU law cases must not be seen as primarily aimed at praising or criticising the past jurisprudence of the Court of Justice. More importantly, it highlights many of the current and future challenges to be faced by the Court while, at the same time and by looking at its past jurisprudence, providing important clues to how such challenges may be successfully answered in the future. It is impossible to do justice in this introduction to the richness of the comments that the reader will find in this volume. Hopefully we were able to trigger your curiosity and highlight how this book is more about the future than the past.

I

Case 26/62, *NV Algemene Transport- en Expeditie Onderneming van Gend en Loos v Nederlandse Administratie der Belastingen*

1

Van Gend en Loos, 3 February 1963—A View from Within

PIERRE PESCATORE

We have the habit of reading and citing judicial rulings in excerpts, as if they were legislative texts. This is a mistake. Judicial rulings are products of litigation and cannot be understood but by asking some more persistent questions, which I will pose regarding the ruling in *Van Gend en Loos*: What is it about? What caused the dispute? What brought the Dutch *Tariefcommissie* to refer the preliminary reference? What were the arguments of the parties, and, finally, what was the opinion of the Advocate General?

The Precedents of the Case and the Problem Laid Down Before the Court

It is 1960. The Member States still have, every one of them, their own customs tariff, with Benelux having a separate one. The three Member States of the Benelux union decide—God knows why—to re-classify their customs tariff which leads to the re-allocation of a chemical product, *l'ureeformaldehyde*, from a category taxed at 3 per cent *ad valorem* to a category taxed at 8 per cent. *Van Gend en Loos*, being an importer of this product, lays down a complaint concerning this increase with the tariff administration which, naturally, rejects the complaint. The applicant subsequently seized the competent court, the *Tariefcommissie*, arguing that Article 12 of the EEC Treaty provides that Member States must refrain from introducing new customs duties and from increasing the duties applicable in their commercial relations. This is a so-called standstill clause, which was applicable from the moment of entry into force of the Treaty.

Presented with this challenge, the judge is faced with a provision of the Dutch constitution regarding the internal effect of international treaties. Its content is quite clear:

> Statutory regulations in force within the Kingdom shall not be applicable if such application is in conflict with provisions of treaties that are binding on all persons, entered into prior or subsequent to the enactment of such statutory regulation.

Through this provision, the Constitution recognises the primacy of international treaties in respect of national law, subject to one condition: the provisions of the relevant treaty must be likely to 'bind all persons'. With a bit of liberty one could read this as meaning 'applicable to all' or as 'concerning everyone'. This led the *Tariefcommissie* to refer to the Court of Justice two preliminary questions, of which the first, the sole interesting in this context, reads:

> Does Article 12 of the Treaty have direct application in national law in the sense that nationals of member states may on the basis of this article lay claim to rights which the national court must protect?

As for the observations submitted to the Court by the parties who wished to be heard, namely the applicant, the Dutch and Belgian governments (Luxembourg cautiously abstained from intervening) and the German government, I will limit myself to raise the points which are important for a proper understanding of the answer given. The Dutch government, being first in line, raised a preliminary question of great importance by contesting the admissibility of the preliminary reference in a case where, by virtue of the nature of the dispute, an action for treaty infringement was still possible. The provisions at issue were numbered 169 and 170 at the time.

As for the substance of the case, the three governments duly stressed that Article 12 is exclusively addressed to the Member States. From this they deduced that such provision cannot possibly have a direct effect. The German government was particularly explicit concerning this point by stating that in Germany 'a legal provision fixing a customs duty contrary to the stipulations of Article 12 would be perfectly valid'.

The Advocate General, Karl Roemer, based his analysis on the nature and scope of the 'obligation' created by Article 12 of the Treaty, in order to conclude, based on a strictly textual analysis, against the direct effect of the relevant provision. The obligation is, in his conviction, designed like a serpent that bites his own tail: it is created by the Member States, and its effect should thus be limited to the States themselves.

It is in this state that the Court found the case file when it started its *délibéré.* Before examining its decision, it seems useful to pose the question whether the Court had relevant precedents before it. The answer is yes. Actually, it had two such precedents.

In the case *Groupement des Industries sidérurgiques luxembourgeoises v Haute Autorité de la CECA*, the Luxembourg government had, as an intervening party, contested the direct effect of Article 4 of the ECSC Treaty, since this provision included the clause 'within the conditions stipulated by this treaty' and these conditions were never fixed for the policy area involved in the dispute.

This argument by the government elicited a sharp answer from the judges. Effectively, after having referred to a previous ruling, in which the Court had characterised the article as forming part of the 'fundamental treaty provisions', the Court added: 'For the same reasons, the provisions of Article 4 are sufficient of themselves and are directly applicable when they are not restated in any part of the Treaty' (ruling of 23 April 1956).

In order to fully understand the ruling in *Van Gend en Loos*, it is necessary to mention yet another case which was ruled upon just before it, but which is a bit blurred in obscurity by virtue of the glory of its closest successor. This is the case *Commission v Luxembourg and Belgium* (sic)[1] of 14 December 1962 (also known as the case involving the *Pain d'épice.*) In this case the Court dealt with sly customs and fiscal practices of the Member States, intended to thwart the effect of the treaty provisions. The case involved an

[1] Even though it is not a producer of *pain d'épice*, Luxembourg is part of the Belgian-Luxembourg economic union; before the Court, the Grand Duchy precedes, alphabetically, the Kingdoms.

import tax which was introduced on *pain d'épice*, of which the fabrication is the main outlet for rye. The Court reacted vehemently when faced with this absurd measure of agricultural protectionism. It is in this ruling that we find the expressions that would shape the ruling in *Van Gend en Loos,* and also the ardour of its style. Even Article 12 of the treaty makes an appearance for the sake of the argument, among the 'foundations of the treaty'.

As for our ruling, written in a time which did not yet discover the joy of numbering and subtitles, we can discern three sets of answers to the question posed: concerning the principles (1), on the substance of the reference (2), and on the preliminary question brought up concerning the relation between the infringement procedure against Member States and the preliminary reference procedure (3).

Certain commentators have criticised the confused reasoning of our ruling and its apodictic rather than demonstrative character. However, anyone who took the trouble of reading as a preface the ruling in *Pain d'épice* will understand that the Court reacted in this manner against the first manifestations of systematic opposition of the governments regarding the loyal execution of their obligations and against their ignorance of the judicial revolution brought about by the Community treaties in the banality of international law. The observations of the Belgian, Dutch and German governments are ample proof of this.[2] As regards the 'loose' style it favours the legibility of the ruling and the force of inherent conviction to its paragraphs, as if it were pages taken from the *Pensées* by Pascal. The interpreter here has the freedom to find the coherence of the argument starting from the middle of the *exposé,* rather than from its beginning or its conclusion.

The Answers on the Principles

The crux of the argument is contained in the expression of a *new legal order*, for the benefit of which the Member States have limited their sovereign rights, and of which the subjects are not only the Member States but also their nationals. This legal order finds its lawful origin in an international treaty, which explains the qualification of this new order as being 'of international law', omitted in later formulations, where the accent was rather placed on the *autonomy* of community law. After having asked clemency for international law,[3] I will now draw attention to the fact that the autonomy is already strongly emphasised in the ruling of the Court, where it reads 'community law, independent of Member State legislation'.

The administration of the sovereign rights, separated from national sovereignties and reaggregated in the framework of the Community, to pursue the common objectives—namely the creation of a *common market*—is entrusted to institutions endowed with their exercise, both in the interest of the *Member States* as *their citizens.* But how can this

[2] Please note that the Rapporteur in the case *Pain d'épice* was none other than Robert Lecourt, who had only just resigned from the French government as a protest against the anti-community drift which it had taken. As for the ruling in *Van Gend en Loos,* it should not be forgotten that it coincided with the start of the personal diatribe of General de Gaulle against the Community, the *volapük supranational* and the rest.

[3] The Court has always been timid regarding international law. This way, it deprives itself of valuable possibilities, such as the GATT Agreement of 1947, or the Vienna Convention on the Law of Treaties, of 29 March 1969, even though this was after *Van Gend en Loos.*

dichotomy be justified? I will try to decipher the reasoning of the Court, starting from the general to the more concrete, and will let the Court speak for itself:

a) The preamble of the treaty, according to the Court, *refers to people, not only to governments*, to which it adds a bit further that all that is *fundamental* in the system must have real effect for the citizen—a distant evocation, maybe even unconscious, to the ruling of 23 April 1956 and casting its shadow, (who knows?), on the subsequent reliance on the argument of *l'effet utile*;[4]
b) the sovereign rights given up by the Member States were those of their nationals, and they remain those of their nationals, even after their transfer to the Community and their reaggregation in the hands of the institutions. In my opinion, this is the strongest argument of all, drawn from the doctrine of State succession;[5]
c) in responding to the rather short thesis put forward by the Advocate General concerning the obligations of the Member States, the Court notes that the creation of a common market '*the functioning of which is of direct concern to interested parties in the community, implies that this treaty is more than an agreement which merely creates mutual obligations between the contracting states*';
d) following up this same argumentation, the Court proceeds to a more exhaustive analysis holding that every obligation entails rights and vice versa, and that those who carry the responsibility of implementing the treaty have corresponding rights, *which become part of their legal heritage*;
e) the Court also draws attention to the democratic character of the Community, due to the presence, in its institutional structure, of the European Parliament and the Economic and Social Council, in the functioning of which the nationals of the Member States, gathered in the Community, are *called upon to contribute*;
f) to which it adds, thinking—in all modesty—of itself and its functioning, that the insertion of Article 177 (now Article 234) concerning the procedure of preliminary ruling links the national jurisdictions to the application of Community law, in order to ensure the uniform interpretation. This evidently implies the existence of individual rights stemming from community law and finding its application even at the level of national law.

There has rarely been a legal argumentation as well developed as this one, and presented to individuals and their judges with such elegance and persuasive power.

The Answers on the Substance of the Reference

Having said this, the Court turns its attention towards the substance of the problem raised by the Tariefcommissie, namely, the substantive content of Article 12 of the treaty.

The Court develops its argument starting from Article 9 of the treaty, which states that the community is based on a customs union—a truth often forgotten these days, when in

[4] See in this regard also my contribution to the *Mélanges Rodrigues Iglesias*, Berlin, 2003, 'Monisme, dualisme et "effet utile" dans la jurisprudence de la Cour de justice de la Communauté européenne'.

[5] Regarding this question, see my contribution to the *Mélanges Wiarda*, Köln, 1988, 'La Cour de justice des Communautés européennes et la Convention européenne des droits de l'homme'.

reality this customs union, based in its turn on Article XXIV of GATT, is the base upon which, throughout the years, the economic and monetary union have been constructed! As such, Article 12, by virtue of its qualification as standstill clause, is the first manifestation of such union. This entails, according to the Court, a '*clear and unconditional prohibition, which is not a positive, but a negative obligation*'.

Disregarding this final part, which has a *parfum civiliste*, the reasoning raises two characteristics that will lastingly serve as a standard for the identification of provisions endowed with this famous *direct effect*: first, their unconditional character, of which is derived the second corollary stating that every prohibition has, *by its very nature*, direct effect. It seems from the ensuing that the drafters of the ruling had some difficulty in placing Article 12 in the summa division of positive and negative obligations, due to the presence, in the text, of the words 'to abstain from' which introduced the suspicion of discretionary power. This shade is, however, swept away by the final sentence of the paragraph, stating that *the fact that it is the Member States who are made the subject of the negative obligation does not imply that their nationals cannot benefit from this obligation.*

It can be deduced that according to this interpretation all that is fundamental is likely to have direct effect, much like the provisions of a constitution.

The Answers on the Preliminary Question

It is in the last place that the Court tackles the question of admissibility raised by the governments who intervened in the procedure. Despite this sprain to procedural logic, this was practically necessary since, as we shall see, it was not possible to examine this question before having resolved the principal questions dealt with in the first set of answers.

The Court, rather strangely, does not put to use the systematic element that it had developed at the very beginning of its reasoning, where it held that, in order to interpret the treaty, one should take into account its *spirit, general scheme and wording*, (the somewhat archaic term 'general scheme' refers precisely to the system). Be that as it may, the Court refuses to interpret Articles 169 and 170 as excluding the preliminary ruling procedure; in essence, this interpretation would render the system of preliminary rulings practically inoperable. The infringement procedure of Member States and the preliminary rulings are, according to the Court, not mutually exclusive, but *complementary*: the former is placed in the hands of the Commission, the second in those of the national judge, to which all individuals must have access in cases where rights bestowed upon them by the Community legal order are violated.

This statement is summed up in a formulation which has since then become famous. The Court held that the vigilance of individuals concerned to protect their rights amounts to an effective supervision in addition to the supervision entrusted by Articles 169 and 170 to the diligence of the Commission and the Member States. This formulation is prophetic, since we would see later on that the preliminary reference—managed with great care by the Court (always emphasising that in the framework of the preliminary ruling it is not its task, but rather the task of the national judge to solve the conflict between national law and Community law)—will effectively become the infringement procedure for the European citizen.

The rejection, by the Court, of the preliminary exception brought up by the national governments has greatly contributed to the unexpected success of this form of reference, a success which has not failed to worry the governments of the Community.[6]

Having said this, let us remind ourselves of the final statement of the ruling in *Van Gend en Loos*, which reads: 'it follows from the foregoing considerations that, according to the spirit, the general scheme and the wording of the Treaty, Article 12 must be interpreted as producing direct effects and creating individual rights which national courts must protect.'

[6] Giorgio Gaja, in his article 'The growing variety of procedures concerning preliminary rulings', published in the *Liber Amicorum Gordon Slynn of Hadley*, 2000, vol 1, has enumerated no less than 12 new variants of the preliminary ruling, which have in common that they weaken the model of Art 177 (which in the meanwhile has become art 234): by making the reference optional for the Member States, by excluding the access to the Court of First Instance by way of this reference, by transforming the decision of the Court into an advisory opinion. The negativism of the governments remains virulent, despite the proclamation of the 'Community of law' which remains, in spite of that, a fascinating statement.

2

The Continuous Significance of *Van Gend en Loos*

BRUNO DE WITTE

The names of the parties in this case (a Dutch transport company litigating with the Dutch tax administration) may seem rather exotic or even off-putting, but under the abbreviated name of the applicant firm, *Van Gend en Loos*, the judgment in Case 26/62 has become famous and is still today, 44 years later, one of the most often cited of all ECJ judgments. It is mentioned in the early chapters of all EU law textbooks. It is worth noting, though, that this judgment did not gradually become a *grand arrêt* in the course of time, but was an instant hit. The judgment, delivered on 5 February 1963, was commented on and praised by one of the members of the Court, Robert Lecourt, in the newspaper *Le Monde* a few weeks later.[7] In the subsequent months, a number of judges, legal secretaries of the Court and members of the Commission's legal service spoke and wrote about the judgment and emphasised its innovative character, thus helping to pave the way for the following year's 'twin' judgment in *Costa v ENEL*. A gathering at which many of these statements were made was the October 1963 congress of the FIDE *(Fédération internationale pour le droit européen)*, the recently established association grouping the little world of legal practitioners and academics who were interested in EC law at that time. This second congress of the association was devoted to the question of self-executing provisions of international treaties and its application to the European Community treaties, and *Van Gend en Loos* was on everybody's lips there.[8] Further indication of the immediate interest provoked by this judgment can be found in the European Court's own list of *notes de doctrine* (now available online), which mentions 26 annotations of Case 26/62 in the year 1963 alone. These even include three English-language annotations (in the *American Journal of Comparative Law*, the *International and Comparative Law Quarterly* and in the very first issue of the new *Common Market Law Review)*, despite the fact that no English-language country was then a member of the EEC. So, it was not only the language used by the Court but also the resonance given to the judgment by an active group of Community lawyers which quickly transformed a rather technical dispute on the payment of import duties by a Dutch firm into a foundational moment of the European Community legal order.

[7] R Lecourt, 'L'Europe dans le prétoire', *Le Monde*, 23 February 1963, 1.

[8] I draw these facts from a very useful legal-historical study by A Vauchez, 'L'Europe et son "triangle magique". Retour sur des arrêts "fondateurs" (*Van Gend en Loos* et *Costa v ENEL*)' in O Costa and P Magnette (eds), *Une Europe des élites?* (Bruxelles, Presses de l'Université de Bruxelles, 2007).

In this contribution, I will touch on three questions that may help us to re-situate this judgment in the evolution of EC law. Those three questions refer to three different periods in time. What was the significance of the *Van Gend en Loos* judgment at the time it was decided? What was its impact on the nature of European law during the decades after the ruling was delivered? And is it still a relevant and 'living' judgment today?

The Birth of a New Doctrine

The major doctrinal novelty of *Van Gend en Loos* was not the discovery that EEC law *could* have direct effect. Self-executing provisions of international treaties were not an unknown phenomenon prior to 1963. Indeed, the reason why the referring Dutch court (which was the *Tariefcommissie*, a specialised customs court) sent a request for interpretation to Luxembourg was that the Dutch Constitution specified, since the early 1950s, that treaty provisions could, depending on their terms, be self-executing within the Dutch legal order. The Dutch court wanted to hear from the European Court of Justice whether Article 12 EEC was one such self-executing treaty provision.[9] Many other monist legal systems, inside and outside Europe (most prominently, the USA since 1829[10]), recognised the possibility for national courts to directly enforce international treaty norms, though these courts rarely used that power in practice.[11]

So, the crucial doctrinal contribution of the *Van Gend en Loos* judgment was another one. It was the affirmation that whether specific provisions of the EEC Treaty had direct effect was to be decided centrally by the European Court of Justice itself, instead of by the various national courts according to their own views or national habits on the matter. It claimed this power against the arguments of intervening governments who had contested the Court's jurisdiction to answer a preliminary question which did not deal with the substantive meaning of Article 12 EEC Treaty but with its possibly self-executing character.

The ECJ did not only *claim* an interpretative monopoly on this question, it also *used* this self-awarded power in a most expansive manner. It might be said that whereas the presumption with ordinary international agreements was (and perhaps still is) that they do not have direct effect, the Court reversed that presumption as far as Community law is concerned.[12] The Court's generous granting of the 'direct effect' label was obvious already in *Van Gend en Loos* both in the general interpretative approach it adopted and in its specific application to the case of Article 12 of the EEC Treaty.

At the *general* level, the Court did not openly contradict what was the received wisdom at the time, namely that the self-executing nature of a treaty provision had to be deduced from the intention of the Contracting Parties. However, the Court did not try to reconstruct the actual, subjective, intention of the drafters of the EEC Treaty (which, at the time, was not easily available anyway), but rather chose to base itself on 'the spirit, the

[9] On the Dutch constitutional law background of the *Van Gend en Loos* reference, see M Claes, *The National Courts' Mandate in the European Constitution* (Oxford, Hart Publishing, 2006), 74.

[10] Chief Justice Marshall's opinion for the Supreme Court in *Foster and Elam v Neilson* (1829).

[11] See, on this reluctance of national courts to declare treaty provisions to be self-executing, M Claes, above note 9, 70–3.

[12] R Alonso García, *Sistema jurídico de la Unión Europea* (Madrid, Thomson Civitas, 2007), 195–6.

general scheme and the wording' of that Treaty. It held that the Treaty, because of its essential aim of creating a common market in which traders and workers could freely move and operate, was intended to confer enforceable rights on individuals. Turning then to the *specific* case of Article 12 of the EEC Treaty, which imposed a standstill obligation on the *Member States*,[13] the Court held that the fact that this rule was addressed to the states did not prevent it from being invoked by *individuals*, the important thing being that Article 12 contained a negative obligation for whose application no further intervention on the part of the states or the EEC institutions was required.[14]

In later cases, the Court went, of course, much further. Whereas it continued to insist on the criteria of clarity and unconditionality, which it had enunciated in *Van Gend en Loos*, it soon started to extend the benefit of direct effect to a growing range of Treaty articles dealing with the common market, even those that (unlike Article 12 EEC) *did* seem, from their wording, to require national or Community implementing acts and even those that left to the Member State a power to derogate from the common market freedoms. The crucial period for making direct effect a pervasive characteristic of Community law was, in fact, the early 1970s, when, at the end of the transitional period which the Treaty text had provided for, the Court decided that the central provisions guaranteeing the free movement of goods, persons and services had acquired direct effect and could be invoked by individuals despite the relative inertia of the states and the EC institutions to put in place the common market through legislative measures. The second major expansion of the direct effect doctrine occurred slightly later in the same decade; it consisted in extending the direct effect doctrine to other sources of Community law, more particularly and most controversially to directives and international agreements concluded by the Community. But this is another story, which will be recounted in other contributions to this volume. What can be observed here is that the *Van Gend en Loos* ruling undoubtedly laid the foundations of the general direct effect doctrine that would allow those later developments, but those developments did not flow 'naturally' from the 1963 judgment and required many further moments of judicial creativity.[15]

[13] This Article can no longer be found in the current text of the EC Treaty; it was repealed by the Treaty of Amsterdam for being obsolete (since it referred to the 'transitional period' which was long past).

[14] This is the relevant passage from the judgment:
'*Attendu que le texte de l'article 12 énonce une interdiction claire et inconditionnelle qui est une obligation non pas de faire, mais de ne pas faire;*
Que cette obligation n'est d'ailleurs assortie d'aucune réserve des Etats de subordonner sa mise en oeuvre à un acte positif de droit interne;
(...) Que le fait, par cet article, de désigner les Etats membres comme sujets de l'obligation de s'abstenir n'implique pas que leurs ressortissants ne puissent en être les bénéficiaires.'
When quoting from the judgment, I use the French text which, as is well known, is the version of the judgment that was discussed and approved by the judges. The official English text of the judgment was written only much later, upon the accession of the UK and Ireland to the European Communities, and does not correctly translate the French version on every point.

[15] See, on this crucial evolution of the doctrine in the 1970s, P Craig, 'Once Upon a Time in the West: Direct Effect and the Federalization of EEC Law' (1992) *OJLS* 453.

The Changing Meaning and Historical Importance of Direct Effect

Van Gend en Loos created a distinction between two types of European Community norms: those with and without direct effect. Whereas all norms of EC law have *primacy* over national law, only some norms have *direct effect*. Indeed, in *Van Gend en Loos* the Court did not say that 'Community law' had direct effect, but rather that Article 12 of the EEC Treaty had direct effect; and on later occasions, it confirmed that other norms, contained in the EEC Treaty, in a directive or even in a regulation[16] did *not* have direct effect. This distinction made much impression at first. In a book-length analysis published in 1970, Leontin-Jean Constantinesco referred to it as the *summa divisio* in Community law.[17] The problem, though, is that the distinction between the two categories is not immediately apparent from the language of the provisions themselves. The *Van Gend en Loos* judgment itself had immediately made clear that a norm could have direct effect even though it neither contained the word 'right' nor the word 'individual'. In other words, there were no obvious signposts in the terms of a legal provision that would signal its direct effect.

The idea that direct effect implied the granting of *rights* to individuals was prompted by some of the language used in the *Van Gend en Loos* judgment, which was itself prompted by the language used by the referring Dutch court. Indeed, the *Tariefcommissie* had asked '*si l'article 12 du Traité C.E.E. a un effet interne, en d'autres termes, si les justiciables peuvent faire valoir, sur la base de cet article, des droits individuels que le juge doit sauvegarder*'. The words '*en d'autres termes*' seemed to imply that the Dutch court needed a clear answer as to whether Article 12 contained rights for individuals. The ECJ obliged, but with some ambiguity, since it held in the *dispositif* of its judgment that Article 12 '*produit des effets immédiats et engendre dans le chef des justiciables des droits individuels que les juridictions internes doivent sauvegarder*'. This sentence could be read as not excluding the possibility that other provisions than Article 12 EEC Treaty could have *effet immédiat* without necessarily creating individual rights.

Such a disjunction between direct effect and the attribution of individual rights occurred in the later practice of the European Court of Justice. It became clear, in the course of the years, that Community norms could, before a national court, be used as a sword or as a shield; or, to use a frequently used pair of French expressions, that they could either have an *effet de substitution* (where the EC law norm was directly applied on behalf of the individual party, instead of the inadequate national norm) or an *effet d'exclusion* (where the EC law norm merely served to exclude the application of a norm of domestic law—often of administrative or criminal law—but without taking the place of the inadequate national norm). In addition, the ECJ affirmed in a few cases (such as *Costanzo)* that this double effect of Community norms could take place not only when a case was brought before a national court, but also when member state administrations are dealing

[16] Contrary to scholarly wisdom, EC regulations do not always and entirely have direct effect. For a case in which the ECJ, quite reasonably, found that a provision of a regulation lacked direct effect, see Case C-403/98 *Monte Arcosu* (2001) ECR I-103.

[17] LJ Constantinesco, *L'applicabilité directe dans le droit de la CEE* (Paris, LGDJ, 1970), ch 1. The book was re-edited in 2006 (Brussels, Bruylant).

with Community law. Also in this non-judicial (or pre-judicial) context, there is a duty for national authorities to apply directly effective norms of Community law.

This expanding interpretation is reflected in what I consider the most appropriate current definition of direct effect as being 'the obligation of a court or another authority to apply the relevant provision of Community law, either as a norm which governs the case or as a standard for legal review'.[18] Whilst explaining why this is the best definition, corresponding most closely to the European Court's case law, Sacha Prechal notes that this definition is not firmly established, and that some writers continue to advocate a more narrow definition in which direct effect necessarily implies the attribution of rights to individuals. There is, in fact, since the adoption of the Amsterdam Treaty, a strategic reason for pro-integrationist minded scholars to advocate a return to a more narrow definition. The EU Treaty, as amended by the Treaty of Amsterdam, excludes the direct effect of decisions and framework decisions adopted under the Third Pillar.[19] By adopting the narrow definition of direct effect, applying it only to what happens when Community law directly confers rights on individuals, one could also limit the exclusionary effect of Article 34 EU Treaty and allow for national courts to use framework decisions as a standard for the review of national measures (that is, give them direct effect in the broad sense). However, I agree with Prechal that this strategic consideration cannot outweigh the disadvantage of a *retour en arrière* towards a strict rights-based definition of direct effect.

It is interesting to note in this context that it took until 1997 (with the conclusion of the Amsterdam Treaty) for the assembled governments to try and check the expansion of the direct effect doctrine. Although the intervening governments in *Van Gend en Loos* strongly disagreed with the Court's innovative approach, they had never tried to collectively overrule the Court on this point. It may have helped that direct effect, for a long time, appeared to the governments as 'lawyer's business'. Indeed, the doctrine was primarily directed at national courts rather than at the governments. It is remarkable to note (as many political scientists did) how easily the national courts in all the member states have accepted the basic principle established by the Court of Justice, namely that the ECJ could legitimately tell national courts which EC law norms had, or did not have, direct effect.

The prominent role given to individuals and firms by the direct effect doctrine has not only modified their own legal status in Community law, from passive subjects to actors in their own right. In *Van Gend en Loos*, the European Court also referred, in a famous phrase, to the beneficial impact of its new direct effect doctrine on the European integration process as a whole: '*la vigilance des particuliers intéressés à la sauvegarde de leurs droits entraîne un contrôle efficace qui s'ajoute à celui que les articles 169 et 170 confient à la diligence de la Commission et des Etats Membres*'. The Court was prescient. We now know that this prediction became true, and that many 'individuals' (which, in actual fact, were usually business firms) used the direct effect doctrine in order to attack protectionist trading rules and, later, other national rules that they considered to be incompatible with Community law. They thus contributed to making the rules of Community law stick. Thereby, they also made the European integration project more valuable for the Member States' governments: the fact that, very often, rules adopted by the EU institutions will be

[18] S Prechal, 'Direct Effect, Indirect Effect, Supremacy and the Evolving Constitution of the European Union' in C Barnard (ed), *The Fundamentals of EU Law Revisited—Assessing the Impact of the Constitutional Debate* (Oxford, Oxford University Press, 2007) 35, at 37–8.

[19] See Art 34(2)(b) and (c) EU Treaty.

enforceable on the initiative of individuals offers an additional guarantee that the agreements reached by the national governments inside the Council, or inside an Intergovernmental Conference, will not be dodged by some foul-playing Member States.

The Present Relevance of the Direct Effect Doctrine

Lenaerts and Corthaut recently noted: 'It may be surprising, but over 40 years after *Van Gend en Loos* or *Costa v ENEL* the debate on how and when individuals can invoke EU law has not abated.'[20] This is indeed surprising if one compares EU law with national legal orders where there is no such thing as a 'direct effect doctrine': although the question whether individuals can rely on a particular national legal norm before a court does occasionally arise, national legal orders do not recognise this as a major doctrinal issue but rather as one of ordinary judicial prudence. Former ECJ judge Pescatore (who had been very active, judicially and extra-judicially, in expanding the doctrine in the late 1970s) referred to this curious difference in a famous article written in 1983, in which he called the direct effect doctrine 'an infant disease' that would soon cease to be of importance, once the Community legal order would have 'grown up' to become more of a federal state-like order.[21] In 2000 and in 2002, Sacha Prechal wrote some articles in which she developed Pescatore's point and argued that the direct effect doctrine had ceased to be a useful prism through which to look at the domestic judicial application of EU law.[22]

Still, it would seem that the existence of a special doctrine of direct effect continues to be justified by the fact that the domestic judicial enforcement of EU norms is different from that of international treaty norms, but also from that of norms of domestic origin in certain respects. *First*, because the existence of direct effect is a matter of interpretation of EU law to be settled by the European Courts of Justice rather than by the national courts separately (the main point established by the Court in *Van Gend en Loos*); therefore, different national habits as to when a legal norm is 'ripe' for judicial enforcement have to give way to a common European doctrine developed by a central body situated in Luxembourg. *Secondly*, because of the existence of certain sources of Community law (namely, directives and international agreements concluded by the EC) which obey special and rather arcane rules regarding their domestic judicial enforcement; national courts must in certain cases refrain from applying norms of directives or international agreements that seem sufficiently clear by their terms, because they are not fit for enforcement for other reasons, according to the European Court. This is notoriously, but very controversially, the case with provisions of a directive when they impose obligations on individuals; and with provisions of the WTO Agreement even when their significance has been spelled out by the WTO's dispute settlement organs. *Thirdly*, the direct effect doctrine remains a characteristic of the Community law part of the EU legal order and does not extend to norms of primary and secondary EU law belonging to the second and

[20] K Lenaerts and D Corthaut, 'Of Birds and Hedges: The Role of Primacy in Invoking Norms of EU Law' (2006) *EL Rev* 287 at 287.

[21] P Pescatore, 'The Doctrine of Direct Effect: An Infant Disease of Community Law', (1983) *EL Rev* 155.

[22] S Prechal, 'Does Direct Effect Still Matter?' (2000) *Common Market Law Review* 1047; S Prechal, 'Direct Effect Reconsidered, Redefined and Rejected' in J Prinssen and A Schrauwen (eds), *Direct Effect—Rethinking a Classic of EC Legal Doctrine* (Groningen, Europa Law Publishing, 2002) 17.

third pillar. Even though some of those norms of secondary EU law can, on their face, lend themselves to application by national courts, such application is either excluded by the terms of the EU Treaty (in respect of decisions and framework decisions of the third pillar) or it is not subject to guidance by the European Court of Justice (CFSP measures not being covered by the preliminary references procedure). These various factors continue to provoke debates about the evolution of the direct effect doctrine, and thereby continue to provide renewed occasions for reflection on the significance of the 1963 judgment that started it all.

3

Van Gend en Loos: The Foundation of a Community of Law

FRANZ C MAYER*

Introduction

The 1963 decision of the European Court of Justice (ECJ) in *NV Algemene Transport- en Expeditie Onderneming Van Gend en Loos v Nederlandse administratie der belastingen*,[23] only the second preliminary reference decision of the Court, is considered to be one of the most important decisions, if not *the* most important decision, of European Union law.[24] The facts of the case, with seemingly technical details of a 3 or an 8 per cent tariff on a substance called ureaformaldehyde, still appear rather unspectacular. *Van Gend en Loos* is generally known for its statements on direct applicability and effect of EC law, on the nature of European law and on the role of the ECJ. These elements together explain the importance of *Van Gend en Loos* for the development of a community of law (*Rechtsgemeinschaft*).

The Facts of the Case

On 9 September 1960, not even three years after the EEC Treaty came into force, the then[25] Dutch company Van Gend en Loos imported from Germany into the Netherlands a chemical product by the name of ureaformaldehyde, a substance used for making glue—and ran into problems, some of them apparently related to the fact that the administrative practice on customs duties for that product was not consistent. The Dutch revenue authorities decided to charge an import duty of 8 per cent of the value of the goods according to the Dutch Tariff Ordinance of 1 March 1960. Van Gend en Loos relied on a previous Tariff Ordinance of 1947, where the tariff had been just 3 per cent, and filed a written objection with the Dutch Inspector of Customs and Excise. The company

* Professor, University of Bielefeld, Law Faculty. I wish to thank Edgar Lenski for useful comments on an earlier version of this text.

[23] Case 26/62 *NV Algemene Transport- en Expeditie Onderneming Van Gend en Loos v Nederlandse administratie der belastingen* [1963] ECR 1 (English special edition).

[24] Contemporary commentators already acknowledged the importance: see, eg, SA Riesenfeld and RM Buxbaum [case note] (1964) 58 *AJIL* 152: 'one of the most important judgments rendered by that tribunal during the first decade of its existence'.

[25] Today, the company is part of the logistics services provider Deutsche Post World Net, see www.vgl.nl.

claimed that by increasing the import duty to 8 per cent the Government of the Netherlands had violated Article 12 of the EEC Treaty, which contained a 'stand-still clause' concerning the increase of duties.[26]

The Inspector of Customs and Excise dismissed the objection. *Van Gend en Loos* then filed an appeal against this decision with the Dutch Tariff Commission (*Tariefcommissie*). This body, which is actually an administrative tribunal, found that the case seemed to raise a problem relating to the interpretation of the EEC Treaty. In accordance with Article 177(3) of the EEC Treaty (now Article 234(3) EC), it made a preliminary reference to the European Court of Justice, seeking a ruling on the following two questions:

1. Does Article 12 of the EEC Treaty have 'direct application within the territory of a Member State', or, put differently, can nationals of such a State 'on the basis of the article in question, lay claim to individual rights which the courts must protect'?
2. In the event of an affirmative reply, does the application of a charge of 8 per cent constitute a prohibited increase in the sense of Article 12 of the EEC Treaty or not?

Direct Applicability and Direct Effect

The *Van Gend en Loos* case was the starting point for the ECJ to develop the principle that certain Community provisions are automatically part of national legal orders of the Member States (direct applicability) and that individuals may invoke these provisions in front of national courts and authorities (direct effect).[27] In this case, the ECJ decided against the Advocate General and against the Member States that the article in question was directly applicable.

The Advocate General: Yes, in Principle, but not Today

Probably the first thing one will notice when looking at the history of the case is the divergence between Advocate General *Karl Roemer* and the Court on the question of direct applicability of Article 12 of the EEC Treaty. Until today, such a divergence is, normally, evidence of an important or at least an interesting case. Here, the Court and the Advocate General agreed in principle, but not on Article 12.

The Advocate General did emphasise that European law does not just consist of contractual relations between a number of States considered as subjects of the law of nations. But as far as Article 12 of the EEC Treaty was concerned, he came to the conclusion that this provision did not have direct internal effect, just like Article 30 of the EEC Treaty (now Article 28 EC) (!). Eric Stein suggests that 'Advocate General Roemer may have reflected the view of the German courts, which recognize treaty-derived rights of

[26] This is the original 1957 wording of Art 12 of the EEC Treaty, which since then has been replaced by Art 25 EC: 'Member States shall refrain from introducing between themselves any new customs duties on imports or exports or any charges having equivalent effect, and from increasing those which they already apply in their trade with each other.'

[27] See on the terminology issue JA Winter, 'Direct applicability and Direct Effect. Two Distinct and Different Concepts in Community law' (1972) 9 *CML Rev* 425.

individuals only if the intention to that effect appears "with full clarity" ... from the content, purpose, and scheme ... of the treaty'.[28]

The Member States: A Double No-no

The Member States' governments could have had no interest in direct applicability of primary law, as this would have introduced the individuals as relevant players in the European integration context and weakened the control of the governments on European law.[29]

Thus, it is not surprising that the government of the Netherlands and the Belgian government tried to prevent the Court from making statements on this issue by challenging the jurisdiction of the ECJ.[30] They argued that the question did not raise problems of interpretation of the Treaty, but of its application within the context of the constitutional law of the Netherlands. And they maintained that the Court had no jurisdiction to decide whether the provisions of the EEC Treaty prevail over Dutch law.

The ECJ: Asserting Constitutional Law Jurisdiction

The ECJ dismissed the objection of the governments and followed the lead of the European Commission.[31] The Court claimed that it did not have 'to adjudicate upon the application of the Treaty according to the principles of the national law of the Netherlands', but to simply interpret 'the scope of Article 12 of the said Treaty within the context of Community law and with reference to its effect on individuals'.

In affirming its jurisdiction on this point, the Court rejected, as far as Community law is concerned, the traditional public international law approach whereby each contracting party is able to determine itself the effect and applicability of a treaty to private parties.

The ECJ used a trick when it sustained that it was merely interpreting European law, as the question of direct applicability necessarily has a complementary element related to the Member States' legal order.

On the substance, the Court could not rely on some explicit treaty provision in this matter. The founding treaties do not deal with the question of direct effect or applicability, with the exception of Article 249 EC (ex-Article 189 of the EEC Treaty), which states that regulations are 'directly applicable in all Member States'. The Court thus was able to establish the criteria for direct applicability starting out from a broad concept of directly applicable rules. The criteria established concern all the rules of Community law and are independent of their denomination by the Treaty and their form. The wording of a provision must be 'clear and unconditional', in addition, it must not be 'qualified by any reservation on the part of States which would make its implementation conditional upon

[28] E Stein, 'Lawyers, Judges, and the Making of a Transnational Constitution' (1981) 75 *American Journal of International Law* 1, at note 20.

[29] See on the Member States in *Van Gend en Loos* K Alter, *Establishing the Supremacy of European Law* (Oxford, Oxford University Press, 2001) 185.

[30] What may be considered surprising is why the other four Member States did not join Belgium and the Netherlands here.

[31] E Stein, 'Lawyers, Judges, and the Making of a Transnational Constitution' (1981) 75 *American Journal of International Law* 1, at 8.

a legislative measure enacted under national law'. The Court subsequently adapted the latter condition in order to make directives (Article 249 EC) directly applicable and effective, under certain conditions.[32] The addressee is not a decisive feature of direct applicability: according to the Court in *Van Gend en Loos*, Community law also confers on individuals legal rights which 'arise not only where they are expressly granted by the Treaty, but also by the reason of obligations which the Treaty imposes upon the Member States'.

In the 1963 case, Article 12 of the EEC Treaty was considered clear and unconditional in its terms and not requiring further action on the part of the State in order to become effective.

In the Long Run …

Today, most primary law provisions are considered to have direct effect and to be directly applicable. This appears so self-evident that the Treaty establishing a Constitution for Europe signed in 2004, which constituted to some extent a restatement of European law and which, inter alia, introduced for the first time a primacy clause into primary law, didn't even bother to mention the direct effect/applicability issue.[33] The same is true for the 2007 Treaty of Lisbon.

Over the years, the ECJ has granted direct effect and direct applicability to secondary law,[34] to the law of the Association Agreements,[35] but not to WTO law.[36]

The Nature of European Law and of the European Construct

Decided in a time when the EEC had just six Member States and just four official languages, *Van Gend en Loos* still is one of the most important decisions of EU law because of its assessment of the nature of European integration law.[37] Together with the decision in the case of *Costa v ENEL* one year later,[38] which established the principle of primacy of European law, *Van Gend en Loos* initiated the departure from a classical public international law reading of

[32] Case 9/70, *Grad v Finanzamt Traunstein* [1970] ECR 825; Case 41/74, *Van Duyn*, [1974] ECR 1337; Case 148/78, *Ratti* [1979] ECR 1629; Case 8/81 *Becker v Finanzamt Münster-Innenstadt* [1982] ECR 53.

[33] It should not be ignored, though, that there is a critical discussion of the usefulness of principle of direct effect (not direct applicability): see P Pescatore, 'The Doctrine of "Direct Effect": An Infant Disease of Community Law' (1983) 8 *EL Rev* 155; S Prechal, 'Does Direct Effect Still Matter?', (2000) 37 *CML Rev* 1047.

[34] See, eg, Case 152/84 *Marshall* [1986] ECR 723 and the cases above, n 32.

[35] See, eg, Case 12/86 *Demirel* [1987] ECR 3719.

[36] See for a recent case Case C-377/02 *Van Parys v Belgische Interventie- en Restituiebureau* [2005] ECR I-1465. See for exceptions, some kind of 'indirect effect', Case 70/87, *Fediol* [1989] ECR 1781 and Case C-69/89 *Nakajima* [1991] ECR I-2069.

[37] The issues are closely related, of course: the specific nature of European law, in the Court's narrative, is the precondition for direct applicability.

[38] Case 6/64 *Costa v ENEL* [1964] ECR 585 (English special edition).

the founding treaties, towards a constitutional law understanding.[39] The ECJ achieved this shift of paradigms by asserting the special nature of European law.[40]

Beyond Public International Law?

Reflecting on the question of direct applicability of Article 12 of the EEC Treaty, the ECJ started out from the general idea that in order 'to ascertain whether the provision of an international treaty extend so far in their effects it is necessary to consider the spirit, the general scheme and the wording of the provisions'.

Interestingly, the Court did not examine the intention of the contracting parties,[41] which is, considering the statements of the governments in the case, not that surprising. Instead, the ECJ created the teleological approach that would later be associated with *effet utile*: the Court argued that 'the objective of the EEC Treaty, which is to establish a common market, the functioning of which is of direct concern to interested parties in the Community, implies that this Treaty is more than an agreement which merely creates mutual obligations between the contracting parties'. The Court supported its opinion by referring to the Preamble of the Treaty and the independent powers of the EEC organs, the exercise of which affects individuals.

The conclusion of the ECJ was that 'the Community constitutes a new legal order of international law for the benefit of which the States have limited their sovereign rights, albeit within limited fields, and the subjects of which comprise not only Member States but also their nationals'.

This description marks the departure from classical public international law,[42] but without totally cutting the ties. The formula used by the Court to describe the European construct, however, has evolved over the years, replacing the reference to international law with a reference to constitutional law: from a new 'legal order of international law' (1963),[43] followed by the formula 'own legal system' (1964),[44] and the concept of the Treaty as 'the basic constitutional charter' (1986)[45] towards 'the constitutional charter of a Community based on the rule of law' (1991).[46] Until today, the constitutional dimension of the European legal order does emphasise the autonomy of European law, but it does not clearly state a separation between EU law and the legal order of the Member States. Rather, this interpretation holds out European law as the overarching legal order within a

[39] See in that context E Stein, 'Lawyers, Judges, and the Making of a Transnational Constitu-tion' (1981) 75 *American Journal of International Law* 1.

[40] E Stein, 'Lawyers, Judges, and the Making of a Transnational Constitution' (1981) 75 *American Journal of International Law* 1, at 24, indicates that this argument orginated at the Commission's legal service.

[41] See in that context the famous decision by the Permanent Court of International Justice, Advisory Opinion of 3 March 1928, *Jurisdiction of the Courts of Danzig*, PCIJ Series B, no 15, at 17, which states that an international agreement may create individual rights, enforceable by national courts—according to the intention of the contracting parties.

[42] Direct effet or direct applicability alone were nothing alien to public international law—if the contracting parties wished to grant this.

[43] Case 26/62 *Van Gend en Loos* [1963] ECR 1.

[44] Case 6/64 *Costa* [1964] ECR 585.

[45] Case 294/83 *Les Verts v Parliament* [1986] ECR 1339, para 23. The French language version is *Charte constitutionnelle de base*, in German *Verfassungsurkunde der Gemeinschaft.*

[46] Opinion 1/91 *EEA* [1991] ECR I-6079, para 1.

community of law, which at the same time is taken up and complemented by the Member States' respective legal orders, forming a non-unitary, multilevel system of public power.[47]

In *Van Gend en Loos*, the Court remained careful not to push it too far: thus—in most language versions—'sovereign rights' instead of 'sovereignty'; thus 'limitation' instead of 'transfer'. The peculiar twofold approach to European integration, where elements of public international law are still around while something distinct has already emerged, remains a hallmark of European integration until today, even with the words 'new legal order of international law' having faded away from ECJ language: it is captured in the title of the 2004 effort to reform the foundations: a *Treaty* establishing a *Constitution.*

An Intended Legal Revolution?

The interesting question, in retrospect, is, whether the judges knew what they were doing. This question leads to a certain history deficit in European integration research: social sciences and law have tended to neglect to work together with historians on a better understanding of what really went on during the foundational period.

We do know that shortly before the judgment, the Community had entered a political crisis with the breaking off of the negotiations with Britain on membership in January 1963.[48] But we do not know whether the judges took a conscious decision to push the legal development because of the political standstill. Most of the individuals who were in charge in these early years are not available any more. Thus, we have no first-hand account of what was going on in the Court in 1963.[49]

But there are hints which help to reconstruct the situation. My assumption is that the step taken in *Van Gend en Loos* did not appear that dramatic to the judges in 1963.

First of all, *Van Gend en Loos* may simply be read as an attempt to deal with a dilemma: the six founding Member States had quite different views of the relationship between domestic and international law, ranging from monism to dualism.[50] What the Court did in *Van Gend en Loos* may be interpreted as the simple attempt to get away from the miasma of public international law theory and to create a clean slate, conceptually and methodologically detached from classical public international law constraints.

Second, *Van Gend en Loos* was probably not totally out of step with all the Member States' views on European integration. Although some governments did voice their concerns during the procedure, it was not the case that all six governments went to the ECJ to clearly say that the ECJ risked totally misinterpreting the Treaty. One explanation here is offered in a note on *Van Gend en Loos* written by the head of the German

[47] See in that context FC Mayer, 'Multilevel Constitutional Jurisdiction', in A v Bogdandy and J Bast (eds), *Principles of European Constitutional Law* 2nd edn (Oxford, Hart, 2009) forthcoming.

[48] 'Sk.' [case note] (1963) 1 *CML Rev* 88.

[49] See the references on Dutch ECJ Judge Donner's statements in 1980 (AM Donner, *Rechtsgeleerd Magazijn Themis* (1980) 354, at 359), though, in M Claes and B De Witte, 'Report on the Netherlands', in JHH Weiler *et al* (eds), *The European Courts and National Courts* (Oxford, Hart, 1998) 171, at note 33.

[50] Pierre Pescatore, who witnessed the negotiation of the treaties, stated in 1965 that at the time of the negotiation, there was no awareness of the huge differences between the Member States as far as the constitutional structures related to international law and the mentalities of the respective national legal community on this issue were concerned, quoted in M Claes, *The National Courts' Mandate in the European Constitution* (Oxford, Hart, 2006) 46. Advocate General Roemer, in his Conclusions in *Van Gend en Loos*, claims the opposite and takes the divergences between the national legal orders as an argument against direct applicability.

delegation that negotiated the EEC Treaty, Carl Friedrich Ophüls.[51] He suggests that in *Van Gend en Loos* the Court simply reiterates what was already the 'predominant view' during the negotiations and when concluding the Treaty. At least for the German government, this seems to be correct, as Ophüls is right when he points to the fact that the Court uses almost the same words in *Van Gend en Loos* as the official memoranda of the German government accompanying ratification of the founding treaties in the 1950s.[52]

In brief: *Van Gend en Loos* was more about reaction than about action. And it may truly have appeared to the judges—or at least to some of them—that they were just spelling something out that was already present when the EEC was founded.

The Role of the ECJ

What is probably as important in *Van Gend en Loos* as the question of *what* was decided is the question of *who* took the decision.[53] By claiming not only jurisdiction, but in a more general sense the authority to decide upon direct effect and applicability and upon the legal nature of the European construct, the ECJ also made a strong statement on itself, its self-understanding and the future role it aspired to.

It is in particular the emphasis the ECJ put on the preliminary reference procedure and the need for uniform interpretation of European law that made it clear that it intended to play an important role in the shaping of European law. *Van Gend en Loos* already contains core elements of the characteristics of this role that would be further developed in countless decisions over the next decades.

The Importance of Member State Courts

The ECJ needed and still needs the national courts, as they bring most of the important cases to Luxembourg, by means of the preliminary reference procedure. At the same time, the ECJ wants to keep national courts under control, in order to secure the uniform interpretation of European law. Thus, the ECJ has to keep a difficult balance between accommodating the Member State courts and controlling them.

These two aspects are both present in *Van Gend en Loos*. The self-perception as the ultimate umpire, the guardian of European law who is constantly monitoring what national courts do, becomes visible in *Van Gend en Loos* when the Court emphasises the need to secure uniform interpretation of the Treaty by national courts and tribunals. This point is brought up when the ECJ mentions Article 177 of the EEC Treaty (now Article 234 EC) as an indication that Member States had acknowledged that European law 'has an authority which can be invoked by their nationals' before national courts.

Here are two examples of how the ECJ nurtured the national courts in *Van Gend en Loos*:

[51] CF Ophüls [case note] (1963) 16 *Neue Juristische Wochenschrift* 1751. See also an earlier publication by Ophüls on the constitutional understanding and the federal aspects of the Schumann plan: CF Ophüls, 'Juristische Grundgedanken des Schumanplans', (1951) 4 *Neue Juristische Wochenschrift* 289.

[52] *Bundestagsdrucksache 417/51* for the ECCS Treaty, *Bundestagsdrucksache 3440/2. Wahlperiode 1953* for the EEC Treaty.

[53] B De Witte, 'Direct effect, Supremacy, and the Nature of the Legal Order', in P Craig and G de Búrca (eds), *The Evolution of EU Law* (Oxford, Oxford University Press, 1999) 179, at 181; M Claes, *The National Courts' Mandate in the European Constitution* (Oxford, Hart, 2006) 73.

When the Belgian government challenged the jurisdiction of the ECJ on the grounds that the answer to the first question would not have any bearing on the result of the proceedings brought in the Dutch Court, the European Court rejected this objection, considering it sufficient 'that the question raised should clearly be concerned with the interpretation of the Treaty'. The ECJ clearly stated here that it was up to the national court to decide upon the relevance of Community law in a case before it. This constituted a friendly signal towards the national courts, attributing them their own role in the European court system and already implying the idea of the national courts as European law courts.[54]

The ECJ's decision on the substance of the second question in *Van Gend en Loos* seems to be inspired by the same approach, consisting of giving national courts some responsibility of their own.[55] The Court left the application of Article 12 of the EEC Treaty, in accordance with its interpretation of the article, to the national court, which had to decide whether the product in question was charged with an import duty higher than that with which it was charged on 1 January 1958, the entry into force of the EEC Treaty.

Interpreting National Law Without Interpreting National Law

Another characteristic of ECJ case law in the realm of the preliminary reference procedure is already on display in *Van Gend en Loos*, something that may be coined 'indirect interpretation'. The Court has always refused to directly interpret Member State law, and has instead insisted on dealing with abstract questions.[56] If necessary, the ECJ rephrases the references just the way it did in the *Van Gend en Loos*.

With respect to the second question, the governments of Belgium and the Netherlands argued that the placing of a product in a particular tariff classification was exclusively a matter of Dutch law and consequently fell outside the jurisdiction of the ECJ under Article 177(1) of the EEC Treaty (now Article 234(1) EC). The ECJ used a strategy it had already chosen in its very first preliminary reference decision in the 1962 *Bosch* case[57] and claimed that it would look at the 'real meaning of the question', which was tantamount to rewriting the reference question submitted by the Dutch court.

[54] On this idea and the 'dédoublement fonctionnel' see CF Ophüls [case note] (1963) 16 *Neue Juristische Wochenschrift* 1751.

[55] In order to answer the second question referred to the ECJ, the Court had to examine two things: what were the duties actually applied at the date of entry into force of the Treaty, and had duties been increased contrary to the prohibition contained in Art 12 of the EEC Treaty. As to the first point, the Belgian and the Dutch government argued that, when the EEC Treaty entered into force, the rate of 3 per cent was not applied but that, in fact, the authorities imposed a tax of 10 per cent—the tax for glue, as this was the primary use of ureaformaldehyde—so that there was actually no 'increase' under the new tariff. The Court followed this argument and held that 'regard must be had to the customs duties and charges actually applied at the date of entry into force of the Treaty'. As far as the alleged increase was concerned, it did not result from an increase in the tariff but was a consequence of the new classification of the product in the new customs tariff. Here, the ECJ held it of little importance 'how the increase in customs duties occurred when, after the Treaty entered into force, the same product in the same Member State was subjected to a higher rate of duty'.

[56] The national courts do not always endorse the ECJ's strategy. See in that context the *Arsenal* case in Great Britain, where the English High Court decided to ignore a preliminary ruling of the ECJ (Case C-206/01 *Arsenal Football Club* [2002] ECR I-10273), stating that the ECJ had no jurisdiction to make findings of fact or reverse the national court on its findings of fact, [2002] EWHC 2695 (ch), All ER (2003) vol I, 137. This decision was overruled by the Court of Appeal: Court of Appeal (Civil Division), 21 May 2003, *Arsenal Football Club v Matthew Reed* (2003) EWCA Civ 96.

[57] Case 13/61 *Bosch* [1962] ECR 45 (50) (English special edition).

The Individual as an Agent of the ECJ and European Law

Finally, an approach that has been used again and again by the ECJ is already present in *Van Gend en Loos*: empowering the individual with a view to strengthen European law. In the words of Miguel Poiares Maduro, 'the "subjectivation" of the Treaties' with a view to enhance effectiveness and legitimacy of Community law.[58]

The governments argued in *Van Gend en Loos* that only Member States or the Commission, according to Articles 169 and 170 of the EEC Treaty (now Articles 227 and 228 EC), could oblige a Member State to enforce the Article 12 obligation. The Court rejected this objection and pointed to the function of Article 177 EEC Treaty (now Article 234 EC), which goes beyond ensuring the uniformity of European law, as this procedure also constitutes a 'direct judicial protection of the individual rights of nationals' in circumstances where no other procedure is available.

Conclusion

Van Gend en Loos already contains numerous elements of what would become hallmarks of ECJ decisions in the ensuing years: the ECJ's understanding of the principle of direct effect/applicability, the claim of a new legal order distinct from traditional public international law, the core role of the ECJ in shaping this new legal order. Probably the judgment did create an expectation that the public international law paradigm would be completely overcome at some point—that has not happened yet.

But *Van Gend en Loos* remains a decision which indicates what distinguishes the European Union from other forms of international co-operation. This is particularly visible in a WTO panel report that may be read as a 'counter *Van Gend en Loos*', with the panel using almost identical words as the ECJ, albeit with a different purpose: 'Neither the GATT nor the WTO has so far been interpreted by GATT/WTO institutions as a legal order producing direct effect. Following this approach, the GATT/WTO did *not* create a new legal order the subjects of which comprise both contracting parties or Members and their nationals.'[59]

There is one major point that distinguishes *Van Gend en Loos* from the other fundamental ECJ decision, *Costa v ENEL*: *Van Gend en Loos* has basically remained uncontested by the Member States. The Member States could have changed the treaties, 'correcting' the ECJ, many times. They did not do it,[60] with the exception of the provision on framework decisions in the EU Treaty (Article 34 EU), which states explicitly, that framework decisions shall not have direct effect.

[58] MP Maduro, *We The Court* (Oxford, Hart, 1998) 9.

[59] United States, Sections 301–310 of the Trade Act of 1974, *Report of the Panel 22.12.1999, WT/DS152/R*, paras 7.72, 7.73, emphasis in the original text. See in that context A Tancredi, 'EC Practice in the WTO: How Wide is the 'Scope for Manoeuvre'?, (2004) 15 *European Journal of International Law* 933; A v Bogdandy, 'Law and Politics in the WTO', (2001) 5 *Max Planck UNYB* 610 at 624.

[60] French President de Gaulle suggested to modify the ECJ's jurisdiction in light of *Van Gend en Loos* and *Costa v ENEL*, though, see the reference in K Alter, *Establishing the Supremacy of European Law* (Oxford, Oxford University Press, 2001) 187.

And even the highest courts of the Member States did accept the principle of direct applicability, albeit some courts had more difficulties in doing so then others.[61] A 1967 decision of the German Constitutional court comes closest to a model national court endorsement of *Van Gend en Loos* when it even endorses the concept of a distinct legal order.[62] In that sense, the *acquis* embodied in *Van Gend en Loos* appears to be effectively consolidated.

On the other hand, the distinction between direct applicability and primacy is suggested mainly because of the two distinct cases in 1963 and in 1964, but the distinction is artificial. The Court simply did not have to decide upon the primacy issue in *Van Gend en Loos*, because the Dutch Court hadn't asked about primacy—as the Dutch legal order itself already attributed primacy to international law.[63] The question of primacy is present, though, in the statements of Member States and of the Advocate General. In that reading *Van Gend en Loos* is a decision on direct applicability *and* on primacy, and the reach of primacy remains contested from the Member State level.[64] This is were open questions remain.[65]

Without *Van Gend en Loos*, European law would look different today. It would not have become the *Rechtsgemeinschaft*, the community of law, that founders such as Carl Friedrich Ophüls or Walter Hallstein were aiming for and that we still have today.[66] The assessment of Eric Stein, written two decades after the decision, is still correct another 25 years later: 'It is safe to say, with the benefit of hindsight, that had the Court followed the Governments, Community law would have remained an abstract skeleton, and a great variety and number of Treaty violations would have remained undisclosed and unredressed.'[67]

[61] See on that the references in B De Witte, 'Direct Effect, Supremacy, and the Nature of the Legal Order', in P Craig and G de Búrca (eds), *The Evolution of EU Law* (Oxford, Oxford University Press, 1999) 179, at 195.

[62] BVerfGE 22, 293. For other examples see Cour de cassation, Le Ski, JT 1971, 460 (Belgium); Cour de cassation, Jacques Vabre, D 1975 II, 497 (France).

[63] See on that M Claes and B De Witte, 'Report on the Netherlands', in JHH Weiler *et al* (eds), *The European Courts and National Courts* (Oxford, Hart, 1998) 171, at 172 *ff*.

[64] On the link between direct effect and primacy see JHH Weiler, *The Transformation of Europe* (1991) 100 *Yale Law Journal* 2403 at note 49; see also K Alter, *Establishing the Supremacy of European Law* (Oxford, Oxford University Press, 2001) 18.

[65] See, eg, the Polish Constitutional Tribunal's decision on *Poland's Accession to the EU*, K 18/04, 11 May 2005, rejecting the concept of a supranational organisation, but even there, the direct effect issue and the idea of an autonomous legal system remain uncontested.

[66] See in that context FC Mayer, 'Europa als Rechtsgemeinschaft', in GF Schuppert *et al* (eds), *Europawissenschaft* (Baden-Baden, Nomos, 2005) 429.

[67] E Stein, 'Lawyers, Judges, and the Making of a Transnational Constitution' (1981) 75 *American Journal of International Law* 1, at 6.

4

Pluralism in *Marbury* and *Van Gend*

DANIEL HALBERSTAM

'Great cases, like hard cases, make bad law', Oliver Wendell Holmes, Jr, famously remarked in his first Supreme Court dissent.[68] For Holmes, 'great cases are called great, not by reason of their real importance in shaping the law of the future, but because of some accident of immediate overwhelming interest which appeals to the feelings and distorts the judgment'.[69] On this account neither *Marbury v Madison*[70] nor *Van Gend en Loos*[71] would qualify. *Van Gend* was a case of great principle without greatly interesting facts. And *Marbury* was a great political battle that nevertheless produced a case of great principle.

But by any measure other than Holmes's, *Marbury* and *Van Gend* are great cases—often called the greatest within their respective systems. Both have foundational significance for the legal systems they helped establish. Both confront the deepest challenge to any legal order: competing claims of ultimate authority. But these cases do not definitively resolve the great problem of pluralism. Instead, both decisions brilliantly capture the devilish subtlety of the pluralist problem and inaugurate regimes of accommodation that, as we shall see, have followed surprisingly similar lines.

Fighting Congress and the President in *Marbury*

Marbury came out of a pitched battle between the incoming Democratic-Republican administration of President Thomas Jefferson and the outgoing Federalist administration of President John Adams.[72] This was political drama at its best. The Federalists, still in control of Congress after having lost the autumn elections, passed a series of judicial reform acts in February 1801.[73] In an effort to mute the force of Jefferson's political 'Revolution of 1800', the lame duck Congress expanded the ranks of the federal judiciary to enable lame duck President John Adams to lodge dozens of Federalists on the bench in

[68] *Northern Securities Co v United States*, 193 US 197, 364 (1904).

[69] *Ibid.*

[70] 1 Cranch (5 US) 137 (1803).

[71] Case 26/62 [1963] ECR 1.

[72] See Bruce A Ackerman, *The Failure of the Founding Fathers* (Cambridge, Mass: Belknap, 2005); George Lee Haskins and Herbert A Johnson, *Foundations of Power: John Marshall, 1801–15* (New York, Macmillan, 1981) (History of the Supreme Court of the United States vol II).

[73] Act of 13 February 1801, 2 Stat 89 (1801); Act of 27 February 1801, 2 Stat 103 (1801).

the waning days of his administration.[74] One such 'midnight judge' was ardent Federalist supporter William Marbury, whose judicial commission had been approved and sealed but not delivered by the outgoing Secretary of State (and freshly appointed Chief Justice) John Marshall.

As soon as Thomas Jefferson took office and his party assumed the majority in Congress, the Jeffersonians worked furiously to undo the handiwork of the outgoing Federalists. In the spring of 1802, the new Congress repealed the year-old Federalist law that had created the 16 federal appellate circuit courts (albeit not the law that created Marbury's office of justice of the peace).[75] By eliminating the offices of the freshly appointed circuit courts, the Jeffersonians effectively ousted many of the newly appointed Federalist judges without the formal impeachment proceedings that would have demanded a showing of bad behaviour. The new judiciary act also directly attacked the Supreme Court. The law reinstated the onerous requirement that the Justices 'ride circuit' to decide appellate cases all across the country. Finally, to insulate itself from immediate legal challenge, the Jeffersonians altered the frequency of Supreme Court sessions, precluding the Court from hearing any cases before 1803.

Less than two weeks after finally hearing Marbury's petition on 11 February 1803, the Supreme Court struck back with a shrewd opinion for a unanimous Court. The Court's lengthy declaration that Secretary of State James Madison (who had refused to appear in court) was legally obligated to deliver Marbury's commission as well as the holding that the judiciary could lawfully review the constitutionality of congressional action would require no co-operation by the Executive Branch or Congress for its execution. A creative reading of the Constitution and Section 13 of the Judiciary Act of 1789 meant that Congress had improperly conferred jurisdiction on the court in this case. The Court accordingly dismissed the case, fully executing its own judgment and establishing the principle of judicial review for the future.

There is an important coda to this story. On 2 March 1803, six days after *Marbury v Madison* was handed down, the Supreme Court decided *Stuart v Laird*.[76] At issue was the Jeffersonian law dismantling the circuit courts and imposing the duty to 'ride circuit' on the Justices. The constitutionality of the 1802 law, in particular the requirement to ride circuit, was highly questionable. John Marshall worked behind the scenes to gauge his colleagues' willingness to resist this encroachment as well, but did not find the unified front needed to counter the assault. The Chief Justice proceeded to recuse himself, allowing Associate Justice William Paterson to pen a perfunctory opinion upholding the new law. At least this way, the Chief Justice was spared the embarrassment of having to turn his back on *Marbury*. The Supreme Court could retain the principle of judicial review announced in *Marbury* while quietly accommodating the *force majeure* of Jeffersonian politics in *Stuart*.[77]

[74] To prevent Thomas Jefferson from appointing a Supreme Court justice in the event of retirement, the law also reduced the number of judges on the Supreme Court from six to five effective upon the next retirement. Act of 13 February 1801, 2 Stat 89.

[75] Act of 29 April 1802, 2 Stat 156.

[76] *Stuart v Laird*, 1 Cranch (5 US) 299 (1803).

[77] Cf Akhil R Amar, *America's Constitution: A Biography* (Random House, New York, 2005).

Disaggregating the State in *Van Gend*

Van Gend followed a similar path of opportunity and cunning. Adjudication under the old European Coal and Steel Treaty had been trickling along without much distinction for the better part of a decade. Not a single watershed case challenging conventional wisdom about the relationship between national and international legal orders is to be found in the over 70 reported judgments on the ECSC from 1954 to 1961. Then, in *de Geus v Bosch and van Rijn*,[78] the first question for an interpretation of the 1958 Treaty on European Economic Community came to the Court under the then-novel preliminary reference procedure of Article 177 EEC (now 234 EC). The stage was set for change.

Advocate General Lagrange immediately recognised the importance of a procedure that was 'designed to play a central part in the application of the Treaty':

> The progressive integration of the Treaty into the legal, social and economic life of the Member States must involve more and more frequently the application and . . . interpretation of the Treaty in municipal litigation . . . and not only the provisions of the Treaty itself but also those of the Regulations adopted for its implementation will give rise to questions of interpretation and indeed of legality. Applied judiciously—one is temped to say loyally—the provisions of Article 177 must lead to a real and fruitful collaboration between the municipal courts and the Court of Justice of the Communities with mutual regard for their respective jurisdictions.[79]

De Geus held that the Treaty *cum* regulation creates immediately applicable law within the domestic legal orders of the Member States. Presaging *Van Gend*, Advocate General Lagrange went one step further: 'Since the Treaty, by virtue of its ratification, is incorporated into the national law, *it is the function of national courts to apply its provisions*, except when powers are expressly conferred on Community organs.'[80]

In the very next reference action, *Van Gend en Loos*, the Court issued its constitutional juggernaut on direct effect, holding that the Treaty of Rome creates rights for individuals that Member State courts must protect. To be sure, international law had long known so-called 'self-executing' treaties, which can confer justiciable rights on individuals. Also, the Permanent Court of International Justice had long confirmed that international law may provide individuals with rights that states must recognise within their domestic legal orders,[81] and that states are not excused from their international legal obligations by virtue of domestic rules of law (whether they be rules of ordinary legislation or of a domestic constitution).[82]

But *Van Gend* was different. By directly ordering Member State courts to apply Community law, the European Court of Justice drafted these state institutions into the immediate service of the Community. This stands in marked contrast to traditional international law, in which the corporate structure of the state remains intact. State

[78] Case 13/61 [1962] ECR 45.

[79] *Ibid.* at 56.

[80] *Ibid.* at 65 (emphasis added).

[81] Jurisdiction of the Courts of Danzig, Advisory Opinion, 1928, PCIJ, Series B, No 15, 17, 18: '. . . it cannot be disputed that the very object of an international agreement, according to the intention of the contracting parties, may be the adaptation by the parties of some definite rules creating individual rights and obligations and enforceable by national courts.'

[82] Treatment of Polish Nationals and Other Persons of Polish Origin or Speech in the Danzig Territory, Advisory Opinion, 1932, PCIJ, Series A/B, No 44, 24.

violations of international law generally only create disputes among states. And even where individuals are allowed to sue states directly, as under Chapter 11 of the NAFTA[83] or the ECHR,[84] the outcome of the litigation is a judgment against the state in its corporate capacity.

To be sure, on one view, the NAFTA and ECHR dispute provisions might seem more dramatic than the pallid request for a preliminary reference on a question of Treaty law from a Member State court. After all, under NAFTA and the ECHR the international tribunal is completely seized with the legal dispute between an individual and a state, completely resolves the case, and orders a remedy. The Rome Treaty's reference procedure, in contrast, merely provides for Member State courts to pose questions of interpretation to the European Court of Justice.

And yet, the seemingly mild indirection of the reference procedure radically disaggregates the state. *Van Gend* holds that Member State courts owe the Community a duty of obedience that is not mediated by the national political branches, national laws, or even the national constitution. The ECJ does not simply pour the answer to a question of Treaty interpretation into the black box of the domestic legal order with whatever consequences for non-compliance this may have under international law. Instead, the ECJ communicates directly with the national court insisting that 'national courts must protect' the 'individual rights' the ECJ finds.

The constitutional disaggregation of the state gives the practical institutional punch to the normative assertion of integrating national and supranational legal systems. The drama of supremacy, for instance, which soon unfolded in *Costa v ENEL*,[85] was not the assertion that national law must yield to Community law. This would have been true with regard to international law as well. The drama lies in the fact that, as an institutional matter, 'superior' Community law is directly infused into the national process of adjudication. All this flows naturally from *Van Gend.*

Van Gend couples the constitutional disaggregation of the state with a normative recalibration of the Community system, that is, the normative turn to the individual.[86] *Van Gend* reads the Treaty as recognising the individual, along with the Member States, as the immediate subject of rights and responsibilities. The transfer of 'sovereign rights' from the Member States to the Community is matched by the idea that 'the nationals of the states [are] brought together in the Community [and] called upon to cooperate in the functioning of the Community'.[87] Here, too, the Court disaggregates the 'peoples' of each state, which are referred to in the preamble's 'ever closer union among the peoples of Europe' only in their corporate capacity. The individual is both legally freed from the

[83] North American Free Trade Agreement, US–Can–Mex, 17 December 1992, 32 ILM 605, 639 (1993) (Chapter 11). For a review of cases, see Jack J Coe, Jr, 'Taking Stock of NAFTA Chapter 11 in its Tenth Year: An Interim Sketch of Selected Themes, Issues, and Methods' (2003) 36 *Vanderbilt Journal of Transnational Law* 1381.

[84] Convention for the Protection of Human Rights and Fundamental Freedoms, 4 November 1950, ETS 5, 213 UNTS 221. For a synopsis of the introduction of individual suits, see, eg, Dinah Shelton, 'The Boundaries of Human Rights Jurisdiction in Europe' (2003) 13 *Duke Journal of Comparative and International Law* 95.

[85] Case 6/64, *Flaminio Costa v ENEL* [1964] ECR 585 (holding that Community law trumps subsequent national law). See also Case 106/77, *Simmenthal* [1978] ECR 629 (holding that Community law trumps national constitutional rule on jurisdiction).

[86] See Daniel Halberstam, *The Bride of Messina: Constitutionalism and Democracy in Europe*, 30 Eur L Rev 30[6] (2005), 775.

[87] [1963] ECR 12.

constitutional confines of her Member State and endowed with what Robert Cover would have called an immediate 'jurisgenerative' capacity at the supranational level of governance.[88]

As in the case of *Marbury*, non-compliance with the judgment in *Van Gend* would have been devastating. Fortunately, however, the Court at the time laboured, in Eric Stein's famous words, '[t]ucked away in the fairland Duchy of Luxembourg and blessed . . . with benign neglect by the powers that be and the mass media'.[89] Moreover, the reference came from the Netherlands, which already had adopted monism as the guiding principle of its own legal system. The judges therefore knew that the Dutch court would carry out their judgment. And so, on a creative reading of Articles 12 and 177 of the EEC Treaty, the ECJ in *Van Gend*, too, could establish a great principle at little cost.

There is a coda to *Van Gend* as well. One year later, the French government boycotted European Council meetings, returning only after the 'Luxembourg compromise' preserved the rule of unanimity for taking any Community decisions and for passing secondary legislation.[90] This way, whatever the European Court of Justice would import into the Member States' legal orders would at least have the formal approval of all the Member States. The ECJ never adjudicated the Luxembourg compromise, which surely violated the spirit, if not the letter, of the Treaties as much as the dismantling of the circuit courts did with regard to the constitution of the United States. As in the United States, this would not be the last compromise to mitigate the clash of pluralism. Instead, it was only the beginning of a continuing process of mutual accommodation.

Confronting Pluralism: Interpretive Pluralism, Systems Pluralism, and Mutual Accommodation in the United States and Europe

In both the United States and Europe the mutual accommodation of pluralism remains with us to this very day. In the United States, the extent of the Supreme Court's power of judicial review is still hotly debated, as are the limits of Congress's and the President's powers to implement their own vision of the Constitution and retaliate against a recalcitrant Court. In the European Union, the scope of supremacy of Community law over national law and the scope of rights that European law and national constitutions afford individuals within the Member States remain unsettled.

In the United States, this institutional stalemate is due to the fact that multiple institutions can lay immediate claim to interpreting the constitution. Although Article III strongly supports the hierarchical superiority of the Supreme Court vis-à-vis lower federal courts and state courts, there is no similarly clear suggestion regarding the Congress, the President, or even the people themselves. Call this *interpretive* pluralism.

A quick contrast with continental systems illustrates the point. The standard European model of judicial review formally privileges a specialised tribunal with a monopoly over

[88] Cf Robert Cover, 'Foreword: Nomos and Narrative' (1983) 97 *Harvard Law Review* 4.

[89] Eric Stein, 'Lawyers, Judges, and the Making of a Transnational Constitution' (1981) 75 *American Journal of International Law* 1.

[90] Cf JHH Weiler, 'The Transformation of Europe' (1991) 100 *Yale Law Journal* 2403, 2423–31.

constitutional interpretation. As originally conceived of by Hans Kelsen, these 'constitutional courts' would operate outside and, indeed, above the remainder of the legal system, rendering opinions and judgments that completely bind the constitutional judgment of all other actors throughout the system. Although many features of Kelsen's model have been modified, the formal recognition of the legitimacy of judicial constitutional review by a specialised constitutional court remains. As Alec Stone Sweet sums it up: 'New European constitutions expressly provide for the supremacy of constitutional courts with respect to constitutional interpretation. European academics and constitutional judges will state as much in one breath . . .'[91]

Although portions of *Marbury* might be read as making the analogous claim of supreme authority on behalf of the Supreme Court in the United States, *Marbury* itself did not definitively resolve this question. To be sure, in ordinary times a justified practice of deference to the Supreme Court prevails. But throughout the Court's history, US constitutional theory and practice have nonetheless allowed multiple competing institutions to lay claim to being authoritative interpreters of the Constitution. In keeping with the pragmatic tradition of the common law, the question in the United States has therefore always been one of finding the proper form of mutual accommodation. *Marbury*—especially when coupled with *Stuart v Laird*—provides a masterful initiation into this continuing conundrum. *That* is why the case is truly great.

The European Union is also a pragmatic legal order, as opposed to a formally ordered one. To be sure, as a matter of Treaty law, the European Court of Justice is the only institution charged with 'ensur[ing]' that the law be observed.[92] And yet, meshing this Treaty system with the existing constitutional structures of the Member States, as *Van Gend* did, yields a situation of *systems* pluralism that shares some of the theoretical and practical features of the *interpretive* pluralism that *Marbury* inaugurated so dramatically in the United States.

Comparative scholarship on *Van Gend*, however, has tended to juxtapose supremacy and direct effect in the Member States with US federal supremacy in the several States. This comparison certainly has its virtues.[93] And the apparent parallelism is obvious. But ultimately, the relationship between federal and state law, as well as that between the federal Supreme Court and the state judiciary, are fully ordered in the United States. Put another way, there is no real practical or theoretical doubt about federal legal (and judicial) supremacy in the United States—at least not since the Civil War, which dispelled any remaining confederate illusions about the nature of the United States Constitution.[94]

Unlike state resistance to federal power in the United States, however, the unsettled relation between the European and Member State legal orders (and their respective judiciaries) will continue for the foreseeable future. In Europe, this is not a troubling disturbance of the rule of law as state defiance of federal rule was in the United States. The

[91] Alec Stone Sweet, 'Why Europe Rejected American Judicial Review: And Why It May Not Matter' (2003) 101 *Michigan Law Review* 2744, 2779.

[92] Art 220 EC.

[93] For an excellent analysis in this regard, see Franz C Mayer, *Kompetenzüberschreitung und Letztendscheidung* (2000).

[94] See, eg, Charles Warren, 'Legislative and Judicial Attacks on the Supreme Court of the United States' (1913) 47 *American Law Review* 1 and 161. I should mention the brief episode during the Civil Rights era, in which the Southern Manifesto reawakened the old idea of confederation and interposition, which provoked the Supreme Court's counterpunch in *Cooper v Aaron*.

uneasy relationship between European and Member State legal orders is not a matter of unlawful constituent state recalcitrance that must be overcome. Not even the constitutional treaty sought to change this in any radical way.[95] In short, like interpretive pluralism in the United States, systems pluralism in Europe is an essential feature of the legal order.[96]

How, then, does each system manage its own brand of pluralism? This is the neglected yet highly relevant comparison between *Van Gend*, *Marbury*, and their respective progenies. The answer is that each system seems to manage its pluralism with three interrelated principles in mind: voice, expertise, and rights. The first asks which institution has the better claim of representing the relevant political will; the second asks which institution has the superior institutional structure, capacity, or knowledge to address the substantive issue at hand; and the third asks which institution will better protect basic rights. These three questions overlap, of course, and they can only be sketched out in their crudest form in the pages that remain. But a quick glance nonetheless suggests the potential fruitfulness of this comparison.

Voice

One might think that in the case of interpretive pluralism claims of democratic voice invariably cut in favour of the political branches. That would be mistaken. As Bruce Ackerman, for one, has argued, the judicial counter-majoritarian difficulty may be reconceived as an inter-temporal difficulty with democratic claims on both sides of the ledger.[97] Viewed thus, judicial review involves the relative democratic credentials of a current parliamentary majority confronting the constitutional politics of the past. Ackerman aside, the relative democratic pedigree of the two sides can be subject to many forms of analysis, including analysing the deliberateness or the deliberative nature of the purported democratic choices on both sides, or examining the citizenry's working assumptions regarding institutional functions (such as judicial review), constitutional substance, or interpretive method.

Depending on the circumstances and the issue, a voice-based argument can cut in favour of the Judiciary, the President, Congress, or, as Larry Kramer has argued,[98] the people themselves. Suffice it to say that the pragmatic accommodation of interpretive pluralism in the United States since *Marbury* has repeatedly reflected the relative democratic pedigree of the competing claims of constitutional substance, method, and authority.

In the case of systems pluralism, one might similarly be tempted to think that claims of voice invariably favour the nation state, not Europe. This, however, would be mistaken as well. As an initial matter, there is, of course, a plurality of democratic wills in the European Union, which Kalypso Nicolaidis has aptly termed a 'demoicracy,' and which requires some

[95] See Mattias Kumm, 'The Jurisprudence of Constitutional Conflict: Constitutional Supremacy in Europe before and after the Constitutional Treaty' (2005) 11 *European Law Journal* 262.

[96] Cf, eg, Neil Walker, 'The Idea of Constitutional Pluralism' (2002) 65 *MLR* 317; Neil MacCormick, *Questioning Sovereignty* (Oxford, Oxford University Press, 1999).

[97] See Ackerman, above n 72; Bruce Ackerman, *We The People: Foundations* (Cambridge, Mass: Belknap, 1991).

[98] Larry Kramer, *The People Themselves: Popular Constitutionalism and Judicial Review* (New York, Oxford University Press, 2004).

assessment of the relative legitimacy of each will's claim within the system.[99] Second, systems pluralism itself is the product of the deliberate openness of Member State constitutional systems to supranational integration, which entails a specific national democratic commitment to accommodating a collective political will beyond the state. Third, even in terms of the strictly national political will, as Don Regan argues in his contribution to this volume, yielding to certain supranational norms may augment the quality of national democracy itself.

Here, too, then, the practice of accommodation may depend—and has depended—on analysing the relative democratic pedigree of competing norms, actors, and decisions. Consider in this regard, for example, the European Communities Act of 1972, which essentially precludes an *inadvertent* violation of Community law on the part of the UK while suggesting a less accommodating position in cases of specific and deep disagreement backed by a deliberate expression of the domestic democratic will.[100] One might read one prong of the Italian accommodation in *Granital* along these lines as well.[101] The German Maastricht opinion,[102] for all its faults, may be similarly understood as coming to an accommodation between the two legal orders based on an assessment of the relative democratic claims that may be made on behalf of each. And the brewing problems with the European Arrest Warrant may be similarly affected by the deliberateness with which the two sides have chosen their competing positions.[103]

Expertise

In the United States, the relative institutional capacity of the Congress, the President, the Court, or even the people themselves figures prominently in the daily paradigm of assessing the strength of judicial review. For example, on the one hand, many argue that the scholarly attributes of the Supreme Court place this institution in a superior position to ascertain the meaning of the Constitution.[104] On the other hand, the daily judicial deference to Congress is based on the assumption that the legion of facts necessary to answer constitutional questions are better ascertained and evaluated elsewhere.

Debates over adjusting the nature and severity of judicial review in the United States frequently focus on relative institutional capacity. Scholars debate, for instance, whether the Supreme Court has (or courts, more generally, have) the capacity to balance meaningfully competing interests or whether they should limit themselves to ensuring the absence

[99] Kalypso Nicolaidis, 'We, the Peoples of Europe . . .' (November/December 2004) *Foreign Affairs* 97.

[100] European Communities Act 1972, c 68 (England); *R v Secretary of State for Transport, ex parte Factortame Ltd* (1991) 1 All ER 70.

[101] Here, the Italian Constitutional Court generally allows lower courts to disapply national law in face of conflicting European law. One exception to this rule, however, is when the national law appears to violate fundamental principles of community law. This can be understood to mean that unless the national legislator deliberately takes on a core aspect of the Community legal order, the national legislator will not be deemed to have made a sufficiently salient democratic decision to oppose European law. If, on the other hand, the national legislator does invoke its full powers, then the matter will go to the Constitutional Court itself. See *Granital SpA v Amministrazione finanziaria*, Corte Cost, 8 June 1984, n 170, 66 Racc uff corte cost 367 (1984), 1984 Giur Cost 1988.

[102] 89 BVerfGE 155 (1993).

[103] Anneli Albi, 'Supremacy of EC Law in the New Member States: Bringing Parliaments into the Equation of "Cooperative Constitutionalism"' (2007) 3 *European Constitutional Law Review* 25.

[104] The classic argument is Alexander Bickel, *The Least Dangerous Branch: The Supreme Court at the Bar of Politics* (Indianapolis, Bobbs-Merrill, 1962).

of discrete, constitutionally obnoxious reasons for action.[105] Conversely, certain institutions might claim specific subject-matter expertise, as the Presidency has most recently in matters of national security in order to escape the watchful eye of the judiciary and the controlling hand of Congress. The specific accommodation on that issue is still out. In the meantime, it is certain, that accommodation in the face of interpretive pluralism in the United States will continue to depend on arguments from relative expertise.

In Europe, too, arguments from expertise have been a staple ingredient of legitimacy claims and the process of mutual accommodation. Indeed, the original idea of the Community grew out of Jean Monnet's dirigiste vision of an expert bureaucratic administration operating far above politics. One even detects a hint of this old idea in the language used in the French constitution to record the accommodation of Community powers: the Community's powers are notably referred to as narrow expertise-based '*compétences*' in contrast to the more broadly political '*pouvoirs*' of either the president or the French parliament.[106]

Insofar as the Community has progressed beyond this simple idea of apolitical knowledge and expertise, arguments about relative strength in structure and capacity nevertheless remain central to evaluating competing claims of authority. The principle of subsidiarity, for example, centrally addresses this very question and has figured prominently in legal as well as political efforts to accommodate the clash of legal orders.[107] One form of pragmatic constitutional accommodation on this score can be found in the Subsidiarity Protocol, which brings about a direct exchange of views on the matter among the national and European legislators.[108]

Rights

In the United States, rights tend to mean courts. And yet, interpretive pluralism has historically left room for multiple institutions to argue for their superior authority in protecting rights. For many years Congress, for example, successfully claimed the position of a co-ordinate expositor of rights under Section 5 of the 14th Amendment. Only recently has the Supreme Court struck down this claim, asserting the Court's monopoly on defining the content of rights even under the 14th Amendment.[109] So far, Congress has not mounted any serious resistance to this consolidating move on the part of the Supreme Court. But this complacence may ultimately be due to the Court's own pragmatic restraint: so far the Court seems to have spared central Congressional civil rights initiatives, such as Title VII of the Civil Rights Act and the Voting Rights Act, from its searching standard of review.

[105] See, eg, Richard H Pildes, 'Avoiding Balancing: The Role of Exclusionary Reasons in Constitutional Law' (1994) 45 *Hastings Law Journal* 711, 715; T Alexander Aleinikoff, 'Constitutional Law In the Age of Balancing' (1987) 96 *Yale Law Journal* 943, 949, 951; Jeremy Waldron, *Rights in Conflict, in Liberal Rights: Collected Papers 1981–1991*, 203 (Cambridge, Cambridge University Press, 1993).

[106] Cf, eg, Constitution du 4 Octobre 1958, Arts 88.1 and 2 with 7 and 25.

[107] Kumm, above n 95, too, proposes using this principle in solving the stand-off between the constitutional systems.

[108] Stephen Weatherill, 'Using national parliaments to improve scrutiny of the limits of EU action' (2003) 28 *EL Rev* 909.

[109] For a critical assessment, see, eg, Robert C Post and Reva B Siegel, 'Legislative Constitutionalism and Section Five Power: Polycentric Interpretation of the Family and Medical Leave Act' (2003) 112 *Yale Law Journal* 1943.

In the European Union, fundamental rights still tend to mean domestic constitutional rights, or, perhaps by now, domestic constitutional rights as supervised by the European Convention on Human Rights. Accordingly, one element of the constitutional standoff between the Community and Member State legal orders famously turned on Member State resistance regarding rights protection. Here, the European Court of Justice only garnered the deference of Member State courts to the ECJ's (and the Community's) claim of superior authority by incorporating central aspects of Member State constitutional rights into Community law itself. To take the best known example, Germany's Constitutional Court will now defer to the European Court of Justice on case-by-case rights protection while keeping a watchful eye on the ECJ's overall track record on rights generally.[110] The European Court of Justice, in turn, has not only incorporated general rights protection into its own jurisprudence, but also begun to defer to specific domestic claims of legislative rights protection that exceed a European-wide standard, even when those protections run up against free movement claims.[111]

Most interesting is the possible shift in accommodating the respective boundaries of European and Member State jurisdiction over rights. According to cases like Mary Carpenter, for example, the European Court of Justice could investigate virtually any Member State's legislative, administrative, or adjudicative act that might negatively affect the exercise of an individual's rights to free movement under the EC Treaty. As the Carpenter case illustrated,[112] jurisdiction under this rubric was potentially vast. It led to ECJ fundamental rights review of Mary Carpenter's residency rights on the reasoning that her residency in the UK provided emotional support to her husband, who exercised free movement rights by working throughout the EU. With the recent *Chen* case,[113] the already vast potential of ECJ fundamental rights review has expanded even further, as the ECJ might now intervene to protect all fundamental rights of all EU citizens.

To date, the European Court of Justice has not regularly exhausted its vast power over fundamental rights protection, most likely for reasons of mutual accommodation. As a general matter, Member States' fundamental rights records have been fair, at least when coupled with protection through the European Court of Human Rights in Strasbourg. There has been little need for the European Court of Justice to intervene, except where the fundamental right did indeed have a particular connection to free movement.

With the accession of Member States with more questionable fundamental rights records, however, the current state of mutual accommodation might be shifting. The European Court of Justice might begin to review fundamental rights claims—especially those coming from the new Member States—more aggressively. Indeed, the ECJ may have laid the foundation for such intervention in the recent *Pupino* case,[114] in which the Court read a European framework directive under the third pillar to protect basic rights of criminal procedure. The ECJ specifically made reference to the ECHR in this decision, as if to lend its own institutional support to what has become an important (but increasingly overworked) ally in this venture.

[110] 73 BVerfGE 339 (1986) (Solange II).

[111] Case C-36/02, *Omega Spielhallen- und Automatenaufstellungs-GmbH v Oberbürgermeisterin der Bundesstadt Bonn*, 2004 ECR I-9609.

[112] Case C-60/00, *Mary Carpenter v Secretary of State for the Home Department*, 2002 ECR I-6279.

[113] Case C-200/02, *Zhu and Chen v Secretary of State for the Home Department* [2004] ECR I-9923 (finding right of residency for mother of EU citizen).

[114] Case C-105/03, *Criminal Proceedings against Maria Pupino* [2005] ECR I-5285.

The new accommodation on rights in Europe may be just this: (1) the Member States (and the European Court of Human Rights) will continue to refrain from reviewing fundamental rights violations involving European law as long as the ECJ generally provides an acceptable level of rights protection; (2) conversely, however, the European Court of Justice will only continue to refrain from aggressively reviewing all fundamental rights claims within its jurisdiction as long as Member States (with the help of a functioning European Court of Human Rights) maintain a general satisfactory level of fundamental rights protection.[115] In the case of new Member States with sketchy human rights records that may slip by an increasingly overburdened European Court of Human Rights, the ECJ may begin to reach more broadly than it traditionally has done with regard to the old Member States. In sum, each level will focus on reviewing only those rights violations that strike at the core of their respective legal systems but only as long as the other level generally protects rights adequately within its own primary sphere of operation.

Conclusion

Van Gend is often casually compared to *Marbury* simply because in each case the high court declares itself to be the final arbiter of central government law. But there is a good deal more to the comparison than that. Both cases serve up what is perhaps the most profound and complex issue of their systems: multiple competing claims of ultimate legal authority. Both decisions make important claims for central judicial authority. And yet, in so doing, each inaugurates a regime of mutual accommodation among the competing actors lasting to this very day.

To be sure, the nature of the competition in the two cases is rather different. In the United States, the competition is mostly horizontal and institutional, that is between the Court, the President, and Congress, as well as the people themselves. And the object is interpreting a single object: the Constitution. In Europe, the competition is mostly vertical and systemic, that is between the legal orders of the European Union and its Member States. To be sure, in Europe there is also competition among different institutions to interpret the Union's foundational charter. But this institutional competition is ultimately based on a deeper, systemic competition, that is, a battle about which legal system trumps the other(s) in cases of conflict.

And yet, despite these differences, the practice of accommodating *interpretive* pluralism in the United States shares important features with the practice of accommodating *systems* pluralism in Europe. By juxtaposing accommodation in the two systems, we may understand these practices far better than if we limit ourselves to only one or the other legal order. In particular, we recognise that actors in both systems seem to rely on considerations of voice, expertise, and rights to manage the pluralist stand-off.

[115] See, eg, Case 380/05, *Centro Europa 7 Srl v Ministero delle Comunicazioni e Autorità per le Garanzie nelle Comunicazioni et al*, nyr (12 September 2007) (Opinion of Advocate General Maduro).

II

Case 6/64, *Flaminio Costa v ENEL* and Case 106/77, *Amministrazione delle Finanze dello Stato v Simmenthal SpA*

1

The European Court of Justice and the Doctrine of Supremacy: *Van Gend en Loos*; *Costa v ENEL*; *Simmenthal*

NIAL FENNELLY[1]

The European Community could not have functioned if its treaties and laws had not taken precedence over the laws and constitutions of the Member States. Without the principle of supremacy, the treaty would, according to one writer, 'rapidly have become a dead letter and in all probability the Community would have been dissolved long ago'.[2]

The treaties did not provide for direct effect, still less for supremacy. They established the Court of Justice, which filled the gap. The great decisions are *Van Gend en Loos*,[3] in 1963, *Costa v ENEL*,[4] in 1964, and *Simmenthal*[5] in 1976.

The Member States had previously proceeded on the assumption that they had bound themselves by classical international agreements: these were binding in international law; they had no implications for their domestic legal systems or for individuals. The decisions in *Van Gend en Loos* and *Costa v ENEL* radically affected the essential character of the Community and its relations with its Member States. The constitutional systems of the Member States were fundamentally and permanently altered.

Van Gend en Loos established the principle that treaty provisions are capable of having direct effect and of being relied upon by individuals in national law. It requires very little reflection to conclude that such provisions must necessarily be accorded primacy over conflicting provisions of national law. The special contribution of *Costa v ENEL* was precisely that. It established the principle of primacy.

The resulting relationship was described by the Court in 1991 in its Opinion[6] on the Agreement creating the European Economic Area as follows:

> As the Court of Justice has consistently held, the Community treaties established a new legal order for the benefit of which the States have limited their sovereign rights, in ever wider fields, and the subjects of which comprise not only the Member States but also their nationals ... The essential characteristics of the Community legal order which has thus been established are in

[1] Judge at the Supreme Court of Ireland.

[2] David T Keeling, 'In Praise of Judicial Activism. But what does it mean? And has the European Court of Justice ever practised it?' *Scritti in Onore di Giuseppe Federico Mancini, vol II* (Milano, Dott. A. Giuffré Editore, 1998.)

[3] Case C-26/62 *NV Algemene Transport- en Expeditie Onderneming Van Gend & Loos v Nederlandse Administratie der Belastingen* [1963] ECR 1.

[4] Case 6/64 *Costa v ENEL* [1964] ECR 585.

[5] Case 106/77 *Amministrazione delle Finanze dello Stato v Simmenthal* [1978] ECR 629.

[6] Opinion 1/91 delivered pursuant to Article 228(1) of the Treaty. [1991] ECR I-6079, para 21.

particular its primacy over the law of the Member States and the direct effect of a whole series of provisions which are applicable to their nationals and to the Member States themselves.

Direct Effect: *Van Gend en Loos*

The facts underlying the decision in *Van Gend en Loos* were not such as to set the blood racing. They were unpromising material for a decision of historic significance. The contemporaneous circumstances were no less promising. The case was decided on 5 February 1963, barely five years after the entry into force of the Treaty of Rome and three weeks to the day after President de Gaulle had unilaterally placed a veto on the negotiations on entry of the United Kingdom into the Community. De Gaulle was profoundly attached to the notion of a *Europe des patries*, which would, in truth, have been much closer to the desires of most eurosceptics.

Van Gend en Loos was an importer of urea formaldehyde from the Federal Republic of Germany into the Netherlands. The adoption of the Brussels nomenclature had the effect of increasing the import duty on an import consignment in 1960 from 3 per cent to 8 per cent. Van Gend en Loos argued that the imposition of this increase constituted an infringement of Article 12 of the Treaty, a standstill provision, which prohibited any increase in existing duties.

Van Gend en Loos argued that Article 12 was a self-executing provision requiring no implementing act at either national or Community level. Crucially, it submitted that the article conferred protection on individuals adversely affected by Member State action infringing it. Individuals could invoke Article 12 in the national court.

The Dutch government argued that only the Commission or another Member State pursuant respectively to Articles 169 (now 226) or 170 (now 227) could complain of an infringement by a Member State.

The case raised very directly the respective roles and jurisdictions of the national courts and the Court of Justice. Individuals had no right of access to the Court of Justice in respect of Member State action. Direct effect would be meaningless in the absence of a competent jurisdiction with the power to give it effect.

Advocate General Roemer, in his somewhat cautious Opinion, expressed the view that 'the effect of an international agreement depends in the first place on the legal force which its authors intended its individual provisions to have, whether they are to be merely programmes or declarations of intent, or obligations to act on the international plane or whether some of them are to have a direct effect on the legal system of the Member States'. He emphasised the absence of any provision for a declaration of nullity of national legal rules. This, in his view, would have been essential if it had been intended to make the direct application of the Treaty prevail over national law.

The Court of Justice, nonetheless, made its now historic pronouncement that:

> The conclusion to be drawn from this is that the Community constitutes a new legal order of international law for the benefit of which the states have limited their sovereign rights, albeit within limited fields, and the subjects of which comprise not only Member States but also their nationals. Independently of the legislation of Member States, Community law therefore not only imposes obligations on individuals but is also intended to confer upon them rights which become part of their legal heritage.

Taken on its own, this passage contains no more than a proclamation of a result. A closer look at the reasoning whereby the Court reached this conclusion is that the Court had regard to:

> the fact that the function of the Common Market was of direct concern to interested parties in the Community;
> this implied that the Treaty is more than an agreement which creates obligations between the contracting states;
> the preamble of the Treaty refers not only to governments but to peoples;
> the Community institutions were endowed with sovereign rights, the exercise of which affects both Member States and their citizens.

Perhaps more compellingly, the Court drew attention specifically to the role and purpose of the Article 177 (now 234) mechanism:

> In addition, the task assigned to the Court of Justice under Article 177, the object of which is to secure uniform interpretation of the Treaty by national courts and tribunals, confirms that the states have acknowledged that Community law has an authority which can be invoked by their nationals before those courts and tribunals.

Van Gend en Loos, then, established the principle of direct effect. While this, in itself, represented a major step on the road to recognition of the special status of the Treaty, it did not explicitly address the issue of conflict with national law. Yet, it seems clear that, for Article 12 of the Treaty to prevail, it had to have the effect of overruling the tariff ruling applied by the Dutch authorities. The Court did not rule expressly on supremacy until it made its decision in *Costa v ENEL*.

Costa v ENEL: The Factual Background

What was Mr Costa's problem? On its face, it was the mere fact that he had received an electricity bill for 1,925 lire from ENEL, the then recently established Italian nationalised electricity undertaking. But there was more to it than that. Mr Costa had been a shareholder in Edison Volta, one of the companies affected by the Italian nationalisation law of 6 December 1962. His objection to the nationalisation, insofar as it was legally formulated at all, was that the law contravened a number of articles of the Treaty Establishing the European Economic Community, the Treaty of Rome. Since it is the only treaty involved, I will simply call it that. The articles invoked were: Article 93 (now 88) on state aids; Article 102 (now 97) on distortion of competition; Article 53 (repealed) on establishment; Article 37 (now 31) on state undertakings.

Mr Costa made his objection before the Giudice Conciliatore in Milan. The true bone of contention, of course, was not Mr Costa's electricity bill or even the applicability of the various articles cited. The referring court provided the Court of Justice with scant information on the issues raised and correspondingly little guidance was ultimately provided as to their correct interpretation. The apparently trivial dispute about a modest electricity bill provided a platform for the proclamation of the most fundamental principle of all regarding the relationship between national law and the Treaty.

The Italian Courts

It is particularly instructive to recall the path taken by Mr Costa's dispute through the Italian courts. The Giudice Conciliatore referred the matter on the one hand to the Italian Constitutional Court and, on the other, to the Court of Justice. The former procedure casts useful light on the significance for the Member States, at the relevant time, of the manner of implementation of the treaty and its integration into national law.

The Treaty prescribed no particular method of implementation. Article 247 merely provided:

> The Treaty shall be ratified by the High Contracting Parties in accordance with their respective constitutional requirements.

At the risk of anachronism, it might be pointed out that the Constitution of Ireland established sovereign and exclusive legislative, executive and judicial organs of government. Ireland simply could not have contemplated membership of the Community when it joined in 1973 without the most radical amendment of its Constitution. That required a popular referendum which expressly accorded primacy to the treaties and measures adopted thereunder.

In Italy, however, as observed by Advocate General Lagrange in his Opinion, the Treaty of Rome had been 'ratified by an ordinary law not having the character of a constitutional law and as such not having the power of derogating from either the rules or the principles of the [Italian] Constitution'.

The Advocate General observed that particular problems of conflict with the Treaty appeared to arise in those Member States which had constitutional courts, namely Germany and Italy.

The Italian Constitutional Court started from the point identified above, namely that the Treaty had been ratified by an ordinary law. It had no other or greater status in Italian law. So far as Mr Costa's complaints were concerned, therefore, the effect of the law on nationalisation of electricity would have to be considered on the basis that it was a later potentially inconsistent law. It would have effect, therefore, in accordance with the normal rules concerning the succession of laws in time. In other words, to the extent that the later law was found to be inconsistent with the earlier one (ratifying the Treaty), its effect would be to repeal it. A further consequence was that there was no need to inquire into whether the later law on nationalisation infringed the 'obligations assumed by virtue of the Treaty'. For the same reason, it was pointless to refer questions of interpretation to the Court of Justice.

Finally, if it were indeed to be the case that Italy had infringed the Treaty, that was not a matter for the Italian courts, but rather should be made the subject matter of an infringement action brought by the Commission in the Court of Justice against Italy as a Member State. This classic international-law approach had already at the date of the decision of the Constitutional Court (24 February to 7 March 1964) been significantly overtaken by the decision of the Court of Justice in *Van Gend en Loos.*

Costa v ENEL: The Decision

The opinion of Advocate General Lagrange took a notably more positive approach to the Treaty than that of Advocate General Roemer in *Van Gend en Loos.* He cited, without naming the case, *Van Gend en Loos*, for its adoption of direct effect of Articles 12 and 31: 'They are, to use the hallowed expression, "self-executing".' Having expounded the need to protect individual rights, he referred to the decision of the Italian Constitutional Court. He thought that there would be "disastrous consequences" if that precedent were maintained and that it 'would risk ... the functioning of the system of institutions established by the Treaty and, as a consequence, the very future of the Common Market'.[7]

Clearly, *Van Gend en Loos* had provided a springboard from which the Court could jump to the next stage. It repeated the reference to limitation of 'sovereign rights' and that the Member States had bound 'both their nationals and themselves'. Turning to address more directly the Italian government's argument (which reflected the decision of the Constitutional Court) it declared:

> The integration into the laws of each Member State of provisions which derive from the Community, and more generally the terms and the spirit of the Treaty, make it impossible for the states, as a corollary, to accord precedence to a unilateral and subsequent measure over a legal system accepted by them on a basis of reciprocity. Such a measure cannot therefore be inconsistent with that legal system. The executive force of Community law cannot vary from one State to another in deference to subsequent domestic laws, without jeopardizing the attainment of the objectives of the Treaty ...[8]

The Court built upon the precedent of *Van Gend en Loos* in two remarkable following passages:

> The law stemming from the Treaty, an independent source of law, could not, because of its special and original nature, be overridden by domestic legal provisions, however framed, without being deprived of its character as Community law and without the legal basis of the Community itself being called into question.
>
> The transfer by the states from their domestic legal system to the Community legal system of the rights and obligations arising under the Treaty carries with it a permanent limitation of their sovereign rights, against which a subsequent unilateral act incompatible with the concept of the Community cannot prevail. Consequently Article 177 is to be applied regardless of any domestic law, whenever questions relating to the interpretation of the Treaty arise.

Implications of Supremacy: *Simmenthal*

The decision in *Costa v ENEL* did not persuade the Italian government or at least some Italian courts that, in the event of conflict with national law, immediate precedence had to be accorded to Community law. The imposition of charges at point of import for veterinary and public health inspection of meat products was contested by the importer, Simmenthal, as being incompatible with Treaty provisions on the free movement of goods. These questions were referred to the Court of Justice pursuant to Article 177 of the Treaty, resulting in a decision favourable to Simmenthal: Case 35/76 *Simmenthal SpA v Italian Minister for Finance*.[9] The referring court, the Pretore di Susa, in application of the answers provided by the Luxembourg Court, made an order for repayment of the charges.

[7] Page 605 of the report.
[8] Page 594 of the report.
[9] [1976] ECR 1871.

The Italian fiscal authorities objected that the Pretore did not have the power simply to refuse to apply a national law because it appeared to conflict with Community law. The law would either have to be changed by the legislature or declared unconstitutional by the Italian Constitutional Court. The Pretore thus made a second reference to the Court of Justice.

Advocate General Reischl, relying heavily on the precedents of *Van Gend en Loos* and *Costa v ENEL*, advised the Court that:

> in the case of directly applicable Community provisions, conflicting national provisions which were adopted subsequently may no longer be applied; this position applies with immediate effect and it is not necessary to await repeal by a legislature or a declaration by a constitutional court that they are unconstitutional.

The judgment of the Court was even more emphatic. It insisted that direct applicability meant that: 'Rules of Community law must be fully and uniformly applied in all the Member States from the date of their entry into force'; they 'render automatically inapplicable any conflicting provisions of current national law'; 'every national court must ... apply Community law in its entirety ... and must accordingly set aside any provision of national law which may conflict with it, whether prior or subsequent to the Community rule.'[10] The provision for direct inapplicability directly answered the concern which Advocate General Roemer had expressed in *Van Gend en Loos* that the Treaty would have had to provide for the annulment of national laws.

Some Comments

The judgments in *Van Gend en Loos* and *Costa v ENEL* represented, not just in their time but permanently, a giant leap on the road to European integration. That proposition would not be disputed either by the friends or enemies of the Court. The decision in *Simmenthal (2)* does not so much break new ground as draw the inevitable conclusions from the first two. Though these judgments did not attract particular controversy in their time, they have been subjected retrospectively to the most searching analysis and sometimes the most severe criticism.

The authors of these decisions were visionaries. In 1995, the late Judge Giuseppe Federico Mancini explained[11] how the expression 'une certaine idée de l'Europe', a phrase coined by former Judge Pierre Pescatore and based in turn on General de Gaulle's invocation of 'une certaine idée de la France',[12] encapsulated the 'synergy produced by the coming together of men who, though steeped in different cultures and legal traditions, shared a common set of values'.

Before embarking on the debate between merits, on the one hand, of the visionaries ('judicial activists') and, on the other, of strict constructionists, it is worth recalling that these decisions were made by the Court of Justice of a Community of only six Member States. It is, therefore, legitimate to ask whether the Member States who have joined the Community and now the Union since 1964 can convincingly complain that they are

[10] Paras 13–21 of the judgment.

[11] Giuseppe Federico Mancini, 'Crosscurrents and the Tide at the European Court of Justice' (1995) 4 Irish Journal of European Law 120, 195.

[12] Charles de Gaulle, *Mémoires de Guerre, L'Appel* 1940–42. Vol 1 (Paris, Librairie Plon, 1954).

bound by these decisions. Those States which have subsequently joined have done so with their eyes open. They have accepted the *acquis communautaire.* In particular, they must be deemed to have been fully aware of these two historic cases.

It is nonetheless worthwhile to consider the justification, at the level of legal analysis, of the conclusions reached in these cases. There are two possible approaches.

The visionary approach has undoubtedly triumphed. It proceeds from the premise, established in *Van Gend en Loos*, that 'the Community constitutes a new legal order of international law' and that, as established in *Costa v ENEL*, 'the law stemming from the Treaty' constitutes 'an independent source of law' of a 'special and original nature'. The consequence was that it was not possible for the Member States 'to accord precedence to a unilateral and subsequent measure over a legal system accepted by them on a basis of reciprocity'.

Once the premise, so expressed, is accepted, the conclusion is compelling. The relevant Treaty provisions are 'self-executing'. They apply automatically. Advocate General Lagrange was certainly correct. He predicted 'disastrous' consequences, if the contrary approach were to be adopted. The entire system envisaged by the Treaty would be set at naught. If Member States were to have the power to supersede directly effective Treaty provisions by adopting and enforcing later inconsistent laws, the legal system established by the Treaty would be at the mercy of the laws of the individual Member States. Community rules, by their very nature, must be uniform. They must apply equally in every Member State. Without uniform application, the very notion of the Community would become meaningless.

It is, nonetheless, legitimate to ask whether the premise underlying the judgment of the Court was legally justified. The Court has been widely and eloquently accused of unilaterally expanding its own power. Was the Court guilty of the logical fallacy of reasoning from its own assumption of the desired result? That would have been an extreme example of the doctrine of *effet utile.*

To answer that question, it is necessary to go back to *Van Gend en Loos*, and the principle of direct effect. Supremacy of Community law was, if not in pure logic, in practical reality an inevitable corollary of that doctrine.

On these issues, the Treaty is silent. It does not provide either that its provisions are to have direct effect or that they are to take priority over conflicting provisions of national law. The Court was left to rely on only two practical and material Treaty provisions. The Treaty ordained that regulations adopted by the institutions should be directly applicable. It also established the novelty, for an international agreement, of the procedure of reference for preliminary ruling pursuant to Article 177 (now Article 234).

It is difficult to discern any purpose in the Article 234 procedure except that the courts of the Member States are obliged to apply Community law. The Treaty, however, says nothing about the obligations of the courts of the Member States, whether or not they have referred questions to the Court of Justice. Equally, the Treaty says nothing about the direct effect or applicability of its own provisions. On the other hand, if regulations are to be directly applicable, why should the same not apply to Treaty articles expressed in terms so clear that they can only have been intended to be effective? Such arguments may be compelling, but they are, at most, inferences. They lead logically to the conclusion that Treaty provisions were intended to have direct effect and, consequently, that they should have primacy over conflicting national legal provisions. However, they find little express support in the words of the Treaty.

The Court of Justice built a great and enduring edifice on the slim foundation of Article 189 (now 249) and Article 177 (now 234). The European Union's character as an international federal polity derives in no small measure from the critical decisions of the Court of Justice in the cases discussed in this Chapter. This has not silenced its critics, but the Court continues to earn the respect of lawyers throughout the world for its achievements and the breadth of its vision.

2

Costa v ENEL and *Simmenthal*: Primacy of European Law

INGOLF PERNICE*

Introduction

Case 4/64, *Costa v ENEL*, decided by the European Court of Justice on 15 July 1964, has become one of the most famous pieces of European jurisprudence. Implicitly, the Court had already accepted the concept of primacy the year before in Case 26/62, *Van Gend & Loos*, stating that provisions of the EEC Treaty, like the standstill clause of the former Article 12 instructing Member States not to increase import duties on goods imported from other Member States, could produce direct effect and be invoked before the national courts by the individual concerned against conflicting provisions of national law. The doctrines of direct effect and primacy go, indeed, hand in hand. It was made very clear in *Costa v ENEL* that:

> The law stemming from the Treaty, an independent source of law, could not, because of its special and original nature, be overridden by domestic legal provisions, however framed.[13]

Thus, national courts shall give precedence to European law in any case of conflict. This is the basis of what has become the 'supremacy',[14] or as others like Koen Lenaerts and Piet van Nuffel call it: 'primacy' of Community law,[15] one of the most fundamental but also controversial principles of European law.

The ECJ has given a series of important arguments for this approach, and confirmed the principle in various cases developing an established jurisprudence, though with some important modulation. More than 40 years later, the basic arguments seem to be as valid as in 1964, and the primary law of the Union more and more confirms the approach taken by the Court. Scholars widely regard the Court's early decisions as the first step towards the 'constitutionalisation' of the European Union. This view may, however, be questioned if one looks at the original concepts and provisions of the Treaty as well as at the European Summit of June 2007. The conclusions of that summit appear all the more surprising, since some national supreme or constitutional courts are reluctant to unconditionally

* Professor Dr jur, Chair for public, international and European Law of the Humboldt University of Berlin, managing director of the Walter Hallstein Institute for European Constitutional Law (WHI) of the Humboldt University of Berlin (www.whi-berlin.de).

[13] Judgment of the Court of 15 July 1964, Case 4/64 *Flaminio Costa v ENEL*, ECR 1944, 1.

[14] See S Wetherill, *Cases and Materials on EU Law*, 7th edn (Oxford, Oxford University Press, 2006) 89.

[15] Koen Lenaerts and Piet van Nuffel, *Constitutional Law of the European Union*, 2nd edn (London, Sweet & Maxwell, 2005), § I-019.

accept the primacy of European law. The argument of this contribution is that this reluctance should be understood to reflect precisely the pluralistic character of the EU construction as a composed system which is not based upon hierarchies but upon the close co-operation between European and national courts. Both European and national courts are, within the limits of their respective competencies, mutually guardians of Community law, of the limits of the competencies conferred to the Union, and of the common European values.

ECJ Jurisprudence of Primacy

Regarding the principle of primacy, it is worth reading the reasoning of the Court's leading case again and again. In *Costa v ENEL* the ECJ is developing basically three important arguments for establishing the principle of primacy of European law: a structural, a material and a textual argument. The reasons given are far more than just grounds for the decision taken in this case. The judgment rather establishes and explains the very nature of the European legal order as a system composed of two complementary bodies of law, European and national, applicable to the same citizens.

The Autonomy and Special Character of European Law

First, the structural argument is based upon the autonomy and the specific character of Community law.[16] The Court argues:

> By contrast with ordinary international treaties, the EEC Treaty has created its own legal system which, on the entry into force of the Treaty, became an integral part of the legal systems of the Member States and which their courts are bound to apply.

By creating a Community of unlimited duration, having its own institutions, its own personality, its own legal capacity and capacity of representation on the international plane and, more particularly, real powers stemming from a limitation of sovereignty or a transfer of powers from the States to the Community, the Member States have limited their sovereign rights, albeit within limited fields, and have thus created a body of law which binds both their nationals and themselves.

European law, thus, is considered an autonomous, new and specific legal system based upon a transfer of sovereign rights to the European institutions with 'real powers'. Its binding force upon the Member States and their nationals is not derived from national law or decisions of the Member States whatsoever, but due to the Treaty itself, which created a system which *ipso iure* forms an integral part of the legal system of each Member State.

[16] See René Barents, *The Autonomy of Community Law*, 2004.

Reciprocity and Non-discrimination

Secondly, and explaining further its first argument, the Court adds a more material consideration, referring to reciprocity and the principle of non-discrimination, as found in the terms of the Treaty.

> The integration into the laws of each Member State of provisions which derive from the Community, and more generally the terms and the spirit of the Treaty, make it impossible for the States, as a corollary, to accord precedence to a unilateral and subsequent measure over a legal system accepted by them on a basis of reciprocity. Such a measure cannot therefore be inconsistent with that legal system. The executive force of Community law cannot vary from one State to another in deference to subsequent domestic laws, without jeopardising the attainment of the objectives of the Treaty set out in Article 5(2) and giving rise to the discrimination prohibited by Article 7.

The Court, thus, seems to refer to the very foundation of validity of law and its effective recognition: in any social system, but particularly in a 'Community of law', as the Court develops in its later case law[17] taking up a very fundamental concept developed by Walter Hallstein,[18] in a system which is based upon voluntary recognition of the binding force of law and does not, at its level, dispose of any means for physical coercion, law is respected because—and as long as—it is equally applied in all cases, to all individuals which are covered by the terms of the provision in question. For every individual, the trust in the full respect of equally applicable terms of law by all the others justifies its own obedience. There cannot be privileges nor discrimination. It is ultimately the reciprocity of such mutual trust among citizens as much as among their Member States which allows a legal system to function, at the national level as well as the European.

In this light, the ECJ rightly sees one of its fundamental functions under Articles 220 and 234 in safeguarding the equal application of the European law in all Member States and, thus, the unity of the European law. The Court's right to interpret European law and its exclusive power to judge upon the validity of its provisions under Article 230 and, according to the *Foto-Frost* decision,[19] under Article 234 EC is indeed the result of European law being recognised as law.

Terms of the Treaty

These considerations in some way correspond to the concept of a social contract[20] based upon the idea of egality and reciprocity;[21] they are supported by further references to the terms of the Treaty. The Court argues in two ways: one is to underline that where

[17] Judgment of the Court of 23 April 1986, Case 294/83 *Parti écologiste 'Les Verts' v European Parliament* [1986] ECR 1339 (ground 23).

[18] Walter Hallstein, *Der unvollendete Bundesstaat*, 1969, 33 *ff*; Franz C Mayer, 'Europa als Rechtsgemeinschaft' in GF Schuppert, I Pernice and U Haltern (eds), *Europawissenschaft*, 2005, 429 *ff*.

[19] Judgment of the Court of 22 October 1987, Case 314/85 *Foto-Frost v Hauptzollamt Lübeck-Ost* ECR 1987, 4199.

[20] Extending this approach: Ingolf Pernice, Franz Mayer and Stephan Wernicke, 'Renewing the European Social Contract. The Challenge of Institutional Reform and Enlargement in the Light of Multilevel Constitutionalism' in Mads Andenas and John Gardener (eds), *Can Europe Have a Constitution?* (2001) *Kings College Law Journal* 12, 60.

[21] See more in detail Ingolf Pernice, *Das Verhältnis europäischer zu nationalen Gerichten im europäischen Verfassungsverbund*, Berlin 2006, 23 *ff*.

derogations are allowed, the Treaty expressly so provides, the other is the provision for regulations in Article 198 EEC which has, meanwhile, become Article 249 EC.

> Wherever the Treaty grants the States the right to act unilaterally, it does this by clear and precise provisions (for example Articles 15, 93(3), 223, 224 and 225). Applications by Member States for authority to derogate from the Treaty are subject to a special authorization procedure (for example Articles 8(4), 17(4), 25, 26, 73, the third subparagraph of Article 93(2), and 226) which would lose their purpose if the Member States could renounce their obligations by means of an ordinary law.
> The precedence of Community law is confirmed by Article 189, whereby a regulation 'shall be binding' and 'directly applicable in all Member States'. This provision, which is subject to no reservation, would be quite meaningless if a State could unilaterally nullify its effects by means of a legislative measure which could prevail over Community law.

While it is true that the Treaty does not explicitly provide for the primacy of European law, express provisions for specific derogations indicate that the power for Member States to derogate from the Treaty seem to confirm the principle as a general rule. More important, however, is the reference to Article 189. This provision shows that the direct effect of provisions of European law is part of its system, expressly agreed upon, and not merely a praetoric development by the ECJ. The significance of this provision cannot be overestimated: no (other) international convention or organisation, so far, is empowered to legislate with direct effect, creating rights and obligations of the citizens. This power, to be regarded as an expression of the sovereign rights conferred to the Union by the Treaty, is a specific characteristic by which the European construction is distinguished from other arrangements in kind, not only gradually.

Conclusion

After all, the Court concludes with a functional argument: what is at stake is the legal base and, ultimately, the functioning of the Union:

> The obligations undertaken under the Treaty establishing the Community would not be unconditional, but merely contingent, if they could be called in question by subsequent legislative acts of the signatories.
>
> . . .
>
> It follows from all these observations that the law stemming from the Treaty, an independent source of law, could not, because of its special and original nature, be overridden by domestic legal provisions, however framed, without being deprived of its character as Community law and without the legal basis of the Community itself being called into question.

In some way the ECJ, indeed, concludes from what it considers the 'terms and the spirit' of the Treaty, the principle of primacy is the logical consequence from the establishment of the European Community by the Member States as an instrument for action in the common interest at a supranational level and a legal system which is supposed to function effectively. Given the objectives of the Treaty, the terms in which it was drafted and the role accorded to the Court of Justice in Article 164 EEC which is now Article 220 EC, to ensure the observation of the law in the interpretation and application of the Treaty, there was no alternative to asserting the principle of primacy.

The reasoning developed in *Costa v ENEL* has been repeated and confirmed in the later case law,[22] where the Court has made clear that primacy even extends to national constitutional law[23] and would even, as stated in Case 106/77 *Simmenthal*, 'preclude the valid adoption of new national legislative measures to the extent to which they would be incompatible with Community provisions'.[24]

Primacy and the Positive Law

Though no clear express provision on the principle of primacy has been introduced into the Treaties up to now, some attempts exist to include it implicitly into the primary law. The Protocol (no 30) annexed to the 1997 Treaty of Amsterdam on the application of the principles of subsidiarity and proportionality refers in paragraph 2 to the *acquis communautaire* and confirms that the principles established by the ECJ on the relationship 'shall not affect the principles developed by the Court of Justice regarding the relationship between national and Community law'. In 2004, the Treaty establishing a Constitution for Europe was signed in Rome including, in Article I-6, a provision under which:

> the Constitution and law adopted by the institutions of the Union in exercising competences conferred on it shall have primacy over the law of the Member States.

Even though this provision remained unclear as to whether the 'law' includes national constitutional law, this provision was considered to be a major achievement in clarity and transparency. Yet, after the peoples of France and the Netherlands had rejected the Constitutional Treaty, the compromise found on the reform of the European Union in June 2007 did not retain this clause. Instead the Draft IGC Mandate attached to the Conclusions of the European Council[25] provides for a Declaration concerning the primacy of EU law as follows:

> Whilst the Article on primacy of Union law will not be reproduced in the TEU, the IGC will agree on the following Declaration: 'The Conference recalls that, in accordance with well settled

[22] See, eg, Judgment of the Court of 19 June 1990, Case C-213/89 *R v Secretary of State for Transport, ex parte Factortame Ltd and others* [1990] ECR I-02433 (ground 20): 'The Court has also held that any provision of a national legal system and any legislative, administrative or judicial practice which might impair the effectiveness of Community law by withholding from the national court having jurisdiction to apply such law the power to do everything necessary at the moment of its application to set aside national legislative provisions which might prevent, even temporarily, Community rules from having full force and effect are incompatible with those requirements, which are the very essence of Community law'.

[23] Judgment of the Court of 17 December 1970, Case 11/70 *Internationale Handelsgesellschaft mbH v Einfuhr- und Vorratsstelle für Getreide und Futtermittel* [1970] ECR 1125 (ground 3): 'Recourse to the legal rules or concepts of national law in order to judge the validity of measures adopted by the institutions of the Community would have an adverse effect on the uniformity and efficacy of Community law. The validity of such measures can only be judged in the light of Community law. In fact, the law stemming from the Treaty, an independent source of law, cannot because of its very nature be overridden by rules of national law, however framed, without being deprived of its character as Community law and without the legal basis of the Community itself being called in question. Therefore the validity of a Community measure or its effect within a Member State cannot be affected by allegations that it runs counter to either fundamental rights as formulated by the constitution of that State or the principles of a national constitutional structure.'

[24] Judgment of the Court of 9 March 1978, Case 106/77 *Amministrazione delle Finanze dello Stato v Simmenthal SpA* [1978] ECR 629 (ground 17).

[25] www.consilium.europa.eu/ueDocs/cms_Data/docs/pressData/en/ec/94932.pdf, 16.

> case-law of the EU Court of Justice, the Treaties and the law adopted by the Union on the basis of the Treaties have primacy over the law of Member States, under the conditions laid down by the said case-law.'

This solution does not seem to have the same authority as an express Treaty provision. It makes clear, however, that *Costa v ENEL* is not questioned but confirmed by the European Council.

Judicial Constitutionalisation of the Treaty

The jurisprudence was interpreted by scholarship as originating the process of 'constitutionalisation' of the European Union up to the Treaty establishing a Constitution for Europe.[26] Joseph HH Weiler stresses that 'the second "constitutionalizing" doctrine, supremacy' gives the principle of direct effect as developed in Van Gend & Loos the 'full impact'. Regarding direct effect he observes that:

> The implications of this doctrine were and are far reaching. The European Court reversed the normal presumption of public international law whereby international legal obligations are result-oriented and addressed to states. Public international law typically allows the internal constitutional order of a state to determine the method and extent to which international obligations may, if at all, produce effects for individuals within the legal order of the state.[27]

The question is, however, whether it was the Court which reversed that presumption, or the Member States—and their peoples—themselves, in establishing the European Economic Community according to the specific powers and procedures provided for in their respective constitutions such as Article 24(1) of the German Grundgesetz.[28] Indeed, the EEC Treaty in paragraph 2 of its Article 189 (which is now Article 249), as the Court referred to in *Costa v ENEL*, expressly states that 'a regulation shall have general application. It shall be binding in its entirety and directly applicable in all Member States'. This conception does not follow the traditional thinking of international law. But as a lesson drawn from the horrors of two world wars, it reflects the new and—compared with the traditional doctrine of national sovereignty—the revolutionary approach put forward in 1950 by Jean Monnet and Robert Schuman to merge certain sovereign powers at a supranational level by establishing a common European authority as a device for preserving peace and promoting prosperity. From the beginning, European integration was meant to constitute a new kind of political organisation, leaving behind nationalism and the structures of the Westphalian system which has failed to preserve peace in Europe.

[26] Eric Stein, 'Lawyers, Judges and the Making of a Transnational Constitution' (1981) *American Journal of International Law* 1, 10 *ff*; G Federico Mancini, 'The Making of a Constitution for Europe' (1989) *CML Rev*, 595, 599 *ff*; Koen Lenaerts, 'Constitutionalism and the many Faces of Federalism' (1990) American Journal of Comparative Law, 205, 208 *ff*; Joseph HH Weiler, 'The Transformation of Europe', (1999) *Yale Law Journal*, 2403, 2413 *ff*.

[27] Weiler, *Transformatio* (note 26), 2413.

[28] More details regarding the specific 'integration clauses' in national constitutions can be found in Anneli Albi, 'Europe: Articles in the Constitutions of the Central and Eastern European Countries' (2005) *CML Rev* 399 *ff*.; see also the national reports on European law and national constitutions, in *FIDE XX Congress London 2002*, published by the British Institute of International and Comparative Law, London, vols I (2002) and II (2003), as well as Jaqueline Dutheil de la Rochère and Ingolf Pernice, General report, *ibid*, vol II, 1, 12 *ff*.

Thus, the peoples of the Member States, represented by their governments acting in the form of an international treaty and by their respective parliaments—if not by referendum—can be regarded as having conferred limited legislative and other powers upon the European institutions established by the EEC Treaty within a 'Community based on the rule of law' (Rechtsgemeinschaft), as Walter Hallstein put it, which has little in common with traditional international organisations.

In *Van Gend & Loos* and *Costa v ENEL*, consequently, the Court just gave effect to what was the new and specific nature of the European Community, and exposed what this means in practice. The specific nature was subsequently acknowledged by the German Federal Constitutional Court which in a Decision of 18 October 1967 called the EEC Treaty 'in some way the Constitution of this Community'.[29] This qualification does indeed reflect what was already laid down in the explanatory memorandum to the German act of ratification of the EEC Treaty in 1957. The memorandum said that the Treaty not only, like a trade agreement, establishes rights and obligations of the States party to the agreement but also rather creates a European body of a constitutional nature. Public authority, the memorandum exposes, is partly transferred from the Member States to the European Economic Community.[30]

In a judgment of 13 April 1986, the European Court of Justice followed this line and called the EEC Treaty the 'basic constitutional charter' of the Community.[31] In its Opinion 1/91 on the Draft Agreement creating the European Economic Area the Court clearly explained the difference from international treaties:

> The context in which the objective of the agreement is situated also differs from that in which the Community aims are pursued. The European Economic Area is to be established on the basis of an international treaty which merely creates rights and obligations as between the Contracting Parties and provides for no transfer of sovereign rights to the inter-governmental institutions which it sets up. In contrast, the EEC Treaty, albeit concluded in the form of an international agreement, none the less constitutes the constitutional charter of a Community based on the rule of law. The Community treaties established a new legal order for the benefit of which the States have limited their sovereign rights and the subjects of which comprise not only Member States but also their nationals. The essential characteristics of the Community legal order which has thus been established are in particular its primacy over the law of the Member States and the direct effect of a whole series of provisions.[32]

[29] BVerfG, 1 BvR 248/63 und 216/67, Decision of 18 October 1967 EG-Verordnungen, (www.servat.unibe.ch/law/dfr/bv022293.html) II.2.c.: 'Der EWG-Vertrag stellt gewissermaßen die Verfassung dieser Gemeinschaft dar. Die von den Gemeinschaftsorganen im Rahmen ihrer vertragsgemäßen Kompetenzen erlassenen Rechtsvorschriften, das "sekundäre Gemeinschaftsrecht", bilden eine eigene Rechtsordnung, deren Normen weder Völkerrecht noch nationales Recht der Mitgliedstaaten sind. Das Gemeinschaftsrecht und das innerstaatliche Recht der Mitgliedstaaten sind "zwei selbständige, voneinander verschiedene Rechtsordnungen"; das vom EWG-Vertrag geschaffene Recht fließt aus einer "autonomen Rechtsquelle"' (Sammlung der Rechtsprechung des Gerichtshofs der Europäischen Gemeinschaften Bd VIII S 97 [110]; Bd X S 1251 [1270]).

[30] Law of 27.7.1957 on the Treaties of 25.3.1957 establishing the European Economic Community and the European Atomic Community, sub 'D Vertrag zur Gründung der Europäischen Wirtschaftsgemeinschaft I Grundzüge', Deutscher Bundestag, 2 Wahlperiode 1953 Drucksache Nr 3440, Anlage A S 108: 'Der Vertrag regelt nicht nur wie ein Wirtschafts- und Handelsabkommen Rechte und Pflichten der beteiligten Staaten untereinander . . . Der Vertrag ruft vielmehr ein europäisches Gebilde verfassungsrechtlicher Gattung ins Leben. Hoheitsfunktionen auf dem Gebiet der Wirtschaft werden aus der Zuständigkeit der Vertragsstaaten ausgegliedert und der Europäischen Wirtschaftsgemeinschaft übertragen.'

[31] Judgment of the Court of 23 April 1986, Case 294/83 *Parti écologiste 'Les Verts' v European Parliament* ECR 1986, 1339 (ground 23).

[32] Opinion of the Court of 14 December 1991, Opinion 1/91, European Economic Area, [1991] ECR I-6079.

Conceptualising the European Treaties as 'constitutional', therefore, corresponds to their very nature and function: they establish, organise and legitimise the exercise of supranational public authority, define the division of powers between the Member States and the European institutions and the legal status of the citizens, organise the decision-making procedures, the participation of the citizens in the exercise of these powers and the necessary devices for judicial review. This is what constitutions are about,[33] and this is the reason why the Treaty establishing a Constitution for Europe rightly used the term Constitution for what was, from the beginning, intended to be the legal basis of an ever closer Union of the peoples of Europe.

'Constitutionalising', in this light, rather means the process of developing these very functions of the Treaties: consolidating and completing its terms, in particular with a view to the fundamental rights of the individuals, and developing the institutional basis of democratic legitimacy and accountability, the principles of subsidiarity and proportionality, judicial review and effective action in the spheres of European competences.

Hence, to abandon all the clarifications introduced by the Treaty establishing a Constitution for Europe would appear as an enormous step back. Yet, in order to meet the difficulties of certain Member States (or governments) to conceptualise a constitution without the implication that this would lead to a European 'super-state', the Draft IGC Mandate, in point 3, states:

> The TEU and the Treaty on the Functioning of the Union will not have a constitutional character. The terminology used throughout the Treaties will reflect this change: the term 'Constitution' will not be used, the 'Union Minister for Foreign Affairs' will be called High Representative of the Union for Foreign Affairs and Security Policy and the denominations 'law' and 'framework law' will be abandoned, the existing denominations 'regulations', 'directives' and 'decisions' being retained. Likewise, there will be no article in the amended Treaties mentioning the symbols of the EU such as the flag, the anthem or the motto.[34]

As the acquis of the presently existing EU is not questioned but further developed by incorporating the substance of the Constitutional Treaty in the future primary law, this statement will not, however, affect the achievements of the ECJ case law. The reference to this case law regarding the principle of primacy,[35] in particular, confirms that the compromise found in Brussels is not intended to reverse the relationship between national and European law as established by the Court since *Costa v ENEL*.

Reaction of National Constitutional Courts

Possibly as a result of the 'absolutist' approach taken by the ECJ in the *Simmenthal* case, many national Supreme or Constitutional Courts are reluctant to unconditionally accept the primacy of European law. While the principle has not yet been violated in practice,

[33] For this argument see in more detail Ingolf Pernice, 'Multilevel Constitutionalism in the European Union' (2002) *EL Rev*, 511, 527–9.

[34] See note 25 above, 16.

[35] *Ibid*, with the text quoted.

these national Constitutional and Supreme Courts have made clear that from a Member States' point of view the national constitutions are and ultimately remain the highest mandatory reference.

The German Federal Constitutional Court

It was the German Federal Constitution Court which took the lead as early as in its *Solange* jurisprudence of 1974 and 1986, confirmed by the *Maastricht* decision in 1993.[36] On the basis of co-operation among the European and national courts it reserves itself the right to judge upon the applicability of European provisions in Germany if evidence is given for a substantial and general disregard, by the European institutions, of the minimum requirements for the protection of fundamental rights or of a clear *ultra vires* act. The Danish Højesteret[37] and the Czech Constitutional Court[38] basically follow this line.

The French Conseil Constitutionnel

The French Conseil Constitutionnel acknowledges, in particular with a view to Article I-5 of the Constitutional Treaty, that the French Constitution remains at the top of the French

[36] References and the wording of this case law and relevant decisions from other Member States can be found on the internet under: www.ecln.net/index.php?option=com_content&task=view&id=17&Itemid=35. For an analysis of the case law see Ingolf Pernice, *Verhältnis* (note 9), 21–43.

[37] Judgment of 6 April 1998, i sag I 361/1997, German translation (1999) EuGRZ, 49, 52: 'The Danish courts therefore may declare a Community measure inapplicable for Denmark, if the extraordinary situation arose that it is possible to conclude with the necessary degree of certainty that the measure after having been confirmed by the European Court of Justice is founded on an application of the Treaty which exceeds the limits of the sovereign powers transferred by the act of accession' (translation by the author).

[38] Judgment of 8 March 2006, Pl US 50/04 *Sugar Quota Regulation II* (http://test.concourt.cz/angl_verze/doc/p-50–04.html): 'The Czech Republic conferred these powers upon EC organs. In the Constitutional Court's view, this conferral of a part of its powers is naturally a conditional conferral, as the original bearer of sovereignty, as well as the powers flowing therefrom, still remains the Czech Republic, whose sovereignty is still founded upon Art 1 para 1 of the Constitution of the Czech Republic. In the Constitutional Court's view, the conditional nature of the delegation of these powers is manifested on two planes: the formal and the substantive plane. The first of these planes concerns the power attributes of state sovereignty itself, the second plane concerns the substantive component of the exercise of state power. In other words, the delegation of a part of the powers of national organs may persist only so long as these powers are exercised in a manner that is compatible with the preservation of the foundations of state sovereignty of the Czech Republic, and in a manner which does not threaten the very essence of the substantive law-based state. In such determination the Constitutional Court is called upon to protect constitutionalism (Art 83 of the Constitution of the Czech Republic). According to Art 9 para 2 of the Constitution of the Czech Republic, the essential attributes of a democratic state governed by the rule of law, remain beyond the reach of the Constituent Assembly itself.
Direct applicability in national law and applicational precedence of a regulation follows from Community law doctrine itself, as it has emerged from the case law of the ECJ. If membership of the EC brings with it a certain limitation on the powers of the national organs in favour of Community organs, one of the manifestations of such limitation must necessarily also be a restriction on Member States' freedom to designate the effect of Community law in their national legal orders. Art 10a of the Constitution of the Czech Republic thus operates in both directions: it forms the normative basis for the transfer of powers and is simultaneously that provision of the Czech Constitution which opens up the national legal order to the operation of Community law, including rules relating to its effects within the legal order.
The Constitutional Court is of the view that—as concerns the operation of Community law in the national law—such approach must be adopted as would not permanently fix doctrine as to the effects of Community law in the national legal order. A different approach would, after all, not correspond to the fact that the very doctrine of the effects that Community acts call forth in national law has gone through and is still undergoing a dynamic development. This conception also best ensures that which was already mentioned, that is, the conditionality of the transfer of certain powers.'

internal legal system, even if the Treaty is named 'Constitution'.[39] Thus, also the transposition into national law of a Community directive is seen as a requirement of the national Constitution, and, as long as this Constitution does not expressly provide otherwise it remains the exclusive competence of the ECJ to judge upon the validity of a Community directive.[40]

The Spanish Tribunal Constitucional

In Spain, the Tribunal Constitucional distinguishes between two categories, 'primacía', which is attributed to European law under Article 93 of the Spanish Constitution, and 'supremacía', which is reserved to the Constitution.[41] The first regards the application of European law within the national system, both seen as co-existing and complementing each other. The second focuses on the position of the Constitution at the top of the system of law applicable in Spain. Having confirmed that supremacy of the Spanish Constitution is not questioned by the primacy so recognised, the Tribunal Constitucional nevertheless relies, in the exceptional case of a conflict, upon the exit clause of Article I-60 of the Constitutional Treaty.[42]

[39] Décision no 2004–505 DC du 19 novembre 2004 Traité établissant une Constitution pour l'Europe, www.conseil-constitutionnel.fr/decision/2004/2004505/2004505dc.htm: qu'en effet, il résulte notamment de son article I-5, relatif aux relations entre l'Union et les Etats membres, que cette dénomination est sans incidence sur l'existence de la Constitution française et sa place au sommet de l'ordre juridique interne.'

[40] Decision no 2004–496 DC of the Conseil Constitutionnel of 10 June 2004—Loi pour la confiance dans l'économie numérique, www.conseil-constitutionnel.fr/decision/2004/2004496/2004496dc.htm (ground 7): 'la transposition en droit interne d'une directive communautaire résulte d'une exigence constitutionnelle à laquelle il ne pourrait être fait obstacle qu'en raison d'une disposition expresse contraire de la Constitution; qu'en l'absence d'une telle disposition, il n'appartient qu'au juge communautaire, saisi le cas échéant à titre préjudiciel, de contrôler le respect par une directive communautaire tant des compétences définies par les traités que des droits fondamentaux garantis par l'article 6 du Traité sur l'Union européenne.'

[41] Declaration DTC 1/2004 of 13 December 2004, on the Treaty establishing a Constitution for Europe, www.ecln.net/documents/Decisions-Spain/2004-european-constitution.pdf, 11: 'Que la Constitución es la norma suprema del Ordenamiento español es cuestión que, aun cuando no se proclame expresamente en ninguno de sus preceptos, se deriva sin duda del enunciado de muchos de ellos, entre otros de sus arts. 1.2, 9.1, 95, 161, 163, 167, 168 y disposición derogatoria, y es consustancial a su condición de norma fundamental; supremacía o rango superior de la Constitución frente a cualquier otra norma, y en concreto frente a los tratados internacionales, que afirmamos en la Declaración 1/1992 (FJ 1). Pues bien, la proclamación de la primacía del Derecho de la Unión por el art I-6 del Tratado no contradice la supremacía de la Constitución.
Primacía y supremacía son categorías que se desenvuelven en órdenes diferenciados. Aquélla, en el de la aplicación de normas válidas; ésta, en el de los procedimientos de normación. La supremacía se sustenta en el carácter jerárquico superior de una norma y, por ello, es fuente de validez de las que le están infraordenadas, con la consecuencia, pues, de la invalidez de éstas si contravienen lo dispuesto imperativamente en aquélla. La primacía, en cambio, no se sustenta necesariamente en la jerarquía, sino en la distinción entre ámbitos de aplicación de diferentes normas, en principio válidas, de las cuales, sin embargo, una o unas de ellas tienen capacidad de desplazar a otras en virtud de su aplicación preferente o prevalente debida a diferentes razones . . . En suma, la Constitución ha aceptado, ella misma, en virtud de su art. 93, la primacía del Derecho de la Unión en el ámbito que a ese Derecho le es propio, según se reconoce ahora expresamente en el art. I-6 del Tratado.'

[42] *Ibid*, 12: 'En el caso difícilmente concebible de que en la ulterior dinámica del Derecho de la Unión Europea llegase a resultar inconciliable este Derecho con la Constitución española, sin que los hipotéticos excesos del Derecho europeo respecto de la propia Constitución europea fueran remediados por los ordinarios cauces previstos en ésta, en última instancia la conservación de la soberanía del pueblo español y de la supremacía de la Constitución que éste se ha dado podrían llevar a este Tribunal a abordar los problemas que en tal caso se suscitaran, que desde la perspectiva actual se consideran inexistentes, a través de los procedimientos constitucionales pertinentes, ello aparte de que la salvaguarda de la referida soberanía siempre resulta a la postre asegurada por el art I-60 del Tratado, verdadero contrapunto de su art. I-6, y que permite definir en su real dimensión la

The Polish Constitutional Court

But far more radically, the Polish Constitutional Court in its judgment on the membership of the EU of Poland highlights the supremacy of the national Constitution and says that in case of conflict a solution must be found by the Polish constitutional legislator, including a revision of the Constitution:

> The accession of Poland to the European Union did not undermine the supremacy of the Constitution over the whole legal order within the field of sovereignty of the Republic of Poland. The norms of the Constitution, being the supreme act which is an expression of the Nation's will, would not lose their binding force or change their content by the mere fact of an irreconcilable inconsistency between these norms and any Community provision. In such a situation, the autonomous decision as regards the appropriate manner of resolving that inconsistency, including the expediency of a revision of the Constitution, belongs to the Polish constitutional legislator.

Such a collision may in no event be resolved by assuming the supremacy of a Community norm over a constitutional norm. Furthermore, it may not lead to the situation whereby a constitutional norm loses its binding force and is substituted by a Community norm, nor may it lead to an application of the constitutional norm restricted to areas beyond the scope of Community law regulation. In such an event the Nation as the sovereign, or a State authority organ authorised by the Constitution to represent the Nation, would need to decide on: amending the Constitution; or causing modifications within Community provisions; or, ultimately, on Poland's withdrawal from the European Union.[43]

Conclusion

Constitutional or Supreme Courts see the basis for the application of European law within the national constitution, and obviously do not feel pre-empted from taking position, in cases of doubt, upon answering, in cases of doubt, questions of applicability of European provisions to national cases. Yet none of the courts claims such competence as a matter of frequent use, but clearly as an exceptional device in extremely serious cases.

A Non-hierarchical Community of Law

Article 31 of the German Grundgesetz provides that in case of conflict federal law breaks state law, and it would be for the Federal Constitutional Court to declare void provisions of state law in conflict with federal law.

No such hierarchy or right of interposition is given to the European Court of Justice. However, it is also clear that national courts may not, according to the judgment of the

primacía proclamada en este último, incapaz de sobreponerse al ejercicio de una renuncia, que queda reservada a la voluntad soberana, suprema, de los Estados miembros.'

[43] Judgment of 11 May 2005, K 18/04, Poland's Membership In The European Union (The Accession Treaty), www.trybunal.gov.pl/eng/summaries/documents/K_18_04_GB.pdf (grounds 1 and 13).

ECJ in *Foto-Frost*, decide upon the validity of provisions of European law.[44] In *Costa v ENEL* the ECJ rightly confirms this view with regard to Article 177 EEC, which is now Article 234 EC:

> This provision gives the Court no jurisdiction either to apply the Treaty to a specific case or to decide upon the validity of a provision of domestic law in relation to the Treaty, as it would be possible for it to do under Article 169.

Contrary to what the court says in the last phrase quoted though, Articles 226 and 228 EC do not give the ECJ the power to declare a national law void but the power to state a violation of European law. Like the absence of any provision for the exercise, by European institutions, of physical forces of coercion by police or other armed forces, in enforcing European law, this limitation of the powers of the European Courts is one of the characteristics of the new kind of political organisation: it is voluntary, based upon the respect of the rule of law and the co-operation among the authorities of the Union and of the Member States.

As far as the Court had created the impression that Community law excluded even the valid entry into force of conflicting national law, namely in its judgment of 9 March 1978, Case 106/77, *Simmenthal*,[45] it seized the opportunity as early as 1991 to stress that in cases of conflict the national provision would not be invalid but national courts would have to disapply the conflicting national provision.[46] The Court was far more explicit in the case of *IN.CO.GE.'90 Srl*, where the Commission relied upon the *Simmental* doctrine, arguing that the national provision in question could not validly enter into force and, therefore, was non-existent because it was adopted subsequently to the conflicting provision of Community law:

> It cannot therefore, contrary to the Commission's contention, be inferred from the judgment in Simmenthal that the incompatibility with Community law of a subsequently adopted rule of national law has the effect of rendering that rule of national law non-existent. Faced with such a situation, the national court is, however, obliged to disapply that rule, provided always that this obligation does not restrict the power of the competent national courts to apply, from among the various procedures available under national law, those which are appropriate for protecting the individual rights conferred by Community law.[47]

European and national law, therefore, co-exist as formally autonomous bodies of law, they are components of the composed constitutional system of the EU, a system with shared powers and responsibilities The principle of primacy only applies in cases of conflict, with the result that the conflicting provision of national law is inapplicable in this case only, but

[44] Judgment of the Court of 22 October 1987, Case 314/85 *Foto-Frost v Hauptzollamt Lübeck-Ost* [1987] ECR 4199 (ground 15).

[45] Judgment of the Court of 9 March 1978, Case 106/77, *Amministrazione delle Finanze dello Stato v Simmenthal SpA* Italy [1978] ECR 629, in particular ground 17, quoted above, with note 24, and ground 18: 'Indeed any recognition that national legislative measures which encroach upon the field within which the Community exercises its legislative power or which are otherwise incompatible with the provisions of Community law had any legal effect would amount to a corresponding denial of the effectiveness of obligations undertaken unconditionally and irrevocably by Member States pursuant to the Treaty and would thus imperil the very foundations of the Community.'

[46] Judgment of the Court (Sixth Chamber) of 7 February 1991, Case C-184/89 *Helga Nimz v Freie und Hansestadt Hamburg*, [1991] ECR I-297 (ground 19).

[47] Judgment of the Court of 22 October 1998, Joined cases C-0/97 to C-22/97 *Ministero delle Finanze v IN.CO.GE.'90 Srl* [1998] ECR I-6307 (ground 21).

not invalid. The impact of the European norm, thus, is reduced to the degree that is necessary to ensure its uniform application throughout the Union. The fact that it is ultimately the national authorities that disapply the relevant provisions gives them a special responsibility—and control.

This ultimate control is what distinguishes the Union from a hierarchical federal system: the co-operation between the authorities at the European and at the national level, which includes the co-responsibility for the safeguard of the common values and fundamental rights of the citizens as well as the limits of Community competence and the principles of subsidiarity and proportionality. The mere fact that national Constitutional or Supreme Courts may refuse the application of a measure because of a clear and serious breach of such rights or principles will compel the European authorities to observe the limits of their powers. On the other hand, the respect of the law, including the values, rights, and principles mentioned, as the fundamental condition of the functioning of the Union, will compel the national Courts not to abuse their prerogative in their own national interest.

The principle and the practice of close co-operation between the European and national courts thus seem to comply best with the constitution of the Union as a community based upon the rule of law as opposed to a Union based on coercive power. The courts at both levels, thus, are altogether the guardians of the law, and of the functioning of the European Union consolidating and developing it as a legal unit in the spirit of multilevel constitutionalism.[48]

[48] The concept was first developed in I Pernice, 'Constitutional Law Implications for a State participating in a Process of Regional Integration. German Constitution and "Multilevel Constitutionalism"', in Riedel (ed), *German Report on Public Law Presented to the XV. International Congress on Comparative Law*, Bristol, 26 July to 1 August 1998, 40–65; see also I Pernice, 'Multilevel Constitutionalism and the Treaty of Amsterdam: European Constitution-Making Revisited' (1999) *CML Rev* 703–50.

3

Conflicts and Integration: Revisiting *Costa v ENEL* and *Simmenthal II*

HERWIG CH HOFMANN

This short Chapter revisits the cases of *Costa v ENEL*[49] and *Simmenthal II*[50] and their effect on the development of the specific nature and the constitutional order of the EU. *Costa v ENEL* and *Simmenthal II* are cases well known for their impact on defining the legal parameters which govern the legal system of the EU/EC. These cases are true classics in the history of case law of the ECJ and thus have been discussed to great detail in legal writing. I will not attempt within this Chapter to do justice to the nuances and the ongoing debates in this literature. Instead, this Chapter will focus on a more rarely addressed but nonetheless central aspect of the cases: it will argue that the specific contribution of *Costa v ENEL* and *Simmenthal II* to the development and definition of the Community legal system arises from a fruitful and productive tension. This tension results from a dichotomy between, on one hand, a rule of conflicts, and, on the other, the notion of the integration of legal systems.

Initially, the principle of supremacy, as outlined in these cases, seems to be establishing a hierarchy of norms between EC and national law. It introduces a conflicts rule giving precedence to Community law over national legal provisions in cases of conflict.[51] The cases, however, equally establish the notion of integration, which, according to *Costa v ENEL* and *Simmenthal II*, is based on the E(E)C Treaty having 'created its own legal system' which upon entry into force 'became an *integral part* of the legal systems of the Member States'[52] and is 'applicable in the territory of each of the Member States'.[53]

The establishment of the principle of supremacy therefore has not led simply to the superimposition of a new level of public power over that of the Member States. The ECJ's approach in its case law from *Costa v ENEL* to *Simmenthal II* led to a unique system of shared sovereignty, in which hierarchic relations are only elements within a wider

[49] Case 6/64 *Costa v ENEL* [1964] ECR 585.

[50] Case 106/77 *Amministrazione delle Finanze dello Stato v Simmenthal SpA (Simmenthal II)* [1978] ECR 629.

[51] This is the point of view from which the cases had predominantly been discussed in the first 20 years after *Costa v ENEL*. See, eg, Samkalden, 'Annotation *Costa v ENEL* 6/64' [1964] *CML Rev* 213–20; MA Dauses, 'Anmerkung zu Urteil des EuGH vom 9 März 1978' RS 106/77 [1978] *Juristenzeitung* 512–13; D Carreau, 'Droit communautaire et droits nationaux: concurrence ou primauté? [1978] *Revue Trimestrielle de Droit Européen* 381–418; D Freestone, 'The Supremacy of Community Law in National Courts' 42 *MLR* [1979] 220–3; G Droesse, 'Das *Simmenthal II*-Urteil des EuGH in der italienischen Rechtsprechung und Literatur' [1983] *Europarecht* 272–83; B de Witte, 'Retour à "*Costa*": La primauté du droit communautaire à la lumière du droit international' [1984] *Revue Trimestrielle de Droit Européen* 425–54.

[52] Case 6/64 *Costa v ENEL* [1964] ECR 585, para 8 (emphasis added).

[53] Case 106/77 *Simmenthal II* [1978] ECR 629, para 17.

structure of jointly exercising public powers. The Chapter is committed to exploring this unique method of sharing sovereignty within the tension between *conflicts* and *integration.*

Supremacy as a Rule of Conflict

One of the essential legal issues the founding Treaties' texts had not explicitly addressed was whether the traditional rules of public international law could be applied within the Community legal system. In other words, whether the ECSC and E(E)C Treaties had created a new kind of legal order, which was a third type of law not fitting into the traditional dualism of national and public international law.[54]

It was thus left to the ECJ to analyse these questions in greater detail. Initially, the European Court of Justice was cautious. In an early staff case arising under the ECSC, *Humblet v Belgian State*,[55] the Court found that it 'is evident from the Treaty' which has the 'force of law in the Member States' that where Member State's legislative or administrative measures are 'contrary to Community law', a Member State is obliged 'to rescind the measure in question'.[56] Essentially, although the Court in *Humblet* found that ECSC law took 'precedence over national law', it left it to the Member States to define in which way Community law could take effect in Member States.[57] *Humblet* was thus based on a rather 'traditional' public international law understanding of the conflicts question of the relation of Community law to the law of the Member States.

The change of parameters came in the case of *Costa v ENEL* in which the Court held a firm position in what Advocate General Lagrange had characterised as a question of the constitutional relations between the Community and the Member States.[58] The Court found that Member States had delegated to the Community the power to define the relationship between Community law and the law of the Member States. The reasoning given by the Court is well known: Community law 'stemming from the Treaty' was 'an independent source of law' which could not 'be overridden by domestic legal provisions, however framed'.[59] In contrast to *Humblet*, *Costa v ENEL* establishes that the Community

[54] This can be explained by the fact that the Treaties of Paris and Rome were created against a background of sovereign states in Europe. Under the classic notion of territorial sovereignty states acted either in the framework of national law or public international law. Public international law was the 'law of contracts' between sovereign states.

[55] Case 6/60 *Humblet v Belgian State* [1960] ECR English special edition 559.

[56] Case 6/60 *Humblet v Belgian State* [1960] ECR English special edition 559, at 569. In *Humblet* the notion of supremacy of Community law was discussed before *Van Gend en Loos* had established direct effect of EC law.

[57] One could argue that when understanding 'force of law' in *Humblet* as referring to law in general and not as a 'loi formelle', *Humblet* was in fact a first step towards a non-traditional understanding of the role of Community law vis-à-vis Member State law (to this effect see: B de Witte, 'Retour à "*Costa*": La primauté du droit communautaire à la lumière du droit international' [1984] *Revue Trimestrielle de Droit Européen* 425–54 at 426). Generally, however, the earlier commentators seem to have understood the relevance of the term to stand for law in the more narrow sense of a 'loi formelle', which indicates a more traditional reading of the case in line with public international law. See, eg, H-P Ipsen, *Europäisches Gemeinschaftsrecht* (Tübingen, Mohr, 1972), 296.

[58] Opinion of Advocate General Maurice Lagrange in Case 6/64 *Costa v ENEL* [1964] ECR 1171 (French edition).

[59] Case 6/64 *Costa v ENEL* [1964] ECR 585, para 13. It subsequently would be 'impossible for the States, as a corollary, to accord precedence to a unilateral and subsequent measure over a legal system accepted by them on a basis of reciprocity' (para 10). The ECJ summarised that '[t]he transfer by the states from their domestic legal

legal order itself defines when and how it takes precedence over the law of the Member States. This is *Costa v ENEL*'s well-understood central innovation to the former strict dichotomy of public international law on one hand and national law on the other. With the integration of Community law 'into the laws of each Member State',[60] precedence was given to co-operatively created law over unilateral acts of the Member States.

The principles established in *Costa v ENEL* were confirmed and further developed in the case law of the ECJ, most notably in *Simmenthal II*.[61] Based on *Costa v ENEL*, the Court in *Simmenthal II* held that 'in accordance with the principle of precedence of Community law', EC law can 'render automatically inapplicable any conflicting provision' of law of the Member States.[62] Member States were obliged to 'set aside' national law 'which might prevent Community rules from having full force and effect'[63] because Community law was 'an integral part of' 'the legal order applicable in the territory of each of the Member States'.[64]

From this perspective, the case law from *Costa v ENEL* to *Simmenthal II* transformed the understanding of how conflicts between Community law and Member States' law would be decided. The cases established an autonomous vertical Community rule of conflicts: they declared the supremacy of any provision of Community law, including single case decisions of administrative nature, over any form of Member State law, including general principles of national constitutional law. Community law thus itself defines its rank within the legal system of its Member States.

The goal of this transformation was openly stated in *Costa v ENEL* and *Simmenthal II*. Community law, which was collectively established through the Community method, was given primacy over unilaterally set national law, precisely with the goal to empower EC law to confer rights and obligations not only on states as subjects of public international law but also on individuals. If states could unilaterally, through their constitutional provisions or otherwise, impede the exercise of the rights of individuals, such rights would not exist. The innovative factor of the Community legal organisation and one of its arguments for supremacy is thus the joint exercise of powers as shared sovereignty.[65] Through this approach, the cases of *Costa v ENEL* and *Simmenthal II* had become essential building blocks in integrating EC law into national law and the central move towards what is often loosely referred to as 'constitutionalisation'.

system to the Community legal system of the rights and obligations arising under the Treaty carries with it a permanent limitation of their sovereign rights, against which a subsequent unilateral act incompatible with the concept of the Community cannot prevail' (para 14).

60 Case 6/64 *Costa v ENEL* [1964] ECR 585, para 9. Community law in this sense consists of explicit 'provisions which derive from the Community' but also 'and more generally the terms and the spirit of the Treaty'.

61 Case 106/77 *Amministrazione delle Finanze dello Stato v Simmenthal SpA (Simmenthal II)* [1978] ECR 629.

62 It further stated that EC law precludes 'the valid adoption of new national legislative measures to the extent to which they would be incompatible with Community provisions'. Case 106/77 *Simmenthal II* [1978] ECR 629, para 17.

63 Case 106/77 *Simmenthal II* [1978] ECR 629, para 22.

64 'Any recognition that national legislative measures which encroach upon the field within which the Community exercises its legislative power or which are otherwise incompatible with the provisions of Community law' 'would amount to a corresponding denial of the effectiveness of obligations undertaken unconditionally and irrevocably by Member States … and would thus imperil the very foundations of the Community' (Case 106/77 *Simmenthal II* [1978] ECR 629, para 17).

65 Article I-6 of the Treaty establishing a Constitution for Europe thus includes an explicit reference to the principle of supremacy as restatement of established case law.

Integration

Integration leading away from public international law towards the Community system of shared sovereignty changed the EC as much as the Member States. The former evolved from an international treaty to a legal order of a constitutional nature. The latter gradually opened themselves to the exercise of public power from outside their territory. Thereby, the old dichotomy of public international law and national law with its distinguishing feature of territorial reach of national law became increasingly less important. The dichotomy was replaced by an evolving network of structures for the exercise of public power in a system of shared sovereignty. The first and most visible aspect thereof was the creation of a judicial network of courts. The second aspect of shared sovereignty, the integration of the legislative and executive power, became increasingly structured in networks which have often evolved beyond formally set rules in the founding Treaties. Both developments are aspects of the important element of 'integration' which was stressed in *Costa v ENEL* and *Simmenthal II*, but continues to receive much less attention than the conflicts rule of supremacy. I will address these two aspects of integration separately.

Judicial Network

The development of shared sovereignty through a network of courts is exceptionally well exemplified by *Costa v ENEL* and *Simmenthal II*. As many of the important cases in the EC legal history, both reached the ECJ as references for a preliminary ruling under Article 234 EC (ex Article 177). In both cases the defendants argued primarily procedural aspects calling into question the right of national courts to request a preliminary ruling.

In *Costa v ENEL*, the Italian government had submitted that the reference for preliminary ruling was 'absolutely inadmissible' because the referring Italian court was not entitled to issue a decision to stay procedures and to refer the question to the ECJ directly on Article 234 EC. Instead, it was obliged to apply Italian law, which only allowed for preliminary references to the Italian Constitutional Court.[66] The ECJ answered rather categorically with a general statement on the nature of E(E)C law. It held that the question whether the national court could directly rely on Article 234 EC (ex 177) for a reference for preliminary ruling was governed by Community law. Otherwise, as was already noted above, unilaterally set national law would be capable of overriding Community law.[67] This pattern was repeated in *Simmenthal II*,[68] where the Court held that the right of requesting

[66] For the background of the Italian courts' multiple requests for references, see Samkalden, 'Annotation *Costa v ENEL* 6/64', [1964] *CML Rev* 213–20 at 214.

[67] Case 6/64 *Costa v ENEL* [1964] ECR 585, paras 10, 14: it would be 'impossible for the States, as a corollary, to accord precedence to a unilateral and subsequent measure over a legal system accepted by them on a basis of reciprocity' (para 10). The 'transfer by the states from their domestic legal system to the Community legal system of the rights and obligations arising under the Treaty carries with it a permanent limitation of their sovereign rights, against which a subsequent unilateral act incompatible with the concept of the Community cannot prevail' (para 14).

[68] The Amministrazione delle Finanze dello Stato had argued that according to Italian constitutional law, Italian legislative provisions violating EC law were unconstitutional. Only the Italian Constitutional Court had

a preliminary reference cannot be impeded by Member States' law because such provisions would risk creating unequal application of Community law in the Member States. As a result, courts from all levels would have the right to refer cases to the ECJ for preliminary ruling under Community law.

In *Costa v ENEL* and *Simmenthal II*, the ECJ thereby reinforced the importance and role of a network of courts established by Article 234 EC (ex 177) with the goal of holding both European and national actors accountable. It was thus assured that the relations between the courts were non-hierarchic in so far as national law could not—against the explicit wording of Article 234 EC—request the exhaustion of national remedies prior to a request for preliminary ruling by the ECJ. The result is a system in which the national judge is also a Community judge and supremacy of Community law does not imply inferiority of national courts. Equally, the ECJ, in cases of a request for preliminary ruling, only decides the Community law aspects of cases. The final decision of the case rests with a national judge. By establishing a rule of conflicts and reinforcing the role of a network of courts, *Costa v ENEL* and *Simmenthal II* strengthened the jurisdictions of both the national courts and the ECJ vis-à-vis the executive powers. Also, in some dimensions, individuals were put on the same level as Member States. Individuals were empowered by Article 234 EC in combination with the principles of supremacy and direct effect to enforce Community law and to request the review of the compliance of national provisions with Community law.

Executive Networks

The second and more hidden element of integrating legal systems arising from the interpretation of Community Law established in *Costa v ENEL* and confirmed in *Simmenthal II* is the role of executive networks for joint exercise of shared sovereignty. Unlike the judicial network, the executive network was the product of a rather fluid and evolutionary development in several historic phases. This is the real legacy of *Costa v ENEL*'s notion of declaring Community law an 'integral part of the legal systems of the Member States'.[69] The effect of this opening of Member States to the exercise of public power from outside of their territory might be illustrated in a simplified step-by-step presentation by looking at vertical, horizontal and diagonal integration.

Vertical Integration

The main effect of the principle of supremacy established by the ECJ in *Costa v ENEL* and *Simmenthal II* initially was to establish a rule for vertical conflicts between Community and national law. This vertical conflicts rule held that any form of directly applicable Community law would render inapplicable conflicting national law irrespective of its rank

the right to declare unconstitutional and thus set aside acts of Italian law. Therefore the Pretore de Susa was obliged to refer the case to the Italian Constitutional Court and not to the ECJ (Case 106/77 *Simmenthal II* [1978] ECR 629, para 6).

[69] Case 6/64 *Costa v ENEL* [1964] ECR 585, para 8.

in the national hierarchy of norms.[70] This general principle of vertical conflicts has, in principle, been accepted by the courts of the Member States.[71]

However, despite *Costa v ENEL* and *Simmenthal II*'s effect to open the Member States' legal systems, implementation of law was still state-bound. The effects of the exercise of public power from the European level remained limited to the individual Member State. The national legal heritage, of which supranational law had become part, was still exercised exclusively within the territory of each individual Member State.[72]

The vertical nature of this conflicts rule makes it seem, therefore, at first sight that a hierarchical relationship between EU/EC law and Member State law had been created by *Costa v ENEL* and *Simmenthal II*. This, however, would be a simplistic and incomplete reading as the reality is more complex. Supremacy of EU/EC law developed over time into a far less hierarchic and more network oriented structure.

Horizontal Integration

The second major development was the 'horizontal' opening of Member States' legal systems. Since the mid 1970s, ECJ case law increasingly focused on the obligation of the Member States to mutually recognise legal acts of other Member States, especially where such was necessary to allow for the exercise of fundamental freedoms within the EC.[73] Mutual recognition led to trans-territorial effect of the law of one Member State in another Member State. That effect was ordered by Community law and thus necessarily based on the notion of supremacy. The *Simmenthal* cases powerfully demonstrate this. The *Simmenthal* saga straddles both the horizontal and the vertical aspect of supremacy. In *Simmenthal I*, the underlying question was whether in order to allow for the exercise of the free movement of goods, the Italian authorities were obliged to *horizontally* recognise a veterinary certificate issued by the French authorities.[74] EC law therefore required, in a 'horizontal conflicts' case, that the law of France have effect in Italy. After the ECJ in a preliminary ruling had affirmed this, *Simmenthal*

[70] It is, however, important to recall that European law was acceptable to Member States *inter alia* because it was not completely alien to the national systems. In European integration, states allowed public power to be exercised also from outside of their legal systems under the condition of being able to participate in its creation and implementation. Member States' executives had become key figures in agenda setting, the legislative procedures as well as the creation of common rules for implementation. With deepening integration to which there is no opt-out, Member States were accepting EC law only because they were fully integrated into the legislative and implementing process (JHH Weiler, 'The transformation of Europe', 100 *Yale Law Journal* [1991] 2403–83 at 2413–23).

[71] The latter in some instances requiring only an exceptional *ultra vires* role in reviewing the ECJ. For an overview see K Lenaerts and P Van Nuffel, *Constitutional Law of the European Union*, 2nd edn (London, Thomson Sweet & Maxwell, 2006), paras 17–015–17–046. This interpretation of EU/EC law has equally not been challenged in any of the many Treaty amendments from the Single European Act to the Treaty of Nice. In Article I-6 of the Treaty establishing a Constitution for Europe, the primacy rule was explicitly spelt out.

[72] In administrative terms, this corresponded to the model of implementation and indirect administration of Community law in each and every Member State separately. C Joerges, 'The Legitimacy of Supranational Decision Making' [2006] 44 *Journal of Common Market Studies* [2006], 779–802 at 791–3.

[73] This horizontal opening is most closely associated with Case 120/78 *Rewe Central AG (Cassis de Dijon)* [1979] ECR 649, which required Member States to mutually accept each other's legislative and administrative decisions in the absence of harmonising legislation from the European level (paras 8, 14).

[74] Case 35/76 *Simmenthal I* [1976] ECR 1871 then provided for the obligation of a Member State to accept the veterinary certificates of another Member State in the case of an investigation procedure harmonised by a directive.

II was a case about the consequences of such a ruling on Italian law. The local judge, the Pretore de Susa, needed to know whether he had the right to set aside Italian law which had been found to be incompatible with EC law.[75] As a result, the ECJ found that the supremacy of Community law obliged Member States to allow for trans-territorial effect of other Member States' law within their legal system. Thereby, Member States had opened their territory to the application of public power not only from the Community level, but also horizontally from other Member States.[76]

The Move Towards an Integrated Legal System—The Age of Subsidiarity as Conflicts Rule

An often unnoticed element of the cases of *Costa v ENEL* and *Simmenthal II* is that they laid the ground for establishing the fabric of the Community legal system not only by means of a hard supremacy rule of conflicts, but also through a unique system of integration of law from multiple levels. In the process of deepening and widening European integration, additional and more sophisticated tools became necessary to avoid the emergence of too many situations of hard conflicts between national and Community law. Instead of creating rules for solving such conflicts, the idea was to prevent them through, for example, the principle of subsidiarity.[77] Subsidiarity initially was designed as a kind of a meta-principle for the vertical distribution of legislative powers between the European and the national levels.[78] In reality however, subsidiarity played a much less important role in the distribution of legislative competences. Instead, the invocation of the principle of subsidiarity practically much more heavily influenced the distribution of powers between legislation and implementation. The emergence of subsidiarity as a constitutional notion thereby historically goes hand in hand with the development of a system of decentralised yet co-operative administrative structures. These forms of co-operation have mostly taken the form of executive networks with participants from the Member States, the Community institutions and private parties.[79]

[75] Case 35/76 *Simmenthal I* [1976] ECR 1871; Case 106/77 *Simmenthal II* [1978] ECR 629, para 3.

[76] Horizontal effect can also mean an effect of law applied between private parties. The horizontal effect due to the primacy of EU/EC law arises not only between states but also between individuals. A national measure might for example be inapplicable in the relation between individuals of one or of several Member States, not only if it is incompatible with Community law in substance. It may also be inapplicable if it was adopted violating procedural rules laid down by Community law for the adoption of national provisions. See: C-441/93 *Pafitis* [1996] ECR I-1347, C-194/94 *CIA Security International* [1996] ECR I-2201, paras 45–54; C-443/98 *Unilever Italia* [2000] ECR I-7535, paras 31–52 and C-159/00 *Sapod Audic* [2002] ECR I-5031, paras 48–52. See for limitations of this rule C-226/97 *Lemmens* [1998] ECR I-3711, para 35.

[77] Subsidiarity was designed to add an additional level of control for the exercise of public power in the EU. Article 5(2) EC.

[78] The ECJ rarely entered into an in-depth debate over the merits of subsidiarity-related arguments—mainly due to respect for the legislative discretion of the Community legislator. This made subsidiarity a legally rather weak tool. See eg C-84/94 *Working time directive* [1996] ECR I-5755; C-233/94 *Deposit guarantee schemes* [1997] ECR I-2405; C- 376/98 *Germany v EP and Council (Tobacco advertising)* [2000] ECR I-8419; C-377/98 *Biotechnological Inventions* [2001] ECR I-7079. A more thorough analysis was only undertaken in C-154/04 *Alliance for Natural Health* of 12 July 2005, paras 101–6.

[79] See for further details the contributions to HCH Hofmann and A Türk (eds), *EU Administrative Governance* (London, Edward Elgar, 2006) and M Egeberg, 'Europe's Executive Branch of Governments in the Melting Pot: An Overview' in M Egeberg (ed), *Multilevel Union Administration* (London, Palgrave, 2006) 1–16.

The impact of this development becomes clearer when taking a step back and looking at the emergence of the integrated executive. In the EU-specific system of integration, executive activity goes beyond implementing activity.[80] It also expands to administrative co-operation in agenda setting[81] and policy making[82]—in all phases of the 'policy cycle'. Structures of integrated executive for all three policy phases operate in large parts beyond the institutions and procedures established by the founding treaties. They have developed in an evolutionary way differing in each stage of the policy cycle and in each policy area, creating a rich diversity of administrative actors on the European levels and their forms of interaction.[83] As a consequence of these developments, the originally more or less distinct vertical and horizontal relations between the European level and the Member States as well as between Member States' law have been transformed into a network of complex relationships.[84]

European integration has therefore led to an opening of the Member States to the exercise of public power from outside of their territory, be this from the European level or from other Member States. At the same time, their branches of government are involved in the creation, implementation and adjudication of European law and other Member States' Europeanised law. Member State and EU structures are thus not only subject to EU/EC law, they also jointly create and implement it. This is now a central notion to EU/EC law of being an integral part of Member State law. This network structure is the essence of the notion of shared sovereignty and the supremacy of co-operatively created Community law over unilateral and Member States' acts.

[80] In this phase, institutions' activities range from single case decisions and preparatory acts thereof to acts of administrative rule-making and the amendment of specific provisions in legislation where so authorised. In many policy areas, the development of the integration of EU and national administrative proceedings has led to 'composite proceedings' to which both national and EU administrations contribute. Diverse structures undertake implementation decisions and administrative rule-making in the various policy areas. Amongst these developments are 'Comitology' committee procedures, in certain policy areas expanded to what is now known as the 'Lamfalussy' procedures. Agencies and their administrative networks play an ever-increasing role. Implementing networks may also include private parties acting as recipients of limited delegation. Administrative networks that have been created and adapted to the needs of each policy area integrate the supranational and national administrative bodies within structures designed to conduct joint or co-ordinated action. In practice, these forms of co-operation consist of obligations of different intensity. They range from obligations to exchange information either on an ad hoc or on a permanent basis to network structures which have been developed to include forms of implementation such as individually binding decisions.

[81] In the phase of agenda setting, national administrations can play a central role in shaping the Commission's policy initiatives. This takes place mainly through expert groups which are generally composed of national civil servants, but also independent experts. These groups are used to test ideas, build coalitions of experts and pre-determine policy incentives later to be formally presented by the Commission as initiative.

[82] The presence of the national executive actors in the EU's decision-making process is mostly felt within the Council working parties supporting COREPER. Here, the national civil servants have to balance their national mandate against the need to reach a consensus in pursuance of EU tasks. Such interaction, albeit to a lesser extent, also exists through the 'Open Method of Co-ordination'.

[83] See with more detail: HCH Hofmann and A Türk (eds) *EU Administrative Governance* (London, Edward Elgar, 2006).

[84] Also, structures have been developed which link European networks with participants from non-EU Member States.

Conclusion: Conflicts and Integration—The Future of Supremacy within a Network

The concentration on supremacy as a central element of vertical conflicts provision gave birth to an understanding of the EU/EC as a multi-level legal system in which the EU/EC legal order has been superimposed on the Member States' legal systems. Questions of constitutionalisation of the legal order have therefore often been viewed from the perspective of the relation between these two distinct yet hierarchically linked legal systems. However, when looking at the evolving network structure of exercising public power within the EU, it seems that the content and impact of these cases would be severely underestimated if they were only reviewed for this 'vertical' dimension. Instead, the content and the effect of *Costa v ENEL* and *Simmenthal II* go far beyond that. They did not only allow for a network of courts, in which any level of Member States' courts were able to interact with the ECJ on the European level under Community rules. This essentially allowed individuals to effectively challenge the validity of EC law as well as the compliance of Member State rules with EC law. The latter reflects the needs of individuals in pluralistic societies, whose interests are not necessarily limited to the territorial limits of single Member States. The cases also led a dynamism requiring the reinforcement and development of networks of the executive branches of power. The effect of this was an exercise of public power not in two separate levels but instead in a more integrated system. The integration of the new Community legal order into the national legal systems thus prompted the development of elaborate network structures for integration of Member States' and Community interests. Most of the developments have taken place in forms not established by the treaties. This leads to a view of the European law not in the form of two superimposed structures with one being the European level[85] and the other being the Member States, each exercising public power only within their respective territories and competencies. Instead, the European legal system has evolved into a three-dimensional structure with complex vertical, horizontal and composite relations of the actors therein. This has consequences not only for our understanding of the role of the EU/EC and the Member States in Europe but also for the analysis of key aspects such as accountability.

It might be too early to determine the true effect of the developments spurned by *Costa v ENEL* and *Simmenthal II* due to the fact that the process of integration is continuing in directions which had not been envisaged in prior times. It is a continuing evolutionary process with a dynamic institutional development. Without the dichotomy of, on one hand, supremacy and, on the other hand, judicial, legislative and executive integration, one could have imagined a much less vibrant, more intergovernmental and more compartmentalised approach to 'integration through law'. The strength of the current integration process was initiated with the parallel approach of creating both conflicts rules as well as fostering procedural and substantive legal integration. This is the remaining legacy of *Costa v ENEL* and *Simmenthal II.*

[85] With the territorial reach of the EU as described in Article 299 EC.

4

From *Costa v ENEL* to the Treaties of Rome: A Brief History of a Legal Revolution

MORTEN RASMUSSEN

With the *Costa v ENEL* ruling in July 1964, the European Court of Justice completed what can only be termed a revolution in European law.[86] By establishing the supremacy of European law inside the legal systems of the Member States, albeit in the areas in which the latter had granted the European Communities (EC) competences, the European Court of Justice (ECJ) secured the effectiveness of the legal mechanism established with the *Van Gend en Loos* ruling a year earlier.[87] In the latter case the ECJ not only assumed authority to rule on what part of the Treaties of Rome—and later secondary legislation—had direct effect but also chose a very broad reading of Article 177 allowing preliminary references from national courts that dealt explicitly with the junction between national and European law. As a consequence the ECJ turned treaty obligations directed towards Member States into rights for Member State citizens. The rest is history. National courts would over time embrace these fundamental principles, thus allowing the ECJ to develop a comprehensive and strong case law and binding their respective governments to respect it. A European rule of law had been established.

The history of the European legal revolution has long been shrouded in legend. In the legal circles of the ECJ, as well as in legal academia, an oral tradition emerged and was carefully nurtured by judges and jurists involved in the revolution.[88] The EC had to be saved from the politicians, so the story went, by means of the rule of law. Charles de Gaulle's take over of power in France in 1958, and later the economic and political crisis of the 1970s, meant that Member States systematically undermined and attacked the very treaties[89] they themselves had solemnly signed in Rome in March 1957. The ECJ simply established and upheld the rule of law, enforcing the treaties on recalcitrant Member

[86] Aff 6/64 *Flaminio Costa v ENEL* (1964) *Recueil* 1194.

[87] Aff 26/62 *NV Algemene Transport- en Expeditie Onderneming van Gend en Loos v Nederlandse Administratie der Belastingen* (1963) *Recueil* 0003.

[88] Eg Robert Lecourt, *L'Europe des Juges* (Brussels, Bruylant, 1976), Pierre Pescatore, *The Law of Integration* (Leyden, 1974), Pierre Pescatore, 'Aspects judiciaires de l'acquis communautaire' (1981) *Revue Trimestrielle de droit Européen* 23, 617–51 and Federico Mancini, 'The Making of a Constitution for Europe' (1989) 24 *CML Rev* 595–614.

[89] In 1958 two new treaties were added to the existing the Treaty of Paris on the ECSC: the Euratom Treaty and the European Economic Community (EEC) Treaty.

States. Had the court not done so, the EC would have fallen into ruin.[90] While contemporary legal and social science scholars have abandoned the normative element of the oral tradition and view the revolutionary rulings in a much more critical light, there have been no attempts to reconsider the legal revolution on the basis of new sources and in the context of recent historical research on the early history of the EC. Both legal and social science literature on the ECJ repeats the same story based on the same few, standard analyses of the revolutionary jurisprudence, which again are based on a mixture of public sources and the oral tradition.[91] It is high time to challenge this tradition.

In contrast to the oral tradition on the legal revolution, the EC can, from 1958 to the Luxembourg compromise in January 1966, best be characterised as a pragmatic economic community under construction with a vague and undecided political dimension. While economic interests in establishing the Common Market and setting up a number of common policies were shared by all six Member States, the open-ended political objective of the EC allowed political actors in sharp disagreement on the political purpose of the Community to join forces in the pragmatic development of common policies. Nationalist French president Charles de Gaulle found the EEC a very suitable framework for the modernisation of the French economy and the securing of income of French farmers, and co-operated closely with the Commission to secure this by establishing common European policies. Similarly, federalist inclined civil servants and politicians, most prominently Walter Hallstein and Sicco Mansholt, joined the institutions of the EC that on the basis of the Treaties of Rome did not at all look like a potential future European federation, but which nevertheless by many were considered the first step in that direction. These divergent political forces co-existed with great uneasiness in the early life of the Community, but together they nevertheless managed to establish the Common Market and a Common Agricultural Policy. With the Luxembourg compromise, however, the open-ended political dimension of the EC narrowed considerably. On the one hand, the informal introduction of the right of veto represented a dramatic defeat of the federal aspirations of the Hallstein Commission; on the other hand, de Gaulle had to accept that no revision of the Treaties of Rome would be possible.[92] The EC continued to be dominated by the Member States that created it, but crucially maintained its supranational institutional elements that in the long term contributed to the development of a complex European political system.[93]

In this context, I will argue that the ECJ, for reasons explored below, sided with the Hallstein Commission. A federalist inclined coalition of judges in the ECJ, officials in the legal service of the Commission and a transnational network of jurists developed and

[90] For the use of the 'ruin' argument see in particular Robert Lecourt, *L'Europe des Juges* (Brussels, Bruylant, 1976).

[91] Eric Stein, 'Lawyers, Judges and the Making of a Transnational Constitution' (1981) 75 *American Journal of International Law* 1, 1–27 is the standard work. But even a highly critical work such as Hjalte Rasmussen, *On Law and Policy in the European Court of Justice* (Dordrecht/Boston/Lancaster, Martinus Nijhoff Publishers, 1986) relies on the oral tradition for factual information about the 1950s and 1960s.

[92] N Piers Ludlow, *The European Community and the Crises of the 1960s. Negotiating the Gaullist challenge* (London and New York, Routledge, 2006) is the standard work today. However, a wealth of new archive-based historical literature has been published over the last decade.

[93] For the argument that the EC already in the 1960s began to develop central features of a European political system see Morten Rasmussen and Ann-Christina Lauring Knudsen, 'A European Political System in the Making, 1958–1970. The Relevance of Emerging Committee Structures' (2008) 14 *Journal of European Integration History* 1.

promoted a federal solution for Europe through law. To European idealists this might well constitute a heroic defence of the Community against the Gaullist attack. However, considering the unsettled political nature of the Community before 1966 and the degree of active French involvement in the establishment of the common policies, the legal revolution looks rather more like an ideologically driven push for federalising the EC. It is important to point out that this argument does not necessarily claim that the ECJ acted outside its role as a court, only that the ECJ in its jurisdiction in the legal revolution consistently chose one particular interpretation of the EEC Treaty over the alternatives. Tracing the history of the legal revolution backwards from the *Costa v ENEL* ruling over the *Van Gend en Loos* ruling to the negotiations on the Treaties of Rome, I will provide new insights into the legal and political dynamics behind it and finally discuss how to interpret this important episode in European Union history.[94]

On 24 February 1964 the first major challenge to the European legal system and the authority of the European Court of Justice was launched by the Italian Constitutional Court. In the case of *Flaminio Costa v ENEL*, a shareholder in a recently nationalised electricity company refused to pay his bill, claiming the nationalisation law to be in breach of both the Italian Constitution and Article 31 of the EEC Treaty. The Milan Court handling the case sent a preliminary reference both to the Italian Constitutional Court and the ECJ. Ruling on the case first, the Italian Constitutional Court followed Article 80 of the Italian Constitution, according to which treaty law enters into force only after an act of the Italian parliament, and consequently ruled the nationalisation law constitutional on the basis of the principle *lex posterior derogate priori*. As the case accordingly was one of Italian constitutional law, the Milan Court was also reproached for sending a preliminary preference to Luxembourg. This doctrine would stand for more than a decade until the Italian Constitutional Court in a series of rulings from 1975 to 1977 finally gave European law supremacy over Italian law.[95]

In the legal service of the Commission, the ruling of the Italian Constitutional Court was considered a most serious threat not only to the establishment of a European legal system, but to the very existence of the EC. The ruling potentially undermined the reciprocity between the Member States on which French EC membership rested according to Article 55 of the French Constitution. It also threatened to create a permanent imbalance between the four Member States, which according to the legal service for constitutional reasons or through their jurisprudence had already accepted the supremacy of European law (that is, France, the Netherlands, Belgium and Luxembourg), and the two Member States with dualist constitutions (Germany and Italy).[96] Furthermore, a real

[94] To write the early history of the ECJ has proved a most difficult and arduous task. The archive of the European Court of Justice is sealed off from the public indefinitely. Private archives are few and relatively poor, mainly due to the vow of secrecy sworn by judges of the ECJ. Instead, a history of European law must overwhelmingly rely on sources from the Commission and the Council archives as well as Member State archives.

[95] *Costa v ENEL & Soc Edisonvolta*, Judgment No 14, 7 March 1964, 87 Foro Italiano 87, I, 465 and Alec Stone Sweet, *The Judicial Construction of Europe* (Oxford, Oxford University Press, 2005), 82–3.

[96] On the basis of available Commission documents, it seems clear that the legal service counted France among the countries that would easily adopt to the supremacy of European law due to the fact that Article 55 of the French constitution explicitly gave international law primacy over national law. This proved not to be the case as the *Conseil d'Etat* in two judgments in 1965 and 1967, on the *Shell Berre* case and the *Petitjean* case respectively, rejected the jurisprudence of the ECJ. The position of the Conseil d'Etat lasted until 1989. Karen J Alter, *Establishing the Supremacy of European Law—The Making of an International Rule of Law in Europe* (New York, Oxford University Press, 2001), 138–40.

danger existed that lower Italian courts would follow the ruling of the Constitutional Court and ignore European law. The director of the legal service, Michel Gaudet, recommended pressuring the Italian Constitutional Court to revise its position with all means available, both at the political level and through legal contacts.[97] What was a stake in the larger picture was how to convince national courts and judiciaries to accept the new principles of European law. In this political context the ECJ had to find a fitting response to the challenge.

In the proceedings of the case before the ECJ, the advocate representing the Commission, Giuseppe Marchesini, repeated these arguments.[98] This was a conscious strategy to provide the ECJ with an opportunity to express its opinion on the problems of the relationship between European law and national legal systems.[99] Advocate General Maurice Lagrange dedicated a substantial part of his intervention to the doctrinal question of how to assure the integration of European law into the Member States. Lagrange concluded that the consequences would be disastrous for the Community if the principles of the Italian Constitutional Court ruling were maintained. The choice for Member States that maintained the *lex posterior derogat priori* principle was either to change their constitution, following the example of the Dutch constitution that gave international law supremacy over national law, or alternatively, to leave the EC.[100] The Italian government, represented by Ricardo Monaco, reiterated the argument of the Italian Constitutional Court. The preliminary reference was argued to be inadmissible. If the Italian government had broken European law, which was claimed not to be the case, such a breach was subject to the infringement procedures outlined under Articles 169 and 170.[101]

In the *Costa v ENEL* ruling, the ECJ followed and even went beyond the recommendations of the Commission and the Advocate General. The ECJ considered the Milan Court's use of preliminary reference perfectly adequate and ruled that the Italian nationalisation law was not illegal under European law. In doing so, the ECJ added a doctrinal principle of major importance in what constituted its most audacious ruling yet. Under international law, a treaty was traditionally considered to prevail over the provisions of municipal law of the Contracting Parties. This was, however, only the case at the international level, and Articles 169 and 170 of the EEC Treaty were exactly designed to address such cases. The ECJ controversially ruled that European law had *internal primacy*, thereby conferring to

[97] Historical Archive of the Commission (HAC).BAC 371/1991.759, Aufzeichnung für den Herrn Präsidenten. Betr: Urteil Nr 14/1964 des Italienischen Verfassungsgerichtshofs; Durchsetzung des Gemeinschaftsrechts in Italien. JUR/EWG/3832/64; HAC.BAC 371/1991.624, Arrêt de la Cour de Justice dans l'affaire 26/62; HAC.BAC.371/1991757, Note à l'attention de Monsieur le Président de la Commission. Objet: Procédure devant les Cours constitutionelles des Etats membres relatives aux lois de ratification du Traité de Rome. JUR/CEE/1008/64-MG/mk, and HAC.BAC.371/1991.757, Note à l'attention de Monsieur le Président de la Commission et de Messieurs Levi-Sandri et Rey. Objet: Procédures devant les jurudictions italiennes concernant les rapports entre le droit communautaire et le droit national. JUR/CEE/1456/64-GM/mk.

[98] HAC.BAC.371/1991. 758, Rapport présenté conformément à l'art 18 du statut de la Cour de Justice des Communautés Européennes dans l'affaire 6/64 and 805 HAC.BAC 371/1991, no 758, Davanti alla Corte di Giustizia delle Comunità Europee, nel procedimento no 6/64. JUR/CEE/1924/64-I.

[99] HAC.BAC.371/1991.757, Note à l'attention de Monsieur le Président de la Commission et de Messieurs Levi-Sandri et Rey. Objet: Procédures devant les jurudictions italiennes concernant les rapports entre le droit communautaire et le droit national. JUR/CEE/1456/64-GM/mk.

[100] HAC.BAC 371/1991.758, Conclusions de M l'Avocat général Maurice Lagrange dans l'affaire 6/64, prononcées à l'audience du 25 juin 1964.

[101] HAC.BAC.371/1991.758, Rapport présenté conformément à l'art 18 du statut de la Cour de Justice des Communautés Européennes dans l'affaire 6/64.

national courts the task to enforce EC rules over conflicting national legislation.[102] It was argued that Member States had in fact already accepted this principle with the ratification of the Treaties.[103] Confronted with the silence of the EEC Treaty on supremacy, the ECJ cited the special nature of the EC and the need for an effective legal system to reach the treaty objectives. To justify the former notion, the ECJ cited the Community's 'unlimited duration', its 'own institutions', 'personality', 'legal capacity' and capacity of 'representation on the international plane' as well as the 'real powers stemming from a limitation of sovereignty or transfer of powers from the states to the community'. If Member States through subsequent legislative acts called European law into question, this would make their unconditional commitment to the EC contingent. It would also render Article 189, which gave regulations direct effect, meaningless, thus jeopardising the attainment of the objectives of the treaty set out in Article 5(2) and finally, as a result of the uneven application of European law, give rise to discrimination on the basis of nationality, as prohibited by Article 7.[104]

By establishing the internal primacy of European law over national law, the ECJ had responded to the challenge from Rome and done so with the establishment of a doctrinal principle that would become the central pillar in the constitutionalisation of the Treaties of Rome. Internal Commission documents clearly testify how dangerous the ruling by the Italian Constitutional Court was perceived in European legal circles. In purely legal terms, however, both contemporary observers as well as scholarly contributions have since seen the ruling as the logical continuation of the jurisprudence of the *Van Gend en Loos* ruling rendered a year earlier. While this legalist interpretation clearly underestimates the tactical dimension of the ECJ ruling, it testifies to the common legal vision behind the two rulings. To trace the historical roots of the legal revolution, I will now turn to the *Van Gend en Loos* case.

In 1960 the Benelux countries transposed their common tariff to the new Brussels nomenclature by the means of an international protocol, which was later adopted by the Dutch parliament. The changes in classification under the new system resulted in tariff increases for a number of products. As a result, a Dutch firm that imported chemicals from Germany and refused to accept an increase in the duties charged went to court. The claim was that the Benelux protocol constituted a breach of the standstill of tariffs in Article 12 of the EEC Treaty. The Dutch administrative court, the *Tariefcommissie*, sent a preliminary reference to the ECJ to learn first whether Article 12 had direct effect and secondly, if this was the case, whether the Dutch law was illegal. If this was the case under Dutch constitutional law, Article 12 would also be supreme to national law.[105]

[102] Bruno de Witte, 'Direct Effect, Supremacy, and the Nature of the Legal Order' in Paul Craig and Gráinne de Búrca (eds), *The Evolution of EU Law* (Oxford and New York, Oxford University Press, 1999), 182–3.

[103] This important point was proposed by Hans-Peter Ipsen at a seminar organised by the Wissentschaftliche Gesellschaft für Europarecht in Bernsheim-Auerbach on 10 July 1964, two and a half weeks before the ruling. ECJ judges AM Donner and Walter Strauss were present, listening eagerly to Ipsen's analysis. Interview with Dr Hans Jürgen Rabe, 11 January 1994, conducted by Karen Alter. I would like to express my gratitude for having been allowed to consult the interview. For this seminar see also Institut für Zeitgeschichte, München, Nachlasse ED94, Walter Strauss, no 328, 'Wissenschaftliche Gesellschaft für Europarecht. Teilnehmer am Kolloquium der Wissenchaftlichen Gessellschaft für Europarecht am 10 und 11 Juli 1964' and 'Das Verhältnis des Rechts der Europäischen Gemeinschaften zum nationalen Recht. 10 Juli 1964'.

[104] Aff 6/64 *Flaminio Costa v ENEL* (1964), *Recueil* 1194.

[105] Importantly the Dutch Supreme Court had by a judgment on 18 May 1962 given its blessing to the first preliminary reference made under the EEC Treaty. Bruno de Witte, 'Direct Effect, Supremacy, and the Nature of the Legal Order' in Paul Craig and Gráinne de Búrca (eds), *The Evolution of EU Law* (Oxford and New York,

In the ruling the ECJ decided that although Article 177 prohibited the interpretation of national law, it had the right to interpret all relevant points of European law explicit or implicit in the preliminary reference. Furthermore, Article 12 was given direct effect because the language constituted an unqualified, negative obligation. While used sparingly in the EEC Treaty, the concept of direct effect was not new. Council regulations had direct effect and Articles 85 and 86 on competition policy were also considered to apply with direct effect until a common competition policy had been established.[106] The controversial part of the judgment was that the ECJ had assumed the authority to interpret which of the provisions of the EEC Treaty held direct effect and moreover, done this in such a generous way that numerous treaty provisions could be expected to attain the same status as Article 12. The ECJ had thereby turned the Treaties of Rome into a potential bill of rights for Member State citizens.[107]

To reach this conclusion, the ECJ performed a somewhat unorthodox interpretation of the general purpose and nature of the EEC Treaty. Since the Danzig ruling in 1928 by the Permanent Court of Justice, scholars of international law had held that direct effect could only be created if the contracting parties of an international treaty clearly stated this was their intention. Traditionally under international law, the intentions of the contracting parties can only be reached through a very close reading of the provisions of the treaty in question. However, instead of carefully exploring the intention of the contracting parties, the ECJ found it opportune to develop a broader framework for an analysis of 'the spirit, the general scheme and the wording of these provisions', which allowed for what can only be characterised as a highly selective reading of the EEC Treaty.[108]

The ECJ claimed that 'the Community constitutes a new legal order of international law for the benefit of which the states have limited their sovereign rights, albeit within limited fields, and the subjects of which comprise not only Member States but also their nationals'. Therefore Community law 'not only imposes obligations on individuals but is also intended to confer upon them rights which become part of their legal heritage'. This conclusion was underpinned by reference to the preamble of the Treaties of Rome, which referred to an ever closer union between the European peoples (and not states). The Community institutions, it was emphasised, were 'endowed with sovereign rights' and 'nationals ... are called upon to cooperate in the functioning of this community through the intermediary of the European Parliament and the Economic and Social Committee'. Finally, the existence of Article 177, to secure a uniform interpretation of European law, demonstrated that the contracting parties had intended their national citizens to invoke European law before courts and tribunals.[109]

Given the innovative nature of the ruling, it is striking that it contradicted not only the positions of three Member States (Germany, the Netherlands and Belgium), but also the

Oxford University Press, 1999), 177–214, 180. For the details of the case see also HAC.BAC.371/1991.620, Note à M Jean Rey, Président du Groupe Juridique et à M Caron, Président du Groupe du Marché Intérieur. Objet: Observations de la Commission devant la Cour de Justice au sujet des demandes préjudicielles de la 'Tarifcommissie' néerlandaise.

[106] See Historical Archive of the Council of Ministers CM3.179. Historique des négociations.

[107] Renaud Dehousse, *The European Court of Justice—The Politics of Judicial Integration* (London, Macmillan, 1998), 46–7.

[108] Eric Stein, 'Lawyers, Judges and the Making of a Transnational Constitution' (1981) 75 *American Journal of International Law* 1, 1–27, 9–10.

[109] Aff 26/62 NV *Algemene Transport- en Expeditie Onderneming van Gend en Loos v Nederlandse Administratie der Belastingen* (1963) *Recueil* 0003.

recommendations by Advocate General Karl Roemer. While the Member States questioned the jurisdiction of the ECJ in a case that clearly was one of application and not interpretation of the EEC Treaty, both Member States and the Advocate General agreed that the EEC Treaty should be considered a traditional international treaty and consequently that Article 12 should remain an obligation directed to the Member States.[110] The position of three of the most pro-European Member States remains an enigma, although new research demonstrates that at least the German position might be the result of an administrative hiccup. Apparently, this position was developed by the law departments of the various ministries, with Ulrich Everling,[111] a young and lower-ranking specialist in EC law at the Ministry of Economy, as the main protagonist. When the pro-European State Secretary of the Foreign Ministry, Karl Carstens, later learned about what had happened after the ECJ had ruled on the case, he had become furious. Future German positions before the ECJ would in the following years pass Cartens' desk in the Foreign Ministry.[112] What is central in this context, however, is the position of the Commission.

In perhaps the most audacious position ever presented before the ECJ, the Commission advocate Leendert van der Burg not only argued that the court had jurisdiction in the case, unless private individuals were to be completely barred of access to the court,[113] but also concluded that national courts were bound to ensure that European law applied directly and even prevailed over conflicting national law, even if the latter was of a later date. Article 12 was therefore self-executing. The Commission defended this radical view on European law by citing the 'special character' of the EC. First, the EC had independent institutions with real powers, delimited by the three Treaties of Rome, but with direct effect not only on Member States, but also on ordinary Member State citizens. Secondly, EC legislation had immediate effects independent of the Member States. This was obviously the case for regulations, but Member States were ultimately also legally responsible for the implementation of directives. Finally, the contracting parties had created an independent court with the declared intention of establishing an effective and uniform application of European law throughout the Community.[114]

The Commission's innovative position had been prepared by the legal service. However, exceptionally for a legal case, the Commission Collegium had endorsed it at the 204th meeting on 31 October 1962.[115] In the memorandum distributed before the meeting, Gaudet outlined three possible scenarios for the European legal system, depending on the ruling in the case at hand. In the first two scenarios, European law would develop into traditional international law. Unless explicitly specified in the Treaties, there would be no direct effect and European law would depend on the application by national parliaments

[110] HAC.BAC.371/1991.621, Stellungnahme der Regierung der Bundesrepublik Deutschland. E 2, 11 01 98; HAC.BAC.371/1991.621, Mémoire du Gouvernement du Royaume des Pays-Bas. Affaire 26/62, n 71; HAC.BAC.371/1991.621, Mémoire de l'Etat Belge, Réf. D. 123/E.L./N.126/S.F.1; and HAC.BAC 371/1991.622, Rapport d'audience Dans l'affaire 26/62.

[111] He would later go on to be judge of the ECJ in 1980.

[112] Billy Davies, *The Constitutionalisation of the European Communities: West Germany between Legal Sovereignty and European Integration 1949–1974*, Dissertation, King's College, 2007, 170–3.

[113] The ECJ had earlier barred individuals from suing the Community institutions under Art 173. Hjalte Rasmussen, 'Why is Article 173(2) Interpreted against Private Plaintiffs?' (1980) 5 *ELR*, 112–27.

[114] HAC.BAC.371/1991.620, Mémoire de la Commission de la Communauté Economique Européenne. JUR/CEE/2750/62, vdB/mb. og HAC.BAC.371/1991.622, Rapport d'audience Dans l'affaire 26/62.

[115] HAC.BAC.371/1991.620, Questions prejudicielles posées à la Court de Justice par la 'Tariefcommissie' néerlandaise en vertu de l'article 177 – CEE (doc. S/06803/62). Projet de P.V. 204ème réunion Commission.

and the goodwill of national governments and administrations. These models were rejected as not conforming to the fundamental features of the EC and because they would completely remove any legal protection of national citizens in the policy fields with which the EC was concerned. Instead, Gaudet recommended what he termed a legal innovation, a third option, namely the establishment of a legal system where all the stipulations of the treaties were directly applicable and supreme vis-à-vis national legislation. This solution built on the original features of the Community, which had already been ratified by the Member States. It would secure the legal rights of individuals, who would be able to enforce the application of European law before national courts and thus create a necessary supplement to Articles 169 and 170. The Commission would consequently be obliged to recommend the ECJ to rule that Article 12 not only had direct effect but also primacy vis-à-vis national legislation. Gaudet admitted that these two principles constituted profound innovations in most of the Member States, touching upon questions of constitutionality and that they might be met with opposition from national courts. It would be essential to convince both the political authorities and national judiciaries about the necessity of these innovations for the functioning of the Common Market. However, as Gaudet pointed out: 'mieux vaut la surprise devant les exigences juridiques de la Communauté que le doute sur la signification même de la Communauté.'[116] Apparently, Commission President Walter Hallstein and the rest of the Commission concurred.

From the little we know about the ECJ's internal deliberations on the *Van Gend en Loos* case, the vote inside the court was extremely close, most likely a narrow majority of four against three.[117] One central document from the ECJ's internal decision-making process has survived, namely a memorandum by Alberto Trabucchi in which he proposes that the ECJ establishes a system of European law with direct effect. Trabucchi's legal argument turned around the necessity of furnishing Member State citizens with legal rights. He found the question so important that the ECJ should take a firm and clear position. The only real solution would be one that conformed with the special nature of the Community, namely to give Article 12 direct effect with the doctrinal consequences this would have. He expressed his concern that this might raise constitutional problems for certain countries and therefore the ECJ should limit itself to direct effect to avoid too much opposition from national judiciaries.[118]

According to the memorandum, the view inside the court actually seemed to go in the direction of confirming European law as traditional international law, while emphasising the contractual nature of the Treaties of Rome. This was the view of Luxembourg judge Leon Hammers, who was the *rapporteur* on the case, and of the President of the Court, André M Donner.[119] The document reveals nothing about the position of the other

[116] HAC.BAC.371/1991.620, Note à M Jean Rey, Président du Groupe Juridique et à M Caron, Président du Groupe du Marché Intérieur. Objet: Observations de la Commission devant la Cour de Justice au sujet des demandes préjudicielles de la 'Tariefcommissie' néerlandaise.

[117] Interview de Pierre Pescatore / Pierre Pescatore. Sanem: CVCE [Prod.], 12.11.2003. CVCE, Sanem (19:22, Editing, Original Sound Track). Centre Virtuel de la Connaissance sur l'Europe, Château de Sanem, L-4992 Sanem (Luxembourg).

[118] The document is included in Giuseppe Perini, *Alberto Trabucchi guirista europeo*, unpublished dissertation, Universita' Degli Studi di Padova, 2005 with permission of the ECJ President, Rodriguez Iglesias. Giuseppe Perini, who is also the grandson of Alberto Trabucchi, has kindly made the document available.

[119] This is supported by the memory of Pescatore: interview with Pescatore by this author conducted in February 2006. Here he claimed that both Hammes and Donner were opposed to the doctrine of direct effect. For an example of Hammes' thinking on European law and the relation to national law before the *Van Gend en*

judges. According to Pierre Pescatore, who has gone furthest in reconstructing the decision-making process, a careful reading of the *Van Gend en Loos* ruling shows the distinct style of writing of Robert Lecourt.[120] Indeed, Pescatore argues that it was Lecourt who from his entering into the court was the main driving force behind the legal revolution and that his contribution is evident in most of the important rulings from 1962 onwards, in particular in *Van Gend en Loos* and *Costa v ENEL*, where he was the *rapporteur* in the latter case.[121] Although the evidence is fragile, it seems likely that Trabucchi and Lecourt were the legal minds behind the *Van Gend en Loos* ruling. At this time, we have no evidence on which to determine the position of the other three judges: Italian Rino Rossi, German Otto Riese and Belgian Louis Delvaux.[122]

In light of the Commission's position, it is clear that the ECJ ruling was not completely out of step with the political forces in the Community, despite the fact that three traditionally pro-integration Member States expressly opposed the introduction of direct effect. To what extent did the ECJ overtake the arguments of the Commission in the ruling? Did the intellectual basis of the *Van Gend en Loos* ruling come from the legal service of the Commission, as Eric Stein[123] has claimed, or was Lecourt the decisive figure, as argued by Pescatore?[124] This is a most difficult question to answer conclusively due to the lack of primary sources from the internal deliberations of the court. Trabucchi does not mention the Commission position (or Lecourt, for that matter) in his internal memorandum. What is perhaps more important than the intellectual copyrights of the

Loos ruling, see HAC.CEAB.1.1035, Charles-Léon Hammes, Président de Chambre à la Cour de Justice des Communautés Européennes Professeur à l'Université de Bruxelles, Recherche des Points d'Impact du Droit Communautaire dans le Domaine des Droits Nationaux.

[120] Pescatore worked alongside Lecourt from 1967 to 1979 and is very likely able to detect Lecourt's style of writing. Unfortunately, Lecourt has left neither private archive nor private papers behind, which will make it difficult to confirm Pescatore's linguistic analysis with primary sources.

[121] Pierre Pescatore, Commission européenne, DG X 'Information Communication, Culture, Audiovisuel', *40 ans des Traités de Rome—Colloque universitaire organisé à la mémoire d'Emile Noël—Actes du colloque de Rome 26–27 mars 1997* (Brussels, Bruylant), 72–6 and 108–9 and Pierre Pescatore, Robert Lecourt (1908–2004), Eloge funèbre par Pierre Pescatore ancien Juge de la Cour, à l'audience solennelle du 7 mars 2005 (2005) *Revue trimestrielle de droit européen* 3, 589–796.

[122] We can only speculate as to the positions of the three remaining judges. It is striking that Otto Riese left the ECJ immediately after the *Van Gend en Loos* judgment. The new German judge Walter Strauss began the day after the judgment. However, Riese allegedly left the ECJ because he was disappointed about not becoming president. He took a position at the University of Lausanne as a director of the Institute of European Studies, which has recently been founded. Nicole-Céline Braun, *La Fonction Supranationale. Présidents – Membres – Juges des Communautés Européennes. Etude comparée des personalités & des Collegès (1952–1967).* Dissertation, Fondation Nationale Des Sciences Politiques Cycle Superieur d'études Politiques, 1967, 246. Braun interviewed all the judges of the 1960s to write her dissertation.

[123] Eric Stein, 'Lawyers, Judges and the Making of a Transnational Constitution' (1981) 75 *American Journal of International Law* 1, 1–27, 24.

[124] There are two important traces of Lecourt's legal thinking before the *Van Gend en Loos* ruling. Pescatore claimed that Lecourt in his first case at the ECJ as rapporteur in the joined Cases 2/62 and 3/62 (*Commission v Luxembourg and Belgium*)—the so-called 'pain d'épice', inserted the first notion of the EC as a special organisation. Pierre Pescatore, Robert Lecourt (1908–2004), Eloge funèbre par Pierre Pescatore ancien Juge de la Cour, à l'audience solennelle du 7 mars 2005 (2005) *Revue trimestrielle de droit européen*, no 3, 589–796. For Lecourt's thinking before he was nominated as judge, see Michel Mangenot, *Une Europe improbable. Les hauts fonctionnaires français dans la construction européenne 1948–1992* (PhD dissertation, Université Robert Schuman de Strasbourg, 2000), 467 in which he cites an article by Lecourt in *Le Monde* from 23 February 1962. Here Lecourt argued that the Establishment of the Common Market would not only happen from the political level, but also from below. For the latter process, law would play a central role. There is a remarkable similarity between his *Le Monde* article from 1962 and the legal logic of the *Van Gend en Loos* and *Costa v ENEL* rulings as well as his later writings on the topic.

legal argument underlying the *Van Gend en Loos* ruling is the degree to which the legal service of the Commission and the ECJ held similar views on European law. One explanation of this is the close links that existed between the ECJ and the legal service of the Commission.[125] However, this explanation overlooks the extent to which the broader context, in which both the ECJ and the Commission operated, shaped the views of the leading protagonists.

The influence of federalist ideology was one striking factor. The Hallstein Commission, which adopted Gaudet's memorandum in the *Van Gend en Loos* case, was dominated by European-minded personalities such as Jean Rey, who was directly responsible for the legal service and who in 1967 as Commission president strongly supported the legal revolution.[126] Other such members included Sicco Mansholt, a leading Dutch socialist and federalist, as well as Walter Hallstein himself, who also held a background as a professor of law. The leader of the legal service, Gaudet, whom we saw played a crucial role in developing the Commission position in the *Van Gend en Loos* case, had for more than a decade been a close associate of Jean Monnet and remained in close contact with him.[127] Likewise, Lecourt had been a prominent member of the Mouvement Républicain Populaire (MRP) and a firm supporter of the European policies of Robert Schuman during the first half of the 1950s. He was also a member of Monnet's Action Committee for the United States of Europe from 1955 onwards.[128] Finally, Trabucchi, although he was never part of the Italian federalist movement, showed sympathy from early on for considering the EC as a new legal phenomenon that might eventually integrate the various national legal systems around a core of European values.[129]

Another crucial factor shaping and supporting the legal revolution was the existence of comprehensive transnational networks of European minded jurists. These networks had developed during the 1950s and had been closely involved in the negotiations of the failed European Political Community from 1952 to 1954.[130] In the first half of the 1960s, the various networks established national associations on European law[131] and founded a European umbrella organisation, Fédération International pour le Droit Européen

[125] The two institutions worked together to document national responses to European law with the Le Centre de documentation du Service juridique des Exécutifs européens en liaison avec le Service de documentation de la Court de justice des Communautés européennes. HAC.BAC 24/1967, 147, 1961–1964. At times there was also direct (although secret) communication between Commission and ECJ officials on important legal questions. For example, during the *Costa v ENEL* case, Lecourt's référendaire, Roger Chevallier, and legal councillor of the legal service of the Commission, Gerhard Berb, discussed the nature of the ruling of the Italian Constitutional Court. HAC.BAC 371/1991.757, Note à l'attention de MM Gaudet, Marchisini concernant l'arrêt de la Cour constitutionelle italienne no 14, du 7 mars 1964.

[126] HAC.BAC 118/1986, 998, 28, 1962–1968, La Construction Juridique Communautaire, Rapport de la première décennie de la CEE, JUR/CEE/816, 26 juin 1967.

[127] Michel Dumoulin (ed), *The European Commission, 1958–72. History and Memories* (Brussels, European Commission, 2007), 224–5.

[128] Raymond Poidevin, *Robert Schuman. Homme d'État 1886–1963*, Imprimerie nationale, Paris, 1986 and Eric Roussel, Jean Monnet.

[129] Giuseppe Perini, *Alberto Trabucchi guirista europeo* (dissertation, Universita' Degli Studi di Padova, 2005) 68–75.

[130] Antonin Cohen, Constitutionalism without Constitution: Transnational Elites Between Political Mobilization and Legal Expertise in the Making of a Constitution for Europe (1940s–1960s), (2007) 32 *Law & Social Inquiry* 32, 1, 109–35.

[131] The French 'Association française des Juristes européens' had already been established in 1953. The other associations were set up in the first half of the 1960s; Nederlandse Vereniging voor Europees Recht, Associazione Italian dei Giuristi Europei, Association Belge pour le Droit Européen, Wissentschaftliche Gesellschaft für Europarecht and Association luxembourgeoise des Juristes européens.

(FIDE). During the 1960s the national associations and FIDE organised a large number of conferences attended both by academics and practitioners of European law, including officials from the Commission and ECJ judges. The national associations also promoted the teaching of and research in European law at national universities, and during the first half of the 1960s they established new academic journals devoted to the study of European law.[132] These activities were largely financed by the Commission, which considered them a crucial tool for securing the support of national judiciaries of the European legal order, essential for the provision of Article 177 cases to the ECJ.[133] The associations of European law would serve to promote European law and the ECJ in numerous ways. Crucially, members of the national associations who served as advocates and national judges were behind important preliminary references sent to the ECJ.[134] Secondly, while the networks of European-minded jurists were small in their respective national context, they would become vocal promoters of European law and firm supporters of the jurisprudence of the ECJ. National judiciaries were not easily convinced about the virtues of a European legal order, and in Germany, for example, it took decades of intense lobbying by jurists such as Hans-Peter Ipsen, Gert Nicolaisen and CP Ophüls to secure the grudging acceptance of central features of European law by the German judiciary.[135] Finally, the ECJ and the legal service of the Commission used the various conferences and seminars of the associations as sounding boards when considering important cases.[136]

A strong transnational alliance between the Commission, the ECJ and transnational networks of jurists sharing a common federalist ideology, clearly acted together to promote a particular vision of European law. This alliance helps explain the similarity of views by the legal service of the Commission and the ECJ demonstrated in the *Van Gend en Loos* case, but also the audacity with which these institutions promoted them. Nevertheless, the breach that the *Van Gend en Loos* judgment represented with traditional international law and the opposition of three Member States meant that only a slim majority in the ECJ supported the new direction. Thus, while the *Van Gend en Loos* judgment was shaped by the broader structural factors just mentioned, it ultimately depended on the very recent nomination of Trabucchi and Lecourt. Without their nominations and contributions the ECJ most likely would not have introduced direct effect and the trajectory of the European legal order would have been fundamentally different.

Trabucchi and Lecourt replaced respectively Nicola Catalano and Jacques Rueff, who both stepped down during their term; the former had actually just seen his term

[132] Leading journals were Rivista di diritto europeo (1961), Common Market Law Review 1964, Cahiers de droit européen (1965), Revue trimistrielle de droit Européen (1965), Europarecht (1966).

[133] For a general memorandum on the links between the Commission, the national associations and FIDE consult: HAC.CEAB 2. 2936, 179, 1962–1964. Note à Messieurs les Membres du Conseil d'Administration du Service Juridique des Exécutifs Européens, de M Gaudet, R Krawielicki, Th Vogelaar,

[134] Antoine Vauchez, Une élite d'intermédiaires. Genèse d'un capital juridique européen, *Actes de la recherche en sciences sociales*, février 2007 and Antonin Cohen, Constitutionalism without Constitution. Transnational Elites between Political Mobilization and Legal Expertise (1940s–1960s), (2007) 23 *Law & Social Inquiry* 1.

[135] Billy Davies, *The Constitutionalisation of the European Communities: West Germany between Legal Sovereignty and European Integration 1949–1974*, Dissertation, King's College, 2007.

[136] Karen Alter, *Jurist Social Movements in Europe: The Role of Euro-Law Associations in European Integration (1953–1975)*, Paper presented at the Conference on The Historical Roots of European Legal Integration, Copenhagen University, 26 October 2007.

renewed.[137] The nomination of Trabucchi is shrouded in the occasional mystery of Italian politics. He was apparently nominated because his brother became Minister of Economy. Being a lawyer of private law and professor at *Universita' degli studi di Padova*, he was certainly an unlikely choice for a position as European judge.[138] Rueff had been the leading figure behind the new economic policies of de Gaulle, designed to prepare France for the Common Market, and finally resigned in 1962 due to his new responsibilities. The French president first opted for René Cassin but the President of the ECJ, Donner, found the nominee too old.[139] This was a remarkable rejection and possibly one with political connotations.[140] Although Cassin was 75 years old at the time, he went on three years later to become President of the European Court of Human Rights in Strasbourg from 1965 to 1969. Instead, Lecourt was chosen and readily accepted the offer.[141] We do not know why de Gaulle nominated a renowned European to the ECJ, considering his negative views on supranational Europe.[142] Having been the *Ministre des Territoires d'Outre-Mer* and leader of the ministers from the MRP in the government, Lecourt had left the Debré government on 24 August 1961 in protest at the Prime Minister's leadership style, and his fellow party members quickly followed him.[143] It is strikingly ironic that the nomination of Lecourt arguably constitutes de Gaulle's most lasting contribution to European integration and with an effect in complete contrast to the European policies he pursued during the 1960s.

While the nominations of Trabucchi and Lecourt were decisive in allowing the activist road taken by the ECJ from 1963 onwards, the legal revolution ultimately depended on the

[137] Historical Archive of the Council of Ministers (HACM) CM2/1961.622, Lettre de M AM Donner, President de la Cour de Justice des Communautés européennes, adressée au: Président de la Conférence des Représentants des Gouvernements des Etats membres; HACM.CM2/1961.622, Note, Objet: Renouvellement d'un certain nombre de membres des Institutions européennes, Bruxelles, le 25 septembre 1961; HACM.CM2/1961.622, Telegramme de Catalano pour Calmes Secrétarire Général Conseil Bruxelles, Luxembourg le 5 octobre 1961.

[138] President Donner's welcome was also somewhat frosty. See *Cour de Justice, Audiences solennelles 1959–1963*, Library of the European Court of Justice, Luxembourg, 26–8. According to Giuseppe Perini, the other judges quickly changed their mind with regard to Trabucchi's abilities. Giuseppe Perini, *Alberto Trabucchi guirista europeo* (unpublished dissertation, Universita' Degli Studi di Padova, 2005), 57–9.

[139] I have not yet been able to confirm this on the basis of the Council and Commission archives. Nicole-Céline Braun, *La Fonction Supranationale. Présidents—Membres—Juges des Communautés Européennes. Etude comparée des personalités & des Collegès (1952–1967)* (Dissertation, Fondation Nationale Des Sciences Politiques Cycle Superieur d'études Politiques, 1967), 115. This information was later left out of the book: Nicole-Céline Braun, *Commissaires et juges dans les communautés européennes, (Librairie Générale de Droit et de jurisprudence)* (Paris, R Pichon and R Durand-Auzias, 1972).

[140] Cassin had been the legal advisor of the Free French government of Charles de Gaulle during the Second World War. From 1944 he was vice-president of the *Conseil d'Etat* and in 1960 he became a member of the *Conseil Constitutionel*, which de Gaulle had established to control the French judiciary in his new Fifth Republic. AW Brian Simpson, *Human Rights and the End of Empire, Britain and the Genesis of the European Convention* (Oxford, Oxford University Press, 2001), 365 and Michel Mangenot, *Une Europe improbable. Les hauts fonctionnaires français dans la construction europénne 1948–1992* (Dissertation, Université Robert Schuman de Strasbourg, 2000), 465–6.

[141] HAC.CEAB2.1137, Telex de Robert Lecourt, pour Monsieur M Couve de Murville, Président de la Conférence des Représentants des Gouvernements des Etats Membres, Luxembourg, le 18 mai 1962; HAC-.CEAB2.1137, Telex de M Couve de Murville aux bons soins de: Monsieur Roger Reynaud, membre de la haute autorité de la CECA., Luxembourg, 17.05.62.

[142] Charles de Gaulle's papers remain inaccessible to the public.

[143] Pierre Pescatore, Robert Lecourt (1908–2004), Eloge funèbre par Pierre Pescatore ancien Juge de la Cour, à l'audience solennelle du 7 mars 2005 (2005) *Revue trimestrielle de droit européen* 3, 589–796 and Nicole-Céline Braun, *La Fonction Supranationale. Présidents—Membres—Juges des Communautés Européennes. Etude comparée des personalités & des Collèges (1952–1967)*, PhD dissertation, Fondation Nationale Des Sciences Politiques Cycle Superieur d'études Politiques, 1967, 115.

way the EEC Treaty had been designed. One major legal innovation, namely the system of preliminary references as outlined in Article 177, as well as a number of legal details in the EEC Treaty, proved to be essential to the constitutionalisation of the EC.

In the negotiations on the Treaties of Rome, the so-called *Groupe de rédaction* from October 1956 to March 1957 dealt with all legal questions, including what was believed by the governments to be a small revision of the ECSC Court of Justice. Led by Italian ambassador Roberto Ducci, the committee was mostly constituted by European-minded jurists from the six states engaged in the negotiations and from the ECSC, among them such important figures as Nicola Catalano (l'Avvocatura dello Stato, Italy and later ECJ judge), Pierre Pescatore (Legal advisor, Foreign Ministry, Luxembourg and later ECJ judge), Michel Gaudet (Director of the legal service, ECSC and later Director of the Legal Service of the EC), Ernst Wohlfarth (German Ministry of Justice and later Director of the Legal Service of the Council) and Jean Jacques de Bresson (magistrat détaché, Quai d'Orsay, France). In an article on the work of the committee, Pescatore has emphasised the autonomy and wide reaching tasks of the *Groupe de rédaction* and how its proposals were almost all accepted at the political level of the negotiations.[144] Recent historiography on the negotiations on the Treaties of Rome does confirm the significant autonomy of the *Groupe de rédaction*, in particular in purely legal matters, but in contrast to Pescatore's claim also demonstrates how the Member States not only decided the main outline of the competences of the institutions and the nature of the decision-making process, but also kept a firm grip on detail.[145] Nevertheless, the latitude given the *Groupe de rédaction* on purely legal matters and the nature of the compromises made inside the committee would become fundamental to the revolutionary jurisprudence of the ECJ from 1963 onwards.[146]

Most importantly the continuation of the broad features of the ECSC ECJ ensured that European law still had roots in French administrative law and thereby shared a number of characteristics with internal state law. Considering how General Advocate Maurice Lagrange had already argued in 1954 that the ECSC ECJ was a constitutional court in embryo, this was no minor triumph.[147] Building on this the *Groupe de rédaction* added a large number of small and discrete legal innovations that highlighted the inner state character of European law and the potential of the ECJ as a constitutional court.[148] The most important innovation was the revision of the ECSC's system of preliminary references. Article 41 of the Treaty of Paris had only offered the ECJ to rule on the validity of acts. However, with the introduction of Article 177, the ECJ could now also address questions of interpretation. The proposal came from Catalano, who knew preliminary references from the Italian Constitutional system. With the support of the German and Benelux delegations, the proposal was accepted probably without the French representative Bresson quite understanding the potential of this new invention. It appeared after all

[144] Pierre Pescatore, Les Travaux du 'Groupe Juridique' dans la Négociation des Traités de Rome (1981) XXXIV *Studia Diplomatica* 1–4, 159–78 and Historical Archives of the European Union, Florence, Serie 09, Collection Melchionni/Ducci. INT. 63. 21.05.1984 Pierre Pescatore.

[145] Anne Boerger de Smedt, *Aux Origine de l'union européenne. La genèse des institutions communautaires (CECA, CED, CEE et EURATOM). Un equilibre fragile entre l'ideal européen et les interets nationaux*, 464–635.

[146] Pierre Pescatore, Les Travaux du 'Groupe Juridique' dans la Négociation des Traités de Rome, (1981) XXXIV *Studia Diplomatica* 1–4, 159–78, 175–6.

[147] Maurice Lagrance, La Cour de Justice de la Communauté européenne du charbon et de l'acier, (1954) 70 *Revue du droit public et de la science politique en France et à l'étranger* 2, 417–35.

[148] *Ibid.* Pescatore discusses several other examples of this in his article.

to be a relatively weak legal instrument.[149] Another example was the creation of Article 189 on the legislative acts of the Council which gave regulations direct effect. The existence of legislative acts with immediate effect was repeatedly used to justify the special nature of the Community, most prominently in the Commission position on *Van Gend en Loos* and in the *Costa v ENEL* judgment.[150]

However, despite the ambiguousness legal nature of the new ECJ caused by using the ECSC as model and promoted by the *Groupe de rédaction*, the contracting parties would probably have characterised the EEC and EURATOM treaties as traditional international treaties. Although French ambitions to completely remove the court of the institutional set up of the EEC was resisted by the other governments there were very few examples of a desire on the side of the contracting parties to endow European law with direct effect and almost no mentioning of the supremacy of European law, which under traditional international law would have to be formulated explicitly to be applied as general principles. Instead, the mechanisms of enforcement of European law in the Member States were Articles 169 and 170, which allowed the Commission and Member States to raise infringement cases, but did not have direct consequences inside the legal order of the Member States and contained no specific sanctions against the perpetrator. This understanding of the Treaties of Rome is confirmed by a closer analysis of the negotiations.

During the entire negotiations, a consensus existed between the governments involved that the objective was to create two economic communities, not a political union.[151] This attitude reflected the fear that the new project would suffer a fate similar to the European Defence Community, which had been rejected in the French national assembly in 1954. This did not necessarily mean that many negotiators did not have a federalist European outlook or that many did not consider the two new communities an important first step in the direction of a European federation. However, agreement existed that common institutions should consequently not go beyond what was strictly necessary for the accomplishment of the economic objectives, and that federalist rhetoric should be avoided. The final EEC Treaty reflected these concerns. A new institutional balance was struck in favour of the Council and the institutional provisions were placed at the end of the treaty. Likewise, there was no reference to a federal or political Europe, only a vague reference to the objective of creating 'an ever closer union among the peoples of Europe'.[152] Considering the nature of the EEC Treaty it is quite clear that the contracting

[149] Bresson later claimed to have fought against the article. Michel Mangenot, *Une Europe improbable. Les hauts fonctionnaires français dans la construction europénne 1948–1992* (Dissertation, Université Robert Schuman de Strasbourg, 2000), 475–6. Unfortunately, there are no traces of Bresson and the work of the Groupe de rédaction in the archives of the Quai d'Orsay.

[150] Pierre Pescatore, Les Travaux du 'Groupe Juridique' dans la Négociation des Traités de Rome, (1981) XXXIV *Studia Diplomatica*, 1–4, 159–78, 171–2.

[151] Only the Dutch government wanted the new Communities to include strong supranational institutions, but these wishes (eventually with few exceptions) had to bow to French reluctance.

[152] Although Jean-François Denieau has claimed that everybody had forgotten the preamble until right before the signature and that he invented the famous line, the true story is perhaps somewhat duller. Jean-François Deniau, *L'Europe Interdite* (Éditions du Seuil, Paris, 1977), 64–5. The *Groupe de rédaction* and the *Groupe du Marché Commun* prepared the preamble during the last month of negotiations in early 1957, and the famous line was added during a meeting between the heads of delegations on 16 and 17 February 1957. HACM.NEGO.CM3.182, Groupe de Rédaction, Projet de rédaction de préamble et des dispositions initiales du Traité Institutiant le Marché Commun, Bruxelles, le 10 janvier 1957, MAE 62 f/57 ssw; HACM.NEGO.CM3.126, Comité des Chefs de Délégation Réunion des 16/17.2.1957, Projet d'ordre de jour, Bruxelles, le 14 février 1957, Ch Del 322, Annexe, MAE 506 f/57 mr; HACM.NEGO.CM3.126, Ausschuss der Delegationsleiter, Entwurf eines Protokolls über die Sitzung des Ausschusses der Delegationsleiter am 17 und 18 Februar 1957 in Paris, Ch Del

partners had purposely cut the political dimension of the Community down to an absolute minimum. Furthermore, powers were centralised in the Council leaving the Commission somewhat weaker than the High Authority in the ECSC and keeping the European Assembly outside the decision making process.

Considering the ambiguous outcome of the negotiation as regard the ECJ, it would be fortuitous to claim that the contracting parties' intention had been to set up a traditional system of international law, however. It is quite plausible that the intention of the contracting parties of international treaties can seldom be established in the broad meaning explored here. Instead, the analysis demonstrated the complexity of a set of negotiations during which created a European legal order with important similarities with traditional international law, while at the same time maintaining and strengthening traits of internal state law. This ambiguity gave room for the audacious interpretations of the ECJ during the legal revolution, while also explaining the internal division of the ECJ and the surprised, if not shocked, response of the Member State governments.

Conclusion

What is perhaps most striking about the legal revolution is how accidental it was. The central *Van Gend en Loos* ruling was a narrow decision that depended on two new judges, whose nomination less than a year before had been far from straightforward. Furthermore, for the ECJ to launch its revolutionary jurisprudence depended not only on a particular reading of the EEC Treaty, which was shared with the legal service of the Commission, but also on a number of legal elements in the EEC treaty, most notably Article 177, inserted by the *groupe rédaction* during the negotiations of the Treaties of Rome. Arguably European law could easily have remained traditional international law with the consequences this would have had for the EC. While historical accidents and unintended consequences (if seen from the perspective of the contracting parties) may have played a fundamental role, this is not to claim that structural factors were not important and could not later potentially have reversed a more conservative jurisprudence. Most importantly, the history outlined above demonstrates the importance and effectiveness of a transnational coalition of pro-European jurists working to further a federal Europe constituted by the Hallstein Commission, the ECJ and well-organised transnational networks of jurists.

Placing the legal revolution in the broader context of the history of the EC, the 'ruin myth' promoted in legal circles cannot be sustained. This is not to deny that ECJ judges such as Lecourt probably saw European politics of the 1960s in this light. However, while sharp disagreements existed between de Gaulle and the Hallstein Commission over the political dimension of the EC, France was one of the central actors behind the establishment of common policies and the success of the early Community. The choice was not

356, MAE 613 d/57 arz/ls; HACM.NEGO.CM3.182, Groupe du Marché Commun, Projet de rédaction pour le Préambule et les Articles I A 3 et observations relatives à l'Article 3 bis et à l'insertion d'une disposition unique concernant la Politique économique générale soumis sur la base de la discussion, and HACM.NEGO.CM3.182, Comité des Chefs de Délégation, Projet de rédaction pour le Préamble et les Articles 1 à 6 adoptée par le Comité des Chefs de délégation le 16 février 1957, Bruxelles, le 25 février 1957 Ch Del 352 (remplace le doc Ch Del 533), MAE 586 (rev) f/57 mts.

necessarily between either constitutionalisation on the one hand and a scenario of 'ruin' on the other, as the Luxembourg compromise also demonstrated by keeping the EEC Treaty intact. Therefore the legal revolution can best be interpreted as an example of how federalist political forces inside the Community institutions tried to push the EC towards a federation by the means of law. Arguably the constitutionalisation of the Treaties of Rome was as much (or little) against the intention of the contracting parties as the intergovernmental Europe promoted by de Gaulle.

What did the legal revolution mean to the institutional balance obtained with the Luxembourg compromise? Historians and social scientists have often overlooked the importance of the constitutionalisation of the treaties and concluded that the informal introduction of the right to veto meant that the Luxembourg compromise was a French victory. In retrospect, however, what stands out is that the Treaties of Rome and the jurisprudence of the ECJ were clearly left intact. Admittedly, the constitutionalisation of the treaties had only a limited practical effect during the 1960s and 1970s, in particular in Italy and France where respectively the Italian Constitutional Court and the Conseil d'Etat continued to ignore it. However, as Joseph Weiler has correctly pointed out with the introduction of majority voting as part of the Single European Act in 1986, the binding nature of European law was suddenly felt by the Member States.[153] Today nobody would dispute that constitutionalisation has been fundamental in shaping the European polity.

Turning towards a normative assessment of the legal revolution, what was at stake for the future Europe? While we should certainly not be blind to the self-empowerment which the legal revolution represented for the ECJ and the Commission, the constitutionalisation also reflected a simple democratic choice on behalf of the citizens of the Community. By creating a Common Market, the Member States had embarked on a project that was fundamental in nature, not only for the material well-being but also for the economic and political freedoms of their citizens. European legislation would inexorably place important obligations on Member State citizens and if a European legal system did not secure access to raise questions of European law before national courts and the ECJ, this would place the legal rights of the individual in the hands of national governments and administrations. The constitutionalisation clearly drew the logical legal consequence of the nature of the European project vis-à-vis national citizens.

The dilemma, of course, was that in doing this, a small elite of jurists in the ECJ and the Commission, in a new institutional system without any other democratic legitimacy than that represented by the elected governments in the Council, deliberately chose what must be characterised as a radical interpretation of the Treaties of Rome. However, would a weaker legal system as claimed by judges and legal scholars not have turned the EU into a loose intergovernmental organisation unable to solve the economic and political problems of Europe? While this question is extremely difficult to answer, legal scholars have certainly been too focused on law and decision-making procedures when expounding how weak Europe would have become, as if co-operation between Member States and progress in the Community depended solely on a strong legal system and smooth decision-making procedures. To the historian such a view builds on a superficial understanding of what drives Member States' co-operation. Did, for example, the success of the SEA merely

[153] Joseph HH Weiler, 'The Transformation of Europe' (1991) *Yale Law Journal* 100, 2403–83.

depend on the introduction of majority voting or did it not rather rest on a deeper consensus between Member States' governments about the importance of the Single Market project?

III

Case 11/70, *Internationale Handelsgesellschaft mbH v Einfuhr- und Vorratsstelle für Getreide und Futtermittel* and Case 4/73, *J Nold, Kohlen- und Baustoffgroßhandlung v Commission of the European Communities*

1

The Incorporation of Fundamental Rights in the Community Legal Order

JOSÉ NARCISO CUNHA RODRIGUES[1]

One of the first cases in which the question of fundamental rights was raised was an annulment action against the High Authority of the European Coal and Steel Community, Case 1/58, *Stork*.[2]

The applicant argued that, in the contested decisions of the High Authority, the rights of the individual which are protected under almost all the constitutions of the Member States had remained a dead letter.

Starting from a dichotomy between Community law and national law, the Court decided in three steps: first, it stated that the High Authority was only required to apply Community law and consequently it was not competent to apply the national law of the Member States. Secondly, it confirmed that under Article 31 of the ECSC Treaty, the Court was only required to ensure that the law was observed in the interpretation and application of the Treaty and of rules laid down for the implementation thereof. Thirdly, it held that, since it was not normally required to rule on provisions of national law, the High Authority was not empowered to examine a complaint that it had infringed principles of German constitutional law when it adopted its decision.

The Court's concern was to mark out the boundaries between the ECSC and the Member States. However, that judgment opened up a long controversy about the supremacy of Community law.[3]

Thus, in Joined Cases 36, 37, 38 and 40/59, *Geitling v High Authority of the ECSC*,[4] the applicants relied on German case law relating to the interpretation of Article 14 of the German Basic Law guaranteeing private property.

The Court insisted that it was not its function to ensure the observance of rules of internal law, even constitutional rules, in force in one or other of the Member States. Moreover, it held that Community law, as it arises under the ECSC Treaty, does not contain any general principle, express or otherwise, guaranteeing the maintenance of vested rights.

The dichotomy between Community law and internal law can be seen again here. Case 40/64 *Sgarlata v Commission*[5] was an annulment action in the field of the common

[1] Judge at the Court of Justice of the European Communities. I should like to thank Mr Timothy Millett for his assistance in establishing the English version of this text.

[2] [1959] ECR 17.

[3] See Joseph Weiler, *Methods of Protection: Towards a Second and Third Generation of Protection, in Human Rights and the European Community : Methods of Protection* (Baden-Baden, Nomos, 1991) 576

[4] [1960] ECR 423.

[5] [1965] ECR 215.

agricultural policy. The applicants argued that the Commission's interpretation of *locus standi* did not give growers of citrus fruit in the Community sufficient legal protection, either at national or at Community level. More precisely, they alleged that, if recourse to Article 173 of the EEC Treaty were to be refused as a result of a restrictive interpretation of its wording, individuals would be deprived of all protection by the courts, both under Community law and under national law, which would be contrary to the fundamental principles governing all the Member States.

Holding the case inadmissible, the Court took a narrow view of that allegation, merely stating that those considerations, 'which would not be discussed here', could not be allowed to override the clearly restrictive wording of Article 173, which it was the Court's task to apply. In any event, the Court also stated that the reference price constituted a general criterion, adopted in the public interest, which limited the powers whereby the Commission and the Member States could discourage the importation of the products in question by measures for safeguarding the common agricultural market. That *obiter dictum* may be read as meaning that general principles were not lacking since protection against the powers of the institutions and of the Member States was ensured by the reference price.

The first judgment in which the Court applied a general principle of law which can be regarded as a fundamental right appears to be Joined Cases 18 and 35/65 *Max Gutmann v Commission.*[6] The case was an action for the annulment of a decision by the Commission of the European Atomic Energy Authority rejecting a complaint by the applicant official against two earlier decisions suspending him and transferring him.

The applicant had alleged a breach of the rule *non bis in idem.* The Court considered that that rule prohibited not only the imposition of two disciplinary measures for a single offence but also the holding of disciplinary proceedings more than once with the regard to a single set of facts.

Those were still the days of the establishment of the concept of supremacy and the creation, within a body of law based on economic freedoms, of methods corresponding to those built up in the different national laws.[7]

The preliminary ruling delivered in case 11/70 *Internationale Handelsgesellschaft*[8] appeared then as a foreseeable development. The spirit of the time can be discerned in the order of reference itself. The national court made the following observation: 'Although Community regulations nos 120/67 and 473/67 are not German laws, but legal rules pertaining to the European Economic Community which belong neither to public international law nor to the internal law of the Member States …, in accordance with Article 24, paragraph 1, of the Basic Law, by rectifying the EEC Treaty, the Federal Republic did not give up the application of elementary fundamental rights laid down in the Basic Law within the European Economic Community.'

The order of reference went on: 'It is necessary to start from the idea that the German legislature agreed to enter the European Economic Community only because it supposed

[6] [1966] ECR 103 and [1967] ECR 1961.

[7] Case 29/69 *Stauder v Ulm* [1969] ECR 419 carried out the first review in terms of fundamental rights, but did not find that they had been breached. The Court held that, interpreted in a certain way, the provision at issue contained 'nothing capable of prejudicing the fundamental human rights enshrined in the general principles of Community law and protected by the Court'.

[8] [1970] ECR 1125.

that the law of the Community of States would be of the same nature as German constitutional law, that is to say that the essential structural principles of internal law would be protected in Community law.'

The defendant in the main action made the point in a more indirect way when it submitted that the Court of Justice could not assess the validity of measures taken by Community institutions by reference to rules of national law, even constitutional law, or to the fundamental rights enshrined therein. Nevertheless, it argued, the fundamental right to free expression and free choice in commercial decisions, enounced by the German Basic Law, constituted an element of that common fund of fundamental values which formed part of Community law.

The Court of Justice replied to those arguments in a passage entitled 'The protection of fundamental rights in the Community legal system'. The 'rhetorical' character of that title clearly announced the importance of the passage that was to follow. It included several findings of major interpretative significance:

a) First, the Court reaffirmed the supremacy of Community law and its rank as an autonomous source of law. It gave two reasons for this: on one hand, because recourse to the legal rules or concepts of national law in order to judge the validity of measures adopted by the institutions of the Community would have an adverse effect on the uniformity and efficacy of Community law. On the other hand, because the law stemming from the Treaty, an independent source of law, could not because of its very nature be overridden by rules of national law, however framed, without being deprived of its character as Community law and without the legal basis of the Community itself being called in question.
b) Secondly, the Court considered that an examination should be made as to whether any analogous guarantee inherent in Community law had been disregarded. As a result, the Court held, on the one hand, that respect for fundamental rights forms an integral part of the general principles of law protected by the Court of Justice and, on the other hand, that the protection of such rights, whilst inspired by the constitutional traditions common to the Member States, must be ensured within the framework of the structure and objectives of the Community.

Those findings mark a break with the process in which the Court had been declining to analyse the question of fundamental rights.

The approach in *Internationale Handelsgesellschaft* was also that the autonomy of Community law required the inspiration from the constitutional traditions common to the Member States to be carried out 'within the framework of the structure and objectives of the Community'. That dual framework (structure and objectives) was based on a realistic vision of the differences between the Member States and the Community, particularly as regards the organisation of power, democratic participation, the role of the institutions and the historical importance of the economy in the field of legislation. However, as certain authors have pointed out,[9] the accent was placed less on fundamental rights as subjective, individual rights than on fundamental rights as instruments of integration.

Furthermore, the Court remained strictly within the dichotomy between Community law and national law, declining to undertake the review of the compatibility of acts

[9] See Weiler, 583.

adopted by the Community institutions with the constitutional law of the Member States. The Court persisted in a unilateral analysis of relations between the Community legal order and the national legal orders.

In Case 4/73 *Nold v Commission*,[10] a coal wholesaler sought the annulment of a Commission decision authorising new terms of business by Ruhrkohle AG. The applicant claimed that the terms of business of Ruhrkohle and the way they were applied infringed certain fundamental rights enshrined in the national constitutions and received into Community law. This was alleged to be the case in respect of the right of property ownership, the protection of which was ensured in particular by Article 14 of the German Basic Law and by the constitution of the Land of Hesse.

The applicant alleged that its exclusion from the coal trade was equivalent to expropriation because it deprived it of 'actual possession'. The applicant also alleged the infringement of the following rights in the case: the right to free development of the personality, the right to freedom of economic action and the principle of proportionality. In addition to the German constitution, the applicant relied on the constitutions of other Member States and various international treaties, including in particular the European Convention for the Protection of Human Rights and Fundamental Freedoms of 4 November 1950 (ECHR) and the Protocol to that Convention of 20 March 1952.

The defendant answered that it was not for the Court of Justice to interpret and apply rules of domestic law of a Member State, even those appertaining to the Constitution. Moreover, it argued, the ECSC Treaty contained no general principle of law, written or unwritten, guaranteeing the maintenance of acquired positions.

In its judgment of 14 May 1974, the Court of Justice held that, as it had already stated, 'fundamental rights form an integral part of the general principles of law, the observance of which it ensures' and that 'in safeguarding these rights, the Court is bound to draw inspiration from the constitutional traditions common to the Member States'.

From those considerations the Court drew the inference that it could not 'uphold measures which are incompatible with fundamental rights recognized and protected by the constitutions of those States'. That postulate, inserted as it is in the specific context of a complaint (that is, that the terms of business applied by a company and approved by the Commission in breach of fundamental rights) raises interesting theoretical questions. Although it cannot be read as laying down a principle, at the very least it was the beginning of a line of case law, consolidated later, whereby the Court extended the review of compliance with fundamental rights to national measures when these were adopted in implementation of Community law.[11] Compliance with fundamental rights was no longer a limit to the power of the Community institutions alone. Likewise, for the first time, the Court made reference to international instruments.

The judgment established a hierarchy of sources between fundamental rights acknowledged in the constitutions of the Member States and international instruments concerning the protection of human rights. In the case of the former, the Court is bound to draw inspiration from the constitutional traditions common to the Member States and not to

[10] [1974] ECR 491; followed in later decisions, in particular Case 136/79 *National Panasonic* [1980] ECR 2033.

[11] That case law has been confirmed in Joined Cases 60 and 61/84 *Cinéthèque* [1985] ECR 2605, paragraph 26, and Case 5/88 *Wachauf* [1989] ECR 2609, paragraph 19.

uphold measures which are incompatible with those fundamental rights.[12] In the case of the latter, the Court is subject to a lesser requirement: 'International treaties for the protection of human rights on which the Member States have collaborated or of which they are signatories can supply guidelines which should be followed within the framework of Community law.'

Thus the Court drew a distinction between an 'obligation', albeit attenuated by the term 'inspiration' (as regards the common constitutional traditions) and mere 'guidelines' (in the case of international treaties). The Court added that 'rights of this nature are protected by law subjected always to limitations laid down in accordance with the public interest'; and that, within the Community legal order, it seems legitimate that 'these rights should, if necessary, be subject to certain limits justified by the overall objectives pursued by the Community, on condition that the substance of these rights is left untouched'.

This finding laid down a 'horizontal provision limiting fundamental rights'.[13] The limits are justified by 'the overall objectives pursued by the Community', and are subject to the conditions that the substance of the rights is left untouched and that the principle of proportionality is respected[14]. This structure is drawn from the ECHR as regards the first two rules and, as regards the principle of proportionality, from the constitutional principles prevailing in certain Member States. It proved to be a source for later case law both weighting the relative importance of rights and defining a hard core of fundamental rights which do not admit any possibility of graduation.[15]

Schmidberger[16] is the most recent case in which the Court has spelt out this distinction between absolute and relative prerogatives. *Internationale Handelsgesellschaft* and *Nold* are informed by a paneuropean vision. Those judgments are typical of a period when, after the autonomous, supranational framework of Community law had been established, it had to be endowed with the principles inherent in the rule of law.

Tracing the presence of fundamental rights in the case law of the Court of Justice over the years, one would find that, before 1969, fundamental rights were considered to be outside the jurisdiction of the Court or otherwise not necessary to resolve the dispute. From 1969 onwards, fundamental rights were analysed as being included in the general principles of Community law, of which the Court ensures the observance. From 1974/

[12] A question may arise as to the common standards from which the Court claims to draw inspiration. It appears that the judgment does not envisage an assessment of those standards in hierarchical order or even on a sort of mathematical average. The term 'inspiration' allows the choices to be linked solely to the specific tension of the judicial function.

[13] A statement confirmed later by Case 44/79 *Hauer* [1979] ECR 3727 and Case 5/88 *Wachauf* [1989] ECR 2609.

[14] See A Tancredi, *L'emersione dei diritti fondamentali assoluti nella giurisprudenza comunitaria*, Rivista di Diritto Internazionale, Milano, vol LXXXIX, 2006, fasc 3, 649.

[15] This line of reasoning was worked out in more detail, for example with regard to the social function of property, in Case 44/79 *Hauer* [1979] ECR 3727.

[16] Case C-112/00 [2003] ECR I-5659. The request for a preliminary ruling came from an Austrian Court. The applicant in the main action was a German undertaking engaged in international road transport, and it was claiming damages from the Austrian authorities because its lorries had been prevented from using the Brenner motorway by a demonstration combined with the Austrian rules on movement of lorries at weekends and bank holidays. The Court held that, 'unlike other fundamental rights enshrined in the ECHR, such as the right to life or the prohibition of torture and inhuman or degrading treatment or punishment, which admit of no restriction, neither the freedom of expression nor the freedom of assembly guaranteed by the ECHR appears to be absolute but must be viewed in relation to its social purpose' (paragraph 80).
On the limitation of fundamental rights, see also Case C-368/95 *Familiapress* [1997] ECR I-3689, paragraph 26, and Case C-60/00 *Carpenter* [2002] ECR I-6279, paragraph 42.

1975, the Court refers explicitly to the ECHR.[17] Starting in 1989, the ECHR is cited as having a 'particular significance'.[18] From 1990 onwards, the Court of Justice cites actual decisions of the European Court of Human Rights.[19]

With hindsight it seems clear that the first judgments in this development both demonstrate and result from a dialogue with German case law. The *Solange I* judgment[20] of the German Constitutional Court has been seen as an answer to *Internationale Handelsgesellschaft*, but it is rather an echo of it, since objectively the prior Community case law was already a reaction to that country's case law. As is well known, *Solange I* decided that, so long as respect for fundamental rights at the Community level was not ensured by the Court of Justice, the German Court would exercise review over Community law.

That decision expressed a *continuum* in relation to other decisions regarding the rank of Community law and started from the premise that, in its then state of development, Community law, in particular the case law of the Court of Justice, was not capable of ensuring a standard of fundamental rights corresponding to that of the German Basic Law.[21]

Later (in 1986) *Solange II*[22] moved towards the presumption of a guarantee, whilst not putting back in question the principle of a reserve of competence: 'So long as the European Community, and in particular the case law of the Court of Justice, guaranties overall effective protection of fundamental rights in relation to the public powers of the Communities which may be considered as essentially comparable to that of the imperative guarantee of fundamental rights in the Basic Law, and in particular protects in a general way the substance of fundamental rights, the Constitutional Court will not exercise its jurisdiction in relation to the applicability of secondary Community law'.

The same Court's judgment in *Maastricht* (1993)[23] has been analysed as a step backwards,[24] but its judgment of 9 January 2001[25] appears to confirm *Solange II*, in the sense that the German Constitutional Court made it clear that it would ensure the observance of European fundamental rights, when it upheld the fundamental right to a lawful judge in a case where another German court had failed to fulfil its obligation to make a reference for a preliminary ruling under Article 234 of the EC Treaty.

These repercussions of the concept of 'equivalent protection' have had echoes in the constitutional case law of other Member States, in particular Austria, Italy, Spain and, most recently, France.[26] They represent contributions to the construction of what might be called a

[17] Case 36/75 *Rutili* [1975] ECR 1219. See also Case 136/79 *National Panasonic v Commission* [1980] ECR 2033, paragraph 19.

[18] Joined Cases 46/87 and 227/88 *Hoechst v Commission* [1989] ECR 2859, paragraph 13, and Case C-260/89 *ERT* [1991] ECR I-2925, paragraph 41.

[19] See, eg, Case C-7/98 *Krombach* [2000] ECR I-1935, paragraph 39.
After hesitations due to a certain reading of the Court's Opinion 2/94 [1996] ECR I-1759, the accession of the European Union to the ECHR appears to be a settled aim: see Article I-9 of the draft European Constitution. In that connection, it may be said that the Intergovernmental Conference went further than the preparatory Convention, in whose view the Union should only 'endeavour' to proceed to accession.

[20] BVerfGE 37, 271.

[21] See Willy Zimmer, *De nouvelles bases pour la coopération entre la Cour constitutionnelle fédérale et la Cour de justice de Luxembourg (à propos de BVerfGE, 7 juin 2000, Solange III)*, Europe, 11e année, no 3, March 2001, 4.

[22] BVerfGE 73, 339.

[23] BVerfGE 89, 155.

[24] The same Court's decision *Solange III* of 7 June 2000 appears to follow the *Maastricht* decision, but that conclusion is not free from doubt.

[25] 1 BvR 1036/99.

[26] As regards Spain and Italy, see Jasone Astola Madariaga, *Los derechos fundamentales y el derecho comunitario*, Cuadernos Europeos de Deusto, 18/1998, 126.

'constitutional arch'[27] linking the Community court to the national courts and which will be completed only when the Court of Justice has defined a concept of 'protection of fundamental rights' which is ensured throughout the Community legal order, whatever the extent of the Court's jurisdiction.[28] That protection may be exercised, where necessary, by the courts of the Member States under the supervision of the Community court. This is recognised by the judgments of the Court of Justice in *Union de Pequeños Agricultores*[29] and *Segi v Council*,[30] albeit that certain reservations might be expressed about those judgments.

The European Court of Human Rights has also subscribed to the idea of equivalent protection.[31] The Joint Declaration by the European Parliament, the Council and the Commission, of 5 April 1977, concerning the protection of fundamental rights and the European Convention for the Protection of Human Rights and Fundamental Freedoms,[32] after mentioning the case law of the Court, referred to the rights guaranteed by the constitutions of the Member States and to the ECHR. That citation bears out the interaction between case law and legislation and the importance of *Internationale Handelsgesellschaft* and *Nold* in the development of Community law.[33] These are also

[27] This expression is used in the sense in which the Court has frequently referred to the Treaty as the 'basic constitutional charter', *cf* Case 294/83 *Les Verts v European Parliament* [1986] ECR 1339, Case C-2/88-IMM *Zwartveld* [1990] ECR I-3365 and Opinion 1/91 [1991] ECR I-6079.

[28] At the present time, the Treaty on European Union in particular leaves the Court's jurisdiction in various respects incomplete.

[29] Case C-50/00 P [2002] ECR I-6677, paragraphs 40 and 41. The Court held that, 'where natural or legal persons cannot, by reason of the conditions for admissibility laid down in the fourth paragraph of Article 173 of the Treaty, directly challenge Community measures of general application, they are able, depending on the case, either indirectly to plead the invalidity of such acts before the Community Courts under Article 184 of the Treaty or to do so before the national courts and ask them, since they have no jurisdiction themselves to declare those measures invalid ... to make a reference to the Court of Justice for a preliminary ruling on validity. Thus it is for the Member States to establish a system of legal remedies and procedures which ensure respect for the right to effective judicial protection.'

[30] Case C-355/04 P, 27 February 2007, paragraphs 51 and 52. The Court held that, as stated in Article 6 TUE, the Union is founded on the rule of law and respect for human rights as general principles of Community law and that, to reply to the right to effective legal protection, the possibility of referring a case to the Court for a preliminary ruling must be open in relation to all provisions adopted by the Council, whatever their nature or form, which were intended to produce legal effects in relation to third parties.

[31] According to that Court, 'protection of fundamental rights offered by Community law is equivalent to that ensured by the mechanism of the [ECHR]': judgment of the European Court of Human Rights of 30 June 2005, *Bosphorus*, point 165.

[32] OJ C 103, 27 April 1977, 1.

[33] References to the ECHR have increased over time. See C-249/96 *Grant* [1998] I-621, C-297/88 and C-197/89 *Dzodzi* [1990] I-3763 and C-540/03 *European Parliament v Council* [2006] ECR I-5769.
A considerable number of judgments have been delivered in the field of fundamental rights. Among the more significant, see the following. In the field of freedom of expression: C-150/98 P *Economic and Social Committee v E* [1999] ECR I-8877, C-274/99 P *Connolly v Commission* [2001] ECR I-1611, C-340/00 P *Commission v Cwik* [2001] ECR I-10269, C-101/01 *Lindqvist* [2003] ECR I-12971, C-71/02 *Herbert Karner Industrie-Auktionen GmbH* [2004] ECR I-621. Regarding the protection of family or private life: C-122/99 P and C-125/99 P *D v Council* [2001] ECR I-4319, C-60/00 *Carpenter* [2002] ECR I-6279, C-413/99 *Baumbast* [2002] ECR I-7091, C-54/03 *European Parliament v Council* [2003] ECR I-5769, C-482/01 *Orfanopoulos* [2004] ECR I-5257, C-154/04 and C-155/04 *Alliance for Natural Health* [2005] ECR I-6451 and C-1/05 *Jia*, 9 January 2007. Concerning the inviolability of the home: 46/87 and 227/88 *Hoechst v Commission* [1989] ECR 2859. Regarding the right to property: C-20/00 and C-64/00 *Booker Aquaculture* [2003] ECR I-7411 and C-347/03 *Regione Autonoma Friuli-Venezia* [2005] ECR I-3785. As to the right to human dignity: C-377/98 *Netherlands v European Parliament and Council* [2001] ECR I-7079. On the subject of personal liberty: C-299/95 *Kremzow* [1997] ECR I-2629. As to the rights of the defence: C-28/05 *Dokter* [2006] ECR I-5431, and regarding the status of victims in criminal proceedings: C-105/03 *Pupino* [2005] ECR I-5285.
On the role of the Court of Justice, see Gianmario Demuro, *Corte di Giustizia delle comunità europea e Corte europea dei diritti dell'uomo*, Rassegna di diritto pubblico europeo, Ano II, no 1, 85 R *ff*.

demonstrated by the Single European Act (1986),[34] the Treaty of Maastricht (1992)[35] and the Treaty of Amsterdam (1997).[36]

In this way, recognition has been achieved of an 'autonomous' system of protection of fundamental rights at the European level. That system comprises its own standards, its own areas of competence,[37] a capacity of dialogue with the constitutional traditions common to the Member States, observance of the established body of Community law in the field of human rights, in particular as supplied by the ECHR, and the ability to develop within its specific theoretical context.

It is possible for the Court of Justice to refer a case back to the protection ensured by the Member States when a question is outside the scope of Community law.[38] However, deciding whether a question of fundamental rights is within or outside that scope is actually one of the most acute problems. The Court has attempted to set out general criteria and, on occasion, has adopted a broad interpretation of the facts,[39] but the principle has never been ruled out.[40]

In conclusion, it is possible to make the following assessment of this development. Community case law was criticised in particular for placing economic integration above the individual for too long. I would not subscribe to that view. I would submit that the internal coherence of Community case law is more apparent today as we have more of a perspective than previously. The Court could not have asserted individual rights without first establishing a system of protection based on the supremacy of Community law. Moreover, in a democratic society, an economic community could only have been a community governed by the rule of law.

Once the direct effect and supremacy of Community law had been established, it was necessary to proclaim fundamental rights as an attribute of the individual. Hence it is not excessive to maintain that the establishment of fundamental rights as individual rights transformed the nature of economic freedoms in a qualitative way. It may be said that nowadays fundamental rights may themselves be subject to a so-called functionalist method in two respects: by reinforcing their social impact and by deepening the subjective dimension of economic freedoms.[41] That development is still a legacy of *Internationale Handelsgesellschaft* and *Nold*.[42] Those judgments have led to:

[34] Which incorporated in its preamble the decision of the Member States jointly to promote democracy, on the basis of the fundamental rights recognised in the constitutions and the laws of the Member States, in the ECHR and the European Social Charter, in particular freedom, equality and social justice.

[35] With Article F(2) TEU, according to which the Union shall respect fundamental rights, as guaranteed by the ECHR and as they are result from the constitutional traditions common to the Member States, as general principles of Community law.

[36] The Treaty amended Article F(1) TEU (and renumbered it Article 6(1) TEU) to the effect that the Union is founded on the principles of liberty, democracy, respect for human rights and fundamental freedoms, and the rule of law, principles which are common to the Member States.

[37] These areas of competence refer to the Community as a whole, and may thus be complemented by the courts of the Member States according to the principle of equivalent protection.

[38] See Case C-309/96 *Annibaldi* [1997] ECR I-7493 and, although the lack of connecting factor may be subject to discussion, Case C-109/01 *Akrich* [2003] ECR I-9607, paragraphs 58 to 60.

[39] For instance, according to certain commentators, Case C-60/00 *Carpenter* [2002] ECR I-6279.

[40] See, eg, Joined Cases 60 and 61/84 *Cinéthèque* [1985] ECR 2605, and Case C-299/95 *Kremzow* [1997] ECR I-2629.

[41] *Cf* Helen Toner, 'Impact assessments and fundamental rights protection in EU law', (2006) *ELR* June, 316 *ff*.

[42] In that sense, the European Council at Cologne assumed that the present state of development of the Union required the establishment of the Charter of fundamental rights which could show the citizens of the Union the importance and the extent of fundamental rights.

a) the incorporation of fundamental rights rooted in European culture, particularly those recognised in the ECHR;
b) the reassertion and reinforcement of the principle of supremacy of Community law by way of the 'constitutionalisation' of fundamental rights;
c) the search for criteria allowing fundamental rights of equal rank to be brought into balance;
d) the assessment of civil, political, social, cultural and economic rights in the unified context required by a well ordered democratic society;
e) openness to the inclusion of new rights, such as environmental and consumer rights;
f) the treatment, in the same theoretical context, of new rights inspired by technological innovation, such as those connected with bioethics; and
g) putting the principle of 'equivalent protection' at the service of the autonomy of the Community legal order as a whole.

The Charter of Fundamental Rights of the European Union[43] crowns that development and represents the end of functionalism at the exclusive service of economic freedoms, the abandonment of the concept of the individual as a factor of production, the implementation of the necessary dialogue between civil, political, culture, social and economic rights, and the assertion of new generations of rights. In that context, citizenship is the new frame of reference and the gravitational pole for establishing a method in case law.

Fundamental rights will contribute to the expansion of the status of citizenship, not only as a result of the central function attributed to it in Article 17(1) EC, but also by virtue of the line set out by the Court in *Grzelczyk*[44] and subsequently reiterated, which is that citizenship is destined to be the fundamental status of nationals of the Member States.

For all these reasons, we are drawing towards the completion of what I have termed the 'constitutional arch'.[45]

[43] Nice, 7 December 2000, OJ 2000 C 364, 1.

[44] Case C-184/99 [2001] ECR I-6193. Moreover, citizenship offers fresh perspectives as regards the concept of the scope of Community law, of which the importance for fundamental rights cannot be underestimated.

[45] Moreover, the Court made this clear, in the particular circumstances of Case C-540/03 *European Parliament v Council* [2006] ECR I-5769. That case concerned Council Directive 2003/86/EC on the right to family reunification (OJ 2003 L 251, 12). The second recital to the Directive states that it respects the fundamental rights and observes the principles recognised in particular in Article 8 of the ECHR and in the Charter of Fundamental Rights of the European Union. The Court held that 'while the Charter is not a legally binding instrument, the Community legislature did, however, acknowledge its importance by stating … that the Directive observes the principles recognized not only by Article 8 of the ECHR but also in the Charter' (paragraph 38 of the judgment). It seems nevertheless inevitable that the rules of the Directive will one day be interpreted in light of the relevant provisions in the Charter.

2

Primacy, Fundamental Rights and the Search for Legitimacy

TAKIS TRIDIMAS

In the evolution of the European Community, *Internationale Handelsgesellschaft*[46] occupies a distinct position. In earlier cases, fearful of subordinating the EC Treaty to the laws of Member States, the ECJ had refused to accept that the Community was bound by the fundamental rights guaranteed by the national constitutions.[47] It is, in fact, ironic that an early, almost primitive, form of constitutional assertion by the ECJ was the denial of fundamental constitutional values. *Internationale Handelsgesellschaft* marked the rights of passage. In its judgment, the Court made pronouncements of profound constitutional importance. On the one hand, it reiterated the supremacy of Community law and took the principle of primacy to its outmost limits: Community law takes precedence even over the most revered provisions of the national constitutions. On the other hand, the Court reassured the Member States that the Treaty shares their constitutional values and ensures ideological continuity. At the same time, the Court took care to safeguard the autonomy of Community law. The national constitutional traditions provide 'inspiration' for respect of human rights in the Community legal order. There their function ends. The balance to be struck where fundamental rights conflict with each other and the application of general principles borrowed from the national constitutions to specific cases is a matter for the Court, since the protection of human rights must be secured 'within the framework of the structure and the objectives of the Community'.[48]

To be sure, the Court arrogated itself important functions as it is the concrete effects of human rights that matter. However, one could hardly advocate a different view. *Internationale Handelsgesellschaft* is not a paradigm of unwarranted judicial activism. The assertion that the Community is bound by fundamental rights finds justification in the constitutional traditions of the Member States. It 'flows logically from the nature of the process of European integration'.[49] As Mancini and Keeling note, it is hardly conceivable that 'the national parliaments would have ratified a Treaty which was capable of violating the fundamental tenets of their own constitutions'.[50] Once it is accepted that human rights

[46] Case 11/70, *Internationale Handelsgesellschaft mbH v Einfuhr- und Vorratsstelle für Getreide und Futtermittel*, [1970] ECR 1125.

[47] See, eg, Case 1/58 *Stork v High Authority* [1959] ECR 17 at 25–6; Joined Cases 36, 37, 38 and 40/59 *Geitling v High Authority* [1960] ECR 423 at 438–9; Case 40/64 *Sgarlata v Commission* [1965] ECR 215 at 227.

[48] *Internationale Handelsgesellschaft*, para 4.

[49] See per Poiares Maduro AG in Case C-380/05 *Centro Europa 7 Srl v Ministero delle Comunicazioni e Autorità per le Garanzie nelle Comunicazioni*, Opinion delivered on 12 September 2007, para 20.

[50] Mancini and Keeling, 'Democracy and the European Court of Justice' (1994) 57 *MLR* 175 at 187.

form part of the Community legal order and bind the Community institutions, their protection must be ensured within the four corners of the Community polity. It would simply not be possible to apply mechanically fundamental rights as recognised in one or another national legal system without taking into account the specific qualities of Community law.

If *Internationale Handelsgesellschaft* reconciled the primacy of Community law with respect for national constitutional traditions, *Nold*[51] made the first step towards the establishment of Community standards for human rights protection. The Court identified as an additional source of human rights, apart from the constitutional traditions of the Member States, international treaties on which the Member States have collaborated or of which they are signatories. Such Treaties, the Court stated, 'can supply guidelines which would be followed within the framework of Community law',[52] thus acknowledging implicitly the ECHR as a source of rights in the Community legal order.[53]

In *Nold* the Court also laid down the formula on the basis of which human rights would be protected. It held that the right to property and the right to practice freely a trade or profession do not constitute unfettered prerogatives but must be viewed in the light of their social function. They should, where necessary, be subject to certain limits justified by the overall objectives pursued by the Community, on condition that the substance of those rights is left untouched.[54]

The political implications of *Internationale Handelsgesellschaft* and *Nold* were enormous. First, they effected a significant transfer of powers inter-judicially, namely from the constitutional courts of the Member States to the ECJ. National courts were precluded from testing the validity of Community measures vis-à-vis domestic standards of fundamental rights and, within the scope of the Treaty, had to defer to the authority of the ECJ. Secondly, the rulings strengthened the Court's power vis-à-vis the other branches of Community 'government'. The ECJ could now question Community action on grounds of compatibility with fundamental rights. The resonance of fundamental rights granted the Court an enormous input of legitimacy. By defending individual liberty, which is seen as the traditional province of the judiciary, the ECJ could now play an important role in public discourse.[55] Thirdly, the judgments opened the way for extending the Court's jurisdiction to national measures. In *Wachauf*[56] and *ERT*[57] the ECJ held that it had jurisdiction to control the compatibility with fundamental rights of national measures implementing and, more generally, falling within the scope of Community law. This development further extended the powers of the judicial branch over the political authorities of the Member States.

[51] Case 4/73 *Nold* [1974] ECR 491.

[52] *Ibid*, para 13.

[53] The first express reference to the Convention was made in Case 44/79 *Hauer v Land Rheinland-Pfalz* [1979] ECR 3727.

[54] *Nold*, para 14.

[55] JHH Weiler, 'Human Rights, Constitutionalism and Integration: Iconography and Fetishism', (2001) 3 *International Law Forum du Droit International* 228.

[56] Case 5/88 *Wachauf* [1989] ECR 2609.

[57] Case C-260/89 [1991] ECR I-2925.

Internationale Handelsgeselschaft: Would an Alternative Outcome Be Possible?

While *Van Gend en Loos* and *Costa v ENEL* defined the '*essential conditions*'[58] of Community law, in incorporating fundamental rights into the Treaty, *Internationale Handelsgeselschaft* completed its content. In short, the judgment was a cornerstone of the constitutional deal. It would be impossible to conceive the European Union in its current state of evolution without that judgment just as it would be hard to conceive its development without *Van Gend en Loos* and *Costa*.

If the ECJ had refused to accept that the Community is bound by fundamental rights, national courts would have intervened to fill the resulting gap in judicial protection thus subordinating Community action to national constitutional standards. Indeed, given that fundamental rights permeate all areas of legislative and administrative activity, Community law would continuously have to yield to national law and primacy become a dead letter. Furthermore, the uniformity of Community law would have also suffered, '*lead[ing] inevitably to the destruction of the unity of the Common Market and the jeopardizing of the cohesion of the Community*'.[59]

Without a firm grounding on the rule of law, which includes respect for fundamental rights, the ECJ would have found it difficult to make the transition to the third-generation primacy cases and colonise the law of remedies. *Simmenthal, Factortame*, and *Francovich*[60] concretise the principles of primacy and direct effect. They are specific illustrations of the right to judicial protection, bred in a culture of fundamental rights which would simply be unable to flourish in the absence of *Internationale*. How could national political and judicial authorities accept state liability in damages for breach of Community obligations if the Community institutions themselves were above judicial scrutiny? Lack of legitimacy would also make it impossible for the ECJ to adopt an expansive interpretation of Community competence and build the edifice of the internal market.

In *Internationale*, the ECJ could have taken a more nation-friendly view of the European project. It could have held that the principle of primacy does not extend to the national constitutions. But this would have turned the avenue opened in *Costa v ENEL* into a cul-de-sac. It could conceivably have acknowledged that, despite the principle of primacy, national constitutional courts have ultimate power to determine the limits of Community competence and may test the validity of Community measures vis-à-vis domestic standards of fundamental rights, thus surrendering *competenz-competenz* to national courts. Such an approach, however, would also have undermined primacy. By setting itself at the apex of the judicial pyramid, the ECJ hijacked the constitutional agenda and set in motion a dialogue with the national constitutional courts from a position of relative strength.

Internationale Handelsgeselschaft facilitated a constitutional consensus which has since been the basis for the constitutionalisation of Community law. Recognition of fundamental rights as binding norms of Community law was the main instrument for the

[58] P Pescatore, *L'Ordre Juridique des Communautés Européennes* (Presses Universitaires de Liège, 1975), 227.

[59] Case 44/79, *Hauer v Land Rheinland-Pfalz*, [1979] ECR 3727, para 14.

[60] Case 106/77 *Simmenthal* [1978] ECR 629; Case C-213/89 *Factortame* [1990] ECR I-2433; Joined Cases C-6 and C-9/90 *Francovich and others* [1991] ECR I-5357.

legitimisation of the EC legal order, the acceptance of supremacy and the embracement of the preliminary procedure by national courts. This consensus is by no means complete. Judgments such as *the German Maastricht* case, *the Danish Maastricht* case, and *Thoburn*[61] indicate that national courts accept their own version of primacy, internalised and conditioned by the exigencies of the national constitutions. A journey through the case law of national supreme courts suggests that the overwhelming majority of them reserve to themselves residual jurisdiction to determine the outer limits of Community competence.[62] Thus, on the issue of *competenz-competenz*, an agreement to disagree has enabled the symbiosis of the ECJ and the national courts.

Still, in the 50-year history of the Community, there has been remarkably little disagreement between the ECJ and national constitutional courts on substantive issues and, where such disagreement has ensued, it has been containable. This has been the result of two converging factors. On the one hand, national courts have shown a willingness to make the European project work and abide by the Court's leadership. One might argue that, in doing so, they remain faithful to the choices of national governments, which after all have been willing participants to European integration. On the other hand, the ECJ itself has shown a considerable degree of flexibility and adaptability by reinventing itself as the self-appointed guardian of national constitutional traditions and the ECHR.

From the Case Law to the Charter

The protection of fundamental rights is an area where the ECJ led the way and the politicians followed by endorsing judicial developments. By the end of the 1980s, the road towards the formalisation of fundamental rights had begun in earnest. Article 6(2) of the TEU expressly acknowledged that the Union is bound by fundamental rights as guaranteed by the ECHR and as they result from the constitutional traditions common to the Member States. This was followed by the entrenchment of the Union values by the Treaty of Amsterdam,[63] the Charter, and the EU Constitutional Treaty. The Reform Treaty maintains the fundamental aspects of the aborted Constitutional Treaty by providing for a legal basis for EU accession to the ECHR and also by granting binding force to the Charter, albeit in a somewhat circuitous way and subject to Protocol 7, which limits its application in the United Kingdom.[64]

Despite the formalisation of fundamental rights through their entrenchment in written texts, it is the ECJ that will continue to set the agenda. The Court's attitude towards the Charter may here deserve closer attention. Given the non-binding nature of the Charter, the ECJ until recently had conspicuously refrained from referring to it even where express

[61] *Brunner* [1994] 1 CMLR 57; *Norup Carlsen v the Prime Minister* [1999] 3 CMLR 854; *Thoburn v Sunderland City Council* [2002] EuLR 253.

[62] See the survey provided in 'The Future Role of the European Court of Justice', HLCEC, 6th Report of Session 2003–04 (HL Paper 47, 2004).

[63] See Article 7 TEU, added by the Treaty of Amsterdam and amended by the Treaty of Nice, which provides for a political enforcement mechanism in the event of a serious and persistent breach by a Member State of the principles referred to in Article 6(1) TEU.

[64] See Article 6(1) TEU, as amended by the Reform Treaty, which grants to the Charter the same legal value as the founding Treaties although the Charter itself is annexed to the draft Treaty in the form of a Declaration (Declaration 11).

reliance was placed upon its provisions by the parties to the proceedings or the national court making the reference. It has now begun a trend of referring to it although in none of the cases has a reference to the Charter been material to the Court's reasoning.[65] Numerous references have been made by Advocates General[66] and some have been made by the CFI.[67] Such references have had mostly, if not invariably, a subsidiary character. The Charter has been used to support and reinforce a result that would have been reached even in its absence. In some cases, the Charter has been an integral part of the CFI's reasoning but never the sole decisive factor and, where particular prominence has been granted to it, it has been in relation to provisions which reflect existing general principles of law deriving from the case law, or the constitutional traditions common to the Member States, or international treaties. In *max.mobil*,[68] the CFI relied on Article 41(1) of the Charter, which provides for the duty of good administration, to support the proposition that the Commission is under a general duty to undertake a diligent and impartial examination of a complaint even in the absence of specific provisions granting rights to complainants. It also referred to Article 47(1) of the Charter, which reaffirms the right to a judicial remedy, to conclude that a complainant could challenge the Commission's decision dismissing a complaint.[69] In *Jégo-Quéré*,[70] the CFI referred to Article 47(1), alongside Articles 6 And 13 ECHR, to stress the paramountcy of the right to an effective remedy and procure a more liberal interpretation of *locus standi* under Article 230(4) EC than that dictated by the case law of the ECJ.[71]

Unfulfilled Expectations?

The Court's reliance on fundamental rights has been criticised as utilitarian: it is not based on a genuine concern to uphold rights but has been used as an excuse to expand the ECJ's influence to the detriment of Member States.[72] Whilst it is correct that reliance on fundamental rights has enabled the Court to expand its jurisdiction and influence, a balanced reading of the case law would make it hard to argue that the expectations raised in *Internationale* and *Nold* have not been fulfilled.

[65] Case C-540/03 *Parliament v Council*, judgment of 27 June 2006, para 38 (respect for private and family life); C-432/05 *Unibet (London) Ltd and Unibet (International) Ltd v Justitiekanslern*, judgment of 13 March 2007, para 37 (Article 47, right to an effective remedy and a fair trial); Case C-303/05 *Advocaten voor de Wereld VZW v Leden van de Ministerraad*, judgment of 3 May 2007, para 46 (Article 20, equality before the law; Article 21, principle of non-discrimination; Article 49, principle of legality of criminal offences and penalties).

[66] See, eg, Case C-173/99 *BECTU* [2001] ECR 4881, at 4891 (Tizzano AG); Case C-353/99 P *Council v Hautala* [2001] ECR I-9565, paras 80–83 (Léger AG); Case C-413/99 *Baumbast and R* [2002] ECR I-7091 (Geelhoed AG); Case C-160/03 *Spain v Eurojust*, Opinion of Poiares Maduro AG delivered on 16 December 2004; Joined Cases C-387/02, C-391/02 and C-403/02 *Berlusconi*, Opinion of Kokott AG delivered on 14 October 2004; C-36/02 *Omega Spielhallen*, Opinion of Stix-Hackl AG delivered on 18 March 2004.

[67] See, eg, Case T-77/01 *Territorio Histórico de Álava—Diputación Foral de Álava v Commission*, judgment of 11 January 2002, para 35 (Article 47).

[68] Case T-54/99 *max.mobil Telekommunikation Service GmbH v Commission* [2002] ECR II-313; reversed on appeal: C-141/02 P *Commission v T-Mobile Austria GmbH*, judgment of 22 February 2005.

[69] Ibid *max.mobil Telekommunikation Service GmbH v Commission* paras 48 and 57.

[70] Case T-177/01 *Jégo-Quéré v Commission* [2002] ECR II-02365, reversed on appeal C-263/02 P *Commission v Jégo-Quéré*, judgment of 1 April 2004.

[71] Ibid, Case T-177/01, *Jégo-Quéré*, paras 42 and 47.

[72] J Coppel and A O'Neill, 'The European Court of Justice: taking rights seriously?' (1992) 29 *CML Rev* 669.

In fact, the most remarkable development in the case law in recent years has been the strengthening of the Court's jurisdiction in the field of fundamental rights. The ECJ has widened and deepened its fundamental rights jurisdiction in a number of ways. First, it has expanded the scope of application of fundamental freedoms which has, in turn, broadened the range of national measures subject to the Court's human rights control.[73] It has asserted jurisdiction where a measure is likely to constitute a potential impediment to intra-Community trade even if it is not as such a restriction on a fundamental freedom. The procrustean bed of *Karner* grants to the ECJ universal jurisdiction on fundamental rights.[74] The ECJ also understands the concept of national measures implementing Community law, which are subject to fundamental rights review, widely.[75]

Most importantly, the ECJ has elevated fundamental rights to core Community values accepting that their protection may take priority over free movement.[76] Finally, the ECJ is more prescriptive as to the standards of review. In an increasing number of preliminary references, it prefers to provide the referring court with a ready-made solution rather than defer to national standards of review. The outcome provided by the ECJ often upholds the national measure whose compatibility with Community law is contested. Thus, the Court provides leadership without necessarily stifling national choice.[77]

All in all, the ECJ continues to practise assertive constitutionalism except that now nation-building through economic integration has given way to nation-building through fundamental rights. This has enhanced its role as the Supreme Court of the Union and, at the same time, brought it closer to the ECtHR and national constitutional courts. There is little doubt that the success of the ECJ in constructing the edifice of European law and attaining the constitutionalisation of the Treaties owes much to the approval, encouragement and co-operation of national courts. As the Maastricht decisions of the German Constitutional Court[78] and the Danish Supreme Court[79] show, however, such co-operation cannot be equated with submission. Primacy means different things to different courts. The ECJ has the delicate task of embracing the national legal orders and addressing the sensitivities of the national supreme courts without endangering the fundamental principles of Union law. The case law has responded to that challenge.

[73] See, eg, Case C-60/00 *Carpenter v Secretary of State for the Home Department,* 11 July 2002; Case C-109/01 *Secretary of State for the Home Department v Akrich,* judgment of 23 September 2003.

[74] Case C-71/02 *Herbert Karner Industrie-Auktionen GmbH v Troostwijk GmbH,* judgment of 25 March 2004. See also the Opinion of Poiares Maduro AG in Case C-380/05 *Centro Europa 7 Srl v Ministero delle Comunicazioni e Autorità per le Garanzie nelle Comunicazioni,* Opinion delivered on 12 September 2007, at paras 21–2. The Advocate General tentatively suggested that a serious and persistent breach of fundamental rights by a Member State may amount to a systemic shortcoming in their protection which may in turn amount in itself to a breach of the Treaty rules on free movement and citizenship.

[75] See Joined Cases C-20 and C-64/00 *Booker Aquaculture Ltd v The Scottish Ministers,* [2003] ECR I-7411.

[76] See, eg, Case C-112/00 *Schmidberger, Internationale Transporte und Planzüge,* judgment of 12 June 2003; Case C-36/02 *Omega Spielhallen- und Automatenaufstellungs v Oberbürgermeisterin der Bundesstadt Bonn,* judgment of 14 October 2004; and in a different context Case C-224/01 *Köbler v Austria,* judgment of 30 September 2003.

[77] See, eg, Case C-112/00 *Schmidberger, Internationale Transporte und Planzüge,* judgment of 12 June 2003; Case C-36/02 *Omega Spielhallen- und Automatenaufstellungs v Oberbürgermeisterin der Bundesstadt Bonn,* judgment of 14 October 2004; and in a different context Case C-224/01*Köbler v Austria,* judgment of 30 September 2003.

[78] *Brunner* [1994] 1 CMLR 57.

[79] *Hanne Norup Carlsen and Others v the Prime Minister* [1999] 3 *CMLRev* 854.

Judgments such as *Schmidberger* and *Omega Spielhallen*[80] show that the Court promotes an integration model based on value diversity which views national constitutional standards not as being in a competitive relationship with the economic objectives of the Union but as forming part of its polity. In that respect, general principles of law are not only an instrument of empowerment of supranational government but also an instrument of legitimacy. The judgment of the ECtHR in *Bosphorus*[81] is an endorsement of the ECJ's enhanced presence in human rights. In some respects, the approach of the Strasbourg Court resembles that of the German Constitutional Court: it views the ECJ as an agent of its own standards which operates under a double conditional and reversible endorsement granted to it by the national courts and the ECtHR. Despite the fact that the case law of the ECJ and the ECtHR are not always in harmony, there can be no doubt that both courts share the same liberal underpinnings. They both understand democracy in the same way, namely not merely as majoritarianism but as 'tolerance, pluralism, and broadmindedness'.[82] They adopt a pluralist vision of democracy which includes the right to be different. To be sure, the two courts share a substantive idea of the rule of law viewing the Convention and the EU Treaties not merely as procedural documents but as including also substantive standards of justice.

New Challenges

Despite the enhanced resonance of fundamental rights, important challenges lie ahead. The following points may be made in this context.

Recent Community measures combatting terrorism through financial sanctions test the Community judiciary to the limit. How are the courts to balance the fight against terrorism with respect for fundamental rights? Whilst it is not possible to examine this topic within the confines of the present contribution, it is worth highlighting the judgment of the CFI in *Organisation des Modjahedines du peuple d'Iran v Council*.[83] In that case, distinguishing its previous judgments in *Kadi* and *Yusuf*,[84] the CFI annulled a Council decision freezing the assets of the applicant on grounds of lack of reasoning and breach of the right to a fair hearing. The judgment contains the most thorough analysis of the right to a hearing in the case law of the ECJ and the CFI. Broadly speaking, it evinces that, in common with the US Supreme Court[85] and the House of Lords,[86] the CFI is prepared to question measures combatting terrorism on procedural grounds and put the brakes on the concept of the 'emergency constitution'.

80 Above, note 76.

81 Judgment of 30 June 2005, application no. 45036/98.

82 See, eg, *Smith and Grady v United Kingdom* (2000) 29 EHRR 493, judgment of 27 September 1999, para 87.

83 Case T-228/02 *Organisation des Modjahedines du peuple d'Iran v Council*, judgment of 12 December 2006. See also the following line of cases: C-229/05 P *PKK and KNK v Council*, judgment of 18 January 2007; C-355/04 P *Segi and Others v Council*, judgment of 27 February 2007; T-327/03 *Stichting Al-Aqsa, established in Heerlen (Netherlands) v Council*, judgment of 11 July 2007; T-47/03 *Sison v Council*, judgment of 11 July 2007.

84 Case T-315/01 *Kadi v Council and Commission* and T-306/01, *Yusuf and Al Barakaat International Foundation v Council and Commission*, judgments of 21 September 2005, not yet reported (appeals pending, Cases C-402/05 P and C-415/05 P).

85 *Humdan v Rumsfeld* 126 SCt 2749.

86 See *S and X v Secretary of State for the Home Department* [2005] 2 AC 68.

A final point refers to the expansion of Community competence in the post-internal market era. In recent years, the European Union's presence on areas hitherto considered to fall within the core of national sovereignty (for example, immigration and criminal law) has increased through intense legislative activity under the Third Pillar. In parallel, we experience a partial communitarisation of EU law through the exportation of Community disciplines to the third pillar. These developments suggest that the ECJ will have an increasingly important role to play in protecting fundamental rights against both the Union and the Community. The more powers that the Community or the Union acquire, the greater the need for fundamental rights safeguards. An interesting juxtaposition between Union competence and fundamental rights protection occurred in the *European Arrest Warrant* case[87] where the Court rejected the claim that the Framework Decision on the European Arrest Warrant violates the principle of legality of criminal offences and penalties and the principle of equality. Whilst, in terms of formal reasoning, the judgment is correct, the introduction of the European Arrest Warrant lowers, at least in some respects, the level of protection of the accused and, in that sense, the expansion of Union competence adversely affects the protection of fundamental rights. Whilst the expectations raised in *Internationale Handelsgesellschaft* have not remained unfulfilled, the need for judicial vigilance appears higher than ever.

[87] Case C-303/05 *Advocaten voor de Wereld VZW v Leden van de Ministerraad* [2007] ECR I-3633.

3

Internationale Handelsgesellschaft, Nold and the New Human Rights Paradigm

MATTIAS KUMM[88]

The story about how the ECJ, from *Stauder*[89] to *Internationale Handelsgesellschaft*[90] and *Nold*[91] has developed its own human rights jurisprudence is a staple element in European scholarship. It is part of the narrative describing the role of the ECJ in the constitutionalisation of EC law. By holding that fundamental rights are an integral part of the general principles of law the observance of which the Court ensures, the ECJ has accomplished two things: to incorporate a central feature of modern constitutions into the corpus of EC law and to help strengthen the authority of EC law against potential challenges before national courts in the name of domestic constitutional rights. So much that is right has been written about this, that I will not focus on trying to uncover a new nuance with regard to any of the obvious themes, be it the complex interaction between the ECJ and German courts, the subtle shift in doctrine between *Internationale Handelsgesellschaft* and *Nold* or the future of the ECJ's doctrine in light of changes relating to the Charter of Fundamental Rights or accession to the ECHR.

Instead the focus of this chapter is an aspect of *International Handelsgesellschaft* and *Nold* that is both fundamental and yet seems to have escaped commentators' attention. In *Nold* and *International Handelsgesellschaft* the ECJ develops the outlines of a conception of human rights that departed from a number of widely held conventional assumptions about what human or constitutional rights are and how they operate in legal practice. It is a mistake to believe that in *Nold* and *Internationale Handelsgesellschaft* the ECJ in the early 1970s merely Europeanises a well-established understanding of human rights, as has been recognised by Member States. Instead the ECJ reconceives constitutional and human rights practice in an interesting and challenging way. The traditional legalist paradigm of human and constitutional rights is effectively replaced by a rationalist human rights paradigm.

In order to substantiate and clarify the claim that the ECJ embraces a new human rights paradigm, the first part this chapter will highlight the central features of the ECJ's conception of human rights and its tension with conventional understandings of human rights. A second part will briefly point to some basic questions on the conceptual, institutional and doctrinal level that such a paradigm shift gives some urgency to. Clearly,

[88] Professor of Law, NYU School of Law.
[89] Case 26/69, [1969] ECR 419.
[90] Case 11/70, [1970] ECR 1161.
[91] Case 4/73, [1974] ECR 491.

a substantial monograph, rather than a short essay, would be necessary to more fully develop the themes, substantiate and perhaps qualify the arguments that are made in this essay. But the point of this essay is modest. It is to make aware of a number of mutually reinforcing features in the ECJ's human rights practice, that give rise to number of distinct questions, that have not received the attention they deserve.

From Legalism to Rationalism: The New Human Rights Paradigm

There are three main features that distinguish the ECJ's human rights jurisprudence from traditional conceptions of human or constitutional rights. They relate to the scope (1), structure (2) and the sources (3) of human rights respectively. Taken together they amount to a shift from a legalist human rights paradigm to a rationalist human rights paradigm.

The Scope of Human Rights: From Things Fundamental to Things Mundane

The scope of human rights protection is traditionally believed to be limited to interests deemed fundamental. Human or fundamental rights generally become part of the debate when the discussion turns to torture, the death penalty, arbitrary police detention, religious coercion, censorship and the like. Typically the lists found in a constitutional Bill of Rights or a Human Rights Treaty are a response to specific historical experiences of blatant disregard of fundamental human interests. One of the reasons that neither the Member States drafting the Treaties of Rome nor the ECJ in its jurisprudence during the 1960s embraced human rights as a matter of concern for EC law is that the EC as an institution primarily concerned with the establishment of a common market was not active in an area that was believed to raise human rights concerns in any serious way. If by the early 1970s the Court changed its mind, it was not because the EC had significantly expanded its competencies—a significant expansion of the EU's competencies would occur only much later in the context of the Maastricht Treaty and beyond—but because its understanding of human rights had changed. Instead of a set of narrowly circumscribed interests deemed fundamental *any kind of liberty interests* would enjoy *prima facie* protection as a right. Human rights were not just about combating the worst kind of dictatorships or government atrocities, human rights were in play the moment the law restricted individual liberty. The language of human rights would play a role not just to point to atrocities and fundamental concerns but to raise complicated questions concerning the most mundane matters.

Both *Internationale Handelsgesellschaft* and *Nold* illustrate this shift. *Internationale Handelsgesellschaft* was a case concerning the forfeiture of a deposit lodged in connection with the issue of export licences for maize meal. The plaintiff had failed to export the quantities of maize he had obtained a licence for, by all indications because it turned out to be more profitable to sell to a domestic buyer. Unter EC rules failure to export after obtaining the licence meant forfeiture of the deposit, unless the failure to export was the result of *force majeure*. That regime, the plaintiff claimed, violated his general right to freedom of action and economic liberty. In *Nold* the issue was whether EC rules relating to the distribution of fuels could require companies to meet a certain volume of sales requirements in order for them to qualify as a direct wholesaler with a right to direct purchase from a selling agency. The plaintiff believed that his denial of that status based on its reduced sales volume was a violation of its fundamental right to freely practice their trade and profession.

It is not at all clear that these types of interests would warrant protection as fundamental rights. The European Convention of Human Rights did not recognise either a general right to liberty,[92] nor a right to freely pursue a trade or profession. Even a right to property could only be agreed upon after difficult negotiations in a separate Protocol. And the situation was not all that different in Member States. To the extent that the original six Member States recognised judicially enforceable constitutional rights at all in 1970, it was not obvious that these types of economic interests enjoyed protection. It is true that any liberty interests and certainly interests related to the freedom to pursue a trade and profession enjoyed *prima facie* protection as judicially enforceable constitutional rights *in Germany*, where both of these cases originated. But even there the Federal Constitutional Court recognised a general right to liberty only as a result of a highly controversial interpretation of a clause guaranteeing the free development of personality.[93] It is striking that the Court did not make much of an effort to find out what the various constitutions of Member States or the European Convention of Human Rights actually had to say about the issue. Indeed, the Advocate General in *Internationale Handelsgesellschaft* introduced as uncontroversial the idea that the general principles of law the Court recognises ought to include a fundamental right 'that the indivdual should not have his freedom of action limited beyond the degree necessary for the general interest'.[94] There might be good jurisprudential reasons to endorse such an expansive approach to the scope of rights.[95] But it was audacious in 1970 to claim that such a right was legally recognised as part of the common constitutional tradition. On the other hand there is no question that an expansive approach to defining the scope of rights effectively furthers the purpose to appease national constitutional courts that the ECJ's protection does not fall below the protection offered by national constitutional rules. If the German constitutional court recognises such interests as worthy of constitutional protection prima facie, adopting a more narrow approach might not be good policy for an ECJ trying to persuade the national courts to abstain from reviewing EC law on national constitutional grounds.

In both cases the Court ultimately concluded that there was no violation of a right. But it reached that conclusion not by determining that there were no interests here that could plausibly qualify as warranting protection as fundamental rights. Instead, the Court acknowledged that fundamental rights guaranteed as general principles of EC law might well be in play, and then immediately focused on the justification of the restrictive practices. *Internationale Handelsgesellschaft* and *Nold* thus established a pattern that the

[92] Art 5 of the convention does mention liberty, but that is interpreted much more narrowly, see for example M Janis, R Kay, A Bradley, *European Human Rights Law* (Oxford University Press, Oxford, 2000), ch 7.

[93] See BVerfGE 6, 32 (Elfes). Art 2, Sect 1 of the German Basic Law posits: 'Everyone has the right to the free development of their personality.'

[94] Case 11/70, Opinion of Mr Advocate General Dutheillet de Lamotte of 2 December 1970, ECR 1140.

[95] For a discussion of these issues see M Kumm, 'On the Structure and Domain of Constitutional Justice' (2003) *ICON* 574–96.

Court would follow in practically every case involving human rights claims. The Court does not generally spend a great deal of time addressing the question whether a particular restriction infringes on a right, nor does it waste much time classifying the interest (is it a general liberty interest, does it concern the freedom to pursue a trade or profession, is it a property right?). Its focus of analysis is on the justification of whatever infringement has taken place. If an infringement of a right can be justified, there is ultimately no violation of the right.

What Do you Have in Virtue of Having a Right? From Trumps to Proportionality

The key question then becomes what type of justification is sufficient to justify an infringement of a right. What do you have in virtue of having an interest that the ECJ recognises as a right? In post-Second World War constitutional texts and international human rights documents the first paragraph of an article would traditionally define the scope of the protected right, whereas the second paragraph would define the specific conditions under which an infringement of a right could exceptionally be justified. More generally fundamental rights are conventionally believed to take general precedence over countervailing policy concerns, subject only to limited exceptions. Correspondingly, legal theorists have describe rights as firewalls[96] and trumps.[97]

Yet the ECJ takes a very different approach that it applies to rights across the board. This approach is already on display in *Nold* and *Internationale Handelsgesellschaft.* An act infringing a right is justified, if it meets the proportionality requirement. Even though the ECJ in its earlier decisions—and even in some later ones—is not as clear and precise as it might be about what exactly this test involves, even in early decisions it is possible to distinguish the familiar three main prongs of the test. The first concerns the question whether the measure at issue furthers a legitimate purpose. With regard to the forfeited deposits at issue in *Internationale Handelsgesellschaft*, for example, the Court first established that they furthered a legitimate purpose: the deposit served as an instrument to ensure that the Commission was well informed about overall volume of export and import, thus providing valuable information on the structure of the market the Commission was charged to help regulate. Second, the measure has to be necessary. It is necessary if there are no other equally effective means to achieve the same goal. In *Internationale Handelsgesellschaft* the Court found the rule regarding its forfeiture was necessary, in that alternative means, such as penalties imposed ex post, were not equally effective. Finally, the Court examines whether the burden imposed is excessive or disproportionate when compared to its benefits. The Court held that the system of deposits and the rules on forfeiture were not a disproportionate burden on the exporter, both because of the relatively modest amount of the deposit and the fact that in case of *force majeure*—which the Court suggested should be interpreted liberally—the deposit was not forfeited.

There are three structural features of the Court's analysis worth noting at this point. First, interests protected as rights and countervailing policy considerations compete on the same level and are subject to the same equation within proportionality analysis. There is

[96] J Habermas, *Between Facts and Norms* (1997).

[97] R Dworkin, 'What Rights do we have?', in *Taking Rights Seriously* (1978), 266. See also R Dworkin, 'Principle, Policy, Procedure' in *A Matter of Principle* (1985), 72.

no built-in priority for claims that involve an infringement of the scope of a right. Second, it has now become clearer why the Court is not very concerned with the question how it should characterise the infringed right. The point of classification, which is usually to apply a rights-specific set of rules relating to the determination of its limits, is absent. All rights are subject to the same limitation: proportionality. As the Advocate General put it his Opinion in *Internationale Handelsgesellschaft*: all human-rights-related questions 'concerning the internal legality of the disputed measures are linked to one and the same problem, namely whether or not these measures comply with a principle of "proportionality", under which citizens may only have imposed on them, for the purposes of the public interest, obligations which are strictly necessary for those purposes attained'.[98] Third, and most importantly, there is nothing specifically law-like about the proportionality test. The test provides little more than a structure for reasoned policy-assessment. There is no legal authority that directly guides or constrains its application. The test specifies the necessary and sufficient conditions that a policy has to meet in order to qualify as good policy even when they impose burdens on certain individuals. If, all things considered, there are good reasons that support a regulatory measure, it will be proportional. If there are no such reasons, the measure is not proportionate. Proportionality has become the lawyers framework to engage in policy analysis in a way that is neither directly guided or constrained by legal authority. Courts engaged in this type of rights reasoning are no longer enforcers of a political will that has previously created and defined a set of legal rights. Such a court has transformed itself into a veto-holding junior-partner in the joint legal-political enterprise of developing and enforcing rational policies that reflect equal respect and concern for each individual. An expansive scope of rights in conjunction with an open-ended proportionality test is the central feature of the rationalist human rights paradigm. As will become clear it is a human rights paradigm that leaves little space for meaningful guidance or constraint by legal authority.

Sources of Law: Legal Basis, Inspiration or False Consciousness?

The sources of post Second World War human rights law are generally legal texts such as constitutions or human rights treaties. No doubt these texts reflect widely held moral beliefs about what rights ought to be respected by political communities whenever they are engaging human beings. But human rights became legal rights in Europe the same way as other more mundane rights: by having the relevant political actors entrench them in legal documents. It is part of the common constitutional tradition of Member States that human rights, to they extent that they are judicially enforced, are enforced only if and to the extent that a constitution or a Treaty, duly interpreted, so establishes. That was a practice the ECJ radically departed from when it started to establish its own human rights jurisprudence in *International Handelsgesellschaft* and *Nold.*

Of course the Court did not explicitly announce a new rationalist human rights paradigm that authorised it to sit as the ultimate arbiter of the EU's policies using proportionality as a general conceptual framework to structure its policy assessment. As is often the case when courts make their most innovative decisions, the ECJ too relied on the most conventional and unassuming concepts and arguments to justify its innovation: it

[98] See Opinion of Mr Dutheillet de Lamothye, Case 11/70, p 1146.

was doing no more than to recognise human rights as general principles of EC law. And it would do so drawing inspiration from the common constitutional tradition of Member States and any international obligations they had signed up to. This is the ECJ's sources formula: general principles, common constitutional traditions, international Treaty law. Sources abound, legal guidance and constraint is assured, and a complex, novel but ultimately not unfamiliar legal field is established. But even though the sources' formula is endlessly repeated by the ECJ, and since the Treaty of Amsterdam has been formally entrenched in EU law, it is misleading in more ways than one. Sources of law have had a negligible role to play in guiding or constraining the Court's human rights jurisprudence and are unlikely to play a much more important role in the future.

The first point is that human rights in the jurisprudence of the Court are not conceived of as a discrete set of reasonably specific rules or principles, each of which needs to be traced to a particular source. Instead the issue is to find a 'source' for the one abstract principle that then serves as the foundation for all further explication of human rights by the Court. To illustrate the point, this is how the Advocate General framed the issue in *International Handelsgesellschaft*: all rights-related questions 'concerning the internal legality of the disputed measures are linked to one and the same problem, namely whether or not these measures comply with a principle of "proportionality", under which citizens may only have imposed on them, for the purposes of the public interest, obligations which are strictly necessary for those purposes attained.' This leads to one central question: 'But a prior question is immediately raised, as to what legal source this principle must be taken in order to be applied against a measure issued by the Community authorities.'[99] The task, as the Advocate General frames it, is to search for a source of a principle that is so abstract that it incorporates wholesale the whole rationalist human rights conception that was described above. To propose that such an abstract and jurisgeneratively productive principle could be law if traced to a source is no different than searching for a legal source for the proposition that courts should not enforce anything as law that is not just. It is a remarkable way to think about sources in connection to human rights.

It is even more remarkable given the role that general principles have played in modern legal systems and international law. General principles of law have historically been used a shorthand for 'natural law concepts' or 'rules recognized by the legal conscience of civilized peoples'.[100] But given the deep suspicion towards these kinds of ideas during most of the positivist 20th century, general principles have in modern legal systems and international law only been used as a residual 'source' of last resort. They have mostly been used to legitimise the use of relatively specific common-sense rules and maxims that are obvious and uncontentious, widely shared or that are very closely linked to other explicitly codified rules and maxims. The resuscitation of the idea of general principles in this highly abstract form seems, at first sight, to be a remarkable revitalisation and reformulation of a non-positivist conception of law.

But of course the Court's formula emphasises that human rights as general principles are inspired by the constitutional traditions common to the Member States. They are not abstractly derived from a conception of law. There is a positive basis for what the Court is doing after all: the Court merely refers to and makes productive use for European

[99] See Opinion of Mr Dutheillet de Lamothe, Case 11/70, p 1146.

[100] See I Bownlie, *Principles of Public International Law* 5th edn (Oxford University Press, Oxford, 1998), 15.

purposes of constitutional commitments shared by Member States. But do Member States' constitutional commitments really reflect a rationalist conception of rights?

As a matter of *constitutional ethos* a rationalist conception of human rights very plausibly informs the constitutional self-understanding of people in liberal democracies in Europe. Something like the rationalist conception of human rights is deeply connected to the enlightenment constitutional tradition and reflected both in formulas used in the American Declaration of Independence and the Universal Declaration of Human Rights. Which Member of the EU would dispute, either in 1970 or today, that any citizens may have legal obligations imposed on them only for the purposes of furthering the public interest, and only to the extent necessary and appropriate to further those interests? Clearly this is part of the European constitutional tradition as it emerged among EU Members after the Second World War.

A completely different question is whether there is a common constitutional tradition to accept such a principle *as a condition for constitutional legality, subject to constitutional enforcement by a court.* Institutionally this amounts to a massive empowerment of the judicial branch. Is it up to a court to enforce such a principle? Certainly the answer given by the French and American Revolutionaries and founders of the modern constitutional tradition was a resounding 'no'. The French suspicion of the judiciary as an institution is well known and has left its own historical mark on constitutional practice in France, where the Universal Declaration of Human Rights was discovered as a legal document that is subject to enforcement by the constitutional council as late as the 1970s. The function of the Declaration was originally to serve as a reference for legislators and citizens, not courts. In the US too, the Bill of Rights was enacted as a contentious afterthought and Amendment to the Constitution originally negotiated in Philadelphia, in order to secure its ratification by some of the more recalcitrant states. The prevailing view was that the Bill of Rights primarily secured what had previously been recognised as the rights of Englishmen in British practice and supplemented by a few specific and limited American guarantees, most importantly the 1st Amendment. The purpose of the Bill of Rights was not to codify the whole panoply of human rights—including the right to freely pursue happiness—that are captured by the Declaration of Independence's majestic clauses.[101] Furthermore the constitutions and human rights treaties written after the Second World War that were subject to judicial enforcement are widely conceived as carefully negotiated legislative acts involving a great many specific compromises and rules. Modern constitutional bills of rights and modern human rights treaties are conventionally believed to provide a great deal more specificity and guidance to courts than the abstract principle the ECJ establishes as the foundation of its human rights jurisprudence. In this sense it is unconvincing to claim that the human rights practice of the ECJ is grounded in principles that enjoy general recognition in Member States.

But there is another way of understanding the Court's formula relating to the inspiration it draws from the common tradition of Member States and international human rights treaties. Perhaps the ECJ is not inspired by the constitutional traditions of Member States in endorsing a highly abstract principle. Perhaps the ECJ is inspired by the way Member States' constitutional actors interpret and specify this principle in concrete

[101] This is confirmed by the 9th Amendment of the US Constitution: 'The enumeration of in the Constitution, of certain rights, shall not be construed to deny or disparage others retained by the people.'

contexts.[102] Unfortunately there is little indication that that is how the ECJ actually refers to Member States' practice either in *Internationale Handelsgesellschaft* and *Nold* or the ECJ's jurisprudence more generally. Member States and international practice is relevant mainly in two ways. First, if a national court makes a reference and indicates that an EC act falls within the scope of a right in that Member State, the ECJ will also recognise it as also falling within the scope of a right under EC law. No national court will outdo the ECJ with regard to the interests it protects as rights. Here the Court unequivocally adopts a maximalist approach. Second, the Court will often draw on Member States and ECHR practice in order to demonstrate that rights are not conceived as absolute, but can be subjected to proportional restrictions related to legitimate public interests. In *Nold* and *International Handelsgesellschaft* the Court does so only by schematic reference, but in later cases the Court occasionally makes more of a comparative effort.[103] This form of comparative engagement amounts to little more than a demonstration that the Court's rationalist conception of rights is not in principle less protective than anything that Member States recognise. Comparative engagement serves apologetic purposes: even though Member States have a written Bill of Rights, nothing in those texts preclude the kind of proportionality analysis the ECJ engages in. On the other hand comparative engagement does not generally constrain or guide the application of the proportionality test. On the contrary: when it comes to the application of the proportionality test, the Court generally insists that it should focus on the issue as it arises in the EU context, rather than distracting itself by an unhelpful focus on other Member States or the ECHR. In *Nold* and *International Handelsgesellschaft* and many later decisions the ECJ emphasises that what counts as proportional needs to be assessed in light of the structure and the objectives of the community as they apply to the community context. When the Court applies the proportionality test to a particular piece of regulation, it makes little sense for the Court to draw heavily on the constitutional experience of Member States, because the difference in context may very well make a difference.[104] It follows that within the rationalist conception of rights there is only limited space for the kind of inspiration by Member States' constitutional traditions that would amount to meaningful legal guidance or constraint. The core inspiration it receives amounts to little more than the confirmation that the rationalist conception of rights in fact also informs the texts and practices of Member States' constitutional tradition and international human rights treaties. 'Your texts don't make much of a difference' is the critically apologetic tenor of the ECJ engagement with Member States' constitutional traditions.

This leads to the next point: nothing said above means to imply that the ECJ is in fact doing something that no other constitutional or international courts are doing. The ECJ is not a fringe outlier court in the methodology it adopts. The rationalist conception of human rights is conceptually deeply at odds with a legalistic conception of human rights.

[102] Indeed the ECJ has, as far as I am aware, never explicitly embraced the very abstract formula that was the focal point of the Advocate General's opinion, even though it captures well much of what the court is in fact doing.

[103] See, e.g., Case 44/79 [1979] ECR 3727 *Hauer v Land Rheinland-Pfalz*.

[104] This also implies that national courts need to be careful when they assess whether the ECJ's jurisprudence provides equivalent fundamental rights protection of national constitutions. A regulation that the Federal Constitutional Court might have struck down if it took the form of a German statute as a violation of a constitutional right might well be rightly upheld as an EC regulation by the ECJ. Such a result is not necessarily an indication that the ECJ does not take rights seriously. It is just as possible that the context of the EU might be different in a way that makes a difference for the purpose of assessing the proportionality of a measure.

Most citizens, constitutional drafters of post Second World War human rights texts and lawyers probably believe in some version of a legalistic conception of human rights, rather than a rationalist one described here. But a closer analysis of what courts are actually doing in many jurisdictions is likely to reveal that constitutional texts are less important than is conventionally believed. Basic structural features of human rights analysis characteristic of the rationalist paradigm—proportionality analysis in particular—are a quasi-universal feature of European human and constitutional rights practice and in many jurisdictions the scope of rights have been interpreted expansively and the specific wording of limitation clauses have not played a significant role.[105] This is certainly true with regard to German constitutional rights practice.[106] It is not implausible that an evolution of the Federal Constitutional Courts' understanding of constitutional rights played a significant role in its doctrinal shift from *Solange I* to *Solange II*. Contrary to its position in *Solange I*[107] the Court in its *Solange II* decision[108] did not insist on the existence of a written Charter of Rights in Europe as a precondition for recognising equivalence of human rights protection on the European level. By the mid-1980s, when *Solange II* was decided German jurisprudence had developed in the direction of a rationalist human rights paradigm, a development that was still in its infancy in 1974, when *Solange I* was decided. Lists of rights and their limitations, unless they exceptionally take the form of clear-cut rules,[109] had simply not contributed to provide much determinacy and clarity. On the other hand the German Constitutional Court had become quite comfortable applying the proportionality principle across the board.[110] Under those circumstances the Court had become less resistant to the idea that the ECJ, even without a textual basis, is essentially engaging in the same practice as the Federal Constitutional Court.[111]

By embracing a rationalist conception of human rights the ECJ is by no means an outlier. But there are two reasons why the ECJ's jurisprudence exemplifies more explicitly a rationalist conception of human rights than other national constitutional practices. First, the absence of a constitutional text meant that the ECJ could not even pretend that its jurisprudence was grounded in ordinary interpretation of legal texts, even though its sources formula did its best to cover that up. Second, the ECJ had strategic reasons to adopt as expansive a conception of human rights as possible, to undercut any claims by national courts and scholars that domestic courts provided more expansive protection.

If human rights texts are in fact less important role than a legalist believes, what is the significance of the European Charter of Fundamental Rights? It is unlikely that the European Charter of Fundmantal Rights, once it becomes valid law in the European Union, will lead to the establishment of a more legalistic conception of human rights. On

105 For such a claim see D Beatty, *The Ultimate Rule of Law* (Oxford University Press, Oxford, 2004).

106 See R Alexy, *A Theory of Constitutional Rights* (Oxford University Press, Oxford, 2002).

107 BVerfGE 37, 271 (1974).

108 BVerfGE 73, 339 (1986).

109 Eg Art 102 Basic Law: 'The death penalty is abolished.'

110 This development is subjected to serious analysis in R Alexy, *A Theory of Constitutional Rights* (Oxford University Press, Oxford, 2002), which first appeared in German in 1985, the year that *Solange II* was decided.

111 Of course, this is not the only explanation for the shift. Other relevant factors are very plausibly the changes in the ECJ's practice between these decisions. Compare the ECJ addressing the human rights issues in *Internationale Handelsgesellschaft* (that led to *Solange I*) and compare it to *Hauer* (leading to *Solange II*). And of course personalities matter. The Rapporteur in *Solange I* had been replaced by the more integration-friendly Judge Frowein as Rapporteur for *Solange II*.

the contrary, the Charter confirms, rather than replaces, the ECJ's rationalist conception. There are three reasons for this. First, as the Reform Treaty makes clear, the Charter complements and does not seek to replace the ECJ's jurisprudence on general principles.[112] Second, the Charter itself clarifies in its Preamble that its purpose is not to establish anything new, but merely to strengthen already existing rights by making them more visible in the Charter. Third, a general limitations clause referring to the principle of proportionality has substituted the traditional post Second World War practice of writing rights-specific limitation clauses.[113] This amounts to a codification of the rationalist paradigm. No doubt the Court will cite the Charter and refer to its provisions where they are pertinent. Furthermore the infringements of interests specifically singled out and listed in the Charter might lead to somewhat closer scrutiny by the Court. But the basic rationalist structure of the Court's jurisprudence will remain unchanged. Indeed, it is not obvious that a single case would be decided differently by the ECJ with or without the Charter. The Charter will certainly not meaningfully guide or constrain the Court, the way a legalist might imagine it. Consequently the decisions by the United Kingdom and Polish Governments to deny the Charter legal force in their jurisdiction are also likely to have few if any legal consequences.

Implications

Neither the critical discussions of the ECJ's formula relating to sources nor the general contrast between the legalist and the rationalist paradigm of human rights should suggest that there is something inherently misguided or wrong about the rationalist conception of human rights. What it does suggest is that challenges and concerns relating to the rationalist model of human rights need to be confronted and addressed. In order for that to happen, it is necessary first to acknowledge that we should not think or talk about the ECJ's human rights practice as if it conformed to the legalist paradigm. Rights as they are understood by the ECJ are not just about things fundamental, they are also about things mundane. An infringement of a right does not establish a presumption that the acts is a violation of a right, it merely triggers the Court's assessment of whether the measure meets the proportionality requirement. And sources doctrine does not play a significant role to guide and constrain judicial decision making. Rights discourse in a rationalist paradigm is about assessing justifications for the actions of public authorities from the perspective of individuals burdened by those actions.

The justification of the ECJ's rights practice would have been less obfuscating if it had justified its practice along the following lines, rather than using the misleading sources formula: 'All Member States share a commitment to human rights, democracy and the rule of law as a foundation of legal and political order. In order to forge a closer Union Member States have established common institutions with wide-reaching regulatory authority, whose laws claim to be the supreme law of the land. For such a claim to deserve

[112] Art 6, Sect 3 Draft Treaty Amending the Treaty on the European Union and the Treaty Establishing the European Community (Treaty of Lisbon).

[113] Art 52, Sect 1 2nd sentence states: 'Subject to the principle of proportionality, limitations may be made only if they are necessary and genuinely meet objectives of general interest recognized by the Union or the need to protect the rights and freedoms of others.'

recognition these laws must meet certain requirements relating to human rights. These requirements are not met, when a law places restrictions on an individual without being justified by a legitimate purpose pursued by necessary and proportionate means. This is a general standard underlying the common tradition of constitutional and human rights in Europe, that also applies to EC law. In order to ensure the effective and uniform application of EC law, the competence to determine whether this standard has been met with regard to EC law lies exclusively with the ECJ and the ECFI.'

What, then, are the major challenges and concerns that need to be confronted and addressed, once a rationalist human rights paradigm is acknowledged? Here it must suffice to briefly highlight some issues. Many of the institutional and doctrinal questions raised are not new and have been discussed in the context of general discussions about the ECJ as a court. But these questions appear in a new light and might require reassessment once the nature of the task the ECJ has carved out for itself by adopting a rationalist human rights paradigm has become apparent.

The first set of questions present direct challenges to a rationalist conception of rights, in which the real work in deciding concrete cases is done within the framework of proportionality analysis. Are there really rational standards available that allow for a meaningful distinction between measures that are proportional and those that are not? Call this the incommensurability challenge. Even if there are such standards, their specific content is likely to be subject to considerable disagreement, either abstractly or on application. To the extent that is the case, it is not clear why courts rather than politically accountable actors should have a comparative institutional advantage in assessing the proportionality of publicly endorsed policies. Furthermore this conception of rights seems to be insufficiently specific and determinate to provide either citizens or political actors with much guidance. Finally it is questionable whether a structure of rights that puts proportionality front and centre can adequately reflect the commitments central to the liberal constitutional tradition. In the liberal tradition rights are generally conceived as 'trumps'[114] over countervailing considerations of policy, or as 'firewalls'[115] providing strong protections against the demands made by the political community. Does a conception of human rights that focuses on proportionality analysis, allowing rights to be overridden whenever sufficiently weighty general interests are at stake, actually do justice to the idea of liberal rights? This is a question with important practical ramifications. If everything is subject to proportionality analysis, what explains, for example the categorical prohibition of torture, even in circumstances when a great deal might be gained by torturing a criminal suspect? And was a recent German Constitutional Court decision wrong, when it struck down a law which authorised shooting down a civilian plane about to be used as a platform for a terrorist attack in cases where the number of persons saved is considerably greater than the number of persons killed?[116] If such an authorisation was one day provided by EC law, would it stand? A better understanding of the place and limits of the proportionality requirement is called for, to more convincingly address these and other issues.[117]

[114] R Dworkin, 'What Rights Do We Have?' in *Taking Rights Seriously* (Oxford University Press, Oxford, 1978), 266.

[115] J Habermas, *Faktizität und Geltung* (Suhrkamp, 1992).

[116] BVerfGE 115, 118 (2005).

[117] For an attempt to do so see M Kumm, 'Political Liberalism and the Structure of Rights: On the Place and Limits of the Proportionality Requirement' in G Pavlakos (ed), *Law, Rights, Discourse: The Legal Philosophy of Robert Alexy* (2007), 131, at 153–62.

The second type of issue concerns questions relating to the institutional structure of the court and the way that judicial opinions are written. If European courts as adjudicators of rights are engaged in the kind of open-ended assessment of policies that the proportionality test calls for, it becomes inevitable that they will have to engage and pass judgment on complex policy questions that may involve controversial empirical and moral judgments. Taking for granted that the ECJ should have an important role to play along these lines, how should an openly rationalist, non-legalistic understanding of its task influence the style that opinions are written in? Should courts not, in the interests of transparency and clarity, be required to write more elaborately reasoned, discursive opinions, rather than using the cryptic formulations that often cover up difficult choices and competing reasons that the court confronts? Of course the more elaborately reasoned opinions of the Advocate General provide some degree of compensation[118] and the ECJ has become somewhat more discursive in recent years. But more might be called for. Indeed the case for allowing dissenting and concurring opinions might also have to be reassessed. And if a court were to more openly address its internal controversies, it would also be necessary for more politically exposed judges to be immunised from political blowback. Like their brethren on most constitutional courts it might be a good idea to appoint them for a longer term (say 10–12 years), without the possibility of reappointment. An open recognition of the court's role in rational policy assessment under its non-legalist conception of human rights might require a reevaluation of these questions and support a change in practice.

On the doctrinal level the central question is how to regulate the division of labour between the political branches and the court respectively. Embracing a rationalist conception of human rights, the ECJ has put itself in a position to assess any and every policy on any and every ground—that's what proportionality means in practice—for so long as it is presented with a case in which the plaintiff claims that his rights have been violated. This presents two connected dangers. The first is to do too much: to assume a role in second-guessing political and administrative judgments that are unsupported by any plausible comparative institutional advantage a court may have. This is the danger of juristocracy.[119] The second is to do too little. Once the scope of rights is as broad as the court has acknowledged and the standards it applies require engagement with rational policy assessment, an overburdened court, particularly one with a crowded docket, may shy back from any kind of meaningful scrutiny. Once a court is charged with monitoring practically everything it might not do a good job at monitoring anything. This is the danger of a court that goes through the motions intoning the rhetoric of proportionality while practically rubber-stamping any decision that the political branches make. There are few today that claim the ECJ is guilty of the former. But there have been some suggesting that it is guilty of the latter.[120] Whatever the case may be, these are questions that require considerably more attention than they have received so far. The ECJ is, of course, aware of these concerns and, using the Strasbourg Court's formula of a margin of appreciation, accords some degree of deference to political branches all the time. But what are the

[118] See M Lasser, *Judicial Deliberations: A Comparative Analysis of Judicial Transparency and Legitimacy* (Oxford University Press, Oxford, 2004).

[119] See R Hirschl, *Towards Juristocracy*, (HUP 2004).

[120] For the claim that the ECJ may be subject to such a charge, see J Coppel, A O'Neill, 'The European Court of Justice; Taking Rights Seriously?' 29 (1992) *CML Rev* 669.

circumstances under which deference is due? What are the circumstances under which little or no deference is due? Is the same level of deference due to EC institutions as to Member States' actions that fall under the scope of EC law, as the ECJ has recently suggested? Given the scope and depth of inquiries a court committed to a rationalist paradigm of human rights has to engage in, these are issues that deserve a great deal more attention than they have received in the past.

4

The ECJ's fundamental rights jurisprudence— a milestone in transnational constitutionalism

BRUN-OTTO BRYDE*

When the European Court of Justice declared in 1970: 'respect for fundamental rights forms an integral part of the general principles of law protected by the Court of Justice. The protection of such rights, whilst inspired by the constitutional traditions common to the member states, must be ensured within the framework of the structure and objectives of the community',[121] it took a decisive step both in the transformation of the Rome treaties into a constitution and in the protection of the European citizens' human rights. In 1974[122] these rights were additionally based on 'the international treaties for the protection of human rights on which the member states have collaborated or of which they are signatories', especially the European Convention on Human Rights, and the development of fundamental rights thereby linked to the wider project of a harmonised human rights sphere in Europe. With this jurisprudence the Court developed a system of human rights protection that could (and should) become an example for other international systems of government.

Constitutionalisation

The proclamation of the existence of an unwritten catalogue of fundamental rights in the community legal order has been an important third step in the constitutionalisation of Europe[123] through judicial action by the Court of Justice. This step came a couple of years

* I thank Andrea Kramer and Astrid Wallrabenstein for their assistance.

[121] ECJ Internationale Handelsgesellschaft/Einfuhr- und Vorratsstelle Case 11/70 [1979] ECR 1125 at 1135; repeated in Einfuhr- und Vorratsstelle für Getreide und Futtermittel / Köster Case 25/70 [1979] ECR 1161; one year earlier the court had already declared in passing the possibility that the European legal order contains a set of unwritten fundamental rights in Stauder (Case 29/69 [1969] ECR 419): 'interpreted in this way the provision at issue contains nothing capable of prejudicing the fundamental human rights enshrined in the general principles of community law and protected by the court'), cf also the Opinion of General Advocate Römer.

[122] ECJ *Nold/Kommission* Case 4/73 [1974] ECR 491 *ff.*

[123] A Peters, *Elemente einer Theorie der Verfassung Europas* (Duncker and Humblot, Berlin, 2001) 401 *ff*; T Giegerich, *Europäische und deutsche Verfassung im transnationalen Konstitutionalisierungsprozess* (Berlin, Springer, 2003) 262 *ff*; GF Mancini, 'A Constitution for Europe' (1989) *CML Rev* 595; MP Maduro, 'The Double

later than the decisive first two steps—direct effect in *van Gend en Loos*[124] and supremacy of community law in *Costa/ENEL*[125]—but it is a logical consequence of these seminal decisions. If the citizens of Europe are directly affected by decisions of the European Communities and if community law has primacy over national constitutions including their guarantees of fundamental rights, then there is a potential gap in the protection of human rights which the Court decided to close.

A rather common reading of this jurisprudential development sees it as defensive action by the European Court of Justice.[126] According to this view, the Court invented fundamental rights to fend off the threat of national constitutional courts, which threatened to review community legislation in order to protect the fundamental rights of their citizens. The following is a narrative often told in classrooms: the German Constitutional Court claims the right to review community legislation against the standard of German fundamental rights 'as long as' there is no catalogue of rights at European level (*Solange I*),[127] the European Court of Justice invents such a catalogue, and the German Court acknowledges this invention with a new doctrine waiving its right to review 'as long as' there is adequate protection on the community level (*Solange II*).[128] Unfortunately, this narrative does not fit with the sequence of events. *Solange I* is from November 1974, *Internationale Handelsgesellschaft* from 1970, *Nold* from May 1974 and the first reference to the doctrine in *Stauder* is already from 1969.[129] Therefore the basis for the German Constitutional Court's argument in *Solange II*, the recognition of European fundamental rights by the European Court of Justice, was already established when it decided *Solange I* (as is clearly pointed out by the dissenters[130]); and the condition set in *Solange I* ('As long as the integration process has not progressed so far that community law receives a catalogue of fundamental rights decided by Parliament') was still not met when *Solange II* was decided. Not the European Court of Justice, but the Bundesverfassungsgericht has changed its jurisprudence.

Yet the common perception that the Court's development of an unwritten fundamental rights catalogue reacted to a perceived threat for the community legal order is not without foundation. The potential of conflict between the European Court of Justice's insistence that community law took precedence over national constitutional law including fundamental rights and the national constitutional courts' mandate to protect those rights obviously did exist. In 1967, the German Constitutional Court appeared to reserve a right

Constitutional Life of the Charter of Fundamental Rights' in EO Eriksen, JE Fossum and AJ Menendez (eds), *The Chartering of Europe* (Baden-Baden, Nomos, 2003) 199, 206.

[124] ECJ, *van Gend en Loos* Case 26/62 [1963] ECR 1.

[125] ECJ, *Costa v ENEL* Case 6/64 [1964] ECR 585.

[126] J Coppel and A O'Neill, 'The European Court of Justice: Taking Rights Seriously', (1992) 29 *CML Rev* 669, 670 *ff*; Mancini (above note 123 at 611), J Kühling, 'Fundamental Rights' in A v Bogdandy and J Bast (eds), *Principles of European Constitutional Law* (Oxford, Hart, 2006) 501, 504 *ff*; A Stone Sweet, *Governing with Judges* (Oxford, Oxford University Press, 2000) 171.

[127] BVerfGE 37, 271 *ff*.

[128] BVerfGE 73, 339 *ff*.

[129] Cf G Nicolaysen, 'Historische Entwicklunglinien des Grundrechtsschutzes in der EU' in S Heselhaus and C Nowak, *Handbuch der Europäischen Grundrechte* (Munich, Beck, 2006) 1, 16.

[130] BVerfGE 37, 293 *ff*: this dissent by justices Rupp, Hirsch and Wand (worth reading again) contains a remarkably comprehensive analysis of the European case law, not just references to the recent cases expressly recognising fundamental rights on the community level but also to the older jurisprudence protecting rights with the help of general principles (rule of law, proportionality, good faith, non-discrimination).

to review European law in an obiter dictum.[131] In addition, there was a heated argument in legal scholarship whether national fundamental rights could be mobilised to challenge community acts. This discussion was a virulent one only in Germany,[132] much more subdued in Italy,[133] and hardly existent in the other four founding member countries. This can be explained partly by the fact that at that time only Italy and Germany had a fully developed system of constitutional review. However, when the founding father of German European law scholarship, Hans Peter Ipsen, addresses the rather extensive German literature worrying about the lack of protection of fundamental rights in European law in 1972,[134] he suspects a different reason. He begins with the rather polemical—but not completely incorrect—statement that one reason for the interest this subject raises in Germany can be excluded, namely the existence of actual threats to fundamental rights of community citizens in practice: if one looks through the literature of the time, there is indeed a remarkable absence of any concrete cases where the existence of a catalogue of rights would have changed the outcome. This is not astonishing. On the one hand, at this early stage the activities of the communities were much more restricted than today to relatively few policy fields, in which there was no potential for violations of human rights comparable to that in nation states. More importantly, the court had developed effective mechanisms for the protection of rights on the basis of basic freedoms and general principles of the rule of law.[135] For Ipsen the alleged concern for fundamental rights is therefore a disguise for the opposition to supranational power as such. If one can argue that the transfer of powers to international organs cannot compromise the protection of fundamental rights and that national courts should thus be able to refuse the national application of community law in their country if it violates national fundamental rights, then the very essence of the supranational law model developed by the European Court of Justice in *Van Gend en Loos* and *Costa* is threatened.

There is evidence that this threat was perceived quite clearly in Luxembourg. Certainly Pescatore, then a judge of the Court, described these discussions as 'threatening' in his seminal article, in which he countered the critics of the alleged fundamental rights deficit by claiming that the community already possessed an unwritten catalogue of fundamental rights.[136] The view that the development of fundamental rights was at least partly instigated by the Court's desire to stop any attempt to use the noble cause of fundamental

[131] BVerfGE 22, 293, 298 *f*. The decision confines itself to the pronouncement that the Federal Constitutional Court cannot be invoked directly by constitutional complaint against Regulations of the Council and Commission of the EEC but adds: 'There is thus no decision as to whether and to what extent the Federal Constitutional Court can measure Community law against the fundamental-rights norms of the Basic Law in the context of a procedure admissibly brought before it—a question which clearly depends on decision of the further reaching preliminary question whether and in what sense one may speak of a binding of the EEC organs by the fundamental-rights order of the Federal Republic of Germany or—putting it the other way—whether and to what extent the Federal Republic of Germany was able in transferring sovereign rights pursuant to Article 24(1) Basic Law to free the Community Organs of such binding' (English translation: Decisions of the Bundesverfassungsgericht Vol 1/I *International Law and Law of the European Communities* 1952–1989 (Baden-Baden, Nomos 1992) 182 *ff*).

[132] For references to contemporary literature cf HP Ipsen, *Europäisches Gemeinschaftsrecht* (Tübingen, Mohr, 1972) 716 *ff*; P Pescatore, 'Les droits de l'homme et l'integration Europeenne' (1968) *Cahiers de droit européen*, 629, 632 *ff*.

[133] Cf Pescatore, 635 *f*.

[134] Ipsen (above note 132) 716 *ff*.

[135] *Ibid*, Nicolaysen (above note 129) 20 *ff*; Justices Rupp, Hirsch and Wand, diss op BVerfGE 37, 293 *ff*; I Pernice, *Grundrechtsgehalte im Europäischen Gemeinschaftsrecht* (Baden-Baden, Nomos, 1979) 27 *ff*.

[136] Pescatore, 636: 'danger pour l'efficacité du droit communitaire'.

rights for the ignoble purpose of defending the sovereign nation state against European integration therefore has some merit. If this was the case, the defence has proven both fruitful and effective, and there is a certain dialectical justice in the fact that those who tried to derail the constitutionalisation of Europe mobilising fundamental rights as an argument moved the Court to a further step of constitutionalisation.

Such a (legitimate) social science perspective on the relationship between national and European actors in the development of European fundamental rights law should not, however, detract from the fact that the position both of the critics and the answer of the Court were well founded.

Whatever the motives of individual participants in the debate, the concern for fundamental rights at the supranational level is more than a cover for nationalism. It highlights a real problem. Even in the absence of concrete cases, the conflict between a comprehensive protection of fundamental rights against violations by state power at the national level and the transfer of regulatory power to a supranational level without comparable protection is obviously serious. And the Court's answer, too, even if also caused by the wish to thwart a potential threat, was not just defensive, but creative and expanded the protection of fundamental rights in Europe. Even if one places *Internationale Handelgesellschaft* and *Nold* in the framework of the competition by the European Court of Justice and national constitutional courts about judicial supremacy, the jurisprudential achievement of the Court is an impressive step in the development of a human rights culture in Europe.

Creativity

A purely defensive understanding of the decisions therefore fails to do justice to the Court's jurisprudential achievement. The Court was both courageous and inventive.

When Advocate General *Römer* claimed in his Opinion in *Stauder* that the general principles of Community law include the fundamental rights common to the legal systems of the member countries, the only authority he gave was a general reference to a view which, according to him, is broadly held in literature.[137] The fact that he does not include more specific references is no coincidence, because in reality there was very little material on which this doctrine could be based. The most important scholarly work which one could rely on stems from the ranks of the Court itself, that is, *Pescatore*'s above-mentioned article.[138]

However, while the Court's decision had innovative power, it was still based on sound jurisprudence.

The Court introduces fundamental rights into the community legal order as general principles of law and thereby links the new doctrine to a well-established concept both in international law and in community law. The Court had already recognised a whole set of

[137] Advocate's General Opinion, *Stauder* Case 29/69, [1969] ECR 427, 428.

[138] Cf above note 132: English: 'Fundamental Rights and Freedoms in the System of the European Communities' (1970) 18 *American Journal of Comparative Law* 343 *ff.* German: 'Die Menschenrechte und die europäische Integration' (1969) *Integration* 103.

principles related to the protection of human rights under this heading (for example, rule of law,[139] proportionality,[140] principle of justice and certainty,[141] *ne bis in idem*,[142] equality of treatment and non-discrimination[143]).

The introduction of fundamental rights was also a logical conclusion from other steps the Court had undertaken to transform the international law treaty system of the Rome treaties into a novel legal order. The European Court of Justice creatively takes up the critique that a system of government directly affecting the lives of citizens cannot deprive them of their fundamental rights and responds to the critique with an expansion of these rights to the supranational level.

Still, the claim that the community legal system contains a catalogue of fundamental rights is clearly a courageous step. In international law, at this point in time (and unfortunately this has not changed much until recently) nobody had seriously considered including human rights under the general principles of law (a rather elusive and not very productive source of general international law). Even the legal systems of the member countries provided less guidance then it might appear today. While it is true that all systems contained some kind of fundamental rights, only in Italy and Germany could they be used by constitutional courts to review legislation. The French Conseil Constitutionnel took the decisive step to include the human rights declarations incorporated in the preamble into its review programme only in its seminal decision of 7 July 1971.[144] In 1969/70 the European Court of Justice could not really draw on well-developed fundamental rights jurisprudence in all member states. It referred instead to a common culture from which it deduced the authority to hold the community organs responsible to keep in line with this culture.

With *Nold* the Court based its jurisprudence on a second authority: international human rights treaties and especially the European Convention of Human Rights. The argument that a common commitment to internationally recognised human rights by states should also influence a new supra-national legal order created by them is convincing.[145] However, it is by no means necessary as evidenced by the fact that until today the argument has not generally been accepted in international organisations. Furthermore, the situation in the member countries was less than clear. France had ratified the convention just days before the court's decision,[146] and the declaration according to Article 25 (old version) opening the way for individual complaints was made only in 1973 by Italy and even later (1981) by France. Thus, in the early 1970s the Convention was by no means an undisputed review standard for state action by national courts and not yet an important part of the Member States' legal culture.

In this legal environment the decision was indeed daring. While it fills a potential gap in fundamental rights protection for some countries, for others it provides a level of protection not yet found at the national level. The decision cannot rely on well-developed

[139] ECJ, *Meroni* Case 9/56 [1958] ECR 133.

[140] ECJ, *Federation Charbonnière de Belgique* Case 8/55 [1955] ECR 292.

[141] ECJ, *Klöckner and Hösch* Cases 17 and 21/61 [1967] ECR 325.

[142] ECJ, *Gutmann* Cases 18 and 35/65 [1966] EJR 61.

[143] ECJ, *Groupement des hauts fourneaux* Case 8/57 [1958] EJR 245.

[144] Décision no. 71–44 DC du 16 juillet 1971.

[145] Kühling (above note 126) 517 *f.*

[146] 3 May 1974 (this explains the cautious wording in *Nold*: '*on which the member states have collaborated* or of which they are signatories').

fundamental rights jurisprudence in the Member States, but creatively develops such jurisprudence in a productive dialogue with the member countries and international human rights institutions.

Expanding Protection of the European Citizens' Fundamental Rights

With *Internationale Handelsgesellschaft* and *Nold* the court had found a doctrinal basis from which it could develop all rights relevant for the activity of the communities. Starting cautiously with the rights that are most relevant in economic regulation—freedom of occupation and property—in the following years a comprehensive list of rights came to be recognised.[147] The importance of human rights in the European legal order goes much beyond those cases of invalidating community acts. Similarly to other (constitutional) courts, the European Court of Justice uses fundamental rights to interpret law,[148] a method that avoids outright confrontation with the lawmaker and still gives fundamental rights an adequate protection. An additional use of fundamental rights is their application in the relationship to the Member States. This use is both expansive when the Court requires respect for European fundamental rights in the application of community law by the Member States,[149] but it is also protective of national fundamental rights cultures when it allows fundamental rights as a defence against prima facie violation of market freedoms as in the famous *Brenner Autobahn* case where freedom of assembly was recognised as a justification for a restriction of the free movement of goods.[150] In sum, the European Court of Justice has worked effectively to transform the European legal order into an order which is inspired by fundamental rights.

The Court's jurisprudence was accepted and supported by the political organs, first in the common declaration by Parliament, Council and Commission of 1977,[151] then in Article 6(2) of the Treaty on European Union, which restated the position of the Court. When the Cologne European Council decided to establish a convention drafting a Charter of fundamental rights, its mandate was to codify the Court's jurisprudence (even if it went much beyond this mandate eventually).

But the Court's fundamental rights jurisprudence did not convince all its critics. Similarly to the discussions preceding *Internationale Handelsgesellschaft* and *Nold*, genuine concern about human rights, conflicts about supremacy and eurosceptic resistance to European integration are often difficult to disentangle in this criticism.

[147] Cf the extensive commentaries and handbooks that have proliferated in the last years: D Ehlers (ed), *Europäische Grundrechte und Grundfreiheiten* 2nd edn (Berlin, de Gruyter, 2005); S Heselhaus and C Nowak, *Handbuch der Europäischen Grundrechte* (Munich, Beck, 2006); HD Jarass, *EU-Grundrechte* (Munich, Beck, 2005).

[148] JHH Weiler and N Lockhardt, 'Taking Rights Seriously: The European Court and its Fundamental Rights Juriprudence' (1995) *CML Rev* 51, 579 583 *ff*; for a recent example cf Advocate General Maduro's opinion *Ordre des Barreaux* C 305/05.

[149] ECJ, *Wachauf* C 5/88 [1989] ECR 2609; *ERT* C 260//89 [1994] ECR I 2925.

[150] ECJ, *Schmidberger* C 112/00 [2003] ECR I 5659. Unfortunately, the Court abandons this correct approach with relation to labour disputes and constitutionally protected rights of collective action in ECJ, *Laval* C-341/05 and *International Transport Workers* C-438/05.

[151] OJ 1977 C103.

On the one hand, there have been continuing doubts about the normative stringency of unwritten rights.[152] This concern was one of the reasons inspiring the decision to draw up a Charter of Fundamental Rights and its inclusion into the projected Constitution.[153]

At a practical level this concern was never completely convincing. Fundamental rights are open-textured norms that acquire normative density only through case law in most constitutional systems. In many countries judge-made catalogues are developed on the basis of just a handful of guarantees.[154] In addition, the European Court of Justice, by increasingly relying on the European Convention on Human Rights, could work with a text. By this means, the Court developed a review framework for the relevant fundamental rights. This development was taken up and refined by European law scholarship. While in the beginning textbooks restricted themselves to the recognition of fundamental rights, the last years have witnessed a profusion of lengthy treatises and handbooks given doctrinal polish to the Court's case law.[155]

On the other hand, a much more strident criticism concerns the effectiveness of the Court's control function. According to a relatively widely held belief the European Court of Justice, while inventing rights, does not use them effectively to control community legislation.[156] This critique is overstated and fails to do justice to the Court's practice.[157] In addition, it is almost certainly based on wrong comparisons.

If one compares the European Court of Justice's activities with some constitutional courts—or the Strasbourg Court—the list of cases in which the violation of fundamental rights is the decisive reason for a decision is indeed small. But it is exactly this comparison that is misdirected.

The European Court of Justice is not a specialised constitutional court but a court of general jurisdiction in European law, even if it also acts as the Union's constitutional court. In the first place, this means that the Court has a lot of business that does not involve human rights, while the fundamental rights question is regularly at the centre of the case in constitutional courts and human rights courts. More importantly, a court of general jurisdiction—even if it has constitutional powers—often does not need to invoke fundamental rights, because it can protect the citizens' rights just by deciding cases correctly under ordinary law.

The reasons for a limited relevance of fundamental rights questions in the court's early jurisprudence remain true to a certain extent until today. While the scope of the European policy fields has continually expanded, thereby increasing the potential for violations of fundamental rights through community action as well, it remains limited to mainly socio-economic functions. The economic fundamental rights, which protect economic freedoms and which were established in *Internationale Handelsgesellschaft* and *Nold*, are

[152] Cf D Kraus, 'Grundrechtsschutz in der europäischen Union' in R Grote and T Marauhn, EMRK/GG Konkordanzkommentar (Tübingen, Mohr, 2006) 139 *ff* with references.

[153] Maduro, 201 *f*; A Wallrabenstein, 'Die Grundrechte, der EuGH und die Charta' (2000) *Kritische Justiz* 381.

[154] Eg human dignity (Israel), (substantive) due process (USA).

[155] Cf n 147 above.

[156] J Coppel and A O'Neill, 'The European Court of Justice: Taking Rights Seriously' (1992) *CML Rev* 669 *ff*; more moderate: B de Wittte, 'The Past and Future Role of the European Court of Justice' in P Alston (ed), *The EU and Human Rights* (Oxford, Oxford University Press, 1999) 859–69.

[157] Weiler and Lockhardt; Maduro, 208; I defended the Court's record myself as counsel for the German *Bundestag* in the Maastricht proceedings before the German Constitutional court: B-O Bryde and A Randelzhofer, 'Stellungnahme des Deutschen Bundestages' in I Winckelmann, *Das Maastricht-Urteil* (Berlin, Duncker & Humblot, 1994) 271, 281 *f*, 349 *ff*.

exactly those rights that national constitutional courts use with restraint as well, allowing for a wide margin of appreciation of the lawmaker. Pleas that the national courts should step in because the European Court of Justice fails to protect fundamental rights regularly assume a state of national constitutional law that plainly does not exist.[158] The European Court of Justice would be ill-advised to adopt an over-activist approach in this field just to silence its critics.[159]

This situation is likely to change with the move of the Union into areas like police and judicial co-operation in criminal matters in which more sensitive civil liberty questions are routinely at stake. It is therefore no coincidence that the European mandate has renewed the concern of national constitutional courts with the role of fundamental rights in European law.[160] But the European courts appear to take up this new challenge.[161] The sensitive question of the fight against terrorism caused a very illustrative use of fundamental rights. The Court of First Instance declared a council decision void[162] and in an even more ambitious decision the European Court of Justice insisted on the rule of law even in the face of binding Security Council sanctions.[163] When the Union expands its competences in this direction, it is exactly in the same dangerous position with respect to fundamental civil liberties as nation states. For that reason, successful invocations of fundamental rights become much more likely than in the classical socio-economic fields of community action. Retrospectively the European citizens are lucky that the European Court of Justice invented fundamental rights when there was no urgent need for them. Their invention in face of international terrorism, which has stretched the commitment to the rule of law in many countries, might have been much more difficult.

The European Court of Justice as Actor in the Harmonisation of European Human Rights

With its jurisprudence the European Court of Justice is also part of the enterprise of building a harmonised system of human rights protection in Europe.

The importance of the court's reference to the European Convention of Human Rights in *Nold* can hardly be overstated. The practical advantages are obvious. The protection of fundamental rights through unwritten case law is not impossible, but at least continental jurists very much prefer to work with texts they can expound and instead of inventing law judges prefer to invoke precedents. By basing the community fundamental rights system

[158] Compare Scholz's claim that the duty to publish warning on cigarette packages violates the very essence of fundamental rights and thus mobilises the *Solange* exception ('Wie lange bis *Solange III*?' (1990) *Neue Juristische Wochenschrift* 941 and BVerfGE 95, 173 *ff* that shrugs of this position under (ordinary) German constitutional law (let alone the core protection of fundamental rights).

[159] On the Court's judicial restraint cf Maduro, 210 *f*.

[160] BVerfGE 113, 273; Cour d'Arbitrage (Belgium) 124/2005 13–7-05; cf also General Advocate Ruiz-Jabaro opinion Case C 303/05; the rather superficial response given to the serious questions raised by the Belgian Constitutional Court by the ECJ (C 303/05) is, however, not likely to encourage the dialogue between national constitutional courts and the ECJ.

[161] Cf General Advocate Maduro's Opinion *Ordre des Barreaux* C 305/05, clearly stressing the need to protect counsel's privacy.

[162] CFI, *Modjahedines/Council* T-228/02; cf also ECJ *PKK and KNK/Council* Case 229/05.

[163] ECJ, *Kadi* C-402/05.

on the twin foundation of comparative law and international treaties, especially the European Convention of Human Rights, the court attains this position. As a result, legal scholarship in Europe can base fundamental rights arguments in European law on the text of the European Convention on Human Rights and the jurisprudence of the European Court of Human Rights and need not wait for a case in which the Court invents a new right.

But the importance of the Court's work with the convention goes beyond this practical advantage and also contributes to the wider European human rights culture. If one looks at the different ways the members of the convention have adopted it into their national legal systems, the emphasis is usually placed on the different degrees of obligation. Those states that give constitutional status to the convention (Austria) or follow a monist system, in which international obligations take precedence over national law (Switzerland) appear to be more strictly bound than those that treat it only as ordinary law (Germany). In this context, it is easily overlooked that obligation comes with an advantage. The states that use the convention as a domestic standard for constitutional review are not only less likely to run into conflicts between constitutional and international law.[164] They also gain influence on the interpretation of the convention because their courts expound the meaning of the convention in their own decisions. Case law, which takes its departure from the text of the convention, is more likely to influence the interpretation at the international level. Similarly, by using the European Convention on Human Rights as a review standard the European Court of Justice belongs to those courts whose jurisprudence is of special importance for the interpretation of convention rights and therefore Europe-wide. Because it draws on both the national constitutions and the European Convention on Human Rights, the court holds a strategic position in the enterprise of harmonising the European human rights system.

This is an important task. At least at first glance, the human rights situation in Europe looks very complex if not confusing. All European countries have their own national catalogue of rights, today regularly protected by national courts. On a continental level there is the European Convention on Human Rights and in the European Union the European Court of Justice has developed unwritten fundamental rights. With the adoption of the Charter of Fundamental Rights,[165] the European bill of rights acquired a written form. The Constitution would have made the situation even more complex because both the Charter and the European Convention on Human Rights would have become binding instruments conjointly with the unwritten fundamental rights.

An outside observer might be forgiven if he suspected that such a number of human rights catalogues was less a wealth but rather a source of conflicts. However, in practice there is very little. National courts, Strasbourg, and Luxembourg have managed to develop a very harmonious concert in the protection of human rights. One reason is the close substantial similarity of the rights systems. In addition, the courts try to avoid conflict by harmonising their jurisprudence. The international courts do this by giving a margin of appreciation to national legal systems, the national courts by interpreting their law in

[164] This is not an empirical statement: there is no reliable evidence that the status of the convention in national law correlates strongly with compliance.

[165] OJ 2000 C 364/1; Callies, 'Die Europäische Grundrechts Charta', in Ehlers (ed), *Europäische Grundrecht und Grundfreiheiten*, 2003; Wallrabenstein, 'Die Grundrechte, der EuGH und die Charta' (2002) *Kritische Justiz*, 381 *ff*.

conformity with the international instruments. But in this harmonisation process the European Convention on Human Rights holds a pivotal place: it is the only continent-wide binding text and in addition it has inspired the fundamental rights law in all European countries.[166] In this development the European Court of Justice has played a major role. With its acceptance of the European Convention on Human Rights as a source for developing its own fundamental rights jurisprudence it very much contributed to the convention's central role in the harmonisation process.

Beyond the Union: the European Court of Justice and the Development of International Human Rights Law

The importance of the Court's decisions should go beyond European law.

At international level, the problem the Court was confronted with in 1970 poses itself with increasing urgency. The Court's decision was based on the argument that a transnational legal order with effect on the citizens of the member countries should provide them with a comparable level of protection of their fundamental rights. Today, this argument can be made for many international organisations.[167]

But the state of the law concerning the binding force of human rights for international organisations is unsatisfactory. In international law, human rights are protected by treaties which sociologically are bills of rights of the international community.[168] Legally, however, these treaties are binding for most, but not all states. International organisations are not parties to these treaties. Because of the overlapping, but not completely identical membership it is difficult to construe their binding nature for international organisations. It is, however, of crucial importance to guarantee that international organisations are bound by human rights. UN sanctions,[169] decisions of the WTO,[170] or decisions of the IMF or World Bank[171] must comply with international human rights standards. This is not doubtful for those human rights that form part of customary international law and even more for those rules that are *jus cogens* and have *erga omnes* application. But it falls short of the application of the ensemble of human rights treaties, which should also be possible.

Here, the international law community could learn from the European Court of Justice. The argument that the transfer of powers from states to international actors cannot deprive the citizens of the member countries of the protection of human rights applies

[166] B-O Bryde, 'The Internationalization of Constitutional Law' in T Groß (ed.), *Legal Scholarship in International and Comparative Law* (Frankfurt, Lang, 2003). 191 *ff.*

[167] S Cassese 'The Globalization of Law' (2005) 37 *New York University Journal of International Law and Politics* 973, 984.

[168] B-O Bryde, 'Verpflichtungen Erga Omnes aus Menschenrechten' *33 Berichte der Deutschen Gesellschaft für Völkerrecht* (Heidelberg, Müller, 1994) 165 *f.*

[169] A Clapham, 'Sanctions and Economic, Social and Cultural Rights' in V Gowlland-Debbas (ed), *United Nations Sanctions and Interantional Law* (The Hague, Kluwer, 2001) 131 *f*; JA Frowein, 'The UN Anti-Terrorism Administration and the Rule of Law' in PM Dupuy, B Fassbender, MN Shaw and K-P Sommermann, *Festschrift für Christian Tomuschat*, Kehl, Engel, 2006, 785; Bossuyt, E/CN.4/Sub.2/2000/33.

[170] Here the discussion and practice are most advanced: Cassese, 984; E-U Petersmann, 'Constitutionalism, International Law' and 'We the Peoples of the United Nations' in H-J Cremer, T Giegerich, D Richter and A Zimmermann (eds.), *Tradition und Weltoffenheit des Rechts (Festschrift für Helmut Steinberger)* (Berlin, Springer, 2002) 291, 307 *f.*

[171] U Suchsland-Maser, *Menschenrechte und die Politik multilateraler Finanzinstitute* (Frankfurt, 1999) 127 *ff.*

similarly to the international level. In addition, the Court's jurisprudence provides the doctrinal instruments to solve this problem. The Court construed unwritten fundamental rights as part of general principles and thereby invoked a concept well known to general international law. In addition, it used an innovative method to ascertain those rights. While relying on comparative law and the treaties concluded by the member states it incorporates neither national constitutional law nor international treaties wholesale into the community legal order. Rather it uses these sources as an inspiration to autonomously develop a level of fundamental rights protection adequate for a transnational authority. With a comparable argument, it should be possible to bind international organisations to the human rights standards that the vast majority of their members have subscribed to either in their national law or as members of international human rights treaties.

Unfortunately, at the international level the actor to implement such a programme is often missing. The International Court of Justice, for example, can only deliver advisory opinions for UN organs, not binding decisions (UN Charter, Article 96). And in most international organisations there is no access at all, not even indirectly, by those individuals or corporations whose rights are infringed on. With an increase of binding decisions of the Security Council this state of the law appears no longer acceptable.[172] The measures taken by the Security Council in combating terrorism are a good illustration. In view of the human rights standards accepted by the international community, it seems hardly tolerable that an international organ can order sanctions against specifically named individuals and organisations without any possibility for those affected to have controlled whether they are listed there correctly.[173]

The European Court of Justice has developed the doctrine with which these problems can be solved. Also for this reason *Internationale Handelsgesellschaft* and *Nold* remain important even after 25 years. The process of the constitutionalisation of the international legal order, which has been started so effectively at the European level, should find its succession at the wider international level.[174]

[172] J Dugard, 'Judicial Review of Sanctions', in Gowlland-Debbas (ed.), 83 *ff.*

[173] This logic informs the ECJ's decision in Kadi (C-402/05); cf also GA Maduro's opinion in this case; for critiques of the CFI's decision in *Yusuf*, Case T-306/01; cf S Hörmann, 'Völkerrecht bricht Rechtsgemeinschaft?' (2006) 44 *Archiv des Völkerrechts* 267; Frowein, 795.

[174] B-O Bryde, 'International Democratic constitutionalism' in R St John Macdonald and DM Johnston, *Towards World Constitutionalism* (Leiden, Nijhoff, 2005) 103, 115.

IV

Case C-260/89, *Elliniki Radiophonia Tiléorassi AE (ERT) and Panellinia Omospondia Syllogon Prossopikou v Dimotiki Etairia Pliroforissis and Sotirios Kouvelas and Nicolaos Avdellas and others*, and Case 5/88, *Hubert Wachauf v Bundesamt für Ernährung und Forstwirtschaft*

1

Wachauf and the Protection of Fundamental Rights in EC Law

FRANCIS G JACOBS

One of the purposes of this Chapter is to illustrate the theme that the same case can be seen differently from different viewpoints. I am asked to consider this theme from the viewpoint of an Advocate General, and I take as an example a case concerning the protection of fundamental rights in EC law, *Wachauf*.[1]

The *Wachauf* case is frequently cited as the case which established an important principle of Community law: the principle that Member States are obliged, as a matter of Community law, to observe fundamental rights whenever they implement Community law. But, if that can be said with the benefit of hindsight, it may not have been how the case first presented itself when it reached the ECJ. Indeed the questions referred to the ECJ in that case had no apparent connexion with that principle. The questions—as set out below—were of a somewhat dry and highly technical character, and made no reference to fundamental rights. Yet the case did come to represent an important advance in the case law in that field.

It had already been established by the ECJ that the Community institutions themselves were obliged, as a matter of Community law, to observe fundamental rights. Even that proposition, which now seems, again with the benefit of hindsight, rather obvious, was the outcome of a lengthy period of gestation of the case law of the Court of Justice.

That part of the story can be recalled briefly. There were in the original EEC Treaty no general provisions requiring observance of fundamental rights. It may have been thought that such issues were unlikely to arise in a treaty on economic matters, and that human rights issues were rather for the Council of Europe and its European Convention on Human Rights. So, although a fundamental right to equal treatment can be regarded as underlying some provisions of the Treaty—notably the prohibition of discrimination on grounds of nationality and the principle of equal pay for men and women for equal work—there were, and remain, no general provisions on fundamental rights of the kind found in national constitutions.

Originally—in the first decade of the Treaty—when Community measures were challenged before the Court on the grounds of conflict with fundamental rights, the Court seemed reluctant to entertain such challenges: the Court appeared to consider that to accept such challenges, based on provisions of national law or national constitutions, might prejudice the primacy of Community law.

[1] Case 5/88 [1989] ECR 2609. It was one of my first Opinions at the Court. The name of the case suggests the maxim *Vigilantibus non dormientibus jura subveniunt*, a maxim appropriate to the outcome of the case.

However, in 1970 in the *Internationale Handelsgesellschaft* case the Court qualified its position, perhaps recognising that in fact its earlier stance might prejudice the primacy of Community law, as Community legislation expanded and increasingly raised issues of fundamental rights, and as national courts showed themselves increasingly concerned about the possible impact of the legislation on such rights. Reasserting the primacy of Community law, the Court of Justice held that Community law could not be overridden by rules of national law. It was therefore not possible to test the validity of Community law measures by reference to fundamental rights protected by the constitutions of the Member States. However—and here came the breakthrough—the Court continued:

> respect for fundamental rights forms an integral part of the general principles of law protected by the Court of Justice. The protection of such rights, whilst inspired by the constitutional traditions common to the Member States, must be ensured within the framework of the structure and objectives of the Community.

Thus the Court on the one hand created a *Community* guarantee of fundamental rights, inspired by the constitutional traditions common to the Member States, and therefore broadly equivalent to them. On the other hand, the Court claimed for itself the position of guardian of those rights, within the system of Community law, and the right to decide the scope of protection by reference to the legitimate public-interest concerns of the Community.

The new approach was exemplified in 1979 in *Hauer*,[2] a case which in some respects foreshadowed *Wachauf*. The measure challenged in *Hauer* was a Council regulation which, with a view to controlling wine surpluses, prohibited the new planting of vines for a period of three years. It was contended that the prohibition infringed the right of property and the rights to trade. The Court accepted that the right of property was guaranteed in the Community legal order in accordance with values common to the constitutions of the Member States. The Court also accepted that the European Convention on Human Rights, which guarantees property rights in its First Protocol, had a special significance in the Community legal order. However the challenge to the Regulation was ultimately rejected.

Thus by the time of the *Wachauf* case, decided in 1989, it was firmly established that the Community institutions were bound, in the exercise of their powers, to respect fundamental rights recognised, in particular, by the constitutional traditions of the Member States and by the European Convention on Human Rights.

But what of the Member States when implementing Community law? That was the issue which fell to be decided in *Wachauf*.

While very understandable, it is perhaps too easy for textbook writers to say, as they tend to, that the issue in *Wachauf* was whether Member States are obliged, as a matter of Community law, to observe fundamental rights whenever they implement Community law. That can be said only with the benefit of hindsight.

Indeed, as a general proposition, it is all too easy to read cases in this way, and this point, perhaps familiar to all lawyers involved in litigation, was constantly brought home to me when I served as Advocate General at the ECJ. Time and again, once the Advocate General has delivered the Opinion, the contours of the case are reasonably clear. That does not mean that they were clear beforehand. Rather, if they are clear when the Opinion is delivered, it is often because the Advocate General has done the necessary groundwork.

[2] Case 44/79 [1979] ECR 3727.

The dispute in *Wachauf* arose out of EC legislation designed to reduce milk production. Under that legislation, producers were encouraged to give up milk production. Farmers who undertook, under the 'outgoers' scheme', to discontinue definitively the production of milk and milk products could claim compensation from the national farm agency. Mr Hubert Wachauf, a dairy farmer, applied for compensation, on the expiry of his tenancy, for the definitive discontinuance of milk production pursuant to the German law implementing the EC provisions. The application had to be accompanied by the landlord's written consent to the discontinuance of milk production.

The German agency refused to grant Mr Wachauf the compensation requested, since the landlord[3] of the farm in question had withdrawn the consent which he had originally given.

Mr Wachauf brought an action against the decision of the Federal Office before the Administrative Court, Frankfurt-am-Main.

That court referred the following questions to the Court of Justice:

1. Is an agricultural production unit having neither dairy cattle nor facilities (such as milking parlours) capable of being used exclusively for milk production a 'holding' within the meaning of Article 12(d) of Council Regulation (EEC) No 857/84 of 31 March 1984 (Official Journal L 90, 1.4.1984, p 13)?
2. Is the surrender of leased property upon the expiry of the lease a case having 'comparable legal effects' within the meaning of Article 5(3) of Commission Regulation (EEC) No 1371/84 of 16 May 1984 (Official Journal L 132, 18.5.1984, p 11), if the leased property is an agricultural undertaking without dairy cattle and without any facilities capable of being used only for milk production (for example, milking parlours) and where the lease provided for no obligation on the part of the lessee to engage in milk production?

From the terms of the questions referred, two points can be made: first, on what the questions did ask, second, on what they did not.

First, on what the questions did ask, the case was apparently a highly technical case on the interpretation of the EC legislation on the milk market, in this case on the outgoers' scheme. Such cases were, and are, customarily assigned by the Court to a three-judge chamber, the smallest composition of the Court and one used for highly technical cases of little apparent general significance. In contrast, most of the cases which reach the Court were (and are) assigned to larger (often substantially larger) formations: today, either five or 13 judges, or, most exceptionally, all 27 judges. In accordance with the normal practice, the *Wachauf* case was assigned to a three-judge chamber.

We may recall that there were at the time relatively large numbers of references on the milk market schemes. They tended, contrary to the normal practice, all to be allocated (by the President of the Court) to one particular Judge as Judge Rapporteur, and therefore also to the same three-judge chamber. The milk cases were not, however, consistently allocated (by the First Advocate General) to the same Advocate General, but were shared out among the Advocates General. There was, however, a specific and rather technical body of case law on the subject.

[3] In fact it seems that the landlord may have been a landlady, namely Princess Sayn zu Wittgenstein. However, in accordance with normal usage, the masculine term can be understood as embracing the feminine.

Second, but perhaps more significant, it should be noted what the questions referred in *Wachauf* did *not* ask. There was no mention, in the national court's questions, of fundamental rights, and nothing in the terms of the questions to suggest that any such issue arose.

That was, however, clearly the underlying concern of the referring court, the Administrative Court of Frankfurt-am-Main, as was apparent from that court's reasoning set out in its order referring the case to the ECJ. Moreover that court had played an important part in previous cases in raising questions of fundamental rights. It was no doubt that concern which prompted the reference. Here the essential problem was whether a tenant farmer, who by his own efforts had built up a dairy herd and had attracted a valuable milk quota as a result, was adequately protected under the scheme. In this case, the national court took the view that if the questions referred were answered in the affirmative, then an issue would arise as to whether certain rules of the outgoers' scheme were compatible with constitutional guarantees. In particular, there might be doubts about the rule requiring the landlord's consent to a tenant's participation in the scheme, and about the rule that, on the expiry of the tenancy, the quota reverts with the land to the landlord, with no provision for compensation.

Although the creation of milk quotas was not intended to create a commodity, there could be little doubt that as a matter of economic reality such quotas had acquired a value. As I put it in my Opinion, a milk quota was an 'intangible asset … which can properly be regarded as having an independent economic value'.

The underlying issue was therefore whether a tenant farmer in the position of Mr Wachauf was entitled to compensation for the asset which he had created by his own efforts. There was no provision for compensation in such circumstances. But did Community law require the payment of compensation, in order to guarantee the fundamental rights of the tenant farmer?

At this point, a further clarification was needed. Once the issue of compensation had been identified, it seemed to be assumed on all sides that, in the absence of provision for compensation in such circumstances, it was the Community legislation which had to be tested for compliance with fundamental rights. That indeed had been the issue in the previous cases, such as *Hauer*.

However, it seemed to me that the decisive issue in the present case was different: where Community measures were implemented by the national authorities, it was their actions which had to be tested, and tested as a matter of Community law. As I put it in my Opinion:

> Although the Court's case-law has hitherto been concerned with respect for property rights by the Community legislator itself, the same principles must in my view apply to the implementation of Community law by the Member States, since it appears to me self-evident that when acting in pursuance of powers granted under Community law, Member States must be subject to the same constraints, in any event in relation to the principle of respect for fundamental rights, as the Community legislator.

The Court of Justice took the same view, apparently even taking it for granted that similar guarantees were required of Member States. After observing that:

> Community rules which, upon the expiry of the lease, had the effect of depriving the lessee, without compensation, of the fruits of his labour and of his investments in the tenanted holding would be incompatible with the requirements of the protection of fundamental rights in the Community legal order,

the Court added:

> Since those requirements are also binding on the Member States when they implement Community rules, the Member States must, as far as possible, apply those rules in accordance with those requirements.

Thus the obligation of Member States, when implementing Community rules, is taken as self-evident.

I would add that in my view, by the words 'as far as possible', the Court did not mean that the national authorities had any freedom of manoeuvre in this respect. On the contrary, the Court appears to have meant 'in so far as the Community rules, properly interpreted, make it possible for the Member States to respect fundamental rights'. If that were not possible—if the rules could not be so interpreted—then the Community rules themselves would be unlawful.

These points follow from a later passage in the judgment, where the Court held, first, that the Community rules in question did leave the national authorities sufficient room to enable them to apply the rules consistently with fundamental rights, either by giving the lessee the opportunity of keeping all or part of the reference quantity (or quota) if he intends to continue milk production, or by compensating him if he undertakes to abandon such production definitively; and held secondly that the submission that the rules in question conflicted with the requirements of the protection of fundamental rights in the Community legal order must therefore be rejected.

Thus the *Wachauf* case established definitively that Member States, when implementing Community rules, are bound, as a matter of Community law, to respect fundamental rights—a point which is especially significant because it is normally the Member States, rather than the Community institutions, which implement Community rules.

It is quite another question whether, as the Court of Justice subsequently held in *ERT*,[4] Member States have similar obligations where they derogate from the economic freedoms of the Treaty. I confess to some doubts on this point, and it is of interest that, in contrast to the *Wachauf* principle, it was not reflected in the EU Charter of Fundamental Rights. The Charter states that it is addressed to the institutions of the Union, and to the Member States only where they are implementing EU law.

Has the Court gone too far in *ERT*—and in subsequent cases such as *Familiapress*?[5]

It might seem that, where a Member State relies successfully on an express derogation from the Treaty, it has shown that it acts within its own competence. Why then should those acts be subject to review by the ECJ for compliance with human rights as a matter of Community law? The assumption underlying this extension of the Court's human rights case law must be that where a Member State relies on an express derogation, it is not acting outside the field of Community law even where the conditions for the derogation are otherwise wholly satisfied. It still remains for the ECJ to check for compliance with human rights.

A first objection to that view is that there are in issue here two independent grounds of challenge: one based on EC law whether the express conditions for the derogation are satisfied, which the ECJ alone can authoritatively resolve; the other based on human rights, which is not here a matter of EC law but can quite well be handled by the national

[4] Case C-260/89 [1991] ECR I-2925.

[5] Case C-368/95 [1997] ECR I-3689.

courts (and if necessary by the European Court of Human Rights). That objection is supported by the fact that in *ERT* itself the ECJ left it to the national courts to decide whether the Greek television monopoly could be justified under Articles 46 and 55 of the Treaty having regard to freedom of expression.

Indeed if it were truly a question of EC law whether any measure relying upon a derogation from the Treaty was also a matter of EC law because of a human rights issue, and it was therefore necessary for the ECJ to intervene, the ECJ would have to settle the difficult question of the appropriate standard of protection which EC law affords to human rights in such cases. Although some authors have suggested that in such cases the national standard of protection should apply, that would undermine the need for the ECJ's view that human rights apply here as a matter of EC law. On the other hand, it would not be satisfactory for the ECJ to seek to determine the standard itself. That would risk involving the ECJ in almost every area of public life in the EU Member States and transforming the ECJ into a second human rights court. This risk has indeed become more apparent in some subsequent cases on EU citizenship where issues of citizenship seem to become confused with issues of human rights.

The *ERT* line of case law, then, seems to overlook the point that there are in such cases two separate and independent issues: one based on EC law and one based on human rights. In contrast, in *Wachauf* there was a single issue, which was whether the manner in which the EC scheme was implemented was compatible with human rights. It was for the ECJ, as the ultimate authority on the interpretation of EC law, to interpret the EC legislation so as to ensure compliance with those rights.

Conclusions

Looking back on the *Wachauf* case with the privilege of hindsight, I will conclude with some general observations.

First, the case provides an interesting exercise in identifying, as described above, the true issue to be decided.

Second, the case provides a good illustration of how an apparently highly technical case can give rise to a significant constitutional pronouncement. Indeed, it must be rare for the judgment of a three-judge chamber to be of such general importance. However, no criticism can in my view be made of the allocation of the case to the smallest composition of the Court, since when the question had once been identified the answer was indeed self-evident.

Third, the case forms part of a development of the Court's case law in a sequence which is not yet closed. In particular, how far can and should the principle extend: should it apply only where the Member States are implementing Community law, or should it be wider?

Fourth, the theme illustrates one of the more remarkable shifts in the case law, if one compares the Court's earliest endeavours with some of its most recent pronouncements. Having initially, as shown above, routinely rejected challenges based on fundamental rights, the Court has recently seemed in some cases to look for such issues even where they were not necessary to its decision, and where the cases could adequately be decided on the basis of, for example, free movement. More positively, the Court has in recent cases such as *Schmidberger*[6] and *Omega*[7] satisfactorily addressed, in my view, new issues

[6] Case C-112/00 [2003] ECR I-5659.
[7] Case C-36/02 [2004] ECR I-9609.

where the fundamental economic freedoms of the Treaty appear to conflict with human rights of the type protected by the European Convention.

Fifth, the case marks a stage in the development of the Court's case law which has proved significant in establishing the Court's credentials as a court taking full account of fundamental rights. In earlier cases the Court was criticised for paying 'lip service' to human rights or for not 'taking rights seriously'. The earlier cases do not appear to have resulted in any successful outcomes for challenges based on human rights In *Wachauf*, because of the nature of the proceedings, the Court itself was not required to give a remedy but left that to the national court, which duly made an award of compensation. So the case may have been the first in which there was an effective remedy based on a fundamental rights challenge.

Sixth, the case law, taken in the round, can also be seen, with hindsight, as meeting some of the concerns of national courts and of the European Court of Human Rights. The ECJ's case law on the protection of fundamental rights, developed in such cases as *Wachauf* and notably *Bosphorus*[8] itself, satisfied the European Court of Human Rights in its own *Bosphorus* case that the protection of human rights in Community law was equivalent to the protection provided under the European Convention on Human Rights. The Strasbourg Court concluded that it was therefore unnecessary for it to undertake its own review of Community measures where they had already been reviewed by the European Court of Justice.

The *Wachauf* case was a step, perhaps small but certainly necessary, in that progression.

[8] Case C-84/95 [1996] ECR I-3953.

2

Looking Back at *ERT* and its Contribution to an EU Fundamental Rights Agenda

DAMIAN CHALMERS[9]

Introduction

In the modern world fundamental rights do a number of things. They seek to secure a good life for individuals by protecting them against arbitrary or oppressive intervention and by requiring states to realise certain goods for them. They also act as a marker for government, setting out what it can and cannot do. Beyond these roles, they are frequently deployed as a legitimation tool. As fundamental rights collectively set out a description of the good life, arguments by the polity or government that these are about realising these serve as one of the easier routes to self-justification. These claims lead to another dimension of fundamental rights, namely they act as points of debate. We may, thus, all agree that the good life is a good thing but understandings of what it is and how we are to realise it will differ significantly. A polity's claim to realise the good life carries the potential, therefore, to stir debate about its claims and its *modi operandi*. In this, fundamental rights serve not merely as points of debate but also as points of continual critique as fundamental rights are idealisations, which remind citizens both of their expectations of a government and of its inability to fulfil these obligations completely. Finally, fundamental rights have a powerful symbolic dimension. They serve to remind the political community in totemic fashion of what it is and what it aspires to.

In unitary states, these dimensions are taken for granted, as fundamental rights have a certain indefeasible quality. In European Union law, they have never had that indefeasibility. EU fundamental rights are not yet set out in any constitutional document, have a limited material and personal scope, and have to compete with other national and international human rights instruments. They have therefore had to struggle for each one of these qualities, and have acquired them unevenly. The central argument of this essay is that the *ERT* judgment was the first moment when an institutional authority raised the question whether EU fundamental rights should have the qualities of national fundamental rights.[10] Prior to *ERT*, fundamental rights acted as no more than judicial constraints on EC policy enactment, be this carried out by EC institutions or Member States. This language of constraint on EU policy making cannot explain the *ERT* judgment which, by stating that Member States were bound by EU fundamental rights when acting within the

[9] London School of Economics and Political Science.

[10] Case C-260/89 *ERT v DEP* [1991] ECR I-2925.

field of EC law, suggested a new territorial remit for EU fundamental rights, namely that of the single market. Any measure potentially compromising transnational market activity would fall within the field of EC law insofar as it would be caught by the economic freedoms and therefore have to be justified under EC law. To be sure, this was an odd and uncertain jurisdiction within which fundamental rights must be enjoyed. It created, however, a terrain of action in which EU fundamental rights could be treated in a self-standing manner, and thus allowed them the possibility to acquire the different dimensions of national fundamental rights.

This essay will consider the extent to which this has happened in the 16 years since and why none of these dimensions has been developed successfully. It will argue that the human rights agenda suggested by *ERT* depended upon a much thicker European constitutionalisation agenda than either public opinion or national governments were willing to countenance. This has been reflected in the recent IGC negotiations for the Reform Treaty where the Union has moved away from a position where it is founded on fundamental rights and these are incorporated into the main Treaty text to a position where it merely commits itself to the legal recognition of them. This paper concludes by considering how this new politics of recognition will affect the place of fundamental rights in EU law, suggesting it will cast their primary role as a point of external reference for EU law in which the Union adopts a more modest role and in which it considers how its policies affect the Good Life, as institutionalised by EU fundamental rights, rather seeking for these to constitute it.

Fundamental Rights and Judicial Protection of the Individual

It is a truism that most administration within the EU legal field is done by national authorities. The Union, with its tiny bureaucracies, relies overwhelmingly on national, regional and local officials for the application, enforcement and policing of EU law. It could also be argued that the majority of law making is also done by national authorities. Outside the specialised and contained fields of competition, external trade and agriculture and fisheries, the instruments of choice—Directives, Framework Directives and Decisions, and Recommendations—rely for their legal effects upon national laws whose normative force is recognised by EU law. In addition, many national laws regulate situations diagonally with Union laws.[11] That is to say that national regulatory, contract and property laws will not implement Union laws, but will have to respect Union norms that cut across their government of a particular situation.[12]

The dictum of the *ERT* judgment that all national measures falling within the field of EC law must be governed by EC fundamental rights norms subjected, in effect, all these measures to a new civil liberties regime. The remit is enormous. Dutch and French

[11] On this see C Schmid, 'Diagonal Competence Conflicts between European Competition Law and National Law. The example of book price fixing' (2000) 8 *European Review of Private Law* 155.

[12] The most obvious example of this is where national laws come into contact with the economic freedoms. In such circumstances, the national law usually applies but must be aligned in such a way that it complies with the EC norm.

estimates suggest that 30 per cent of all legislation within the Netherlands is either EU law or implements EU law.[13] There are no reliable estimates on national measures touched by or falling within the field of EC law, but it is not unreasonable to suspect that it is great again. *ERT* created a dual regime, therefore, in which commensurately significant parts of policy and legislation in national territories were to be governed either by exclusively national arrangements or by EU fundamental rights norms and institutional arrangements. This new regime obviously raised questions of pedigree and comparative institutional performance—should highly sensitive matters be ruled on by the Court of Justice or local bodies? How did a judicially enforced unwritten bill of rights compare with the myriad of national forms of fundamental protection?

These hoary questions, whilst important, are probably irresoluble. After 16 years, a couple of more pragmatic questions can be addressed to evaluate performance. One is the standard of review, namely beyond simply the rhetorical, how do the courts interpret fundamental rights norms? The other is the co-ordination of the EU law regime with national regimes. To say that a measure falls outside the EU law is not to say that there is an absence of protection. It is simply to say that, given all Member States have institutional mechanisms dedicated to the protection of fundamental rights, it is governed by a different set of choices and arrangements. Such dual regimes are always going to lead to charges of inconsistency, but a more realistic point of critique is to consider how the regimes align themselves with each other and the principles for allocating cases between regimes.

In relation to the standard of review, the Court of Justice has faced two challenges. The first is that the EU has never been able to articulate a vision of the Good Life that would inform its choice of fundamental rights and their interpretation. Reasons are provided for its having fundamental rights, namely protection of supremacy of EC law and fundamental rights being a good thing, but if one ponders their mission, one stares at an institutional vacuum. This leads to bizarre debates about whether the EU should take a maximalist or minimalist approach to fundamental rights with one assumed to be a very strong protection of the individual and the other a weaker one. Yet this debate cannot even be begun until one has some sense as to what 'protection of the individual' means, as it is too crude and too libertarian to assume it is simply about placing constraints on government. The absence of a fundamental right ethic is particularly apparent when the Court of Justice is faced with ruling on sensitive matters that are strongly informed by powerful national constitutional or cultural traditions.

The consequence has been a patchwork case law. One hallmark is the very rare overturning of measures by the judiciary. In many instances, notwithstanding the structures of Article 234 EC, the Court of Justice will rush to indicate that a national measure complies with EU law. It will rarely indicate that a national measure conflicts with EU law, and the number of measures where this appears to be the case are very rare indeed.[14] Moreover, it is very difficult to find many Union legislative measures that have been struck down for violation of fundamental rights. No Directive, for example, has ever been struck

[13] M Bovens and K Yesilkagit, 'De invloed van Europese richtlijnen op de Nederlandse wetgever' (2005) 10 *Nederlands Juristenblad* 2005; Conseil d'Etat, Rapport Public 2006, 19.

[14] There are only eight cases where there is some indication this is the case. Case 5/88 *Wachauf v Bundesamt für Ernährung und Forstwirtschaft* [1989] ECR 2609; Case C-368/95 *Vereinigte Familiapress Zeitungsverlags- und Vertreibs Gmbh v Bauer Verlag* [1997] ECR I-3689; Case C-60/00 *Carpenter v Secretary of State for the Home Department* [2002] ECR I-6279; Case C-442/00 *Angél Cabellare v Fondo de Garantía Salarial* [2002] ECR I

down by the Court on those grounds. Judicial intervention is rare. Another hallmark is an unpredictable and weak standard of review. In difficult cases, the Court of Justice has either enunciated the basic rights and indicated the matter to be exclusively one for the national court[15] or simply deferred to the national constitutional settlement.[16] In the instances where it has appeared to strike down national measures, it has tended to repeat formulaically the case law of the ECHR.[17] This has been problematic partly because of the erratic choice of standard of review, but also for the unquestioning obedience to the case law of the European Court of Human Rights, a body which, it must be remembered, has to respond to the demands and needs of a wider number of Member States and which has less guarantee of judicial independence than the Court of Justice.

The other difficulties have been to do with the co-ordination of the EU system with national systems of protection. There are here both formal and a substantive difficulties.

The formal difficulties have to do with the allocation of jurisdiction between the two systems. At the moment, it is determined by the reach of the phrase 'within the field of EC law', which sets out the scope of the EU jurisdiction with the national regime governing everything outside this field. There are a lot of uncertainties to this test. Within the EC pillar, the remit is determined largely by the ambit of the economic freedoms. If a measure falls within Articles 28, 39, 43, 39 or EC respectively it can only be justified if, inter alia, it respects fundamental freedoms. The challenge, however, is that each of these provisions is developed in an ad hoc manner through case law. In the period since *ERT*, the range of Article 28 EC shrank following the *Keck* judgment, and then expanded. The range of the other provisions has, by and large, been broadened since then, albeit often in ways that have led to some legal uncertainty.[18] Whilst a case may be made for this in terms of trade liberalisation, the demands of this seem a highly contingent and unpredictable basis around which to apportion fundamental rights protection.

The other uncertainty concerns the third pillar. Following the Treaty of Amsterdam, the jurisdiction of the Court of Justice was extended to the third pillar and the question arose to what extent it could import its case law from the EC pillar to that pillar. In recent years, it has suggested that it is mindful to do that,[19] yet, with regard to fundamental rights, the Court has developed an ambiguous test. It has stated that Union institutions are bound, as are Member States when they implement Union law,[20] a seemingly different test from that 'acting within the field of Union law'. This ambiguity is likely to be institutionalised by the proposed Reform Treaty which proposes to bring the pillars together, and establishes that the principles for the allocation of jurisdiction are set out in Chapter 7 of the European Union Fundamental Rights and Freedom. This provides that Member States are bound by

-11915; Case C-276/01 *Steffensen* [2003] ECR I-3735; Joined Cases C-465/00, C-138/01 and C-139/01 *Österreichischer Rundfunk and Others* [2003] ECR I-4989; Case C-109/01 *Secretary of State for the Home Department v Akrich* [2003] ECR I-9607; Joined Cases C-482/01 & C-493/01 *Orphanopoulos et al v Land Baden-Württemberg* [2004] ECR I-6237.

[15] Case C-260/89 *ERT v DEP* [1991] ECR I-2925.

[16] Eg Case C-36/02 *Omega Spielhallen v Oberbürgermeisterin der Bundesstadt Bonn* [2004] ECR I-9609.

[17] Eg Case C-60/00 *Carpenter v Secretary of State for the Home Department* [2002] ECR I-6279 Case C-442/00 *Angél Cabellare v Fondo de Garantía Salarial* [2002] ECR I -11915; Case C-109/01 *Secretary of State for the Home Department v Akrich* [2003] ECR I-9607; Joined Cases C-482/01 & C-493/01 *Orphanopoulos et al v Land Baden-Württemberg* [2004] ECR I-6237.

[18] See D Chalmers *et al*, *European Union Law* (Cambridge, CUP, 2006) 508–13 and Chapters 15–17 and 19.

[19] Case C-105/03 *Pupino* [2005] ECR I-5285; T-47/03 *Sison v Council*, Judgment of 11 July 2007.

[20] Case C-354/04P *Gestoras Pro Amnistía et al v Council* [2007] ECR I-1579; C-355/04P *Segi et al v Council* [2007] ECR I-1657; Case C-303/05 *Advocaten voor der Wereld v Leden van de Ministerraad*, [2007] ECR I-3633.

Union fundamental rights when they implement Union law.[21] An Explanatory Memorandum from the Secretariat, to which recourse is required, provides that implementing is to be interpreted as meaning the same as the *ERT* formula.[22] Further uncertainty is piled on by the third pillar providing for a number of exemptions from judicial control. The Court of Justice, in particular, is to have no jurisdiction to review the validity or proportionality of operations carried out by the police or other law enforcement services of a Member State or the exercise of the responsibilities incumbent upon Member States with regard to the maintenance of law and order and the safeguarding of internal security.[23] Even if this exemption does not apply to national courts, they cannot be guided by the jurisprudence of the former. Beyond this, there is uncertainty to what extent police and security services can be bound by fundamental rights in Union law with institutional practice very uneven.[24]

The substantive difficulties follow from national courts not playing ball according to the rules of the game as set out by the Court of Justice. This has taken a number of forms. The most exclusive defiance has been provided by the Italian Constitutional Court which has argued that it has exclusive jurisdiction to rule on fundamental rights set out in the Italian Constitution, irrespective of whether the matter falls within the field of Union law. It sees these as a reserved core of activity for itself around which EU law and its institutions must navigate.[25] The British courts have reserved for themselves the right to check the parameters of EU fundamental rights law insisting that these will only bind British authorities if they are implementing EC law or relying on a derogation granted by EC legislation.[26] Finally, there is the practice of the German and French courts who do not seek to patrol actively the jurisdiction of the Court of Justice, but instead offer interpretations of particular rights, notwithstanding that the circumstances of the case may fall within the remit of EU law, and make it clear that these interpretations are to prevail rather than any interpretation by the Court of Justice.[27] Such widespread recalcitrance suggests little possibility of a European constitutional dialogue between national constitutional courts and the Court of Justice. There are few referrals to the Court of Justice by national constitutional courts and little evidence of their weaving its case law into their deliberations. Instead, the situation is one where the Court of Justice has been unable to impress its authority on national constitutional courts either in setting out a division of duties or in their taking its views into account in making decisions. And, in this, they beg the question why they should. As non-majoritarian institutions, the central justification for their powers lies in their being prudent guardians of the ethical settlements underlying national political communities and national legal systems. A strong case has to be made why they should give up these duties of guardianship, and simply a pedigree of 'Europe'

[21] Article 51(1). The text is available at OJ 2000, C 364/1.

[22] CHARTE 4473/00, 46.

[23] Article 35(6) TEU.

[24] N Grief, 'EU Law and Security' (2007) *32 EL Rev*, 357.

[25] *Admenta v Federfarma (Italian State Council)* [2006] 2 CMLR 1177.

[26] This test seems narrower than the *ERT* test. *R v MAFF ex parte First City Trading* [1997] 1 CMLR 250; *R v Secretary of State for the Environment, Transport and Regions ex parte IATA* [1999] 1 CMLR 1287; *Marks and Spencer v CCE* [1999] 1 CMLR 1152.

[27] For Germany see the views of the Financial Court of Hamburg in the 'Bananas' litigation, 27 EuZW (1995) 413. For France see the view of the Constitutional Council on the compatibility of the secularity of the Republic with EU law, *Re EU Constitutional Treaty and the French Constitution (French Constitutional Council)* [2005] 1 CMLR 750.

and an impoverished meaning of the ethics of fundamental rights, which is all that EU law offers at the moment, should probably not be sufficient.

Fundamental Rights as a Marker and Justification of EU Government

ERT marked a subtle but significant shift in the relationship between EU government and fundamental rights. Prior to *ERT*, the position was that set out in the 1977 Joint Declaration of Council, Commission and Parliament, namely that the EC institutions and EC law respect fundamental rights.[28] As has been said elsewhere, it was a policy of non-violation. The principle of non-violation could not explain the *ERT* judgment. Instead, it sets the EU as a body that promotes respect for human rights by other bodies, in this instance the Member States. The shift is rooted not simply in the *ERT* judgment, but in a number of institutional practices that developed from the early 1990s onwards. Development policy, accession and external trade policy were all realigned so that rhetorically, at least promotion of fundamental rights was an element of all the EU external relations policies.[29] The presence of a double standard where fundamental rights were imposed on non-EU states but were not required of Member States[30] and of the *ERT* judgment, which provided both a legal basis and a justification for EU institutions to develop internal human rights policies, has led to a gradual shift in which a general orientation to develop fundamental rights has emerged, albeit in a patchwork fashion.

The headline step was the Treaty of Amsterdam. Article 6 TEU provided not merely that the Union respect fundamental rights,[31] but was now founded on them. Provision was also made for sanctions leading to expulsion of Member States for serious violations of fundamental rights.[32] The difficulties of developing an internal policy were exposed, however, with the halting response in 1999 by other Member States to the entry of the explicitly racist Freedom Party into the Austrian Government. Whilst sanctions were taken, they were taken outside the framework of the Union decision-making procedures and there was a strong eagerness to bring Austria back into the fold.[33] As with many matters of Union policy, more significant developments were occurring in the undergrowth of the institution decision-making procedures, most notably the activities of the Parliament and the Council. From 1993 onwards, the European Parliament Committee on Citizens' Freedoms and Rights published an annual report on human rights in the European Union. In 1996, the Commission appointed a Comité des Sages to consider how fundamental rights could be incorporated into the Amsterdam Treaty. Ignored by the IGC,

[28] OJ 1977, C 103/1.

[29] On the development see P Alston et al (eds), *The EU and Human Rights* (Oxford, OUP, 1999) 553–756.

[30] Eg Opinion of the Economic and Social Committee on 'The European Union and the External Dimensions of Human Rights Policy', OJ C 206/117. For a withering critique see A Williams, *EU Human Rights Policies: A Study in Irony* (Oxford, OUP, 2004) ch 4.

[31] The previous position in Article F TEU.

[32] Article 7 TEU.

[33] U Sedelmeier, M Merlingen and C Mudde, 'The right and the righteous? European norms, domestic politics and the sanctions against Austria' (2001) 39 *Journal of Common Market Studies* 59.

this pushed for the adoption of a civic and social rights agenda by the Union.[34] The Commission followed up this report by establishing an independent group of experts chaired by Professor Simitis, who reaffirmed in early 1999 the need for a human rights agenda, but one that treated civil and social rights as indivisible.[35] The 1999 German initiative leading to the establishment of an EU Charter of Fundamental Rights emerged alongside these initiatives to develop a human rights policy. The Charter, proclaimed in December 2000, was not concerned to promote a human policy but to render EU fundamental rights more visible to the citizen and, in so doing, legitimate the Union. The Charter provided, however, a springboard for these Institutions by providing a series of rights that could only be realised through legislative action[36] and by setting out a field of action for these rights, namely the actions of Union Institutions and implementing actions of Member States.

The first body to realise this was the European Parliament. The Committee on Citizens' Rights and Freedoms requested that a Network of Independent Experts be established to assess the protection given to these rights by Member States.[37] National responses to 11 September, with all their associated civil liberties concerns, gave this an added impetus, and in 2002 the Network of Independent Experts was established to provide an annual report on the state of fundamental rights in the Union, help the Commission develop policy and provide the Commission with specific information on fundamental rights issues when requested.[38] Alongside this, the Commission committed itself in 2001 to carry out assessments of the impact on Charter rights of any significant legislative proposal.[39] In brief time, the Union had gone to a situation where it was monitoring human rights situations in Member States, thinking how to develop a human rights policy of its own and, formally at least, orienting all its policies so that these contribute or at least do not impair the rights and principles in the Charter.

Whilst significant, these actions were the self-organising ones of the Commission and the Parliament. The seminal moment in the definition of a Union human rights policy was December 2003, when the European Council agreed to replace the moribund European Monitoring Centre on Racism and Xenophobia with a Human Rights Agency specifically so that the latter could collect and analyse human rights data with a view to enabling Union policy to be defined in this field. The European Union Agency for Fundamental Rights came into being in March 2007.[40] It illustrates some of the tensions in enabling Union policy to be defined by fundamental rights. The tasks of the Agency are fourfold: collect and standardise data for policy development; issue opinions to the Union institutions and Member States when implementing Community law; publish reports on

[34] Comité des Sages, 'For a Europe of Civic and Social Rights' (EC Commission, 1996).

[35] Report of the Expert Group on Fundamental Rights, 'Affirming Fundamental Rights in the European Union: Time to Act' (DG V, EC Commission, 1999).

[36] This was recognised in the version of the Charter adopted by the Constitutional Treaty which held that a number of principles in the Charter were only judicially cognisable in relation to implementing acts, Article II-112(5) CT.

[37] European Parliament, On the Situation as Regards Fundamental Rights in the European Union, 2000/2231(INI).

[38] The Network was based upon a service contract between the Commission and the University of Louvain. It was disbanded with the establishment of the Fundamental Rights Agency. Details of its work can be found at http://ec.europa.eu/justice_home/cfr_cdf/index_en.htm#.

[39] EC Commission, Application of the Charter of Fundamental Rights of the European Union SEC (2001) 380/3.

[40] Regulation 168/2007 establishing a European Union Agency for Fundamental Rights, OJ 2007, L 53/1.

fundamental rights; develop relations with civil society. All these are associated very much with the creation of a government of fundamental rights. Yet there are clear constraints. The Agency's remit only really applies to the first pillar. It can only issue opinions on legislative proposals when requested by the Union institutions, and whilst it can publish reports, it is unclear to what extent it can condemn or monitor national practices.

The extent to which fundamental rights informs and guides Union policy making is thus very opaque. Current mechanisms such as impact assessment give no guidance as to the depth of internal evaluation or critique taking place. They do not really spread to the national administration of Union's policies. This ambivalence and hesitancy has become more apparent with the development of external mechanisms, such as the Fundamental Rights Agency. Looking at it, it is not yet clear whether its opinions will guide Union policy or whether it will be excluded from sensitive matters and its opinions and information relegated to background context.

Fundamental Rights as Points of Legitimation, Critique and Debate

ERT opened up the possibility of fundamental rights acting to legitimise on the Union on the grounds of its promotion of them. Even if the extent of that activity is highly contestable, it is not clear that this would generate support. Resistance has culminated in the reaction to the European Union Charter on Fundamental Rights at the 2007 June European Council launching the IGC on the Lisbon Treaty.

The United Kingdom and Poland insisted on a Protocol that would limit the effects of the Charter on the judicial review of national measures:

> The Charter does not extend the ability of the Court of Justice, or any court or tribunal of the United Kingdom, to find that the laws, regulations or administrative provisions, practices or action of the United Kingdom are inconsistent with the fundamental rights, freedoms and principles that it reaffirms.[41]

In addition, the Polish government has entered a unilateral Declaration stating:

> The Charter does not affect in any way the right of Member States to legislate in the sphere of public morality, family law as well as the protection of human dignity and respect for human physical and moral integrity.

The legal effects of both are uncertain. A unilateral Declaration does not even have any interpretive force. Whilst a Protocol does have legal status, the use of the wording 'extend' does not preclude the invocation of the Charter to review British or Polish measures.[42] More important are the broader symbolic effects. When set against the Irish and Maltese opt-outs from EU law for their abortion laws as well as the jealous guardianship of the monopoly of interpretation of their constitutions by national constitutional courts, these

[41] OJ 2007, C 357/156.

[42] So much is admitted in the Protocol which states that only rights in Title IV of the Charter (solidarity rights) are not justiciable.

cannot be seen as isolated steps but as a broader assertion of the importance of national community over broader European values, however distorted the ethics of the former might seem.

Fundamental rights can be seen as an attempt to legitimate the European Union in processes that lie beyond the institutions of the nation state. The European Union, it is argued, creates a direct link between the European Union and its citizens through strengthening individual autonomy. Her public autonomy is strengthened through processes of representation and participation which are informed by the discourse of the EU Charter, whilst the very same rights protect her private autonomy.[43] However, there is little evidence that individuals want these goods to be offered to them by the European Union. Analyses of public opinion suggest the strongest indicators of support or resistance for the European Union are the economic benefits or loss created by integration and a strong sense of national or sub-national identity. Support comes most strongly from economic winners and those with a strong sub-national identity, whilst resistance is most marked amongst economic losers and those with a strong national identity who see a strong cultural threat from integration.[44] There is little space for fundamental rights discourse within this matrix. Even where a particularly salient issue arises, therefore, it appears to have little effect on perceptions of European integration. Two cases in point were the wide-ranging debates surrounding the Polish laws on abortion and the Romanian laws prohibiting homosexuality—both of which had to be reformed prior to accession. One would have expected these to rally liberals to the cause of European integration and social conservatives to oppose it. Surveys showed these to have negligible effects on public perceptions of the European Union.[45]

Yet, whilst it may be difficult to discern these broader effects amongst public opinion, it is possible to observe a sea change amongst political elites of which the most obvious manifestation was the incorporation of the Charter into Part II of the Constitutional Treaty. Fundamental rights have become since *ERT* a much more central part of the European policy making discourse. This is witnessed also in the increased activities of the European Parliament and Ombudsman in this field, both of whom are, increasingly, willing to challenge the actions of the other EU institutions for non-compliance with fundamental rights obligations.[46] There is also the proliferation of groups with strong human rights interests in or observing Brussels, most notably Statewatch, ILGA, the European Social Forum, the European Disability Forum, the European Network against Race, ECRE and Amnesty International. To be sure, it may be argued that many of these groups were present before the *ERT* judgment and that a judgment concerned with the relationship between national law and fundamental rights is conceptually distinct from the activities surrounding Brussels policy making. Yet the *ERT* judgment deserves some

[43] J Habermas, *The Postnational Constellation* (Cambridge, Polity, 2001) ch 4 esp 100 *ff*.

[44] M Gabel, 'Economic Integration and Mass Politics: Market Liberalization and Public Attitudes in the European Union' (1998) 42 *American Journal of Political Science* 936; S Carey, 'Undivided Loyalties: Is National Identity an Obstacle to European Integration' (2002) 3 *European Union Politics* 387.

[45] J Bielasiak, 'Determinants of Public Opinion Differences ion EU Accession in Poland' (2002) 54 *Europe Asia Studies* 1241.

[46] Recent attempts by the European Parliament to strike down legislation for non-compliance with fundamental rights include Joined Cases C-317/04 and C-318/04 *Parliament v Council*, [2006] ECR I-4721; Case C-540/03 *Parliament v Council*, [2006] ECR I-5769. For an example of the Ombudsman's practice see Summary of decision on complaint 1155/2004/TN against the European Commission regarding European School, Annual Report of the European Ombudsman 2005 (Brussels, European Ombudsman, 2006) 68–80.

credit here, for, perhaps more than any other judgment, it helped to make fundamental rights both more salient and more present in the legal and political activities surrounding the European Union.

In that regard, the contrast between the attention given to fundamental rights by the narrow EU public sphere and the ignoring of it in wider political and legal communities is striking. It symbolises probably both the greatest success and the greatest failure of the *ERT* legacy. In that regard, the response of the recent IGC to the status of the Charter was instructive. The Charter will not be included in the Lisbon Treaty. Instead a reference will be made to it in a new Article 6(1):

> The Union recognises the rights, freedoms and principles set out in the Charter of Fundamental Rights ... which shall have the same legal value as the Treaties.

On its face, the new treatment seems legally irrelevant, as the reference will give the same legal value to the Charter as if it were incorporated into the Treaty itself. It tells us, however, something very powerful about how national governments wish the future treatment of fundamental rights by the EU. The development of fundamental rights is not to be a central mission of or founding justification for the Union. The new provision is, indeed. a retrenchment from the current situation in which the Union is 'founded' on fundamental rights. Instead, fundamental rights is to be a second-order quality which conditions all the work of the European Union. The dream of EU fundamental rights having the same indefeasible quality as national fundamental rights is gone. They have been unable to develop those qualities since *ERT* and the statement of the European Council both drives a stake through the heart of that agenda and is an acknowledgment of this cold reality.

This is not a return to the days of where EU policy should simply not violate fundamental rights. The new agenda talks, instead, of a recognition of fundamental rights. This involves, on the one hand, acknowledgment that the wide-ranging policy agenda of the Union in areas such as development, policing, crime, asylum necessarily generates many fundamental rights concerns, and that the Union must develop an approach to accommodate these. Recognition suggests, on the other hand, also a more intimate relation than simply a commitment not to violate. It implies that fundamental rights are at one level external to the Union, as one cannot recognise oneself, but also implies that they are something seen as sufficiently significant that the Union must justify itself by reference to them. For a failure of explicit justification amounts, for all practical purposes, to a declaration that the rights are invisible, and thus violates the duty of recognition. The duty of recognition suggests, therefore, that fundamental rights become what Bengoetxea and others have termed a source of external justification in Union law.[47] To be sure, EU law must not violate them, but they—in this case the Charter—institutionalise a practical morality in whose terms the Union must justify its policy choices and must develop its narratives to bring coherence and to make sense of its enterprise.

[47] J Bengoetxea *et al*, 'Integration and Integrity in the Legal Reasoning of the European Court of Justice' 43, 60–3 in G de Búrca and J Weiler (eds), *The European Court of Justice* (Oxford, OUP, 2001).

Conclusion

At the affective level, constitutions are about both recounting a collective way of life and providing an imaginary for what a collective way of life could be.[48] Fundamental rights, with their powerful imagery, perhaps do this more than other constitutional instruments. They rely on supporting narratives suggesting collective sacrifice, common rites of passage and mutual indebtedness, narratives that are not present in European Union law. Without these, it is unsurprising that the suggestive elements for EU human rights posed by *ERT* have not been realised. *ERT* has, instead, been part of a process of institutional socialisation that has elevated fundamental rights discourse within EU policy making. Bringing that to the fore is no mean achievement. It might mean that fundamental rights are predominantly about EU institutional reflexivity and critique and about providing a reference point for the understanding of EU actions beyond crude utilitarian calculations rather than the generation of some postnational nirvana. Yet, to be a source of institutional modesty and reflection is something of value, and there are few other legal tools that have successfully provided that in EU law.

[48] This view is most present in the work of P Kahn, *The Cultural Study of Law* (Chicago, University of Chicago Press, 1999). For similar views with regard to the EU see U Haltern, 'Pathos and Patina: The Failure and Promise of Constitutionalism in the European imagination' (2003) 9 *ELJ* 14.

3

Wachauf and *ERT*: On the Road from the Centralised to the Decentralised System of Judicial Review

ZDENĚK KÜHN*

In Western societies of the 20th and early 21st centuries the bill of rights plays a new key role in legitimising the government. As a side effect, the courts in Europe of our time hold in effect a sort of veto power over many important political decisions. With the collapse of the original strictly conceived model of separation of powers, courts are no longer unwilling and mechanical enforcers of rules made by political process in the parliament. The judicialisation of politics and society seems to be 'a partial aspect of societal evolution'.[49] Some talk about 'the secular papacy', that is, the judiciary of the Modern West playing the role of the 12th-century papacy of the medieval Western world.[50] Others criticise the rise of 'juristocracy' and the fall of popular politics.[51]

In short, in Europe at the onset of the 21st century politics has become deeply judicialised and the judiciary has become profoundly involved in the issues which used to be the sole domain of 'pure' politics.[52] At the same time, the expansion of 'New Constitutionalism' also means that the crucial question is who gets the final say about what fundamental rights mean. In this chapter, I argue that the most important consequence of the *Wachauf* and *ERT* judgments is an inconspicuous move from the centralised system of the fundamental rights review in most Member States to the decentralised system based on the co-operation of national ordinary courts and the European Court of Justice. To what extent this move in the fundamental rights arena might be workable remains to be seen.

* Associate Professor, Charles University Law School, Prague, the Czech Republic; Justice of the Supreme Administrative Court of the Czech Republic. PhD, Charles University Law School (2001); LLM, University of Michigan Law School (2002); SJD, University of Michigan Law School (2006). I owe my thanks to Jan Komárek for his helpful comments on one of the earlier drafts. The usual disclaimer applies.

[49] G Teubner, 'Juridification: Concepts, Aspects, Limits, Solutions' in G Teubner (ed), *Juridification of Social Spheres* (Berlin, W de Gruyter, 1987) 3, at 27. Cf generally A Stone Sweet, *Governing with Judges. Constitutional Politics in Europe* (Oxford, Oxford University Press, 2000).

[50] R Badinter, S Breyer (eds), *Judges in Contemporary Democracy: An International Conversation* (New York, NYU Press, 2004) 67, at 79.

[51] R Hirschl, *Towards Juristocracy: The Origins and Consequences of the New Constitutionalism* (Cambridge, Harvard University Press, 2004).

[52] RA Miller, 'Lords of Democracy: The Judicialization of "Pure Politics" in the United States and Germany' (2004) 61 *Washington Lee Law Review* 587.

Wachauf

It is not surprising that the phenomenon of 'New Constitutionalism' started to influence emerging constitutionalisation of the European Communities in the 1960s and 1970s. As both Weiler and Maduro claim, creating a sort of European constitution (including limiting the Union by the protection of fundamental rights) was required by the need not only to legitimate but also to control the increasing power of the Union.[53] The fact that the ECJ stated that the Union itself shall be restrained by human rights was thus a necessary (and generally welcome) consequence of assuming direct effect and primacy of European law in the early 1960s.

Still, one can plausibly argue that the actual importance of decisions like *Internationale Handelsgesellschaft*[54] is much overstated. In practical terms what matters most for the application of EU law in Member States is the question whether while implementing EU law the national authorities of the Member States are required, as a matter of EU law, to observe (EU) fundamental rights.[55] In *Wachauf* the ECJ unequivocally replied that they are:

> Since those requirements [of the protection of fundamental rights in the Community legal order] are also binding on the Member States when they implement Community rules, the Member States must, as far as possible, apply those rules in accordance with those requirements.[56]

The principle elaborated in *Wachauf* becomes practical typically in the situation when '[t]he Community regulations in question accordingly leave the competent national authorities a sufficiently wide margin of appreciation to enable them to apply those rules in a manner consistent with the requirements of the protection of fundamental rights'.[57]

53 Cf JHH Weiler, *The Constitution of Europe: 'Do the New Clothes Have an Emperor?' and Other Essays on European Integration* (Cambridge, Cambridge University Press, 1999); MP Maduro, 'The Importance of Being Called a Constitution: Constitutional Authority and the Authority of Constitutionalism', (2005) 3 *International Journal of Constitutional Law* 332.

54 Case 11/70 *Internationale Handelsgesellschaft mbH v Einfuhr- und Vorratsstelle für Getreide und Futtermittel* [1970] ECR 1125.

55 F Jacobs, 'Human Rights in the European Union: The Role of the Court of Justice' (2001) 26 *EL Rev* 331, at 333.

56 Judgment of the Court (Third Chamber) of 13 July 1989, case 5/88 *Hubert Wachauf v Bundesamt für Ernährung und Forstwirtschaft* [1989] ECR 2609. The Court followed the advice of its Advocate General Sir Francis Jacobs who reasoned 'that when implementing Community law it is also incumbent upon Member States to have regard to the principle of respect for the right to property which, as the Court has recognised ..., is guaranteed in the Community legal order in accordance with the ideas common to the constitutions of the Member States, which are also reflected in Art. 1 of the first Protocol to the European Convention on Human Rights. *Although the Court's case-law has hitherto been concerned with respect for property rights by the Community legislator itself, the same principles must in my view apply to the implementation of Community law by the Member States*, since it appears to me self-evident that when acting in pursuance of powers granted under Community law, Member States must be subject to the same constraints, in any event in relation to the principle of respect for fundamental rights, as the Community legislator.' AG opinion, para 22 (emphasis added). The Advocate General referred to the earlier case, when the ECJ held that 'where community rules leave Member States to choose between various methods of implementation, the Member States must comply with the principle stated in Article 40(3)' ['a specific enunciation of the general principle of equality which is one of the fundamental principles of community law']. See Case 201 and 202/85 *Marthe Klensch and others v Secrétaire d'État à l'Agriculture et à la Viticulture* [1986] ECR 3477, paras 9 and 10.

57 *Wachauf*, para 22.

I cannot avoid comparing the *Wachauf* principle with the principle of the constitutionally conforming interpretation.[58] If the European rule as applied in a Member State conflicts with the requirements of fundamental rights, even though it can be applied consistently with those requirements, it is natural that it is not the European rule but the national measure which shall be blamed. Following this logic of 'constitutionally conforming interpretation', what shall be eliminated is not the European rule itself but its (incorrect) national application.

Seen in this way, the *Wachauf* principle reemphasises a quasi-federal structure of the interference between EU and national law. The ECJ follows its *Simmenthal* ruling[59] and associates itself with ordinary national courts rather than with constitutional tribunals in the task of making European law supreme. The reason why the ECJ established that national implementing legislation shall be reviewed against the framework of 'European' fundamental rights rather than national constitutional law can be easily found in a well-known requirement of uniform application of European law. Standard European textbooks refer to the notion of agency[60] which is typical for the structure of powers within Europe: a Member State acting on behalf of the Community, either by enacting general rules by national laws, applying national laws, or by applying EU rules.[61]

The rule of interpretation consistent with fundamental rights is one of the key factors of the 'New Constitutionalism'. It can be seen as a prerequisite to any rational system of judicial review. If the *Wachauf* rule is seen in this view, it promotes the efficient practice of judicial review of European rules because it eliminates, in a greater number of cases, the need to set aside or nullify European rules which could operate in conflict with fundamental rights on the local level via their national application.

Yet, deciding against what standards national implementing measures shall be reviewed might also be a question of power. The *Wachauf* principle might thus strengthen the power of the ECJ which could impose uniformly its version of fundamental rights via national ordinary courts. As one leading expert on comparative constitutionalism noted, making interpretation consistent with fundamental rights is often much more lasting and pervasive than simply annulling the law for its unconstitutionality.[62] It is for the simple reason that interpreting (unlike annulling) would often remain virtually unnoticed by other important political players. While interpreting European rules and their national

[58] Cf Germany, where it is referred to as the principle of the constitutionally conforming interpretation (Verfassungskonforme Auslegung). P Sachs (ed.), *Grundgesetz: Kommentar* (München, Beck, 1996) 61–2. The Federal Constitutional Court held that 'if a rule allows several readings, but only one reading leads to a constitutionally permissible construction, the reading consistent with the Basic law is obligatory': BVerfGE 49, 148 (157). In Germany, the first decision which established this doctrine was BVerfGE 2, 266 (282), quoted in Sachs at 61, note 61.

[59] Case 106/77 *Amministrazione delle Finanze dello Stato v Simmenthal SpA* [1978] ECR 629, para 26 ('National courts must protect rights conferred by provisions of the Community legal order and that it is not necessary for such courts to request or await the actual setting aside by the national authorities empowered so to act of any national measures which might impede the direct and immediate application of community rules').

[60] P Craig, G de Búrca, *EU Law. Text, Cases and Materials* 3rd edn (Oxford, Oxford University Press, 2003) 339 *ff.*

[61] Cf on this D Halberstam, 'Of Power and Responsibility: the Political Morality of Federal Systems' (2004) 90 *Virginia Law Review* 731 (comparing a European 'fidelity' approach and an American 'entitlements' scheme, ie philosophical concepts which are behind different systems of governance).

[62] A Sajó, 'Constitutional Adjudication in Light of Discourse Theory' (1995) 17 *Cardozo Law Review* 1193 at 1208 ('constitutional tribunals have more of a chance to provide lasting and unsupervised determinations of the law by interpreting the law rather than voiding it').

implementations consistently with fundamental rights, the ECJ considerably expands the impact of its case law throughout national legal orders.

On the other hand, if the power is gained, then it must be lost somewhere else. The most likely candidate is a national constitutional court. Whereas traditionally in most Member States the *national* law might be struck down for its conflict with fundamental rights by the national constitutional court only, in *Wachauf* the ECJ requires implicitly constitutional scrutiny by *all* national courts. Thus, although an ordinary court is obliged to refer to its constitutional court any law which it interprets as in conflict with the national constitution, in order for the latter to adjudicate its constitutionality, an ordinary court should not do so in the area where the Member State acts as the agent of the EU. Instead, it must interpret the national measure consistently with the protection of fundamental rights as well as the implemented European rule.

The problem does not rest only with the issue of centralised review. There are few European countries which follow the system of decentralised judicial review exercised by all courts. For instance, all Scandinavian nations, where until recently judicial review did not exist or was not practised, opted to follow the decentralised model—most recently in Finland in 2000. Up to now, Scandinavian courts have shown high respect to their legislatures, especially if compared with activist constitutional courts of the German type. For instance, Swedish courts strike down laws only very exceptionally, consistent with the Swedish Constitution which states that parliamentary acts may be set aside only if their conflict with the constitution is 'obvious and apparent'. Generally, Scandinavian political parties oppose further judicial empowerment, and are certainly against the introduction of any type of constitutional court.[63] Thus in Scandinavia the *Wachauf* principle challenges the overall understanding of the self-restrained judiciary and its role vis-à-vis the national legislature. The experience of Great Britain shows, however, that the transformation of judicial power does not require an enormous amount of time.[64]

The *Wachauf* principle seems to be generally recognised now. Last but not least, it has been codified by the Charter of Fundamental.[65] The principle is consistent with the logic of 'uniform interpretation' of European law,[66] which dates back to the very beginning of the ECJ's case law. Viewing it in this way, the answer to the novel question presented by *Wachauf* was, to use the words of its Advocate General, 'rather obvious—obvious in any event, as is so often the case, with the benefit of hindsight'.[67] Curiously, *Wachauf* was decided by the smallest unit of the Court—a chamber of three judges.

Were *Wachauf* decided otherwise, it would have undermined the logic of 'uniform interpretation' as made in the earlier case law. We must remember that the EU judicial

[63] A Husa, 'Guarding the Constitutionality of Laws in the Nordic Countries: A Comparative Perspective', (2000) 48 *Am J Comp L 345* (2000).

[64] Cf. D Nicol, *EC Membership and the Judicialization of British Politics* (Oxford, Oxford University Press, 2001).

[65] Charter, Art 51(1): 'The provisions of this Charter are addressed to the institutions and bodies of the Union with due regard for the principle of subsidiarity and to the Member States only when they are implementing Union law. They shall therefore respect the rights, observe the principles and promote the application thereof in accordance with their respective powers.'

[66] The object of Art 234 (ex 177) is 'to secure *uniform interpretation* of the Treaty by national courts and tribunals'. Case 26/62 NV *Algemene Transport- en Expeditie Onderneming van Gend en Loos v Netherlands Inland Revenue Administration* [1963] ECR 1 (emphasis added). For a recent innovative reassessment cf J Komárek, '"In the Court We Trust"—But Should We? On the need for hierarchy and differentiation in the preliminary ruling procedure' (2007) 32 *EL Rev* 467.

[67] Jacobs, above n 55, at 334.

system is particularly vulnerable to inconsistencies: that is why it highlights the *ideal* of uniformity[68] so much. In addition, the problem is not purely theoretical: any different answer would be likely to create serious disparate impacts in practice throughout the Union. While some countries practise abundant constitutional fundamental rights reviews (the activist German Federal Constitutional Court is a primary example), the level of judicial protection of fundamental rights is significantly weaker in some others.[69]

ERT: Expanding the Reach of the ECJ

Two years after *Wachauf*, in 1991, the ECJ was dealing with the question whether Member States' actions are subject to (EU) fundamental rights review wherever they derogate from the Treaty or wherever such actions restrict the exercise of common market freedoms. The ECJ had been engaged with this question before *Wachauf*, and it appeared that the question was answered in the negative despite the opposite advice of its Advocate General Sir Gordon Slynn. The reason for this rejection in *Cinéthèque* was the premise that the question of fundamental rights review (at least under such scenario as in *Cinéthèque*) 'falls within the jurisdiction of the national legislator'.[70]

In 1991 the Court clarified its opinion in *ERT*[71] when a Greek law which granted exclusive rights for carrying out radio and television broadcasts to ERT came under review. Parties of the dispute before a Greek court disputed the law by the Community rules on the free movement of goods and the rules on competition as well as the freedom of expression under the European Convention. The Court's Advocate General Lenz did not consider the argument by the Convention relevant for this case, when he referred to *Cinéthèque* for further support:

> The rules of the Convention are to be regarded as part of the Community legal order. . . . That right [freedom of expression] must therefore be respected *by the Community institutions*. It is however also clear that it is not primarily the Court of Justice which is called upon to judge alleged or actual infringements by the Member States of the human rights protected by that Convention (that is a matter for the institutions designated by the Convention on Human

[68] R Sacco, 'Diversity and Uniformity in the Law' (2001) 49 *American Journal of Comparative Law* 171 (dealing with the side effects of one-sided attempts at uniformity).

[69] Few people would claim, however, that the situation in the latter states is necessarily inferior to those belonging to the former group. Cf C Neal Tate, T Vallinder (eds), *The Global Expansion of Judicial Power* (New York, New York University Press, 1995) 345–68 (dealing with Sweden).

[70] Case 60 and 61/84 *Cinéthèque SA v Fédération National des Cinémas Français* [1985] ECR 2605 (the Court was dealing with the two cases which challenged section 89 of French Act 82–652 of 29 July 1982 on audiovisual communication which prohibited the sale or rental of a movie while the movie was still being shown in the theatres unless a minimum period of time from the date of issuance of the performance certificate had elapsed. The decree was primarily challenged as being contrary to Arts 30 and 34 of the EEC Treaty on the free movement of goods, and to Art 59 of the EEC Treaty on freedom to provide services. After holding that the French legislation was compatible with Arts 30, 34 and 59 of the EEC Treaty, the Court considered in its para 26 the argument that the French legislation was contrary to the principle of the freedom of expression: 'Although it is true that it is the duty of this Court to ensure the observance of fundamental rights in the field of Community law, it has no power to examine the compatibility with the European Convention of national legislation which concerns, as in this case, an area which falls within the jurisdiction of the national legislator').

[71] Case C-260/89 *Elliniki Radiophonia Tiléorassi AE and Panellinia Omospondia Syllogon Prossopikou v Dimotiki Etairia Pliroforissis and Sotirios Kouvelas and Nicolaos Avdellas and others* ECR [1991] I-2925 (hereinafter *ERT*).

> Rights); in particular, it does not fall to the Court to examine the compatibility of the rules of the Member States with the Convention on Human Rights (this has been *clearly established* in the case-law; see the judgment in [*Cinéthèque*]).[72]

However, comparing both the opinion of the Advocate General and that of the Court, we could easily see that the solution made by *Cinéthèque* was far from 'clearly established'. After reviewing the Greek derogation from the free movement of services and the rules on competition the Court reached the opinion that the protection of (EU) fundamental rights is applicable even if the Member State derogates from the Treaty in the interest of a conflicting national policy:

> As the Court has held [referring, inter alia, to *Cinéthèque*], it has no power to examine the compatibility with the European Convention on Human Rights of national rules which do not fall within the scope of Community law. On the other hand, where such rules do fall within the scope of Community law, and reference is made to the Court for a preliminary ruling, it must provide all the criteria of interpretation needed by the national court to determine whether those rules are compatible with the fundamental rights the observance of which the Court ensures and which derive in particular from the European Convention on Human Rights.
>
> In particular, where a Member State relies on the combined provisions of Articles 56 and 66 in order to justify rules which are likely to obstruct the exercise of the freedom to provide services, such justification, provided for by Community law, must be interpreted in the light of the general principles of law and in particular of fundamental rights. *Thus the national rules in question can fall under the exceptions provided for by the combined provisions of Articles 56 and 66 only if they are compatible with the fundamental rights the observance of which is ensured by the Court.*
>
> It follows that in such a case *it is for the national court, and if necessary, the Court of Justice* to appraise the application of those provisions having regard to all the rules of Community law, including freedom of expression, as embodied in Article 10 of the European Convention on Human Rights, as a general principle of law the observance of which is ensured by the Court.[73]

The conclusion of the ECJ does bring a plethora of questions. First, what rules appear to be within the scope of Community law? Moreover, unlike the *Wachauf* type of situation where a Member State acts as the agent of the Union (it does something required by EU law by means conflicting with EU fundamental rights), it is a different matter if the same Member State seeks to justify the derogation from the Treaty by national measure while applying national policy[74] or even a competing national fundamental right.[75] Why must it argue before the ECJ that its derogation is also consistent with (EU) fundamental rights? If the Member State successfully defends proportionality, reasonableness etc. of its derogation from the Treaty, why should not the issue of fundamental rights be left to the national

[72] Paras 49 and 50 of the AG opinion (emphasis added).

[73] *ERT*, paras 42–44 (emphasis added).

[74] Cf Weiler, above n 53, at 126; JHH Weiler and SC Fries, 'A Human Rights Policy for the European Community and Union: The Question of Competences', in P Alston (ed), *The EU and Human Rights* (Oxford, Oxford University Press, 1999), 147 at 164.

[75] Cf C Kombos, 'Fundamental Rights and Fundamental Freedoms: A Symbiosis on the Basis of Subsidiarity' (2006) 12 *European Public Law* 433, analysing the *ERT* type of disputes and distinguishing a classical *ERT* type—the EU fundamental right used as a restriction to derogation from EU law, a hybrid type—derogation itself is based on some competing fundamental right (such as *Familiapress* analysed below), and a hard type—a heteromorphous right (the right peculiar to a specific state) is forming the basis of that derogation (such as German-styled human dignity in case C-36/02 *Omega Spielhallen- und Automatenaufstellungs-GmbH v. Oberbürgermeisterin der Bundesstadt Bonn* [2004] ECR I-9609).

bodies empowered to review national measures against the backdrop fundamental rights (if there are such bodies)? As famously stated by Sir Francis Jacobs:

> So I would suggest that such acts [derogations from the Treaty by Member States] are subject to the Community principle of non-discrimination on grounds of nationality, and to the principle of proportionality, both of which are vital, from the point of view of Community law, in defining the scope of Member States' obligations under the Treaty; but are not subject, as a matter of Community law, to the principle of respect for fundamental rights. If that is right, then the Court of Justice must be taken to mean that *the national court must have regard to fundamental rights, but not that the exercise of that function is itself a matter for review by the Court of Justice.*[76]

Others approve the *ERT* line of case law. They are worried how 'the state of the common market' would look like 'if each Member State could determine by reference to its own laws and values – without any reference to Community law – what was or was not covered by the prohibition and its derogation.' That is why the derogation should be fully controlled by EU law.[77] I am not entirely persuaded. Limiting the review to the basic principles of European law, and at the same time leaving the substantial portion of fundamental rights review to the national bodies would not endanger the common market. On the other hand, it is definitely true that if the open-ended doctrines of proportionality and like are applied by the ECJ, moderate but full fundamental rights review does not really represent a much bigger encroachment on Member States interests.[78]

ERT was followed by *Familiapress* in 1997. In this case the Court was dealing with the Austrian law which prevented the importation of periodicals lawfully produced and marketed in another Member State by reason of their containing prize puzzle competitions or games. The Court decided that this was the derogation from Article 30 of the Treaty (quantitative restrictions on imports and all measures having equivalent effect are prohibited between Member States) and analysed it against the backdrop of applicable tests. The Court referred to *ERT* and rephrased it that 'where a Member State relies on overriding requirements to justify rules which are likely to obstruct the exercise of free movement of goods, such justification must also be interpreted in the light of the general principles of law and in particular of fundamental rights', which include freedom of expression enshrined in Article 10 of the Convention.[79]

Let us consider the practical consequences of the *Familiapress* ruling. Because the European Convention had been granted constitutional status in Austria,[80] the Court's conclusion might change little in Austria. In fact, fundamental rights protection was not

[76] Jacobs, above n 55, at 338.

[77] Weiler and Fries, above n 74, at 163. See also *ibid*, at 164: 'Is it so revolutionary to insist that when the Member States avail themselves of a Community law created derogation they respect too the fundamental human rights, deriving from the constitutional traditions of the Member States, even if the European Community construction of this or that right differs from its construction in this or that Member State?' See also K Lenaerts, 'Fundamental Rights in the European Union' (2000) 25 *EL Rev* 575, 590 *ff.*

[78] See Weiler and Fries, above n 74, at 164.

[79] Case C-368/95 *Vereinigte Familiapress Zeitungsverlags- und vertriebs GmbH v Heinrich Bauer Verlag* [1997] ECR I-3689, paras 23 and 24.

[80] See the federal constitutional act of 4 March 1964, BGBl [Bundesgesetzblatt]1964/59. In detail M von Grünigen, 'Die österreichische Verfassungsnovelle über Staatsverträge vom 4. März 1964', (1965) 25 *Zeitschrift für ausländisches öffentliches Recht und Völkerrecht* 76.

even sought by the referring Austrian court[81] (perhaps the Austrian court considered it natural that the Austrian Act must be subject to that scrutiny). In fact, the *Familiapress* type of ruling 'might give teeth to the European Convention in those countries which have after decades not yet incorporated it into national law';[82] the number of these countries, however, is steadily declining.[83]

On the other hand, what makes the difference in Austria (and most other Member States) is the shift of the final word from the Austrian Constitutional Court to the ECJ. Whereas under a normal scenario the Austrian court would refer the issue of the conflict between the law and fundamental rights to its constitutional court, under the *ERT* line of case law 'it is for the national court, and *if necessary, the Court of Justice* to appraise the application of those provisions having regard to all the rules of Community law, including freedom of expression'.[84]

The *ERT* type of case law did not find its way to the Charter of Fundamental Rights.[85] Although the history behind Article 51 of the Charter is haphazard, there are clear indications that its framers did not intend to deviate from the Court's case law.[86]

Prospects

The impact and the problems of the transfer of final say in the fundamental rights issues made by *Wachauf* and *ERT* should not be underestimated. For instance, from the point of view of the new Member States of Central and Eastern Europe the most discussed issue is not whether their constitutional courts can set aside the European rule for its unconstitutionality: constitutional courts more or less easily agree that this is a task for the ECJ and its review under (EU) fundamental rights.[87] In contrast, reviewing national laws for their conflict with fundamental rights, including those implementing European rules, is

[81] Cf. *Familiapress*, the opinion of AG Tesauro (para 26: 'Although it is not the subject of a specific question by the referring court, I feel that the issue of the compatibility of the national provision under discussion with Article 10 of the European Convention for the Protection of Human Rights and Fundamental Freedoms, which was raised during the course of the procedure, merits a response on the part of the Court.').

[82] Weiler and Fries, above n 74, at 164. That is why Weiler and Fries argue that what shall be applied in the *ERT* type of case law is the core of the ECHR rights. See also Weiler, above n 53, at 126. On the other hand, Arnull is right, after observing decisions of the ECJ, that 'where Member States have sought to rely on a Community law derogation, the ECJ has encountered difficulty in offering national courts meaningful advice on the application of the general principle of respect for fundamental rights'. A Arnull, 'From Charter to Constitution and Beyond: Fundamental Rights in the New European Union' (2003) *PL* (winter) 774 at 780 (quoting examples). See also D Chalmers, 'Competition and Industrial Property: Television and the Court of Justice' (1992) 17 *EL Rev* 248 (commenting on ERT, Chalmers found it 'extremely regrettable that the Court stated that the matter as to whether the television monopoly breached any general principle of law was one for the national judge to decide').

[83] See E Stein, 'International Law in Internal Law: Toward Internationalization of Central-Eastern European Constitutions?' (1994) 88 *American Journal of International Law* 427.

[84] See quotation of *ERT* above n 73 (emphasis added).

[85] For the text see above n 65.

[86] G de Búrca, 'The Drafting of the European Union Charter of Fundamental Rights' (2001) 26 *EL Rev* 126 at 137; P Eeckhout, '&The EU Charter of Fundamental Rights and the Federal Question' (2002) 39 *CML Rev* 945, 977–79. Against Jacobs, above n 55 at 338, and Arnull, above n 82 at 781.

[87] The Czech *Sugar Quota Case II* of 8 March 2006 (Pl. US 50/04) approved the current standard of EU fundamental rights which neither is 'of a lower quality than the protection accorded in the Czech Republic', nor does the standard 'markedly diverge from the standard up till now provided in the domestic setting by the Constitutional Court'. The *Sugar Quota II*, part VI.B (full English translation available at the Court's website

another issue. Although the ECJ designated decentralised review as the basic paradigm for the judicial enforcement of European law within the national legal orders,[88] this sensitive issue is rarely associated with the fundamental rights arena. Most constitutional courts of the new Member States seem willing to keep this power in the fundamental rights arena exclusively for themselves.

In light of these considerations, it is worth noting that in most New Member States the previous communist paradigm of the judiciary's unconditional observance of the entire legal system (including various substatutory directives and regulations) seems to have been replaced by the paradigm of a rigid adherence to centralised judicial review. Slovakia is the most extreme example. The Slovak Constitution vests in its Constitutional Court the exclusive competence to review any possible conflict of rules.[89] In fact, as Slovak judges operate within a completely centralised system of judicial review, they only acquired the power of judicial review on 1 May 2004 when they became part of the decentralised European judiciary and, thus, obliged to apply European law.

In the Czech Republic the Constitutional Court proclaimed in 2002 that centralised fundamental rights review is a necessary condition of the rule of law which can never be altered (thus making centralised review 'a part of the essential attributes of a democratic state governed by the rule of law'[90]). The Court argued by the Czech legal system 'which does not contain judicial precedent with the quality and binding nature of a source of law'.[91] It remains to be seen how these approaches would be reconciled with the requirements of the *Wachauf/ERT* line of case law. In any case, the practical significance of the *Wachauf/ERT* line of case law will, for similar and other[92] reasons, be low in Central and Eastern Europe for the time being.

If we 'fall into the trap of thinking of the Community as an entity wholly distinct from the Member States' (as all of us often do),[93] we could easily condemn the *Wachauf/ERT* line of case law as an improper interference with the hierarchy and structure of the national legal order. But if we avoid this 'trap', it is too easy to underestimate sensitive conflicts which are likely to occur by the rigorous application of the *Wachauf/ERT* line of case law and the expansion of EU law. These conflicts[94] might occur either between the Court of Justice and national courts including constitutional courts or even between national constitutional courts and national ordinary courts. Vulnerable relations between some national constitutional tribunals and their ordinary courts might play the role in this

www.concourt.cz). Cf a more complicated approach by the Polish Accession Treaty Case (part III.18.5), the decision K 18/04 of 11 May 2005, published in Polish in Orzecznictwie Trybunalu Konstytucyjnego. Zbiór urzędowy [Collection of Decisions of the Constitutional Tribunal. Official Collection], 2005, ser. A, nr. 5, item 49. A basic English summary is available at the Tribunal's website.

88 *Simmenthal* above n 59.

89 See Art 125 para 1 (a) and Art 144 para 2 of the Slovak Constitution as amended in 2001.

90 The *Sugar Quota II*, above n 87: 'the delegation of a part of the powers of national organs may persist only so long as these powers are exercised in a manner ... which does not threaten the very essence of the substantive law-based state. In such determination the Constitutional Court is called upon to protect constitutionalism. According to Art 9 para 2 of the Constitution, the essential attributes of a democratic state governed by the rule of law, remain beyond the reach of the Constituent Assembly itself.'

91 The judgment Pl. US 36/01 (The Bankruptcy Trustee Case) of 25 June 2002, English translation available at www.concourt.cz.

92 Cf Z Kühn, 'Worlds Apart. Western and Central European Judicial Culture at the Onset of the European Enlargement' (2004) 52 *American Journal of Comparative Law* 531.

93 Weiler and Fries, above n 26, at 161.

94 One might of course add potential tensions between the ECJ and the ECHR.

(especially if keep in mind that 'certain tensions among the courts constitute a necessary component of every system of centralised judicial review'[95]). Let us take a recent case *Cordero Alonso* as an example.[96]

In *Cordero Alonso* the Court of Justice interpreted the prohibition of discrimination differently from the earlier judgment of the Spanish Constitutional Tribunal.[97] On the one hand, the ECJ avoided answering expressly the question made by a referring court whether the Spanish administrative and judicial institutions, when applying the national rule transposing the content of Directive 80/987, are bound by the prohibition of discrimination 'deriving from Community law, as defined by the interpretation thereof given by the Court', 'notwithstanding that that interpretation does not coincide with the interpretation in the case-law of the Spanish Constitutional Court of the equivalent fundamental right' in the Spanish Constitution.[98] On the other hand, the ECJ's answer, although not made expressly, is clear: 'the national court must disapply a national rule which, in breach of the principle of equality *as recognised in the Community legal order*, precludes the payment' described in the judgment. 'That obligation persists regardless of whether or not the national court has been granted competence under national law to do so.'[99] Thus the national ordinary court must follow the meaning of discrimination as made by the ECJ and ignore the respective judgment of its national constitutional court.[100]

The logic of European integration empowered the national ordinary courts and disempowered national constitutional courts by the European-style decentralised judicial review of national law for its compliance with EU law.[101] Because, as a practical matter, but also due to subsidiarity and legitimacy requirements, the *ERT* type of cases would require

[95] L Garlicki, 'Constitutional Courts versus Supreme Courts' (2007) 5 *International Journal of Constitutional Law* 44 at 63. One might fairly judge that a recent 'Red Star' case (the first reference coming from new Member States) was a futile attempt of a national judge in Hungary to circumvent her own national constitutional court (the latter already ruled on the issue). See the order of the ECJ of 6 October 2005, Attila Vajnai [2005] ECR I-8577. Cf on this M Bobek, 'A New Legal Order, or a Non-Existent One? Some (Early) Experiences in the Application of EU Law in Central Europe' (2006) 2 *Croatian Yearbook of European Law & Policy* 265, 266–67; M Bobek, 'On the Application of European Law in (Not Only) the Courts of the New Member States: 'Don't Do as I Say'?' (2007–2008) 10, *Cambridge Yearbook of European Legal Studies* 1 – 34.

[96] Case 81/05 Anacleto *Cordero Alonso v Fondo de Garantía Salarial (Fogasa)* [2006] ECR I-7569.

[97] *Ibid*, para 23 (the referring court observed that, in its judgment No 306/1993 of 25 October 1993, the Constitutional Tribunal held that the principle of equality before the law under that scenario is not infringed because there is no different treatment of identical situations).

[98] *Ibid*, para 25.

[99] *Ibid*, paras 47 and 46.

[100] Other interesting questions might soon be referred to the ECJ. For instance, what is the national ordinary court supposed to do if it opines that the national measure implementing EU law is in conflict with both EU and national fundamental rights? Shall it set aside the national law (or refer the issue to the ECJ)? Or shall it refer the law to its national constitutional court to decide the issue from the point of view of the national constitution, and then, in case of the negative answer, follow the EU track prescribed by the *Wachauf* and *ERT* line of case law? In addition, if the Charter would ever become binding, then the issue of Art 53 would bring another interesting problem to the *Wachauf/ERT* line of case law. Despite the scholarly writings which do not take Art 53 at its face value (JB Liisberg, 'Does the EU Charter of Fundamental Rights Threaten the Supremacy of Community Law?' (2001) 38 *CML Rev* 1171, I Pernice, 'Integrating the Charter of Fundamental Rights into the Constitution of the European Union: Practical and Theoretical Proposition' (2003) 10 *Columbia Journal of European Law* 5, 30 *ff*) one should notice that precisely this provision has got a very important role in making the ultimate position of the Spanish Constitutional Tribunal in the Constitutional Treaty case. See FC de la Torre, 'Tribunal Constitucional (Spanish Constitutional Court), Opinion 1/2004 of 13 December 2004, on the Treaty establishing a Constitution for Europe' (2005) 42 *CML Rev* 1169, at 1180, at 1197.

[101] There are even opinions that the centralised model of constitutional review seems to be in crisis, also due to the EU integration. Cf V Ferreres Comella, 'The European Model of Constitutional Review of Legislation: Toward Decentralization?' (2004) 2 *International Journal of Constitutional Law* 461.

a wide margin of national discretion,[102] the burden of responsibility to balance conflicting rights, values, policies and principles is effectively placed on *all* national courts which would challenge some deeply embedded conceptions of the judiciary and the separation of powers in many Member States.[103]

At the same time the logic of 'New Constitutionalism' and the overall judicialisation shifted the important last word of the acceptance or veto power over any European rule on national high courts, especially constitutional courts. Thereby in some sense national constitutional courts appeared on the European scene even stronger. The lead was taken by the German Federal Constitutional Court in its (in)famous 'Maastricht' decision,[104] which on legalistic basis protects German sovereignty within the Union from the uncontrollable expansion of the Union's power at the expense of the nation states.[105] Thus enforcing the *Wachauf/ERT* line of case law against national constitutional courts requires a delicate balancing rather than confrontation.[106]

[102] Cf JA Sweeney, 'A "Margin of Appreciation" in the Internal Market: Lessons from the European Court of Human Rights' (2007) 34 *Legal Issues of Economic Integration* 27 at 49 (arguing that 'the idea of a judicially recognised "margin of appreciation", where Member States' morals and public policies come into conflict with free movement rights, can play an important role in an essentially contested EU'.).

[103] A Barav, 'Omnipotent Courts', in D Curtin, T Heukels (eds), *Institutional Dynamics of European Integration. Essays in Honour of Henry G Schermers Vol II* (Dordrecht, M Nijhoff, 1994) 265. Not all judges enjoy the new powers that they have acquired in the area of Community law. For instance, some English judges hesitated, or even openly protested, the use of this power in some delicate matters of national policies. Cf *ibid* at 300, quoting Hoffman J, according to whom '[i]n applying the Treaty as interpreted by the Court, the national court has to be aware of another division of powers: not between European and national jurisdiction, but between legislature and judiciary'.

[104] BVerfGE 89, 155 (1993), in English (1994) 33 *International Law Materials* 388. The German decisions seem to be followed by most constitutional courts of the new Member States. See W Sadurski '"Solange, chapter 3": Constitutional Courts in Central Europe—Democracy—European Union' EUI LAW 2006/40 LAW Working Papers, available at http://hdl.handle.net/1814/6420.

[105] National constitutional courts thus claim the power which, if truly exercised, would destroy the complex design of the European Union. For the comparison with the role of nuclear weapons during the Cold War see JHH Weiler and U Haltern, 'Constitutional or International? The Foundations of the Community Legal Order and the Question of Judicial Kompetenz-Kompetenz' in A-M Slaughter, A Stone Sweet and JHH Weiler (eds), *The European Court and National Courts—Doctrine and Jurisprudence* (Oxford, Hart, 1998) 362. All relevant parties know about the impact of powers they claim, while at the same time they know that their real strength lies not in their actual use, but merely in their potential to be used.

[106] Cf a famous Irish abortion case which preceded ERT by several months: Case C-159/90, *Society for the Protection of Unborn Children v Grogan* [1991] ECR I-4685.

4

'All the guidance', *ERT* and *Wachauf*

PEDRO CRUZ VILLALÓN[107]

Citing *Wachauf*,[108] *ERT*[109] famously proclaims the Community's commitment to fundamental rights: 'It follows that, as the Court held in its judgment in Case C-5/88 *Wachauf v Federal Republic of Germany* (1989) ECR 2609, paragraph 19, the Community cannot accept measures which are incompatible with observance of the human rights thus recognized and guaranteed'.[110]

Let's place to one side the fact that, as is frequently the case, the point made in *Wachauf* was not exactly the same as in *ERT*.[111] More relevant to our purpose is the link made by the ECJ between the two judgments here under consideration. The main significance of this link is that it inaugurates, one might say, a 'conventionality'[112] review of national law by the ECJ.[113]

[107] Universidad Autónoma de Madrid.

[108] Judgment of the Court (Third Chamber) of 13 July 1989. *Hubert Wachauf v Bundesamt für Ernährung und Forstwirtschaft* (Case 5/88).

[109] Judgment of the Court of 18 June 1991. *Elleniki Radiophonia Tiléorassi AE and Panellinia Omospondia Syllogon Prossopikou v Dimotiki Etairia Pliroforissis and others* (C-260/89, TJCE 1991/213), paragraph 41.

[110] In general, on the role of fundamental rights in the jurisprudence of the ECJ, AG Chueca, *Los derechos fundamentales en la Unión Europea*, 2nd edn, Barcelona, Bosch, 1999; N Colneric, 'Protection of Fundamental Rights through the Court of justice of the European Communities', www.competition-law.ox.ac.uk/iecl/pdfs/working2colneric.pdf; S Douglas-Scott, 'The EU and Human Rights', ch 13 in *Constitutional Law of the European Union*, 431–78; D Kraus, Konkordanzkommentar zum europäischen und deutschen Grundrechtsschutz, Tübingen, Mohr-Siebeck, 2006, 97–154. J Kühling, Grundrechte, in A v Bogdandy (ed.), *Europäisches Verfassungsrecht. Theoretische und dogmatische Grundzüge*, Berlin, Springer, 2003, 583–630; K Lenaerts, *Respect for fundamental rights as a constitutional principle of the European Union*; P Pescatore, 'La Cour de Justice des Communautés Européennes et la Convention Européenne des Droits de l'Homme', in F Matscher and H Petzold (eds.), *Protecting Human Rights: The European dimension*, 2nd edn, 1990, 441–55 ; M Pi Llorens, *Los derechos fundamentales en el ordenamiento comunitario*, 1999; A Rodriguez, *Integración europea y derechos fundamentales*, 2001; GC Rodríguez Iglesias and A del Valle Gálvez, *El Derecho comunitario y las relaciones entre el Tribunal de Justicia de las Comunidades Europeas, el Tribunal europeo de Derechos Humanos y los Tribunales Constitucionales nacionales*; A Salinas de Frías, *La protección de los derechos fundamentales en la Unión Europea*, Granada, 2000; G Tesauro, 'The role of the court of justice in the protection of fundamental rights', in N Colneric, D Edward, J-P Puissochet and D Ruiz-Jarabo Colomer (eds.), *Une communauté de droit. Festschrift für Gil Carlos Rodríguez Iglesias*, 2003, 103–10; A Vitorino, 'La Cour de justice et les droits fondamentaux depuis la proclamation de la Charte', *ibid.*, 111–26 ; JH Weiler, 'Fundamental rights and fundamental boundaries: On the conflict of standards and values in the protection of human rights', 1995, in *The Constitution of Europe*, 1999, 102–29.

[111] See below, '*Wachauf*: A common task'.

[112] I am wholly aware of the inaccuracy, and even arbitrariness of limiting to the European Convention on Human Rights a standard of control which is or may be much broader and deeper (the ECHR as 'minimum standard'). The ECHR is clearly not all for this purpose, in spite of the ECJ's proclamation of its 'special significance' (*ERT*, 41). It should suffice to refer to the opinion of Advocate General Jacobs in *Konstantinidis*, in which the absence of a reference to human dignity in the ECHR leads him to a deeper inquiry (paras. 35–39). Nevertheless, and further to the obvious simplicity of the expression, the preeminence of the ECHR in the matter could excuse this abuse of language.

[113] Cf M Ruffert, 'Die Mitgliedstaaten als Verpflichtete des Gemeinschaftsgrundrechte', *EuGRZ* 1995, 518–30.

ERT and *Wachauf*, in effect, signal the moment in which the ECJ widens its projection of fundamental rights over Community law itself by extending it to the law of Member States. In much the same way as there had been an evolutionary period between the years 1969–79[114] (in which the ECJ moved from ignoring—or at least showing reticence[115] towards—fundamental rights when adjudicating on Community law to its recognition as 'general principles of fundamental (community) law'), a later period (1989–1991) can be identified, in which fundamental rights also come to be applied by the ECJ as parameters of national law.[116] *ERT* and *Wachauf* may not be the only judgments invoked in this respect,[117] but they offer significant illustrations.

These judgments represent each of the two situations in which 'at least' the ECJ considers itself competent to control the 'conventionality' of national law. Here it must be borne in mind that the ECJ is supreme only as judge of EU law, not of the law of Member States; this notwithstanding the fact that the primacy clause necessarily makes ECJ's interpretations of EU law, binding even if indirectly, with respect to national law. But in the *ERT* and *Wachauf* cases the ECJ pronounces itself, or so it seems, 'almost' directly on the 'conventionality' of national law itself. Nevertheless, a particular circumstance is required before this quasi-direct form of control of national law can be assumed. These circumstances indicate how this kind of control comes to be presented in an 'individualised' way, that is, as identified with a limited number of cases, two at least: (1) when national law implements Community law (as was the case in *Wachauf*), and (2) when the state invokes an exception to the four basic freedoms (as was the case in *ERT*).[118]

In the following I wish to examine the contemporary importance of these developments.[119] But before doing so, we should first return to the factual circumstances of *ERT* and *Wachauf* to assess the extent to which the type of control asserted can be understood to apply in an individualised manner. To that effect *Steffensen*[120] could be a good case. Finally, the *Bosphorus* case,[121] when examined by the ECtHR, allows for a conclusive reflection.[122]

[114] From *Stauder* (12 November 1969) to *Hauer* (13 December 1979) passing through *Internationale Handelsgesellschaft* (17 December 1970) and *Nold* (14 May 1974). Cf Rodríguez, 188, Chueca Sancho, 88, Pi Llorens, 25.

[115] Kraus, 101, 'reserviert ... eher abgelehnt'.

[116] While the 'first phase' was very positively received, the same cannot be said of the second. Kühling, 'more difficult to evaluate', 606.

[117] Weiler, 119 cites '*Rutili*, *Cinéthèque*, *Klensch*, *Wachauf*, the Advocate-General in *Grogan*, and *ERT*'; Rodríguez, 111, cites *Rutili* before *ERT*.

[118] Weiler, 120, 'two types of situations'; Kühling, 607, 'zwei Situationen'.

[119] The relevance of the question is tellingly described by Kühling, 606: 'The axis and anchoring ground of the important discussion around the future vertical extension of the fundamental rights of the Union'. The German expressions 'Gemeinschaftsgrundrechte', or 'Unionsgrundrechte', accurately convey the specificity of the fundamental rights 'in' the EU.

[120] Judgment of 10 April 2003 (C-276/01).

[121] Judgment of 30 June 2005 (Case of *Bosphorus Hava Yolları Turizm ve Ticaret Anonim Şirketi v. Ireland*).

[122] The consequences of the eventual accession of the EU to the ECHR as well as the binding effect of the European Charter of Fundamental Rights are not to be considered here.

Wachauf: A Common Task

Briefly, Hubert Wachauf was a farmer who had developed a dairy business on land leased as a farm. Since Wachauf had provided the livestock as well as the rest of the necessary equipment himself, when the leasing contract expired, the question arose whether the dairy quota, or the indemnification for the abandonment of production, should revert to the land owner and not to the lessee, as could be deduced from the applicable Community norm.[123] In which respect it is to be kept in mind that the relevant German legislation[124] only allowed for the lessee to keep the diary quota 'with the authorisation' of the lessor, which ultimately did not happen in that case. The national court viewed this as an expropriation without indemnification and, as such, a violation of fundamental rights.

Paragraph 19 of *Wachauf*, the one cited by *ERT* in our opening remark, reads as follows: '... Community rules which, upon the expiry of the lease, had the effect of depriving the lessee, without compensation, of the fruits of his labour and of his investments in the tenanted holding would be incompatible with the requirements of the protection of human rights in the community legal order. Since those requirements are also binding on the Member States when they implement Community rules, the member States must, as far as possible, apply those rules in accordance with those requirements.' This statement summarises the doctrine of the ECJ at the moment when the judgment in *Wachauf* was rendered.

As can be seen, the answer of the ECJ refers exclusively to Community law: a hypothetical interpretation of Community law whereby a lessee in the circumstances of Mr Wachauf would end up with the deprivation of the fruits of his labour and investment would be contrary to fundamental rights.

But this is not a result necessarily derived from Community law (paragraphs 20 and 21). According to Council Regulation 857/84 Member States are entitled to decide that all or part of the quota, or of the indemnification, benefits the lessee, in subtraction of the whole amount of the quota or of the indemnification. The final conclusion of *Wachauf* is that the states keep a sufficient 'margin of appreciation' in implementing Community law so as to avoid a result that would clearly contravene fundamental rights (paragraph 22). And the ECJ has already stated in paragraph 19 that when implementing Community law the states, exactly in the same way as the EC, must apply the said norms in conformity with fundamental rights. The ECJ concluded that the argument raised by the national court, that the relevant Community law is in breach of fundamental rights, was rejected (paragraph 23).

In this light, *Wachauf* is a paradigmatic case of interpretative adjudication of EC law in conformity with fundamental rights, particularly an interpretative judgement in which a given interpretation of the norm is discarded as unconstitutional. Consequently it is difficult to see in *Wachauf* a shift in the law subject to review, that is, a shift from EU law to national law.[125] The question nevertheless is that, in the circumstances of the case, the

[123] Council Regulation No 857/84 and Commission Regulation (EEC) No 1371/84.

[124] German Law of 17 July 1984 on compensation for the discontinuance of milk production.

[125] The language of the Advocate General in this case is closer to a direct censure by the ECJ of the national law. Jacobs proposes an answer which involves a clear prohibition to the Member State, based upon the respect of the principle of equality and the right of property, to adopt a norm such as the German relevant provision. This opinion has possibly influenced the understanding of *Wachauf*.

imagined—and at the same time 'rejected'—norm is in no way a purely hypothetical one, but a very plausible consequence of the provisions of the national law implementing EU law. From this perspective, it is rather difficult not to see in *Wachauf* a censure, implied but clear, of national law. Furthermore, the ECJ is instructing the national court to follow its own example when doing its part of the job, that is, to enact national law in conformity with fundamental rights. Finally, and in the same vein, the ECJ is suggesting that the interpretation it proposes in paragraph 19 should also be followed by the national court. In general, it would be more appropriate to see here an invitation for both courts to collaborate, rather than the sheer substitution of one court by the other.[126] In conclusion, *Wachauf* highlights in particular the possibilities as well as the duty of national courts to engage in an interpretative judgment in conformity with fundamental rights of the relevant national provisions, especially in cases where the states clearly enjoy a 'margin of interpretation'. The ECJ is here keen on avoiding the impression that it is controlling national law,[127] though, as we shall see, this may not be the case two years later.

ERT: A Leading Role for the ECJ

More than in the high-sounding words of our opening citation, the key statement in *ERT* is found in its following paragraph: ' . . . On the other hand, where such (ie national) rules do fall within the scope of Community law, and reference is made to the Court for a preliminary ruling, it must provide all the criteria of interpretation[128] needed by the national court to determine whether those rules are compatible with the fundamental rights the observance of which the Court ensures and which derive in particular from the European Convention on Human Rights.'

Let us recall that ERT, which has been enjoying the monopoly of television broadcasting in Greece, impugned before the national court the creation of a local TV station in Thessalonika. By means of a preliminary reference, the national court directed as many as 10 questions to the ECJ. Eight of them concerned the interpretation of the norms which, by exception, permit the states to depart from the 'basic market freedoms', singularly in this case the free movement of services. In the last two questions, however, the national court directly seeks a review of the Greek television monopoly in the light of the freedom of expression proclaimed in Article 10 ECHR. The answer given by the ECJ to these two last questions (paragraphs 41 to 45 of *ERT*) exposes in the most complete form the doctrine of the ECJ with respect to its review of the 'conventionality' of national law.[129]

It is interesting to note that the ECJ does not see himself in the least compelled to comment on the fact that the national court is asking for a direct and autonomous review of the 'conventionality' of national law, that is, the Greek broadcast monopoly in the occasion. The explanation, however implicit, may be found in our opening citation of

[126] In general terms, the *Wachauf* approach has been widely accepted. Cf Kühling, 608.

[127] The *Wachauf* doctrine is to be successively confirmed in, for instance, case C-186/96 of 17 December 1998, also on regulation of diary production; and C-540/03, 27 June 2006, on the regrouping of minors (C-540/03) is more interesting.

[128] 'All the guidance', as shall be later said: *Steffensen*, para 70.

[129] 'The most complete statement' according to Advocate General Jacobs in his opinion in *Konstantinidis*, which in para 42 reproduces these five paragraphs of *ERT*.

ERT: the review of the 'conventionality' of national law does not necessarily have to be made as an indirect control through the adjudication on EC law. The only requirement is that the relevant national law finds itself within the 'scope of Community law'. The ECJ does not elaborate any further on this category, but the general idea seems to be that a national provision falls within the scope of application of EC law, wherever the latter has any say on the matter regulated by national law. As a result, 'some' Community law (and this is the function that Articles 56 and 66 of the EEC Treaty play here) has to be invoked for the ECJ to review the 'conventionality' of national law. But the answer of the ECJ is not disguised as an interpretation of the invoked Community law, which is only there to show that the reviewed national provision finds itself within the 'scope of application' of Community law.[130] Under these circumstances, the ECJ's job is clear: it is supposed to offer 'all the interpretative criteria', 'all the guidance', that the national court needs in order to adjudicate on the 'conventionality' of national law. Interestingly enough, the ECJ (paragraph 45) does not consider it necessary to give any specific guidance on the 'conventionality' of the Greek television monopoly; it simply instructs the national court to examine such a monopoly in the light of Article 10 ECHR, without additional assistance.

The 'scope of Community law' doctrine and the 'all the guidance' doctrine are the basic categories provided by ERT, the second of which, as already seen, is of no consequence for the case. The answer to the question posed by the Greek court is based, on the contrary, on a systematic interpretation of the EC norms concerning the basic market freedoms, and their possible exceptions (the eight first questions of the Thessalonika court). The potential of the 'all the guidance' doctrine shall have to be sought in later ECJ judgments.[131]

Steffensen or, a Touchstone

Twelve years after *ERT*, we read in *Steffensen*: 'It is for the national court ... to assess, in the light of all the factual and legal evidence available to it, whether or not the results of analyses of samples of a manufacturer's products are to be admitted as evidence . . . In that regard, . . . the national court must consider whether such evidence must be excluded in order to avoid measures incompatible with compliance with fundamental rights, in particular the right to a fair hearing before a tribunal as laid down in Article 6(1) of the European Convention for the Protection of Human Rights and Fundamental Freedoms' (paragraph 80). In this way, the doctrine laid out in paragraph 42 of *ERT* is not only reiterated (paragraph 70) but also effectively applied.

Joachin Steffensen, director of a sausage factory, had been fined by the German authorities on the basis of a national law implementing Council Directive 89/397/EEC of 14 June 1989, which harmonised the general principles governing official inspection of foodstuffs. Article 7(1) of the Directive provided in its second subparagraph that 'Member

130 *ERT* is certainly of no help in trying to restrict the review of 'conventionality' of national law by the ECJ to the singular situations represented by *Wachauf* and *ERT* itself.

131 The impact of *ERT* on the ECJ jurisprudence is clearly more relevant than the one of *Wachauf*: 29 quotations of *ERT*, 9 of *Wachauf*, since 1997.

States shall take the necessary steps to ensure that those subject to inspection may apply for a second opinion' on the samples taken. The German Local Court referred to the ECJ, through a preliminary reference, two questions on the interpretation of that subparagraph.

The first question is of no particular interest. It simply asked whether the Directive created, by itself, a right to this 'second opinion', regardless of the provisions of the relevant national law. This was obviously purely a question of interpretation of the Directive. In contrast, the second question posed by the national court went far beyond that. It inquired whether the Directive implicitly prohibited the national courts from accepting as evidence the incriminatory results of an analysis of the samples taken in cases, such as this one, where the person fined had not been offered the opportunity to request a 'second opinion'.

This second question asks whether the absence of a 'second opinion' has consequences for the right to a fair trial. If so, a fine imposed on the basis of a sample which could not be the object of a second opinion could arguably be in breach of fundamental rights. Thus construed, the question is related to the well-known doctrine 'fruits of the poisonous tree'. Despite Germany's submission that procedural law falls within the competence of Member States, on this occasion the ECJ gave the national court 'all the guidance' in order to ensure that the 'adversarial principle' was respected (see the opening quotation of *Steffensen*). In paragraphs 69 to 80 the ECJ undertook an inquiry into the jurisprudence of the ECtHR on Article 6.1 ECHR and recognised that the ECtHR does not specify which evidence is admissible and which is not. However, invoking *Mantovanelli v France*, the ECJ highlighted the importance of the adversarial principle, as it would give the person fined the opportunity to impugn the conclusions of a technical opinion submitted by the administration.

From a purely formal point of view *Steffensen* is simply a preliminary ruling 'on the interpretation of the second subparagraph of article 7(1) of Council Directive 89/397/EEC of June 14 1989 on the official control of foodstuffs'. But in fact no interpretation of the Directive appears in the answer to the second question posed by the German court. The mention of Article 7(1) here serves only to comply formally with the requirement derived from the 'scope of application' doctrine. With that, the ECJ is in a position to address the difficulties of the national court regarding the respect to the adversarial principle in the circumstances of the case. Although it is ultimately for the national court to decide, it seems clear that the ECJ is giving the national court precise instructions in answer to the question posed: in the circumstances of the case, the results of the 'first opinion' are not to be taken into account.

The difficulty posed by the German court arose neither from the EU Directive nor from the relevant German provision. The latter included a requirement that the inspected person keep a portion, duly sealed, of the sample obtained. This provision is obviously intended only to make possible the receipt of a reliable second opinion. In the circumstances of the case, no portion of the sample came to the hands of Mr Steffensen (paragraph 25). This problem did not arise from the relevant legal provisions, however, but only from the actual circumstances of the case.

Steffensen is a good example of the extraordinary extension reached by the 'scope of application' doctrine. It also shows how the ECJ is ready to 'help' the national court resolve all the problems of 'conventionality' that may arise within such a scope.[132] Under these circumstances, the conduct of the national courts in making this type of preliminary reference to the ECJ could very well be criticised. The preliminary reference in *Steffensen* was, with respect to the second question concerned, very much a spontaneous initiative of the national court. It was a question on which the national court could have resolved by itself, without resorting to the ECJ, and possibly even without resorting to the German Federal Constitutional Court. The entire responsibility cannot be placed on the ECJ when it accepts jurisdiction over a purely 'conventionality' question, even if it is vaguely disguised under the 'scope of Community law' doctrine.

Conclusion: The *Bosphorus* Perspective

The ECtHR ruling in the *Bosphorus* case[133] sheds light on the ECJ's doctrine on review of the 'conventionality' of national law. It is clear that *Bosphorus* has created a situation of considerable privilege for the acts of Member States implementing Community law: in the absence of state discretion, these acts appear to enjoy a presumption of 'conventionality', even if that can be rebutted on a case-by-case basis. On the contrary, when state discretion concurs, state acts are subject to the same scrutiny as if they had no connection to Community law, or as if they were acts of a non-EU Member State.[134]

This is certainly not the occasion for a critique of the *Bosphorus* doctrine, or for inquiring on the logic of the distinction between both types of Member State acts. The functional proximity of the categories of 'state discretion' and 'margin of appreciation' highlights the existence of a common playing field of both European jurisdictions: for the moment at least, the ECtHR keeps asserting its jurisdiction in such cases, even in concurrence with a previous decision of the ECJ. More intriguing is the notoriously secondary role of the national—even constitutional—courts in the review of the 'conventionality' of national laws, as a result of the 'joint action' of the ECJ and the ECHR.

The 'scope of application' doctrine, given the reach it has attained, is to be considered in this light. It would be nonsense to ask the ECJ for a kind of 'reverse *Bosphorus*', in favour of the ECtHR. But perhaps it would make some sense to ask for a kind of 'reverse *Solange II*',[135] as an indirect consequence of *Bosphorus*. Such a 'reverse *Solange II*' ('*Solange*' in the sense of the 'current state of the European integration') could well lead to a gradual

[132] It clearly appears that the ECJ has not limited its control to the conventionality of national law to the 'two' assumptions that strictly represent *Wachauf* and *ERT*, and that Kuhling considers 'inconvenient' ('nicht angezeigt'), 609–10). All this regardless of the fact that there have been cases in which the ECJ has declared its lack of jurisdiction (*Anibaldi* C-309/96 of 18 December 1977) and that the ECJ in *Konstantinidis* (C168/91) did not follow Advocate General's Jacobs in his view of the *civis europeaum*.

[133] See the separate opinions, only partially concurrent. C Eckes, Does the ECHR provide protection from the European community?—The Case of Bosphorus Airways, *European Public Law*, 13, 47–67. A Haratsch, Die Solange-Rechtsprechung des EGMR—Das Kooperationsverhältnis zwischen EGMR und EuGH—ZaöRV 66 (2006), 927–47. N Lavranos, Das So-Lange-Prinzip im Verhältnis von EGMR und EuGH—Anmerkung zu dem Urteil der EGMR v. 30.06.2006, Rs. 450 36/98, EuR 2006, 79–92.

[134] It remains the case that a state would be fully responsible under the Convention for all acts falling outside its strict international legal obligations. The numerous Convention cases cited by the applicant at paragraph 117 above confirm this. Each case (in particular, the *Cantoni* judgment, at § 26) concerned a review by this Court of the exercise of state discretion for which EC law provided (157).

[135] BVerfGE 73, 339, 387.

abandonment by the ECJ of the 'scope of application' doctrine, in favour of the national courts. The probability of conflicting judgments of the ECJ and the ECtHR would diminish. Such contradictions would shift to the 'dialogue' between national courts and the ECtHR. But these, with exceptions,[136] have long been considered usual.

The concurrence of the two jurisdictions would surely continue whenever national law implements EU law (*Wachauf*). Here the more or less direct review of the 'conventionality' of national law by the ECJ is very much justified, even if a conflict between the two European Courts—to a much lesser degree—may still occur. The important thing is that national—constitutional—courts take on, without unnecessary limitations, their share in the preservation of fundamental rights in all those matters where Community law is not really in question. *Bosphorus* provides a good excuse that will enable the ECJ to retreat from *ERT* to *Wachauf*.

[136] Case *Görgülü v Germany*, 26 May 2004. C Grabenwarter, 'Das mehrpolige Grundrechtsverhältnis im Spannungsfeld zwischen europäischem Menschenrechtschutz und Verfassungsgerichtsbarkeit', in: P-M Dupuy, B Fassbender, MN Shaw and K-P Sommerman (eds.), *Völkerrecht als Wertordnung. Common Values in International Law. Festschrift für/Essays in Honour of Christian Tomuschat*, 2006, 193–206.

V

Case 283/81, *Srl CILFIT and Lanificio di Gavardo SpA v Ministry of Health* and Case 314/85, *Foto-Frost v Hauptzollamt Lübeck-Ost*

1

CILFIT and *Foto-Frost* in their Historical and Procedural Context

DAVID EDWARD[1]

The judgments of the Court of Justice in *CILFIT*[2] and *Foto-Frost*[3] are frequently misunderstood. They have been cited as examples of judicial activism by which the Court is alleged to have stretched the limits of its own jurisdiction at the expense of the national courts, especially the supreme courts. The opposing point of view is that these cases do no more than exemplify the normal judicial function of interpretation where the text is open to doubt and there is a practical problem to be resolved: one may disagree with the result, but that is no reason to question the motives that led to that result.

In order to understand why the two cases were decided as they were, it is important to place them in context.

The Legislative Background

The ECSC Treaty (like the later EEC and Euratom Treaties) provided that 'the Court shall ensure that in the interpretation and application of this Treaty … the law is observed'.[4] It also provided, in a very sketchy way, for a system of preliminary references to the Court of Justice from national courts, giving the Court exclusive competence to rule on questions of validity (not interpretation):

> La Cour est *seule compétente* pour statuer, à titre préjudiciel, sur la *validité* des délibérations de la Haute Autorité et du Conseil, dans le cas où un litige porté devant un tribunal national mettrait en cause cette validité.[5]

The wording implies, but does not expressly impose, a duty on national courts to refer any live issue of validity to the Court of Justice.

When the Rome Treaties were negotiated in 1956, Nicola Catalano, a member of the drafting committee who became a Judge of the Court of Justice in 1958, proposed a form

[1] Judge of the Court of First Instance 1989–92 and of the Court of Justice 1992–2004. Professor Emeritus of the University of Edinburgh.

[2] Case 283/81 *Srl CILFIT e Lanificio di Gavardo SpA v Ministero della Sanità* [1982] ECR 3415.

[3] Case 314/85 *Foto-Frost v HZA Lübeck-Ost* [1987] ECR 4199.

[4] Article 31 ECSC; *cp* Articles 164 EEC and 136 Euratom.

[5] Article 41 ECSC (emphasis added).

of words that, in part, followed the terms of the ECSC Treaty and, in part, foreshadowed the eventual text of Article 177 EEC (now Article 234 EC) and Article 150 Euratom:

> La Cour est *seule compétente pour statuer en dernière instance* sur toute question concernant *l'interprétation ou l'application* du présent Traité, ainsi que des mesures prises en son exécution. Lorsqu'une telle question est soulevée, suivant les règles de procédure nationale devant *une juridiction de dernière instance* d'un des États membres, cette juridiction, si elle estime qu'une décision sur ce point est nécessaire pour rendre son jugement, demande à la Cour de statuer sur cette question et se conforme à l'arrêt de celle-ci.

In this formulation, validity was not expressly mentioned.

The drafting committee then produced three versions. The first version followed the lines of Article 41 of the ECSC Treaty, but giving the Court exclusive competence for interpretation as well as validity. The second version followed the Catalano proposal—giving the Court exclusive competence at last instance and imposing an obligation to refer on national courts of last instance. The third version was very close to what became Article 177 EEC. The final form of Article 177 differed, first, in making explicit the distinction between (i) interpretation of the treaty, (ii) validity and interpretation of acts of the institutions, and (iii) interpretation of statutes of bodies established by the Council; and, second, in imposing the duty to refer on courts and tribunals, 'against whose decisions there is no judicial remedy under national law', irrespective of their status in the national hierarchy.[6]

Thus, in the choice between exclusive competence and shared competence, the drafting committee opted for shared competence both for interpretation and for validity, balanced by an unequivocal obligation to refer imposed on national courts whose decisions are final. The unequivocal nature of that obligation is, if anything, clearer in the original language texts than in English.[7] The obligation to refer is conditional only to the extent that the national court must 'consider that a decision on the question is necessary to enable it to give judgment'.

The text of Article 177 gave rise to controversy on two issues:

(1) In what circumstances is a national court whose decisions are final entitled not to refer a question to the Court of Justice?
(2) May a national court whose decisions are not final decide on the validity of an act of a Community institution?

CILFIT was concerned with the first question, *Foto-Frost* with the second.

[6] For the evolution of Article 177, see Schulze and Hoeren (eds.), *Dokumente zum Europäische Recht*, vol II, pp 373–439 (emphasis added).

[7] French: *cette juridiction est* ***tenu*** *de saisir la Cour de justice*; Dutch: *is deze instantie* ***gehouden*** *zich tot het Hof van Justitie te wenden*; German: *so ist dieses Gericht zur Anrufung des Gerichsthof* ***verpflichtet***; Italian: *tale giurisdizione è* ***tenuta*** *a rivolgersi alla Corte de giustizia*; English: *that court or tribunal* ***shall*** *bring the matter before the Court of Justice.*

The Jurisprudence before *CILFIT*

In *da Costa*[8] the Netherlands Tariefcommissie referred two questions identical to those it had referred in *Van Gend en Loos*.[9] The propriety of the reference was not in question since, at the stage of making the second reference, the Tariefcommissie had not yet received the answer to *Van Gend en Loos*. Once *Van Gend en Loos* had been decided, the Commission urged that the *da Costa* reference should be dismissed for lack of substance, but the Court rejected that solution.

In his Opinion, Advocate General Lagrange started from the position he had already taken in *Fédéchar*,[10] that where the text is clear it requires no 'interpretation'. His solution was an application of the theory of the *acte clair*, which had been adopted by the French *Conseil d'État* (and, to a lesser extent, by the *Cour de cassation*) in order to get round the rule that the French executive has exclusive competence to interpret treaties. By holding that treaties did not require interpretation when the meaning was clear, the French courts restricted the power of the executive to interfere with the role of the judiciary.[11] Parallels to the doctrine of *acte clair* existed in Italian and German statute law as regards the obligation to refer questions of constitutionality to the Constitutional Court.

In its judgment in *da Costa*, the Court started from the 'unrestricted' nature of the obligation imposed by the third paragraph of Article 177. It did not endorse *acte clair* or any comparable approach. It relied instead on two concepts—(i) the authority of a ruling of the Court, and (ii) the '*cause*' of the national court's obligation to refer—holding that the authority of a prior ruling may deprive that obligation of its *cause*, and so empty it of its content.[12] The Court added: 'Such is the case especially[13] when the question raised is materially identical with a question which has already been the subject of a preliminary ruling in a similar case.'

Notwithstanding the Court's rejection of the *acte clair* doctrine, the French *Conseil d'État* persisted in applying it, not least in its refusal to accept that the provisions of directives might have direct effect,[14] although the Court had, in the meanwhile, stressed that 'the particular objective of the third paragraph [of Article 177] is to prevent a body of national case law not in accord with the rules of Community law from coming into existence in any Member State'.[15]

In the meanwhile, the Court of Justice had declined, on grounds of jurisdiction (*compétence*), to answer questions that did not fall within the scope of Article 177—*Mattheus* and *Foglia v Novello*.[16]

[8] Joined cases 28 to 30/62 *Da Costa en Schaake NV, Jacob Meijer NV, Hoechst-Holland NV v Nederlandse Belastingadministratie* [1963] ECR 31.

[9] Case 26/62 *Van Gend en Loos v Nederlandse Belastingadministratie* [1963] ECR 1.

[10] Case 8/55 *Fédération Charbonnière de Belgique v High Authority* [1954–56] ECR 245 at 277–8.

[11] See the Opinion of Advocate General Capotorti in *CILFIT* [1982] ECR 3435.

[12] There is no precise equivalent of *cause* (Latin *causa*) in common law terminology, so the English translation is not entirely satisfactory ('the authority of an interpretation ... may deprive the obligation of its *purpose* and thus empty it of its substance').

[13] Translating *notamment*, which can mean anything from 'for example' to 'especially'.

[14] See the list of cases in the Opinion of Advocate General Capotorti in *CILFIT*, 3437.

[15] Case 107/76 *Hoffmann-La Roche v Centrafarm* [1977] ECR 957, point 5.

[16] Case 93/78 *Mattheus v Doego Fruchtimport und Tiefkühlkost* [1978] ECR 2203; Case 104/79 *Foglia v Novello* [1980] ECR 745, and (subsequently) Case 244/80 *Foglia v Novello II* [1981] ECR 3045.

The extent of the duty to refer became what Advocate General Capotorti described as a 'lively controversy in progress among legal writers and discernible in decisions of national courts'.[17] It was also the subject of a Written Question in the European Parliament. The Commission's answer was that:

> National courts are not required, under Article 177 of the EEC Treaty, to stay proceedings and systematically refer to the Court of Justice all questions concerning the interpretation of Community law which are submitted to them. They can decline to make a reference and decide the matter themselves in cases where such questions are perfectly straightforward and the answer is obvious to any lawyer with a modicum of experience.[18]

CILFIT—The Issue and Submissions

It was in that context that the Italian Court of Cassation referred *CILFIT* to the Court of Justice. The underlying question of Community law was whether, for the purpose of import levies, wool was an 'animal product' within the scope of the relevant Community regulation. The Italian Ministry of Health had decided that wool did not come within the scope of the regulation and this decision had been upheld by the Court of Appeal. Before the Court of Cassation, the Ministry argued that 'the factual circumstances are so obvious as to rule out the possibility of their being capable of any other interpretation, and that obviates the need to refer the matter for a preliminary ruling to the Court of Justice'.

Ironically, when the substantive issue was referred to the Court of Justice two years after the first reference, a chamber of three judges was able to answer the question in 13 paragraphs—wool was not an animal product for the purposes of the Regulation.[19] But, perhaps because the answer was obvious, this was a good case in which to test the nature and extent of the duty to refer.

The question referred by the Court of Cassation was:[20]

> Does the third paragraph of Article 177 … impose an obligation to refer that does not allow the national judge to make any assessment[21] of whether the question raised is well-founded or is the obligation conditional, and if so within what limits, on first finding a reasonable interpretative doubt?

Before the Court, the claimants argued that the *acte clair* theory was inept in the context of Community law. They drew attention to the technical nature of Community law, to the fact that national courts do not have access to all the sources, and to the uncertainties 'due to the sometimes complex interaction between national law and Community law'. They added that allowing supreme courts a discretion to refer would involve 'the risk of creating an atmosphere of tension between national courts and Community institutions' and might promote discord.

[17] Advocate General Capotorti in *CILFIT*, 3433.

[18] Answer to Written Question by Mr Krieg No 608/78 (OJ 1979 C 28), quoted under 'Facts and procedure' in *CILFIT*, 3425.

[19] See Case 77/83 *Srl CILFIT e Lanificio di Gavardo SpA v Ministero della Sanità* [1984] ECR 1257.

[20] As the English translation of the question in *ECR* does not quite convey the sense of the original, an alternative translation is offered.

[21] In the original, *delibazione*—tasting or sampling.

The governments and the Commission, on the other hand, while recognising the importance of uniform interpretation and application, urged the adoption of an *acte clair* approach, each using a somewhat different formula. The Danish Government and the Commission drew attention to the fact that Community texts are drafted in several languages, and the Commission added that they frequently reflect political compromises with the result that 'the exercise of discretion by a national court in relation to Community legislation calls for much greater caution than recourse to the theory of the *acte clair* in a national context'. The Commission suggested that recognition by the Court of the national court's margin of discretion 'would bear witness to its confidence in national courts'.

CILFIT—The Advocate General's Opinion

In his Opinion, Advocate General Capotorti rejected all the arguments based on the text of Article 177 except the 'simple fact' that

> the only unequivocal indication which may be derived from the text ... is the difference between the provisions of the second paragraph and those of the third.

He rejected the *acte clair* approach advocated by his predecessor Lagrange, not only on theoretical grounds, but also because of the way in which the *Conseil d'État* had used *acte clair* to avoid making a reference in circumstances where it clearly ought to have done so. Rejecting the statutory test in Italian constitutional law of whether the point is 'manifestly unfounded', he stressed 'the specific technical and formal characteristics of Community law ... (different language versions; novelty of the content and terminology of Community law)' as well as 'differences in the methods of interpretation adopted by the Court of Justice and those on which national courts rely, stemming from the differences between the legal spheres in which the former and the latter operate'.

In conclusion, the Advocate General advocated a hard line approach, pointing out that national courts already have a 'wide margin of discretion' in determining whether a ruling on the interpretation of a provision of Community law is really necessary to enable them to give judgment.

CILFIT—The Court's Judgment

Against that background, the Court was faced with a limited choice. It could give effect to the words of the Treaty and insist on the unconditional obligation to refer, or it could find a way of introducing an element of discretion for which the Treaty did not provide. If the Court had been intent on stretching the limits of its jurisdiction at the expense of the national courts, it would have chosen the first (strict constructionist) alternative. In the event, it opted for a limited variant of the second, going further than the Advocate General but less far than had been proposed by the Commission and the intervening governments.

The Court began by stressing the discretion (*pouvoir d'appréciation*) of the national courts, including courts of last resort, to decide whether a decision on the question of

Community law is necessary to enable them to give judgment. If they so decide (but not otherwise), the Treaty unequivocally requires courts of last resort to refer.

The Court then recalled its decision in *da Costa*, limiting the obligation to refer where the question raised is 'materially identical with a question which has already been the subject of a preliminary ruling in a similar case'. To this, it added a further limitation 'where previous decisions of the Court have already dealt with the point of law in question, irrespective of the nature of the proceedings which led to those decisions, even though the questions at issue are not strictly identical'. In effect, the Court adopted a doctrine of precedent that involves considering the *ratio decidendi* of a previous case rather than its formal relationship to the case in hand.

Finally, the Court envisaged the situation where 'the correct *application* of Community law may be so obvious as to leave no scope for any reasonable doubt as to the manner in which the question raised is to be resolved'. The use of the expression 'application of Community law' is significant, since it focuses on the essential function of the national court, which consists in applying Community law to concrete cases. Of course, application may require prior interpretation but even if it does, the first task of the national court is to determine whether the text *could* apply to the fact situation before it, even if there is a doubt as to its interpretation.

It is at this point in its reasoning that the Court introduced what have come to be called 'the *CILFIT* criteria':

- if the correct application of Community law appears obvious to the national court, it must be convinced that it would be equally obvious to the courts of other Member States and to the Court of Justice;
- the national court must take account of 'the characteristic features of Community law and the particular difficulties to which its interpretation may give rise'. These are:
    - that Community legislation is drafted in several languages, all equally authentic;
    - that Community law uses terminology peculiar to it;
    - that legal concepts do not necessarily have the same meaning in Community law and the national law of the Member States;
    - andthat provisions of Community law must be construed in their textual, purposive and temporal context.

CILFIT—Discussion

The difficulties and criticisms to which *CILFIT* has given rise stem from two statements in the judgment: first, that the national court 'must be *convinced* that the matter is equally obvious to the courts of the other Member States and to the Court of Justice',[22] and second, that 'an interpretation of a provision of Community law involves *a comparison of the different language versions*'.[23]

Some critics read these statements literally, suggesting that national courts have to engage in an exhaustive linguistic and jurisprudential comparison of all the language texts

[22] *CILFIT*, point 16.
[23] *CILFIT*, point 18.

and speculate about the way in which the national courts of other Member States (about which they may have no reliable information) would look at the matter. That interpretation of the judgment cannot reflect the intention of the Court.

In those passages the Court was drawing attention to a point made by *all* those who submitted observations (claimants, governments and Commission)—namely, that Community texts are not monolingual and cannot be interpreted according to purely national canons of interpretation. One can concede that the Court's phraseology is not ideal, without going to the opposite extreme of absurd literalism. Moreover, the critics do not do justice to the judgment as a whole.

Perhaps the most important point to note is that the Court rejected the doctrine of *acte clair*, as it had already done in *da Costa* 20 years before. So it is deeply regrettable that the expression '*acte clair*' has entered the vocabulary of Community law, particularly in the United Kingdom, whether for reasons of linguistic snobbery[24] or because it is thought to be useful as legal shorthand. As shorthand, it is seriously misleading because it oversimplifies the problem with which the Court was faced and the answer it gave.

The proper question for the national court is *not* whether the law is 'clear', precisely because of the 'characteristic features and difficulties' of Community law, which were foreshadowed in the submissions to the Court and the Advocate General's Opinion and would have been self-evident to anyone acquainted with academic discussion of the problem. As explained by the Court, the question for the national court is more sophisticated and is reflected in the more recent wording of Article 104(3) of the Court's Rules of Procedure.

First, the court should consider whether the 'question' is materially identical to a question on which the Court has already ruled[25] or whether the point of law has already been dealt with.[26] Next, the court should consider whether there is 'scope for any *reasonable doubt* as to the manner in which the question raised is to be resolved'.[27] It is in this last context that the national court should take account of the '*CILFIT* criteria'. Read in that context, they are caveats rather than strict criteria and, indeed, read fairly, they are no more than common sense.

Foto-Frost—The Background

Foto-Frost presented the same kind of problem as *CILFIT*. Both cases were concerned with interpretation of the text of Article 177 and in both cases the relevant part of the text appeared, at first sight, to be unambiguous. The court's task was to divine the intention of the Treaty makers.

The case concerned the import by Foto-Frost into the Federal Republic (West Germany) via Denmark and the United Kingdom of binoculars made at the Carl Zeiss factory in Jena in the GDR. Indirect import was necessary because of an agreement between Foto-Frost and the West German Zeiss company based at Oberkochen. The question was

24 *Omne ignotum pro magnifico est.* Tacitus, *Agricola* 30.
25 *Da Costa*, cited at *CILFIT*, point 13.
26 *CILFIT*, point 14.
27 *CILFIT*, point 16.

whether import duties were payable. In the past, Foto-Frost had been exempted from payment of duties by the West German customs authorities. On this occasion the customs authority asked the Commission for a ruling on whether duty should have been charged and, if so, whether Foto-Frost was now liable to pay it.

The Commission ruled that import duties should have been paid, and that although Foto-Frost had been granted exemptions on previous occasions, it ought to have known that this was wrong: Foto-Frost was therefore liable for the import duty. The Commission also held—it later conceded wrongly—that Foto-Frost had failed to comply with the requirements concerning customs declarations.

In the reference to the Court of Justice by the Hamburg Finance Court the main point at issue was the validity of the Commission's decision. The first question was whether the Finance Court could review the validity of the decision and, if it found it to be invalid, determine whether payment of duty could be waived. On the assumption that the answer was No, subsequent questions asked whether the Commission's decision was valid and whether payment could be waived.

Foto-Frost—The Issue and Submissions

The question whether a national court could review the validity of an act of a Community institution was, as Advocate General Mancini said, 'one of the thorniest (*tra i più scabrosi*) that the Court has ever had to tackle'. Essentially, the choice was between literal interpretation of the text and the workability of the system.

On the one hand, there was the text of Article 177 as compared with Article 41 of the ECSC Treaty. The ECSC Treaty expressly gave the Court exclusive competence to rule on the validity of acts of the institutions; the EEC Treaty did not. The legislative history described above shows that the possibility of giving the Court exclusive competence, either in the short formula of the ECSC Treaty or as part of a longer formula, was one of the choices before the drafting committee. How could it be argued that the Treaty makers intended the Court to have exclusive competence when that option had clearly been rejected?

On the other hand, from the point of view of uniform and fair application of Community law, there was the unappealing prospect of national courts throughout the Community declaring Community regulations, directives and decisions invalid without control by any Community authority unless and until the case reached a court that was bound to refer under the third paragraph of Article 177. On several occasions, German administrative and finance courts had asserted the power to declare Community acts invalid and on at least one occasion had done so. Lurking in the wings was the judgment of the German Constitutional Court in *Solange I*.[28]

Academic opinion was divided, but the submissions to the Court of Justice were not. Foto-Frost, the German government and the Commission all submitted that the Court must have exclusive jurisdiction on issues of validity. The German government gave no

[28] *Internationale Handelsgesellschaft mbH v Einfuhr-und Vorratsstelle für Getreide und Futtermittel* [1974] 2 CMLR 540.

reasons for its view. (No other government intervened.) The Commission attached particular importance to the effectiveness of its decisions, such as the decision in issue.

Foto-Frost—The Advocate General's Opinion

In his Opinion Advocate General Mancini examined the arguments on either side. He rejected arguments based on *dicta* of the Court (in *Schwarze*[29] and *Granaria*[30]) that were said to support the contention that the Court did not have exclusive competence. He accepted that 'the arguments based on the wording of Article 177 are solid ones', but he felt that 'they also lead to such dangerous and anomalous results as to overshadow the undeniable uneasiness which one feels in rejecting them'. Since the authors of the Treaty could not have overlooked the consequences of a literal interpretation, 'the "elliptical" wording of Article 177 is attributable to a singular but not impossible oversight'.

He went on to identify four anomalies that would arise if the Court did not have exclusive competence to declare Community acts invalid—two legal and two practical.

The first legal anomaly would be that inferior national courts would be free to declare Community acts invalid, whereas the highest courts could not do so since they would be bound to refer the matter to the Court of Justice. The second would be the threat to the coherence of the Community legal order if national courts of all the Member States were free to declare Community acts invalid. The Advocate General stressed the underlying logic of Article 189 EEC (now Article 249 EC) that acts of the Community institutions must be applied uniformly through the Community.

The first practical anomaly would be that the national court would be faced with a task for which it is 'ill equipped or, in any case, very much less well equipped than the Court of Justice'. '[T]o review the validity of Community measures is a delicate task necessitating perfect knowledge of the relevant provisions, which are often drafted in an unpalatable, even esoteric, jargon, or of economic data to which there is no ready access'. The second practical anomaly would be that 'the national court could never put temporal limits on the effects of the judgment by which it declares a measure to be invalid ... which would have potentially disruptive [economic] consequences on the functioning of the common market'.

The Advocate General's conclusion was that his solution was 'not irrefutable, but certainly reasonable and, in any event, more satisfying than the opposite view'. Having said that, he accepted that a national court does not have an obligation to refer where it concludes that the Community act is valid (because there is then no 'question' to refer). He also accepted that there should be an exception to the general rule in summary or interlocutory proceedings, where protection of the trader requires suspension by the national court of the operation of the Community act. This had already been explicitly recognised by the Court in *Hoffmann-La Roche v Centrafarm*,[31] and was supported by the Commission in its submissions.

[29] Case 16/65 *Firma G Schwarze v Einfuhr- und Vorratsstelle für Getreide und Futtermittel* [1965] ECR 877 at 886.

[30] Case 101/78 *Granaria BV v Hoofdproduktschap voor Akkerbouwprodukten* [1979] ECR 623, point 4.

[31] Above note 15, at point 4.

Foto-Frost—The Court's Judgment

The Court began by saying that the text of Article 177 did not settle the question whether national courts could declare a Community act invalid. Like the Advocate General, it accepted that national courts can reject arguments of invalidity where these are unfounded since 'by taking that action they are not calling into question the existence of the Community measure'. The Court then advanced four reasons why national courts do not have competence to declare a Community act invalid:

- the main purpose of Article 177 is to ensure uniform application of Community law;
- divergences between national courts would jeopardise the unity of the Community legal order and detract from legal certainty;
- the coherence of the system of judicial protection requires that the power reserved to the Court under Article 173 [Article 230 EC] should likewise be reserved to the Court under Article 177 [234];
- the Court is in the best position to decide on the validity of Community acts:
  - because the institution(s) the validity of whose acts are in question can participate in the proceedings in order to defend the validity of those acts; and
  - because the Court can require non-participating Member States and institutions to provide any necessary information.

Foto-Frost—Discussion

The judgment in *Foto-Frost* is perhaps somewhat peremptory in its tone, and may be thought to rely too much on formulaic pronouncements such as 'the very unity of the Community legal order' and 'the necessary coherence of the system of judicial protection'. That may explain some of the unfavourable reaction to the judgment. Nevertheless, there is an underlying seam of common sense which is better expressed in the Advocate General's Opinion and some of the academic writing.

The question at issue was not one to which there was an obvious answer. There was a strong textual argument in favour of recognising the competence of national courts to declare Community acts invalid. The arguments against were essentially practical: the Community system would not work, and certainly would not work fairly, if national courts—particularly lower courts—were free to declare acts of the institutions inapplicable within their jurisdiction. Support for these arguments could be found in the Treaty, notably the inferences that could be drawn from Articles 173 and 189. So the method of interpretation chosen by the Court was certainly 'purposive' but it did not do violence to the Treaty text.

Assessment

Two questions arise. First, are *CILFIT* and *Foto-Frost* 'good law'? Second, looking ahead, do they provide an adequate basis for the future relationship between the Court of Justice and the courts of 27 or more Member States?

As regards the first question, neither *CILFIT* nor *Foto-Frost* can reasonably be said to be an example of judicial activism. In both cases, there was a genuine problem of interpretation to be resolved, on which professional and academic opinion had differed. *CILFIT* gave greater leeway to the national courts than a strict reading of Article 177 would have required: *Foto-Frost* gave less. The Court could have reached a different decision but there was a rational legal justification for both judgments.

In practice, the relationship between the Court of Justice and the national courts, including the supreme courts, has worked reasonably well—as well, at any rate, as could reasonably have been expected in a federal or quasi-federal system.[32] Tension has, on the whole, been avoided by the exercise of common sense on both sides. The judgments in *CILFIT* and *Foto-Frost*, far from creating tension or failing to show confidence in the national courts, have been helpful in drawing a workable line of demarcation of competences.

Perhaps the best vindication of *CILFIT* and *Foto-Frost* as sound interpretations of the will of the Treaty makers lies in the fact that, despite repeated academic and political urgings, and despite recommendations by the Due Working Party on the future of the Community court system,[33] the text of Article 234 was not altered by the Treaty of Nice, nor was any amendment on this point suggested in the Draft Treaty establishing a Constitution for Europe or the Treaty of Lisbon.

As regards the future, the question is not so much whether *CILFIT* and *Foto-Frost* should be reconsidered, but whether the strict requirements of Article 234, as interpreted in those judgments, should be reconsidered. In seeking to answer that question, it is as well to accept that there will always be a degree of tension between national courts and the Court of Justice. Similar tensions exist *within* national systems: judges of first instance often resent the way in which their judgments are reversed or criticised by the courts of appeal, and judges of the courts of appeal are often heard to say that the supreme court is too remote from the practicalities of everyday judicial life.

Whatever rules may be made, it is inevitable that national courts will sometimes feel that they should allowed to get on with deciding cases rather than being forced to refer them to the Court of Justice. This will be true particularly of supreme courts, not least because their cases are likely to be already several years old and a reference to Luxembourg will only add further delay. Bearing in mind the requirements of the ECHR, it is legitimate for national courts to ask whether the further delay involved in a reference is really necessary.

Again, it is as well to recognise that, while uniform application of the law is an ideal that all courts should aim to achieve, complete uniformity is frequently unattainable in

[32] See, eg, the comparative study of EU and US practice in Matthew T King, *Towards a Practical Convergence: The Dynamic Uses of Judicial Advice in United States Federal Courts and the Court of Justice of the European Communities* (2002) 63 *University of Pittsburgh Law Review* 703.

[33] *Report by the Working Party on the Future of the European Communities' Legal System*, January 2000, 15–16, http://ec.europa.eu/comm/dgs/legal_service/docs/due-_en.pdf.

practice. Thus, it is accepted in the United States that one of the grounds on which the Supreme Court will grant *certiorari* is that a conflict exists on a point of law among the various federal circuits. Divergences of view with divergent results are part of the reality of judicial life.

Having said that, it is important also to recognise the dangers of giving free rein to national courts. These were graphically illustrated by Case C-129/00 *Commission v Italy*,[34] which concerned the perennial problem of repayment of taxes and duties levied contrary to Community law (*répétition de l'indu*). The Court of Justice had repeatedly stated (notably in *Comateb*[35] and *Dilexport*[36]) that Member States must not impose on the taxpayer the obligation to prove that the cost of an unlawful tax or duty has not been passed on to third parties. Nevertheless, the Italian courts, and especially the Corte Suprema di Cassazione, interpreted Italian law in such a way as effectively to create a presumption that the cost of the tax or levy had been passed on and that it was up to the taxpayer to prove the contrary.

The Commission took the almost unprecedented step of launching an infringement action against Italy on the ground that the national case law—largely the case law of the supreme court—and administrative practice based on that case law, were contrary to Community law. The Court found in the Commission's favour, stressing that:

> A Member State's failure to fulfil obligations may, in principle, be established under Article 226 EC whatever the agency of that State whose action or inaction is the cause of the failure to fulfil its obligations, even in the case of a constitutionally independent institution.[37]

The cases of *Köbler*[38] and *Traghetti del Mediterraneo*,[39] raising the issue of state liability for the actions of national courts, also illustrate the potential for greater conflict where national courts appear not to be prepared to accept the lines of demarcation of competences established by the Court of Justice.

The advantage of maintaining the existing text of Article 234 as interpreted in *CILFIT* and *Foto-Frost* is that, at the very least, it reminds national courts of their duty to apply Community law in accordance with the case law of the Court of Justice and to seek guidance from the Court if they are in doubt as to what the law is. Delay is less of a problem than it used to be since Article 104(3) of the Rules of Procedure now enables the Court to give a quick answer where it can be deduced from existing case law or admits of no reasonable doubt.

If it is accepted that the texts provide the basis for a reasonable working relationship between the Court of Justice and national courts, it may be wise to be guided by the maxim 'If it works, don't fix it'.

[34] Case 129/00 *Commission v Italy* [2003] ECR I-14637.

[35] Joined Cases C-192/95 to 218/95 *Société Comateb and others v Directeur général des douanes et droits indirects* [1997] ECR 165.

[36] Case 343/96 *Dilexport Srl v Amministrazione delle Finanze dello Stato* [1999] ECR I-579.

[37] *Commission v Italy*, point 29, citing Case 77/69 *Commission v Belgium* [1970] ECR 237, point 15.

[38] Case C-224/01 *Gerhard Köbler v Republik Österreich* [2003] ECR I-10239.

[39] Case C-173/03 *Traghetti del Mediterraneo SpA v Repubblica italiana* [2006] ECR I-5177.

2

The Classics of EU Law Revisited: *CILFIT* and *Foto-Frost*

PAUL CRAIG

The decisions in *CILFIT*[40] and *Foto-Frost*[41] are most certainly classics of the ECJ's jurisprudence, which have served to define and shape the nature of the relationship between the Community courts and national courts under Article 234.

The Three Limbs of *CILFIT*

The decision in *CILFIT* is, of course, best known for what the ECJ said in relation to the *acte clair* doctrine. It should nonetheless be recalled that the ECJ's holding in that respect was but part of a more general ruling concerning the nature of the relationship between national courts and the ECJ under Article 234. The ECJ held that national courts or tribunals against whose decisions there was no judicial remedy under national law must, where a question of Community law was raised before them, comply with their obligation to make a reference, unless the question raised was irrelevant, or the Community provision in question had already been interpreted by the Court, or where the correct application of Community law was so obvious as to leave no scope for any reasonable doubt.[42] The three criteria, relevancy, prior ECJ ruling and *acte clair* were grounded in an admixture of normative and practical considerations.

The *relevancy criterion* flowed from the very wording of Article 234, which requires that a decision on the question raised is necessary to enable the national court to give judgment. In *CILFIT* the ECJ made it clear that the courts or tribunals referred to in Article 234(3) have the same discretion as any other national court or tribunal to ascertain whether a decision on a question of Community law is necessary to enable them to give judgment, with the consequence that they are not obliged to refer a question concerning the interpretation of Community law raised before them if that 'question is not relevant, that is to say, if the answer to that question, regardless of what it may be, can in no way affect the outcome of the case'.[43]

[40] Case 283/81 *Srl CILFIT and Lanificio di Gavardo SpA v Ministry of Health* [1982] ECR 3415.
[41] Case 314/85 *Firma Foto-Frost v Hauptzollamt Lübeck-Ost* [1987] ECR 4199.
[42] See, more recently, Case 495/03 *Intermodal Transports BV v Staatssecretaris van Financien* [2005] ECR I-8151.
[43] Case 283/81 *Srl CILFIT*, para 10.

In normative terms, this clearly made sense in the light of the wording of Article 234, and also served to ensure that answers to questions of Community law were grounded, in the sense that there really was a 'case or controversy' relating to the Community legal issue, which would frame the ECJ's response. In practical terms, the relevancy criterion served to prevent the ECJ from using its scarce judicial resources on the resolution of disputes where Community law was irrelevant, thereby also preventing the 'strategic' deployment of Community law argument in national courts as a delaying tactic by litigants.

The *CILFIT* judgment also developed the pre-existing law in relation to *the effect of a prior ECJ ruling* on the existence of an obligation to refer by national courts of last resort. It reaffirmed the earlier *Da Costa* ruling,[44] and confirmed that the authority of an interpretation under Article 234 already given by the Court could deprive the obligation to refer of its purpose and thus empty it of its substance.[45] The ECJ in *CILFIT*, however, extended this aspect of *Da Costa*, making it clear that this could also be so not only where the question raised was materially identical with a question that had already been the subject of a preliminary ruling in a similar case, but also where previous decisions of the Court had already dealt with the point of law in question, 'irrespective of the nature of the proceedings which led to those decisions, even though the questions at issue are not strictly identical',[46] subject to the caveat that the national court might still choose to refer if it wished to do so, more especially where it was unclear about a specific facet of the earlier ruling. An earlier decision could therefore be relied on by the national court in a subsequent case, irrespective of whether the former decision had arisen in for example proceedings under Articles 226 or 230, where the later case took the form of an Article 234 action. The ECJ in *CILFIT* also made it clear that this could be so even though the two cases might not be strictly identical, provided that the essence of the legal point arising in the second case had been answered in the earlier decision.

There were once again normative and practical considerations that influenced the ECJ in this respect. In normative terms, the authority of the Court's decisions was thereby enhanced, since they became authoritative rulings for all national courts.[47] The ECJ's rulings were no longer only of 'bilateral' relevance for the national court that requested the ruling. They would henceforth have a 'multilateral' impact on all national courts. The reverse side of the same coin was equally significant. It was precisely *Da Costa* as affirmed and extended by *CILFIT* which turned national courts into Community courts of general jurisdiction in their own right. Once the ECJ had issued a ruling on a particular point it was then for national courts to apply this ruling in subsequent cases and they should only trouble the ECJ where they felt unsure about some aspect of the prior ruling. EU law without *CILFIT* would therefore have looked and been very different, at least so far as the nature of the overall Community legal architecture was concerned. The result of *CILFIT* and *Da Costa* was that national courts became 'enrolled' as part of a network of courts adjudicating on Community law, with the ECJ at the apex of that network. They become 'delegates' in the enforcement of EC law, and part of a broader Community judicial hierarchy.

[44] Cases 28–30/62 *Da Costa en Schaake NV, Jacob Meijer NV and Hoechst-Holland NV v Nederlandse Belastingadministratie* [1963] ECR 31.

[45] Case 283/81 *Srl CILFIT*, para 13.

[46] *Ibid*, para 14.

[47] H Rasmussen, 'The European Court's *Acte Clair* Strategy in *CILFIT*' (1984) 9 *EL Rev* 242.

The normative considerations driving *Da Costa* and *CILFIT* were reinforced by those of a practical nature. Even though these rulings were given at a time when the ECJ was not subject to the same workload problems as it is now, it would nonetheless have been regarded as wasteful for all concerned if the national court was obliged to refer, and the ECJ was obliged to hear a case where it had resolved the substance of the legal issue in a prior case. A judicial system could not be supposed to exist on such terms. The national courts would not see the sense of a system which placed pressure on them to allow issues to be litigated again, where the ECJ had already given a considered judgment. There is of course inherent in this regime the risk that a national court might misinterpret past ECJ authority. Any system of precedent inevitably entails certain 'error costs', the possibility of mistakes by national courts. The benefits are, however, very significant and include the increased volume of Community law which can be litigated, mostly correctly, at any one time, and also the important symbolic advantage which flows from the recognition that the national courts are part of a Community judicial hierarchy. It should be noted that a study found a high rate of national implementation of ECJ rulings, 96.3 per cent.[48]

It was, however, the third limb of *CILFIT*, which was concerned with the *acte clair* doctrine, that proved to be most controversial. The ECJ held, as is well known, that even where there was no prior ruling a national court of last resort was permitted not to refer where 'the correct application of Community law may be so obvious as to leave no scope for any reasonable doubt as to the manner in which the question raised is to be resolved'.[49] This conclusion was tempered by the imposition of strict conditions that had to be satisfied before the national court could legitimately conclude that the matter was indeed *acte clair*. These conditions required the national court to be satisfied that the matter would be regarded as equally obvious in the different language versions; it had to be mindful that Community law used its own terminology, and that legal concepts did not always bear the same meaning in different legal systems; the national court was also required to interpret particular provisions in the light of Community law as a whole. The current indications are that the ECJ is content with the formulation in *CILFIT* and shows no inclination to modify the ruling to any significant degree.[50] It is true that in *Intermodal*[51] the ECJ declined to extend the *CILFIT* conditions, holding that a national court was not required to ensure that the matter was equally obvious to bodies of a non-judicial nature, such as administrative authorities. Subject to that caveat, the ECJ reaffirmed the *CILFIT* condition that before declining to refer a national court must be convinced that the matter was so obvious that there was no scope for any reasonable doubt as to the way in which the question should be resolved, and more especially that the matter was equally obvious to other national courts and to the ECJ.[52]

[48] S Nyikos, 'The Preliminary Reference Process: National Court Implementation, Changing Opportunity Structures and Litigant Desistment' (2003) 4 *European Union Politics* 397.

[49] Case 283/81 *Srl CILFIT*, para 16.

[50] Case C-461/03 *Gaston Schul Douane-expediteur BV v Minister van Landbouw, Natuur en Voedselkwalitiet* [2005] ECR I-10513, paras 15–25; Case T-47/02 *Danzer and Danzer v Council* [2006] ECR II-1779, paras 36–37.

[51] Case 495/03 *Intermodal Transports*, para 39.

[52] *Ibid*, paras 38–9.

The rationale for the *CILFIT* ruling was debated and contested in the academic literature. Mancini and Keeling[53] followed Rasmussen,[54] who maintained that the judgment was based on an astute strategy of 'give and take'. This theme was developed by Mancini and Keeling, who argued that the ECJ's strategy was to concede to national courts the power not to make a reference when the matter was clear, but then to restrict the circumstances in which 'the clarity of the provision may legitimately be sustained to cases so rare that the nucleus of its own authority is preserved intact'.[55] The Court hoped thereby to induce national supreme courts to use willingly the mechanisms for judicial co-operation provided by the Treaty, and reduce the risk that Community law might be the subject of divergent interpretations.

The wisdom of this strategy was, however, questioned by those such as Arnull, who argued that national courts still controlled the application of the *CILFIT* criteria for *acte clair* and could therefore manipulate them if they wished to do so.[56] Advocates of this view therefore questioned the desirability of this aspect of the *CILFIT* ruling and implicitly if not explicitly argued against any relaxation of the conditions laid down by the ECJ. Others took a different view. There were those such as Advocate General Jacobs who argued that national judges should not have to consider all the official language versions of Community acts.[57] Rasmussen went further, and argued that the *CILFIT* conditions should be modified, this being one way to meet the practical workload problems currently besetting the ECJ.[58] On this view *CILFIT* should be modified so as to give more power to national courts to resolve cases, even where the legal issues involved in such cases were not straightforward. This expanded vision of *acte clair* would serve in effect as the method for demarcating the line between those cases that warranted attention by the ECJ, and those that could be left for determination by the national courts.

It is helpful once again to distinguish the normative and practical considerations that underlie the *acte clair* doctrine and the reactions to it. In normative terms there is much to be said for the basic proposition that 'clear' cases can be decided by national courts, even those of last resort, without recourse to the ECJ. The national courts operate once again as the delegates of the ECJ for the application of Community law, and the latter can then utilise its time in deciding more problematic cases. This of course begs the question of what constitutes a 'clear case'. Lawyers can and indeed do argue about the meaning of just about anything. This reductionist point should not, however, be pressed too far. The reality is that the *CILFIT* conditions were designed to ensure that, so far as possible, national courts would not regard cases as *acte clair* unless they really were free from significant interpretive doubt. It is, however, questionable whether the injunction on national courts to consider all different language versions of the relevant text is either necessary or desirable in an expanded Community, with the increase in the number of official languages. To this extent it may well be desirable to loosen the *CILFIT* conditions. It is, however, doubtful whether the doctrine should be changed over and beyond this. It is more specifically questionable whether it should be changed in the manner suggested by

53 F Mancini and D Keeling, 'From *CILFIT* to *ERT*: The Constitutional Challenge Facing the European Court' (1991) 11 *Yearbook of European Law* 1.

54 H Rasmussen, 'The European Court's *Acte Clair* Strategy in *CILFIT*' (1984) 9 *EL Rev* 242.

55 Mancini and Keeling, 4.

56 A Arnull, 'The Use and Abuse of Article 177' (1989) 52 *MLR* 622.

57 Case C-338/95 *Wiener v Hauptzollamt Emmerich* [1997] ECR I-6495.

58 H Rasmussen, 'Remedying the Crumbling EC Judicial System' (2000) 37 *CML Rev* 1071, 1109.

Rasmussen, for the following reason. We should undoubtedly think broadly of possible strategies to ease the workload of the ECJ. Part of this strategy might be to leave more cases to be resolved by national courts, although I doubt whether this is the optimal solution. In any event, whatever view one takes on this particular issue, it is inappropriate to attempt to effectuate this change by liberalisation of the *acte clair* doctrine, because it distorts its foundations. A matter does not become *acte clair* in any meaningful sense of that term merely because one decides that the matter is not worthy of the attention of the ECJ. A criterion that provides that the ECJ will hear cases based on the importance or significance of the issue being litigated, with other cases being left to national courts even if they are not straightforward, is qualitatively different from the concept of *acte clair*.

There are also practical considerations underlying the *acte clair* doctrine in something like its present form. In practical terms it allows straightforward cases to be disposed of expeditiously by national courts, thereby saving costs for litigants and the court system alike. There is inevitably the possibility of error costs, but, as we have seen, that is always so whenever a matter is left for the disposition of national courts. The danger of incorrect constructions by national courts becoming embedded should not, however, be overstated. If a national court were minded to do this intentionally in a particular case it would be subject to the possibility of damages liability pursuant to *Köbler*.[59] This would be *a fortiori* so if the national court were more systematically to interpret matters as *acte clair* where they did not warrant this appellation, and there is the further possibility that the Member State might be subject to an enforcement action under Article 226.[60] In any event, the matter might still come before the ECJ via a different court from the same legal system, or from a different legal system. It would also be open to the ECJ to correct aberrant interpretations by national courts, in the context of a case on a related point that has come before it, although the implications of this for prior decisions at national level would be subject to *Kühne*.[61]

The Limits of *Foto-Frost*

The decision in *Foto-Frost*[62] is central to the relationship between national courts and the ECJ under Article 234. The ECJ's conclusion that national courts had no power to invalidate a Community norm of their own volition was based on a variety of arguments.

The ECJ accepted that Article 234 did not settle the issue. It accepted also that it was open to national courts to conclude, after listening to the arguments advanced by the parties, that the Community measure challenged was valid. The principal argument advanced by the ECJ for holding that national courts could not invalidate a Community norm was that it would thereby jeopardise the uniformity of Community law: 'divergences between courts in the Member States as to the validity of Community acts would be liable to place in jeopardy the very unity of the Community legal order and detract from the

[59] Case C-224/01 *Köbler v Austria* [2003] ECR I-10239.

[60] See the Commission reasoned opinion in relation to Sweden, C(2004) 3899.

[61] Case C-453/00 *Kühne & Heitz NV v Produktschap voor Pluimvee en Eieren* [2004] ECR I-837.

[62] Case 314/85 *Firma Foto-Frost*. See also Case C–27/95 *Woodspring DC v Bakers of Nailsea Ltd* [1997] ECR I-1847; Case C-461/03 *Gaston Schul*, paras 15–25; Case C-344/04 *R on the application of IATA and ELFAA v Department of Transport* [2006] ECR I-403, paras 27–32.

fundamental requirement of legal certainty'.[63] This was backed up by a secondary argument based on the analogy between Articles 230 and 234: since Article 230 gave the ECJ exclusive jurisdiction to declare void an act of a Community institution in a direct action, the coherence of the system required that where the validity of a Community act was challenged indirectly via Article 234 before a national court the power to declare the act invalid should also be reserved to the Court of Justice.[64] The third and final strand of the argument was that the ECJ was best placed to decide on the validity of Community acts. This was because the Protocol on the Statute of the Court of Justice allowed Community institutions whose acts were challenged to participate in the proceedings to defend the validity of the acts in question, and also allowed the ECJ to gather information from Member States and institutions which were not participating in the proceedings.

There is of course an interesting analogy and contrast between *CILFIT* and *Foto-Frost*. The former, as we have seen, stands for the proposition that national courts may decide cases for themselves either where there has been a prior ECJ ruling on the issue, or where the matter is *acte clair* in the sense considered above. *Foto-Frost* read together with the *ICC* case[65] stands for the proposition that national courts should follow prior ECJ rulings declaring a Community act to be void, but cannot decide on the invalidity of a Community act in the absence of an ECJ ruling on the point, notwithstanding the fact that the invalidity may be clear, although they may be able to give interim relief.

The interesting issue is whether *Foto-Frost* should be relaxed so as to enable national courts to invalidate a Community norm. One's view on this issue depends in part on how far one is convinced by the nature of the arguments advanced by the ECJ in *Foto-Frost*. Thus some have questioned the need for uniformity, which is the ECJ's principal argument. I do not share these doubts. There would be considerable practical and conceptual problems if Community norms were to be regarded as invalid in some national systems and not in others. These problems would be exacerbated in an expanded Community of 27 Member States. The procedural advantages of having such matters litigated before the ECJ, allowing participation by the Community institution whose acts are challenged and the gathering of salient information from other Community institutions and Member States, should also not be underestimated. I am therefore unconvinced by arguments that the *Foto-Frost* limitation on national courts should be removed.

This does not, however, mean that matters cannot be improved. We need to press a little further to understand why and how this might be achieved. We should not lose sight of the reason why Community norms are challenged indirectly via the national courts. The primary reason is of course that the limits of standing for direct actions preclude any claim being brought under Article 230, with the consequence that the only method of challenge for an individual claimant is an indirect action via Article 234. If the standing limits under Article 230 were to be relaxed, then it would be open to individuals to proceed directly before the CFI, and many would naturally choose to do so. The validity of the Community measure could then be determined by an expert Community court, with the procedural advantages for the parties to the litigation mentioned by the ECJ in *Foto-Frost*. The liberalisation of the standing rules for direct actions would therefore

[63] Case 314/85 *Firma Foto-Frost*, para 15.

[64] *Ibid*, para 17.

[65] Case 66/80 *International Chemical Corporation v Amministrazione delle Finanze dello Stato* [1981] ECR 1191.

significantly reduce the incidence of indirect challenge to Community norms in national courts, and hence reduce also any difficulties faced by litigants as a result of the *Foto-Frost* limit on national courts. This change would, moreover, have the added benefit that such cases would be heard by the CFI, rather than the ECJ, thereby helping to reduce the work load of the latter.

3

Cilfit and Foto-Frost: *Constructing and Deconstructing Judicial Authority in Europe**

DANIEL SARMIENTO[66]

CILFIT and *Foto-Frost* stand as landmark cases that have fashioned the relationship between national and community courts. They both contribute to establish the scope of the preliminary ruling procedure by covering the lacunae left by both the TEC and the TEU, but they also expand the powers that both Treaties grant to national and community courts. They are creative and activist judgments necessary at their time, but with different abilities to stand the course of years. In this Chapter I will argue that *CILFIT* and *Foto-Frost* were delivered in a specific context that has drastically changed in recent times. The main weaknesses of the judgments will be underlined in view of the present circumstances, not without making some proposals of change for the coming years. I will support a new approach to *CILFIT* based on the constitutional relevance of cases before national courts, complemented by a strict support of *Foto-Frost.* Overall, the case for a stronger role for the European Court of Justice will be made, but only in a judicial context in which national courts can establish a discursive rapport on European constitutional issues. Contrary to what federal judicial systems prove, in which the ultimate arbiter of constitutional issues is a sole and only voice, I believe the process of European integration requires exactly the opposite perspective: the ECJ should stand as an ultimate arbiter in issues foreign to constitutional matters, yet develop a real dialogue with its national counterparts in cases which involve a principle of European constitutional law. If such thesis proves correct, *CILFIT* and *Foto-Frost* could still stand as the landmark cases they struggle to be today, contributing to shape the relation between community and national courts for 50 more years.

* Many thanks to Ricardo Alonso García, Victor Ferreres Comella and Jan Komárek for valuable comments. The usual disclaimer applies.

66 University Complutense of Madrid.

Daniel Sarmiento

Diversity and Authority: Delivering *CILFIT* and *Foto-Frost* in the 1980s

In 1982 the ECJ introduced a major reform in Article 234 TEC (then Article 177 TEEC) by transforming the obligation of national courts of last instance to make references to the ECJ into a discretionary decision. The Court was drawing inspiration from case-law developed by the French Conseil d'Etat, known as the *acte clair* doctrine, by which national courts could solve cases of EC law by their own authority when 'the correct application of Community law may be so obvious as to leave no scope for any reasonable doubt as to the manner in which the question raised is to be resolved'.

This was the contribution of the ECJ in the *CILFIT* case,[67] but it was preceded 19 years earlier by another relevant decision that complements the former. In *Da Costa*,[68] the Court exempted national courts of last instance from making references when the case was 'materially identical with a question which has already been the subject of a preliminary ruling in a similar case'. But while *Da Costa* introduced an exception to the obligation imposed by Article 234 TEC when the ECJ had previously made a decision on an identical case, *CILFIT*'s innovation was much more radical. After all, according to *CILFIT* national courts of last instance could avoid making the reference even *without* a previous decision from the Luxembourg Court, thus transforming them into ultimate arbiters of clear questions of Community law.

The radical appearance of *CILFIT* was nuanced by the ECJ in the same judgment, introducing a series of conditions that national courts were to fulfil before implementing EC law by their own authority. These requirements were supposed to act as a counterbalance to the *acte clair* doctrine, involving that the national court or tribunal 'must be convinced that the matter is equally obvious to the courts of the other member states and to the court of justice', followed by a 'a comparison of the different language versions' and the interpretation 'in the light of the provisions of Community law as a whole' of the relevant provisions.

Despite the strict requirements introduced in *CILFIT*, the soul and body of the judgment remained in its first dictum: the ability of national courts of last instance to implement EC law by their own authority when the result 'may be so obvious as to leave no scope for any reasonable doubt as to the manner in which the question raised is to be resolved'. Being thus the normative nucleus of *CILFIT*, the ECJ had contributed to reverse a clear and unconditional obligation provided by Article 234 TEC. The reasons that pushed the Court to make such a decision are still a matter of debate among legal scholars and practitioners,[69] but the rationale behind *CILFIT* could be sketched in the following terms: first, the Court considered the time had arrived for a decentralised implementation of EC law, particularly by sharing the task with national courts of last instance. Thirty years after the creation of the Community, national courts were ready to assume a prominent role in the judicial implementation of European rules, sending thus a message

[67] Case 283/81 *Cilfit and Others* [1982] ECR 3415.

[68] Joined Cases 28/62 to 30/62 *Da Costa* [1963] ECR 31.

[69] Rasmussen, H, 'Remedying the Crumbling EC Judicial System' (2000) *CML Rev* 37; Trimidas, T, 'Knocking on Heaven's Door. Fragmentation, Efficiency and Defiance in the Preliminary Reference Procedure' (2003) *CML Rev* 40.

of confidence and trust that would ultimately enhance the relationship between community and national courts. Second, *CILFIT* was the first of many judgments designed to implant mechanisms of docket control by the ECJ, in view of the rapid growth of preliminary rulings and the gradual expansion of the Community to new Member States. Third, the generous terms of the first *CILFIT* test and the strict requirements of the second were ambiguous enough to grant a huge discretion to the ECJ at the time of shaping its relationship with national courts. *CILFIT* is an ambivalent judgment that walks in two separate directions, and the Court is able to choose freely which route to take with ample discretion.

Five years after *CILFIT* the ECJ delivered *Foto-Frost*,[70] confirming its exclusive jurisdiction to review community acts in the course of proceedings before national courts. The terms of *Foto-Frost* are clear and unconditional: the ECJ is the only court in the whole Union to determine the validity of both EU and EC acts, imposing on national courts the obligation of making a reference to the Court whenever they have doubts concerning the community provision they must implement. EU lawyers are unanimous about the importance and necessity of *Foto-Frost* in order to mantain the unity and coherence of the community legal order, but in 1987 the argument was not so obvious. Advocate General Mancini's Opinion in the *Foto-Frost* case is a good example of the fears and doubts the ruling posed to the Court, and despite Mancini's support of the Court's decision, he expressed his opinion 'subject to one exception, a number of doubts and, above all, no little apprehension as to how a judgment in accordance with that proposal would be received'.

Foto-Frost was a hard case due to the ambiguous terms of Article 234 TEC, where the obligation to make references was established only for national courts of last instance, granting thus discretionary power to inferior courts. In a literal interpretation of the provision, it could be argued that decisions on the validity of community acts were only to be delivered by the ECJ when they arose before a national court of last instance, but not when the matter was to be decided by inferior courts. In the latter case, national courts had the power, but not the obligation, of making the reference to the ECJ. This interpretation of Article 234 TEC was indirectly supported by previous case law of the Court and the practice of national courts,[71] but the decision in *Foto-Frost* walked in the opposite direction and created an unconditional monopoly of the ECJ to review all community acts, imposing thus a new obligation on inferior national courts. The rationale behind *Foto-Frost* is hierarchy and authority, subject only to one exception: the faculty of national courts to question the validity of community acts in the context of interim measures prior to the ECJ's preliminary ruling.

Centralising and Decentralising the Union's Judicial System: The Search for an Equilibrium and the Quest for Authority

CILFIT and *Foto-Frost* are the best testimony of the ECJ's struggle to deal with its role as the ultimate authority of EC law in a fragile institutional context. While *CILFIT* stands as

[70] Case 314/85 *Foto-Frost* [1987] ECR 4199.

[71] Case 101/78 *Granaria v Hoofdproduktschap voor Akkerbouwprodukten* [1979] ECR 62.

the paradigm of decentralisation and the enhancement of fluid and supportive relations with national courts, *Foto-Frost* is an unambiguous sign of judicial authority underlining the *secondary* role that national courts can play at times when implementing EC law. *CILFIT* devolves powers to national courts, as *Foto-Frost* takes them away.

The logic of the Court's decision can be better understood from the perspective of institutional politics; particularly an institutional analysis of judicial co-operation among courts of autonomous legal systems, where no procedures enable one court to review the decisions of the other. Such is the case of the ECJ in its relation with national courts: the former stands as a supreme interpreter of EC law, but the Treaties have excluded an appeal against national court decisions on points of community law. The only course of judicial communication (and control) between both courts is the preliminary ruling procedure, and *CILFIT* and *Foto-Frost* show how the Court has made an intense use of the mechanism in order to shape its role as the ultimate interpreter of EC law. Using a stick and carrot strategy, the Court has contributed to reinforce its position by handing down judgments that underline the vertical nature of its relation with national courts (*Foto-Frost*), followed by decisions stressing horizontal traits (*CILFIT*).[72]

But despite the horizontal appearance of a judgment like *CILFIT*, the practice of the Court has shown a nuanced but constant inclination towards a vertical approach to national courts. In fact, the Court's policy of dialogue and deference towards national courts has commonly hidden a burst of authority that reinforces the Court's position in the arena of European judicial politics.[73] For instance, *Da Costa* is apparently a generous decision with national courts, exempting them from the obligation of making a reference when the ECJ has previously solved 'materially identical' cases. However, this judgment constitutes the proclamation of a community doctrine of binding precedent for national courts; but hardly binding for the Court. On further occasions, when the Court has claimed its lack of jurisdiction and devolved a matter to national courts, as was the case in *UPA*,[74] this deferral was followed by the creation of a strict obligation for national courts to make preliminary references. This is also the case of *CILFIT*, in which the Court apparently relaxed the obligations as provided by Article 234 TEC, only to accompany such exemption by a list of harsh and deliberately ambiguous conditions to be fulfilled by national courts of last instance. In such terms, the Court was apparently granting further powers to national courts, but *CILFIT* was drafted in such a way that would enable the ECJ to relax or, if circumstances proved fit, toughen its implementation. What seemed to be a further step in the spirit of judicial co-operation tacitly involved another step in the reinforcement of the Court's authority. In a subtle but effective way, the ECJ had fashioned the faults and lacunae of Article 234 in order to transform the preliminary ruling into the closest thing to a European appeal that disciplines the role and decisions of national courts when implementing EC law.

The result of this analysis proves to be rather contradictory: *CILFIT*, traditionally considered a fundamental judgment in the design of co-operative relations between the ECJ and national courts, also hides a hierarchical agenda that struggles to confirm the

[72] Alter, K, *Establishing the Supremacy of European Union Law. The Making of an International Rule of Law in Europe* (Oxford, Oxford University Press, 2001) 38.

[73] Mancini, GF, *Democracy and Constitutionalism in the EU* (Oxford, Hart Publishing, 2001) 23; Craig, P and De Búrca, G, *EU Law* 2nd edn (Oxford, Oxford University Press, 1998) 407–8.

[74] Case C-50/00 P *Unión de Pequeños Agricultores v Council* [2002] ECR I-6677.

authority of the European Court. On the other hand, the paradigm of self-assertions of judicial authority (*Foto-Frost*) finds no foundation in the Treaties and is the result of a creative interpretation of Article 234 TEC by the ECJ, despite the public awareness of its solid aims. Looking at *CILFIT* and *Foto-Frost* in this fashion helps us understand the difficulties of the Court in establishing its role of supreme interpreter of EC law in an institutional context where the founding constitution (the Treaties) have kept silent over the issue. Seen this way, *CILFIT* and *Foto-Frost* seem much more fragile than usual, and we can raise serious doubts over their ability to face the challenges before EU law in the coming years. A challenge that must be dealt with both a creative and realist perspective of the political, social and economic setting in which the future Union will operate. A context the ECJ may well start to envision by adapting *CILFIT* and *Foto-Frost* to the difficulties I will now portray.

Challenging *CILFIT*

Twenty-five years after *CILFIT*, the statistics show a worrying lack of preliminary rulings from national courts of last instance. At first sight this could be a coherent portrayal of the aims pursued by *CILFIT*, but the practice of national courts proves quite the contrary. A brief look at the reports of national case law will show an alarming amount of decisions making questionable interpretations of EC law, where no reference to the ECJ was made due to *CILFIT*. It seems that some national jurisdictions have assumed that *CILFIT* is a general rule that exempts them from making references to the ECJ, transforming thus the exception into the main rule. The inactivity of the courts has forced the Commission and Member States to reconsider the limitation established by Article 68 TEC, whereby the power to raise references under Title IV of the Treaty are limited to national courts of last instance.[75] A limitation that also applies to Spain under Article 35 TEU, in areas sensitive to fundamental rights such as police and judicial co-operation in criminal matters.

Good proof of the national courts' difficulties in handling *CILFIT* are a series of judgments delivered in 2003 and 2004, whereby the ECJ confirmed Member State liability for breach of EC law due to judicial action, followed by the first infringement procedure aimed at judicial decisions contrary to EC law. In *Köbler*[76] and *Commission v Italy*[77] the Court took a significant step by exerting pressure over national courts of last instance, in two cases in which the *CILFIT* doctrine enabled Austrian and Italian courts to hand down manifestly illegal judgments. The *Köbler* saga evidenced a structural problem in the activity of national courts, particularly located in courts of last instance, leading legal scholars to reflect over the convenience of the *CILFIT* doctrine in such a critical context.

[75] 'Adaptation of the provisions of Title IV of the Treaty establishing the European Community relating to the jurisdiction of the Court of Justice with a view to ensuring more effective judicial protection', COM(2006) 346 final.

[76] Case C-224/01 *Köbler* [2003] ECR I-10239.

[77] Case C-129/00 *Commission v Italy* [2003] ECR I-14637.

Afterall, *Köbler* and *Commission v Italy* were not well received by national courts,[78] and the delicate equilibrium described in the previous section of this paper could have been severely damaged due to *CILFIT*'s deterioration.

At this point, *CILFIT*'s reconsideration has been a common cause of concern among EC lawyers. There is a generalised feeling that national courts have got *CILFIT*'s message wrong, either voluntarily or involuntarily. Even members of the Court have stressed their worries about the convenience of this doctrine, proposing reforms or its overruling.[79] Advocate General Ruiz-Jarabo, in the *Gaston Schul* case, openly said *CILFIT* was an 'outrageous' judgment,[80] while academic writers have recently proposed the creation of a right of appeal against decisions of national courts of last instance before the ECJ.[81] The unsolved consequences of *Köbler* add further worries over the future of a judgment like *CILFIT*, particularly after the incorporation of twelve new Member States with inexperienced courts in the area of EC law.

Having regard to the lack of references and the risks underlying *Köbler*, the Court's implementation of *CILFIT* could be reinterpreted and made stricter, thus recovering the normative value of Article 234(3) TEC. This measure could overload the Court's docket, but such fear could be solved by minor reforms. In fact, the institutional arrangements introduced by the Nice Treaty empower the Council to grant jurisdiction to the Court of First Instance to hear preliminary rulings in specialised areas. Although such decentralisation of the procedure has not been yet implemented, its future adoption could well contribute to strengthen the obligation to make references provided by Article 234 TEC, followed by a subtle overruling of *CILFIT*. Sharing competence over preliminary rulings with the CFI would enable the ECJ to make use of the strict conditions included in the second *CILFIT* test, changing thus the perception embedded today in national courts of last instance and taking away part of the unnecessary pressure exerted by *Köbler*. *CILFIT* still has a future, but not in the fashion tolerated by the ECJ in the past 25 years.

Challenging *Foto-Frost*

Unlike *CILFIT*, the terms of *Foto-Frost* have been strictly followed by national courts, keeping intact the ECJ's monopoly over questions of validity of Community acts. However, there is also a considerable pressure over *Foto-Frost*, casting doubts over its

[78] See Wattel, PJ, '*Köbler, CILFIT* and *Welthgrove*: We can't go on meeting like this' (2004) *CML Rev* 41 and Komárek, J, 'Federal elements in the Community judicial system: Building coherence in the Community legal order' (2005) *CML Rev* 42.

[79] Opinion of Advocate General FG Jacobs in Case C-338/95 *Wiener SI* [1997] ECR I-6495; Opinion of Advocate General A Tizzano in Case C-99/00 *Lyckeskog* [2002] ECR I-4839; Opinion of Advocate General C Stix-Hackl in Case C-495/03 *Intermodal Transports* [2005] ECR I-8151 and Opinion of Advocate General D Ruiz-Jarabo Colomer in Case C-461/03 *Gaston Schul Douane-expediteur* [2005] ECR I-1051. Writing extrajudicially, see Lenaerts, K, 'The Unity of European Law and the Overload of the ECJ—The System of Preliminary Rulings Revisited' in Pernice, I, Kokott, J, Saunders, C (eds), *The Future of the European Judicial System in a Comparative Perspective* (Baden-Baden, Nomos, 2006) 219–24.

[80] Opinion of Advocate General D Ruiz-Jarabo Colomer in Case C-461/03 *Gaston Schul Douane-expediteur* [2005] ECR I-1051, 52.

[81] Baquero Cruz, J, 'La procédure préjudicielle suffit-elle à garantir l'efficacité et l'uniformité du droit de l'Union européenne?' in Azoulai, L and Burgorgue-Larsen, L (eds), *L'autorité de l'Union européenne* (Brussels, Bruylant, 2006).

ability to keep its aims 20 years after its conception. Strangely, this pressure has not come from national courts but from the ECJ itself, giving good proof of the challenges facing *Foto-Frost* today.

Having considered the delicate foundations of a judgment like *Foto-Frost*, it may seem surprising to know that the ECJ has exerted further obligations on national courts when facing issues of validity. Such is the case in *Unión de Pequeños Agricultores* (*UPA*),[82] whereby the Court refused to relax the strict standing conditions for private litigants when challenging Community acts in direct actions according to Article 230(4) TEC. Having considered the consequences of this limitation from the perspective of the fundamental right to an effective remedy, the Court kept its strict interpretation of Article 230 TEC, but stressing the terms of *Foto-Frost*. Thus, private parties would still have difficulties to have direct access to community courts, but they should always have the means of posing the question before national courts, and ultimately reach the ECJ through a preliminary reference on validity. But in *UPA* the ECJ stressed that, when a Community act could not be challenged *ex* Article 230 TEC, 'national courts are required, so far as possible, to interpret and apply national procedural rules governing the exercise of rights of action in a way that enables natural and legal persons to challenge before the courts the legality of any decision or other national measure relative to the application to them of a Community act of general application, by pleading the invalidity of such an act'. In other words, *Foto-Frost* has now two normative components: first, its traditional rule on jurisdiction, granting exclusive competence to the ECJ on issues of validity; and second, a positive obligation for all national courts to raise the preliminary ruling when the Community act could not be challenged through a direct action. The terms in which this new obligation are stressed seem to push national courts into an unexpected procedural terrain, forcing them to relax national standing requirements in order to ultimately make the reference. A heavy burden now in hands of national courts, due to the Court's refusal to do exactly what it is now casting in its national counterparts.

Members of the Court have also raised the concerns over *Foto-Frost*'s ability to stand the course of time, even making proposals that undermine the judgment's ability to enforce the Court's institutional position. In *Gaston Schul*,[83] Advocate General Ruiz-Jarabo proposed an exception to *Foto-Frost* when an issue of validity fulfilled the requirements of *Da Costa*. The Court did not follow the Advocate General, but struggled to explain why a national court should raise a reference over a 'materially identical' case previously solved by the Luxembourg court. Further pressure was put by Advocate General Mengozzi in *SEGI*,[84] a delicate case involving the issue of access to the Court in the Second and Third Pillars. In Mengozzi's powerful Opinion (not followed by the Court), the lack of jurisdiction of the community courts on issues of validity (Articles 35 and 46 TEU) was to be supplemented by recognising national courts such powers of review. By stressing the limitations of the ECJ's jurisdiction, Mengozzi was tacitly suggesting that the Treaty on European Union had granted *Foto-Frost*'s powers to both community and national courts, reopening the debate prior to 1985.

We can now see how the apparently crystal-clear simplicity of *Foto-Frost* is hardly a fact. The events of the past years have challenged the logic of a judgment originally designed to

[82] See above note 73.
[83] See above note 79.
[84] Joined Cases C-354 and 355/04 P *Gestoras Pro Amnistía and SEGI* [2007] (unreported).

safeguard the authority of the Court. The growing amount of legislation produced by the Council and Parliament can make us wonder about the ability of the Court to handle its *Foto-Frost* monopoly in the coming years. Criminal and other restrictive legislative acts of the Second and Third Pillars make it ever more difficult to understand the limitations established under Articles 35 and 46 TEU, forcing thus the erosion of *Foto-Frost*'s rationale. An erosion ever more critical once the number of national courts has spectacularly increased due to the incorporation of 12 new Member States. Overall, urgent measures are needed to reinforce the spirit of Foto-Frost, and thus enable the Court to maintain the institutional role once gained, but now may be fading.

Dual Authority: Hierarchical Agendas and a Methodology of Constitutional Discourse

At this point, serious thought is needed in order to re-establish the authority that *CILFIT* and *Foto-Frost* once cast upon the Court. I will suggest that the present circumstances can be solved by a two-fold policy from the Luxembourg court, both vertical and horizontal. Many of the problems underlying *CILFIT* and *Foto Frost* could be corrected by stressing the vertical discourse over national courts, forcing them thus to fulfil their obligations in stricter terms. Decentralising the preliminary reference procedure to the Court of First Instance will contribute to make this new approach possible, at the time *CILFIT*'s second test should be reinforced. A hierarchical approach from community courts would be possible, but only if the discourse becomes horizontal when issues of a constitutional nature are raised before the courts. In this circumstance the ECJ should recover the co-operative rationale underlying Article 234 TEC, granting national courts a considerable margin of action, but having previously made a judgment representative of social, cultural and national sensibilities, where authority is the result of an argumentative discourse, and not a rule of competence. Such context requires a methodology not of constitutional conflict, but of constitutional dialogue, in which all national courts should have the opportunity of having their say, but also a common understanding of the deference the ECJ must be granted.

The criteria to determine what is a constitutional issue will not be easy to identify, but we will always stand before such a case when dealing with fundamental rights, issues of competence between Member States and the EU/EC, or conflicts that have direct consequences on national constitutional provisions. Having located the areas, the methodology of constitutional dialogue should stand over two premises: first, the recognition of the ECJ as the authoritative interpreter of EU/EC law, and therefore its priority to hear and deliver a decision on constitutional issues; second, the obligation of the ECJ to consider all the relevant factors surrounding the case, included the national legal traditions involved (which will ultimately embrace the social and cultural traditions of Member States). The Court's success will enable all national courts to assume a decision based not only on legal, but rational authority as well.[85]

[85] I have made this proposal in *Poder Judicial e Integración Europea* (Madrid, Thomson-Civitas, 2004) 294 *ff.* Also in support of a rational methodology of constitutional conflict, see Kumm, M, 'The Jurisprudence of

Finding the right balance between vertical and horizontal agendas will enable the Court to keep the spirit of *CILFIT* and *Foto-Frost* alive and well. My proposal supports a flexible notion of authority in fundamental issues of constitutional relevance, and a strict approach in all the rest. The logic of federal judiciaries proves quite the contrary, granting a supreme interpreter with the power to give the final decision on fundamental issues. But the process of European integration shows exactly the opposite evolution: a rich cultural tapestry in which 27 sovereign states establish a Union not based on the unity of constitutional identity, but its diversity. The source of legitimacy in Europe is a complex and multilayered process in which all relevant actors have a relevant role to play; a role that becomes vital when the topic of judicial discussion runs into the terrain of constitutional debate.

Keeping *CILFIT* and *Foto-Frost* in such dual context, both horizontal and vertical, will enable the Court, and the Union, to unite in diversity 50 more years, in the same fashion the Treaty of the European Community has so successfully achieved.

Constitutional Conflict: Constitutional Supremacy in Europe before and after the Constitutional Treaty' (2005) 3 *European Law Journal*; Poiares Maduro, M, 'Europe and the Constitution: What if this is as Good as it gets?' in Weiler, JHH and Wind, M (eds), *European Constitutionalism Beyond the State* (Cambridge, Cambridge University Press, 2003).

4

The Juridical *Coup d'État* and the Problem of Authority: *CILFIT* and *Foto-Frost*

ALEC STONE SWEET

As readers of this book well know, the courts—not the Member States—designed the blueprint for legal integration in Europe. As the doctrines of direct effect and supremacy gradually took hold, Article 234 emerged as a kind of central nervous system for the enforcement of EC law and the co-ordination of the EC and the national legal orders. For more than 40 years, this system has successfully managed the myriad complexities of legal integration. It has also heavily conditioned legislative outcomes in a wide range of policy domains, and it has helped to determine the course of European integration more generally (Weiler 1991; Fligstein and Stone Sweet 2002). But the system has never been 'perfected'. It has evolved continuously, often unpredictably, in response to a steady stream of challenges to supremacy arising from litigation of EC law in national courts.

The underlying social logic of the Article 234 system—the key to its success—is that it provides a relatively stable *process* for handling the peculiar problems associated with governing a multi-tiered polity like the EU. This process, however, has not been content-free, because the Court's notion of supremacy is not neutral with respect to the role assigned to national judges. The Court expects national judges to operate as agents of the Community order: when they adjudicate disputes in domains governed by EC law, they are obliged to take decisions with reference, and deference, to that law. As European integration has deepened, the list of duties the ECJ has assigned to national judges, as de facto Community judges, has lengthened.[86] Some judges may inhabit this role naturally and easily, but most will never fully embrace supremacy, at least not as the ECJ conceives it. The Court knows this perfectly well. The Court also knows that it has no means of forcing national judges to accept its jurisdiction or to help it achieve its vision of legal integration. In consequence, the various scholarly accounts suggest, legal integration has proceeded through persuasion, mutual empowerment, and inter-court dialogue (Alter 2001; Slaughter, Stone Sweet and Weiler, eds, 1998).

Some of the anxieties associated with supremacy come to the Court via preliminary references, and the Court has used specific preliminary rulings to clarify its general message. *CILFIT* and *Foto-Frost* are two such cases. Both concern unresolved authority problems created by the Court's bid to constitutionalise the Treaty.

[86] Ultimately, supremacy and direct effect are about enhancing the effectiveness of EC law, but that process has had no ultimate endpoint. Instead, the Court, through Article 234, steadily intrudes on domains previously thought to be immune to its reach; consider the doctrines associated with state liability and effectiveness of remedy.

These problems are not unique to the Article 234 system. Put generically, they are governance situations in which the organ empowered to make the law has no direct, jurisdictional means of obtaining obedience from a second organ, whose exercise of authority is necessary to render the law made by the first organ effective. Such situations have become ubiquitous in Europe. In this chapter, I will focus on how three such situations emerged as a result of what I will call the *juridical coup d'état*.

The Juridical Coup d'État

By the phrase 'juridical coup d'état', I mean a fundamental transformation in the normative foundations of a legal system through the constitutional lawmaking of a court. A 'normative foundation' is a precept of a system's higher law. Although there are differences between Kelsen's conception of the Grundnorm and Hart's (1994) notion of a Rule of Recognition, a juridical coup d'état is a judicial decision that changes both. I conceptualise 'fundamental transformation' restrictively. First, we must be able to infer, reasonably, that the constitutional law produced by the transformation would have been rejected by the founders had it been placed on the negotiating table. Second, the outcome must alter—fundamentally—how the legal system operates, again, in ways that were, demonstrably, unintended by the founders. The transformation will make it impossible for an observer to deduce the new system from institutional design at the ex ante constitutional moment. It will also imply a breach of pre-coup separation of powers orthodoxy. Put differently, traditional separation of powers schemes will fail to model, post-coup, the constitutional roles and limitations conferred on the organs of the state. Last, by 'constitutional lawmaking', I mean the modification of the constitution through adjudication (interpretation and application). A juridical coup d'état constitutes a particular type of lawmaking, one that alters the Basic Norm and a Rule of Recognition.

My notion of the juridical coup d'état raises a range of important issues. First, the question of how to understand an endogenous change in a legal system's Grundnorm, let alone one accomplished through adjudication, is not a simple one. In the first version of his Pure Theory of Law, Kelsen himself equated the idea of 'successful revolution' with a change in the Basic Norm, and used the example of a coup d'état, in which the King is replaced by representative government, as an illustration. After the coup, Kelsen (1934: 54) writes: 'One [now] presupposes a new Basic Norm, no longer the Basic Norm delegating law making authority to the monarch, but [one] delegating authority to the revolutionary government.'

Using these criteria, I can identify three important instances of the *juridical coup d'état* in Europe (perhaps there are more). In 1958, the German Federal Constitutional Court (GFCC) held, in *Lüth*,[87] that since 'constitutional values' (now 'principles') permeate 'all spheres of law', it would henceforth be the duty of the entire judiciary to ensure the compatibility of 'every provision of the private law' with rights. The German Basic Law says no such thing. In 1964 (*Costa*, this volume), the European Court of Justice (ECJ) announced the doctrine of the supremacy of EC law which, in combination with direct effect and Article 234, gradually congealed into the central nervous system mentioned

[87] BVerfGE 7, 198 (1958).

above. The Member States neither provided for the supremacy of the Treaty, nor for the direct effect of the Treaty or of Directives. In 1971, the French Constitutional Council moved to incorporate a charter of rights into the Constitution of the Fifth Republic,[88] knowing full well that the founders had explicitly rejected including such a charter.

Each of these cases constitutes, respectively, the single most important constitutional change in the history of that system. In each, the *juridical coup d'état* provoked systemic change, post-revolution, as its implications materialised and were processed. These changes have been registered on separation of powers doctrines, core components of which have been swept away. And, in each, a specialised constitutional court radically expanded the scope of its own authority, and that of the constitutional law, while generating a set of fundamental authority conflicts. Defined generically, an authority conflict is a governance situation in which the organ empowered to make (or give content to) the law has no direct, jurisdictional means of obtaining obedience from a second organ, whose exercise of authority is necessary to render the law made by the first organ effective. I now turn to how three such situations emerged as a result of what I will call the *juridical coup d'état.*

Cases

Germany

The German Basic Law (1948) gives pride of place to rights provisions and confers on a Federal Constitutional Court (FCC) broad powers—abstract and concrete review authority, as well as jurisdiction over individual constitutional complaints—to protect those rights. The Constitution, however, tells us next to nothing about the status of rights in the private law, or on the scope of the role private law judges ought to play in protecting rights. In 1950, there were good reasons to believe that the Basic Law would not fundamentally alter the relationship between public and private law, and that the latter would retain its autonomy from the former, except at the margins (through concrete review). The founders had rejected proposals to confer judicial review powers on ordinary judges and on the various supreme courts; and they did not stipulate that rights would have effect between private individuals in their legal relations. Academic lawyers dominated the drafting process and, in German doctrine, distinctions between public and private law were considered quasi-absolute. Moreover, the Civil Code (1896) possessed huge prestige, perhaps even the 'real' constitution, given the instability of the public law.

Prior to the *Lüth* case, some judges began to use constitutional rights in their interpretation of certain statutes, without prompting from the FCC, especially in the labor courts. In *Lüth*, the FCC partly legitimised this behaviour. But it went further, requiring that all private law judges employ proportionality analysis to balance (a) rights and (b) other cognisable legal interests (constitutional values inhering in the codes) when the two come into tension in any specific case. According to the Court, the 'value system' expressed by the constitution, and in particular the system of rights, 'affects all spheres of law'. As a result, 'every provision of the private law must be compatible with this system ... and

[88] Council Decision 71/44, *Recueil des Décisions du Conseil Constitutionnel* 29 (1971).

every such provision must be interpreted in its spirit'. When private law judges fail to do so, the FCC asserted, or when they fail to strike a proper balance, they violate 'objective constitutional law', and thus the rights of individuals. Read as a jurisdictional revolution, the ruling created a new cause of action, against the civil law judge, which the FCC would hear through the constitutional complaint procedure.

As subsequently developed, the *Lüth* line of jurisprudence means that 'all private law is directly subject to constitutional rights' (Gardbaum: 20), which means that rights are indirectly effective between individuals. In practice, the difference between direct and indirect effect is negligible (Alexy 2002: 352–65). Indeed, Kumm (2006: 352) goes so far as to argue that if, tomorrow, Germans were to adopt a constitutional amendment designed to make rights *directly* effective between individuals, the amendment 'would change practically nothing'.

By definition, a *juridical coup d'état* is deeply structural, and so are its most important implications. I would emphasise the following in the German case. First, in private law litigation, individuals not only may plead rights; they possess a right to a procedure—proportionality analysis—to determine the scope of their rights in the private law context. Second, the individual complaint procedure has been transformed: after *Lüth*, it becomes a mechanism for monitoring and enforcing the FCC's new constitutional order. My third point is a necessary consequence of the first two. Once rights come into play, the civil judge must reason and decide much as a constitutional judge would. The FCC, for its part, can only properly perform its task—to review how a civil court has balanced rights and other legal values—by intruding on the role of the presiding judge.[89]

Constitutionalist lawyers and judges celebrate the *Lüth* jurisprudence for, in effect, securing and completing the *Rechtsstaat*; but it remains deeply controversial in parts of the private law world.[90] The bottom-line issue is about authority: once the *Rechtsstaat* has been constitutionalised, how can it be defended, given the fragmented structure of judicial authority? The FCC enlists all judges in the project then commands: 'thou shalt balance'. Because, in balancing situations, it is not the doctrine ('thou shalt balance; everything in proportion') but the fact-context that varies, the boundaries between the work of ordinary and constitutional judges will be obliterated, routinely, if the latter is to review the substantive decision-making of the former. Placed in the shadow of the constitutional complaint, civil law judges today record their efforts to arrive at decisions that will satisfy the proportionality requirement. When the FCC overrules them, it is on substantive grounds. It says: 'procedurally you have acted as a good constitutional judge (you have balanced), but you have misinterpreted rights (you have got things out of proportion)'. To repeat, the FCC cannot assess how the private law judge has weighed contending interests, without sifting through the facts and reweighing these same interests.

Sceptics start from the presumption that the civil law judge is in a better position to balance, if balancing there must be. Even the most fervent supporters of *Lüth* acknowledge that balancing is a relatively open-ended exercise in judicial policymaking (Alexy 2002: Postscript). If balancing leads the judge to a choice among at least two (legally defensible) policies, why should the FCC possess the power to impose its preferred policy on the

[89] The comments of Zumbansen (2001) and Hestermeyer (2001), on two recent FCC rulings in this genre, are revealing.

[90] Indeed, the intensity of the scholarly debate about this shows no sign of relenting; see Diederichsen (1998) and Canaris (1999).

courts closest to the dispute—and to the law being interpreted? This issue also emerged in EC law, once the ECJ required national judges to engage in proportionality analysis, as it has, for example, in the adjudication of free movement of goods and indirect sex discrimination claims (Stone Sweet 2004: chs 3, 4).

Though the controversy still rages in Germany, the core of the authority problem can be resolved through the constitutional complaint procedure,[91] as it cannot be in EC law.

France

The founders created the Constitutional Council to help them secure the Government's control over Parliament, which they meant to be virtually absolute. In the *Travaux préparatoires*,[92] efforts to confer upon the Council 'judicial' attributes were blocked (Stone 1990: ch 2). The founders rejected proposals to model the organ on the Austro-German prototype, and they pointedly refused to grant it jurisdiction over rights. Although the Preamble to the 1958 Constitution declares the 'solemn attachment' of the French people to the Preamble of the 1946 Constitution, the drafters of both the 1946 and 1958 constitutions insisted that the preamble was unenforceable as law.[93] In 1971, the Council began to incorporate a set of rights texts, found in the 1946 Preamble, into the 1958 Constitution. By 1979, it had used each of these texts to strike down Government-sponsored statutes adopted by Parliament, and in the 1980s it emerged as a powerful force in French legislative politics.

One expects a *juridical coup d'état* to generate developments that are unforeseeable, and the French case is no exception. In the post-*coup* (Sixth) Republic, for the first time in French history, constitutional rights are enforceable, but not only by the Council.

During the Fourth Republic, the supreme administrative court, the Council of State developed, under the banner of 'general principles of law', various restrictions on administrative action. Most of these principles, including 'individual liberty', 'equality before the law', 'freedom of conscience', and 'non-retroactivity', functioned, *de facto*, as rights. In the 1980s, the Council of State began to convert them into rights, *de jure*, thus securing their permanence and higher law status. It shielded itself by following the Constitutional Council's lead, converting into rights those principles that the latter promoted to a constitutional rung. In 1996, the Council of State took the momentous step of constitutionalising a principle on its own, without prior authorisation by the constitutional judge. For its part, the supreme civil court, Cassation, began to engage in a new form of statutory review in the late 1980s: 'the constitutional correction of legal norms' (Cartier 1995). Ordinary judges are now obliged to interpret provisions of the codes as if they were in harmony with constitutional rights (and, more importantly, with the ECHR). In the presence of a law deemed unconstitutional, all the judiciary can do is correct the law through interpretation, since there is no way for a law, once promulgated, to be annulled.[94]

[91] The gaps in constitutional control that remain can be important in certain cases; see Faller (1990).

[92] *Travaux préparatoires de la Constitution du 4 Octobre 1958*. Paris: Documentation française, 1960.

[93] For the Fourth Republic, see *Débats du 7 Mars, 1946*, Assemblée nationale constituante: 607–39. For the Fifth Republic, see *Travaux préparatoires de la Constitution du 4 Octobre 1958*.

[94] An amendment adopted in July 2008 introduces a procedure for the *ex post* review of the constitutionality of French statutes in force, upon referral by either the Supreme Court (*Cassation*) or the Council of State. See Stone Sweet, 2008.

It is indisputable that the *juridical coup d'état* enhanced the Council of State's authority over the administration, and Cassation's authority over statute. In some meaningful sense, both are now constitutional judges, and both are rights-protecting courts. One could discuss at great length the implications for French separation of powers doctrines that flow from the fact that rights now play a role in the legal order, but yet are outside the Constitutional Council's reach. I will focus instead only on the scope of the latter's authority over the interpretation of rights. Compared to the German Court's position, the Council's authority over the courts is feeble at best. The Council exercises only pre-enforcement abstract review of statutes; there is no formal link between the Council and the judiciary.

In the 1980s, following the examples of the German and Italian constitutional courts, the Council began to issue 'binding interpretations'—rulings declaring that statutory provisions under review could *only* be considered constitutional under one specific interpretation—the narrowest of 'saving constructions' in American parlance. The percentage of decisions containing such pronouncements has increased over time, in some years to as high as 60 per cent. They are meant to bind all public authorities, including judges; to allow otherwise would be to permit a law to be enforced in an unconstitutional way.

The authority problem is obvious: the Council relies on the judiciary to enforce its legal positions, but cannot compel the courts to do so. The position of Cassation has always been that 'there is no legal obligation to follow binding interpretations' (Table Ronde 1995: 279–80). Many civil judges are openly hostile to the idea of being placed under the tutelage of the Council. Their major union, the Professional Association of Judges, went so far as to release a *Communiqué* that called on judges and prosecutors to ignore binding interpretations, which they characterised as 'trivial gloss'.[95] The Council of State also insists that it is not legally bound by the Council's reasoning, although it has sometimes copied binding interpretations into its decisions.

Until the Constitutional Council is given jurisdiction over individual constitutional complaints, the authority problem is irresolvable.

The European Community

In the beginning, the Court aimed direct effect and supremacy -at the Member States. The national courts were not primary targets; instead the Court sought to build them into the mechanism itself. In the early important cases (for example, *Van Gend en Loos*[96]), referring judges showed themselves to be willing partners in the endeavour, all but begging for authorisation to enforce the Treaty against conflicting national rules. The ECJ could not have guessed that supremacy would transform Article 234 into a system that would generate—chronically—massive authority problems which, by their nature, are irresolvable under that system. Today it is obvious that supremacy and direct effect, ultimately, are about the effectiveness of EC law, but 'effectiveness' has had no ultimate endpoint. Instead, the Court steadily intruded on domains previously thought to be immune to its reach; consider doctrines associated with rights, state liability, and effectiveness of remedy.

[95] *Le Monde*, 9 August 1993.

[96] In *Van Gend en Loos* (see this volume), the referring judge exhibited no supremacy anxiety, perhaps due to the strong monism expressed by the Dutch constitution.

The formal story of how supremacy developed has always been accompanied by another set of accounts, stories that are more political science than doctrinal deduction. These accounts seek to explain the evolution of supremacy as strategic choices of the Court, reacting to strategic choices made by national judges. For the most part, they are told by and for academic lawyers, and they dominate the scholarly discourse on supremacy. Although there are differences in approach and focus, there is broad consensus on the basics: that the supremacy saga is a profoundly political process, mediated by constitutional law and Article 234; that this process is relatively open-ended; that it cannot be explained simply in legal terms or any single logic of action; and that it is about the nature and division of judicial authority in Europe. In structure and theme, these stories are also not so different from what one finds in Germany and France, post-*coup*.

I have been asked to comment on *CILFIT* and *Foto-Frost*, two cases that have generated a lively, political science-style debate among academic lawyers. Craig and De Búrca (2003: 439–52) survey and contribute to this political science, and I have learned from and recommend it. I will briefly discuss the cases with reference to two dimensions: supremacy conflict, and case management.

Let me begin with the second dimension, which is an understudied aspect of supremacy politics. These rulings establish parameters for practical decision making within the Article 234 structure. *CILFIT*, in effect, tells national judges that there is now (in 1982) enough redundant case law in the system for them to take greater responsibility for managing EC law in their courtrooms. They are to determine the extent to which EC law is material to any case at bar, and they are to decide how to use that law as precedent, with guidance by the Court on the margins. With the Article 234 docket overloading, the Court says to judges: 'just because a litigant pleads EC law in your courtroom, does not mean that you should file a reference.' The national judge is better positioned to avoid the delays, now growing, entailed by the preliminary reference procedure. If *CILFIT* expands the national judge's discretion to interpret and apply EC law on her own, without a reference, *Foto-Frost* restricts that discretion, requiring a reference when there is good reason to think that the applicable EC law is invalid. *Foto-Frost* significantly reduces the complexity of the national judge's task under Article 234. A litigant can plead invalidity, and the judge can entertain the plea. But she is absolved of having to decide the question, thus escaping a massive investment of resources, with little practical pay off.

More commonly, these cases are recounted as episodes in supremacy politics. If *CILFIT* anoints national judges as full-fledged agents of Community law, it is also a rear-guard, defensive response to an authority conflict. Some national courts, including the French *Conseil d'état* and the German *Bundesfinanzhof*, openly flouted Article 234 requirements, and they applied national law that was clearly invalid under EC law. In *CILFIT*, the ECJ states that a reference is not required in situations of settled law, but requires national judges to ensure that the law really is settled, given strict criteria. The underlying authority problem that afflicts relations between the ECJ and unco-operative court is rooted in the institutional limitations of the Article 234 system, so it cannot be fixed through a preliminary ruling that is, in the end, addressed to the co-operative courts. *Foto-Frost* too looks ineffectual, even beside the point, when considered from the point of view of the complicated *Kompetenz-Kompetenz* questions that have emerged. The Court's ruling comes after some national courts had already stated that they possessed independent authority to assess the validity of EC norms.

These authority conflicts are irresolvable under the present Article 234 system.

A Defence

Consider the null proposition: the *juridical coup d'état* is a theoretical impossibility. The null proposition will be valid if the following statement is true: constitutions that confer upon a court the power of constitutional review impose no meaningful *substantive* constraints on the exercise of that court's review authority. If the null proposition holds, one cannot ask if the terms of any constitutional ruling is 'unfounded' or 'not authorised' by the constitution. Indeed, it would make no sense to ask if the court ever decided a case wrongly, as a matter of substantive law. Although some readers may lean toward the null proposition, many legal theorists, and nearly all European doctrinal authorities, spend a great deal of time asking whether important decisions were, in fact, decided correctly. Why is that?

I would be shocked, but not unhappy, if one day I were to discover that a consensus had formed around the null proposition (but I have no stake in the survival of Continental legal science). If one rejects the null proposition, however, then it would seem that my phrase, *juridical coup d'état*, rings true. Here's what Hans Kelsen writes in his *Pure Theory of Law* (1992: 208–09):

> The principle that a norm of a legal order is valid until its validity is terminated in a way determined by this legal order or replaced by the validity of another norm of this order, is called the principal of legitimacy. The principal is applicable to a legal order with one important limitation only: It does not apply in case of a revolution. A revolution in the broader sense of the word—that includes a *coup d'état*—is every not-legitimate change of this constitution, or its replacement by another constitution. From the point of view of legal science, it is irrelevant whether this change of the legal situation has been brought about by the application of force against the legitimate government, or by members of the government themselves .... Decisive is only that the valid constitution has been changed or replaced in a manner not prescribed by the constitution [that was] valid until then.

Constitutional courts are an obvious and significant part of government in modern constitutional systems of delegated powers. When they delegate to themselves new jurisdictional authority, in 'a manner not prescribed by the constitution', thereby fundamentally changing the structure of delegated arrangements, then we are presumptively in the world of the *juridical coup d'état.*

Kelsen then goes on to discuss why some constitutional transformations are in fact changes in the Grundnorm (when they are deeply structural). It seems impossible to deny that the Grundnorm changed in France when, in the decade of the 1970s, for the first time since the Great Revolution, fundamental rights became enforceable, by an extra-parliamentary body, against statutes duly adopted by Parliament. In the EC, during the period bounded by *Van Gend en Loos* and *Simmenthal II*, we discovered that a host of constitutional orthodoxies (and prohibitions on judicial power) in place in the Member States were legally invalid under the Treaty of Rome. In France and the EC, courts announced new norms governing the system of delegated powers, and these norms replaced old ones. I suspect that Kelsen would not be surprised to learn that systemic transformation was the result. Others, including the many political scientists who deny the power and agency of norms and normative discourse, should be surprised.

Concluding Comments

This chapter has probably raised more questions than it has answered. I will conclude with brief comments on issues that deserve more explicit treatment.

First, my interest in the juridical *coup d'état* is empirical, not normative. Indeed, I take no normative position whatsoever on these developments. Most German and French constitutional lawyers, and most EU law scholars, defend what has happened in the fields of their respective expertise. Many scholars who specialise in legal domains that have been disturbed by these changes have been far more critical. Indeed, each of these *coups* set off doctrinal wars that have not been extinguished to this day. One of my claims is that any attempt to justify these rulings as deductions from the *Grundnorm* or from black-letter constitutional law, will fail, precisely because such rulings altered, fundamentally, the *Grundnorm* itself. As a result, a huge amount of doctrinal activity is devoted to defending the *coup d'état* on functional[97] and other normative grounds. These normative debates are important to me to the extent that they have been important to how the law has subsequently developed, post-*coup*.

Second, in these cases, the juridical *coup d'état* led to a steady growth of judicial power, *vis à vis* that of legislators and executives. Courts are more central to the process through which the constitution and the polity evolves than they would have been had the *coup* not occurred. Although each also produced an authority problem between judges, dealing with it did not diminish the judiciary's centrality. There is no paradox. In each case, the *coup* expanded the reach of rights across the legal system, while leaving intact the system's organisational architecture: a judiciary of independent, functionally differentiated courts. Garlicki (2007) has recently argued that the authority problem inheres in the European model of constitutional review. If so, the *coup d'état* not only exacerbated the problem, it perhaps even made it inevitable.

Third, as this volume is partly concerned with 'the path dependence' of the law, it is worth noting that the juridical *coup d'état* comprises, by definition, what economic historians and 'historical institutionalists' would call a 'critical juncture'—a rupture in norms and practices that starts a social system down a new but unpredictable path (Stone Sweet 2002b). From the point of view of the founders of the constitution, the new path was unintended, and the systemic consequences of the *coup* could not have been foreseen. From the point of view of the judges who propagated the *coup*, the authority problem that emerged was unintended. Yet, in each of our cases, the authority problem itself generated dynamics that have helped propel the system forward.

References

Alexy, Robert (2002), *A Theory of Constitutional Rights*, Oxford, Oxford University Press.
Alter, Karen (2001), *Establishing the Supremacy of European Law*, Oxford, Oxford University Press.

[97] By a 'functional defence', I mean a normative evaluation of a judicial ruling in view of the purported benefits it will provide to society; the good provided may be moral, economic, political, legal, and so on. In each of my three cases, it is the functional defence of the juridical *coup* that counts in the mainstream scholarly discourse on the matter.

Canaris, Claus-Wilhelm (1999), *Grundrechte und Privatrecht—eine Zwischenbilanz*, Berlin, Walter de Gruyter.

Cartier, Marie-Elisabeth (1995), 'La Cour de Cassation et L'application de la Déclaration des Droits de 1789', in *La Cour de Cassation et la Constitution de la République*, Aix-en-Provence, Presses Universitaire d'Aix-en-Provence.

Craig, Paul, and Gráinne de Búrca (2003), *EU Law: Text, Cases and Materials*, Oxford, Oxford University Press.

Diederichsen, Uwe (1998), 'Das Bundesverfassungsgericht als oberstes Zivilgericht—ein Lehrstück der juristischen Methodenlehre', *Archiv für die civilistische Praxis* 171 *ff.*

Faller, Hans-Joachim (1990), Budesverfassungsgericht und Bundesgerichtshof, 115 *Archiv des Offentlichen Rechts.*

Gardbaum, Stephen (2003), 'The "Horizontal Effect" of Constitutional Rights', 102 *Michigan Law Review* 388.

Garlicki, Lech (2007), 'Constitutional Courts versus Supreme Courts', 5 *International Journal of Constitutional Law* 44.

Hart, HLA (1994), *The Concept of Law* 2nd edn, Oxford, Oxford University Press.

Hestermeyer, Holger (2001), 'A Chamber of the Federal Constitutional Court Endorses Private Dentists' Information Service and Directory within the Framework of the Right to Occupational Freedom', 2 *German Law Journal* 18 (1 December). Online at http://www.germanlawjournal.com/article.php?id=112.

Kelsen, Hans (1934), B Litschewski-Paulson and S Paulson trans 1992, *Introduction to the Problems of Legal Theory: a Translation of the First Edition of the Reine Rechtslehre or Pure Theory of Law*, Oxford, Clarendon.

Kumm, Mattias (2006), 'Who is Afraid of the Total Constitution? Constitutional Rights as Principles and the Constitutionalization of Private Law', 7 *German Law Journal* 4. Online at http://www.germanlawjournal.com/article.php?id=724.

Slaughter, Anne-Marie, Alec Stone Sweet, and Joseph Weiler, eds (1998), *The European Court and the National Courts—Doctrine and Jurisprudence: Legal Change in its Social Context*, Oxford, Hart Publishing.

Stone, Alec (1990), *The Birth of Judicial Politics in France*, New York, Oxford University Press.

Stone Sweet, Alec (2002), 'Path Dependence, Precedent, and Judicial Power', in M Shapiro and A Stone Sweet, *On Law, Politics, and Judicialization*, Oxford, Oxford University Press, ch 2.

Stone Sweet, Alec (2004), *The Judicial Construction of Europe*, Oxford, Oxford University Press.

Stone Sweet, Alec (2008), 'Le Conseil Constitutionnel et la Transformation de la République', *Les Cahiers du Conseil Constitutionnel* (25), 65–9.

Zumbansen, Peer (2001), 'Federal Constitutional Court Bans Shock Ads: Free Expression, Fair Competition, and the Opaque Boundaries between Political Message and Social Standards', 2 *German Law Journal* 1 (15 January). Online at http://www.germanlawjournal.com/article.php?id=14.

Weiler, Joseph (1991), 'The Transformation of Europe', 100 *Yale Law Journal* 2403.

VI

Case 22/70, *Commission of the European Communities v Council of the European Communities (European Agreement on Road Transport, ERTA)*; Joint Cases C-466/98, *Commission v United Kingdom*; C-467/98, *Commission v Denmark et al (Open Skies Judgments)* and *Opinion of the Court 2/94 on the Accession by the Community to the European Convention for the Protection of Human Rights and Fundamental Freedoms*

1

The EC External Competencies: From the *ERTA* Case to the Opinion in the Lugano Convention

PAOLO MENGOZZI

In 1994, in its Opinion 1/94, the Court of Justice had hardened its attitude on the existence, in some areas, of an implicit exclusive Community competence, by marking a change from the one adopted in the *ERTA* case, which was definitely open, to a strongly restrictive one. With the judgment in the *ERTA* case (22/70[1]), pronounced on 31 March 1971, the Court, in broad terms, affirmed that 'each time the Community, with a view to implementing a common policy envisaged by the Treaty, adopts provisions laying down common rules, whatever form these may take', in such a matter, 'the Member States no longer have the right, acting individually or even collectively, to undertake obligations with third countries which affect those rules. As and when such common rules come into being, the Community alone is in a position to assume and carry out contractual obligations towards third countries affecting the whole sphere of application of the Community legal system. With regard to the implementation of the provisions of the Treaty the system of internal Community measures may not therefore be separated from that of external relations.'

The language used by the Court became slightly cautious in Opinion 1/76 delivered on 26 April 1977 on the compatibility with the EC Treaty of a 'draft agreement establishing a European laying-up fund for inland waterway vessels'. Stating in this regard, the Court had specified that 'whenever Community law has created for the Institutions of the Community powers within its internal system for the purpose of attaining a specific objective, the Community has authority to enter into the international commitments *necessary* for the attainment of that objective even in the absence of an express provision in that connexion'.[2] However, in this instance, the Court did not overly insist on such an idea of necessity. It simply remarked that the Community's competence to enter into 'the international commitments necessary for the attainment' of a Community objective was in that case reasonable, as necessary in itself, without questioning whether these commitments could be undertaken by the Member States or, for the peculiarity of the situation, should be undertaken because inextricably linked to the attainment of a Community objective.

In Opinion 2/91 delivered on 19 March 1993, the language used by the Court became more mindful in order to control the exclusive competence of the Community to conclude

[1] ECR, 263.
[2] ECR 1977, 357.

Convention No 170 of the International Labour Organization concerning safety in the use of chemicals at work. In this Opinion the Court, expressing a more clearly defined criterion, deemed that the Member States were no longer provided with the power to conclude agreements in a particular area and that, therefore, in the same area the Community had exclusive external competence, in every case where such area was already, *to a large extent*, covered, on an internal level, by Community rules with the objective of achieving complete harmonisation and not containing minimum requirements only.[3]

With Opinion 1/94, delivered on 15 November 1994[4] with reference to the conclusion of the agreements signed on 15 April 1994 in Marrakech at the end of the Uruguay Round, the Court took the above-mentioned strongly restrictive attitude in excluding the exclusive competence of the Community to conclude two multilateral commercial agreements concerning services and the protection of intellectual property. In doing so, definitely taking a new departure in respect of what it had deemed in the past, the Court went on to affirm that there is an external exclusive competence of the Community, based on the previous exercise of powers attributed to it only in the internal plan, only a) if 'it has included in its internal legislative acts provisions relating to the treatment of nationals of non-member countries or expressly conferred on its institutions powers to negotiate with non-member countries', b) if the area has been the object, on a Community level, of a *complete* harmonisation or c) if, in the absence of such harmonisation, the conclusions of the agreement from the Community is 'intrinsically linked', and, therefore, absolutely indispensable to the attainment of the objectives of the Community.

The Court confirmed this rigid attitude in the 'Open skies'[5] judgment which it pronounced on an infringement proceeding brought by the Commission towards some member countries because they had renewed some bilateral agreements concerning air transport concluded with the United States of America before the institution of the Community and in spite of the fact that, in the meantime, the Community had adopted internal legislation in this area with regulations nos 2407/92 of the Council of 23 July 1992 on licensing of air carriers,[6] 2408/92 of the Council of 23 July 1992 on access for Community air carriers to intra-Community air routes,[7] 2409/92 of the Council of 23 July 1992 on fares and rates for air services,[8] 2299/89 of the Council of 24 July 1989 on a code of conduct for computerised reservation systems,[9] as modified by Regulations 3089/93 of the Council of 29 October 1993[10] and 95/93 of the Council of 18 January 1993 on common rules for allocation of slots at Community airports.[11] The Commission assumed that the adoption of these regulations by the Community had given place to an exclusive competence of the latter to conclude international agreements with reference to the whole area of international air transport.

[3] ECR 1993, I-1061, 25.

[4] ECR, I-5267.

[5] Court of Justice, judgments of 5 November 2002, C-475/98, *Commission v Austria*, ECR I-9797, C-471/98, *Commission v Belgium*, ECR I-9681, C-467/98, *Commission v Denmark*, ECR I-9519, C-469/98, *Commission v Finland*, ECR I-9627, C-476/98, *Commission v Germany*, ECR I-9855, C-472/98, *Commission v Luxembourg*, ECR I-9741, C-466/98, *Commission v United Kingdom*, ECR I-9427, C-468/98, *Commission v Sweden*, ECR I-9575.

[6] OJEC L 240 of 24.08.1992, 1.

[7] OJEC L 15 of 23.01.1993, 33.

[8] OJEC L 240 of 24.08.1992, 15 .

[9] OJEC L 220 of 29.07.1989, 1.

[10] OJEC L 278 of 11.11.1993, 1.

[11] OJEC L 14 of 22.01.1993, 1.

After having recalled the different criteria which it had previously used without choosing the one or the ones to be considered preferable,[12] the Court, first of all, proceeded to compare the bilateral agreements which were the object of the infringement proceeding with Regulations 2407/92 and 2408/92. Evaluating those agreements according to the criteria resulting from the *ERTA* judgment it deemed that they could not be regarded as 'affecting those regulations'.[13] Evaluating, then, the same agreements, in the light of the criterion developed in Opinion 1/94, according to which the Community's exclusive competence arises when a complete internal set of rules exists, the Court deemed that these two regulations would not comply with this criterion denying that the discipline of the bilateral agreements conflicted, under this profile, with the Community's exclusive competence.

Passing to a comparison of these bilateral agreements with Regulation 2409/92, with a statement, surely incisive, but certainly not presenting the breadth it could have by completely following the criteria previously expressed in the *ERTA* judgment and in Opinion 2/91, the Court deemed that they conflicted with an exclusive Community competence as they concern fares charged by air carriers other than Community air carriers where they operate on intra-Community routes because 'Regulation 2409/92 has, indirectly but definitely, prohibited air carriers of non-member countries which operate in the Community from introducing new products or fares lower than the ones existing for identical products'.

By adopting Opinion 1/03 delivered on 7 February 2006 concerning the 'competence of the Community to conclude the new Lugano Convention on jurisdiction and the recognition and enforcement of judgments in civil and commercial matters',[14] the Court formally took up the technique it had used in the 'Open skies' judgments to recall the criteria already expressed in the *ERTA* judgment and in Opinions 1/76, 2/91 and 1/94, but, in doing so, it innovated in a substantial way. After having recalled the stand it had taken prior to Opinion 1/94 and in the 'Open skies' judgment, the Court pointed out that the three above-mentioned situations, in its cited judgments, where an exclusive competence of the Community must be recognised, 'are, however, only examples, formulated in the light of the particular contexts with which the Court was concerned'. In so doing, contrary to what it had done in the judgments adopted on 5 November 2002, it took a stand which substantially consists in a concrete renewal and expansion of the broad criterion which it had expressed in the *ERTA* judgment.[15] At point 122 the Court recalled having already recognised in that judgment (point 31) 'to be exclusive Community competence in particular where the conclusion of an agreement by the Member States is incompatible with the unity of the common market and the uniform application of Community law'. It surely added that a) 'where, given the nature of the existing Community provisions, such as legislative measures containing clauses relating to the treatment of nationals of

[12] For a criticism of the method so followed by the Court, see McLean, D, *The ECJ Advisory Opinion No 1/03*, report presented to the Round Table 'The external competence of the European Union and Private International Law', The Court's Advisory opinion on the Lugano Convention, Milan, 16 September 2006.

[13] Court of Justice, 5 November 2002, C-467/98, 92.

[14] ECR 2006, I-1145.

[15] For a remark according to which the Court of Justice has taken 'the principles set out in the *ERTA* judgments seriously' compare Kohler, C, *The European Court's Opinion on the Competence of the Community to conclude the new Lugano Convention*, Report presented to the Round Table 'The external competence of the European Union and Private International Law', the Court's Advisory Opinion on the Lugano Convention, Milan, 16 September 2006, not yet published.

non-member countries or to the complete harmonisation of a particular issue, any agreement in that area would necessarily affect the Community rules within the meaning 'of the above-mentioned ERTA judgment' and 1, at point 126, b) 'it is not necessary for the areas covered by the international agreement and the Community legislation to coincide fully'; however, it also pointed out that 'it is also necessary to take into account not only the current state of Community law in the area in question but also its future development, insofar as that it is foreseeable at the time "where that analysis must be done"'. And, above all, it concluded that 'in short, it is essential to ensure a uniform and consistent application of the community rules and the proper functioning of the system which they establish in order to preserve the full effectiveness of Community law'.

On such a broad criterion which marked a shift from a 'largely harmonised' test towards a more flexible, dynamic 'effect on Community law' test,[16] the Court placed only one limit: in the wake of an adjustment that the Court made according to which, comparing the agreement concluded with existing Community rules, the assessment must be based not only on the scope of the rules in question but also on their nature and content, it specified (at 132) that 'if an international agreement contains provisions which presume a harmonization of legislative or regulatory measures of the Member States in an area for which the Treaty excludes such harmonization, the Community does not have the necessary competence to conclude that agreement. Those limits of the external competence of the Community concern the very existence of that competence and not whether or not it is exclusive.'

The favourable attitude to the acknowledgment of the exclusive competence of the Community to conclude international agreements which, in this way, it showed on a general level, was broadly confirmed by the Court, through the re-examination of the principles listed in its previous case law, to rule specifically on the competence of the Community to conclude the new Lugano Convention. In this respect, evidence of it is constituted by the Court's adoption of the first among the three criteria listed in Opinion 1/94 according to which 'whenever the Community has included in its internal legislative acts provisions relating to the treatment of nationals of non-member countries ..., it acquires exclusive external competence in the spheres covered by those acts'.

Regulation 44/2001, which regulates the area as far as relationship between the Community and the other States of the Lugano Convention is concerned, at its Article 4, paragraph 1, foresees that 'if the defendant is not domiciled in a member State, the jurisdiction of the courts of each Member State shall, subject to Articles 22 and 23, be determined by the law of that Member State'. In spite of the fact that the doctrine unanimously deems that this provision leaves to the Member States the discipline of judicial competence in regards to persons domiciled in non-Member States,[17] the Court attributed to it the function of having given a Community character to the provisions of

[16] See, in this sense, Lavranos, N, *Case Law A. Court of Justice Opinion 1/03*, in *CML Rev* 2006, 1095, recalled by Kohler, above note 15.

[17] For a remark of general character according to which, when Community discipline does not extend to certain aspects of a matter, the Member States maintain their competence to regulate those aspects of that matter in the national order or in the relationship with the non-Member States, see Pocar, F, *La comunitarizzazione del diritto internazionale privato: una 'European conflict of law revolution'?*, in Riv di diritto internazionale privato e processuale, 2000, 880. More specifically, in the sense indicated in the text, see Gaja, G, 'Sulla competenza della CE rispetto alla cooperazione giudiziaria in materia civile' in *Il Corriere giuridico* 2006, suppl 2, 37; Kohler, C, *The European Court's opinion on the competence of the Community to conclude the new Lugano Convention* – Report presented at the Round Table 'The external competence of the European Union and private international law'. In

the Member States concerning such specific subject.[18] In so doing, attributing to the provision a function contrary to which that the drafters of Regulation 44/2001 had attributed to it, the Court was able to affirm that the Community has an implicit exclusive competence in the area because Regulation 44/2001 includes 'provisions relating to the treatment of nationals of non-member countries'.[19]

The stand so taken by the Court is open to discussion. However, it constitutes the manifestation of the Court's will to respond to the fact that the widening of Community law to the discipline of what, broadly speaking, is private international law, is linked to the progressive establishment of an area of freedom, security and justice and to the will of the Member States to place firmly in the Community juridical order the measures adopted in the area of judicial co-operation in the civil area.[20] The near future will clarify if it is a fortuitous attitude linked to the matter on which the Court ruled or if it is really a veritable, definitive reversal of trend.[21]

the same sense see, moreover, the stands taken by the Council and most governments which submitted their observations to the Court, as indicated at point 64 of Opinion 1/03.

[18] On the point see Kohler, above note 15, who recalls that this idea of 'comunitarisation' has been contained in the Commission's and the Parliament's observations before the Court.

[19] See McLean, D, *The EC Advisory opinion 1/03*, 6 *ff.* When taking its stand, the Court may have been encouraged by the fact that, during the procedure which led to the adoption of such opinion, the Council, with *Decision* 2005/790/EC of 20 September 2005, firstly authorised the Commission to negotiate an agreement between the European Community (without the contribution of Member States and therefore in the frame of the extension of an exclusive competence) and the Kingdom of Denmark which extends to Denmark the provisions of Regulation (EC) 44/2001 of the Council, on jurisdiction and the recognition and enforcement of judgments in civil and commercial matters and, then, its own President to designate the person(s) empowered to sign the Agreement on behalf of the Community. One cannot overlook the fact that such encouragement has reached the Court even if during the procedure, as it results from point 64 of the opinion, the Council, in formal consistency with the fact that it 'exceptionally' authorised the negotiation and the signature of the agreement with Denmark, remarked that the regulation at issue, at Article 4(1), leaves the Member States free to determine the jurisdiction of their courts where the defendant is not domiciled in the Community; in so doing, the Council, rather, put forward an argument diametrically opposed to the one on which the Court based the solution given to the problem. Obviously the stand firmly taken by the Council with Decision 2005/790/EC induced the Court to attribute less weight to the stand taken during the procedure by the Council and to consider Decision 2005/790/EC as constituting, beyond all criticisms resulting from the qualification of the authorisation contained therein as 'exceptionally' given, the substantial sign of a maturing, even in the sensitivity of the Council, of a need for the extension of the exclusive competence of the Community to conclude international agreements on jurisdiction and the recognition and enforcement of judgments in civil and commercial matters.

[20] On the same sense see Kohler, above note 15.

[21] For a remark according to which the solution adopted by the Court in opinion 1/03 has been 'strongly pursued by the Commission, even when, according to the principles, a sharing of the Community and of the Member-States in concluding agreements with non Member-States in the area of judicial cooperation should result' and for taking back of this attitude to a more general interest to strengthen the negotiating position in the relationship with Member States, which 'favours the attribution of the competence to an only actor: the Community', see Gaja, G, 'Sulla competenza della CE rispetto alla cooperazione giudiziaria in materia civile', 37. On the possible practical consequences of Opinion 1/03 for the Community's and the Member States' international relations see Eeckhout, P, *General Report on the External Relations of the EU and the Member States (Topic 3) to the 22nd FIDE Congress*, 278. According to this author 'perhaps it is possible to consider distinguishing between the existence of exclusive Community competence and its exercise'; the Community as it does in the field of the common commercial policy, could in some cases simply authorise the Member States to act under its supervision. In the same sense see Mischo, J, *Luxembourg National Report*, 140.

2

Bold Constitutionalism and Beyond

PIET EECKHOUT*

The *ERTA* decision is arguably the single most important judgment the Court has handed down in the field of EC external relations law. It is difficult to overestimate its significance for the EU's external action. This significance is not confined to the history of EC law: today, the principle which the Court established is more relevant than ever before. As the EC's legislative activity grows, so does the EC's exclusive external competence to conclude any international agreement which contains provisions 'affecting' an instrument of Community law. The enormous scope of this exclusive competence is insufficiently appreciated, and the actual practice hardly manages to catch up with its expansion. Many examples could be given, but I will confine myself to just a couple. In the framework of the fight against terrorism various UN Security Council Resolutions imposing sanctions and other measures are implemented by way of EC Regulations. Once such a regulation is in force, there is, following *ERTA*, exclusive EC competence for the adoption of any further UN Resolutions or decisions affecting it (for example a de-listing decision). Of course the Community is not a member of the Security Council, and cannot therefore itself exercise such competence. Nevertheless, those EU Member States which are Security Council members are not in principle acting in their own capacity, but are EC agents which should act in accordance with common positions reached in Brussels.[22] In the field of human rights protection, EC external competence is likewise expanding, in particular since the adoption of the 2000 Directives on non-discrimination.[23] Any international negotiation touching upon issues of non-discrimination on grounds of race, religion, belief, age, etc, comes within the EC's exclusive competence. This includes negotiations in the Council of Europe, again notwithstanding the fact that the Community is not a party to the ECHR, and notwithstanding the Court's ruling in the *ECHR Opinion*, commented upon below. Many other examples could be given of how broadly the *ERTA* logic in principle works.

The significance of *ERTA* does not merely flow from its practical consequences. The judgment established a strong constitutionalist approach to EC external relations law, and was markedly activist and supportive of European integration. Today we are used to the *ERTA* principle, and the approach which the Court adopted may seem legally obvious. In

* Professor of European Law and Director, Centre of European Law, King's College London; associate academic member, Matrix Chambers, London. This contribution builds on the more extensive treatment of the implied-powers case law in P Eeckhout, *External Relations of the European Union – Legal and Constitutional Foundations* (Oxford, Oxford Uuniversity Press, 2004) ch 3.

[22] This follows from Opinion 2/91 *re ILO Convention No 170* [1993] ECR I-1061, para 37.

[23] Directive 2000/43 implementing the principle of equal treatment between persons irrespective of racial or ethnic origin [2000] OJ L 180/22 and Directive 2000/78 establishing a general framework for equal treatment in employment and occupation [2000] OJ L 303/16.

order to safeguard the uniformity and effectiveness of EC legislation, one cannot allow Member States to negotiate and conclude international agreements whose provisions may affect such legislation. The Community needs to be involved with a view to ensuring congruity between internal legislation and international commitments. But we are of course all blinded by more than 30 years of gazing at the judgment and the stream of case law and commentary which sprung from it. The Court could easily have adopted a different approach. The EEC Treaty, as it stood, referred to the conclusion of international agreements in just a couple of articles: essentially on commercial policy and on association. The article on how to conclude such agreements (now Article 300 EC) opened with 'Where this Treaty provides for the conclusion of agreements . . .', suggesting that there was external competence only where the Treaty expressly provided for it. The EEC Treaty did not contain a parallelism principle, in contrast with the EAEC Treaty (Article 101). Advocate General Dutheillet de Lamothe was of the view that implied powers, as known in US law, could not be reconciled with the principle of conferral. It is true that the Court had to find a solution to the problem that the ERTA negotation covered a subject on which the EC had legislated. However, that solution could have been found outside the sphere of exclusive treaty-making competence. The Court could have applied a rule of primacy, as further analysed below. International law obligations could have been dealt with along the same lines as other problems of conflict between Community law and the laws of the Member States.

The Court, instead, chose the path of avoiding potential conflicts by preferring the institutional mechanism of exclusive external competence. It not only confirmed that the Community could act internationally across the entire range of its law-making activities, but harnassed this international capacity by excluding autonomous Member State action in areas where the Community has legislated. The political and even constitutional sensivity of such a bold external competence claim could hardly be overrated. Exclusive competence is exceptional in the Community's constitutional order, and where it affects the external sovereignty of the Member States it is even more delicate.

ERTA created a clear path dependency: international action by Member States which may affect EC law, and by extension international lawmaking in general, is looked at through a competence prism, a prism through which one mainly looks at one type of analysis, ie whether there is exclusive EC competence or not. *ERTA* set the scene for a long series of institutional battles focusing on the external powers of the Community. That approach was strengthened by the Court's confirmation that the common commercial policy also comes within the EC's exclusive competence.[24] At institutional level this perspective has been internalised by the Commission and the Council, who consider fighting for Community, respectively national, competence a core function. The competence battles are now replicated at the level of the relationship between the three EU pillars.[25]

Was the creation of this path dependency justified? *ERTA* was clearly appropriate in its historical legal and political context. The ERTA agreement covered an important element of transport policy, and EC absence from international transport negotiations would have made the development of the fledgling common transport policy even more difficult. The Regulation which triggered exclusive Community competence was next to identical to

[24] Opinion 1/75 *re Understanding on a Local Cost Standard* [1975] ECR 1355.

[25] See, eg, Case C-176/03 *Commission v Council* [2005] ECR I-7879 (environmental penalties) and Case C-91/05 *Commission v Council* [2008] ECR I-3651.

ERTA's content. Moreover, *ERTA* was decided not long after the empty chair crisis, which gave rise to the Luxembourg compromise – a time of political and institutional stagnation. The Court was right, in those circumstances, to make an attempt to safeguard the role of the Community's institutions, and of the Commission in particular.

Did the *ERTA* exclusive competence approach best fit the EC legal system as a whole, and is it still justified, today, to look at the EU's role in international lawmaking exclusively, or at any rate mainly, through the *ERTA* prism? I am not convinced that a resounding yes is the right reply to those questions.

The first point to note is that the term 'exclusive competence' is somewhat deceptive, in that it may suggest that, where such competence is present, the Community alone will be able to conclude the international agreement at hand. In practice that will only rarely be the case. The EC's exclusive competence is limited to those provisions of the international agreement which 'affect' EC legislation. The standard case is therefore that such competence is partial. Other parts of the agreement may come within the Community's concurrent competences, indeed certain provisions may not be within the Community's competence at all. *ERTA* is therefore foundational to the practice of concluding mixed agreements. In this practice, which continues to dominate EC external policies, the question is not so much whether the Community will participate in an international negotiation, and conclude the resulting agreement, on its own. The question is rather whether there is exclusive competence for part of the negotiation and agreement, and as a result whether a mixed agreement is needed.

This is not the place to analyse all the difficulties and problems which 'mixity' causes. But the list is long, and continues to grow. Mixed agreements give rise to difficult questions of delineation of Community and Member States' competences. In most cases there is no express delineation, creating uncertainty for third countries and institutional tension within the Community.[26] Where there is a declaration of competences, it is often vague and not very helpful.[27] At international law level all this leads to complex issues of international responsibility.[28] Where an international agreement provides for its own dispute settlement system, again questions may arise as to the respective positions and roles of the Community and its Member States.[29]

As was mentioned, the legal justification for the *ERTA* approach lies in safeguarding the uniformity and effectiveness of Community law. As the Court phrased it recently in the *Lugano Convention Opinion*, the purpose of *ERTA* competence is 'to ensure that the agreement is not capable of undermining the uniform and consistent application of the Community rules and the proper functioning of the system which they establish'.[30] Let us consider this a little further.

The logic of the Court's reasoning is that Community participation in the international negotiation will ensure that the resulting agreement is consistent with existing EC legislation. Of course, the outcome of that negotiation may also be inconsistent, requiring

[26] As to the latter see, eg, Case C-25/94 *Commission v Council* [1996] ECR I-1469 (FAO).

[27] Eg, the declaration of competences for UNCLOS, see Case C-459/03 *Commission v Ireland* [1996] ECR I-4635 (Mox Plant).

[28] Cf P Eeckhout, 'The EU and its Member States in the WTO – Issues of Responsibility', in L Bartels and F Ortino (eds), *Regional Trade Agreements and the WTO Legal System* (Oxford, Oxford University Press 2006) 449–64.

[29] *Commission v Ireland*, cited above.

[30] Opinion 1/03 *re Lugano Convention* [2006] ECR I-1145, para 133.

the Community to amend internal legislation, but then at least that decision will consciously (one hopes) be taken by the competent Community institutions.[31] Furthermore, a Community agreement is an inherent part of Community law, and thus subject to the Court's jurisdiction. This enables the Court to ensure the uniform interpretation of Community law as a whole – the agreement and internal legislation.

If, by contrast, individual Member States could conclude an agreement which 'affects' Community legislation, there could be conflict or a lesser kind of interference (such as a domestic interpretation of Community legislation in light of the agreement, undermining the uniform application of EC law). The Court of Justice would be unable to interpret the agreement, as it would not be a Community act.

The question is whether such problems could not equally be resolved through conflict rules and principles of co-ordination and co-operation. Community law prevails over inconsistent national law, whatever the origin of the latter. A Member State cannot justify a breach of Community law on the ground of respect for its international obligations, unless those obligations predate EU membership (Article 307 EC). Even under general international law, the EC Treaty obligations cannot be set aside by a later international agreement (unless it were to include all Member States). Primacy, of course, may be regarded as a second-best solution, because it does not avoid conflict or interference, but is simply a method for resolving it. However, Community law contains further instruments. Particularly in the external sphere, Member States are under a strong duty of co-operation with the Community institutions. Instruments of co-ordination and co-operation could be used to avoid conflicts between agreements which Member States conclude and existing Community law.

It is, however, too late in the day to expect the Court to overturn *ERTA*. The doctrine is now so firmly part of the EU's constitution (partly unwritten, no capital) that a reversal appears inconceivable. That does not, however, mean that there is no room for some of the above ideas. Does the Community really have to participate in each and every negotiation and does it need to conclude each and every agreement which 'affects' some EC legislation? The Court has confirmed that exclusive Community competence can also be exercised by the Member States, provided there is a specific Community authorisation.[32] This mechanism, employed in the field of trade policy, could also be useful in other areas of international lawmaking. Where the Community interest is not strong enough to justify Community participation in an international negotiation, the exercise of exclusive Community competence could be delegated to the Member States. One advantage of this approach would be to avoid problems of partial mixity: mixed agreements to which not all the Member States are parties. Such agreements may create problems in that, insofar as they are concluded by the Community they are binding on all Member States, even those which have not concluded them in their own capacity. In turn this requires a clear delineation of the Community's obligations and those of the Member States, which is often hard to achieve in practice.

The *Open Skies* cases illustrate some further points. In these cases the Court did not accede to the Commission's claims of exclusive competence on the basis of *ERTA*, with some limited exceptions. Instead the Court established that the Member States' air traffic

[31] Note the rule in Art 300(3) EC requiring the assent of the European Parliament for agreements entailing amendment of acts adopted under the co-operation or the co-decision procedure.

[32] Case 41/76 *Donckerwolcke v Procureur de la République* [1976] ECR 1921.

agreements violated the right of establishment, by conferring traffic rights on national carriers only. This has led the Council to agree to EC negotiations with the US on a new, Community-wide agreement – something the Commission had been asking for 15 years.[33] It is not exclusive competence which gave rise to the negotiations, but rather the fundamental incompatibility of having, on the one hand, a unified and liberalised internal market in aviation and, on the other, a nationality-based system of external traffic rights. It is deplorable that the Council could not act before the Court had established this, rather obvious, incompatibility. Even so, the episode also indicates that, next to legal rules and principles, institutional capacity and policy definition play an important role. When the Commission argued for EU-wide negotiations with third countries it had little expertise and cacapity in this area, nor did it present clear proposals on how external traffic rights would be allocated under new Community agreements. This made the Member States rather reluctant to agree to a strong Community role in external aviation agreements. Even so, the fundamental incompatibility between the free internal market and carved-up international policies could not be maintained. It is the substantive conflict of those policies with the EC Treaty which is creating a common European policy.

The *ECHR Opinion* is not an *ERTA*---type case in the sense that there was no issue of exclusive competence on the basis of EC legislation being affected. However, it does confirm the path dependency which *ERTA* created, since the question of ECHR accession was looked at through the competence prism. It is worth recalling that the Council's request for an Opinion – precarious, because there was no political consensus on accession at the time – inquired as to the compatibility of accession with the EC Treaty. Much if not most of the debate before the Court concerned issues of institutional compatibility: would accession not undermine the exclusive jurisdiction of the Court of Justice? But the Court decided to focus on competence, rather than substance, with the argument that it could do no more because there was no draft agreement on accession, and therefore no particular arrangements it could examine.

The *ECHR Opinion* created its own path dependency, one which has turned out to be much more negative than *ERTA*. It is a path dependency which in all likelihood the Court did not seek. The sentence in the Opinion which opened this path is: 'No Treaty provision confers on the Community institutions any general power to enact rules on human rights or to conclude international conventions in this field.'[34] This sentence is part of a broader reasoning, and therefore needs to be put in context – but that is rarely done. On the question of competence the Court adopted a classic reasoning, by first stating that external competence can be express or implied. It subsequently uttered the above sentence, which is in itself a rather uncontroversial description of the Treaty. The Court immediately moved on to refer to the possibility of using (current) Article 308 EC, but found, after some analysis, that that provision could not serve as a legal basis, essentially because accession would entail such a modification of the system for the protection of human rights, with fundamental implications for the Community and for the Member States, that it would be of constitutional significance, and thus outwith the scope of Article 308. I have criticised this reasoning elsewhere, and need not here reiterate that critique.[35] Let us

[33] COM (90) 17 final of 23 February 1990.

[34] *ECHR Opinion*, para 27.

[35] P Eeckhout, 'The EU Charter of Fundamental Rights and the Federal Question' (2002) 39 *CML Rev* 981–3.

instead focus on the meaning of the above sentence. It is mostly read as meaning that the Community has no competence to legislate in human-rights matters, or to conclude international agreements pertaining to human rights. The Court, however, never said that. It appeared to accept that Article 308 could in principle be used, were it not for the constitutional significance of ECHR accession.

And yet, ever since, all debates concerning the EU's proper role in the sphere of human rights are tainted, if not dominated, by competence discussions and struggles.[36] It is a sad and sorry story. Human rights are regarded as having a purely negative function, as mere limitations to the activities which the EU undertakes. They are conditions for lawfulness, no more. The EU is not seen as a political actor which could make a positive contribution to the definition of fundamental rights or which could make protection of such rights central to at least some of its policies. And this in times when the EU is increasingly involved in policies in which human-rights protection is a central concern, such as criminal law, immigration and asylum, and the fight against terrorism.

From a constitutional perspective, too, this approach makes no sense. The EC legal order is, in many ways, embedded in the legal systems of the Member States. The protection of fundamental rights is itself a prime instance of this embeddedness, since it was constructed on the foundations of the jurisprudential notion of 'general principles of Community law'. As such, fundamental rights are an integral part of the EC legal system. They are not external, or superimposed, or a given natural law.[37] They are constructed through interaction between Community law and national law. They are embedded in EC law, as are the laws of the Member States in general. This means that the Community (and the EU as a whole) can ill afford not to engage in substantive debates about which rights are considered 'fundamental', their scope, ways of protecting them, judicial and other remedies, etc. A debate about minimum standards of treatment of asylum seekers, embodied in an EC Directive,[38] is at once a debate about the Community's role in protecting fundamental rights. It definitely does not assist that debate to circumvent the fundamental rights discourse because it may raise sensitive issues of Community competence. Doing that also carries the enormous risk of leading to a minimalist policy outcome: we merely need to check that the legislation we adopt conforms to the (minimum) standards of the ECHR – anything going beyond that may lead to a competence dispute.

However, the organic development of EU fundamental rights law may well push back these competence struggles. Indeed, the *ERTA* logic of exclusive competence itself may play a role in that respect. The *Commission v Council* judgment of 1971 continues to be the most authentic 'classic' in the external relations case law.

[36] Eg, the debates on the EU Charter, in particular its horizontal provisions, and on the remit of the Fundamental Rights Agency.

[37] Cf C McCrudden, 'The Future of the EU Charter of Fundamental Rights', Jean Monnet Working Paper No 10/01 (www.jeanmonnetprogram.org) at 25.

[38] Council Directive 2003/9/EC of 27 January 2003 laying down minimum standards for the reception of asylum seekers, [2003] OJ L 31/18.

3

ERTA, *ECHR* and *Open Skies*: Laying the Grounds of the EU System of External Relations

CHRISTOPHE HILLION*

Introduction

This Chapter looks back at the EC external relations case law formulated by the European Court of Justice in its *ERTA*, *ECHR*, and *Open Skies* pronouncements.[39] It underlines the continuing relevance of the rules on external competence allocation that this case law encapsulates. It also points to other notions which those verdicts evoke, namely the notions of 'compliance' and 'coherence'. These have been featuring more prominently in the Court's external relations jurisprudence, and appear to supplement its primary focus on articulating and policing the distribution of competence between the Member States and the Community.

Three Layers in the EC External Competence Construct

The three rulings of the Court reflect different, though complementary, judicial approaches to the rules on allocation of external competence between the Member States and the Community.[40]

* Professor of European Law, Europa Institute, University of Leiden. I greatly benefited from insightful discussions with Marise Cremona, Joni Heliskoski, Rass Holdgaard, and from the suggestions and support of Anne Myrjord. Any remaining mistakes are mine only.

[39] Respectively: Case 22/70 *Commission v Council* [1971] ECR 263; Opinion 2/94 *ECHR* [1996] ECR 1759; and Case C-466/98 *Commission v United Kingdom* [2002] ECR I-9427, Case C-467/98 *Commission v Denmark* [2002] ECR I-9519, Case C-468/98 *Commission v Sweden* [2002] ECR I-9575, Case C-469/98 *Commission v Finland* [2002] ECR I-9627, Case C-471/98 *Commission v Belgium* [2002] ECR I-9681, Case C-472/98 *Commission v Luxembourg* [2002] ECR I-9741, Case C-475/98 *Commission v Austria* [2002] ECR I-9797, and Case C-476/98 *Commission v Germany* [2002] ECR I-9855). For a detailed analysis of this case law see R Holdgaard, *External Relations Law of the European Community—Legal Reasoning and Legal Discourses* (Alphen aan den Rijn, Kluwer Law International, 2008); D Scannell, 'Trespassing on sacred ground: The implied external competence of the European Community' (2001) 4 *Cambridge Yearbook of European Legal Studies* 343, A Dashwood and J Heliskoski, 'The classic authorities revisited' in A Dashwood and C Hillion (eds), *The general law of EC external relations* (London, Sweet & Maxwell, 2000) 3.

[40] The EU system of external relations is also governed by rules on allocation of competence between the Member States and the EU *qua* CFSP & PJCCM, and between the EC and the EU *qua* CFSP & PJCCM; see

In its *ERTA* judgment, the Court introduces its famous *implied powers* doctrine. Through a purposive interpretation of the Treaty provisions on the EC international legal personality, the Court enables the Community to negotiate and conclude external agreements over the whole range of its broadly defined objectives. It also makes this power potentially exclusive, in the sense of a progressive limitation of Member States' autonomous power on the international scene to the benefit of the Community.[41]

Held in the aftermath of the transitional period foreseen in the Treaty for setting the Common Commercial Policy, the *ERTA* decision catalyses the on-going emergence of the Community as law-making actor on the global stage, particularly in the GATT context. It also typifies the role the Court of Justice has played in policing the boundaries between the Member States' and the Community's external competence,[42] by reference to the *effet utile* of Community policies rather than through a textual interpretation of the EEC Treaty.[43]

While the '*ERTA* doctrine' itself is no longer contested, the conditions of its application remain contentious, to the extent that, as rightly recalled by Marise Cremona, they are still 'the subject of both academic discussion, institutional debate and new case law'.[44] Such disagreement is itself aggravated by a changing and more diverse Member States' 'ideology' with respect to the European integration. Indeed, since the implied powers doctrine was established, notions of conferred powers, subsidiarity and proportionality have been inserted into the Community constitutional fabric, both as express organising principles of the EC legal order,[45] and implied in the formulation of various new EC power-conferring provisions.[46] At the same time, new modes of co-operation (eg CFSP) have

further C Hillion, *The European Union and its Eastern European Neighbours: A Laboratory for the Organisation of EU External Relations* (Oxford, Hart Publishing, 2010, forthcoming).

[41] The Court found that the competence of the Community to conclude international agreements arises not only from an express conferment by the Treaty but may equally flow from other provisions of the Treaty and from measures adopted, within the framework of those provisions, by the Community institutions; that in particular, each time the Community, with a view to implementing a common policy envisaged by the Treaty, adopts provisions laying down common rules, whatever form these may take, Member States no longer have the right, acting individually or even collectively, to undertake obligations with non-member countries which affect those rules; that, as and when such common rules come into being, the Community alone is in a position to assume and carry out contractual obligations towards non-member countries affecting the whole sphere of application of the Community legal order; and that, to the extent to which Community rules are adopted for the attainment of the objectives of the Treaty, Member States cannot, outside the framework of the Community institutions, assume obligations which might affect those rules or alter their scope.

[42] In this regard: see, eg, Opinion 1/75 *Local Cost Standard* [1975] ECR 1355; Joined Cases 3, 4 and 6/76 *Kramer* [1976] ECR 1279; Opinion 1/76 *Laying-up Fund* [1977] ECR 741; Opinion 1/78 *Natural Rubber* [1979] ECR 2871; Case 804/79 *Commission v United Kingdom* [1981] ECR 1045; Case 45/86 *Commission v Council (GSP)* [1987] ECR 1493; Opinion 2/91 *ILO* [1993] ECR I-1061.

[43] E Stein writes that 'contrary to the prevailing learned opinion, and to the consternation of some Member Governments, the Court of Justice rejected the principle of enumerated powers in favor of the doctrine that Community power should be coextensive with its internal powers'; E Stein and L Henkin, 'Part I: the International Dimension' in M Capelletti, M Seccombe and J Weiler (eds), *Integration Through Law—Europe and the American Federal Experience* (vol 1, book 3; Berlin/New York, Walter de Gruyter, 1986) 43.

[44] M Cremona, 'Defining competence in EU external relations: lessons from the Treaty reform process', in A Dashwood and M Maresceau (eds), *Law and Practice of EU External Relations* (Cambridge, Cambridge University Press, 2008) 50; M Cremona, 'External Relations of the EU and the Member States: Competence, Mixed Agreements, International Responsibility, and Effects of International Law' (2006) European University Institute: LAW Working Paper 22/06, 2. Michel Petite also points out that reading *ERTA* 'may appear an easy task—applying it in practice is, however, more tricky'; M Petite, 'Current Legal Issues in the External Relations of the European Union' (2006) *EUI LAW Working Paper* 38/06, 7. See also R Holdgaard, 'The European Community's Implied External Competence after the *Open Skies* Cases' (2003) 8 *European Foreign Affairs Review* 370.

[45] Art 5 EC.

[46] Eg EC Articles on culture, public health, and development co-operation.

been introduced in the European integration process, alongside and as an alternative to the Community method. Member States, qua *pouvoir constituant*, have thus sought to harness that process and limit the almost proverbial 'competence creep'[47] phenomenon that it was found to engender, and which was catalysed notably by the Court's competence jurisprudence.

Those efforts bore fruit, notably at judicial level as epitomised by Opinion 2/94 on the Community accession to the ECHR. This *Avis* provides evidence of a new layer in the Court's jurisprudence on competence allocation in the then newly emerging EU system of external relations. Here, the Court explicitly refers to the TEU principle of conferred powers to limit the reach of both EC implied and residual powers based on Article 308 EC,[48] an approach it averted in *ERTA*, despite explicit requests from the Council and AG Dutheillet de Lamothe.[49]

This pronouncement confirms the earlier *WTO* Opinion,[50] which embeds the Community's implied and residual powers into the new EU legal framework. Indeed, the Court's external competence case law post-1/94 appears to be coloured by the tones of the Treaty of Maastricht,[51] by its interpretation by the Member States' judiciary,[52] and perhaps by the difficulties that riddled its ratification. This evolving jurisprudence may have been equally tainted by the imminent 1996 Inter-Governmental Conference (IGC), aimed notably at discussing the possible *communitarisation* of areas of intergovernmental co-operation introduced by the Maastricht Treaty.[53] Observing the division of tasks between the judiciary and primary law makers, the European judges may have found it more apposite to send signals to the 'Masters of the Treaties' than to pre-empt the outcome of their discussions.

The Court of Justice thus not only acts as the *garant* of the Community interest against individual Member States' encroachment, it also preserves, at another (meta) level, the Member States' powers as primary law makers of the EU. Having ensured the unity of the common market and the uniform application of Community law in *ERTA*,[54] the Court also seemingly upholds the EU institutional integrity against Community's abuse of its implied and residual powers, and the substantive and procedural limits to its competence, prescribed by the Treaty. The Court thereby safeguards the overall balance of powers

[47] S Weatherill, 'Competence creep and competence control' (2004) 23 *Yearbook of European Law* 1; A Dashwood, 'The Limits of European Community Powers' (1996) 21 *EL Rev* 113.

[48] *ECHR*, para 23. Indeed, the Court points out in para 30 that Article 308 'being an integral part of an institutional system based on the principle of conferred powers, cannot serve as a basis for widening the scope of Community powers beyond the general framework created by the provisions of the Treaty as a whole and, in particular, by those that define the tasks and the activities of the Community'.

[49] According to AG Dutheillet de Lamothe: '[i]t appears clear from the general scheme of the Treaty of Rome that its authors intended strictly to limit the Community's authority in external matters to the cases which they expressly laid down'; Case 22/70 *Commission v Council* [1971] ECR 263 at 293.

[50] Opinion 1/94 *WTO* [1994] ECR I-5267.

[51] As pointed out by Dashwood, 'in the era of the Maastricht Treaty, there is a clear legal duty to apply Article [308] consistently with the principle of attribution of powers'; A Dashwood, 'Commentary' in A Dashwood and S O'Leary (eds), *The Human Rights Opinion of the ECJ and its Constitutional Implications* (1996) CELS Occasional Paper No 1, Centre for European Legal Studies, Cambridge, 18.

[52] Most notably by the BvfG in its *Brunner* decision, and particularly its para 99.

[53] Art B TEU.

[54] See para 31 of the judgment.

envisaged by the then recent TEU, in due respect of the perceived original intent of the primary law makers.[55] This new layer of case law exemplified by *ECHR* thus supplements the initial *ERTA* jurisprudence.

These two strands of the Court's external competence case law are at work in the *Open Skies* judgments. In line with *ECHR*, these judgements reflect that the external powers case law is coloured by the EU organising principles. The Court here turns its attention to the question of *necessity* of an EC external action in areas of shared competence, in *casu* air transport. Having confirmed its earlier WTO dictum that necessity based on Opinion 1/76 jurisprudence is restricted to the demonstration that the internal competence may be effectively exercised only at the same time as the external competence, the Court questions the necessity of an *ERTA*-based external action.

As a preliminary step, it examines the formulation of the EC power conferring provisions (in *casu*, Article 80(2) EC) to determine the applicability of the *ERTA* doctrine to the domain at hand, thus suggesting that the *ERTA* effect is not automatic but instead a function of the nature of the powers conferred on the Community.[56] Recalling the proverbial rationale of that doctrine, the Court nonetheless finds that the *ERTA* doctrine is in principle applicable to the area of air transport:

> If the Member States were free to enter into international commitments affecting the common rules adopted on the basis of Article 84(2) of the Treaty, that would jeopardise the attainment of the objective pursued by those rules and would thus prevent the Community from fulfilling its task in the defence of the common interest.
>
> ...
>
> It follows that the findings of the Court in the AETR judgment also apply where, as in this case, the Council has adopted common rules on the basis of Article 84(2) of the Treaty.[57]

There follows a meticulous analysis of relevant Community rules to determine whether they could be affected by Member States' international commitments.[58] The Court thereby checks to what extent the *ERTA* effect operates in view of internal Community rules. And in this respect, it clearly defers to the political choices made by the EC law-making authorities upstream, holding that the Council did not intend to establish a complete package of legislation. Equally, the Court shows deference to the *external* policy choices. Hence, having emphasised the Council's power to decide on the extent and the procedure of Community involvement in air transport (Article 80(2) EC), the Court notes that in practice, 'the Council declined to give effect' to the Commission's early initiatives to

[55] In this regard, see Case T-306/01 *Yusuf* [2005] ECR II-3533, and Case T-315/01 *Kadi* [2005] ECR II-3649, where the Court of First Instance shows deference to the Union's constitutional architecture set out by the TEU; see also Joined Cases C-402/05 P and C-415/05 P *Kadi and Al Barakaat International Foundation v Council and Commission* (3 September 2008, nyr).

[56] Para 78. Further: R Holdgaard, 'The European Community's Implied External Competence after the Open Skies Cases' (2003) 8 *European Foreign Affairs Review* 385; and the annotation of J Dutheil de la Rochère and PJ Slot (2003) 40 *CML Rev* 697. Indeed, the EC provisions on development co-operation and humanitarian aid (as well as Art 133(6) EC) suggest that the *ERTA* effect cannot apply to those areas; as indeed confirmed by the Court: eg Joined cases C-181 and 248/91 *Parliament v Council (Bangladesh)* [1993] ECR I-3685 (Humanitarian aid) and Case 316/91 *Parliament v Council (EDF)* [1994] ECR I-625 (development co-operation), and Case 91/05 *Commission v Council (ECOWAS)* (20 May 2008, nyr).

[57] Paras 79–80; this quote refers to the pre-Amsterdam numbering of Article 80(2) referred to earlier in this Chapter. See also paras 74–75, case C-523/04 *Commission v the Netherlands* [2007] ECR I-326.

[58] Paras 90–93, *Open Skies.*

conclude a comprehensive air transport agreement with the USA,[59] and that it subsequently adopted only 'a limited mandate to negotiate with that country'.[60] The Council's assessment of expediency of an EC external action is thus unquestioned,[61] particularly in view of the powers it is granted by the Treaty.[62] The Court thereby suggests that the necessity of a Community external action in the field of shared powers is to be determined by taking account of the formulation of the power-conferring basis, as well as by the actual exercise of that power by the EC political institutions.

The EU judicature thus not only polices the confines of the Community external competence by reference to the principle of conferred powers as it did in *ECHR*, it also oversees the *exercise* of those Community powers, by reference to the notion of necessity, which in turn relates to subsidiarity. Indeed, the Court's assessment of the necessity criterion is seemingly strict, as suggested by its finding that distortions to the flow of services in the internal market which might arise from Member States' bilateral agreements 'do not in themselves affect the common rules adopted in that area', and are 'not (therefore) capable of establishing an external competence of the Community'.[63]

In that, the *Open Skies* judgments confirm *ECHR* which embedded the external powers case law in the EU legal and institutional framework. This Court's approach may also be related to the fact that they were decided in the aftermath of the 'Laeken Declaration' which led to the convening of the Convention on the Future of Europe, in charge of clarifying notably 'the division and definition of powers' as well as the Union's 'institutional set-up'. Again, the Court may have exercised some self-restraint in order not to interfere with the Convention's constitutional mandate.[64]

That said, the *Open Skies* judgments suggest that a balance is being sought between the post-TEU external competence case law that embeds the external powers jurisprudence in the EU constitutional framework (*ECHR* and *WTO* Opinions), *and* Member States' obligation of loyalty derived from Article 10 EC, and which underpins the *ERTA* doctrine. The Court not only recalled the basic rationale of its *ERTA* doctrine in order to apply it to air transport,[65] its detailed analysis of EC rules to determine whether they could be affected by Member States' bilateral commitments also ends up, almost surprisingly, with a conspicuous reminder of *ERTA* and its foundations:

[59] Para 18.

[60] Para 19. See also para 60, where the Court recalls that the Treaty entrusts the Council with the tasks of deciding whether it is appropriate to take action in the field of air transport and to define the extent of Community intervention in that area. The Court also points out that it was after the exercise of the internal competence, that the Council authorised the Commission to negotiate an air transport agreement by granting it a restricted mandate, while taking care to make clear that the system of bilateral agreements would be maintained until the conclusion of a new agreement binding the Community.

[61] The Council's ability to decide whether it is expedient to enter into an agreement with third countries was acknowledged by the Commission in the field of transport in the *ERTA* case; see para 70 of the judgment.

[62] Tizzano AG also insists on the 'necessity' of the Community agreement being assessed by the competent institutions, and following the procedures prescribed; adding that the contrary would lead to uncertainty, arbitrariness into the division of powers between the Community and Member States, and could distort the procedures and the interinstitutional balances set out by the Treaty; paras 51–53.

[63] Para 95: cf the Court's approach to Community harmonising powers based on Art 95 TEU, eg Case 376/98 *Germany v Council and Parliament (Tobacco Advertising)* [2000] ECR I-8419; Case C-491/01 *British American Tobacco* [2002] ECR I-11453; Case C-380/03 *Germany v Parliament and Council* [2006] ECR I-11573.

[64] Indeed, the specific Convention's Working Group 'External Action' had not yet submitted its final report.

[65] See paras 79–80 quoted above.

> Article [10] of the Treaty requires Member States to facilitate the achievement of the Community's tasks and to abstain from any measure which could jeopardise the attainment of the objectives of the Treaty.

In the area of external relations, the Court has held that the Community's tasks and the objectives of the Treaty would be compromised if Member States were able to enter into international commitments containing rules capable of affecting rules adopted by the Community or of altering their scope (see Opinion 2/91, paragraph 11, and also, to that effect, the *AETR* judgment, paragraphs 21 and 22).[66]

That discernible conciliation between the two strands of the ECJ external competence case law becomes more evident in its Opinion on the New Lugano Convention.[67] Here, the Court confirms its post-TEU jurisprudence by emphasising that 'Community enjoys only conferred powers and … accordingly, any competence, especially where it is exclusive and not expressly conferred by the Treaty, must have its basis in conclusions drawn from a specific analysis of the relationship between the agreement envisaged and the Community law in force and from which it is clear that the conclusion of such an agreement is capable of affecting the Community rules'. Building on its *Open Skies* approach, the Court undertakes a 'comprehensive and detailed analysis' to determine whether the Community has the competence to conclude an international agreement and whether that competence is exclusive.[68]

At the same time, the Court's detailed analysis is not simply 'quantitative'[69] as it was in the *WTO* Opinion. Building on *Open Skies*,[70] it takes account 'not only of the *area covered* by the Community rules and by the provisions of the agreement envisaged but also of the *nature and content* of those rules and those provisions, to ensure that the agreement is not capable of undermining the *uniform and consistent application* of the Community rules and the *proper functioning of the system* which they establish' (emphasis added). Moreover, the Court opines that its scrutiny must include not only the current state of Community law but also 'its future development'.[71]

While relying on its post-TEU jurisprudence, the Court reinvigorates its *ERTA* doctrine as well, based on concerns of effectiveness of Community rules.[72] Indeed, it acknowledges the Community exclusive powers to conclude the new Lugano convention, an unusual outcome since the entry into force of the TEU.

[66] Paras 110–111, *Open Skies*. See also paras 74–75, case C-523/04 *Commission v the Netherlands* [2007] ECR I-326.

[67] Opinion 1/03 *New Lugano Convention* [2006] ECR I-1145.

[68] A distinction that had been blurred by the Court *Open Skies* judgments, and which was not explicitly made in *ERTA*.

[69] An expression used by F Hoffmeister, in his case note on *Open Skies* (2004) 96 *American Journal of International Law* 567.

[70] Para 124, Opinion 1/03.

[71] Para 126, emphasis added.

[72] P Eeckhout, 'General Report', FIDE 2006.

From Adjudicating Competence Allocation to Ensuring Compliance and Coherence in EU External Relations

The external relations' case law embodied in *ERTA*, *ECHR* and *Open Skies* has thus far been envisaged through the prism of *competence allocation*, and its significance in the organisation and functioning of the EU system of external relations. However, other and arguably undervalued facets to this case law ought to be looked at. In particular, those pronouncements also hint at the Court's increasing attention to Member States' *compliance* with their Community obligations, including obligations derived from the principle of *co-operation* expressed in Article 10 EC.[73]

In the *Open Skies* verdicts, the Court found that in the exercise of their air transport powers, the Member States had failed to fulfil a number of their obligations under Community law. In *casu*, the clause on ownership and control of airlines, included in the bilateral Open Skies agreements, breached Article 43 EC on the freedom of establishment, for it introduced an unlawful discrimination against other Community nationals by preventing them from benefiting from the treatment which the host state accords to its own nationals.[74] Each Member State concerned therefore had to revise its Open Skies agreement to ensure their compliance with the EC provisions on freedom of establishment. The Court thereby recalled that, when they act within the remit of their powers, the Member States are bound to ensure that their international commitments are consistent with Community law in general.[75]

In the aftermath of the *Open Skies* judgments, the Community adopted a regulation that establishes a procedure for the notification and authorisation of bilateral negotiations conducted by the Member States in the field of air transport.[76] Under this new procedure, Member States' (re)negotiation of their bilateral air transport agreements has been supervised by the Commission for the purpose of ensuring their *consistency* with Community law. But this regulation is more than merely ensuring consistency between Member States' commitments and EC law, it also purports to guarantee *co-operation* between the Member States and the Community institutions in an area where they share competence. Indeed, the preamble of the regulation recalls the Court's well-established jurisprudence on the 'duty of cooperation':

> Where it is apparent that the subject-matter of an agreement falls partly within the competence of the Community and partly within that of its Member States, it is essential to ensure close cooperation between the Member States and the Community institutions, both in the process of negotiation and conclusion and in the fulfilment of the commitments entered into. That obligation to cooperate flows from the requirement of unity in the international representation of

[73] For a detailed analysis of the requirements of compliance and co-operation, see M Cremona, 'Defending the Community Interest: the duties of cooperation and compliance' in M Cremona and B de Witte (eds), *The Constitutional Fundamentals of EU external relations* (Oxford, Hart Publishing, 2008); C Hillion, 'Mixity and Coherence in EU external relations: the significance of the Duty of Cooperation' in C Hillion and P Koutrakos (eds), *Mixed Agreements Revisited* (Oxford, Hart Publishing, 2009, forthcoming).

[74] Paras 131–133.

[75] Also in this sense: Case C-124/95 *Centro-Com* [1997] ECR I-81.

[76] See Regulation 847/2004; OJEU 2004 L 157.

> the Community. The Community institutions and the Member States should take all necessary steps to ensure the best possible cooperation in that regard.[77]

The same preamble also points out that the system the Regulation establishes aims at 'ensur(ing) that a Member State conducting negotiations takes account of Community law, broader Community interests and ongoing Community negotiations'. As a spin-off, the *Open Skies* judgments have therefore led to the setting-up of an EC monitoring mechanism of Member States' bilateral negotiations, as a specific codification of the duty of co-operation in the field of air transport.

The case law similarly points to Member States' obligations flowing from the principle of co-operation, expressed in Article 10 EC, for the purpose of ensuring not only the consistency, but also the *coherence* of the Community's external action. Such obligations were made particularly prominent in two Court judgments of 2005, involving infringement proceedings against Luxembourg and Germany.[78] The Council had authorised the Commission to negotiate a Community agreement in the field of inland waterways transport with several third European States. Despite invitations from the Commission to refrain from doing so, Luxembourg and Germany concluded bilateral agreements in the same area, with the same third countries, while the Commission was itself negotiating.

Having rejected the other Commission's contention that the Community had exclusive external competence in the area concerned, the Court of Justice held that by failing to co-operate or consult with the Commission, those Member States had compromised the achievement of the Community's task and the attainment of the objectives of the Treaty,[79] in violation of their 'duty of genuine cooperation'. The Court further pointed out that:

> The adoption of a decision authorising the Commission to negotiate a multilateral agreement on behalf of the Community marks the start of a concerted Community action at international level and requires, for that purpose, if not a duty of abstention on the part of the Member States, at the very least *a duty of close cooperation between the latter and the Community institutions in order to facilitate the achievement of the Community tasks and to ensure the coherence and consistency of the action and its international representation.*[80]

Hence, prior to the existence of common rules, and thus before any *ERTA* effect occurs in an area of shared powers, Member States are nonetheless bound by specific obligations to ensure that their autonomous actions,[81] though not in conflict with EC substantive law,[82] 'do not prevent the Community from fulfilling its tasks in the defence of the common interest'. What is more, their action ought to facilitate the achievement of the Community's tasks and 'ensure the coherence and consistency of the action and its international

[77] This formulation is typical of the Court's pronouncements related to mixed agreements; see, eg, Opinion 2/91 *ILO* [1993] ECR I-1061; Opinion 1/94 *WTO* [1994] ECR I-5267.

[78] C-266/03 *Commission v Luxembourg* [2005] ECR I-4805; C-433/03 *Commission v Germany* [2005] ECR I-6985.

[79] See also Opinion of Maduro AJ, 1st October 2009 in Case C-246/07 *Commission v Sweden (PFOS)* (pending).

[80] Emphasis added.

[81] See also the Court's judgment in C-459/03 *Commission v Ireland ('MOX plant')* [2006] ECR I-4635.

[82] As pointed out by Dashwood, the scope of EC competence differs from the scope of application of the EC Treaty: Dashwood, above n 51 at 22; A. Dashwood, 'The Limits of European Community Powers' (1996) 21 *EL Rev* 113.

representation'.[83] As the two judgments mentioned above demonstrate, and as it has been confirmed since, such Member States' obligations are enforceable.[84]

Arguably, the Court's concern for the defence of the common interests by way of co-operation among external relations actors, rather than simply through the assertion of exclusive Community powers, could already be detected in *ERTA*. While it is the cradle of the implied powers doctrine, it also contains various other expressions of the duty of co-operation which binds the actors of the external relations system, particularly where the vesting of powers in the Community has not (yet) fully taken effect.[85] For instance, the Court emphasised in broad terms that 'wherever a matter forms the subject of a common policy, the Member States are bound in every case to act jointly in defence of the interests of the Community'.[86] It also pointed out that in the specific circumstances of the case, the Council and the Commission had 'to reach an agreement … on the appropriate methods of cooperation with a view to ensuring most effectively the defence of the interests of the Community'. The Court thereby posits that each actor in the external relations system, namely the Member States, the Commission and the Council, are bound to contribute, through co-operation, to the fulfilment of the Community objectives, and to the defence of its interests.

In the two infringements proceedings mentioned above, the Court goes further by explicitly setting out obligations stemming from the duty of co-operation, and by asserting that these can be enforced. More than policing competence allocation, and ensuring that Member States comply with EC substantive rules, the Court now engages in fostering the coherence and consistency of the Community's external action.[87]

This co-operation jurisprudence suggests a growing Court's acceptance of the plurality that characterises the EU system of external relations. It could also contribute to the development of a more mature legal order, less determined by the usual competence grabbing instinct than by a genuine Community reflex.

Conclusion

The *ERTA*, *ECHR* and *Open Skies* pronouncements encapsulate the core principles of the Court's jurisprudence on competence allocation in the EU system of external relations. The paper suggested that far from being outdated, this composite case law endures in its essentials,[88] as recently demonstrated by Opinion 1/03.[89] Indeed, much of the external relations litigation continues to revolve around those competence-related principles and

[83] Further on the link between the duty of co-operation and the requirement of coherence: C Hillion, '*Tous pour un, un pour tous!* Coherence in the external relations of the European Union' in M Cremona (ed), *New developments in EU external relations* (Oxford, Oxford University Press, 2008).

[84] Eg C-459/03 *Commission v Ireland ('MOX plant')* [2006] ECR I-4635.

[85] Para 81.

[86] Paras 77 and 78, *ERTA*. Although that obligation was partly derived from the provisions of former Art 116 EEC (para 76), which since then has been deleted from the EC Treaty, the Court only referred to this article 'as a subsidiarity point', thereby suggesting that Member States' obligation still stands.

[87] Further: Hillion, above n 83.

[88] Dashwood and Heliskoski, above n 39. To be sure, the Member States have attempted to codify that composite jurisprudence, as suggested by the TCE and the Reform Treaty. Further: M Cremona, 'The draft Constitutional Treaty: external relations and external action' (2003) 40 *CML Rev* 1347; A Dashwood, 'The relationship between the Member States and the European Union/European Community' (2004) 41 *CML Rev*

the conditions of their application. Yet it has become clear, in recent years, that establishing the exclusive competence of the Community is a complex and often unsuccessful enterprise, for legal and/or political reasons. In the EU system of external relations, essentially based on shared powers, the effectiveness of Community policies also depends on compliance with Community law, including with procedural obligations of genuine co-operation.

355 (2004); B De Witte, 'The Constitutional law of external relations' in I Pernice and M Poiares Maduro (eds), *A constitution for the European Union: first comments on the 2003 draft of the European Convention* (Baden-Baden, Nomos Verlagsgesellschaft, 2004) 95.

[89] See also the Court's analysis of the competence question in its ruling in Joined Cases C-402/05 P and C-415/05 P *Kadi and Al Barakaat International Foundation v Council and Commission* (3 September 2008); on the continuing reference to *ERTA* see, eg, Case 45/07 *Commission v Greece (IMO)* (12 February 2009, nyr); and on the defence of the Community interest, see Case C-205/06 *Commission v Austria*, and Case C-249/06 *Commission v Sweden* (3 March 2009, nyr).

4

Constructing the European Polity: *ERTA* and the *Open Skies* Judgments[90]

ROBERT POST

Whatever unification Europe is destined to achieve will owe a great debt to the statesmanlike decisions of European Court of Justice (ECJ). Consistently sidestepping 'the presumptive rule of interpretation typical in international law, that treaties must be interpreted in a manner that minimizes encroachment on state sovereignty', the ECJ has 'favored a teleological, purposive rule drawn from the book of constitutional interpretation.'[91] The Court has forcefully promoted the emergence of a distinctive transnational entity endowed with forms of authority that are both significant and unique.

We presently lack vocabulary to designate the strange polysemic forms of authority this entity actually possesses. It is plainly not a state. It embodies some characteristics of constitutional government, but fails to exemplify others.[92] The entity is commonly referred to as an 'emerging European polity',[93] but the notion of a 'polity' seems to have been elected by default, for it is seldom analysed or defined.

My thesis in this Chapter is that the notion of a 'polity' is especially apt in describing European institutions, for a polity designates a territorial institutional arrangement that enables politics. Politics is the mutual determination of destiny through common action. It is the remarkable achievement of the ECJ to have forged an arena that makes possible the political engagement of European states, institutions and individuals. The Court has

[90] I am grateful for the research assistance of Sandeep Ramesh and Amanda Shanor.

[91] JHH Weiler, *The Transformation of Europe*, (1991) 100 *Yale Law Journal* 2043, 2416.

[92] Dieter Grimm, 'Does Europe Need a Constitution?' in Richard Bellamy (ed), *Constitutionalism and Democracy* (2006) 479–99; Miguel Poiares Maduro, 'The Importance of Being Called a Constitution: Constitutional Authority and the Authority of Constitutionalism' (2005) 3 *International Journal of Constitutional Law* 332.

[93] Francesca Bignami, 'Creating European rights: National Values and Supranational Interests' (2005) 11 *Columbia Journal of European Law* 241, 340; Christian Joerges, 'The Challenges of Europeanization in the Realm of Private Law: A Plea for a New Legal Discipline' (2004) 14 *Duke Journal of Comparative & International Law* 149, 168; Kanishka Jayasuriya, 'Globalization, Law, and the Transformation of Sovereignty: The Emergence of Global Regulatory Governance' (1999) 6 *Indiana Journal of Global Legal Studies* 425, 443; Lisbet Hooghe and Gary Marks, '"Europe with the Regions": Channels of Regional Representation in the European Union' (1996) 26 *Publius*, 73, 90; Paul Pierson and Stephan Leibfried, 'Multi-Tiered Institutions and the Making of Social Policy' in Stephan Leibfried and Paul Pierce (eds) (1995) *European Social Policy: Between Fragmentation and Integration* 11; Philippe C Schmitter, 'The Single European Act, the Maastricht Accord and the Emerging European Polity' in Berhanu Abegaz, Patricia Dillon, David H Feldman, and Paul F Whiteley (eds), *The Challenge of European Integration: Internal and External Problems of Trade and Money* (1994); JHH Weiler, 'On the Judicial Protection of the Human Rights of Non-EC Nationals—A Critique' in Henry G Schermers, et al (eds), *Free Movement of Persons in Europe: Legal Problems and Experiences* (1993), 248. See Carolyn Rhodes and Sonia Mazey (eds), *The State of the European Union: Building a European Polity?* (1995), 3. The idea of a European polity is of course a very old one. Andreas Dorpalen, 'The European Polity: Biography of an Idea' (1948) 10 *Journal of Politics* 712.

been shrewd and capable in establishing the institutional forms necessary for this engagement. In this chapter I shall explore some under-emphasised ways in which the ECJ has nourished the emergence of the institutional structures of a polity by examining the Court's foundational decisions in the justly famous *ERTA* case[94] and its most recent progeny, the *Open Skies* Judgments.[95]

A polity is an institutional structure that enables the conduct of politics. But what is politics? Two great visions of politics come down to us from the 20th century. The first is by the German theorist Carl Schmitt. Politics, writes Schmitt, is fundamentally about the distinction 'between friend and enemy'.[96] 'The friend and enemy concepts are to be understood in their concrete and existential sense, not as metaphors or symbols . . . An enemy exists only when at least potentially, one fighting collectivity of people confronts a similar collectivity.'[97] Politics, for Schmitt, is the form of social solidarity that is produced when the survival of a group is threatened.[98] The 'political community'[99] is the 'decisive entity which transcends the mere societal-associational groupings'[100] because the political community is the solidarity to which we turn to guarantee our very survival.[101] Politics for Schmitt entails the kind of unity necessary to meet external danger.

Hannah Arendt offers a contrasting account of politics. For Arendt politics is the form of social solidarity that enables mutual promises and interdependence. Arendt writes that for 'the men of the American Revolution' power was 'the very opposite of a pre-political natural violence. For them, power came into being when and where people would get together and bind themselves through promises, covenants, and mutual pledges; only such power, which rested on reciprocity and mutuality, was real power and legitimate.'[102] Such mutuality 'became the basis for 'associations'—the gathering-together of people for a specified political purpose'.[103] Politics for Arendt consists of mutual action inspired by common commitments. Politics presupposes not unity, but 'the fact of human plurality'.[104]

The contrast between Schmitt and Arendt is seemingly vivid. For Schmitt, a polity derives from response to external threat; for Arendt it derives from reciprocity and

[94] *Commission of the European Communities v Council of the European Communities*, Clase 22/70, Judgment of 31 March 1971.

[95] Case C-466/98, *Commission v United Kingdom*; C-467/98, *Commission v Denmark*; C-468/98, *Commission v Sweden*; C-469/98, *Commission v Finland*; C-471/98, *Commission v Belgium*; C-472/98, *Commission v Luxembourg*; C-475/98, *Commission v Austria*; C-476/98, *Commission v Germany*; Judgments of 5 November 2002.

[96] Carl Schmitt *The Concept of the Political* 26 (2007).

[97] *Ibid*, 27–8.

[98] 'War is neither the aim nor the purpose nor even the very content of politics. But as an ever present possibility it is the leading presupposition which determines in a characteristic way human action and thinking and thereby creates a specifically political behavior . . . A world in which the possibility of war is utterly eliminated, a completely pacified globe, would be a world without the distinction between friend and enemy and hence a world without politics.' *Ibid*, 34–5.

[99] *Ibid*, 47.

[100] *Ibid*, 45.

[101] 'Were a world state to embrace the entire globe and humanity, then it would be no political entity . . . If, in fact, all humanity and the entire world were to become a unified entity based exclusively on economics and on technically regulating traffic, then it still would not be more of a social entity than a social entity of tenants in a tenement house, customers purchasing gas from the same utility company, or passengers traveling on the same bus. An interest group concerned exclusively with economics or traffic cannot become more than that, in the absence of an adversary.' *Ibid*, 57.

[102] Hannah Arendt, 'On Revolution' 181–2 (1963).

[103] *Ibid*, 182.

[104] Hannah Arendt, 'The Promise of Politics' 93 (2005).

mutuality.[105] For Schmitt the agents of politics are unified collectivities of people, exemplified by states; for Arendt the agents of politics are individual actors, exemplified by citizens who engage with each other voluntarily. Yet underlying these sharp differences lie deep similarities. Schmitt and Arendt each believe that politics can exist only in the presence of human plurality,[106] and only if there is freedom of collective action.[107] For Schmitt this action paradigmatically consists in the need 'to preserve one's own form of existence' from the encroachment of enemies.[108] For Arendt it consists in the freedom to 'interact with one another without compulsion, force, and rule over one another, as equals among equals . . . managing all . . . affairs by speaking with and persuading one another'.[109]

For both Schmitt and Arendt, freedom of collective action can occur only within a spatial ordering. Schmitt regards politics as dependent upon an entity, like a state, which expresses 'the political status of an organized people in an enclosed territorial unit'[110] by deciding 'for itself the friend-enemy distinction'.[111] The possibility of politics is undermined when the 'concrete spatial order of . . . territorial states'[112] is endangered by the loss of 'a clear concept of spatial *nomos*.'[113] For Arendt 'the crucial point about . . . political freedom is that it is a spatial construct'.[114] Politics can occur only in an 'agora, where free men could meet as peers on any occasion' and where there could be 'a public space . . . in the presence of others'.[115] For both Schmitt and Arendt the collapse of 'political space as

[105] We might say, in this regard, that Schmitt looked to the Roman ideal of politics, whereas Arendt admired the Greek polis. 'To the Greek way of thinking, freedom was rooted in place, bound to one spot and limited to its dimensions, and the limits of freedom's space were congruent with the walls of the city, of the polis, or, more precisely, the agora contained within it. Outside those borders lay, first, foreign territory where one could not be free because one was no longer a citizen there or, better, a political man; and, second, the private household, where one could not be free either, because there one had no equals who alone constitute freedom's space. ' Arendt, above note 104, at 170. The Greeks 'believed that whenever the polis dealt with other states, it no longer actually needed to proceed politically, but could instead use force . . . In other words, what we today call 'foreign policy' was not really politics for the Greeks in any real sense' (*ibid*, 129). 'There is no doubt that the concept of foreign policy—of *politics* in foreign relations—and consequently of the idea of a political order beyond the borders of one's own nation or city, is solely of Roman origin. The Roman politicization of the space between peoples marks the beginning of the Western world.' *Ibid*, 189.

[106] If for Schmitt politics would cease were there a single world state that embraced the 'entire globe,' above note 101, so for Arendt politics would cease if 'the fact of human plurality' were to fade away, so that we were left with '*man*' instead of '*men*' (*ibid*, 93). 'If . . . there were to be some cataclysm that left the earth with only one nation, and matters in that nation were to come to a point where everyone saw and understood everything from the same perspective, living in total unanimity with one another, the whole world would have come to an end in a historical-political sense.' *Ibid*, 176.

[107] Schmitt and Arendt differ in their conception of action. Arendt believed that speech was the paradigmatic form of political engagement. Political interaction consisted of 'being able to persuade and influence others,' *ibid*, 168, because 'the most important activity of a free life moves from action to speech, from free deeds to free words' (*ibid*, 124). For Schmitt, by contrast, 'the core of the political idea' was 'the exacting moral decision' which liberal 'freedom of speech and of the press' sought to suspend 'forever in an everlasting discussion'. Carl Schmitt, Political Theology: four chapters on the Concept of Sovereignty 63–65 (2005).

[108] Schmitt, above note 96, at 27.

[109] Arendt, above note 104, at 117.

[110] Schmitt, above note 96, at 19.

[111] *Ibid*, at 30.

[112] Carl Schmitt, 'The Nomos of the Earth in the International Law of the "Jus Publicum Europaeum"'140 (2003).

[113] *Ibid*, 243.

[114] Arendt, above note 104, at 119. See the discussion in note 105, above; Hans Lindahl, Give and Take: Arendt and the Nomos of Political Community (2006) 32 *Philosophy and Social Criticism* 881.

[115] *Ibid*, 123.

such'[116] meant the loss of the possibility of politics. Schmitt and Arendt agree that a successful polity must embody the institutional form of political space.

There is a subtle but significant difference in the way that Schmitt and Arendt conceptualise the space of politics. For Schmitt, political space refers to territory where persons actually live. For Arendt, it refers to a constructed framework where persons can interact with each other. The International Labour Organization, for example, can create a space for Arendtian politics that is not located in any discrete physical region of the globe. This difference is connected to the stakes of politics. For Schmitt, politics touches persons where they physically live and hence where its consequences cannot be avoided. It therefore involves, as Leo Strauss observes, the inescapable question of 'what ultimately matters for man', 'the life-and-death quarrel' that divides 'humanity into friends and enemies'.[117] Because the agora for Arendt can be a metaphoric space, politics need do not involve such high stakes. It is possible for those who participate in the politics of the Governing Body of the ILO in Geneva to return home to lives otherwise untouched by their decision making. It is fair to say, however, that Arendt considered the Greek city-state as the paradigmatic example of an agora; the politics within this territorial agora would necessarily involve the same inescapably serious dimensions as those theorized by Schmitt.

This concurrence of Schmitt and Arendt allows us to offer a minimal definition of a 'polity' as a territorial institutional structure that creates the political space necessary for the conduct of politics. Schmitt's and Arendt's views of politics were of course subtle and continuously in motion, containing many idiosyncrasies and complexities, but for our purposes I will bracket these complexities and simply use Schmitt and Arendt to propose two ideal forms of politics that a polity can facilitate. I shall call these internal politics and external politics. A polity that facilitates internal politics must create a political space that allows for the emergence of common commitments based upon the mutual engagement of a plurality of political actors who are bound to each other in trust and reciprocity.[118] A polity that facilitates external politics must create a political space that expresses collective unity, so that the polity can act in a world that lacks such trust and reciprocity.[119]

[116] *Ibid*, 130.

[117] Leo Strauss, *Notes on Carl Schmitt, The Concept of the Political*, in Schmitt, above note 96, at 101–3. 'The political is a basic characteristic of human life; politics in this sense *is* destiny; therefore man cannot escape politics.' *Ibid*, 94.

[118] Arendt is sometimes interpreted as excluding from politics certain kinds of social and economic questions. I do not mean to endorse this view. See Hanna Fenichel Pitkin, 'The Attack of the Blob: Hannah Arendt's Concept of the Social' (1998); Lawrence J Biskowski, 'Practical Foundations for Political Judgment: Arendt on Action and World' (1993) 55 *Journal of Politics* 867.

[119] I do not mean by this formulation to accept the full paraphernalia of Westphalian sovereignty that Schmitt may be thought to embrace. Consider Yale H Ferguson and Richard W Mansbach, 'Conclusion: The Past and Growing Complexity of Global Politics, in What is the Polity?: A Roundtable' (Spring 2000) 2 *International Studies Review* 3, 29–30:

> [W]e conceive of political space in which a vast array of polities overlap, layer, nest, and interact—coexist, cooperate, and conflict in the context of particular issues that often overlap. Polities regularly share some or all of the same political space. The domain of each polity consists of those persons who identify with it, the resources it can command, the 'reach' it has with respect to adherents located in 'space' in the broadest sense (for example, for firms and markets—even cyberspace), and issues. All polities are 'authorities' and 'govern' within their respective domain. Authority or governance in our definition is effective control or significant influence within a domain. Such authority need not be exclusive (it can be and often is shared), nor need it be regarded as legitimate, although legitimacy is an asset. 'Nested' polities are those that lie partially or wholly within the domain of another polity. They may be completely dominated by the host polity, share some functions with it, or be completely autonomous.

It is plain that a polity that facilitates external politics need not also establish internal politics. Cohesion in external affairs can be achieved without the presence of an agora for internal politics; totalitarian states, for example, regularly engage foreign governments as a collective unity while at the same time suppressing within their borders the plurality of actors necessary for internal politics. A polity that facilitates internal politics, by contrast, may sometimes also need the capacity to engage in external politics. A territorial agora that cannot protect itself from foreign predation will not long survive; the need for unity in defence would seem fundamental. If politics within an agora creates power through promises and mutual pledges, this power would quickly dissipate if participants in the agora were free separately to engage with those outside the agora in ways that were inconsistent with their mutual commitments. However free participants in the agora must remain to re-negotiate common commitments among themselves, these commitments might be gravely damaged were participants in the agora to be unable to join together collectively to support them when facing outwards. In the absence of such solidarity, the trust necessary for internal politics could be fatally undermined.

It would appear, therefore, that in a world of separate and potentially antagonistic polities, serious pressures can drive internal politics also to create an external politics both to uphold the commitments agreed upon within an internal agora and to sustain the integrity of the process by which these commitments are achieved. It follows that there will be a tendency for a polity which prizes internal politics also to develop the capacity to facilitate external politics, in which it functions as a unified territorial unit to protect its internal agora. A complete polity will protect its internal agora from external coercion; it will safeguard the trust necessary for that agora to function by requiring external solidarity in support of the commitments made within the agora.

The European Community began primarily as a commitment to an internal politics. It was an effort among European actors to use promises, covenants, and mutual pledges to generate common political power.[120] There are a plethora of theories about why such an internal agora managed successfully to come into being.[121] My concern in this chapter, however, is to explore the connection between the creation of this internal agora and the formation of a polity empowered to engage in external politics. Although some capacity to engage in external politics was present from the beginning of the Community,[122] it has

[120] In 1951, with the establishment of the European Coal and Steel Community, European states pledged to lay 'the basis for a broader and deeper community among peoples long divided by bloody conflicts; and to lay the foundations for institutions which will give direction to a destiny henceforth shared' (Preamble to Treaty Establishing the European Coal and Steel Community (Paris, 18 April 1951), in *Sweet & Maxwell's European Community Treaties* 3 (2nd edn 1975)). When the European Economic Community was created six years later, these states pledged themselves to 'common action to eliminate the barriers which divide Europe' and to 'concerted action in order to guarantee steady expansion, balanced trade and fair competition' (Preamble to Treaty Establishing the European Economic Community (Rome, 25 March 1957), in *ibid*, 61). In the 1992 Maastricht Treaty on the European Union, European states pledged 'to establish a citizenship common to the nationals of their countries' (Preamble, Treaty on the European Union 4 (1992)).

[121] For a useful summary, see Ben Rosamond, 'Theories of European Integration' (2000).

[122] The EEC Treaty of 1957, for example, authorised the European Community to 'conclude with a third State, a union of States or an international organisation agreements establishing an association involving reciprocal rights and obligations, common action, and special procedures'. Member States agreed to 'coordinate their trade relations with third countries so as to bring about . . . the conditions needed for implementing a common policy in the field of external trade' (Art 238, in *European Community Treaties*, above note 1120, at 122). In Art 111(1) Member States agreed 'in respect of all matters of particular interest to the common market' to 'proceed within the framework of international organizations of an economic character only by common action',

grown more robust and defined as the European polity has matured.[123] There are no doubt many reasons for this trend, but one important cause is the potential dependence of an internal politics on external politics.

Cases like *ERTA* and the *Open Skies* judgments demonstrate that the ECJ has been acutely sensitive to this relationship. These cases turn precisely on how plurality within an internal agora may require unity in external affairs. The ECJ has used law to link these two kinds of politics, and in the process it has forged a stronger and more complete European polity.

Arendt and Schmitt offer fundamentally different accounts of how law would function within a polity. Arendt believes that the political space of a polity is established by law, which 'produces the arena where politics occurs'.[124] Arendt therefore conceptualises law as 'prepolitical' in the sense that it is 'constitutive for all further political action and interaction'.[125] 'Just as the walls of a city, to which Heraclitus once compared the law, must first be built before there can be a city identifiable by its shape and borders, the law determines the character of its inhabitants.'[126] For Schmitt, by contrast, law that defines a polity is produced by the politics of the polity. Law, 'like every other order . . . rests on a decision and not on a norm'.[127] The authority 'to produce law . . . need not be based on law'.[128] Because authority 'remains, whereas law recedes', the persistence of the state in times of emergency 'is undoubted proof of its superiority over the validity of the legal norm'.[129]

A striking fact about decisions like *ERTA* and the *Open Skies* judgments is that they illustrate that Arendt and Schmitt were each, in their own way, correct. The ECJ in these cases regards the 1957 Treaty establishing the European Community as prepolitical and fixed insofar as it defines and limits the agora within which internal European politics can proceed. But the ECJ transcends and modifies the Treaty when defining the authority of the European Community in foreign affairs, and in so doing the ECJ explicitly takes instruction from commitments that have been created within the internal agora of European politics. It explicitly fashions norms of law out of the pledges of politics.

On the surface *ERTA* was a technical and dull case, about as distant from high political theory as it is possible to imagine. *ERTA* involved negotiations for the European Agreement Concerning the Work of Crews of Vehicles Engaged in International Road Transport

ibid, Art 116, *ibid*, 96. Article 113 provided that 'agreements with third countries' implementing a 'common commercial policy' were to be negotiated by the Commission of the European Community, *ibid*, Art 113, *ibid*, 95–6.

[123] So, for example, the most recent European Union Treaty explicitly adopts the objective of enabling the Union 'to assert its identity on the international scene, in particular through the implementation of a common foreign and security policy including the progressive framing of a common defence policy, which lead to a common defence.' Title I, Article B, Treaty on the European Union 8 (1992).

[124] Arendt, above note 104, at 181.

[125] *Ibid*, 180. 'The law is . . . something by which the polis enters into its continuing life, something it cannot abolish without losing its identity.'

[126] *Ibid*, 180–1. 'The crucial point,' Arendt writes, 'is that the law . . . has something violent about it in terms of both its origins and its nature. It comes into being by means of production, not action; the lawgiver resembles the architect of the city and its builder, not the *politikos* and the citizen' (*ibid*, 181). 'We easily forget the spatial character of laws. All laws first create a space in which they are valid, and this space is the world in which we can move about in freedom. What lies outside this space is without law and, even more precisely, without world; as far as human community is concerned, it is a desert.' *Ibid*, 189–90.

[127] Schmitt, 107.

[128] *Ibid*, 13.

[129] *Ibid*, 12.

(the ERTA),[130] which were proceeding under the auspices of the Inland Transport Committee of the United Nations Economic Commission for Europe. The ERTA dealt with prosaic details like the required ages, work periods, and rest periods of drivers engaged in inter-European vehicular transportation. In 1969 the Community had issued Regulation No 543/69,[131] which addressed many of the same issues as the ERTA and which was in some details inconsistent with the ERTA. Regulation No 543/69 governed only transportation within the Member States of the Community.

The *ERTA* case arose in a complicated posture. The Commission of the European Communities (the Commission) had sued the Council of the European Communities (the Council) on the question of whether 'the negotiation and conclusion of the ERTA, involving as it did a matter arising out of the common transport policy and governed by Community law within the territory of the six Member States since Regulation No 543/69 came into force, could only be carried out by the Community'.[132] The contention of the Commission was that neither the individual Member States, nor the Council, which represented the Member States within the Community, were authorised to negotiate an international agreement like the ERTA; only the Commission, which embodied the unity of the European Community, could represent the Community at the bargaining table.[133] In technical legal terms, the question was whether the Community had 'exclusive competence' to negotiate the ERTA. When the many complications and technicalities of the case are set aside, its essential question was whether matters involving international road transportation would, after Regulation No 543/69, have to be negotiated by the European Community, or whether Member States retained authority to negotiate their own separate agreements.

The 1957 Treaty of Rome, which established the European Economic Community, contained a small number of very specific provisions awarding competence to the Community to deal with states outside the Community. None of these provisions encompassed the subject matter of transportation.[134] Transportation policy was explicitly

[130] The present version may be accessed at www.unece.org/trans/doc/2006/sc1/ECE-TRANS-SC1–2006–02e.pdf.

[131] Available at http://eur-lex.europa.eu/Notice.do?mode=dbl&lang=en&lng1=en,en&lng2=bg,de,en,es,fr,ga,it,nl,ro,&val=14803:cs&page=1&hwords=543/69~.

[132] Case 22/70, *Commission of the European Communities v Council of the European Communities (ERTA)* [1971] ECR 263, 269.

[133] Article 113 of the EEC treaty provided that 'agreements with third countries' implementing a 'common commercial policy' were to be negotiated by the Commission. It should be understood that 'the antagonism between the Commission and the Council . . . epitomizes the struggle between supranationalism and intergovernmentalism . . . The Commission has consistently . . . perceived the Council as the bodyguard of national competence, greatly reluctant to recognize and exercise external competence. The Council, i.e. the Member State governments, see the Commission as purely intent on increasing its own, supranational powers.' Piet Eeeckhout, 'External Relations of the European Union: Legal and Constitutional Foundations' 98 (2004).

[134] According to Dutheillet de Lamothe, Advocate-General in *ERTA*:

> Eleven out of the 248 articles of the Treaty of Rome are particularly devoted to prescribing and arranging a Community authority in relationships with third countries or with international organizations.
>
> These are:
>
> —on the one hand, the six articles appearing in Part Three of the Treaty, Articles 111 to 116, which are written into the chapter on Commercial Policy;
>
> —on the other hand, the five articles appearing in Part Six of the Treaty which is devoted to General and Final Provisions, Articles 228–231 and Article 238.
>
> There is in addition a very general provision, but one which may have a certain relevance to the matter: Article 235.
>
> It should be emphasized from the outset that Title IV of Part Two of the Treaty, the only title devoted to

addressed in Articles 74 to 84 of the Treaty, and these provisions, which pledge that 'the objectives of this Treaty shall . . . be pursued by Member States within the framework of a common transport policy',[135] concern only the internal politics of the European polity.[136]

Advocate-General Dutheillet de Lamothe thus opined that the ECJ could not interpret the Treaty to award exclusive competence to the Community to negotiate the AETR without engaging 'in a discretionary construction of the law . . . a judicial interpretation far exceeding the bounds which the Court has hitherto set regarding its power to interpret the Treaty'.[137] Such a holding would recognise 'that the Community authorities exercise, in addition to the powers expressly conferred upon them by the Treaty, those implied powers whereby the Supreme Court of the United States supplements the powers of the federal bodies in relation to those of the confederated States'.[138] It would require 'a teleological interpretation of the Treaty' characteristic 'of a constitutional court', rather than the kind of restrictive interpretation ordinarily accorded to treaties between independent states.[139]

The judgment of the ECJ in *ERTA* is commonly recognised as 'seminal' and 'innovative'[140] because the Court chose to deploy a form of teleological interpretation. But an important question is the nature of the 'telos' which the Court chose to interpret the Treaty to attain. I suggest that in *ERTA* the ECJ was driven by the goal of perfecting the European polity by theorising the circumstances in which the unity of external politics was necessary in order to safeguard the conduct of internal politics.

As a matter of doctrine, the ECJ held that the exclusive external competence of the Community can be inferred not merely from the 'substantive provisions' of the Treaty, but also 'from measures adopted . . . by the Community institutions'.[141] It concluded that the power of the Community to act politically with respect to third countries depended upon the political actions of the members of the European polity vis-à-vis each other:

> Each time the Community, with a view to implementing a common policy envisaged by the Treaty, adopts provisions laying down common rules, whatever form these may take, the Member States no longer have the right, acting individually or even collectively, to undertake obligations with third countries which affect those rules.
>
> As and when such common rules come into being, the Community alone is in a position to assume and carry out contractual obligations towards third countries affecting the whole sphere of application of the Community legal system.

Transport, has no express provision relating to the Community's 'treaty-making power', to use an expression employed by Anglo-Saxon lawyers.
Case 22/70, *Commission v Council*, Opinion of Mr Advocate-General Dutheillet de Lamothe, delivered on 10 March 1971, at 289.

135 Article 74, 1957 Treaty of Rome, above note 120.

136 'The Council . . . contends that since the Community only has such powers as have been conferred on it, authority to enter into agreements with third countries cannot be assumed in the absence of an express provision in the Treaty . . . Article 75 relates only to measures internal to the Community, and cannot be interpreted as authorizing the conclusion of international agreements.' *ERTA* paras 9–10.

137 Opinion of Mr Advocate-General Dutheillet de Lamothe, above note 134, at 289.

138 *Ibid*, 293.

139 'The Court did not follow the traditional interpretation, according to which the competence of an international organization should be interpreted restrictively, but, assuming the function of a constitutional court, it followed a teleological interpretation of the Treaty.' Takis Tridimas and Piet Eeckhout, 'The External Competence of the Community and the Case-law of the Court of Justice: Principle versus Pragmatism' (1994) 14 *Yearbook of European Law* 143, 149.

140 *Ibid*, 149.

141 *ERTA*, paras 15–16.

> With regard to the implementation of the provision of the Treaty the system of internal Community measures may not therefore be separated from that of external relations.[142]

Although the Treaty did 'not expressly confer on the Community authority to enter into international agreements' in the area of transportation,[143] nevertheless the fact that members of the European polity had joined together to create Regulation No 543/69 meant that they had 'vested in the Community power to enter into any agreements with third countries relating to the subject-mater governed by that regulation'.[144] To conclude otherwise would 'be incompatible with the unity of the Common Market and the uniform application of Community law'.[145]

Although the logic of the *ERTA* decision may not be legally or constitutionally transparent, it closely tracks the structure of politics within a polity. The ECJ recognised that the law of the Treaty had created the political space within which Member States could engage with each other to enact Regulation No 543/69. Regulation No 543/69 was the tangible result of the mutual trust and reciprocity of internal politics. The question facing the ECJ was whether the Regulation, as well as the trust necessary for the enactment of future regulations, would be undermined if Member States could separately negotiate with third parties to draft an ERTA that might potentially conflict with the Regulation. The ECJ had no difficulty answering this question. As it opined four years later, to accept the possibility 'that, in relations with third countries, member states may adopt positions which differ from those which the community intends to adopt . . . . would . . . distort the institutional framework, call into question the mutual trust within the Community and prevent the latter from fulfilling its task in the defence of the common interest'.[146]

The legal conclusion of exclusive Community competence thus follows directly from the need to preserve the integrity of internal Community politics. *ERTA* accurately expresses the paradoxical interdependence of internal and external politics. The internal agora of the former, which generates power and legitimacy, must ultimately be sustained by the 'fighting collectivity' of the latter, which guards 'the defence of the common interest'.

The ECJ in *ERTA* does not derive the legal norm of exclusive Community competence from the text of the Treaty, but instead from actual exercise of internal Community politics. The ECJ regards Articles 74–84 of the Treaty as fixed and binding authority that establishes a sphere of 'common action'[147] with regard to the subject of transportation. The ECJ treats these Articles like the 'city wall' invoked by Heraclites; they define the space within which internal politics can proceed. Exclusive Community competence does not arise until members of the Community polity have actually joined together within that agora to enact Regulation No 543/69. The enactment of Regulation No 543/69, rather than the text of the Treaty, is legally decisive. The legal norm of exclusive Community competence flows directly from the historical exercise of collective political will.

The Court's technical disposition of the case depends on this point. At issue in *ERTA* was the question of whether certain 'conclusions' of the Council 'on the attitude to be taken by the Governments of the Member States in the decisive negotiations on the

142 *Ibid*, paras 17–19.
143 *Ibid*, para 28.
144 *Ibid*.
145 *Ibid*, para 31.
146 Opinion 1/75 [1975] ECR 155.
147 Preamble, Treaty Establishing the European Economic Community, above note 120, 61.

ERTA'[148] should be annulled because inconsistent with the role of the Commission as the sole representative of the Community in matters concerning which the Community has exclusive external competence. Although the ECJ held that the enactment of Regulation No 543/69 had created such exclusive external competence, it also ruled that the Council's conclusions should not be annulled because of the complex relationship between their timing and the 'period' when 'the common transport policy was not yet sufficiently developed' to deprive 'Member States' of the 'power to conclude' ERTA.[149] In *ERTA* the ECJ allocated power within the Community on the basis of a sensitive appreciation of the actual historical unfolding of concrete internal political processes.

This approach carried significant advantages for the ECJ's goal of perfecting the European polity. The very reticence of the Treaty on the question of external competence suggests how controversial control over external politics can be in the delicate dance of European integration. By tying the transfer of exclusive competence to specific political commitments, the ECJ was able to invoke bonds of reciprocity and trust generated by those commitments as a justification for transferring competence from Member States to the Community. *ERTA* is in this regard a shrewd and careful opinion. It relies upon power created within the internal agora to authorise the Community to engage in external politics to defend the exercise of that power.

ERTA 'marked a watershed in the definition of the Community's external competence'.[150] It came to stand for the conclusion that the ECJ would infer exclusive external competence, the mark of a fully developed polity, not merely from 'an express conferment by the Treaty', but also from 'the adoption of internal measures'.[151] The goal was to prevent 'the Community's unity of action being compromised by potential divergences between the internal measures and those subsequently adopted externally'.[152] The ECJ has recently and dramatically reaffirmed these principles in the *Open Skies* judgments.

Like *ERTA*, the *Open Skies* judgments involved a highly technical and arcane subject. At issue were bilateral treaties regulating various aspects of commercial air travel between the United States and numerous important Member States, including Germany, the UK, Denmark, Sweden, Belgium, Austria, and Luxembourg. Separate control over commercial air traffic was far more important to Member States than separate control over the road crews that had been at issue in *ERTA*. If the 1957 Treaty had stated that the achievement of 'a common transport policy' was a goal of the Community,[153] it had also specified that such common policy concerned only 'transport by rail, road and inland waterway'[154] and that 'the Council may, acting unanimously, decide whether, to what extent and by what

[148] *ERTA*, para 44.

[149] *ERTA*, para 82. I should also note that the ECJ was highly attuned to the pragmatic consequences of shifting competence in the midst of the ERTA negotiations. 'At that stage of the negotiations, to have suggested to the third countries concerned that there was now a new distribution of powers within the Community might well have jeopardized the successful outcome of the negotiations, as was indeed recognized by the Commission's representative in the course of the Council's deliberations.' *Ibid*, para 86.

[150] Opinion of Advocate General Tizzano on 31 January 2002 in the *Open Skies* judgments, para 63.

[151] Case C-467/98, *Commission v Denmark* [2002], paras 77–78.

[152] Opinion of Advocate General Tizzano on 31 January 2002 in the *Open Skies* judgments, para 64.

[153] Article 74, above note 120.

[154] *Ibid*, at Article 84(1).

procedure appropriate provisions may be laid down for sea and air transport'.[155] Member States jealously guarded their independent prerogatives to regulate commercial air travel.

Starting in 1990 the Commission had 'repeatedly requested a mandate from the Council to negotiate' a common Community 'air transport agreement' with the United States,[156] but it had been continuously rebuffed[157] on the ground that 'the Member States retained their full powers in relations with third countries in the aviation sector, subject to measures already adopted or to be adopted by the Council in that domain'.[158] When the United States in the 1990s initiated forceful diplomatic initiatives to negotiate bilateral treaties with individual Member States, the Commission warned that the proposed treaties were incompatible with 'the Community's external competence'.[159] In 1998 the Commission brought an action against Member States seeking a declaration that Community law had been infringed.

The suit forced the ECJ to intervene in a highly controversial subject. The Commission's first gambit was to urge the ECJ to abandon the *ERTA* framework and to decide the question of exclusive external competence on the basis of abstract legal norms. The Commission contended that the bilateral treaties violated Community law because 'the Community has exclusive competence to conclude an international agreement, even in the absence of Community provisions in the areas concerned, where the conclusion of such an agreement is necessary in order to attain the objectives of the Treaty in that area, such objectives being incapable of being attained merely by introducing autonomous common rules'.[160]

The Commission sought an abstract legal judgment that 'the field of air transport' was inherently 'international' so that it was impossible to separate 'the internal and external markets'.[161] It contended that as a matter of law it was 'necessary to prescribe, through Community measures . . . the treatment to be accorded to third-country carriers and to conclude the corresponding agreements'.[162] The bilateral agreements negotiated by individual Member States would distort 'competition' and destabilise 'the Community market' by allowing 'American carriers to operate on the intra-Community market without being subject to all the obligations of the system established by Community rules, and to compete in this way with their Community counterparts'.[163]

The Commission's argument invoked an old and ambiguous decision, Opinion 1/76, which seemed to hold that if 'the participation of the Community' in an 'international agreement is necessary for attaining one of the Community's objectives',[164] the Community could acquire exclusive external competence even in the absence of an express Treaty

[155] *Ibid*, at Article 84(2). This provision has since been modified to read: 'The Council may, acting by a qualified majority, decide whether, to what extent and by what procedure appropriate provisions may be laid down for sea and air transport.' It is now to be found in the Consolidated Treaty at Article 80(2).

[156] Opinion of Advocate General Tizzano on 31 January 2002 in the *Open Skies* judgments, paras 9–14.

[157] A 'limited mandate' for negotiating with the United States in relation to a specified set of subjects was finally granted in 1996. *Ibid*, at para 12.

[158] *Ibid*, para 11.

[159] *Ibid*, para 20. The Commission also believed that the right of establishment would be violated, as well as the general duty of co-operation created by the old Article 5 (now Article 10). *Ibid.*

[160] Case C-467/98, *Commission v Denmark* [2002], para 45.

[161] *Ibid*, para 46.

[162] *Ibid*, para 46.

[163] *Ibid*, paras 47–48.

[164] *Ibid*, para 56. Opinion 1/76 *re Inland Waterways* [1977] ECR 741. For a discussion of the ambiguities of this opinion, see Eeeckhout, above note 133, at 64–9.

provision and even in the absence of Community legislation that might be 'affected' (in the sense of *ERTA*). Like *ERTA*, Opinion 1/76 rests on the functional interdependence of internal and external politics. But in contrast to *ERTA*, Opinion 1/76 regards this interdependence abstractly. If the genius of *ERTA* was that exclusive external competence would be transferred to the Community only *after* Member States had themselves first demonstrated the need for internal collective action by enacting common legislation, Opinion 1/76 would authorise this transfer solely on the basis of the Court's own legal judgment that exclusive Community competence was necessary to preserve the possibility of internal politics. Because the 'legal' underpinnings of any such judgment would always be controversial, the logic of Opinion 1/76 placed the ECJ in a far more exposed and vulnerable position than did the logic of *ERTA*.

Given the Council's explicit repudiations of the Commission's past efforts to assume Community control over air travel, the ECJ in the *Open Skies* judgments was not about to risk its own political capital by independently inferring the existence of exclusive external competence. It observed instead that community institutions were fully able to mitigate 'any discrimination or distortions of competition' that might be caused by the bilateral agreements of Member States. The Court brusquely concluded that it did not perceive 'a situation in which internal competence could effectively be exercised only at the same time as external competence'.[165]

The ECJ instead sought the safe harbour of *ERTA*. It struck down the provisions in the bilateral agreements that 'affected' Regulation No 2409/92, which addressed the setting of fares and rates on intra-Community routes, and the provisions that 'affected' Regulation No 2299/89, which addressed the use of computerised reservation systems (CRSs). The Court relied on *ERTA* for the conclusion that Regulations Nos 2409/92 and 2299/89 had rendered these particular aspects of the treaties invalid because beyond the competence of the Member States.[166] The Court conspicuously determined that the bilateral treaties did not 'affect' other regulations that had been adduced by the Commission, in particular Regulations Nos 2408/92 and 95/93.

The ECJ was thus careful to tie the question of external competence to actual legislation. It explicitly theorised the project of perfecting the European polity in terms of the progress of internal European politics:

> [E]ach time the Community, with a view to implementing a common policy envisaged by the Treaty, adopts provisions laying down common rules, whatever form these may take, the Member States no longer have the right, acting individually or even collectively, to undertake obligations towards non-member countries which affect those rules or distort their scope; and . . . when such common rules come into being, the Community alone is in a position to assume and carry out contractual obligations towards non-member countries affecting the whole sphere of application of the Community legal system.[167]

The ECJ positioned itself as merely expressing the immanent logic of the Community's own internal politics. It asserted that these politics, not the Court, triggered the need for

[165] *Ibid*, para 62.

[166] 'It follows . . . that, by entering into international commitments concerning air fares and rates charged by carriers designated by the United States of America on intra-Community routes and concerning CRSs offered for use or used in' the Territory of a Member State, the Member State 'has failed to fulfill its obligations under Article 5 of the Treaty and under Regulations Nos 2409/92 and 2299/89.' *Ibid*, para 112.

[167] *Ibid*, para 77.

unity vis-à-vis non-Member States. The Court described the nature of this need in overtly Schmittian terms: 'If the Member States were free to enter into international commitments affecting the common rules adopted . . . that would jeopardize the attainment of the objective pursued by those rules and would thus prevent the Community from fulfilling its task in the *defence* of the common interest.'[168]

If the structure of the *Open Skies* judgments derives directly from *ERTA*, the spirit of these more recent opinions seems quite distinct. The ECJ had in *ERTA* been quite attentive to the ebb and flow of actual internal political engagement. Its conclusion that the Council's conclusions should not be invalidated expressed a nuanced appreciation of complex historical processes. This sensitivity may have been required because European integration was then in its early stages and hence more controversial, or it may have been required because the Court's own position as the promoter of the European polity was more insecure.

The ECJ in the *Open Skies* judgments, by contrast, does not feel the need to deploy an analogously subtle awareness of the actual internal politics of commercial air traffic. It instead treats Community legislation as a purely formal trigger for the transfer of exclusive competence. The Court announces, for example, that if Community legislation contains 'provisions relating to the treatment of nationals of non-member countries', the Community automatically 'acquires an exclusive external competence in the spheres covered by those acts'.[169] The ECJ uses this formal and broad interpretation of the concept of 'affecting' Community legislation to strike down elements of the bilateral treaties.[170]

Far from the close attention to the actual, historical interrelationship between internal and external politics that was the hallmark of *ERTA*, the ECJ in the *Open Skies* judgments seems to regard the existence of Regulations Nos 2409/92 and 2299/89 almost as an excuse for the abrupt transfer of exclusive competence to the Community. The ECJ is concerned that this transfer be complete and formal. It explicitly states that the bilateral agreements are to be set aside even if they explicitly require that Community regulations 'be complied with',[171] for Member States are 'not authorized to enter into' the bilateral agreements on their own, even if the substance of the agreements 'does not conflict with community law'.[172]

This suggests that, appearances to the contrary notwithstanding, the ECJ in the *Open Skies* judgments feels greater independence to pursue its agenda of perfecting the European polity than had the ECJ in *ERTA*. Although in the *Open Skies* judgments the ECJ refuses nakedly to advance this agenda in its own name as it had in Opinion 1/76, it nevertheless feels confident enough to seize upon Community legislation as a mere occasion formally to fuse internal politics with external politics so as to form a single, complete polity. The ECJ no longer seems interested in appropriating the legitimacy created by the actual political will expressed by Community legislation. In *ERTA* the ECJ had sheltered itself under the wings of that legitimacy, but in the *Open Skies* judgments the Court protects its own position instead by striking out on its own path of ostentatiously determining *which* regulations will utterly strip Member States of external competence.

168 *Ibid*, para 79 (emphasis added).
169 *Ibid*, para 83.
170 *Ibid*, para 96.
171 *Ibid*, para 101.
172 *Ibid*.

That is the significance of the Court's exaggerated deference to the rights of Member States in the context of Regulations Nos 2408/92 and 95/93.

The Court in the *Open Skies* judgments thus stakes out a complicated position. It no longer feels the need to push for European integration by harnessing the actual power created by internal political commitments. But neither does it feel free to step too far out in front of internal political developments as it had in Opinion 1/76. Instead in the *Open Skies* judgments the ECJ uses the cover of Community legislation polity to perfect the European polity. Because such legislation will always be distinct and particular, this strategy leaves the ECJ ample room for retreat and manoeuvre should its agenda in particular circumstances prove untenable as the project of European integration negotiates the strong cross-currents of recent decades. It is, on the whole, a masterful performance by a confident and forceful Court.

VII

Case 43/75, *Gabrielle Defrenne v Société Anonyme Belge de Navigation Aérienne Sabena*

1

The Shock Troops Arrive in Force: Horizontal Direct Effect of a Treaty Provision and Temporal Limitation of Judgments Join the Armoury of EC Law

ELEANOR SHARPSTON[1]

Lord Denning famously described the overall impact of EEC law on English law in prophetic terms (entirely appropriate to a maritime nation) in *HP Bulmer Ltd v J Bollinger SA*, when he declared[2]:

> But when we come to matters with a European element, the Treaty is like an incoming tide. It flows into the estuaries and up the rivers. It cannot be held back.

The effect of *Defrenne* on comfortable, traditional English notions of what courts can (or should) do with legislative texts might be regarded as more akin to a tidal rip.

The Defrenne Saga

Gabrielle Defrenne seems an unlikely heroine of Community law. She joined Sabena, the Belgian national carrier, as an air hostess in 1951. In 1963 she was given a new contract of employment which described her duties as 'Cabin steward and air hostess—Principal cabin attendant'. Obviously she was an efficient and valuable member of the flight team. However, on 15 February 1968 she gave up her duties, in accordance with Article 5(5) of her contract of employment, which stated that contracts held by women members of the crew shall terminate on the day on which the employee in question reaches the age of 40 years. When she left Sabena, she received an allowance on termination of service.

Mrs Defrenne brought two separate sets of proceedings. First, she brought an action on 13 March 1968 before the Tribunal du travail of Brussels, seeking compensation for the loss she had suffered in terms of arrears of salary, termination allowance and pension entitlement as a result of the fact that air hostesses and male members of the cabin crew

[1] The views expressed are personal to the author and do not bind the Court at which I serve as an Advocate General. I am grateful to my colleague in chambers, Dr Geert de Baere, and to Miranda Aldrich de Savorgnani (the Middle Temple's 2007 Bristow Scholar) for their assistance in tracking down material and filling in citation references.

[2] [1974] Ch 401 at 418.

performing identical duties did not receive equal pay. She also brought a challenge on 9 February 1970 before the Conseil d'Etat, seeking annulment of the Royal Decree of 3 November 1969 which laid down special rules governing the acquisition of the right to a pension by air crew in civilian aviation.

On 17 December 1970 the Tribunal du travail dismissed her claims for arrears of salary, termination allowance and pension entitlement as unfounded. On 11 January 1971 Mrs Defrenne appealed that judgment to the Cour du travail of Brussels. Her appeal sat in the queue before the national court for over four years.

In the meantime, she lost her case before the Conseil d'Etat. On a reference under what was then Article 177 EC,[3] the ECJ held by judgment of 25 May 1971 in Case 80/70 *Defrenne v Belgium* ('*Defrenne I*') [1971] ECR 445 that a retirement pension established within the framework of a social security scheme laid down by legislation does not constitute consideration which the worker receives from his employer within the meaning of Article 119(2) EEC. The Conseil d'Etat duly dismissed her application by a judgment of 10 December 1971.

With the score standing at 2–0 against her, a less stubborn lady than Mrs Defrenne might have lost heart and given up the fight. Not so: she maintained her appeal before the Cour du travail. Finally, on 23 April 1975 that court upheld the judgment of the Tribunal du travail dismissing her claims in respect of termination allowance and pension entitlement. However, it was persuaded to make a reference to the ECJ in respect of her claim for arrears of salary.[4] It therefore asked the ECJ to rule on the following questions:

> 1.Does Article 119 of the Treaty of Rome[5] introduce directly into the national law of each Member State of the European Community the principle that men and women should receive equal pay for equal work and does it, therefore, independently of any national provision, entitle workers to institute proceedings before national courts in order to ensure its observance, and if so from what date?
>
> 2.Has Article 119 become applicable in the internal law of the Member States by virtue of measures adopted by the authorities of the European Economic Community (if so, which and as from what date?) or must the national legislature be regarded as alone competent in this matter?

Mrs Defrenne and the Commission lodged observations—perhaps surprisingly, Belgium did not. However, both the United Kingdom and Ireland intervened to say, at length and volubly, that Article 119 did not satisfy the criteria for direct effect and introduced no rule on equal pay into the national legal orders of the Member States.[6] The Commission argued that Article 119 *had* become directly effective upon expiry of the (extended) transitional period.[7]

In his opinion, Advocate General Trabucchi treated sex discrimination in the same light as discrimination based on nationality, which was without doubt contrary to the Treaty.

[3] Now Art 234 EC.

[4] Case 43/75 *Defrenne v SABENA* ('*Defrenne II*') [1976] ECR 455.

[5] Now Art 141 EC.

[6] Since the United Kingdom had introduced an Equal Pay Act in 1970, the argument was perhaps less on the actual concept of equal pay as such (although the Equal Pay Act 1970 is less broadly drawn than the then Art 119 EEC) than on the unpalatable notion that Art 119 might be directly effective (let alone horizontally directly effective).

[7] Initially, Member States had until the end of the first stage of the transitional period, ie, until 1 January 1962, to implement the principle of equal pay. However, the Resolution of the Conference of the Member States of 30 December 1961 on the equalisation of rates of pay for men and women workers sought to extend that deadline to 31 December 1964.

He considered that, even though the form of words used ('principle that men and women should receive equal pay') might seem too vague and the meaning of the word 'principle' itself might not be very specific, the purpose of the rule was nevertheless clear: to prohibit any discrimination to the detriment of women with regard to pay.[8] Sex equality was one of the fundamental rights that the Court was bound to safeguard. He took a similarly robust approach to the doubts that one might entertain about the precise definitions of the concepts of 'pay' and 'equal work'.[9] The Member States' resolution extending the deadline for full application of that principle could not amend the Treaty provisions themselves. As for the objections to recognising that Treaty provisions might have 'horizontal' direct effect, 'the decisive factor in determining what the effects of a Community provision are in national law is not the identity of those to whom it is addressed but its nature, which the Court defines on the basis of 'the spirit, the general scheme and the wording' of the provision itself'.[10] His recommendation to the Court was stark in its simplicity: horizontal direct effect and no temporal limitation.

In its judgment, the Court began by making clear the interpretative approach that it intended to take:

> The question of the direct effect of Article 119 must be considered in the light of the nature of the principle of equal pay, the aim of this provision and its place in the scheme of the Treaty.[11]

It began conservatively enough:

> Article [141] pursues a double aim.
> *First* ... the aim of Article 119 is to avoid a situation in which undertakings established in states which have actually implemented the principle of equal pay suffer a competitive disadvantage in intra-Community competition as compared with undertakings established in states which have not yet eliminated discrimination against women workers as regards pay.[12]

Having given precedence to the market-economy concept of a 'level playing field', however, the Court followed Advocate General Trabucchi's social lead:

> *Second*, this provision forms part of the social objectives of the Community, which is not merely an economic union, but is at the same time intended, by common action to ensure social progress and seek the constant improvement of living and working conditions of their peoples, as is emphasized by the Preamble to the Treaty.
> This double aim, which is at once economic and social, shows that the principle of equal pay forms part of the foundations of the Community.

...

> ... in interpreting this provision, it is impossible to base any argument on the dilatoriness and resistance which have delayed the actual implementation of this basic principle in certain Member States.
> In particular, since Article 119 appears in the context of the harmonization of working conditions while the improvement is being maintained, the objection that the terms of this article may be observed in other ways that by raising the lowest salaries may be set aside.

[8] At 486.
[9] *Ibid.*
[10] At 486.
[11] Para 7.
[12] Paras 8 and 9, emphasis added.

> Under the terms of the first paragraph of Article 119, the Member States are *bound to ensure and maintain* 'the application of the principle that men and women should receive equal pay for equal work'.[13]

After that forthright stance, the Court proceeded to draw a careful distinction between 'direct and overt discrimination which may be identified solely with the aid of the criteria of equal pay and equal work referred to in [Article 119]' and 'indirect and disguised discrimination which can only be identified by reference to more explicit implementing provisions of a Community or national character'.[14] The treatment which formed the subject-matter of Mrs Defrenne's complaint fell within the first category. As was shown by the very findings of the judgment making the reference, the national court was in a position to establish all the facts that would enable it to decide whether the female worker was receiving lower pay than a male worker performing the same tasks. The Court concluded that 'in such a situation at least, Article 119 is directly applicable and may thus give rise to individual rights which the courts must protect'.[15]

In so saying, the Court gave very short shrift to the objection that Article 119 should not have 'horizontal' direct effect. It considered that it was 'not possible to sustain any objection that the application by national courts of the principle of equal pay would amount to modifying independent agreements concluded privately or in the sphere of industrial relations such as individual contracts and collective agreements. In fact, since Article 119 is mandatory in nature, the prohibition on discrimination between men and women applies not only to the action of public authorities, but also extends to all agreements which are intended to regulate paid labour collectively, as well as to contracts between individuals'.[16]

However, in a conciliatory gesture towards Ireland and the United Kingdom, who had made much of the possible economic consequences of attributing direct effect to Article 119, the Court was prepared 'to take exceptionally into account the fact that, over a prolonged period, the parties concerned [had] been led to continue with practices which were contrary to Article 119, although not yet prohibited under their national law'.[17] The Court concluded that, 'In these circumstances, it is appropriate to determine that, as the general level at which pay would have been fixed cannot be known, important considerations of legal certainty affecting all the interests involved, both public and private, make it impossible in principle to reopen the question as regards the past. Therefore, the direct effect of Article 119 cannot be relied on in order to support claims concerning pay periods prior to the date of this judgment, except as regards those workers who have already brought legal proceedings or made an equivalent claim'.[18]

[13] Paras 10–16, emphasis added.
[14] Para 18.
[15] Para 24.
[16] Paras 38 and 39.
[17] Para 72.
[18] Paras 74 and 75.

The Commentators

What have the English-language commentators made of the various aspects of the ECJ's ruling in *Defrenne II*?

Some disliked it, root and branch. Philip Allott,[19] under the heading 'The European Court *ordains* equal pay for women'[20] complained that, 'The laconic temerity of the European Court is now one of its settled traditions, and yet each further instance is somehow able to amaze us once again'. Recognising that the implications of the ruling went far beyond its effect on national pay legislation, he singled out four aspects of the decision for critical comment. First, *Defrenne II* shows that a 'teleological element [must be] put in a prominent place in the list of indicators of direct applicability'. Secondly, 'if the Article 119 principle has general direct effect, it will also, and predominantly, affect contractual relations between non-governmental persons'—a point that came in for scathing comment.[21] Thirdly, although legal regulation of equal pay for women was not 'fallow ground' when the Court came to it, the Court had blithely ignored what it did not wish to be influenced by in reaching its decision.[22] But he reserved his fiercest criticism for the fourth element, which he termed the 'legislative aspect' of the Court's decision.[23]

Hjalte Rasmussen, noted for his criticism of what he regards as the ECJ's undue judicial activism, classified *Defrenne II* as one of the examples of 'the most grave judicial policy involvement … where judicial constructions are made squarely disrespectful of the textual indications found in the constitutional documents'.[24] When later he states baldly that, 'The most illuminating European case is probably [*Defrenne II*]'[25] he is not being complimentary. 'It was the blatant policymaking, much more than the socio-economic fact having a crucial impact on the interpretation of the law, that was in the center of the many protests which sounded out in the aftermath of *Defrenne II*.'[26] However, he considers that '*Defrenne II* should … be hailed for its merit that the Court brought itself abreast of the requirements of one crucial parameter of modern constitutional litigation: it accepted the responsibility to mould constitutional doctrine in order to make more acceptable the practical effects of judicial decision'.[27] Put slightly differently—if the Court is going to upset everyone with an innovative ruling on the meaning of a text, at least it had the sense to upset them for the future, not the past.

Two aspects of the Court's ruling provoked not only contemporary commentary, but raised questions that have continued to echo down the years since *Defrenne II* was

[19] (1977) *Cambridge Law Journal* 7–10.

[20] My emphasis.

[21] See below.

[22] 'The Court took the view that the ILO convention obligations [under ILO Convention No 100 of 29 June 1951] did not affect the EEC Treaty obligations, that the Belgian Decree of 1967 [expressly implementing Art 119 but differing in its effect from the interpretation finally given by the Court] was irrelevant and that the Community acts [threats of infringement proceedings and the Equal Pay Directive] could not have altered the effect of Art 119.'

[23] See below.

[24] Hjalte Rasmussen, On Law and Policy in the European Court of Justice: A Comparative Study in Judicial Policymaking (Dordrecht, Martinus Nijhoff Publishers, 1986) at 29.

[25] At 438 (section sub-heading).

[26] At 441.

[27] *Ibid.*

decided: the horizontal direct effect of Article 119 EC (now, Article 141 EC) and the temporal limitation of the effects of a judgment of the Court.

The Court's Ruling on Article 119

Writing in 2006, Antony Arnull[28] comments that '[b]y comparison with the provisions on freedom of movement and competition, those dealing with social policy were fairly anodyne',[29] and goes on to single out Article 119 as the provision that, 'although originally introduced as a result of a French initiative to prevent competition from being distorted by differing national standards on the matter ... has been used by the Court of Justice in a bold and creative way to develop a powerful right to equal pay for equal work'.[30] That article 'formed part of a title of the Treaty which appeared largely programmatic in nature and the argument that it was not directly effective was by no means devoid of merit. The Court evidently regarded the Member States' failure to comply with the obligations imposed on them by Article 119 as wholly unacceptable. It may also have seen itself as acting in accordance with the declarations, referred to by Advocate General Trabucchi at the beginning of his opinion, made by the Heads of State and Government in Paris in 1972.'[31]

For Allott in 1977, however, the Court's boldness and creativity were not welcome features of its ruling. Horizontal direct effect was a wholly unwelcome development. Here, Allott is stinging in his criticism: 'As with the Community's rules of competition ... the Court is content to leave others to work out the consequences of its broad interpretation of superficial and imprecise Community rules imposed upon the complex and urgent legal relationships of the everyday world.' Moreover, 'Article 177 confers on the Court a power to give rulings concerning "the interpretation" of the Treaty. Its ruling in the *Defrenne* case is legislative in that, because Article 119 is plainly not a complete legislative provision on equal pay, the Court gave some general indications as to the substantive effect of the Article.'

Here is indeed the nub of the problem. Seen through the eyes of the common law tradition, instruments enacted by public authorities that set binding parameters governing legal relationships between private parties are drawn like English statutes. They contain careful definitions and detailed rules, each expressing the specific choices that the legislator, elected to Parliament and accountable directly to it, has made. Broad statements of principle, whilst indubitably familiar from international law, have no business imposing legally binding rules whose scope, to English eyes, is vague, uncertain, unascertainable. Comparative law makes English-trained lawyers aware that other legal systems do, perhaps, frame their statutes differently from us—and of course, within their own legal traditions, they are quite free to do so. It was the intrusion, into our own legal system, of binding horizontal direct effect flowing from such an imprecise instrument as a Treaty article that was so very shocking. In that respect, Allott was not necessarily wrong to be appalled. His was an eminently respectable common law reaction.

[28] Anthony Arnull, *The European Union and its Court of Justice* (2nd edition) (Oxford EC Law Library, Oxford, Oxford University Press, 2006).

[29] At 534.

[30] At 535.

[31] At 538: the passage in the Advocate General's opinion to which he refers is [1976] ECR 455 at 483.

On the whole, Allott's reaction was probably shared by many English lawyers of the time—not many other English lawyers were quite like Lord Denning. In 1974, in his 'user's guide' to EC legal drafting, he had already explained (in the inimitable Denning style) that:

> The treaty is unlike any of the enactments to which we have become accustomed. The draftsmen of our statutes have striven to express themselves with the utmost exactness. They have tried to foresee all possible circumstances that may arise and provide for them. They have sacrificed style and simplicity. They have foregone brevity. They have become long and involved ... In consequence, the judges have followed suit. How different is this Treaty! It lays down general principles. It expresses its aims and purposes. All in sentences of moderate length and commendable style. But it lacks precision. It uses words without defining what they mean. An English lawyer would look for an interpretation clause but he would look in vain. There is none. All the way through the Treaty there are gaps and lacunae. They have to be filled in by the judges, or by Regulations and Directives. It is the European way ... Seeing these difficulties, what are the English courts to do when they are faced with a problem of interpretation? They must follow the European pattern. No longer must they examine the words in meticulous detail. No longer must they argue about the precise grammatical sense. They must look to the purpose or intent.[32]

Later (and younger) commentators are either less appalled or have become used to the fact that 'Community law does it differently'. Thus Claire Kirkpatrick, in a thoughtful article, considers (after quoting that same Denning passage) that 'The terms of any dialogue between the UK courts and the ECJ on sex equality would inevitably be unlike those in other Member States which had simply implemented Community obligations largely by reproducing the provisions of Article 119, the Equal Pay Directive and the Equal Treatment Directive into national legislation. Despite accepting that the [Equal Pay Act 1970] and the [Sex Discrimination Act 1975] were the national implementation of Community sex equality obligations in what Lester dubbed "a necessary legal and political fiction",[33] it was clear that this acceptance would require the British courts to mediate two styles of legislative drafting and statutory interpretation which were poles apart.'[34]

Looking back, it seems that the 'shock value' of horizontal direct effect in *Defrenne II* should indeed be attributed to the Court's use of almost pure teleology (purpose over literal wording) and its willingness to contemplate that *any* Treaty provision might operate 'horizontally'[35] than to the possible specific consequences of imposing equal pay for women in contractual relations between private sector employers and employees. The Equal Pay Act 1970 had, after all, already introduced the essence of such a requirement, albeit in a typical English statutory style.[36] *Defrenne II* was worrying because no one really

[32] *Bulmer v Bollinger* (cited in note 1) at 425–6.

[33] A Lester, 'The Uncertain Trumpet. References to the Court of Justice from the United Kingdom: Equal Pay and Equal Treatment without Sex Discrimination' in HC Schermers *et al* (eds) *Article 177 EEC: Experiences and Problems* (TMC Asser Instituut, 1987) 164 at 165.

[34] C Kirkpatrick, 'Community or Communities of Courts in European Integration? Sex Equality Dialogues Between UK Courts and the ECJ' (June 1998) (4)(2) *European Law Journal*, 121–47 at 132.

[35] The Court eventually confirmed the horizontal direct effect of Art 81 EC (ex Art 85) in Case C-453/99 *Courage Ltd v Bernard Crehan* [2001] ECR I-6297.

[36] Section 1(1) and (2) state:

1.—(1) The provisions of this section shall have effect with a view to securing that employers give equal treatment as regards terms and conditions of employment to men and to women, that is to say that (subject to the provisions of this section and of section 6 below) —

(a) for men and women employed on like work the terms and conditions of one sex are not in any respect less favourable than those of the other; and

knew how big—or active—was the genie that the Court had just conjured out of the lamp. And, if the Court could do that with the wording of Article 119, what might it not do with other Treaty provisions, in due course?

Some commentators have sought to place the actual decision in *Defrenne II* in a wider context. Thus, Barnard[37] discusses whether the Court, pursuing 'its own distinctive market-integrationalist agenda',[38] has focused on the 'market-correcting'[39] function of social policy on its 'market-making' dimensions. 'The market-making thesis comprises two limbs: first, the creation of a European-wide labour market, by removing obstacles to the mobility of workers, and secondly, removing distortions to competition by, on the one hand, seeking to harmonise costs on firms and, on the other, preventing social dumping by firms and a race to the bottom by States. The clearest example of the market-making thesis can be found with the inclusion of Article 141 [that is, Article 119] on equal pay in the Treaty'.[40] She concludes, 'It therefore seems that the Community has seen social policy in terms of a dichotomy combining a market-led conception of employment regulation, with some recognition of the market-correcting or social function of such regulation.'[41] I agree with her that the Court may well have had its eye as much on the economic consequences of *not* ensuring that all Member States had to apply equal pay between the sexes as on the social desirability of saying that it was important for them to do so. It was, after all, the economic condition, rather than the social condition, that the Court turned to first in its judgment. That said, *Defrenne II* represents the first real indication from the Court that the social side of establishing a 'common market' might also be important. The fact that the Court attributed a double aim to Article 119; and that it began by stressing the market-economy, 'level playing field' argument, should not detract from the significance of that step.

The Temporal Limitation

In *Defrenne II*, the Court first employed the device of limiting the temporal effect of its judgment. Criticism was not slow in coming. Arnull records that, 'In a paper presented at a conference held in Luxembourg less than six months after *Defrenne* was decided,

(b) for men and women employed on work rated as equivalent (within the meaning of subsection (5) below) the terms and conditions of one sex are not less favourable than those of the other in any respect in which the terms and conditions of both are determined by the rating of their work.
The following provisions of this section and section 2 below are framed with reference to women and their treatment relative to men, but are to be read as applying equally in a converse case to men and their treatment relative to women.
(2) It shall be a term of the contract under which a woman is employed at an establishment in Great Britain that she shall be given equal treatment with men in the same employment, that is to say men employed by her employer or any associated employer at the same establishment or at establishments in Great Britain which include that one and at which common terms and conditions of employment are observed either generally or for employees of the relevant classes.

[37] C Barnard, EC Employment Law 3rd edn (Oxford, Oxford University Press, 2006).

[38] A quotation from Streek, 'From Market Making to State Building? Reflections on the Political Economy of European Social Policy' in Leibfried and Pierson (eds), *European Social Policy: Between Fragmentation and Integration* (Washington DC, Brookings Institution, 1995) 399.

[39] At national level, social policy is traditionally viewed as serving a social justice or social cohesion function that corrects the results that would otherwise be generated by the unfettered operation of market forces.

[40] Barnard, above note 38, at 51, citing Streek, above note 39.

[41] At 53–4.

Hansom[42] argued that the Court had arrogated to itself "a dispensing power which I believe is not known to any modern court of any of the Member States", namely the power to declare what the law is as to the future but to leave the past untouched. That power, he observed, "is inherently the mark of the legislative function and there is an obstinate belief upon the continent of Europe that a court does not have a legislative function". In Hamson's view, the Court had been driven to take this position as a result of its unduly enthusiastic development of the doctrine of direct effect, which might otherwise have produced "chaos".[43]

Allott,[44] having expressed his dismay at horizontal direct effect,[45] continued, '[The Court's] decision ... is also legislative in the more dramatic sense that, while finding that Article 119 has had direct effect since 1 January 1962 (1 January 1973 in the case of the new Member States, including the United Kingdom), the Court was apparently impressed by economic arguments put forward by the British and Irish Governments ...; accordingly the Court purported to exclude the possibility of retrospective claims based on the Article. To regard this part of the ruling as stating a rule of Community law, it would be necessary to show that the Court is a common-law court or else a constitutional court. That is to say, it would be regarded, like the House of Lords, as stating the law in such a way that its statement retrospectively (in respect of past situations) and prospectively constitutes the law. Or else, like the Supreme Court of the United States, its statement of the law would be the interpretation of an existing text which potentially contained the content which, as from now on, is found actually to be present in it. There are strong grounds for regarding the Court as, indeed, falling into both categories and the courts of the original Member States have come close to acknowledging this as a fact. It remains to be seen whether a British court, particularly the House of Lords, would be willing to do as much, or whether it would regard the Court as having exceeded its jurisdiction.'

There was, indeed, a tendency to draw on the US tradition for comfort. One anonymous commentator[46] described the prospect of hundreds of backdated legal actions by disgruntled women workers as 'daunting' and greeted the temporal limitation with relief in the following terms: 'This judicial involvement in administrative policy has been much criticised, but in fact it is a necessary concomitant to [the Court's] legislative actions and represents a welcome acceptance of its responsibility for the practical consequences of an apparent unilateral change in the law by the *ipse dixit* of the Court alone. In this, the Court was in fact following the long-established practice of the US Supreme Court which was dramatically exemplified in the latter's judgments in *Brown v Board of Education*.'[47]

Derrick Wyatt[48] likewise reassured his readers that, 'The phenomenon of the prospective judgment is certainly not alien to the Anglo-Saxon legal tradition: indeed, it has long had a place in the jurisprudence of the Supreme Court of the United States. As the [Supreme] Court said in *Chicot County Drainage District v Baxter State Bank*,[49] "The past

[42] Arnull, above note 28, at 538. The paper cited is Hansom, 'Methods of interpretation—a critical assessment of the results' in *Reports of a Judicial and Academic Conference held in Luxembourg on 27–28 September 1976*, II-15.

[43] Arnull, *ibid.*

[44] Above note 19, at 9.

[45] See above.

[46] (1976) *Journal of Business Law* 296–8.

[47] 347 US 483 (1954) and 349 US 294 (1955).

[48] (1976) *European Law Review* 399–402.

[49] 308 US 371 (1949) at 374.

cannot always be erased by a new judicial declaration. The effect of the subsequent ruling [in that case, as to invalidity] may have to be considered in various aspects, with respect to particular relations, individual and corporate, and particular conduct, private and official. Questions of rights claimed to have become vested, of status, of prior determinations deemed to have finality and acted upon accordingly, of public policy in the light of the nature both of the statute and of its previous application, demand examination."'[50]

In a long and characteristically thoughtful analysis,[51] Judge Koopmans defined the problem as being one that 'arises in cases in which a court gives a new interpretation to a certain rule of law, or to a legal principle (new as compared to its earlier case law, or new as compared to existing practice), and in which citizens, or business corporations, or administrative agencies, had no reason to foresee such a change. The question is then whether rulings of this kind should be considered as part of the rule of law they set out to interpret, and therefore apply retrospectively from the moment this rule of law came into force, or whether they should be considered as "new law", and therefore apply only to future cases. Framed in this way, the question presupposes that the normal system is one of retrospectivity, and this is in fact what most lawyers will take for granted.'[52] He points out that, 'there should be a "clean break with the past" … The "clean break" is easy to see in the *Marckx* case[53] … It is more difficult to discern the "break" in *Defrenne* … there may be a "clean break",[54] but the judgment itself is silent on it, and only implicitly admits it when considering the question of the "temporal effect".'[55] Here, Judge Koopmans puts the logical problem facing courts with chilling clarity: 'either earlier case law gives some indication o[f] the new course to be followed, or the new course is not foreshadowed at all … when we put the problem in these abstract terms, we are bound to deny any necessity of prospective application: either the courts reform having foreshadowed, and retrospectivity is in order, or they don't foreshadow, but then they should stick to the line of their earlier case law. Unhappily, most legal problems resist being defined away in this manner; there is, of course, a "large murky area" between continuing an established interpretation and making a clean break with the past.'[56] The conditions which make courts resort to prospective application are: a clear break with the past, reliance on pre-existing law and the disruptive effect of retrospectivity.[57] Judge Koopmans draws two conclusions. First, 'the practice of giving prospective effect to new case law is not necessarily an indication that the courts trespass upon areas traditionally reserved to legislative authorities'.[58] The second conclusion 'is less reassuring: there is no way of defining a set of criteria that would enable the courts to make their choice between retrospective and prospective application

[50] Wyatt, above note 49, at 401.

[51] 'Retrospectivity Reconsidered' (November 1980) *Cambridge Law Journal* 39(2), 287–303. The short extracts that follow cannot do justice to the quality of the analysis.

[52] At 288.

[53] European Court of Human Rights, 13 June 1979, Series A, No 31.

[54] Judge Koopmans seems to accept that there was, inasmuch as earlier cases had established the possibility of vertical direct effect (individual against State) whereas in *Defrenne II* the direct effect had to do with a situation in the field of private law, of employer against employee.

[55] At 291.

[56] At 292.

[57] He also examines, as a possible fourth criterion, the 'purpose' being served by the new ruling; but concludes that the purpose argument cuts both ways: see pp 295–6.

[58] At 301.

on the basis of fixed standards, and with a clear conscience. On every single occasion they will have to strike the balance between legal certainty on the one hand and equal protection on the other.'[59]

In exploring the temporal limitation of *Defrenne II*, all three commentators implicitly confirm the shrewdness of Allott's more succinct analysis. If the Court *is* rather like the US Supreme Court in the functions that it performs, there is nothing too worrying about it declaring the true meaning of a provision whose interpretation was indeed open to contradictory interpretations and simultaneously, in an appropriate and exceptional case, making that ruling prospective rather than retrospective. All that is required—and for some, that 'all' is a difficult word to swallow—is that one should accept that the Court of Justice of the European Communities fulfils the same function in this respect as the Supreme Court in the United States of America …

Whether it was actually necessary to create and use that power in *Defrenne II* itself is, perhaps, not self-evident. Would there really have been 'chaos' if the Court had not limited the temporal effect of its ruling? As Advocate General Trabucchi pointed out,[60] all claims would in any event have been subject to national rules on limitation. Fixing the exact level of remuneration to which the female claimant would be entitled was a problem that had to be confronted for Mrs Defrenne anyway. It seems, moreover, to be fairly readily ascertainable as being the difference between what she was in fact paid and what she would have been paid had she been a man.[61] To that extent, the Court was perhaps erring on the side of prudence, rather than boldness, in both creating and applying the temporal limitation in *Defrenne II*.

Arnull, from the vantage point of 2006, concludes that '… the device of limiting the temporal effect of a judgment might fairly be described as a stroke of genius, permitting the Court to consolidate the direct effect of sufficiently clear provisions of the Treaty while at the same time satisfying the requirements of legal certainty. It is a device to which the Court subsequently resorted only exceptionally and it has made it clear that it will only do so in the ruling which first established the point in issue and not in later cases where the same point is raised. Indeed, there is a certain irony in the criticisms which the device has attracted. Its effect is to limit the scope of the rights conferred by the Treaty and therefore the extent to which national law is affected, yet many of those who have been most vociferous in attacking the device have at the same time tended to see the Court as too keen to extend the reach of Community law and interfere with the prerogatives of the Member States. Moreover, one of the Member States which was responsible in *Defrenne II* for the birth of the device was later to become associated with critics of the Court who cited the case as an example of excessive activism'.[62] One can only add that, despite such intellectual criticism, Member States in general have not hesitated to ask for temporal limitation of judgments when they are, or claim to be, concerned at the possible negative economic impact of a ruling against them.

[59] At 302.

[60] [1976] ECR 455 at 492.

[61] See, eg, Case C-33/89 *Kowalska* [1990] ECR I-2591 at para 20 and Case C-184/94 *Nimz* [1991] ECR I-I-297 at para 21.

[62] At 540.

Looking Back at *Defrenne II*

Of the elements highlighted by Allott as ones that 'will particularly repay further study', some seem—with the benefit of another 30 years' worth of case law from the Court—to be rather less shocking than he then found them. The teleological approach taken by the Court has become a standard feature of EC law. Similarly, we have become used to seeing the Court use the presence of other international instruments to underpin a teleological step forward rather than as an argument for approaching the unknown conservatively. The Court has consistently kept the Commission's use (or non-use) of infringement proceedings—a matter that lies within the Commission's executive discretion[63]—quite separate from the Court's own analysis, within the context of a reference under Article 234 EC (ex Article 177), of what a particular provision of Community law should mean.[64] It has likewise eschewed being influenced by how Member States have interpreted their obligations under Community law when determining the precise scope of those obligations (although if a Member State's interpretation, though erroneous, was reasonable, that will bar individual claims for damages against the Member State concerned).[65]

Horizontal direct effect and temporal limitation, in contrast, continue to give trouble and food for thought. The Court's recent decision in *Viking*[66] that Article 43 EC is 'capable of conferring rights on a private undertaking which may be relied upon against a trade union or an association of trade unions'[67] was built, in part, on the ruling in *Defrenne II*.[68] There is continuing debate about the ruling in *Mangold*[69] which, in a 'horizontal' context, allowed the claimant to maintain that the prohibition in Community law on age discrimination precluded his employer from treating him adversely in the award of a fixed-term contract.[70]

[63] Case 247/87 *Star Fruit* [1989] ECR 291.

[64] The roots of this approach go back as far as Case 26/62 *Van Gend en Loos* [1963] ECR 1. Some 33 years later, in Case C-194/94 *CIA Security International v Signalson and Securitel* [1996] ECR 2201, the United Kingdom tried (unsuccessfully) to argue that a Member State's failure to respect the standstill period under Directive 83/189/EEC for introducing technical measures that might adversely affect free movement of goods could be sanctioned only through infringement proceedings.

[65] See, eg, Case C-392/93 *R v HM Treasury, ex parte British Telecommunications* [1996] ECR 1631.

[66] Case C-438/05 *International Transport Workers' Federation and Finnish Seamen's Union v Viking Line ABP and OÜ Viking Line Eesti*, judgment of 13 December 2007, not yet reported.

[67] See para 66 of the judgment.

[68] See para 58 of the judgment. For a more innovative approach to the horizontal effect of Treaty provisions on free movement, see the opinion of Advocate General Poiares Maduro in *Viking* at points 29–56. This opinion provoked a classic English response from Professor Alan Dashwood (in a paper presented at the CELS 'round table' on *Viking* and *Laval*, Cambridge, 1 February 2008) that the free movement provisions can clearly be distinguished from the rules on competition and from Art 141 EC (ex Art 119) by their subject matter; that the free movement provisions are essentially concerned with the exercise of public powers and with exceptions whose exercise calls for a balancing act beyond the competence of private parties; and that horizontal direct effect for such provisions should only be recognised in cases where national law permits organisations to exercise a regulatory task either *de jure* or *de facto*.

[69] Case C-144/04 [2005] ECR I-9981.

[70] In Case C-411/05 *Palacios de la Villa* [2007] ECR I-8531, the Court neatly sidestepped the question of whether, in *Mangold*, it had really said that there was a specific principle of Community law, with horizontal direct effect, that prohibits discrimination on grounds of age. The issue was again before the Court in Case C-427/06 *Bartsch*, judgment of 23 September 2008, not yet reported. Again, the Court did not give a specific answer, although paragraphs 24 and 25 of the judgment suggest that the (implicit) answer is probably 'no'.

Once temporal limitation of judgments became available, Member States (unsurprisingly) started to argue that it should be granted in cases in which the financial consequences of losing the argument seemed unpalatable. The Court has occasionally been receptive—most notably, in *Barber*,[71] where it held that private occupational pension schemes (as distinct from the statute-based pension scheme at issue in *Defrenne I*) fall within the definition of 'pay' in Article 119 (now Article 141). An extended line of case law followed on whether particular pensions cases were concerned with level of pension (so that time started to run from *Barber*) or with access to pension (so that time ran from *Bilka*).[72] Temporal limitation has, therefore, sometimes added a further layer of complexity.

Moreover, the Court has since imposed restrictive conditions on when it is prepared to grant temporal limitation. First, such a restriction may be allowed only in the actual judgment ruling upon the interpretation sought.[73] That is because 'there must necessarily be a single occasion when a decision is made on the temporal effects of the requested interpretation, which the Court gives of a provision of Community law. In that regard, the principle that a restriction may be allowed only in the actual judgment ruling upon that interpretation guarantees the equal treatment of the Member States and of other persons subject to Community law, under that law, fulfilling, at the same time, the requirements arising from the principle of legal certainty'.[74] Secondly, such a limitation will be imposed only in very specific circumstances, namely where (a) there is a risk of serious economic repercussions owing in particular to the large number of legal relationships entered into in good faith on the basis of rules considered to be validly in force and (b) it appears that both individuals and national authorities have been led into adopting practices which did not comply with Community law by reason of objective, significant uncertainty regarding the implications of Community provisions, to which the conduct of other Member States or the Commission may even have contributed.[75] The financial consequences which might ensue for a Member State from a preliminary ruling do not in themselves justify limiting the temporal effects of the ruling.[76]

A Postscript

One is tempted to regard *Defrenne II* as part of Community law history—a fundamental decision, certainly, before which one genuflects when teaching or learning EC law at university; but one that, in the specific substantive issues that it addresses, is (surely)

[71] Case C-262/88 *Douglas Barber v Guardian Royal Exchange* [1990] ECR I-1889.

[72] Case 170/84 *Bilka Kaufhaus v Weber von Hartz* [1986] ECR 1607.

[73] Case C-292/04 *Meilicke* [2007] ECR 1835 at para 36—see also (for example) Case 309/85 *Barra* [1988] ECR 355, para 13; Case 24/86 *Blaizot* [1988] ECR 379, para 28; Case C-163/90 *Legros and Others* [1992] ECR I-4625, para 30; Case C-415/93 *Bosman and Others* [1995] ECR I-4921, para 142; and Case C-437/97 *EKW and Wein & Co* [2000] ECR I-1157, para 57.

[74] *Meilicke*, para 37.

[75] See most recently Case C-313/05 *Brzeziński* [2007] ECR I-513, paras 57 and 58.

[76] See Case C-184/99 *Grzelczyk* [2001] ECR I-6193, para 52, and Case C-209/03 *Bidar* [2005] ECR I-2119, para 68. For a detailed and helpful analysis of the possibility of temporal limitation in a recent case, see the Opinion of Advocate General Stix-Hackl in Case C-475/03 *Banca populare di Cremona v Agenzia Entrate Ufficio Cremona* at points 130–86 (opinion of 14 March 2006—the Court did not decide the point after all).

remote from our present world of work. So I certainly thought until the day when, as a barrister in private practice in London, I received instructions from the Equal Opportunities Commission in Hong Kong. Legislation had just been introduced there to promote sex equality, modelled heavily on both English and EC legislative provisions. The Equal Opportunities Commission was backing claims for reinstatement and/or compensation brought by five former airline stewardesses whose contracts with Cathay Pacific had automatically been terminated when they reached 40, whilst their male counterparts continued happily until their 55th birthdays. As Mrs Defrenne's victory against Sabena was relied upon repeatedly by an English barrister (in traditional wig and gown) appearing before a Chinese judge in a Chinese court in a former British colony on the other side of the world in order to show that such a claim was conceivable at all—it was scornfully (indeed, disbelievingly) opposed every inch of the way by counsel for Cathay Pacific[77]—it became evident that the issues, arguments and attitudes were as relevant in 2003 as in the 1970s; and that the Court's ruling in *Defrenne II* not only casts a very long shadow, but also needs to do so.

[77] After a series of preliminary skirmishes in court on procedural matters to get the action started and then to keep it alive, including a spirited attempt by Cathay Pacific to obtain security for costs against the Equal Opportunities Commission as a condition for the individual plaintiffs to be allowed to proceed with their claim, the case settled out of court just before it was due to come on for trial.

2

SABENA is dead, Gabrielle Defrenne's case is still alive: the old lady's testament…

DENYS SIMON[78]

What would European law look like without the judgment in *Defrenne*? This question—the first one, no doubt, that comes into mind in the context of this volume—does not necessarily compel a unanimous answer.

Indeed, one tends spontaneously to ask in relation to *Defrenne* the famous question asked by President Lecourt: 'What would Community law have been without the 1963 and 1964 judgments?'[79] or the one asked more recently by the Director-General of the European Commission's Legal Service: 'What would the Common Market be without *Cassis de Dijon*?' Or, recently, air-transport without *Open Skies*, free movement of students without *Gravier* and free movement of patients without *Geraets-Smits and Peerbooms*?[80]

Thus, why not be content to join the chorus and share this commonly accepted view by asking: 'What would have happened to the principle of equal treatment between men and women without *Defrenne*?' Isn't it by definition one of those judgments which 'have shed vivid light on the judicial panorama of the Community'?[81]

Isn't it one of those guiding lights, a judicial pronouncement about which we have the feeling that it has always been there, a judgment whose text, to paraphrase the poet, is 'very old, and has taken on this gentle air of the elderly'?[82]

However, in the French case-law collections of the 'important judgments' of the Court of Justice *Defrenne* is not considered either as one of the fundamental decisions for the Community legal order[83] or as an essential solution in relation to substantive Community law.[84] The books and treatises on European law, including those on Community social welfare law, do not place it in a privileged position. Similarly, if one refers to the case notes published immediately after the judgment had been handed down by the Court one

[78] Professor of Law, Université de La Réunion.

[79] R Lecourt, in 'L'Europe et le droit, Mélanges en hommage à Jean Boulouis' (1981) *Dalloz*, 349.

[80] M Petite, 'Halte au feu sur la Cour' (2006) 1 *Revue du Droit de l'Union Européene* 5 *ff*, esp 7.

[81] R Lecourt, in 'L'Europe et le droit', above note 80, 349.

[82] A Rimbaud, *Le buffet* 'Poésies', in 'Oeuvres complètes', La Pléiade NRF Gallimard 1972, p 34–5.

[83] J Boulouis et RM Chevallier, 'Grands arrêts de la Cour de justice des Communautés européennes' (1994) *Dalloz* 6th edn.

[84] J Boulouis, RM Chevallier, D Fasquelle, M Blanquet, 'Les grands arrêts de la jurisprudence communautaire, droit communautaire des affaires, marché intérieur, politiques communautaires' (2002) *Dalloz* 5th edn. This book contains a commentary on *Defrenne III* (Case 149/77 *Defrenne v Sabena* [1978] ECR 1365).

would find a very critical approach: 'In spite of the importance that the Community law crowd would have liked to give to *Defrenne*, its particular importance and effectiveness seems to me to be limited'.[85]

Is *Defrenne*, then, a false 'great judgment', its glory usurped and its importance overrated? Does it owe its fame to the natural tendency of lawyers, evident both in case law and in academic literature, to repeat, like an incantation, initial judicial pronouncements and elementary truths, as if the number of occurrences in citations were a definitive guarantee of the pertinence, the quality and the importance of a judgment? Or has it survived the test of time thanks to a subconscious admiration for the obstinate determination of an air hostess who succeeded in obtaining three preliminary references to the Court of Justice[86] and thus joined the club of the habitual applicants of Community law alongside Meroni, the Lüttickes, the Rewes, the Roquettes and the Mulders?

It is to these questions, then, that one should give answers in 'revisiting', 30 years later, a number of the 'presumed important judgments' of the Court. And the lessons from the judicial adventures of Mrs Defrenne seem to be the following.

Defrenne or One of the First Steps towards Equality of the Sexes

Contrary to what is sometimes suggested, *Defrenne II* does not constitute the starting point of the principle of non-discrimination on grounds of sex in Community law, as the Court had already invalidated certain provisions of the Staff Regulations which provided for an unjustified difference in the treatment of men and women.[87] Having been asked to rule on Article 119 EEC (new Article 141) in the first *Defrenne* case, the Court held that the principle that men and women should receive equal pay for equal work was implicit in the Treaty and that the concept of 'pay' included 'any other consideration, whether in cash or in kind, whether immediate or future, provided that the worker receives it, albeit indirectly, in respect of his employment from his employer'.[88] Yet, *Defrenne II* is considered a major step towards equal treatment of men and women. There seem to be two reasons justifying this view.

To begin with, there is the issue of the reach of the principle of equality between men and women, particularly in relation to the Court's reasoning whose implications became evident only after some time had passed. Despite the fact that this question had received little attention at the time, *Defrenne* expresses the Court's conception of the philosophy of the European experiment. It has been suggested that the adoption of Article 119 EEC was not so much the result of a modern conception of sex equality but rather an effort to avoid

[85] C Philip (1977) *Revue Trimestrielle de Droit Européen*, 529 *f*, esp 535.

[86] Case 80/70 *Defrenne v Belgium* [1971] ECR 445 (*Defrenne I*); Case 43/75 *Defrenne v Sabena* [1976] ECR 455 (*Defrenne II*) ; Case 149/77 *Defrenne v Sabena* [1978] ECR 1365 (*Defrenne III*).

[87] Case 20/71 *Sabbatini* [1972] ECR 345. The Court quashed a decision denying the applicant an 'expatriation allowance' because the recipient of the allowance had to be a 'head of household' which was defined in the Regulations as a 'married male official'. See also Case 21/74 *Airola* [1975] ECR 221.

[88] *Defrenne I* para 6. This definition did not *a priori* exclude pension schemes provided that these were not obligatory, ie directly regulated by law without negotiations within the company or department involved and compulsorily applicable to categories of salaries.

a kind of social dumping resulting from the employment, in certain sectors of the economy, of an underpaid female workforce which would have led to the distortion of competition.[89] In fact, the Court expressly referred to this economic dimension of Article 119 stating that 'in the light of the different stages of the development of social legislation in the various member states the aim of Article 119 is to avoid a situation in which undertakings established in states which have actually implemented the principle of equal pay suffer a competitive disadvantage in intra-community competition as compared with undertakings established in states which have not yet eliminated discrimination against women workers as regards pay'.[90]

However, the Court immediately added that 'this provision forms part of the social objectives of the Community, which is not merely an economic union, but is at the same time intended, by common action, to ensure social progress and seek the constant improvement of the living and working conditions of their peoples, as is emphasized by the preamble to the Treaty'.[91] It is 'this double aim, which is at once economic and social' that makes the 'principle' of equal treatment of men and women a 'basic principle' that 'forms part of the foundations of the Community'.[92]

These statements call for two points to be made. On the one hand, the social dimension of the principle of equal treatment means that the only correct interpretation of this principle is one that promotes social progress. Far from merely imposing a mathematical equality, which could be achieved by reducing the salaries of male employees to the same level as the salaries of the female ones, the logic of Article 119 implies that equality of treatment and non-discrimination can only be achieved by increasing the lower salaries[93] and, thus, achieving equality to the top.[94] On the other, elevating equality of treatment to the rank of a basic principle that is part of the foundations of the Community is the first step towards according it the status of a general principle of Community law, and thus, treating it as a fundamental human right.[95] This status was confirmed by subsequent cases, the Community legislature—mainly through directives that dealt with different aspects of equality of treatment—and finally the authors of the Treaty through the provisions on social policy annexed to the Treaty of Maastricht and those on fundamental rights of the Treaty of Amsterdam.[96] More recently, the status of the principle of equal treatment was reaffirmed in the Charter of Fundamental Rights and in the Treaty establishing a Constitution for Europe.[97]

Further, the Court specified the concept of 'principle' in the 'language of the Treaty' in terms that have lost none of their vigour or importance. It explained that the use by

[89] On competition concerns at the time of the *travaux préparatoires* of the Treaties see Rapport Ohlin, 'Les aspects sociaux de la coopération économique européenne' (1956) *BIT Etudes et documents nouvelles* series 46, Geneva. The same idea can be found in the Spaak report. On this point see F Baron, Marché intérieur et droit social dans l'Union européenne, Aix Marseille PUAM 1998, esp paras 303 *f.*

[90] *Defrenne II*, para 9. The same point in made in subsequent cases, eg Case 203/82 *Commission v Italy* [1983] ECR 2525.

[91] *Defrenne II*, para 10.

[92] *Ibid*, paras 12 and 14.

[93] *Ibid*, para 15.

[94] *Defrenne II* inaugurated the Court's consistent case law on this point. See, eg, Case C-373/89 *Rouvroy* [1990] ECR I-4243; Case C-154/92 *Van Cant* [1993] ECR I-3811.

[95] See *Defrenne III.*

[96] See the new Arts 2, 3, 13, 137 and 141 EC.

[97] See mainly Arts II-81 (1) and II-83 of the Charter. Art I-2 of the Constitutional Treaty states that equality is one of the 'values' upon which 'the Union is founded'.

Community law of the term 'principle', which is 'specifically used in order to indicate the fundamental nature of certain provisions', could not in any way be interpreted as amounting to a 'vague declaration' deprived, *per ipsam*, of any normative, obligatory content. On the contrary, the use of the term 'principle' denotes the existence of a normative aspect destined to produce as such, despite its generality, legal effects. These considerations foreshadowed the future structure of the objectives, the values and the principles which govern the Community judicial order. An attempt has been made to show in other contexts how the affirmation of a constitutional dimension of the Community—independently of any formal constitutional text—depended on a rigorous articulation of the common aims and values which bring into the fore the common principles that inform an autonomous and coherent reading of the Community judicial system.[98] *Defrenne* is a particularly telling example, in the field of equality of treatment between men and women, of this jurisprudential development.

The second reason why *Defrenne* is an important case relates specifically to the issue of sex equality: the Court of Justice recognised the need to interpret Article 119 EC as covering not only direct but also indirect discrimination. Indeed, this distinction and its consequences were the target of the most virulent critiques of *Defrenne II*.[99] The Court juxtaposed the two types of differential treatment as follows: contrary to indirect or disguised discrimination, 'direct and overt discrimination' is discrimination 'which may be identified solely with the aid of the criteria based on equal work and equal pay referred to by Article [119]'[100] or discrimination that has its 'origin in legislative provisions or in collective labour agreements and which may be detected on the basis of a purely legal analysis of the situation'[101] and results in 'unequal pay for equal work carried out in the same establishment or service'.[102]

If one accepts this distinction, it seems that, awkwardly, the Court made it to tally with the distinction between direct effect and the absence of direct effect thus justifying the reservations expressed by some academic authors about the solution adopted in *Defrenne*.[103] In fact, the ambiguity of the distinction would be lifted later on, with the Court expressly accepting that Article 119 was directly effective both in relation to indirect or covert discrimination as well as direct discrimination.[104] In any case, there is no doubt that *Defrenne II* was the first case to make formally explicit the differences between direct[105]

[98] See D Simon, *Le système juridique communautaire* 3rd edn (Paris, PUF, 2001), esp paras 51 *f*; 'Y a-t-il des principes généraux du droit communautaire?' (1991) 14 *Droits* 73 *f*; 'Les fondements de l'autonomie du droit communautaire' in *Droit international et droit communautaire, perspectives actuelles* (Paris, Pedone, 2000) 207 *f*. See also J Molinier (ed), *Les principes fondateurs de l'union européenne* (Paris, PUF, 2005); *Le droit de l'Union européenne en principes, Liber amicorum en l'honneur de J Raux* (Rennes, Apogée, 2006); D Simon, Les principes en droit communautaire, in S Caudal (ed), Les principes en droit (Paris Economica 2008) 287 *f*.

[99] Not only by academic authors but also by Advocates-General. See, eg, Advocate General Warner in Case 69/80 *Worringham* [1981] ECR 767, 802 or Advocate General Darmon Case 170/84 *Bilka* [1986] ECR 1607.

[100] *Defrenne II*, para 18.

[101] *Ibid*, para 21.

[102] *Ibid*, para 22.

[103] See, eg, P Rodière, *Droit social de l'Union européenne*, 2nd edn (Paris, LGDJ, 2001), esp 286–7.

[104] See Case 69/80 *Worringham* [1981] ECR 767; Case 96/80 *Jenkins* [1981] ECR 911; Case C170/84 *Bilka* [1986] ECR 1607.

[105] Later defined in the directives as a situation where someone is treated less favourably than another because of one's sex while being in a comparable position.

and indirect discrimination[106] which would later occupy a central place in the case law on equality of treatment.[107]

To these contributions that *Defrenne* made to the issue of sex discrimination,[108] one should add the consequences that it had for the Community judicial system as a whole, which, I think, are much more important than the former.

Defrenne or the Inviolability of the Hierarchy of Norms

Defrenne is a paradigmatic case of the judicial strategy adopted by the Court of Justice in its flamboyant period. Although the Community had not yet been solemnly proclaimed as a Community resting on the rule of law, the Court's concern for the realisation and consolidation of the rule of law was already at the heart of its reasoning.

First, the Court affirmed that a practice followed by the Member States or the Community institutions could not prevail over their obligations flowing from the Treaty: the fact that certain national legal systems were not compatible with Article 119 or that the institutions had been tolerant or at least passive in relation to the failure of Member States to act could not put in doubt the obligations they had undertaken by signing the Treaty. To hold otherwise, the Court tersely stated, 'would be to risk raising the violation of the right to the status of a principle of interpretation',[109] which would be inconsistent with the normative structure of the Community legal order and with the Court's role as the guardian of the rule of law in the interpretation and application of the Treaty according to Article 164 EEC (new Article 220 EC). Thus, although in classic international law the modification of obligations undertaken by signing a Treaty through subsequent practice is far from excluded,[110] the Court vigorously rejected the transposition of this practice in the Community system, inaugurating a consistent line of case law[111] based on the special nature of the Community judicial order.[112] Even clearer is the Court's rejection of any possibility to amend the Treaty without following the formal procedure prescribed therein.

[106] Defined in the directives as a situation where a formally neutral rule is more burdensome for the members of one sex than the members of the other, unless this difference can be objectively justified as pursuing a legitimate aim and the means used to achieve it are necessary and appropriate.

[107] On the importance of this distinction for the case law on equality of treatment see M Darmon and JG Huglo, 'L'égalité de traitement entre les hommes et les femmes dans la jurisprudence de la Cour de justice des Communautés européennes: un univers en expansion' (1992) *Revue Trimestrielle de Droit Européen* 12; P Garrone, 'La discrimination indirecte en droit communautaire: vers une théorie générale' (1994) *Revue Trimestrielle de Droit Européen* 425. For a systematic study of this issue see R Hernu, *Principe d'égalité et principe de non-discrimination dans la jurisprudence de la Cour de justice des Communautés européennes* (Paris, LGDJ, 2003).

[108] For a detailed analysis see O Dubos, 'Principe d'égalité entre les femmes et les hommes' in G Canivet, L Idot, D Simon (eds), *Lamy procédures communautaires*, Etude no 160; D Martin, *Egalité et non discrimination dans la jurisprudence communautaire* (Brussels, Bruylant, 2006).

[109] *Defrenne*, para 34.

[110] Temple de Preah Vihar (*Cambodia v Thailand*) [1962] ICJ 1; arbitral award of 22 December 1963 *France v United States* XVI Reports of International Arbitral Awards 11.

[111] Eg Case 7/71 *Commission v France* [1971] ECR 1003; Case 106/77 *Simmenthal* [1978] ECR 629; Opinion 1/78 [1979] ECR 2871.

[112] On this point see D Simon, 'Les fondements de l'autonomie du droit communautaire' in *Droit international et droit communautaire, perspectives actuelles*, 207 *f.* [stopped here pending decision on translation]

It must be noted that the Member States had by common accord adopted on 30 December 1961, the day before the expiration of the period laid down by Article 119 for making enforceable the obligation for equal treatment, a resolution to delay the immediate coming into force of the 'equal pay for equal work' obligation, adopting instead a step-by-step plan until 31 December 1964. However, the Court, despite the fact that Member States were once again able to find arguments from public international law,[113] held that the Treaty could be amended only in accordance with the formal procedure provided for in what then was Article 236 EEC. Although the Court did not offer detailed reasoning for this conclusion, it can be supported by two types of consideration: first, the need to prevent the unanimous modification of the Treaty outside the prescribed procedural framework as this would undermine the institutional logic requiring the involvement of the different Community institutions in the process, an expression of the unique and autonomous nature of the Community constitutional order; secondly, the need to ensure the conformity of rules of secondary law with primary law, an expression of the principle of hierarchy of norms.[114] Thus, *Defrenne II* is one of the important judgments[115] which confirm the inviolability of Community constitutional law against any attempt to amend it without following the formal procedure and ensure the respect of the principle of hierarchy of norms which is inherent in the rule of law.[116]

Defrenne or the Reach of Direct Effect

Many things have been written on the contribution of *Defrenne* to the doctrine of direct effect of Community law. With the passing of time, there seem to be three points of particular importance.

First, the judgment brings to light—no doubt in a rather elliptical way—the, often misunderstood,[117] reasoning underlying the principle of direct effect. The first step towards the recognition of the direct effect of a primary law provision as the one in question is, in effect, to correctly understand the scope of Article 119 in relation to the 'equal pay for equal work' rule, its objective and its place in the Treaty's system of rules.

Subsequently, the criteria of invocability—clarity, precision, unconditionality, lack of discretion of the community or national authorities—perform a function which precisely becomes clear in *Defrenne*: they can be used to test whether the rule is technically applicable by the national judge. That is an analysis in terms of justiciability. This is why the Court stated that in cases of direct and overt discrimination the national court is 'in a position to establish all the facts which enable it to decide whether a woman worker is

[113] Art 39 of the Vienna Convention of 23 May 1969. See P Sands, 'Article 39', in O Corten et P Klein (eds), Les conventions de Vienne sur le droit des traités, commentaire article par article (Brussels, Bruylant, 2006) 1523 *f* and the bibliography cited therein.

[114] See, eg, Case T-51/89 *Tetra Pak* [1990] ECR II-309.

[115] See also Case 59/75 *Manghera* [1976] ECR 91.

[116] Although it was not necessary for the Court to pronounce on the compatibility of the resolution with the Treaty, it is reasonable to assume that, had it been necessary, it would have found it to be incompatible with the general principle of law that guarantees equality of treatment between men and women as a fundamental right.

[117] A number of discussions of direct effect confuse the foundations of the principle with the practical criteria of invocability.

receiving lower pay than a male worker performing the same tasks'.[118] Thus, it is the capacity of the national judge to give effect to Community law that constitutes the criterion of a rule's technical aptitude to have direct effect.

Second, *Defrenne* constitutes a step towards the relaxing of the three criteria for direct effect. The lack of clarity and precision does not prevent the national judge from directly applying a Community rule whose meaning can be made more clear and precise through interpretation by both the national and Community judicature.[119] The fact that the rule is subject to a condition, that is, implementation within a certain period, does not deprive it of the capability of having direct effect; it rather delays direct effect until the condition has been fulfilled—in this case the expiration of the transition period.[120] The existence of Directives for the implementation of the principle of equal treatment cannot be relied upon to question the direct effect of Article 119, as they are harmonising measures adopted to promote, and not undermine, the effective realisation of the objectives of the Treaty.[121]

Third, *Defrenne* is equally important for the issue of horizontal direct effect. Whether this was fully appreciated at the time is, once again, not clear. The Court held that the obligation of equal treatment of male and female workers that, under Article 119, is addressed to Member States is relevant not only for the national legislature or administration which cannot adopt or maintain discriminatory rules on remuneration; rather, the state is equally bound in its capacity as employer to put in place a system of equal remuneration. Here is the inaugural moment of what later will be described as enlarged vertical direct effect: subsequent case law would explore the further potential of the concept of direct effect, mainly in relation to directives,[122]—the so-called diagonal direct effect—which covers not only public law entities[123] but also private law legal persons that are under the control of the state or possess special powers resembling the powers of public bodies.[124] This considerable extension of the invocability of Community law was completed by the recognition in *Defrenne* that the rules of primary Community law which necessarily create obligations for private individuals[125] are capable of having horizontal direct effect. This is the meaning of the Court's statement that 'the prohibition on discrimination between men and women applies not only to the action of public authorities, but also extends to all agreements which are intended to regulate paid labour collectively, as well as to contracts between individuals'.[126]

118 *Defrenne II* para 23.

119 This idea can be traced back to Case 27/67 *Fink Frucht* [1968] ECR 327. It was clearly articulated in *Defrenne* and subsequently relied on by the Court of Justice in the case law on equality of treatment: Case 96/80 *Jenkins* [1981] ECR 911; Case C-262/88 *Barber* [1990] ECR I-1889.

120 For a similar reasoning see Case 2/74 *Reyners* [1974] ECR 631; Case 59/75 *Manghera* [1976] ECR 91.

121 *Defrenne* paras 60 and 64. See also *Reyners* paras 26 *ff.*

122 Case 152/84 *Marshall* I [1986] ECR 723; Case C-271/91 *Marshall II* [1993] ECR I-4367. See the note of A Rigaux and D Simon in *Europe*, October 1993.

123 Case 103/88 *Fratelli Costanzo* [1989] ECR 1839.

124 Case C-188/89 *Foster v British Gas* [1990] ECR I-3313. For the various possibilities see D Simon *Le système juridique communautaire* 3rd edn (Paris, PUF, 2001), esp para 312 *f.*

125 Case 36/74 *Walrave* [1974] ECR 1405.

126 *Defrenne* para 39. As noted by Advocate General Trabucchi, the invocability of Art 119 means that in horizontal litigation national courts must declare any contractual agreements or collective regulations which have an element of discrimination based on sex to be void.

Defrenne or the Temporal Limit of the Effect of Judgments on Preliminary References

The last major aspect of *Defrenne* is that it introduced a limitation on the temporal effect of the judgments of the Court of Justice making clear that they operate *ex tunc.* Although the declaratory nature of the judgments delivered in preliminary references would point to an effect *ex nunc*, the Court limited, for the first time, the retroactive effect of its rulings: although it stated that taking into account the practical consequences of a judgment cannot go as far as to undermine the objective nature of the law, it found that, exceptionally, individuals should be able to invoke Article 119 only for future claims and not for remuneration periods which precede the date of the judgment.

It has been suggested that this move away from the inherent retroactivity of an interpretative ruling is due to the uncertainty about the reach of the 'equal pay for equal work' rule before the judgment and the risk of serious adverse financial consequences in the Member States. It is only for these reasons that the Community judicature (and no one else) may decide that 'important considerations of legal certainty affecting all the interest involved, both public and private' justify the temporal limitation of the effects of a judgment. The Court, however, introduced 'an exception to the exception' and allowed those workers who had already brought legal proceedings or made similar claims before the judgment in *Defrenne* was given to rely on the case. This solution, which was severely criticised at the time,[127] seems, after all, a balanced and justified approach. Thus, *Defrenne* was registered in the body of the Court's case law as a ruling relevant both for the effects of a judgment in preliminary references about the interpretation of Community law[128] as well as references about the validity of Community acts.[129] Having provoked considerable resistance in certain national jurisdictions that almost degenerated into a 'battle of judges',[130] the principles emanating from *Defrenne* have served as the origin of convergent developments in national legal systems.[131]

[127] See, eg, C Philip, *Revue trimestrielle de droit européen* 1977, 529 *f*, who criticises this type of 'amnesty'. Advocate General Trabucchi was similarly hostile toward the *ratione temporis* limitation of the effects of the judgment.

[128] For a characteristic example see Cases C-197/94 and C-252/94 *Soc Bautiaa* [1996] ECR I-505. In relation to Art 119 see Case C-262/88 *Barber* [1990] ECR I-1889; Case C-109/91 *Ten Oever* [1993] ECR I-4879. For the lack of temporal limitations see Case C-363/93 and Cases C-407–411/93 *Lancry* [1994] ECR I-3957 noted by D Simon *Journal du droit international*, 1995, 435.

[129] Case 4/79 *Providence Agricole de Champagne* [1980] ECR 2823; Case C-228/92 *Roquette Frères* [1994] ECR I-1445, noted by D Simon, Europe 1994 no. 224.

[130] Trib Inst de Lille, 15 July 1981, Case *Roquette, Répertoire Dalloz*, 1982, 615, note J Boulouis; CE (F) 26 June 1985 Case *ONIC, Actualité juridique, Droit administratif, 1985*, 615, concl B Genevois; CE (F) 13 June 1986 Case ONIC, *Revue trimestrielle de droit européen* 1986 concl JC Bonichot; Corte costituzionale (I) 21 April 1989 Fragd, RDI 1989, 103. See also M Walbroeck, 'May the Court of Justice limit the retrospective operation of its judgments?' (1981) *Yearbook of European Law* 115; U Everling, Der Ausschluss des Rückwirkung bei der Feststellung der Ungültigkeit von Verordnungen durch den Gerichtshof der EG, Feschrift für B Börner, 1992, 57 *f*; D Simon, *L'effet dans le temps des arrêts préjudiciels de la CJC: enjeux ou prétexte d'une nouvelle guerre des juges, Liber amicorum* P Pescatore (Baden-Baden, Nomos, 1987), 651 *f*.

[131] CE (F) 11 May 2004, Association AC! et autres, Rec Leb. 197 concl. Devys, Grands arrêts de la jurisprudence administrative n° 118; 25 février 2005 France Telecom Rec Leb 86. For a recent example of the impact of the '*Defrenne* formula' on national case law see CE(F) 16 July 2007 Soc Tropic Travaux Signalisation no. 291545.

The judgment in *Defrenne* appears, after this brief overview of its consequences, like one of those places where, to paraphrase the poet, there are forged 'ces écritures nouvelles encloses dans les grands schistes à venir'.[132]

[132] Saint John Perse, Vents I, 3.

3

Defrenne II Revisited

SÍOFRA O'LEARY*

A Brief Overview of *Defrenne II*

In Case 43/75 *Defrenne v Sabena* (hereafter *Defrenne II*), with reference to the nature of the principle of equal pay in Article 119 EEC (hereafter Article 141 EC), the dual economic and social aims of that provision and its place in the scheme of the Treaty, the Court held that that provision is directly applicable and may give rise to individual rights which national courts must protect.[133] Complainants may rely on Article 141 EC before national courts to challenge legislative provisions and provisions of collective agreements, as well as provisions of individual employment contracts, and those which are incompatible must be disapplied or declared null and void. Although the Court held that equal pay should have been fully secured by the Member States by 1 January 1962, in response to the concerns expressed by some Member States regarding the serious economic consequences of a finding of direct effect, it admitted, for the first time, a temporal limitation on the effects of its judgment.[134]

Defrenne II represents one of the most important jurisprudential milestones in the development of EC law. Although it was neither the first nor the clearest expression of direct effect,[135] nor the first case in which a principle addressed to Member States was deemed to have direct effect, it was the Court's first explicit recognition of horizontal direct effect.[136] In addition, while the scope and substantive detail of the principle of equal

* Référendaire, Court of Justice of the European Communities; Visiting professor, College of Europe, Bruges.
I am grateful to Drs Clare Kilpatrick and JM Fernández Martín for their comments and criticisms. The views expressed are purely personal to the author.

[133] Case 43/75 [1976] ECR 455 was one of a trilogy of preliminary references originating in the complaints of a Belgian air hostess against her employer. Mrs Defrenne complained that the lower pay received by female air hostesses when compared to that received by male cabin stewards doing identical work was contrary to Art 119 EEC. In Case 80/70 *Defrenne v Belgium* [1971] ECR 445 (*Defrenne I*), the Court held that the concept of pay in Art 119 EEC did not cover the retirement pension scheme of which the applicant was a member. In Case 149/77 *Defrenne v Sabena* [1978] ECR 1365 (*Defrenne III*), it held that Art 119 EEC is limited to questions of pay discrimination between male and female workers and cannot be interpreted as prescribing equality in respect of other working conditions. Art 119 EEC was amended and renumbered by the Treaty of Amsterdam. Reference is made hereafter to the renumbered Art 141 EC for the sake of simplicity.

[134] The direct effect of Art 141 EC cannot be relied on in order to support claims concerning pay periods prior to the date of the *Defrenne II* judgment, that is 8 April 1976, except as regards those workers who had already brought legal proceedings or made an equivalent claim.

[135] See Case 43/75, para 18, where the Court's discussion of the direct applicability of Art 141 EC became confused with notions of overt and disguised discrimination.

[136] See further W Van Gerven, 'Contribution de l'arrêt *Defrenne* au développement du droit communautaire' (1977) *Cahiers de droit européen* 131–43.

pay have been elaborated in numerous subsequent cases, *Defrenne II* nevertheless represents the seminal case in the development of EC sex discrimination law. It is also a fundamental milestone in the transformation of what had appeared until then to be an entirely subsidiary and dormant title on social policy in the Treaty of Rome. The judgment vividly brought home the Court's statement in *Van Gend en Loos* to the effect that the vigilance of individuals concerned to protect their rights would be one of the key means to ensure the effective supervision of EC law.[137] It is difficult to identify another case which had the same *potential* to directly affect, even transform, the rights of individual members of the working population. For, while *Bosman* may have transformed Europe's footballing landscape and further developed the law on the free movement rights of migrant job-seekers and workers and while *Baumbast* confirmed that Article 18 EC conferred rights directly on EU citizens, the fact remains that only the rights of a reduced percentage of the Union's population were and are likely to be influenced by these decisions, given the limitation of their personal scope of application by the condition of Member State nationality and their dependence on an element of actual (or potential) migration. In contrast, Article 141 EC applies to all workers in the EU, regardless of any exercise of free movement and regardless, it would appear, of their nationality.

Factors Influencing the Decision in *Defrenne II*

A close reading of the judgment highlights a number of the factors which clearly influenced the Court. First, from a legal perspective, the Court specifically located within the fundamental obligation to interpret and apply the Treaty, assigned to it by Article 220 EC (ex 164 EEC), its refusal to exclude the direct effect of Article 141 EC, despite the fact that the latter was framed in terms of the *principle* of equal pay and addressed to Member States. In this respect, the judgment fits neatly with other decisions, originating in the early 1970s, in which the Court first hinted and then expressly stated that fundamental rights form part of the general principles of law, the observance of which the Court observes. As in *Van Gend en Loos, Walrave & Koch,*[138] *Reyners*[139] or *Van Binsbergen,*[140] the Court was keen to ensure that provisions of the Treaty governing relations between and among persons in daily life gave rise to judicially enforceable rights and obligations.[141]

Secondly, from a political perspective, the Court made little attempt to hide its frustration at the failure by certain Member States to discharge the clear and precise duty imposed on them by Article 141 EC and at the institutions, specifically the Commission, for not reacting 'sufficiently energetically' against this failure to act. In this respect, it was no doubt influenced by the Community's new-found interest in and commitment to social policy objectives. The latter, although grandiosely proclaimed in the preamble to and Title III of the Treaty of Rome, had received little attention until the early 1970s. However, while *Defrenne II* must be regarded not as a redefinition or reorientation of the

137 Case 26/62 *Van Gend en Loos* [1963] ECR 1.
138 Case 36/74 [1974] ECR 1405.
139 Case 2/74 [1974] ECR 631.
140 Case 33/74 [1974] ECR 1299.
141 See further P Davies, 'The European Court of Justice, National Courts and the Member States' in P Davies *et al* (eds), *European Community Labour Law: Principles and Perspectives* (Oxford, Clarendon, 1996) 95.

political and legislative agenda, but rather as itself confirmation of that changing agenda,[142] the line of case law that it spawned no doubt provided a further incentive to rework and extend the provisions on social policy, which eventually culminated, albeit over 20 years later, in fundamental amendments to Article 141 EC and the other social policy provisions introduced by the Treaty of Amsterdam.

Finally, the series of events and, more importantly, the individuals who helped to transform *Defrenne II* from a case of individual female disgruntlement with unequal treatment at the hands of her employer to the jurisprudential milestone described above cannot be dissociated from the widespread mobilisation of women in the 1970s. Gabrielle Defrenne was but one of many thousands, nay millions, of female employees in the then EEC whose employment and pay conditions were less favourable than those enjoyed by male colleagues performing equal work or work of equal value. With the main Belgian union for airline staff refusing to take up what it regarded as 'women's issues', she agreed to allow her situation to form the basis of a test case against Sabena Airlines defended by two formidable Belgian labour lawyers who had for some time been arguing for the direct effect of Article 119 EEC.[143] She was the type of applicant to whom the Court's call to arms in *Van Gend en Loos* had been directed and her lawyers chose her case precisely because of its capacity to procure change.

The Legacy of *Defrenne II*

While in many respects, as we will see below, the Court's subsequent development of the principles established in or derived from *Defrenne II* has often disappointed, it would be wrong to ignore the enduring political and legislative legacy of that case on the one hand and its jurisprudential legacy on the other. For *Defrenne II* marked but the beginning of the Court's journey in uncovering the content and implications of EC law on gender equality.

As regards the political and legislative legacy of the case, by focusing on the Member States' affirmation in the preamble of the EEC Treaty that their essential objective was the constant improvement of the living and working conditions of their peoples, *Defrenne II* transformed the Treaty title on social policy. The Court thus ensured that those social objectives should serve as the backdrop to EC sex equality law and social and employment legislation generally. By 2000, in another equal pay case, it transpired that the economic objective behind Article 141 EC had become secondary to its social aim.[144] Although the Court's sex equality case law reveals a constant tension between this social commitment and the economic imperatives underpinning European integration—a tension still played

[142] See also C Hoskyns, *Integrating Gender* (London, Verso, 1996) 92: 'The Court was responding to events and trends and consolidating them, rather than establishing a new direction, as has sometimes been argued' and Davies, *ibid*, 103. The judgment in *Defrenne II* followed closely on the heels of the expiry of the deadline for the transposition of Directive 75/117 on equal pay (OJ 1975 L45/198).

[143] For further details about the background to and details of *Defrenne I* and *II* see generally Hoskyns, *ibid*, chs 4–5.

[144] Case C-50/96 *Schröder* [2000] ECR I-743, paras 53–57.

out in the first two lines of Articles 136 and in the case law of the Court[145]—it is difficult to see how, without the *Defrenne* trilogy, EC sex equality law or even social and employment law generally, would have developed as they have. The revolutionary nature and effect of the Court's recognition of the horizontal and vertical direct effect of what some had considered a programmatic principle addressed to Member States has also arguably influenced subsequent attempts to amend and extend the social policy provisions of the EC Treaty,[146] and decisions not to give legally binding effect to other instruments enumerating economic and social rights. A distinct wariness of what can become of social provisions in the hands of the Court can be viewed in the careful construction of the general prohibition of discrimination in Article 13 EC[147] and in the price paid for the incorporation into the Draft Constitution of the 2000 Charter of the Fundamental Rights of the European Union, which contains a heterogeneous catalogue of socio-economic rights in its solidarity chapter.[148]

From a jurisprudential perspective, recognition of the direct effect of the principle of equal pay was the spark which ignited the case law on equal pay, in particular, and sex equality generally. Following *Defrenne II*, the Court expressly interpreted equal work as including work of equal value, which was essential if Article 141 EC was to be used to challenge gender-segregated pay structures. It also recognised that Article 141 EC prohibited directly and indirectly discriminatory pay practices, whether intentional or unintentional.[149] While directly discriminatory practices require justification with reference to express derogations in the Treaty and secondary legislation, of which, for Article 141 EC, there are none, those which disparately impact on particular groups of workers have to be objectively justified and proportionate. The question of what constitutes pay became of fundamental importance as applicants sought to have their sex discrimination claims resolved with reference to Article 141 EC rather than the other Sex Equality Directives.[150] By broadly defining what constitutes pay in Article 141 EC, the Court guaranteed its application to a wide variety of benefits regardless of the contractual, statutory or voluntary basis on which those benefits are awarded.[151] The *Defrenne* trilogy also

[145] See, eg, Case C-341/05 *Laval* [2007] ECR I-11767, concerning the compatability with EC law on the free provision of services of industrial action to force a service provider to sign a collective agreement in respect of terms and conditions of employment.

[146] Opposition to the incorporation of new social and employment provisions in the Maastricht Treaty culminated in a Protocol on Social Policy annexed to the Treaty and a Social Policy Agreement annexed to the Protocol to which the United Kingdom was not a party. That Member State had also refused to sign the unbinding 1989 Community Charter of the Fundamental Social Rights of Workers.

[147] No doubt confirmed by the judgment in Case C-144/04 *Mangold* [2006] ECR I-9981, para 75, where the Court recognised that the principle of non-discrimination on grounds of age constitutes a general principle of EC law.

[148] OJ 2000 C364/8. A proviso was inserted in the general provisions (Art II-112(5)) seeking to exclude the possibility of direct effect being accorded purely programmatic policies and principles in the Charter.

[149] See, in particular, in the context of indirect sex discrimination, the fundamentally important decision in Case 170/84 *Bilka* [1986] ECR 1607. The Court's finding, in *Bilka*, that benefits paid to employees under an occupational pension scheme constitute pay and the absence of a further temporal limitation in that case contributed in no small part to determining the contours of the Court's subsequent case law on the application of Art 141 EC in the field of pensions.

[150] A label used in this context to refer principally to Directives 76/207 on equal treatment (OJ 1976 L 39/40) and 79/7 on equal treatment in matters of social security (OJ 1979 L6/24).

[151] See, eg, Case C-262/88 *Barber* [1990] ECR I-1889, where a redundancy payment and a pension paid out under a contracted out occupational pension scheme were held to come within the scope of application of Art 141 EC. The effect of the Court's ruling in that case on other institutional actors in the EC is evidenced by the *Barber* protocol annexed to the Maastricht Treaty.

highlighted the Court's unwillingness to step beyond the jurisdictional limits of Article 141 EC as it refused to recognise a general prohibition of discrimination on grounds of sex and confined that provision to issues of pay.[152] The resulting compartmentalisation of EC sex discrimination law was accentuated or propelled further by the Court's broad definition of pay and by the fact that while the prohibition of discrimination on grounds of sex in the field of pay enjoyed both vertical and horizontal direct effect, provisions of the Sex Equality Directives were limited to vertical direct effect and, indeed, in the case of social security, subject to important derogations such as that on the determination of pensionable age. The generous and purposive interpretation of the principle of equal pay stemming from *Defrenne II* is thus rightly regarded as the foundation of and reason for the development of EC sex discrimination law generally to its current scope and depth.[153]

Great Expectations

The greatest, yet most obvious, expectation which *Defrenne II* created was that there would be an end, at the level of individual employers or collective agreements, to the pay discrimination of female workers, to national legislation or practices which countenanced such differences and, more generally, to the gender pay gap. Because of the temporal limitation on the effects of the judgment, never mind national procedural limitations on retrospective claims, the historical effects of or reasons for pay discrimination were clearly not going to be wiped out overnight. Nevertheless, it might have been expected that over 30 years after this ground-breaking decision, female workers could aspire to receiving the same pay for equal work or work of equal value. Statistics reveal, however, that pay equality remains elusive. On the one hand, the gender pay gap in the EU (excluding the two new entrants in 2007) hovers, on average, around 25 per cent, with the largest gap in the UK (30 per cent) and the smallest in Slovenia (11 per cent).[154] On the other, there is no sign of an end to labour market segregation, itself a major contributor to the gender pay gap.[155] If anything, current employment patterns—outsourcing, increased resort to fixed term contracts and atypical employment forms—appear to accentuate it. EC sex equality law and the case law of the Court on, *inter alia*, Article 141 EC, with its narrow symmetrical or formal approach to equality, seem to have had limited impact in both these respects.

Leaving aside the sometimes inconsistent, disappointing or narrowly conceived case law of the Court on equal pay, examples of which will be discussed in the next section, it is clear that the reasons for the limited impact of EC sex equality law are several. The legislature, for example, whether at Community or national level, has failed to bolster or supplant the Court's work with the legislative framework which the Court itself in

[152] Case 149/77, paras 19–20.

[153] E Ellis, 'The Recent Jurisprudence of the Court of Justice in the Field of Sex Equality' (2000) 37 *CML Rev* 1403, 1403 and G Mancini and S O'Leary, 'New Frontiers of EU Sex Equality Law' (1999) 24 *EL Rev* 331.

[154] Neither do these general statistics provide a sufficiently comprehensive picture given further differences in the pay received by part-time and full-time, manual and non-manual workers, private and public sector workers. The figures are taken from European Commission, *The Gender Pay Gap. Origins and Policy Responses*, July 2006, which is itself based on Eurostat, *Structure of Earnings Survey 2002 (SES)*.

[155] On both these phenomena see further A McColgan, *Just Wages for Women* (Oxford, Clarendon Press, 1997).

Defrenne II regarded as necessary to deal with certain aspects of pay discrimination.[156] In addition, if the Court's consolidation of *Defrenne II* disappoints, part of this may be due to the weight of expectation which proceeded this judgment and to the hopes placed in EC sex equality law by those stymied by the lack of progress in this field at domestic level and opposed to the increasingly deregulatory thrust of national employment policies.[157] Mention must also be made of the little use made by the Commission of the infringement procedure to pursue Member States for their failure to fulfil their Treaty obligations pursuant to Article 141 EC, a provision which, in the Court's own words, 'imposes on states a duty to bring about a specific result to be mandatorily achieved within a fixed period'. Had the Commission pursued infringements in this field as energetically as it has in others, many litigants might have been spared the burden of proving the existence of discrimination and forcing legislative and institutional change at considerable personal, financial and, no doubt, professional cost.[158] The continued segregated nature of the labour market means that the principle of equal pay, on its own, is an insufficient tool for eliminating the gender pay gap since, as we shall see below, identification of an appropriate comparator may prove elusive or, following decisions of the Court, impossible. Moreover, the principle of equal pay in Article 141 EC is an insufficient means to tackle the various factors which are widely regarded as contributing to a devaluation of female labour or its concentration in certain sectors or in certain types of jobs.[159]

Shortcomings in the Jurisprudence on Equal Pay post-*Defrenne II*

While, as we saw, the Court did much to breathe life into Article 141 EC and EC sex discrimination generally, some perceive its recent case law, in particular, as a desertion of its early courageous stance in cases like *Defrenne II*, while others question its commitment to (substantive) equality from the outset. There is certainly tension and confusion in much of the Court's case law about the role and function in EC law of the equal pay principle and the prohibition of discrimination on grounds of sex generally. This section seeks to highlight this tension by focusing on difficulties relating to the choice or availability of comparators in equal pay cases, to the judicial enforcement of the principle of equal pay—most notably the burden of proof in equal pay cases and objective justification of indirect sex discrimination case—and, finally, to the Court's failure to consolidate the fundamental rights underpinnings of EC sex equality law and the substantive vocation of that law which it has championed.

Application of the principle of equal pay depends on a comparison between the work done by a woman and a man and the pay they receive in return. *Defrenne II* suggested, and

[156] See Case 43/75 *Defrenne II* para 19 and the perceptive comments of J Forman, 'The Equal Pay Principle under Community Law' (1982) *Legal Issues of European Integration* 17.

[157] See, eg, the national political, social and legislative background to Case C-167/97 *Seymour-Smith* [1999] ECR I-623.

[158] See L Fletcher, 'Enforcement of EC Sex Equality Law' in T Hervey and D O'Keeffe (eds), *Sex Equality Law in the EU* (Chichester, John Wiley, 1996) 173, 176.

[159] See further McColgan, above note 155 and R Townshend-Smith, *Sex Discrimination in Employment* (London, Sweet & Maxwell, 1989).

the Court later confirmed, that the notion of equal work includes also work of equal value.[160] The choice of an appropriate comparator has proved problematic, however. On the one hand, the Court has given little if any guidance on how the comparator should be chosen.[161] Its case law offers up examples of surprising, unpredictable and even contradictory results.[162] It has at times merged the question of comparability with that of justification, with the purpose of a distinction being relied on to determine the former. Once comparability is excluded, all questions of discrimination and justification lapse.[163]

On the other hand, since the direct effect of Article 141 EC is dependent on the form of discrimination complained of being judicially identified (solely) with the aid of criteria laid down by that provision, a claimant who has to look to another undertaking or indeed industry in order to find an equal pay comparator may find it difficult if not impossible to rely on the direct effect of the principle of equal pay. Basing itself on *Defrenne II*, the Court has stated that the applicability of Article 141 EC is not limited to situations in which men and women work for the same employer.[164] However, the Court has recently been faced with equal pay claims by workers comparing their pay to that received by employees of their former employer who has since dismissed them only to avail of their services through the intermediary of an agency.[165] The express purpose of this operation was to reduce the increased cost of those workers as a result of sex equality law. Since differences in pay in such situations cannot be attributed to a single source and there is thus no body which is *responsible* for the inequality and which could restore equal treatment,[166] the Court has held that these situations do not come within the scope of that provision. The upshot of these cases is that workers cannot rely on the direct effect of the principle of equal pay to counteract cross-sectoral pay inequalities and they are impotent, as Fredman points out, when employers resort to legal devices separating the supervisory and remunerative dimensions of the employment relationship, despite the fact that the purpose of those devices may be precisely to evade the financial consequences of the equal pay principle itself.[167]

Do these decisions, which considerably circumscribe the impact of Article 141 EC, highlight the poor quality of the Court's equal pay jurisprudence, the limits of the principle whose observance it is entrusted to ensure, or simply the Court's failure or unwillingness to transcend those limits? Believing itself to be constrained by the jurisdictional limits of Article 141 EC, the Court in *Allonby* clung to the need for a legislative

[160] Case 43/75, paras 20 and 54.

[161] See, eg, Case C-249/97 *Grüber* [1999] ECR I-5295, para 31, where the Court examined whether the applicant and her comparator were in situations which were in substance and origin similar.

[162] Compare the choice of comparator in Cases C-13/94 *P v S* [1996] ECR I-2143, C-249/96 *Grant* [1998] ECR I-621 and C-423/04 *Richards* [2006] ECR I-3585.

[163] See Cases C-249/97 *Grüber* or C-309/97 *Angestelltenbetriebsrat der Wiener Gebietskrankenkasse* [1999] ECR I-2907.

[164] Case C-256/01 *Allonby* [2004] ECR I-873, para 45. Cf Case 129/79 *MacCarthys* [1980] ECR 1275, para 15 for a narrower approach restricting comparison on the basis of Art 141 EC to the same establishment or service.

[165] See Cases C-256/01 and C-320/00 *Lawrence* [2002] ECR I-7325, para 17, which involved outsourced workers doing work of equal value to that performed by their chosen comparators still working for their previous employers. One wonders whether in *Allonby* the applicant erred in misdirecting her equal pay claim to the agency rather than her former employer.

[166] *Ibid*, paras 46 and 18 respectively.

[167] S Fredman, 'Marginalising Equal Pay Laws' (2004) 33 *Industrial Law Journal* 281. Following Case C-256/01 *Allonby*, once an employer delegates control over terms of employment, the direct applicability of Art 141 EC may no longer apply. See, eg, *DEFRA v Robertson* [2004] ICR 1289 (Court of Appeal, UK).

solution at Community and/or national level to remedy the problems faced by the applicants.[168] But did it fully exploit the 'available interpretative space' offered by Article 141 EC?[169] Could the discrimination in *Allonby* not have been directly ascertained by the national courts on the basis of the facts before them? The Court's language in *Defrenne II* regarding the direct applicability of the principle of equal pay to comparisons in the same establishment or service did not seem to automatically exclude situations where discrimination was judicially identifiable in the context of a triangular employment relationship. It simply acknowledged that a comparison between work done in the same establishment or service was more readily amenable to judicial identification.[170] One of the Court's own Advocates General had previously argued that the limitation of the scope of comparison to the same establishment or service would impose a restriction on the principle of equal pay which has no foundation in Article 141 EC and would limit the scope of application of that principle as regards activities of equal value.[171] The Court itself has indicated that equal value claims can be determined in the context of an adversarial procedure.[172] Yet, in *Allonby*, although willing to impose an independent EU definition of worker in answer to another aspect of the referred case, the Court was unwilling to go beyond the formal boundaries of the atypical triangular employment relationship linking the applicants, their former employer and the agency which now paid them to perform identical work, in the same establishment as their comparators, for their former employer.[173] The issue of the direct effect of Article 141 EC aside, there is no judicial condemnation in *Allonby* of the employer's resort to a legal device clearly at odds with the principle of equal pay, no mention that pay disparities of this type conflict with a principle which Member States are obliged to respect and no remonstrance with the Member States or Community institutions for failing to tackle these disparities. If one contrasts these omissions with the statements of the Court in *Defrenne II* it appears that the times they have indeed been a-changing.

Although *Defrenne II* ensured that individual employees could pursue their claims to equal pay through the national courts, relying directly on Article 141 EC, it also shifted the burden of ensuring and maintaining observance of the principle of equal pay from the Member States, the addressees of Article 141 EC, and the Commission, the guardian of the Treaties, to individual employees. Since 1976, the Court appears to have given judgment in only six infringement actions relating specifically to Article 141 EC. While the direct effect of the principle of equal pay means that individual employees can assert their right against other private parties and the state, it is only when that individual can prove that there has been an interference with their right that the remedial structure of the law comes into play.[174] Despite the multiple difficulties involved in mounting an equal pay case and the

[168] Opinion of Advocate General Geelhoed Case C-256/01 *Allonby*, para 53. This is not the first time the Court has referred to the need for a legislative solution to remedy pay discrimination. See also Case C-249/96 *Grant*, para 48, as regards pay discrimination on grounds of sexual orientation which it held fell outside the scope of application of Art 141 EC.

[169] The phrase is borrowed from J Shaw, 'Gender and the Court of Justice' in G De Búrca and JHH Weiler, *The European Court of Justice* (Oxford, Oxford University Press, 2001) 87, 121.

[170] Compare Case 43/75, paras 21–22 with point 4 of the Opinion of Advocate General Trabucchi, 486.

[171] See Advocate General Verloren van Themaat in Case 143/83 *Commission v Denmark* [1985] ECR 427, 430.

[172] Case 61/81 *Commission v United Kingdom* [1982] ECR 2607, para 13.

[173] See also Fredman, above note 167, 282–3.

[174] S Fredman, 'Transformation or Dilution: Fundamental Rights in the EU Social Sphere' (2006) 12 *European Law Journal* 41, 48.

disincentive of bringing a case against an employer and singling out colleagues for comparison, the onus is on the individual complainant to discharge the burden of proof.[175]

Given this legal and evidential burden, the Court has accepted that the burden of proof may shift when this is necessary to avoid depriving workers who appear to be the victims of discrimination of any effective means of enforcing the principle of equal pay. However, even in this respect its case law continues to waver. As regards a length of service criterion, it first held in *Danfoss* that there was no need for the employer to provide special justification with reference to the particular job in question since 'length of service goes hand in hand with experience and since experience generally enables the employee to perform his duties better'.[176] In later cases, notably *Nimz*, the Court refused to accept length of service on its own as sufficient justification for a pay differential. An employer had to provide proof of the contribution of seniority to performance of the particular job at issue and could not simply rely on a presumption.[177] Asked in a recent case how a national court should understand this apparently divergent jurisprudence, the Court resurrected *Danfoss* and the general principle that an employer is free to reward length of service without having to establish the importance it has in the performance of specific tasks entrusted to the employee and without reference to the circumstances of the individual case.[178] While both trade unions and employers' associations declared victory following the decision of the Court in *Cadman*, the absence of a reference to *Nimz* in the judgment is telling, as is the Court's statement to the effect that its answer constituted only a *clarification* of the case law in this field.

It is commonplace that the purpose of prohibiting indirect discrimination is to tackle hidden obstacles which stand in the way of certain disadvantaged groups, historically, in this context, women. Its success depends on robust scrutiny of the objective justifications advanced by employers and legislators to explain away the adverse impact of their measures, practices and policies, as well as effective policing of the proportionality of those measures.[179] Yet it is in respect of its case law on these two issues that the Court's critics have been most vociferous, chiding its 'inability to articulate a principled way in which to balance the commercial interests of the employer against the interest of the employee not to be discriminated against'[180] and its failure to more strictly police the interference by Member State legislation and legislation of the EC itself with the equality principle. Thus, when confronted with Member State justifications citing national social and employment policies, the Court has emphasised the wide margin of discretion of these parties and accepted that they were reasonably entitled to consider that the measures adopted pursuant to those policies were necessary in order to achieve aims unrelated to any discrimination on grounds of sex.[181] However, in the absence of a stringent standard

[175] Case C-127/92 *Enderby* [1993] ECR I-5535, para 13. See further C Kilpatrick, 'Community or Communities of Courts in European Integration? (1998) 4 *European Law Journal* 121, 133.

[176] Case 109/88 *Danfoss* [1989] ECR 3199, para 16.

[177] Case C-184/89 *Nimz* [1991] ECR I-297, para 14.

[178] Case C-17/05 *Cadman* [2006] ECR I-9583, paras 34–38.

[179] E Ellis, 'Recent Developments in European Community Sex Equality Law' (1998) 35 *CML Rev* 379, 384 et seq.

[180] *Ibid.*

[181] See, eg, Cases C-317/93 *Nolte* [1995] ECR I-4625, para 34; C-167/97 *Seymour-Smith* [1999] ECR I-623, para 77, and C-25/02 *Rinke* [2003] ECR I-8349, paras 40–42.

of justification, indirect discrimination loses much of its bite and certainly any pretension to being an instrument geared to achieving substantive equality.

Finally, although *Defrenne II* is regarded as having triggered a process from which sex equality emerged as a fundamental constitutional principle, the case law of the Court often belies its fundamental status. The Court has not hesitated to limit its scope in the light of the cost of its application for individual employers or the state. Regularly cited examples are the temporal limitations in *Defrenne II* and *Barber*, recognition of economic grounds of justification or market forces in cases of indirect sex discrimination—despite the clear risk that such recognition may allow precisely those factors which have led to the underpayment of women and which are functional to the market being reintroduced to justify their disadvantage[182]—and the unduly broad margin of discretion afforded Member States and the Community when justifying indirectly discriminatory legislation. Equally, although the Court in *Defrenne II* clearly stated that to comply with Article 141 EC it was necessary to raise the lowest salaries, otherwise known as levelling up, its adherence to a formal model of equality has led to its validation of levelling down.[183] Similarly, while the Court did much initially to carve out a degree of protection for pregnant workers and those on maternity leave, its application of the principle of equal pay to those workers is riddled with inconsistency and undue weight attributed to considerations of cost.[184] This case law suggests that the fundamental right not to be discriminated against on grounds of sex has never successfully or completely shaken itself free of the economic imperatives underpinning the Treaty and, despite the Court's lip service to substantive equality or the social objectives of Article 141 EC, the power of the market may continue to subordinate social rights where there is a conflict with efficiency.[185]

Conclusions

There is no doubt that the legacy of *Defrenne II* endures. Fifty years after the signing of the Treaty of Rome, the economic objectives of the EC still resonate as the above case law demonstrates, but they are no longer assured predominance. Recognition in that case of the horizontal and vertical direct effect of the principle of equal pay proved a catalyst for lasting change, not just in individual equal pay cases but also on a broader, legislative scale, as the recent Recast directive on sex equality demonstrates.[186] Furthermore, horizontal direct effect has spread its wings to other Treaty provisions and temporal limitations are regularly requested and sometimes conceded. The Court's case law on Article 141 EC has ensured that female workers have access to a wide range of benefits previously denied them and although its indirect sex discrimination case-law sometimes disappoints, there is

[182] See Advocate General Lenz in Case C-127/92 *Enderby* [1993] ECR I-5535, 5563.

[183] Case C-408/92 *Smith v Avdel* [1994] ECR I-4435.

[184] Compare Cases C-342/93 *Gillespie* [1996] ECR I-475, C-411/96 *Boyle* [1998] ECR I-6401, Case C-191/03 *McKenna* [2005] ECR I-7631 and C-284/02 *Sass* [2004] ECR I-11143, albeit the Court classified the later as an equal treatment case under Directive 76/207.

[185] Fredman, above n 174, 46.

[186] Directive 2006/54 on the implementation of the principle of equal opportunites and equal treatment for men and women in matters of employment and occupation (recast) (OJ 2006 L240/23).

no doubt that it has contributed in no small part to rooting out examples of institutional or structural discrimination which previous generations of female workers accepted or were forced to accept as the norm.

Yet the gender pay gap persists, the labour market remains segregated, work which is predominantly female attracts lower pay and predominantly female workers converge in part-time employment or avail of job-sharing options and extended unpaid childcare leave, with all the employment disadvantages which those choices entail. The fact that the Court's case law post-*Defrenne II* has failed to tackle the different instances and forms of disadvantage and inequality which result from an employment market which is structured in this way are many and varied as we have seen. The limits of the principle whose observance the Court was entrusted to ensure and the legal instruments made available to ensure it rank among those reasons. However, what has given rise to some of the greatest criticism of the Court's sex equality jurisprudence post-*Defrenne II* is the fact that while the Court regularly flirts with the notion that the right not to be discriminated on grounds of sex constitutes a fundamental right and that the objective of EC law in this field is the attainment of substantive and not merely formal equality,[187] too much of its jurisprudence confutes these claims. The Court regularly ignores the fact that many labour market choices—working part-time, job-sharing, resigning in the absence of childcare provision, taking unpaid parental leave—are not choices made freely and out of self-interest by individual female employees but are determined by those employees' responsibility to others in society.[188] It is also guilty of reinforcing some of the very prejudices and stereotypes which disadvantage women in employment and which substantive equality seeks to eradicate.[189]

The Court demonstrates at times a lack of conviction regarding sex equality law, a lack of understanding regarding the different components of that law or a basic paucity or lack of rigour in its legal reasoning. It is for this reason that some critics identify periods of greater and lesser glory in the interpretation and application of EC sex equality law. Were the Court in 2009 to be confronted with the legal and political modern day equivalent of *Defrenne II*, can one be confident that it would decide such a case in the same way? Some decisions nowadays still reflect the commitment of the erstwhile Court to a European ideal, a European social contract of sorts and a desire to protect 'les veuves et les orphélins', however naïve or politically motivated that commitment may have been.[190] However, other judgments display a harder, economic and political realpolitik which is perhaps more closely suited to the mood in the Member States in these times.

In any event, perhaps the most fitting way to conclude a review of *Defrenne II*, over 50 years after the signing of the Treaty of Rome and over 30 after that judgment, is to refer to the recent *Jonkman* case, which was a sequel to the *Defrenne* trilogy. The applicants in that case, former Sabena air hostesses now retired, like Gabrielle Defrenne, continued to

[187] See, eg, Cases C-409/95 *Marschall* [1997] ECR I-6363, para 29 or C-243/94 *Hill and Stapleton* [1998] ECR I-3739, para 42.

[188] See, variously, Cases C-249/97 *Grüber*, C-220/02 *Österreichischer Gewerkschaftbund* [2004] ECR I-5907; 170/84 *Bilka* [1986] ECR 1607 and C-63 and C-64/91 *Jackson and Cresswell* [1992] ECR I-4737.

[189] See, eg, Cases C-476/99 *Lommers* [2002] ECR I-2891 or C-218/98 *Abdoulaye* [1999] ECR I-5723.

[190] Shaw, above note 169, who argues that politics of subsidiarity and sovereignty infuse the Court's jurisprudence on gender equality.

allege sex discrimination as regards the calculation of their statutory pensions.[191] Regardless of the outcome in that case, the fact that the Court received such a reference is vivid testimony to the fact that equal pay is, as yet, unattained. Undoubtedly, these applicants were bolstered in bringing their case by their former colleague's victory, at least in terms of legal principle, in *Defrenne II* and by the Court's sex equality case law developed thereafter. However, their need to bring the case is a stark reminder of what appears to be the continued failure by Member States to respect and guarantee sex equality and even of failure on the part of the Commission to ensure respect for the fundamental right not to be discriminated against on grounds of sex.[192]

[191] Joined Cases C-231/06 and C-233/06 *Jonkman and others* [2007] ECR I-5149. The alleged discrimination essentially lay in the imposition by Belgian legislation of a single global payment of adjustment contributions to cover the periods during which the air hostesses were historically discriminated against, together with interest at the annual rate of 10%. The Court held that Directive 79/7 precludes a Member State from requiring the payment of adjustment contributions to be made together with interest other than that to compensate for inflation. That directive also precludes a requirement that that payment be made as a single sum, where that condition makes the adjustment concerned impossible or excessively difficult in practice. According to the Court, that is the case in particular where the sum to be paid exceeds the annual pension of the interested party.

[192] Was an infringement action by the Commission too much to expect as a means of vindicating the rights of these applicants in this most historically important of social, political and legal contexts? The Commission has not been so bashful in other fields—see Cases C-212/99 *Commission v Italy* [2001] ECR I-4923 and C-119/04 *Commission v Italy* [2006] ECR I-6885, regarding Art 39 EC and the rights of foreign language lecturers in Italian universities.

4

Gender Equality and Social Policy after *Defrenne*

HORATIA MUIR WATT

In holding (albeit prospectively[193]) that gender equality in the workplace was a general principle of Community law, whose purport went beyond the sole issue of equal wages expressly governed by Article 119 of the Treaty of Rome (now 141 EC), the landmark *Defrenne* judgment[194] placed non-discrimination at the heart of the European social model, gave it direct horizontal effect at a time when such a step was considered by Sir Otto Kahn-Freund himself as 'unlikely',[195] and set the scene for the development of Community labour law in terms of 'fundamental personal rights'.[196] An initially modest provision designed to avoid social dumping, Article 119 was thus raised by the Court to the constitutional status which the Treaty of Amsterdam would later endorse and expand. Thirty years on, such a move retains its significance for at least two reasons. First, while social policy has proved in the long run to be the 'sick man of public policy' in Europe,[197] anti-discrimination has remained the focus of judicial and, in its wake, legislative activism, surviving the contemporary neo-liberal policy shift towards the ascendancy of employment over social concerns.[198] Secondly, gender equality has occupied the position of 'a somewhat lonely principle' as one of the few justiciable social rights in Community law.[199]

[193] Introducing prospective overrruling, the Court asserted that such a principle did not exist at the time of the events being litigated before the Belgian referring court.

[194] The *Defrenne* litigation gave rise to no less than three ECJ judgments (Case 80/70, 1971; Case 43–75 1976; aff. 149/77, 1978) of which the third is of particular significance. See too the sequel in ECJ 21 June 2007, aff. C-231 to 233/06, *ONP v Jonkman.*

[195] 'Labour Law and Social Security', vol I, ch VI, in E Stein and L Nicholson (eds), *American Enterprise in the Common Market: A Legal Profile* (Ann Arbour, 1960), 329, asserting that Art 119 does not confer any rights on any individual.

[196] The decisive step was to recognise that the 'elimination of discrimination on grounds of sex forms part of the fundamental rights' under Community law (Judgment, para 27), subsequently to be endorsed by the European Court of Human Rights.

[197] M Poiares Maduro, 'Europe's Social Self: "Sickness unto Death"', in Jo Shaw (ed), *Social Law and Policy in an Evolving European Union*, 2000, 325; A Somek, 'Concordantia Catholica: Exploring the Context of European Antidiscrimination Law and Policy' (2005) 14 *Transnational Legal and Contemporary Problems* 959.

[198] Somek, cited above.

[199] C Hoskyns, *Integrating Gender: Women, Law and Politics in the European Union* (London, Verso, 1996).

Undeniably, the Court's case law since *Defrenne* has contributed to mitigate gender discrimination[200] and has gone a long way towards extending the purport of non-discrimination to other sources of inequality,[201] both in the workplace, widely construed,[202] and beyond the sole issue of wages and its initially restrictive interpretation of the scope of Article 119, while pushing back the limits of gender to encompass sexual orientation.[203] More remarkably still, it has condemned indirect discrimination, which requires looking at the way in which equality is ensured 'in practice'.[204] In turn, this has paved the way for the new 'integrated approach' to discrimination by which the Commission, through 'gender mainstreaming', intends to extend the purview of equality concerns across all EC policies.[205] However, despite, or perhaps because of, the role of gender equality as the cornerstone of European social policy and as a central tenet of integration, several distinct strands of questions arise today as to the fate of the *Defrenne* ruling, in the context of radical economic and social changes in the European and global labour market.[206] Indeed, 30 years after *Defrenne* and the adoption of the Equal Pay Directive (75/117/EEC), women still receive on average only 84 per cent of men's wages and, beyond differences linked to gender, the European labour market is still rife with various forms of inequalities. While the new 'open method of co-ordination'[207] and the Framework Directive (2000/78/EC) certainly offer bright prospects in the battle against social exclusion, it is frequently observed that the formal domain of gender equality under the Treaty provisions still privileges employment and social security, and, despite the constitutional status of non-discrimination, does not always appear to warrant the strict enforcement that benefits the economic requirements of free movement. This situation may stem from the internal inconsistencies within the concept of non-discrimination, if not from the various tensions at the heart of European social policy.

[200] The Court has retained an extensive interpretation of the concept of gender, which encompasses transsexuality and consequently a change of assigned gender (Case C-13/94 *P v S* [1996] ECR I-2143, paras 19–21).

[201] ECJ, *Mangold* (C-144/04, 2005), holding that there is a prohibition to discriminate on grounds of age which constitutes a part of the general principle of equal treatment as a fundamental right under Community law.

[202] The concept of worker has been widely construed (see Case 53/81, *Levin*, 1982).

[203] In *P v S and Cornwall County Council* [1996] C-13/94, the Court broke ground when it held that employment discrimination against transsexuals constitutes direct discrimination incompatible with Art 119 of the Treaty in that 'to tolerate such discrimination would be tantamount . . . to failure to respect the dignity and the freedom to which [transsexuals are] entitled and which the Court has a duty to safeguard'.

[204] Art 141(4) EC now aims to 'ensuring full equality in practice'.

[205] Eg to the insurance market, or in access to goods and services. Gender mainstreaming essentially posits that gender should be taken into account by policy-makers at all stages of the political and policy-making process. Fiona Beveridge, 'Building Against the Past: The Impact of Mainstreaming on EU Gender Law and Policy' (2007) 32(2) *EL Rev* 193.

[206] See C Joerges, 'What Is Left of the European Economic Constitution? A Melancholic Eulogy' (2005) 30(4) *EL Rev* 461 at 462: 'Can the welfare state survive globalisation? Can "the" European social model survive Europeanisation?'

[207] The open method of co-ordination targets 'the reorganisation, improvement, development and evaluation of policy processes, so that a gender equality perspective is incorporated in all policies at all levels and at all stages, by the actors normally involved in policy-making'.

Whither Non-discrimination?

The expansion of the prohibition of gender discrimination to encompass various other forms of unequal treatment has led to a paradoxical, but perhaps largely predictable, conflict between non-discrimination and equality.[208] Since *Defrenne*, the Court has effected a remarkable shift from a formal (or Aristotelian) concept of non-discrimination as articulated in much of the existing EU equality legislation, which merely requires that people in similar situations should be treated equally, to a substantive concept which moves well beyond the 'sameness of treatment' requirement to catch the structural causes of exclusion.[209] This expansive judicial policy has now been championed by the Commission, whose new integrated approach is designed precisely with that end in view.[210] With full employment and human dignity as the horizon, the focus is now put upon eradicating 'the socially entrenched forms of disadvantage which undermine the ability of certain groups to compete on an equal basis'.[211] For instance, one of the causes of disadvantage suffered by women in the workplace may lie in the unequal distribution of childcare responsibilities between women and men outside the labour market; this implies that an employment culture of long and anti-social working hours is likely to have a greater negative impact on women.[212] Similarly, lower pay for part-time work will place women at a particular disadvantage in the labour market, since in many sectors, the part time workforce will be predominantly female.

In this respect, feminist and critical race studies have done much to highlight the stereotypes on which the legal system still rests to a large extent, while emphasising, ofter counterintuitively, the negative impact that protective legislation in the labour market, redistributive of wealth to the workforce as a whole, may nevertheless produce on certain particularly disadvantaged minority groups, including women, ethnic minorities, or young unskilled workers. An obvious implication of this policy reorientation towards a substantive understanding of discrimination is that it clearly cannot be exclusively employment-based and must encompass other areas of social exclusion, such as education and vocational training. While such a swing is obviously welcome, it is not unproblematic, in at least three different ways.

First, while largely compelled by the Court itself,[213] the shift towards a substantive, proactive understanding of discrimination leads inevitably to the acknowledgment of the limits of judicial action in individual litigation in implementing a wider social policy

[208] See Síofra O'Leary and Giuseppe Federico Mancini, 'The New Frontiers of Sex Equality Law in the European Union' (1999) 24(4) *EL Rev* 331; N Bamforth, 'Conceptions of Antidiscrimination Law' (2003) 24 *OJLS* 693; Mark Bell and Lisa Waddington, 'Reflecting on Inequalities in European Equality Law' (2003) 28(3) *EL Rev* 349; H Collins, 'Social inclusion: A Better Approach to equality Issues' (2005) 14 *Transnational Legal and Contemporary Problems* 897.

[209] Beveridge, cited above.

[210] The Commission's 'mainstreaming' policy is designed to ensure the across-the-board integration of employment, labour, social, economic, and human rights policies.

[211] Mark Bell, 'Equality and the European Union Constitution', 33 *Industrial Law Journal* 242 at 247.

[212] *Ibid.*

[213] In its pregnancy jurisprudence, for example, the Court held that 'the result pursued by Directive 76/207 is substantive, not formal, equality'.

designed to go to the roots of structural inequalities.[214] Positive action designed to ensure equal opportunities outside the workplace may be needed to redress past and present disadvantages which persist within the employment field.[215] But it is here that the real difficulties arise, since group-oriented redistributive policies generate dissonance with formal equality principles.[216] As practised in the United States with the constitutional approval of the Supreme Court, affirmative action is designed to reach fixed quotas of minority representation in education and the workforce. By contrast, the European version of positive action stops short of explicit quotas and aims to preserve meritocracy.[217] The Court itself has therefore had to balance positive action and formal equality in its scrutiny of national provisions introducing preference for women as a group, and has done so by allowing only those measures which aim to attain equality of opportunity, not result. Unconditional priority of women over men therefore oversteps the mandate of Article 2(4) and introduces discrimination. Preference is Treaty-proof only when mitigated by a proviso allowing the balance to tilt in favour of a male applicant for specific reasons.[218]

A second difficulty inherent in the notion of non-discrimination is the choice of comparator.[219] Sameness of treatment is clearly an inadequate tool to combat all those disadvantages and exclusions which do not lend themselves to a straightforward comparison of like with like.[220] For instance, the choice of male comparator for pregnancy or pregnancy-linked illness is obviously nonsensical.[221] Grappling with this difficulty, the Court has decided that since only women can be refused employment on grounds of pregnancy, such a refusal constitutes direct discrimination on grounds of sex.[222] A different dilemma arose in respect of the rights of lesbian partners claiming benefits which accrue to heterosexual couples, which highlights the way in which the choice of comparator may lead to asserting equality in unequal treament. Here the comparator is not a man with a female partner, but a male employee who has a partner of the same sex, who would no doubt have been treated equally unfavorably.[223]

[214] See Bell and Waddington, cited above. Individual action has been made, encouraged and facilitated, particularly by providing for a shift in the burden of proof and protecting complainants from victimisation. But individual litigation may not be enough to eradicate deeper social disadvantage.

[215] In *Marschall v Land Nordrhein-Westfalen* (C-409/95, 1997) the Court accepted that 'even where male and female candidates are equally qualified, male candidates tend to be promoted in preference to female candidates particularly because of prejudices and stereotypes concerning the role and capacities of women in working life and the fear, for example, that women will interrupt their careers more frequently, that owing to household and family duties they will be less flexible in their working hours, or that they will be absent from work more frequently because of pregnancy, childbirth and breastfeeding'.

[216] O'Leary and Mancini, cited above.

[217] Collins, cited above.

[218] *Kalanke* (C 450/93, 1995) and *Marschall* cited above.

[219] Aileen McColgan, 'Cracking the Comparator Problem: Discrimination, "Equal" Treatment and the Role of Comparisons' (2006) *European Human Rights Law Review* 6, 650–77.

[220] O'Leary and Mancini, cited above.

[221] The American Supreme Court nevertheless held initially that distinctions concerning pregnancy are not based on sex because the group of non-pregnant persons consists of members of both sexes, employers or, in the alternative, if and when the action of employers is found to be justified, on those female workers who bear children (*Geduldig v Aiello* (1974) 417 US 484 and *General Electric Co v Gilbert* (1976) 429 US 125; see O'Leary and Mancini, cited above).

[222] *Dekker* C-188/88, 1991.]The Court has, however, chosen, somewhat confusingly, to apply a substantive test as regards pregnancy itself and a comparative test as regards those consequences of pregnancy leading to illness and absence from work which continue after the protected period. See O'Leary and Mancini, cited above.

[223] *P v S and Cornwall County Council*, cited above.

Of course there is no real reason—other perhaps than the reluctance of the Court to provoke anew the wrath of Member States on political senstive issues—why, on both these counts, it may not make the appropriate adjustments in order to ensure better adequation of the legal tools at its disposal to the aim of dignity and social inclusion. However, these difficulties may in fact point to a third and deeper problem in relation to the role of the Court in implementing a more demanding conception of equality. In the past, as explained by Mancini, 'equality policy has focused on the development of legal rights, with hard legal rules, backed by the possibility of recourse to the Court of Justice, as the "gold standard"'. The current turn to mainstreaming makes the role of the Court more uncertain and has still to find its place in the jurisprudence of the Court. However, 'it is doubtful whether the Court might prove a meaningful site for action'.[224] The difficulty lies in the fact that Article 3(2) does not contain hard rules defining the duties of the Institutions as far as following an integrated agenda is concerned, nor does it make clear what standard of judicial review is to be applied.[225] It is difficult, therefore, to conclude otherwise than by considering the mainstreaming duty 'as a political rather than a legal obligation',[226] leaving the Court, which may be expected to accord the Institutions a wide margin of discretion, bereft of significant means of control.

Whither European Social Policy?

The fragility of European social policy is largely accountable to Europe's 'constitutional assymetry'. It is within the province of the Member States to regulate social protection and to support full employment by fiscal and monetary policies, while the Community regulates market access.[227] This means, for instance, that the Union cannot directly address employment issues at a European level of governance. One solution to the inevitable tension which results from this assymetry may lie in the contemporary development of 'soft' or non-coercive regulatory tools, emphasising mutual learning and exchange of good practices, on a Community level. Whereas the open method of co-ordination and gender mainstreaming were initially designed as tools to improve its own policy-making, the Commission has succeeded thereby in introducing gender goals and targets for Member States in politically sensitive areas such as social protection.[228] Thus, even if employment policy does not belong to Community competence, it can be discussed, non-binding objectives substantiated, guidelines offered.[229]

But this shift to new forms of regulation, empowering the Community in the field of social policy, is affected by a double paradox, which impacts directly on the present ability of the Court to pursue a progressive agenda in this field. On the one hand, the Commission's new quest for social inclusion through equality mainstreaming may be

[224] O'Leary and Mancini, cited above.

[225] *Ibid.*

[226] *Ibid.*

[227] Joerges and Somek, cited above.

[228] J Zeitlin, 'Comments on Jacobsson and Vifell, Employment Policy Co-ordination: Between Deliberation and Discipline?' (2004), cited by C Joerges, 479.

[229] Joerges, cited above, observing however that this soft methodology is not unproblematic in terms of democracy, since it basically entails entrusting decision-making to 'opaque networks'.

increasedly subordinate to economic concerns, which are likely to infuse the Court's own contribution. On the other, while the resources now offered by the concept of European citizenship can undoubtedly serve to promote the constitutionalisation of social rights much along the same lines as the principle of non-discrimination in *Defrenne*, they also appear to herald the decline of social policy, from which equality concerns are increasingly dissociated.

Community social policy as such is limited to transnational aspects of social protection which favour the cross-border mobility of workers as factors of production.[230] Harnessed to the promotion of transnational business, it is essentially a policy of 'sustainable market dependence'.[231] That is not to say that it does not make considerable room for the assertion of social rights, but, as already apparent in *Defrenne*, the rationale for such rights is as much a utilitarian policy geared to ensure healthy regulatory competition as an intrinsic dignity concern.[232] The later evolution of Community law, carried by the soft regulatory shift towards greater equality and social inclusion, does not bely this rationale: more inclusive labour markets enlarge the workforce; mainstreaming anti-discrimination into employment policy serves to enhance employability.[233] The Lisbon process subordinates gender equality to the 'meta-goals' of the Union, the equality of women as workers and consumers being central to their implementation.[234] Equality concerns in the new areas covered by the open method of co-ordination thus appear largely as 'efficiency' criteria, bereft of any larger vision of citizenship. However beneficial their side effects, such strategies run the risk that 'any on-going commitment to gender equality becomes entirely contingent on the other, economic, goals to which it is linked, rather than becoming embedded in institutional practices in its own right'.[235] Already, policies which support women who do not wish to conform to the utilitarian model—those who choose not to enter the labour market but stay at home to look after children, work unpaid in the home, care for the elderly or supply unpaid labour within their communities—are viewed with disfavour.[236]

Traditionally, the role of the Court has mediated between the demands of the market and the requirements of social inclusion by upholding justifications of obstacles to economic mobility—the newest illustration of its essential role to this effect is in the uncharted area of industrial action with cross-border impact.[237] Recently, it has used Union citizenship as a source of new individual rights and protection.[238] This new legal basis may well serve to improve the status of equality concerns, just as, in *Defrenne*, equal pay between women and men was raised from being an element of labour law, to the status of a fundamental norm of Community law.[239] Indeed, Article 13 offers the

[230] Somek, cited above.

[231] *Ibid*, 961.

[232] Art 191 was initially included in the Treaty of Rome on the instigation of France, so as not to be disadvantaged in regulatory competition in relation to other Contracting States' less protective social policies.

[233] Somek, cited above.

[234] O'Leary and Mancini, cited above.

[235] Somek, cited above.

[236] O'Leary and Mancini, cited above.

[237] In *Viking*, C-438/05 (2007), a strike by Finnish sailors was designed to prevent relocation of the employer to Estonia in order to prevent the reduction of wages.

[238] See, eg, *Sala* (C-85/96), *Grzelczyk* (C-184/99).

[239] O'Leary and Mancini, cited above.

possibility of 'rebranding' anti-discrimination law as part of the citizenship acquis.[240] Thus, the Directives adopted on the basis of this provision (the Racial Equality Directive and the Framework Directive forbidding discrimination on grounds of religion or belief, disability, age and sexual orientation in the field of employment) both evidence and cement the constitutional basis of equality in the workplace and, as has been rightly pointed out, may well indeed improve the status of the Directives before the Court of Justice.[241]

Nevertheless, the choice of Article 13 as legal basis for anti-discrimination policy, rather than the Social Chapter of the Treaty (Title XI[242]) has been criticised.[243] Article 13 applies 'without prejudice to the other provisions of this Treaty', accentuating the fragmentation of the powers of the Community in the field of social policy. The Court of Justice has therefore had to mediate disagreements on the implementation of social policies in areas such as the environment, culture and health.[244] But more deeply, the status of social policy may be at stake. While recourse to Aarticle 13 heralds reinforcement of citizenship, the decision not to rely on Article 137 is seen to convey a negative signal with respect to social policy, implying that anti-discrimination law is becoming 'detached' from its social policy origins, and supplying further indication of the lower priority accorded to developing such policy.[245] It may be therefore that the Court has an essential role to play in the future, in maintaining wherever possible the link it established in *Defrenne* between equality and social concerns, which may now be a condition of the survival of European social policy.

[240] Mark Bell and Richard Whittle, 'Between Social Policy and Union Citizenship: The Framework Directive on Equal Treatment in Employment (2002) *EL Rev* 27(6), 677.

[241] *Ibid.*

[242] Art 137(2), enables the adoption of directives to 'support' and 'complement' the activities of Member States in the fields of improvement in particular of the working environment to protect workers' health and safety; working conditions; the information and consultation of workers; the integration of persons excluded from the labour market; equality between men and women with regard to labour market opportunities and treatment at work, with a view to achieving the objectives (specified in Art 136 EC) of the promotion of employment, an improvement in living and working conditions, proper social protection, dialogue between management and labour, lasting high employment, and the combating of exclusion.

[243] Bell and Whittle, cited above.

[244] *Ibid.*

[245] O'Leary and Mancini, cited above.

VIII

Case 294/83, *Parti écologiste 'Les Verts' v European Parliament*

1

The Basic Constitutional Charter of a Community Based on the Rule of Law

KOEN LENAERTS*

Introduction

The judgment known simply as *Les Verts* constitutes both a cornerstone and a milestone in the jurisprudence of the Court of Justice of the European Communities (the Court of Justice or the Court). Its significance is multi-faceted, and it is indeed striking that so many fundamental points of European law can be found in one case.

As is well known, the case presented the Court with novel questions concerning the interpretation of Article 173 EEC (now Article 230 EC), both with regard to the standing of the European Parliament[1] as a defendant in an action for annulment ('*légitimation passive*') and the admissibility hurdles of 'direct and individual concern' for natural and legal persons.[2] As regards the former, although at the time, the text of the Treaty did not explicitly provide for judicial review of measures adopted by the European Parliament,[3] the Court nevertheless held that it would be 'contrary both to the spirit of the Treaty as expressed in Article 164 [now Article 220 EC] and to its system' if acts of the European Parliament intended to have legal effects vis-à-vis third parties could not be challenged by an action for annulment.[4] It was within this context that the Court proclaimed in paragraph 23:

> [T]he European Economic Community is a Community based on the rule of law, inasmuch as neither its Member States nor its institutions can avoid a review of the question whether the measures adopted by them are in conformity with the basic constitutional charter, the Treaty.[5]

It then declared that by virtue of Articles 230 and 241, on the one hand, and Article 234, on the other, 'the Treaty established a complete system of legal remedies and procedures designed to permit the Court of Justice to review the legality of measures adopted by the institutions'.[6]

* President of Chamber of the Court of Justice of the European Communities and Professor of European Law at the Katholieke Universiteit Leuven. All opinions expressed herein are personal to the author.

[1] Then referred to as the Assembly: see Arts 4, 137–144 EEC.

[2] See Case 294/83 *Parti écologiste 'Les Verts' v European Parliament* [1986] ECR 1339, para 35; Opinion of Advocate General Mancini in Case 294/83 *Les Verts*, para 6, at 1348.

[3] Under Art 173(1) EEC, the Court of Justice was given jurisdiction to review only 'the legality of acts of the Council and the Commission other than recommendations or opinions'.

[4] Case 294/83 *Les Verts*, para 25.

[5] *Ibid*, para 23.

[6] *Ibid.*

As regards the latter conditions of direct and individual concern in relation to the standing of natural and legal persons under the second paragraph of Article 173 EEC (now the fourth paragraph of Article 230 EC[7]), the Court also set down important rulings.[8] This was particularly so in relation to the 'delicate' issue of individual concern.[9] Under the facts of the case, the French political association 'Les Verts—Parti écologiste' brought this action to annul two budgetary decisions of the European Parliament concerning the financing of information campaigns conducted by political parties participating in the 1984 European elections.[10] In essence, the applicant argued that the criteria for the allocation of these funds unlawfully favoured the parties already represented in the European Parliament to the detriment of those groups that would be taking part in the 1984 elections and were therefore not represented.[11] By strict adherence to the prior case law on the matter of individual concern, the applicant did not qualify as such.[12] Yet, the Court reasoned that if only the represented and hence identifiable political groups were individually concerned, this 'would give rise to inequality in the protection afforded by the Court to the various groupings competing in the same elections'.[13] In these circumstances, the applicant was to be considered individually concerned by the contested measures.[14]

Certainly, the foregoing points were not the only important ones in the case. The Court's rulings concerning the legal capacity of the applicant to pursue the action despite its dissolution and subsequent merger into a new political association[15] and the Court's power to review the conditions for the admissibility of an action for annulment of its own motion[16] continue to filter down through the case law. The substantive elements of the case concerning the scope of the budgetary powers wielded by the European Parliament in relation to the financing of the European elections have also not gone unnoticed.[17]

Be that as it may, there are good reasons why the Court's interpretation of Article 173 EEC (now Article 230 EC), upholding judicial review of acts of the European Parliament and affirming standing for parties in the applicant's position, assumes centre stage in the discussion. First, the true 'stakes of the game' underlying this case involved the credibility

[7] Identical to the second paragraph of Art 173 EEC, the fourth paragraph of Art 230 EC provides: 'Any natural or legal person may, under the same conditions, institute proceedings against a decision addressed to that person or against a decision which, although in the form of a regulation or a decision addressed to another person, is of direct and individual concern to the former.'

[8] See Case 294/83 *Les Verts*, paras 31, 37.

[9] R Joliet and DT Keeling, 'The Reimbursement of Election Expenses: A Forgotten Dispute' (1994) 19 *EL Rev* 243, 253.

[10] See Case 294/83 *Les Verts*, paras 1–11. The applicant lodged a total of eight actions challenging various measures of the European Parliament related to the allocation of these funds both before the Court of Justice and the French Conseil d'Etat, all of which were dismissed save the instant case. For further discussion, see Opinion of Advocate General Mancini in Case 294/83 *Les Verts*, paras 1, 3, at 1341, 1344–5; Joliet and Keeling, note 9, at 244–51.

[11] See Opinion of Advocate General Mancini in Case 294/83 *Les Verts*, para 3, at 1344. The applicant put forward seven pleas challenging the contested decisions: Case 294/83 *Les Verts*, para 12. In its examination of the first three, the Court concluded that the decisions infringed Art 7(2) of the 1976 Act concerning the election of the representatives of the Assembly by direct universal suffrage: *ibid*, para 55.

[12] This explains the divergence between the Court's judgment and the Opinion of Advocate General Mancini, who submitted that the action should be deemed inadmissible for lack of individual concern: see Opinion of Advocate General Mancini in Case 294/83 *Les Verts*, paras 9–11, at 1352–6.

[13] Case 294/83 *Les Verts*, paras 35–36.

[14] *Ibid*, para 37.

[15] See *ibid*, paras 13–18.

[16] See *ibid*, para 19.

[17] See *ibid*, paras 39–55. For further discussion, see Joliet and Keeling, note 9.

of the European Parliament and the legitimacy of representative democracy in the Community legal order, so as to guarantee that all political groups could be accorded equal opportunities to present themselves to the voters in the European elections.[18] This may have been made more explicit in the Opinion of Advocate General Mancini, as opposed to the Court's judgment.[19] Still, it should not be missed that the Court sought in *Les Verts* to ensure 'a parliament that is respected and is worthy of respect, an open democracy, a concern for justice and equality'[20].

Second, the timing of the judgment is also of note. Delivered on 23 April 1986, *Les Verts* came only a few months after the signing of the Single European Act in which the Member States failed to amend the Treaty so as to provide the European Parliament with standing under Article 173 (now Article 230) of the Treaty.[21] Thus, it fell to the Court of Justice to uphold the observance of equal judicial protection in the Community legal order notwithstanding the Member States' lack of consensus on the matter.[22] Although the case has beckoned critical remarks in relation to the Court's supposed judicial activism, it has been staunchly defended by scholars who emphasise among other things that the Court's judgment in *Les Verts* was subsequently incorporated by way of the Maastricht Treaty, where it has remained firmly in place ever since.[23]

In any event, the jurisprudential (and doctrinal) heart of *Les Verts* lies in the twofold impact of the famous paragraph 23, espousing both the 'constitutional' nature of the Treaty and the 'complete system of legal remedies and procedures' laid down by the Treaty. Therefore, perhaps it is only now with the benefit of two decades of hindsight that the implications drawn from these two components of *Les Verts* can be revisited and appreciated in a new light. The structure of this discussion is divided into two parts in order to provide some reflection on both points.

[18] See K Lenaerts, 'Some Thoughts About the Interaction Between Judges and Politicians' (1992) *U of Chicago Legal Forum* 93, 113. See also K Lenaerts and T Corthaut, 'Judicial Review as a Contribution to the Development of European Constitutionalism' (2003) 22 *Yeabook of European Law* 1, 34.

[19] See Opinion of Advocate General Mancini in Case 294/83 *Les Verts*, para 6, at 1348.

[20] Joliet and Keeling, note 9, at 244; for further eloquent remarks, see *ibid* at 266. These aspects of *Les Verts* would have important reverberations in *Matthews v United Kingdom* (App no 24833/94) ECHR 18 February 1999, in which the European Court of Human Rights deemed the European Parliament a true 'legislature' for the purposes of Art 3 of Protocol No 1 of the European Convention of Human Rights, thereby concluding that the UK was in breach of this provision by failing to organise European elections in Gibraltar: see paras 36–54, 65. For the aftermath of this case in relation to the action taken by the UK to remedy this violation, see Case C-145/04 *Spain v United Kingdom* [2006] ECR I–7917.

[21] See, eg, V Constantinesco and D Simon, Note (1987) 108 *Journal du droit international* 409, 411; J-P Jacqué, Note (1986) 23 *Revue trimestrielle de droit européen* 500, 503. The Single European Act was signed at Luxembourg on 17 February 1986 and at The Hague on 28 February 1986, but it did not enter into force until 1 July 1987. See Notification [1987] OJ L 169/29.

[22] For further discussion of the interplay between the legislative and judicial routes in relation to *Les Verts*, see Lenaerts, note 18, at 111–13; V Constantinesco and D Simon, Note (1987) *Recueil Dalloz Sirey Jur* 79, 80.

[23] See, eg, A Arnull, *The European Union and its Court of Justice*, 2nd edn (Oxford, Oxford University Press, 2006) 67–8 (and further citations therein). Indeed, the Treaty was amended in accordance with 'the exact language' of the Court's case law: FG Jacobs, 'Constitutional Control of European Elections: The Scope of Judicial Review' (2005) 28 *Fordham International Law Journal* 1049, 1056.

A Community Based on a 'Constitutional Charter': Community Law as a Complete and Coherent Constitutional System

As the Court proclaimed in *Les Verts*, the Community has a 'basic constitutional charter, the Treaty'.[24] Viewed from a comparative perspective, this beckons analogy with the celebrated opinion of Chief Justice Marshall of the US Supreme Court in *McCulloch v Maryland*, in which he proclaimed that 'we must never forget that it is a *constitution* we are expounding'.[25] *Les Verts* made clear that the Court of Justice must heed a similar admonition in its 'expounding' of the Treaty.[26] In other words, *Les Verts* served to highlight the special nature of a constitution and the fact that the Treaty can essentially be considered the constitution of the European Community in a substantive, functional sense.[27] As seen below, the Community legal order contains the classical functions of a constitution in terms of the horizontal division of powers between the European institutions, the vertical division of powers between the Community and the Member States and the protection of fundamental rights, all of which are staunchly guarded by the Court of Justice.[28]

Horizontal Division of Powers

From the horizontal perspective, there is an essential 'institutional balance' in the allocation of powers among the European institutions, which the Court is charged to maintain.[29] In effect, the Court verifies that the institutions are acting in conformity with the rules of the Treaty so as to ensure the validity of measures adopted by them and that the proper legal basis setting forth the decision-making procedure to be followed in the adoption of such measures has been used.

A remarkable example is the *IATA* case,[30] concerning the validity of certain provisions of Regulation No 261/2004 in the field of air transport.[31] By way of a reference for a

[24] Case 294/83 *Les Verts*, para 23.

[25] *McCulloch v Maryland*, 17 US (4 Wheat.) 316, 407 (1819).

[26] In fact, specific attention has been drawn to the interplay between the Court's teleological approach and 'constitutional' interpretation in *Les Verts*: see Arnull, note 23, at 621.

[27] See further K Lenaerts, 'La constitutionnalisation de l'ordre juridique de l'Union européenne' in *Mélanges en l'honneur du Professeur Francis Delpérée. Itinéraires d'un constitutionnaliste* (Brussels, Bruylant, 2007) 815–31; J-L Quermonne, 'L'émergence d'un droit constitutionnel européen' (2006) 58 *Revue internationale de droit comparé* 581. In any case, this point should be seen apart from the debate about the Treaty establishing a Constitution for Europe [2004] OJ C 310/1 [hereinafter Constitutional Treaty], which invites consideration of somewhat different and broader issues outside the scope of this discussion.

[28] Lenaerts, note 27, paras 18–32, at 8–13 (also underscoring important aspects of European citizenship).

[29] It should not be lost from sight that it was in Case C-70/88 *European Parliament v Council* ('*Chernobyl*') [1990] ECR I-2041, the 'companion' case to *Les Verts* in which the Court finally accorded the European Parliament with standing to bring an action for annulment ('*légitimation active*'), that the Court also established the 'institutional balance' among the institutions and its role in maintaining it: see paras 21–27.

[30] Case C-344/04 *International Air Transport Association and European Low Fares Airline Association* ('*IATA*') [2006] ECR I-403.

[31] Reg (EC) No 261/2004 of the European Parliament and of the Council establishing common rules on compensation and assistance to passengers in the event of denied boarding and of cancellation or long delay of flights, and repealing Reg (EEC) No 295/91 [2004] OJ L 46/1.

preliminary ruling from an English court, the Court was confronted with a question concerning the compatability of Article 5 of the Regulation with the co-decision procedure enshrined in Article 251 EC.[32] The applicants in the national proceedings argued that the Conciliation Committee convened in accordance with Article 251 EC was not permitted, without exceeding its powers under this provision, to approve of new amendments to the proposed measure that had not previously been made by the European Parliament at second reading.[33] The idea behind this contention was that the institutional balance under the Treaty would be disturbed, since the amendments adopted by the Conciliation Committee could be approved by a simple majority of the European Parliament, as opposed to an absolute majority of its component members as required in the second reading.[34]

In rejecting this argument, the Court recalled:

> [O]nce the Conciliation Committee has been convened, it has the task not of coming to an agreement on the amendments proposed by the Parliament but, as is clear from the very wording of Article 251 EC, 'of reaching agreement on a joint text', by addressing, on the basis of the amendments proposed by the Parliament, the common position adopted by the Council.[35]

Thus, the text of Article 251 EC did not include any restrictions on the content of the measures chosen so as to enable agreement to be reached on a joint text—the authors of the Treaty having intended by recourse to the word 'conciliation' to make the co-decision procedure effective and to confer a wide discretion on the Conciliation Committee—and hence Article 251 EC could not be read as limiting in principle the power of that Committee.[36]

Certainly, *IATA* does not stand alone. Indeed, numerous examples abound in which the Court has sought to maintain the institutional balance with particular regard to the involvement of the European Parliament in the decision-making process.[37] In any case, it should not be forgotten that at the heart of the inter-institutional litigation consistently brought before the Court concerning the choice of legal basis for a Community measure lies the determination as to the correct decision-making procedure to be followed, thereby explaining its 'constitutional significance' for the horizontal, as well as the vertical, division of powers.[38]

Vertical Division of Powers

From the vertical perspective, the balance of powers between the Community and the Member States is maintained by the system of conferred competences and mechanisms for

[32] The English court referred a total of eight questions, seven contesting the validity of the regulation and one concerning the interpretation of the second paragraph of Art 234 EC: Case C-344/04 *IATA*, para 20. As for the latter question, see further below notes 132–135 and accompanying text.

[33] *Ibid*, para 55.

[34] For further discussion, see Opinion of Advocate General Geelhoed in Case C-344/04 *IATA*, paras 54–99.

[35] Case C-344/04 *IATA*, para 57.

[36] *Ibid*, paras 57–59.

[37] See K Lenaerts and P Van Nuffel, *Constitutional Law of the European Union* 2nd edn (London, Sweet & Maxwell, 2005) paras 14-021–14-022, at 584–6 (and citations to relevant case law therein).

[38] Opinion 2/00 *Cartagena Protocol* [2001] ECR I-9713, para 5. For further discussion of the constitutional implications of the choice of a legal basis, see Lenaerts and Van Nuffel, note 37, paras 5-009–5-012, at 86–90.

controlling the exercise of such competences as set down in the Treaty.[39] In this way, the Court of Justice is accorded the 'constitutional function' to ensure that the Community does not transgress the limits of the competences conferred upon it and encroach upon the competences of the Member States.

The Court's prominent case law concerning Article 95 EC—bestowing competence on the Community to enact harmonisation measures for the establishment and functioning of the internal market—likely stands as the quintessential example. Indeed, it was in relation to this Treaty provision that the Court for the first time struck down a Community measure[40] as *ultra vires* in the *Tobacco Advertising* case.[41] The Court emphasised that Article 95 EC did not confer on the Community legislature 'a general power to regulate the internal market'[42] and laid down the conditions that must be satisfied for recourse to Article 95 EC.[43] In doing so, the Court made clear that, provided these conditions were fulfilled, the Community legislature was not prevented from relying on Article 95 EC on the ground that public health protection was 'a decisive factor in the choices to be made'.[44]

Recently, the Court was confronted with the 'sequel' to this case[45] in *Tobacco Advertising II*[46] concerning Directive 2003/33/EC on the approximation of the laws of the Member States relating to the advertising and sponsorship of tobacco products,[47] which was enacted under the very same Treaty provisions as the previous directive annulled in the first *Tobacco Advertising* judgment.[48] The Court reiterated the requisite conditions for the use of Article 95 EC[49] and found them to be fulfilled in the instant case.[50] The Court confirmed the existence of obstacles to the free movement of goods and services and the risks of distortions of competition, which 'warranted intervention by the Community legislature on the basis of Article 95 EC',[51] and found that the contested provisions were 'intended to improve the conditions for the functioning of the internal market'.[52] Despite

[39] See Arts 5, 7 EC. As for the Union, see Arts 2, 5 EU.

[40] Dir 98/43/EC of the European Parliament and of the Council on the approximation of the laws, regulations and administrative provisions of the Member States relating to the advertising and sponsorship of tobacco products [1998] OJ L 213/9. This directive was based on Arts 57(2), 66 and 100a (now Arts 47(2), 55 and 95) EC.

[41] Case C-376/98 *Germany v European Parliament and Council* ('*Tobacco Advertising*') [2000] ECR I-8419.

[42] *Ibid*, para 83.

[43] See *ibid*, paras 81–117. For further discussion, see K Gutman, 'Note, Case C-66/04, Smoke Flavorings; Case C-436/03, SCE; and Case C-217/04, ENISA' (Winter 2006/2007) 13 *Columbia Journal of European Law* 147, 149–50.

[44] Case C-376/98 *Tobacco Advertising*, para 88. This would be reiterated in subsequent cases. See, eg, Case C-491/01 *British American Tobacco (Investments) Ltd and Imperial Tobacco Ltd* ('*BAT*') [2002] ECR I-11453, para 62; Case C-434/02 *Arnold André GmbH & Co KG* [2004] ECR I-11825, para 32; Case C-210/03 *Swedish Match AB and Swedish Match UK Ltd* [2004] ECR I-11893, para 31; Joined Cases C-154/04 and C-155/04 *Alliance for Natural Health and Others* [2005] ECR I-6451, para 30.

[45] Opinion of Advocate General Léger in Case C-380/03 *Germany v European Parliament and Council* ('*Tobacco Advertising II*') [2006] ECR I–11573, para 2.

[46] Case C-380/03 *Germany v European Parliament and Council* ('*Tobacco Advertising II*') [2006] ECR I–11573.

[47] Dir 2003/33/EC of the European Parliament and of the Council on the approximation of the laws, regulations and administrative provisions of the Member States relating to the advertising and sponsorship of tobacco products [2003] OJ L 152/16; corrigendum, [2004] OJ L 67/34.

[48] See note 40.

[49] See Case C-380/03 *Tobacco Advertising II*, paras 36–43.

[50] See *ibid*, paras 45–88.

[51] *Ibid*, para 68.

[52] *Ibid*, para 81.

the prominence of the case law concerning Article 95 EC, however, it constitutes merely one of a multitude of areas in which the Court is confronted with maintaining the 'constitutional' balance of powers between the Community and the Member States.[53]

Protection of Fundamental Rights

Finally, the 'constitutional' nature of the Treaty can be illustrated by the system of fundamental rights protection in the European Union, for which the Court of Justice continues to play an indisputable role. As regards the European institutions, the Court has sought to ensure utmost respect for fundamental rights whether it be in relation to their executive or legislative tasks.

For instance, in the case *European Parliament v Council*,[54] concerning Council Directive 2003/86/EC on the right to family reunification,[55] the Court stressed that 'a provision of a Community act could, in itself, not respect fundamental rights if it required, or expressly or impliedly authorised, the Member States to adopt or retain national legislation not respecting those rights'.[56] On that basis, the Court proceeded to ascertain whether the contested provisions of the directive violated fundamental rights,[57] thereby underlining in traditional fashion their status as an integral part of the general principles of law whose observance the Court ensures and for which the Court draws inspiration from the constitutional traditions common to the Member States and from the guidelines supplied by international instruments for the protection of human rights on which the Member States have collaborated or to which they are signatories,[58] with the European Convention for the Protection of Human Rights and Fundamental Freedoms (ECHR) receiving special significance in this regard.[59] Moreover, for the first time, the Court cited the Charter of Fundamental Rights of the European Union,[60] highlighting its principal aim and the important role attributed to it by the Community legislature in view of the reference made to it in the preamble of the directive.[61]

[53] Eg, the field of direct taxation is a viable area: see K Lenaerts and L Bernardeau, 'L'encadrement communautaire de la fiscalité directe' (2007) 43 *Cahiers de droit européen* 19–109; K Lenaerts, 'Die gemeinschaftsrechtliche Umrahmung der direkten Besteuerung' in *66. Deutscher Juristentag 2006* (Munich, Beck, 2006). The free movement of goods should also be considered: see J Snell, 'Who's Got the Power? Free Movement and Allocation of Competences in EC Law' (2003) 22 *Yearbook of European Law* 323.

[54] Case C-540/03 *European Parliament v Council* ('*Family reunification*') [2006] ECR I-5769. For detailed discussion, see A Arnull, 'Family Reunification and Fundamental Rights' (2006) 31 *EL Rev* 611.

[55] Council Dir 2003/86/EC on the right to family reunification [2003] OJ L 251/12.

[56] Case C-540/03 *Family reunification*, para 23.

[57] Ultimately, the Court ruled that the contested provisions of the directive did not violate the fundamental right to respect for family life or the principle of non-discrimination: *ibid*, paras 76, 90, 103, 109.

[58] The Court pointed to the International Convention on Civil and Political Rights and the Convention on the Rights of the Child as international instruments of which the Court takes account in applying the general principles of Community law: *ibid*, para 37.

[59] *Ibid*, para 35.

[60] Charter of Fundamental Rights of the European Union, proclaimed in Nice on 7 December 2000 [2000] OJ C 364/1.

[61] Case C-540/03 *Family reunification*, para 38. The significance of the Court's reference to the Charter in this judgment has not been missed and has in fact prompted further discussion on the function of the Charter in relation to the Court's elaboration and recognition of fundamental rights. See, eg, Opinion of Advocate General Poiares Maduro in Case C-305/05 *Ordre des barreaux francophones et germanophone and Others v Council* [2007] ECR I–5305, para 48; Opinion of Advocate General Ruiz-Jarabo Colomer in Case C-303/05 *Advocaten voor de Wereld VZW* [2007] ECR I–3633, paras 78–79. The second case to cite the Charter—and this time outside the

The obligations placed on the Union, as well as on the Member States, to respect fundamental rights were squarely addressed by the judgment delivered by the European Court of Human Rights in *Bosphorus*.[62] Despite a somewhat complex factual and procedural background,[63] the case essentially concerned Ireland's confiscation of the applicant's aircraft pursuant to a Community measure, which was challenged as a violation of the fundamental right to property under Article 1 of Protocol No 1 of the ECHR.

The European Court of Human Rights held that a state's action taken in compliance with its legal obligations flowing from its membership in an international organisation such as the European Union was justified so long as the organisation was considered to protect fundamental rights, 'as regards both the substantive guarantees offered and the mechanisms controlling their observance, in a manner which can be considered *at least equivalent* to that for which the Convention provides'.[64] If equivalent protection was provided by the organisation, then there was a presumption that the state has not infringed its obligations under the ECHR when 'it does no more than implement legal obligations flowing from its membership in the organisation'.[65] However, this presumption was rebuttable in cases where the protection of Convention rights was deemed 'manifestly deficient'.[66] The European Court of Human Rights concluded that the system of fundamental rights protection in the European Union was equivalent to the Convention system, thereby triggering the presumption—which was not rebutted in the case at hand—that Ireland acted in accordance with its Convention obligations.[67]

In sum, the foregoing remarks demonstrate that the Treaty performs the classical functions of a constitution by preserving the balance of powers both horizontally between the institutions and vertically between the Community and the Member States and by ensuring respect for fundamental rights. Although the Court's reference to the Treaty as 'the basic constitutional charter' in *Les Verts* may have seemed somewhat startling at the time, in truth there was nothing revolutionary about it, as the plain, everyday case law of the Court shows. Nevertheless, *Les Verts* stands as the first time that the Court expressly called attention to the 'constitutional' nature of the Treaty,[68] and these famous words

context of the preamble of a Community act making reference to it—is Case C-432/05 *Unibet (London) Ltd and Unibet (International) Ltd* ('*Unibet*'), [2007] ECR I–2271, para 37. For further discussion of this case, see below notes 99–104 and accompanying text.

[62] *Bosphorus Hava Yollari Turizm ve Ticaret Anonim Sirketi v Ireland* (App no 45036/98) ECHR 30 June 2005 (2006) 42 EHRR 1.

[63] For detailed discussion, see S Douglas-Scott, Note (2006) 43 *CML Rev* 243.

[64] *Bosphorus*, para 155 (emphasis added). In the same paragraph, the Court explained that by use of the word 'equivalent', it meant 'comparable' since 'any requirement that the organisation's protection be "identical" could run counter to the interest of international co-operation pursued . . . However, any such finding of equivalence could not be final and would be susceptible to review in the light of any relevant change in fundamental rights' protection'.

[65] *Ibid*, para 156.

[66] *Ibid*.

[67] See *ibid*, paras 159–67. This was so, even though the limited standing accorded to individuals under the fourth paragraph of Article 230 EC was picked out for critical treatment: see *ibid*, para 162; Joint Concurring Opinion of Judges Rozakis, Tulkens, Traja, Botoucharova, Zagrebelsky and Garlicki, para 3; Concurring Opinion of Judge Ress, para 2. For further discussion of this issue, see below nn 80–104 and accompanying text.

[68] See Constantinesco and Simon, note 22, at 81 n 9. Notably, in the Opinion of Advocate General Lagrange in Case 6/64 *Costa v ENEL* [1964] ECR 585, at 605, there were some apparent hints: 'It is certainly true to say that the Treaty of Rome has, in a sense, the character of a genuine constitution, the constitution of the Community.'

would be repeated in subsequent judgments[69] (as well as in the Opinions of the Advocates General[70]) through the present day. Notably, in *Opinion 1/91*, the Court framed the matter slightly differently so as to make clear that the Treaty, 'concluded in the form of an international agreement, none the less constitutes the constitutional charter of a Community based on the rule of law'.[71] It is to the 'rule of law' component so intrinsic to this phrase that the focus of attention now turns.

'A Community Based on the Rule of Law': Community Law as a Complete and Coherent System of Judicial Protection

To recall, the Court announced in *Les Verts* that the European (then Economic) Community is 'a Community based on the rule of law'.[72] This statement constituted the very first time that this principle entered the case law of the Court of Justice, coming well before its explicit mention in Article 6 EU.[73] This was also the very first time that the principle of the rule of law was defined, as setting down the corresponding requirements of judicial protection in the Community.

As the Court ruled, by virtue of Articles 230 and 241 EC, on the one hand, and Article 234 EC, on the other, 'the Treaty established a complete system of legal remedies and procedures' designed to permit the Court to review the legality of acts adopted by the institutions.[74] Thus, natural and legal persons would be protected against the application of general measures that they could not challenge directly before the Community courts, by reason of the admissibility requirements laid down in the fourth paragraph of Article 230 EC.[75] This was because:

> Where the Community institutions are responsible for the administrative implementation of such measures, natural or legal persons may bring a direct action before the Court against implementing measures which are addressed to them or which are of direct and individual concern to them and, in support of such action, plead the illegality of the general measure on which they are based. Where implementation is a matter for the national authorities, such persons may plead the invalidity of general measures before the national courts and cause the latter to request the Court of Justice for a preliminary ruling.[76]

[69] See, eg, C-15/00 *Commission v European Investment Bank* [2003] ECR I-7281, para 75; Case C-314/91 *Weber v European Parliament* [1993] ECR I-1093, para 8; Case 2/88 Imm *JJ Zwartveld and Others*, Order of 13 July 1990 [1990] ECR I-3365, para 16; Case T-306/01 *Yusuf and Al Barakaat International Foundation v Council and Commission* [2005] ECR II-3533, para 260; Case T-315/01 *Kadi v Council and Commission* [2005] ECR II-3649, para 289.

[70] See, eg, Opinion of Advocate General Poiares Maduro in C-160/03 *Spain v Eurojust* [2005] ECR I-2077, para 15; Opinion of Advocate General Ruiz-Jarabo Colomer in C-249/02 *Portugal v Commission* [2004] ECR I-10717, para 40; Opinion of Advocate General Ruiz-Jarabo Colomer in C-315/99 P *Ismeri Europa Srl v Court of Auditors* [2001] ECR I-5281, para 39.

[71] Opinion 1/91 *Draft agreement relating to the creation of the European Economic Area* [1991] ECR I-6079, para 21.

[72] Case 294/83 *Les Verts*, para 23.

[73] Art 6(1) EU provides: 'The Union is founded on the principles of liberty, democracy, respect for human rights and fundamental freedoms, and the rule of law, principles which are common to the Member States.'

[74] Case 294/83 *Les Verts*, para 23.

[75] *Ibid.*

[76] *Ibid.*

In short, *Les Verts* established that there was a complete and coherent system of judicial protection vis-à-vis both the institutions and the Member States. First, the system is *complete* in the sense that several legal remedies and procedures operate before the Community courts and the national courts to ensure the review of the legality of the acts of the institutions and the Member States. Second, the system is *coherent* in the sense that it defines the respective tasks of the Community courts and the national courts in conformity with the allocation of powers laid down by the Treaty. For the purposes of this discussion, the focus will be placed on the acts of the institutions as was the case in *Les Verts* itself.[77] Yet, it should not be overlooked that the Court's pronouncement in *Les Verts* holds true just as much for the Member States. Indeed, the full load of the case law brought to bear on the complete and coherent system of judicial review in relation to Member State action—whether by way of the procedure for infringement actions under Articles 226–228 EC or the preliminary ruling procedure under Article 234 EC—is an equal part of the *Les Verts* legacy.[78]

The 'Complete' System of Judicial Protection

The complete system of judicial protection means that sufficient legal remedies and procedures exist before the Community courts and the national courts so as to ensure judicial review of the legality of the acts of the Community institutions, with the result that when the review of the legality of a Community act cannot be carried out directly by the Community courts for reasons of inadmissibility, it must somehow be brought before the national courts which will refer for a preliminary ruling on validity control of such act. This has likely been one of the most controversial aspects of *Les Verts* in view of subsequent case law that identified gaps in the purportedly 'complete' Community system of judicial protection.

This was clearly illustrated by the saga of *Unión de Pequeños Agricultores*[79] and *Jégo-Quéré*,[80] in which the Court of Justice deemed inadmissible two actions for the annulment of Community regulations because the respective applicants did not satisfy the condition of individual concern under Article 230 EC. Yet, the objection of illegality under Article 241 EC and the preliminary ruling procedure under Article 234 EC provide a sufficient legal remedy for natural or legal persons contesting the legality of a Community act of general application only when there exists a Community or a national implementing measure that will permit such persons to challenge the Community act before the Community court or the national court in an action brought against the implementing measure. As a result, where a Community act of general application requires no implementing measures at Community level or at national level and national law affords no

[77] Indeed, the Court chose to stress this component of *Les Verts* (albeit without explicit reference) when it stated in *Unión de Pequeños Agricultores*: 'The European Community is, however, a community based on the rule of law in which its institutions are subject to judicial review of the compatibility of their acts with the Treaty and with the general principles of law which include fundamental rights.' Case C-50/00 P *Unión de Pequeños Agricultores v Council* [2002] ECR I-6677, para 38.

[78] See generally K Lenaerts, D Arts and I Maselis, *Procedural Law of the European Union*, 2nd edn (London, Sweet & Maxwell, 2006), chs 2–6, at 33–199.

[79] Case C-50/00 P *Unión de Pequeños Agricultores v Council* [2002] ECR I-6677, affirming Case C-173/98 *Unión de Pequeños Agricultores v Council* [1999] ECR II-3357.

[80] Case C-263/02 P *Commission v Jégo-Quéré & Cie SA* [2004] ECR I-3425, setting aside Case T-177/01 *Jégo-Quéré & Cie SA v Commission* [2002] ECR II-2365.

declaratory relief,[81] gaps in the Community system of judicial protection may remain even though the act directly imposes obligations on natural or legal persons or deprives them of some rights.[82]

Taken together, *Unión de Pequeños Agricultores* and *Jégo-Quéré* serve to highlight that there are three possible solutions.[83] The first solution entails a relaxed interpretation of the notion of individual concern, so as to provide standing for natural or legal persons seeking to challenge Community acts of general application. Yet, despite well-known attempts by Advocate General Jacobs in his Opinion in *Unión de Pequeños Agricultores*[84] and by the Court of First Instance (CFI) in its judgment in *Jégo-Quéré* to put forward flexible constructions of individual concern,[85] the Court's affirmation of the CFI's dismissal in *Unión de Pequeños Agricultores*[86] and its setting aside of the CFI's judgment in *Jégo-Quéré*[87] attest to the fact that the Court of Justice is unwilling to embark upon this path, considering the matter beyond its jurisdiction and leaving it to the Member States to amend the Treaty in this regard.[88]

The second solution lies with the national courts. As was emphasised in both *Unión de Pequeños Agricultores* and *Jégo-Quéré*, 'it is for the Member States to establish a system of legal remedies and procedures which ensure respect for the right to effective judicial protection'.[89] Yet, here too, this solution is not watertight and leaves open the risk of some gaps in the system of judicial protection. The degree of judicial protection available to a natural or legal person is in fact made dependent on the ability of the national courts to provide an appropriate legal remedy.[90] Furthermore, the emphasis placed on the national courts appears to constitute only an obligation to make best endeavours, not an obligation to declare an action admissible where the procedural law of the particular Member State does not provide for any form of 'declaratory relief'.[91] Yet, as evidenced by cases such as

[81] Compare, eg, Case C-491/01 *BAT* [2002] ECR I-11453: see further notes 92–93 and accompanying text.

[82] Lenaerts, Arts and Maselis, note 78, para 3–007, at 87–8. Moreover, it would be difficult to argue that there is no gap in the system if the sole form of legal remedy for disputing the compatibility of the Community act at issue with superior Community law was to be subject to administrative or criminal proceedings and to any penalties that may result for having infringed the Community act whose legality is being contested. Such legal remedy would undoubtedly not be sufficient to secure effective judicial protection for the natural or legal person concerned. Compare Case C-432/05 *Unibet* [2007] ECR I–2271, para 64, which is discussed further below at notes 99–104 and accompanying text.

[83] See Lenaerts, Arts and Maselis, note 78, para 3–008, at 88–91.

[84] See Opinion of Advocate General Jacobs in Case C-50/00 P *Unión de Pequeños Agricultores v Council*, paras 60, 103.

[85] See Case T-177/01 *Jégo-Quéré v Commission*, para 51.

[86] Case C-50/00 P *Unión de Pequeños Agricultores v Council*, paras 46–47.

[87] Case C-263/02 P *Commission v Jégo-Quéré*, paras 39, 50. In his Opinion in *Jégo-Quéré*, Advocate General Jacobs resolved himself to adhering to the traditional interpretation of individual concern following the Court's judgment in *Unión de Pequeños Agricultores*, albeit not without expressing concern on the matter: see Opinion of Advocate General Jacobs in Case C-263/02 P *Commission v Jégo-Quéré*, paras 43–47.

[88] Case C-50/00 P *Unión de Pequeños Agricultores v Council*, paras 43–45. At first glance, this could be said to be somewhat ironic, since the Court declined to interpret 'individual concern' in a flexible manner similar to what was done in the *Les Verts* case itself. Yet, with a closer look, the two cases can be considered to stem from markedly different rationales: see Opinion of Advocate General Mengozzi in Case C-354/04 P *Gestoras Pro Amnistía and Others v Council* and Case C-355/04 P *Segi and Others v Council* [2007] ECR I–1579, paras 168–169.

[89] Case C-50/00 P *Unión de Pequeños Agricultores v Council*, para 41; Case C-263/02 P *Commission v Jégo-Quéré*, para 31.

[90] Lenaerts, Arts and Maselis, note 78, para 3–008, at 90.

[91] See Case C-50/00 P *Unión de Pequeños Agricultores v Council*, para 42; Case C-263/02 P *Commission v Jégo-Quéré*, para 32.

BAT[92] and *Omega Air*,[93] for those legal systems that do provide for such declaratory relief, the Court has not hesitated to rule that this route should be taken advantage of to the full.

This leaves the third solution of amending the Treaty pursuant to Article 48 EU, as suggested by the Court in *Unión de Pequeños Agricultores*.[94] The Lisbon Treaty would introduce two important changes in this regard. First, the conditions for standing of a natural or legal person would be widened under Article 263 TFEU in relation to the review of 'a regulatory act which is of direct concern to them and does not entail implementing measures'.[95] Second, under Article 19 EU, 'Member States shall provide remedies sufficient to ensure effective legal protection in the fields covered by Union law'.[96] This provision may have far-reaching implications in terms of prompting the Court to transform the obligation to make best endeavours into an obligation to achieve a particular result, when read against the background of Article 47 of the Charter of Fundamental Rights of the European Union[97] and the relevant case law of the European Court of Human Rights.[98]

In fact, it may be wondered whether one need await the entry into force of the Lisbon Treaty in view of the Court's recent judgment in *Unibet*.[99] In this case, the Court was faced with the interpretation of the principle of effective judicial protection of an individual's rights under Community law in connection with an applicant seeking to contest the compatability of Swedish betting legislation with Community law by way of a free-standing declaratory-type action even though this was not provided for under the Swedish procedural rules.[100]

In relevant part, the Court considered that although the Treaty was not intended to create new remedies in the national courts to ensure the observance of Community law,

[92] Case C-491/01 *BAT* [2002] ECR I-11453, paras 39–41.

[93] Joined Cases C-27/00 and C-122/00 *Omega Air Ltd and Others* [2002] ECR I-2569. Here, the Court did not even consider the issue of admissibility of the reference for a preliminary ruling, which was pursued by way of declaratory relief in the English and Irish courts: see *ibid*, para 39.

[94] See Case C-50/00 P *Unión de Pequeños Agricultores v Council*, para 45.

[95] Art 263(4) TFEU of the Treaty of Lisbon amending the Treaty on European Union and the Treaty establishing the European Community, signed at Lisbon, 13 December 2007 [2007] OJ C 306/1; consolidated versions of the Treaty on European Union and the Treaty on the Functioning of the European Union [2008] OJ C 115/1 [hereinafter Lisbon Treaty]. This had already been included in Art III-365(4) of the Constitutional Treaty. See further Lenaerts, Arts and Maselis, note 78, paras 7–184–7–188, at 325–8. Although the Constitutional Treaty did not enter into force, the changes wrought by this provision have already appeared as part of the parties' arguments in the present case law: see, eg, Case T-142/03 *Fost Plus VZW v Commission*, Order of 16 February 2005 [2005] ECR II-589, para 79.

[96] Art 19(1), second para EU.

[97] The first para of Art 47 of the Charter of Fundamental Rights of the European Union, note 60, provides: 'Everyone whose rights and freedoms guaranteed by the law of the Union are violated has the right to an effective remedy before a tribunal in compliance with the conditions laid down in this Article.' The legally binding force of the Charter would be recognised in the Lisbon Treaty: see Art 6(1) EU; Declaration (No 1) concerning the Charter of Fundamental Rights of the European Union. Under the Lisbon Treaty, the text of the Charter is not included in the Treaties. It has been re-enacted by the European Parliament, the Council and the Commission and published separately in the Official Journal [2007] OJ C 303/1.

[98] Lenaerts, Arts and Maselis, note 78, para 3–009, at 91–2.

[99] Case C-432/05 *Unibet* [2007] ECR I–2271.

[100] *Ibid*, paras 17–29. This case also raised important issues concerning the right to effective judicial protection in relation to the adoption of interim relief suspending the application of national measures until a competent court has ruled whether such measures are compatible with Community law: see *ibid*, paras 66–83. Moreover, the Court explicitly referred to Art 47 of the Charter of Fundamental Rights of the European Union in relation to the principle of effective judicial protection: see *ibid*, para 37, which is discussed further above in note 61.

this would be otherwise 'only if it were apparent from the overall scheme of the national legal system in question that no legal remedy existed which made it possible to ensure, even indirectly, respect for an individual's rights under Community law'.[101] As a result, the principle of effective judicial protection did not require Sweden to provide for a free-standing declaratory-type action that would seek primarily to challenge the compatability of national provisions with Community law to the extent that there existed certain indirect legal remedies that would still allow an individual to challenge the compatability of national law with Community law: first, by way of an action for damages; and second, by way of judicial review of the decision rejecting the individual's application for permission to engage in promoting its betting activities in Sweden.[102]

Importantly, however, the Court emphasised that if an individual 'was forced to be subject to administrative or criminal proceedings and to any penalties that may result as the *sole* form of legal remedy for disputing the compatability of the national provision at issue with Community law, that would *not* be sufficient to secure for it such effective judicial protection'.[103] In this way, *Unibet* does much to ensure that there exist sufficient legal remedies and procedures in the Member States so as to remedy the existing gaps in the complete system of judicial protection.[104]

In any event, such gaps are not confined to the Community legal order but are equally apparent in the second and third pillars of the Union. Indeed, the question of the complete system of judicial protection prescribed by *Les Verts* has already received a much different answer as regards the third pillar of Police and Judicial Co-operation in Criminal Matters (PJCCM), as evidenced by the Court's admission in *Pupino*[105] that 'there is no complete system of actions and procedures designed to ensure the legality of the acts of the institutions in the context of Title VI' of the EU Treaty.[106]

This is aptly demonstrated by the *Eurojust* case,[107] concerning an action for annulment brought by Spain under Article 230 EC against several calls for applications for the recruitment of temporary staff positions issued by Eurojust, a Union body responsible for promoting cooperation among national authorities in relation to the fight against serious crime.[108] In its defence, Eurojust contended that the action was inadmissible because there was no legal basis on which it could be brought.[109] The Court agreed, holding that the action could not be brought under Article 230 EC because that provision did not encompass review of acts adopted by Eurojust.[110] Yet, in response to Spain's argument that

[101] *Ibid*, paras 40–41.

[102] *Ibid*, paras 47–48, 55–61, 64–65.

[103] *Ibid*, para 64 (emphasis added).

[104] See also note 82 and accompanying text.

[105] Case C-105/03 *Pupino* [2005] ECR I-5285.

[106] *Ibid*, para 35. This was so, even though it has been emphasised that these statements, placed in their proper context, only related to the limits placed on the jurisdiction of the Court of Justice, as opposed to the national courts, to review the legality of the acts of the institutions: see Opinion of Advocate General Mengozzi in Case C-354/04 P *Gestoras Pro Amnistía and Others v Council* and Case C-355/04 P *Segi and Others v Council* [2007] ECR I–1579, paras 125–126. In other words, they did not prevent the Court from finding that the principle of conforming interpretation and the duty of loyal cooperation applied in connection with framework decisions adopted in the third pillar: see Case C-105/03 *Pupino*, paras 34–43.

[107] Case C-160/03 *Spain v Eurojust* [2005] ECR I-2077.

[108] See Art 29 EU. Compare Art 85 TFEU of the Lisbon Treaty. The official documents relating to Eurojust are available through its website, http://eurojust.europa.eu/official.htm.

[109] Case C-160/03 *Eurojust*, paras 25–26.

[110] *Ibid*, paras 36–40, 44.

the right to effective judicial protection 'requires that all decisions of a body with legal personality subject to Community law be amenable to judicial review',[111] the Court stressed that the contested acts were not exempt from such review altogether because there was the route of access to the Court of Justice—now the European Union Civil Service Tribunal—under the Staff Regulations and that the Member States were entitled to intervene in such proceedings and to seek appellate relief.[112]

The Court's judgment in this case contrasted sharply with the Opinion of Advocate General Poiares Maduro, which submitted that the action should be declared admissible under Article 35 EU. In particular, the Advocate General drew explicit analogy to *Les Verts*[113] and concluded that this provision must be interpreted to allow certain applicants to bring an action for annulment against any measure adopted in the third pillar that produces legal effects vis-à-vis third parties: '"the very idea of legality", as it must prevail in a Union governed by the rule of law, requires that to be the case.'[114]

Likewise, in *Gestoras Pro Amnistía and Others*,[115] the Court confirmed that it had no jurisdiction to entertain an action for damages in the third pillar.[116] This was so, despite the applicants' professed damages resulting from being placed on a list of terrorist organisations by way of certain common positions adopted by the Council.[117] However, the Court rejected the applicants' argument that they had been deprived of all judicial protection.[118] This was because although its jurisdiction relating to preliminary rulings and actions for annulment under Article 35 EU did not, in principle, include judicial review of common positions, the Court reasoned that since the preliminary ruling procedure was 'designed to guarantee observance of the law in the interpretation and application of the Treaty, it would run counter to that objective to interpret Article 35(1) EU narrowly'.[119] As a result, the Court held that the right to make a preliminary reference must exist 'in respect of all measures adopted by the Council, whatever their nature or form, which are intended to have legal effects in relation to third parties'.[120]

Notably, the outcome of the two aforementioned cases would be much different under the Lisbon Treaty. The Court of Justice would have jurisdiction to review the legality of the acts adopted by Union bodies in the former third pillar by way of actions for annulment

[111] *Ibid*, para 41.

[112] *Ibid*, paras 42–43.

[113] See Opinion of Advocate General Poiares Maduro in Case C-160/03 *Eurojust*, para 20.

[114] *Ibid*, para 21 (citing, by analogy, Opinion of Advocate General Mancini in Case 294/83 *Les Verts*, para 7). The Advocate General further stated that legal proceedings brought on the basis of the Staff Regulations were not a viable substitute: see *ibid*, paras 23–24.

[115] Case C-354/04 P *Gestoras Pro Amnistía and Others v Council* [2007] ECR I–1579. See also Case C-355/04 P *Segi and Others v Council* [2007] ECR I–1657, which was delivered on the same day. Since the relevant part of the Court's findings in the two cases is practically identical, reference will be made only to the former judgment.

[116] Case C-354/04 P *Gestoras Pro Amnistía and Others*, paras 46–48.

[117] See *ibid*, para 1.

[118] *Ibid*, para 51.

[119] *Ibid*, paras 52–53.

[120] *Ibid*, para 53. The Court also pointed out that it had jurisdiction to review the lawfulness of such acts under circumstances where either a Member State or the Commission brought an action pursuant to Art 35(6) EU and placed emphasis on the national legal systems enabling natural and legal persons to challenge the lawfulness of acts of the European Union which included seeking damages where appropriate. *Ibid*, paras 55–56.

under Article 263 TFEU[121] and actions for damages under Article 268 TFEU and the second paragraph of Article 340 TFEU,[122] even if certain limitations remain in relation to the Court's jurisdiction in this field.[123]

As regards the completeness of the system of judicial protection in the second pillar concerning the Common Foreign and Security Policy (CFSP), the situation becomes even more sensitive. At present, as a general matter, the Court of Justice does not have jurisdiction to review the legality of acts adopted in this field. Prompted by the onslaught of cases before the Court of Justice and the CFI concerning natural and legal persons subject to sanctions for being placed on the list of terrorist organisations,[124] scholars have highlighted gaps in the judicial review of CFSP instruments and the still-limited changes introduced by the Constitutional Treaty, since taken over by the Lison Treaty' in this regard.[125] Nonetheless, some progress has been made. Although Article 275 TFEU of the Lisbon Treaty does not provide the Court of Justice with jurisdiction over CFSP acts, it carves out two exceptions, one of which would allow the Court to review 'the legality of decisions providing for restrictive measures against natural or legal persons adopted by the Council' in the former second pillar.[126] This may likely play a prominent role in closing the present loopholes particularly in cases involving the fight against terrorism.

The 'Coherent' System of Judicial Protection

The coherent system of judicial protection means that there exist both direct and indirect routes as far as the review of the legality of Community acts is concerned, each of which implicates important, albeit differing, roles for the Community courts and the national courts as laid down by the Treaty. Through the course of the Court's jurisprudence, the coherence of the system of judicial protection has been developed through three series of cases concerning: first, the power to declare a Community act invalid; second, the inadmissibility of the indirect route of a preliminary ruling on the validity of a Community act where the direct route of the action for annulment is available; and third, illegality resulting from the failure to act on the part of the Community institutions.

[121] Art 263(1) TFEU confers jurisdiction on the Court to 'review the legality of acts of bodies, offices or agencies of the Union intended to produce legal effects *vis-à-vis* third parties'. The Lisbon Treaty also provides for specific arrangements to be made in this regard: see Art 263(5) TFEU.

[122] These provisions appear in almost identical terms to their present counterparts in Art 235 EC and Art 288, second para EC, respectively.

[123] See Arts 72, 276 TFEU.

[124] See, eg, Case C-229/05 P *PKK and KNK v Council* [2007] ECR I–439; Case T-228/02 *Organisation des Modjahedines du peuple d'Iran v Council* [2006] ECR II–4665; Case T-306/01 *Yusuf and Al Barakaat International Foundation v Council and Commission* [2005] ECR II-3533; Case T-315/01 *Kadi v Council and Commission* [2005] ECR II-3649. The latter two judgments were set aside on appeal: see Joined Cases C-402/05 P and C-415/05 P *Kadi and Al Barakaat International Foundation v Council and Commission* [2008] ECR I-6351.

[125] See, eg, T Corthaut, 'An Effective Remedy For All? Paradoxes and Controversies in Respect of Judicial Protection in the Field of CFSP under the European Constitution' (2005) 12 *Tilburg Foreign Law Review* 110; M Garbagnati Ketvel, 'The Jurisdiction of the European Court of Justice in respect of the Common Foreign and Security Policy' (2006) 55 *ICLQ* 77; R Gosalbo Bono, 'Some Reflections on the CFSP Legal Order' (2006) 43 *CML Rev* 337.

[126] Art 275(2) TFEU. The other exception allows the Court 'to monitor compliance with Art 40 of the Treaty on European Union', which essentially concerns the relationship between the policy fields encompassed within CFSP and other areas of Union competence. This had already been included in Art III-376 of the Consitutional Treaty. For further discussion of this provision, see Garbagnati Ketvel, note 125, at 98–117.

The first series of cases concerning the power to declare a Community act invalid was undoubtedly paved by the Court's landmark judgment in *Foto-Frost*,[127] in which the Court established that a national court does not have the power to declare an act of the Community institutions invalid.[128] The Court stressed in relevant part 'the necessary coherence of the system of judicial protection established by the Treaty'.[129] Drawing reference to *Les Verts*, the Court explained that 'requests for preliminary rulings, like actions for annulment, constitute means for reviewing the legality of acts of the Community institutions'.[130] Therefore, since Article 230 EC gives the Court exclusive jurisdiction to declare a Community act void, 'the coherence of the system requires that where the validity of a Community act is challenged before a national court the power to declare the act invalid must also be reserved to the Court of Justice'.[131]

In more recent cases, the Court of Justice engaged in further consideration of *Foto-Frost*. In *IATA*,[132] the Court clarified that 'the fact that the validity of a Community act is contested before a national court is not in itself sufficient to warrant referral of a question to the Court for a preliminary ruling'.[133] Where a lower court considers that the arguments challenging the validity of a Community act are unfounded, it may reject such arguments and conclude that the act is completely valid, since under these circumstances it is 'not calling into question the existence of the Community act'.[134] In contrast, where such a court considers that the arguments challenging the validity of a Community act are well-founded, it must make a preliminary reference to the Court on the act's validity.[135]

Moreover, in *Gaston Schul*,[136] the Court was faced with a question concerning the highest court's duty to refer under the third paragraph of Article 234 EC, namely whether such court was required to seek a preliminary ruling concerning the validity of a Community act under circumstances where the Court of Justice had already declared invalid analogous provisions of another comparable Community act.[137] In essence, the case implicated both *Foto-Frost* and *CILFIT*,[138] in which the Court laid down several exceptions to the highest court's duty to refer under the third paragraph of Article 234 EC.[139] In response, the Court confirmed its ruling in *Foto-Frost* and decided that its ruling in *CILFIT* could not be extended to questions relating to the validity of Community acts

[127] Case 314/85 *Foto-Frost* [1987] ECR 4199.

[128] *Ibid*, paras 15, 20.

[129] *Ibid*, para 16. The Court's rationale was also based on the uniform application of Community law and on its premier position for deciding cases involving the validity of Community acts: see *ibid*, paras 15, 18. For further discussion, see Lenaerts, Arts and Maselis, note 78, para 2–006, at 35–6 and paras 2–056–2–057, at 79–80.

[130] Case 314/85 *Foto-Frost*, para 16.

[131] *Ibid*, paras 16–17.

[132] Case C-344/04 *IATA* [2006] ECR I-403.

[133] *Ibid*, para 28. For discussion of further aspects of this case, see above nn 30–36 and accompanying text.

[134] *Ibid*, para 29.

[135] *Ibid*, paras 30, 32.

[136] Case C-461/03 *Gaston Schul Douane-expediteur BV* [2005] ECR I-10513.

[137] *Ibid*, para 15.

[138] Case 283/81 *CILFIT* [1982] ECR 3415. For another case implicating consideration of both *Foto-Frost* and *CILFIT*, see Case C-495/03 *Intermodal Transports BV* [2005] ECR I-8151.

[139] In this case, the Court established that a court of last resort was excused from its duty to refer where: (1) the question is irrelevant; (2) the question is 'materially identical' to that of a previous preliminary ruling; (3) the question has been decided by previous rulings of the Court although the nature of the proceedings and the questions at issue are 'not strictly identical' (*acte éclairé*); and (4) where 'the correct application of Community law may be so obvious as to leave no scope for any reasonable doubt as to the manner in which the question raised is to be resolved' (*acte clair*). Case 283/81 *CILFIT*, paras 10, 13, 14, 16.

that would excuse the highest court from its duty to make a reference under Article 234 EC.[140] Making reference to *Les Verts*, the Court underlined that the possibility of a national court ruling on the validity of a Community act under such circumstances was 'incompatible with the necessary coherence of the system of judicial protection instituted by the EC Treaty'.[141]

Importantly, *Foto-Frost* has raised particular sensitivities in the fields of Title IV of the EC Treaty concerning visas, asylum, immigration and other policies related to free movement of persons and the third pillar, both of which are subject to special rules limiting the Court's preliminary ruling jurisdiction as compared to Article 234 EC. In the context of Title IV, the Court's preliminary ruling jurisdiction on the validity (and interpretation) of Community acts has been restricted to the highest courts of the Member States under Article 68 EC.[142] As such, questions arise as to whether the *Foto-Frost* rule applies in this field, since among other things, the Court's rationale hinging on the coherent system of judicial protection seems wanting where the lower courts are precluded from making references on the validity of Community acts to the Court of Justice.[143] Yet, this matter may be resolved in accordance with Article 67(2) EC, given the Commission's proposal to align this area with Article 234 EC.[144]

As for the third pillar, the lower courts may also be able to make references even though the Court's preliminary ruling jurisdiction is presently curtailed in this area. Under Article 35 EU, each Member State is required to make a declaration either accepting the Court's jurisdiction for all national courts or for only the highest.[145] To date, although many Member States have submitted declarations allowing their lower courts to make references, several others have either opted for the more restrictive approach or have declined to submit a declaration altogether.[146] As such, the application of *Foto-Frost* in the third pillar raises similarly delicate issues as mentioned above in relation to Title IV of the EC Treaty, since the judicial review of Union acts adopted in this area varies according to the declaration submitted by the Member State concerned and therefore leads to gaps in the coherent system of judicial protection for which there is no remedy provided under the present Treaty framework.[147]

[140] Case C-461/03 *Gaston Schul*, paras 17, 19, 25. Compare the Opinion of Advocate General Ruiz-Jarabo Colomer in Case C-461/03 *Gaston Schul*, paras 80–92, in which he urged the Court to refine *CILFIT* and to carve out an exception to *Foto-Frost* under certain conditions.

[141] Case C-461/03 *Gaston Schul*, para 22.

[142] See Art 68(1) EC.

[143] M Claes, *The National Courts' Mandate in the European Constitution* (Oxford, Hart Publishing, 2006) 578–9. For discussion of the various solutions proffered by scholars, see *ibid*, at 579–83.

[144] See Commission (EC), 'Adaptation of the provisions of Title IV of the Treaty establishing the European Community relating to the jurisdiction of the Court of Justice with a view to ensuring more effective judicial protection' (Communication) COM (2006) 346 final, 28 June 2006.

[145] Arts 35(2) and (3) EU.

[146] According to the 2008 Document prepared by the Court of Justice Research and Documentation Service, available at *http://curia.europa.eu/jcms/jcms/Jo2_7031/*, only 17 Member States have made declarations accepting the Court's preliminary ruling. Spain submitted a declaration allowing only the highest courts to make references, whereas 16 Member States (Austria, Belgium, the Czech Republic, Finland, France, Germany, Greece, Hungary, Italy, Latvia, Lithuania, Luxembourg, the Netherlands, Portugal, Slovenia and Sweden) submitted declarations allowing both the lower and the highest courts to make such references. To date, the remaining 10 Member States have not submitted any declaration or there is no official information available.

[147] See, eg, Opinion of Advocate General Mengozzi in Case C-354/04 P *Gestoras Pro Amnistía and Others v Council* and Case C-355/04 P *Segi and Others v Council* [2007] ECR I–1579, paras 121–132, in which the Court's rationale based on tenets of *Les Verts* was found particularly lacking. However, with the entry into force of the

In *the second series of cases*, the Court of Justice established important rules concerning an individual's recourse to the direct and indirect routes of legality control, which constitute interlocking components of the coherent system of judicial protection. In this context, the coherence requirement operates so as to preclude an applicant from arguing before a national court that a Community act is invalid for the purposes of a preliminary ruling under Article 234 EC under circumstances where the applicant could have directly challenged such act before the Community courts under Article 230 EC.

Starting with *TWD Textilwerke Deggendorf*,[148] the Court held that an applicant who could 'without any doubt' have challenged a Commission decision and who allowed the mandatory time limit laid down by the Treaty to expire was precluded from calling into question the lawfulness of that decision before the national courts in an action brought against the measures taken by the national authorities to implement that decision.[149] To rule otherwise 'would in effect enable the person concerned to overcome the definitive nature which the decision assumes as against that person once the time-limit for bringing an action has expired'.[150]

TWD Textilwerke Deggendorf was followed by several cases that further inscribed the interlocking character of the direct and indirect routes of legality control. In *Wiljo*,[151] concerning a Commission decision addressed to the applicant,[152] the Court decided that the applicant was precluded from challenging the legality of the decision before a national court, since it did not bring an action for annulment against the Commission's decision 'even though it could undoubtedly have done so'.[153] Likewise, in *Nachi Europe*,[154] the Court held that the applicant could not plead before a national court the invalidity of a Council regulation imposing anti-dumping duties on imports of ball bearings, which specifically identified certain manufacturers including Nachi Fujikoshi of which Nachi Europe was a subsidiary.[155] The applicant could 'undoubtedly' have sought the annulment of the Council regulation, since it was associated with Nachi Fujikoshi and its resale prices for the goods concerned were used in connection with the dumping margins assessed for Nachi Fujikoshi, thereby allowing it to be regarded as directly and individually concerned by the provisions of the regulation.[156]

In view of this case law, the applicant is precluded from taking the indirect route of a preliminary ruling on validity only if it could 'undoubtedly' have challenged the validity of a Community act directly through the action for annulment under Article 230 EC.

Lisbon Treaty, the current restrictions on the Court's preliminary ruling jurisdiction in the third pillar (as well as that under Title IV of the EC Treaty) would be eliminated. This was the case under the Constitutional Treaty. See Lenaerts, Arts and Maselis, note 78, paras 22–007–22–008, at 517–18.

[148] Case C-188/92 *TWD Textilwerke Deggendorf GmbH* [1994] ECR I-833. This should not be taken to imply that this was the first case in which this issue had arisen: see citations in *ibid*, paras 13–15, 19, 21–23.

[149] *Ibid*, paras 17, 24.

[150] *Ibid*, para 18.

[151] Case C-178/95 *Wiljo NV* [1997] ECR I-585.

[152] *Ibid*, para 10.

[153] *Ibid*, para 23.

[154] Case C-239/99 *Nachi Europe* [2001] ECR I-1197.

[155] *Ibid*, paras 3–5, 40.

[156] *Ibid*, paras 38–39. Although the case concerned a Community regulation, the Court found that this did not preclude such a measure 'from becoming definitive as against an individual in regard to whom it must be considered to be an individual decision and who could undoubtedly have sought its annulment under Article 230 EC, a fact which prevents that individual from pleading the illegality of that regulation before the national court'. *Ibid*, para 37.

Conversely, under well-settled case law, if there remains doubt on the admissibility of the action for annulment, then access to the indirect route of a preliminary ruling must be left open.[157] Recently, the Court underscored this latter component in *Roquette Frères*.[158] There, by way of national proceedings, the applicant sought to challenge six Community regulations concerning the common organisation of the markets in the sugar sector.[159] The lower instance court dismissed the case on the grounds that Roquette Frères should have brought an action for annulment under Article 230 EC in line with *Nachi Europe*.[160] Roquette Frères appealed, and the national court submitted a reference to the Court on the matter.[161]

In its ruling, the Court considered that the disputed regulations laid down a scheme for basic production quantities of isoglucose allocated to the Member States, which were responsible for distributing such quotas among producers but were given 'some room for manoeuvre' as regards the redistribution of such quotas under the conditions laid down by the Community rules so as to enable new entrants in the market to start up isoglucose production.[162] On that basis, the Court found that a producer could not in principle be considered directly concerned for the purposes of Article 230 EC.[163] Consequently, it could not be argued that Roquette Frères 'undoubtedly' could have brought an admissible action for annulment against the Community regulations, and therefore, it was allowed to plead the illegality of the relevant provisions of these measures before the national court.[164]

Finally, *the third series of cases* implicate the coherence of the system of judicial protection where the alleged illegality results from a failure to act on the part of the Community institutions. In *T Port*,[165] the question arose as to whether a national court was authorised to order interim measures in a situation involving a failure to act by the Commission. In contrast to previous case law concerning the adoption of interim measures by a national court in the context of the implementation of a national measure based on a Community measure whose validity was being contested,[166] the instant case concerned the adoption of interim measures in which the existence and the scope of the applicant's rights hinged on a measure that the Commission had not yet adopted.[167]

In these circumstances, the Court explained:

> The Treaty makes no provision for a reference for a preliminary ruling by which a national court asks the Court of Justice to rule that an institution has failed to act. Consequently, national courts

[157] See, eg, Case C-241/95 *Accrington Beef Co Ltd and Others* [1996] ECR I-6699; Case C-408/95 *Eurotunnel SA and Others* [1997] ECR I-6315. For further references, see Lenaerts, Arts and Maselis, note 78, paras 10–007–10–008, at 357–60.

[158] Case C-441/05 *Roquette Frères* [2007] ECR I–1993.

[159] *Ibid*, paras 1, 26–30.

[160] *Ibid*, paras 31–32.

[161] *Ibid*, paras 33–34.

[162] *Ibid*, paras 42–44.

[163] *Ibid*, para 45.

[164] *Ibid*, paras 47–48. The fact that the applicant was the only isoglucose producer in France and had been assigned the entire basic production quantity allocated under the relevant Community measures did 'nothing to change that finding': *ibid*, para 46.

[165] Case C-68/95 *T Port GmbH & Co KG* [1996] ECR I-6065.

[166] See *ibid*, paras 47–51 (referring to Joined Cases C-143/88 and C-92/89 *Zuckerfabrik Süderdithmarschen AG and Zuckerfabrik Soest* [1991] ECR I-415 and Case C-465/93 *Atlanta Fruchthandelsgesellschaft mbH and Others (1)* [1995] ECR I-3761).

[167] *Ibid*, para 52.

> have no jurisdiction to order interim measures pending action on the part of the institution. Judicial review of alleged failure to act can be exercised only by the Community judicature.[168]

Accordingly, the Treaty did not authorise a national court to order interim measures until such time as the Commission had adopted the requisite act in order to deal with cases of hardship affecting traders such as T Port.[169] With that said, the Court posited various avenues so as to ensure judicial protection for the persons concerned, contemplating that the Member State or the particular trader could bring an action for failure to act before the Community courts under Article 232 EC, in which case interim measures could be adopted by these courts.[170] Specifically, the Court pointed out that such a trader would be able to bring this type of direct action, since it would be the addressee of the measure that the Commission failed to adopt or in the very least directly and individually concerned by it.[171]

This solution suggested in *T Port* should be considered alongside the Court's more recent judgment in *Ten Kate*.[172] This case concerned the possible liability of a Member State arising from the fact that it had refrained from bringing either an action for failure to act or an action for annulment against the Commission in a situation where the parties concerned were unable themselves to bring such actions against the Commission because—contrary to what seemed to have been the case in *T Port*—they were not individually concerned.[173] The Court found that 'neither the wording of Article 230 EC nor that of Article 232 EC imposes any obligation on a Member State to bring an action'.[174] Moreover, such an obligation could not be inferred from the duty of sincere co-operation enshrined in Article 10 EC.[175] Thus, Community law did not impose any obligation on a Member State to bring an action for failure to act or an action for annulment for the benefit of one of its citizens.[176]

At the same time, however, the Court underscored that just as a natural or legal person was able to challenge before a national court the legality of any decision or other national measure relative to the application to him or her of a Community act of general application by pleading the invalidity of such an act, '[t]he same holds true where a natural or legal person invokes a failure to take a decision, within the meaning of Article 232 EC, which it considers to be contrary to Community law'.[177] In this way, consistent with *T Port*, the Court ensured that the indirect route of a preliminary ruling on validity of a failure to act was open to such persons under those circumstances where the direct route of a failure to act was not available.

[168] *Ibid*, para 53.

[169] *Ibid*, para 62.

[170] *Ibid*, paras 58–61.

[171] *Ibid*, para 58.

[172] Case C-511/03 *Ten Kate Holding Musselkanaal BV and Others* [2005] ECR I-8979.

[173] *Ibid*, paras 17, 22. Moreover, an action for damages against the Community would not have enabled the applicants to continue their production activity: *ibid*, para 17.

[174] *Ibid*, para 27.

[175] *Ibid*, para 28.

[176] *Ibid*, para 32. The Court further stated that Community law did not preclude in principle national law from containing such an obligation, provided that the Member State retained a degree of discretion as to the appropriateness of bringing an action so as not to give rise to the risk that the Community courts would be inundated with frivolous actions. *Ibid*, paras 31–32.

[177] *Ibid*, para 29.

Conclusion

In view of the foregoing discussion, it is no exaggeration to point out the difficulty, if not impossibility, of attempting to imagine the course of European law without *Les Verts*. The five crucial sentences of paragraph 23 have made an indelible imprint on the European judicial landscape. For one thing, the Court's characterisation of the Treaty as 'the basic constitutional charter' made clear the constitutional nature of the Treaty and the constitutional functions accorded to the Court of Justice that embody the mainstay of its activities through the present day.

For another thing, the complete and coherent system of judicial protection espoused by the Court of Justice in *Les Verts* continues to provide the benchmark for the Community as well as for the Union. Ironically, the strong criticism that *Les Verts* has received in relation to the apparent 'cracks' in the system attests to its continuing vitality, rather than to its demise. This can be glimpsed as much by the new paths forged in relation to the second and third pillars of the European Union, as by the well-trodden ones in the Community itself that continue to present novel and complex questions involving the direct and indirect routes of legality control. In this way, as evidenced by the steady stream of references to this case by the Court of Justice and the Advocates General, *Les Verts* has become firmly ingrained in the fabric of the Community legal order. It will therefore continue to present ongoing challenges to the Community—and to the Union—to ensure that the standards set by this momentous judgment will not cease to be met in the forthcoming decades.

2

Les Verts v The European Parliament

JEAN-PAUL JACQUÉ[178]

The *Les Verts*[179] case will be remembered in the history of the Court both due to its substantial contribution to the Community's constitutional system and the role of the European Court of Justice in that system, and as an illustration of the European Parliament's dynamic usage of the litigation system.

There is no need to spend too long on the facts. The Parliament put in place a system for financing information campaigns leading up to the European elections of 1984. The sums allocated in the Community budget were to be apportioned between the political groupings in Parliament and political groupings that received more than 5 per cent of the vote in the European elections. Sixty-nine per cent of the allocated funds were distributed each year to the political groupings in Parliament, pro-rated by the number of Parliamentarians in each grouping, and 31 per cent were placed in a reserve fund. After the elections, these reserve funds were to be divided between the groupings that had received at least 5 per cent of the vote in one Member State, or 1 per cent of the vote in at least three Member States. The Parti écologique français 'Les Verts' requested that the Court declare the system void on a variety of grounds, including lack of competence and discrimination.

A Dynamic Use of Litigation by Parliament

In this case, Parliament, as a defender, would normally have taken the position that the complaint was not admissible because Article 173 (now 230) was aimed only at acts of the Council or the Commission. This defence would not have been undermined by the fact that the ECSC treaty created the possibility of annulment actions against acts of Parliament and that, in accordance with the case law of the Court, this route was available as long as the acts challenged concerned the organisation and functioning of Parliament,

[178] Professor emeritus at the Robert-Schuman University in Strasbourg, Director of the Council's legal service. The opinions of the author, who was an employee agent of Parliament during the case, in no way represent those of the institution to which he belonged. Text translated by Dana Kaersvang.

[179] Judgment of 23 April 1986, *Parti écologiste 'Les Verts' v The European Parliament*, Case 294/83, rec. 1339; see Constantinesco and Simon, *Le Parlement devant la Cour: Les Verts*, Dalloz 1987, 77; Daniele, *Il Parlemento europeo dinanzi alla Corte de giustizia*, Il Foro italiano, 1987, col 315–24; Jacqué, *Recours en annulation,campagne d'information pour les élections européennes*, RTDE 1986, 500–11; Jolliet, *Le remboursement des frais électoraux: un contentieux oublié*, Estudios en homenaje al profesor don Manuel Diaz de Velasco, Technos, Madrid, 985–1005; Kovar, *Observations sur l'arrêt Les Verts*, CDE 1987, 314–32; Schermers, *De groene partij*, Ars Aequi, 1986, 770–5; Voelker, *Rechtsschutz Privater genegenüber dem europäischen Gesetzgeber*, Die öffentliche Verwaltung, 2003, 570–77.

because the acts were inextricably linked to the three treaties (ECSC, EEC, and EC).[180] In effect, the action provided for in Article 38 of the ECSC treaty was only open to privileged applicants. Les Verts, therefore, could not have recourse to it. Under such conditions, a wise defence would have been based on inadmissibility under Article 173 EEC. In addition, the case concerned an act of general applicability and, at first glance, les Verts were not directly or individually affected by it. Under such conditions, a defence based on inadmissibility offered Parliament a certain security (although not absolute) and would have permitted it to avoid a debate about the merits, where its position was less solid.

And yet, this approach was not taken. Parliament chose to plead admissibility, thereby opening itself up to the attacks of les Verts just as Saint Sebastian opened himself up to the archers' arrows. This approach, which was far from obvious, was selected for political reasons by the President of the time, Piet Dankert, with full knowledge of the case.[181] Parliament's fundamental objective was to obtain the Court's recognition of its capacity to be sued. This would give it a basis in a similar future case to achieve its real objective, standing to bring suit, which was required to allow it to assert its prerogatives before the Court of Justice. In this case, the Court was not able to avoid the question of Parliament's capacity to be sued because it did not have the opportunity, as it had in prior cases, to hide behind the ECSC treaty, and was obliged to confront the question. At the time, Parliament considered that if the Court recognised its capacity to be the target of a suit, the parallels would make it easier to convince the Court to grant it standing to sue in a subsequent case. In order to attract the Court to this approach, Parliament abstained from raising any objection to admissibility in its written defence.[182] It even overtly declined to argue that the applicant was not directly and individually concerned. Instead, it evoked the supposedly special character of political parties which, it argued, could not be treated as ordinary applicants. The argument was weak, as the jurisprudence on actions brought by regional authorities would soon show, but its primary purpose to was take this position overtly so that the Court would not have the impression that it claimed that it could be sued even while trying to cause the action to fail by sheltering behind other arguments on admissibility. Anyway, taking account of the weakness of its argument on this last point, Parliament could secretly hope that the Court would follow its classic jurisprudence and find that les Verts was not individually concerned. In this sense, the Opinion of Advocate General Mancini gave it full satisfaction, since it proposed to recognise its capacity to be sued but indicated that the action should be declared inadmissible on grounds that the applicant was not individually concerned.

Thus, the case showed an audacious long-term litigation strategy whereby Parliament risked having the regulation annulled, although it was strongly supported by political parties, in the hope of eventually convincing the Court to grant it standing to bring such

[180] Judgment of 10 February 1983, *Luxembourg v The European Parliament*, Case 230/81, rec. 255.

[181] Piet Dankert's successor, Pierre Pfimlin, was aware of the risk that the action would be annulled and reoriented Parliament's arguments, but it was too late to turn back. However, he modified Parliament's defence, leading to the slightly contradictory position noted by Advocate General Mancini in his opinion ('Moreover, it should be said in the first place that the defendant has not assisted the Court in finding the correct solution, even though it did not raise a formal objection of inadmissibility . . . [T]he Parliament dissociated itself more and more clearly from that argument as the case proceeded.').

[182] It reoriented its position to plead that the applicant was not individually affected on the instruction of President Pflimlin. The political groupings had seen which way the wind was blowing and feared that they would have to return the sums they had received. As a result, they put pressure on the President in order to make the defence less open to admissibility.

actions itself. As we now know, the approach would be fruitful but difficult, as demonstrated by the Court's initial refusal to find standing in the *Comitologie*[183] case before the success in the *post-Chernobyl* case.[184] In the latter case, the Court would not base its holding on parallelism, but on the preservation of the institutional balance mentioned in *Les Verts*. But it is likely that *Les Verts* was a first step that made possible the later evolution in Parliament's judicial standing.

A Constitutional Approach

If the Court agrees with Parliament as to its capacity to be the target of a suit, it does so by situating the case in a constitutional context. Therefore, the case is typical of the Court's constructive approach in its first generation jurisprudence. Three essential elements illustrate this point.

1. First, the most important point relates to the holding by the Court that the Community is a **Community based on the rule of law**. By this new step, the Court introduced the concept of the state based on the rule of law, shared by all the Member States, into the law of European integration. It is then easy to reach the conclusion that respect for the rule of law is necessarily accompanied by respect for the hierarchy of laws and, thus, of the subordination of secondary legislation to treaty provisions. This is not a very large shift, since Article 173 already provided for judicial review of legislation in the Community framework. Most important was the extrapolation from a basic principle, the subordination of legislation, to a rule of admissibility through recourse to the new concept of the Community based on the rule of law. In effect, if the treaty provides for judicial review, such review is not available solely under the conditions in Article 173, which does not provide for challenges to acts of Parliament. And yet, in its reasoning, the Court inverted the situation. It is because the Community is a Community based on the rule of law that all acts that affect third parties must be subject to judicial review, regardless of the limits in Article 173. The pre-eminence of the rule of law thus empowers the Court to implicitly revise the treaty so that the Court can play its full role. Subsequently, the idea of the Community based on the rule of law would continue to advance. Not only would it serve as a basis for the Court's progressive construction of a coherent system of jurisdictional review,[185] it would be inscribed by the treaties as one of the principles of the Union and appears today in Article 6(1) of the Treaty of the European Union.

2. A second constitutional element in this case is the principle of balance of powers. On this point, the Court noted that, if actions for the annulment of acts of Parliament having effects on third parties were inadmissible, this would result in permitting Parliament to encroach on the powers of the other institutions and the Member States with impunity. The balance of powers established by the treaty could be altered without any barrier to

[183] Judgment of 27 December 1988, *Parliament v Council*, Case 302/87, rec. 5615.
[184] Judgment of 22 May 1990, *Parliament v Council*, Case C-70/88, rec. I-2041.
[185] In this regard, see the work of Frédérique Berrod, *La systématique des voies de droit communautaires*, Dalloz, 2003.

prevent it.[186] In this context, the admissibility of cases challenging acts of Parliament appeared indispensable in order to preserve the institutional balance that was set out in the treaty through the separation of powers. Reliance on separation of powers was not new to the Court, as it had already used the concept in *Meroni*[187] and *Köster*.[188] Its primary importance is for what followed, as it was on this basis that the Court granted Parliament standing to bring suits, concluding that this was the only means of protecting its prerogatives against the potential overreaching of other institutions. The capacity to be sued is seen as a guarantee against future overreaching by Parliament, while its standing to sue gives it a weapon to fight encroachments from other institutions. Thus is assured the respect of Article 4(1) of the EEC (now Article 7), according to which 'each institution shall act within the limits of the powers conferred upon it by this Treaty'. However, like the cases relating to the seat of Parliament, it was less about the balance of institutional powers than about guaranteeing respect of the division of competencies between the Member States and the Community. The Court estimated that the system of financing put in place by Parliament affected the power to control campaign financing, which was reserved to the Member States in the Act of 20 September 1976 relating to the election of Parliament and universal suffrage.[189]

3. Ultimately, the references to the Community based on the rule of law and the principle of balance of powers are situated in a constitutional framework since the court treated the treaties as a **constitutional charter**. 'The European Economic Community is a community based on the rule of law, inasmuch as neither its Member States nor its institutions can avoid a review of the question whether the measures adopted by them are in conformity with the basic constitutional charter.'[190] This expression was to be used a second time by the Court in its *Opinion relating to the European Economic Area*.[191] The reference permits recourse to a classic system of constitutional control in the Member States and the comparison of the Court to a constitutional court. It is not known how much care went into the selection of the terminology, but it is appropriate to note that the Court avoided using the term 'constitution'. The reference to a constitutional charter refers to the period of the restoration of the monarchy in France, in 1815 and 1830, during which the term 'charter' was used to specify the basis of the law as not emanating from the popular will, but rather as constituting an act of self-limitation by the monarch, generally referred to as *charte octroyée*.[192] By analogy, the rights guaranteed by the treaties were granted by the Member States as 'Masters of the Treaty'. Regardless, this case strongly affirmed the break with international law already evident in the *Costa/ENEL* case,[193] which underlined the specificity of Community law. As a result, a dynamic interpretation of the

[186] 'Measures adopted by the European Parliament in the context of the EEC treaty could encroach on the powers of the Member States or of the other institutions, or exceed the limits which have been set to the Parliament's powers, without its being possible to refer them for review by the Court', para 25.

[187] Judgment of 13 July 1961, Cases 14, 17, 20, 24, 26 and 27/60, rec. 321.

[188] Judgment of 17 September 1970, Case 25/70, rec. 1161.

[189] For this purpose, the Court will have to reclassify the allocations in order to show that the financing of information campaigns done by political parties and groupings could not be differentiated from financing for electoral campaigns.

[190] Para 23.

[191] Opinion of 14 December 1991, Case 1/91, rec. I-6079, in which the Court was even more precise: 'The EEC Treaty, albeit concluded in the form of an international agreement, none the less constitutes the constitutional charter of a Community based on the rule of law.'

[192] Literally, 'granted charter'.

[193] Judgment of 15 July 1964, Case 6/64, rec. 1141.

admissibility provisions in the EEC treaty was rendered easier. The construction of a system of review in a coherent framework, even if it is necessary to go beyond the letter of the treaty, could then be privileged by connection to a strict interpretation of the will of the parties.

The Coherence of the System of Review

The *Les Verts* case was as interesting on the litigation plane as on the constitutional plane. It constituted a stage in the progress of the court in order to construct a coherent system of review, but it was equally significant in the development relating to admissibility of annulment actions.

In so far as, in a Community based on the rule of law, the acts of institutions cannot escape review of their conformity with the treaty, the Court could not but infer the existence of a complete system of judicial review. It emphasises that private parties can attack measures attributable to Community institutions and, in doing so, raise the issue of the invalidity of the acts of general application that provided the bases for such measures. They can equally, when faced with the implementation of national measures, invoke the illegality of these acts before national courts and request that the question be referred to the Court of Justice. Experience shows that this system is not as complete as the Court would like us to believe, since there remains the case of a general act that does not require community or national implementing measures. In this case, the challenge cannot be brought before a national judge and the community judge cannot find it admissible because Article 173 requires that the litigants be individually concerned in order to be able bring the case before the Court. In the *Union de Pequeños Agricultores* case,[194] the Court took account of the gap and sent the case back to the national courts, charging those courts with the responsibility of providing the appropriate recourse. The Treaty Establishing a Constitution for Europe filled this gap in Article III-365, paragraph 4. The Treaty of Lisbon maintains this provision. In any case, the coherence of paths of appeal must naturally drive the Court of Justice to permit acts of Parliament that could be contested by the prejudicial route, as was the case in *Lord Bruce of Donnington*,[195] to also be brought through direct requests for annulment.

On the basis of this assumption of the existence of a complete system of judicial review, the absence of reference in Article 173 to acts of Parliament is explained by historical reasons. If review of the acts of Parliament were not provided for, this was not because the authors of the Treaty excluded it deliberately, but because Parliament did not have the power of decision in the original Treaty. As this situation has since changed, it is fitting to fill the gap and permit Parliament to be sued. The argument is supported *a contrario* by the fact that the ECSC Treaty, which provided for the power of decision, certainly limited to Parliament, provided for the possibility of challenging its decisions. The reasoning,

[194] Judgment of 25 July 2002, Case C-50/00P, rec. I-6677.

[195] Judgment of 15 September 1981, Case 208/80, rec. 2205. It is true that this type of judgment related to interpretation and the Court will only implicitly give Parliament *carte blanche* in relation to the validity of the measure.

however, is not entirely convincing. In effect, from the beginning, Parliament had a power of self-administration on the basis of its internal regulations. In this framework, Parliament could adopt acts having effects on third parties and yet Article 173 did not offer any protection against such acts. It is, however, also true that one could support the view that the authors of the treaty did not envisage such a borderline situation and that, if they had, they would have opened a path for review.

As concerns admissibility, the case clarified the fact that all actions destined to produce legal effects with regard to third parties could be the object of an annulment petition. The mention of articles aimed at producing judicial effects relates to Article 173. The problem was to know if this refers exclusively to the type of acts described in Article 189 (now 249). In the *ERTA* case, the Court emphasised the autonomous character of the notion of the act as used Article 173 in finding that the right of appeal was not limited to compulsory acts aimed at Article 189 of the EEC Treaty, but that

> Since the only matters excluded from the scope of the action for annulment open to the Member States and the institutions are 'recommendations or opinions'—which by the final paragraph of Article 189 are declared to have no binding force—Article 173 treats as acts open to review by the Court all measures adopted by the institutions which are intended to have legal force.
> The objective of this review is to ensure, as required by Article 164, observance of the law in the interpretation and application of the treaty.
> It would be inconsistent with this objective to interpret the conditions under which the action is admissible so restrictively as to limit the availability of this procedure merely to the categories of measures referred to by Article 189.[196]

Under these conditions, no argument can successfully bar the recognition of the reviewability of Parliamentary decisions, so long as they produce effects on third parties.

The internal nature of the Parliamentary decisions at issue cannot be an obstacle to admissibility. In effect, the existence of effects on third parties was not contestable since the financial contributions were destined, in part, to political groupings not represented in Parliament. Certainly, the Court, in applying the principle of institutional autonomy, did not in principle extend its control over purely internal acts carried out in the framework of each institution. However, it does not hesitate to control acts that could produce effects outside of the institution concerned. Thus, in Case 230/81, relating to the seat and place of work of Parliament, the Court did not find the case inadmissible due the internal character of the act. On the contrary, it connected the question of the existence of a reviewable act to an examination of the substance, which presumed that, in the case where the relevant act infringed on o kjkjlkj the competencies of States in the matter of the seat of Parliament, the act was reviewable.[197] Subsequently, the Court has always examined with care the contents of an 'internal' action in order to check whether it produced effects on third parties. In *Netherlands v Council*, it thus judged that an internal act relating to the transparency of the work of the Council could be based on the Council's internal regulatory power even though it may produce effects on third parties.[198] This attitude is

[196] Judgment of 31 March 1971, Case C-22/70, rec. 263.

[197] Judgment of 10 February 1983, *Luxembourg v European Parliament*, rec. 255.

[198] 'The fact that the Decision ... has legal effects vis-à-vis third parties cannot call in question its categorisation as a measure of internal organisation. There is nothing to prevent rules on the internal organisation of the work of an institution having such effects ...' Judgment of 20 April 1996, Case C-58/94, rec. I-2169. See also the Judgment of 15 June 1994, *Commission v BASF and others*, Case C-137/92P, rec. I-2555 accepting that the rights of third parties can prevail in certain dispositions of internal affairs.

not surprising. In effect, to grant total immunity to actions based on the power of internal organisation would permit an institution to unilaterally call into question the institutional balance or the division of competencies between the Community and the Member States. The judicial review of such acts is the consequence of having a Community based on the rule of law.

It remains to discuss the point of whether the applicant was individually concerned by the measure. Advocate General Mancini estimated that the response must be negative since, when the contested measures were adopted, the lists of candidates had not been decided in the Member States and Parliament could not determine which parties would benefit from the appropriations. He was not followed, and it is difficult to avoid the impression that the Court, without saying so explicitly, either wanted to make Parliament pay the price of its victory on admissibility by concluding that les Verts were individually concerned, or, more simply, considered it fitting to put a halt to a situation that did not satisfy elementary criteria of political equity.[199] In effect, the court adopted such an original reasoning, which it did not use again, that it gave the impression that the reasoning was due to the circumstances of the case. It based its position on the fact that certain of the beneficiaries of the financing, the political parties in Parliament, had participated in the decision and were identifiable beneficiaries of it. Under these conditions, to recognise their power to bring an eventual challenge while les Verts were banned from doing so would create an inequality in judicial protection, an inequality which it fell to the Court to correct. To tell the truth, the remedy brought by the Court does not seem aimed at correcting a hypothetical gap since none of the political parties represented in Parliament were involved in the appeal and it would be possible to respond that they were also not directly concerned to the extent that the measure applied to political groupings, the nature and composition of which might vary during the term of office. Moreover, subsequently, the Court has seemed reticent to allow recourse by groupings or parties against internal political decisions, finding that they were not individually concerned. Thus, when non-attached Members of Parliament contested a decision by the Bureau of Parliament relating to the use of budgetary allocations put at the disposal of political parties and non-attached Members, the request was declared inadmissible by an unequivocal order of the Tribunal on grounds that the applicants were not individual concerned: 'That measure applies generally and in the future to the political groupings and non-attached Members. It is therefore capable of affecting future political groupings and non-attached Members as well as those of whom the Parliament was constituted at the time the measure was adopted, even though it does not concern any of them individually.'[200] If the political groupings could not act against such a decision, then the discrimination against third parties envisaged by the Court did not exist and the argument of the

[199] It is this last point that the late Professor Jolliet, Judge Rapporteur in the case, raised in his contribution to the collection in honour of Diez de Valasco: 'If the Court, in resolving the issue of individual concern, had adhered to the traditional criteria and had ignored the novelty of the situation that would have produced the paradoxical result of making the action for annulment available as to the groupings which had no need of it and denying that remedy to the groupings which did need it. Coming immediately after the declaration that the Community is founded on the rule of law, such a "denial of justice" would have make a mockery of the reasoning by which the Court arrived at the conclusion that it had jurisdiction to entertain an action for annulment against a measure of the European Parliament.' English version of Professor Jolliet's test, translated by Keeling, from the text published in French in the *Estudios en homenaje al professor don Manuel Diaz de Velasco* (Madrid, Technos), 985–1005.

[200] Order of 10 January 2005, Case T-357/03, *Gollnisch and others v European Parliament*, rec. II-1.

Court in *Les Verts* was unfounded.[201] In effect, in *Les Verts*, the Court assumed that an application brought by a political group would be receivable in order to find that discrimination existed vis-à-vis third parties. If that assumption was baseless, the application should have been declared inadmissible. It is true that the budgetary allocations only related to the elections of 1984 and had been adopted in 1982, which could, in the case at issue, render the individualisation easier, taking account of the improbable nature of the formation of new groupings in the interval. However, the judgment makes no mention of this fact, which, in other contexts, would not permit a decision in favour of admissibility. Under such conditions, the solution reached in *Les Verts* seems to be an isolated response to a case of a particular kind and has not been followed.

Conclusion

Rereading the case with the knowledge that one has today of Community law can make the observations of the Court seem banal, since they have been incorporated in the treaties. As often, in maters of European integration, the acquired knowledge seems so natural that one forgets the fights that gave birth to it, whether in intergovernmental conferences, through legislative channels, or in the confidential atmosphere of the Court. As René Jolliet wrote, it may in fact have no value as precedent. But one must recognise that the Court brought about a revolution, not only in granting Parliament capacity to be sued and, thus, opening the way to granting it standing to sue and then to the recognition in the treaties of a status for Parliament equivalent to that of the Council and the Commission. Furthermore, this audacious step of the Court, which remains to this day, applies to the Community the notion of a state governed by the rule of law, which implies as much the existence of a coherent system of political review as it implies effective judicial protection of private parties. This constitutional approach constitutes the case's essential contribution to community law today.

[201] It is regrettable that the case, which was brought before the Court by Group of the European Right against the decision of the Bureau of Parliament regarding the division of budgetary allocations for the European elections in Spain and Portugal, did not go beyond provisional measures. It could doubtless have given interesting clarification on this point. See Orders of 18 September and 16 October 1986, Case 221/86R, recs. 2579 and 2969.

3

What Has Been, and What Could Be, Thirty Years after *Les Verts/European Parliament*

ALBERTO ALEMANNO[202]

Introduction

The *Les Verts* judgment went down history not only as the first judicial recognition of the Community as 'a Community based on the rule of law'[203] but also because it identified within it 'a complete system of legal remedies'.[204] While the former statement turned out to be a mere acknowledgment of a pre-existing reality, the latter proved more controversial.

Thirty years after its delivery, this study proposes to analyse the role that this judgment has played within the evolution of the Community remedies system, by provocatively exploring whether the expectations which it has generated have been fully satisfied. In other words, was the Court's dictum a statement of fact, a prediction or a wish?

The Genesis

As is well known, the Court held in *Les Verts* that, despite the fact the European Parliament did not appear in the list of potential defendants as laid down in Article 230 EC,[205] it had jurisdiction to entertain an action for annulment against the acts of the EP.

Contrary to what it might appear prima facie, the outcome reached by the Court in *Les Verts*, though innovative, was not entirely surprising. The solution given had been not only

[202] Associate Professor of Law, HEC Paris; formerly Legal Secretary at the European Court of Justice, Luxembourg.

[203] The Court referred again to the Community Treaty as a 'constitutional charter' in its Opinion 1/91, where the Court distinguished the Treaty from the Agreement establishing the European Economic Area (EEA) between the EC and its Member States on the one hand, and certain Member States of the EFTA (European Free Trade Association) on the other hand. See Opinion of 14 December 1991, ECR 1991–10, at 6102.

[204] Case 294/83 *Les Verts* [ECR] 1339, para 23.

[205] It is by relying on this textual argument that several authors excluded that EP acts could be challenged under Article 230. See, eg, G Vandersanden and A Barav, *Contentieux communautaire*, Brussels, 1977, 135 *ff*. This textual argument was even strengthened by the fact that the ECSC, unlike the successive treaties, expressly provided for the competence of the Court to annul, inter alia, an 'act' of the EP. See Article 38 ECSC.

foreseen by several scholars,[206] but it had also been anticipated by some previous judgments recognising a more relevant role to the Parliament within the European system of legal remedies.[207] Yet, the most significant element proving this *favor* stems from the same European Parliament's line of defence: the EP did not even try to deny that in principle a legal person, such as the applicant association was entitled to bring an action for annulment against an act of the EP.[208] This explains why the Court had to verify on its own motion whether the conditions of Article 230 EC had been fulfilled.[209]

Even though this outcome was not only expected at that time but also convincingly motivated by the concern to subject to review the action of the EP, following the conferral of new powers,[210] this did not prevent the judgment from being labelled a 'judicial revision' of the Treaty.[211] Yet, the judgment has also been welcomed as a further manifestation of a judicial policy designed to achieve a wide interpretation of the Court's jurisdiction.[212] This seems to show at best the very subtle line existing between the courts' exercise of a legitimate gap-filling function and judicial activism.

But how did the Court end up making such ambitious claims in order to come to the conclusion that an action for annulment may also be brought against the acts of the Parliament? In particular, was it really necessary to underline that the EC is 'a Community based on the rule of law' and that the Treaty establishes 'a complete system of legal remedies' to come to this conclusion?

Today it might be tempting to argue that the Court could have convincingly come to the same conclusion by limiting its answer to the reasoning developed in paragraphs 24 and 25. Here, by following closely the logical interpretative steps as suggested in Article 31 of the Vienna Convention on the Law of the Treaties,[213] it first easily overcomes the textual argument opposing the admissibility of the action before engaging into a teleological argument ('both to the spirit of the Treaty … and to its system') in order to finally recognise its jurisdiction upon actions for annulment introduced against acts of the EP intended to have legal effect vis-à-vis third parties.[214] Yet, although this reasoning may well

[206] P Pescatore, 'Reconnaissance et contrôle des actes du Parlement européen' (1978) *Revue trimestrielle de droit européen* 581; JC Masclet, 'Le Parlement européen devant ses juges' (1983) *Revue du marché commun* 518. See also the Editorial of the (1982) *European Law Review* 7.

[207] Case 138/79 *Roquette Frères* [ECR] 3333 (right of the EP to intervene in an Art 230 procedure before the Court); Case 208/80 *Lord Bruce of Donington* [ECR] 2205 (competence under Article 234 to interpret acts of the EP); Case 13/83 *Parliament/Council* [ECR] 1513 (right of the EP to rely on actions for failure to act).

[208] On the contrary, the EP strategically decided not to raise any objection to admissibility, by arguing that political parties should be allowed to bring an action 'against measures which determine under what conditions and in what amount they are to receive, on the occasion of the direct elections, funds from the European Parliament for the purpose of making the latter more widely know'. Para 30.

[209] Para 19 of the judgment.

[210] Initially, the EP could not take binding decisions, other than those concerning its own staff.

[211] V Costantinesco and D Simon, Recueil Dalloz Sirey (1987) *Jurisprudence* 82 and J Jacqué, 'Recours en annulation, capagne d'information pour l'élection du Parlement européen' (1986) *Revue trimestrielle de droit européen* 503.

[212] *Ibid*, 82. See H Schermers and D Waelbroeck, *Judicial Protection in the European Union* (Brussels, Kluwer, 2001) 309 *ff*, 409–10.

[213] Article 31, para 1 (General rule of interpretation) establishes that '[A] treaty shall be interpreted in good faith in accordance with the ordinary meaning to be given to the terms of the treaty in their context and in the light of its object and purpose. On the role of this Treaty in the EC Courts' interpretation, see A Rosas, *The European Court of Justice: sources of law and methods of interpretation* and P Mengozzi, 'The jurisprudence of the Court of Justice and the Court of First Instance of the European Communities' in G Sacerdoti, Y Yanovich, J Boahnes, *The WTO at Ten* (Cambridge, Cambridge University Press, 2006).

[214] Para 25 of the judgment.

have been self-sufficient to validate the solution of the case at hand, the Court felt the need to insert a further premise to its logic. Without such an extra argument this judgment would have been likely to fall into oblivion.[215] And this was not the kind of result expected by its judge-rapporteur,[216] who recently revealed that there was great awareness within the Court that their answer to this point would have assured the judgment a place in the annals of European Community law. This insider information, by contextualising this case within its historical and sociological dimensions, seems to shed some light on the factors that might have led the Court to strengthen its reasoning by adding its highly celebrated (and often quoted[217]) meta-argument according to which, since the Community is based on the rule of law, all its institutions must be subject to judicial review and to this end the same Community established a 'complete system of legal remedies'. But what would enable the system to qualify as 'complete'? According to the Court, the EC judicial system deserves such a qualification because despite the fact that 'natural and legal persons ... cannot contest general measures directly before the court by reason of the special conditions of admissibility laid down in Article 173 ... they may plead the invalidity of [these] measures before the national courts and cause the latter to request the Court of Justice for a preliminary ruling'.[218]

While it is debatable whether this last indication was strictly necessary to the solution of the case at hand, the Court felt the need to illustrate (and to somehow prove) that its previous statement relating to the completeness of the system was well grounded. This illustration is crucial to the extent that it did not only unexpectedly acknowledge (though impliedly) that Article 230 may not always be available to individuals, but it also showed, for the first time, an alternative path aimed at ensuring individuals' judicial protection vis-à-vis acts of the institutions. In so doing, the Court identified Article 234's preliminary reference procedure as a viable solution to the problem raised by the strict conditions of admissibility to Article 230. The Court's case law on the interpretation of Article 230(4) which encourages individual applicants to bring issues of validity of Community measures indirectly before the Court of Justice via the national courts was born.

Thirty Years of Les Verts in the Courts' Case Law

This judicial statement, though ancillary to the solution of the present case, has had a transformational effect on the EC remedies system, by shaping the scope of each specific legal remedy and, accordingly, the mission entrusted to the EC Courts by Article 220. As will be shown below, the EC Courts, because of the approach taken in *Les Verts*, have been encouraged on several occasions to widen the limits of their own jurisdiction in order to ensure the existence of a 'complete system of legal remedies'. In other words, this judgment

[215] This seems to be proved by the same *Les Verts* judgment in so far as its part relating to the substance of the case has been completely overlooked. In the hope of rescuing this part of the judgment from oblivion, René Joliet devoted an article to it in 1994 published in the *European Law Review*. See R Joliet, DT Keeling, 'The Reimbursement of Election Expenses: A Forgotten Dispute' (1994) *EL Rev* 243 *ff*.

[216] *Ibid*, at 244.

[217] *Les Verts* has been quoted in more than 50 judgments and orders during the last 30 years.

[218] Para 23. However, since in the present case the plaintiff could not raise the issue before national courts, the Court felt obliged to reinterpret Article 230.

has generated a powerful rhetoric of completeness which has enlightened (and still does) the Courts' discourse in relation to the interpretation of the scope of the different Community legal remedies and the relationship existing among them.

Several judgments have thus contributed 'to complete' the system by better defining every single legal remedy and allocating functions between the courts of the Member States and the Court of Justice. Thus, for instance, in *Foto-Frost* the Court, facing 'one of the thorniest [question] it has ever had to tackle',[219] had to determine whether national courts may, within the framework of a preliminary reference concerning the validity of Community acts, declare these acts invalid.[220] Although Article 234 EC does not settle this question, but rather leaves open such an option, the Court denied that power by relying on the principle of the uniform interpretation of Community law. Indeed, according to the Court, to recognise such power would enable divergences between courts in the Member States so as 'to place in jeopardy the very unit of the Community legal order'.[221] Under the rhetoric of completeness, this judgment has contributed to this ideal by filling up a clear gap which had been clearly left behind by the drafters of the Treaty when considering the relationship between Article 230 and 234 EC.[222] Similarly, in *European Parliament v Council* the Court, although expressly relying solely on the principle of institutional balance, recognised, despite the silence of the Treaty, the capacity of the European Parliament to bring an action for annulment.[223] Once again the Court, by showing its willingness to fill up a 'legal vacuum'[224] left by the drafters of the Treaty, contributed to 'complete' the system of legal remedies. Paradoxically, however, to achieve that result, it first had to acknowledge that 'the various legal remedies provided [by the Treaty], however effective and diverse they may be, may prove to be ineffective or uncertain' to guarantee that a measure by the Council or the Commission in disregard of the Parliament's prerogatives will be reviewed.[225] The benchmark of completeness sanctioned in *Les Verts* unquestionably required enabling also the Parliament to bring an action for annulment.

A further stretch of the philosophy of completeness initiated in *Les Verts* may be found in *Johnston v Chief Constable of the Royal Ulster Constabulary*.[226] Here the Court held that persons aggrieved by actions or orders of national authorities encroaching on their rights under EC law 'have the right to obtain an effective remedy in a competent court' and that 'it is for the Member States to ensure effective judicial protection as regards compliance with the applicable provisions of Community law'.[227] The rhetoric of completeness extends its argumentative strength as to lead the Court to impose also on Member States the duty to ensure access to justice.

The same pattern of thought has enlightened a series of judgments which not only has sanctioned the autonomy of each legal remedy but has also better defined the relationships existing among them. Thus, for instance, because of the concurrent roles played by

[219] Opinion of AG Mancini delivered on 19 May 1987 in Case 314/85 *Foto-Frost* [1987] ECR 4199, para 4.
[220] Case 314/85 *Foto-Frost* [1987] ECR 4199.
[221] *Ibid*, para 15.
[222] AG Mancini, above note 219, para 4.
[223] Case 302/87 *Parliament v Council* [1988] ECR 5615.
[224] This is the term which has been used by the Parliament in its submission. See *ibid*, para 8.
[225] *Ibid*, para 16.
[226] Case 222/84 [1984] ECR 1651. See also Case 222/86 [1987] 4097, para 14.
[227] *Ibid*, para 18.

Article 230 actions for annulment and Article 234 preliminary reference procedures as to the validity of EC acts, the Court has felt the need to determine their relationship. In *TWD Textilwerke Deggendorf*[228] the Court held that is not possible for the addressee of an EC act who could undoubtedly have challenged that decision to call in question the lawfulness of that decision before the national courts in an action brought against the measures taken by the national authorities in implementation of that decision. As AG Jacobs had elegantly said, 'greater damage to the coherence of the system of remedies would be done if an undertaking were allowed to challenge indirectly, under Article 177, a decision against which the appropriate remedy is clearly a direct action under Article 173'.[229] Once again, it appears from this case that, despite the existence of a 'complete system of legal remedies and procedures', the drafters of the Treaty clearly had not fully considered the relationships existing between Article 230 and Article 234.

At the same time, the imperative of completeness building upon the idea according to which Article 234 should be the solution to the problem raised by the strict conditions of admissibility laid down by Article 230 has oriented the Courts in several other judgments. As will be illustrated below, in these circumstances, the paradigm developed in *Les Verts* (234 may compensate for the limits of 230) has been relied upon by the Courts in order to justify its refusal to expand the interpretation of 'direct and individual concern' under Article 230.

Thus, for instance, in *Area Cova*, in upholding a CFI order declaring inadmissible an action for annulment introduced by a group of Spanish boat owners against a Community regulation, the Court, in justifying its refusal of *locus standi*, held that 'the possibility for individuals to have their rights protected by means of an action before the national courts, which have the power to grant interim relief and, where appropriate, to make a reference for a preliminary ruling ... constitutes *the very essence of the Community system of judicial protection*'.[230] Given that in the specific circumstances of the case it was impossible to bring the matter before any Spanish court, in the absence of any national act of implementation, this latter statement, though presenting itself as a linear application of *Les Verts*, sounded rhetorical and empty.[231]

Therefore, while it is true that the approach undertaken in *Les Verts* has, on the one hand, contributed to the widening of the Courts' jurisdiction under Article 220, on the other hand, it has also offered them an easy (and often unsatisfactorily) justification to explain their refusal to expand the established interpretation of 'direct and individual concern'. As a result, by seeking in Article 234's preliminary ruling procedure a solution to the problem raised by the denial of effective direct access to judicial protection, this judgment has not necessarily played in favour of a broader reading of the admissibility criteria as laid down in Article 230(4). In particular, the rhetoric of completeness as laid down in *Les Verts* combined with the very limited possibility to directly challenge EC

[228] Case C-188/92 *TWD Textilwerke Deggendorf v Germany* [1994] ECR I-833, para 17. For a follow-up of this case law, see also Case C-491/01 *British American Tobacco (Investments) Ltd and Imperial Tobacco Ltd* ('*BAT*') [2002] ECR I-11453, paras 39–41, and, more recently, Case C-432/05 *Unibet (London) Ltd and Unibet (International) Ltd* ('*Unibet*'), ECR 2271, paras 40–41.

[229] Opinion of AG Jacobs delivered on 15 September 1993 in *TWD*, para 20.

[230] Case C-3/00 P *Area Cova v Council* [2001] ECR 983 and Case C-301/99 P, *Area Cova v Commission* [2001] ECR 1005, para 54.

[231] See also Case 321/95 P *Stichting Greenpeace Council (Greenpeace International) v Commission* [1998] ECR 1651, paras 32 and 33.

normative acts before EC Courts, had instead contributed to channel the judicial review of EC acts through Article 234 EC's preliminary ruling procedure. Seen under this perspective, the role played by *Les Verts* does not seem to have necessarily advanced the principle of effective judicial protection and that insofar as judicial review under Article 234 is much less effective than under Article 230 EC. This is because the preliminary reference procedure presents several drawbacks as compared to the action for annulment. Judicial review under the former is not only slow and indirect but also entirely at the mercy, at least in practice, of the national court as to whether the question will be referred to the Court. Hence, it is difficult to believe that Article 234 could complete the system by compensating the lacunas stemming from the set of legal remedies provided for by the Treaty in particular in Article 230(4).

This had become particularly problematic to the extent that more and more judgments have shown that there exist an increasing number of situations in which individuals who are not addressees may be de facto affected by a EC given act, but cannot challenge it under Article 230(4) to the extent they do not satisfy its requirements.

Confronted with such situations, the EC courts reacted unpredictably.[232] On the hand they denied *locus standi* to non-addressees despite their *de facto* individual interest, by often insisting that Community rights 'are fully protected by the national courts which may, if need be, refer a question to this Court for a preliminary ruling under Article 177 EC'.[233] On the other hand, in other cases, the Court recognised *locus standi* to non-addressees by stretching the limits of the *Plaumann* test. This has happened mainly for the following three reasons: either because of the specificities of the field at hand, because of the exceptional character of the circumstances surrounding the case or even because the Courts have been induced by reasons of 'substantial justice'.[234]

Thus, for instance, in *Fediol*, the Court deduced from the numerous substantive and procedural rights conferred to the complaints by the antidumping regulation that their complaint would individualise them under Article 230 EC.[235] The Court had already adopted a similar approach in other fields, such as competition[236] and state aids.[237]

As for the best example of a reasoning grounded on arguments of substantial justice one cannot but refer to *Extramet*.[238] In this judgment, the Court recognised *locus standi* of a non-addressee, despite the fact that it had not participated in the procedure leading to the adoption of the act, by stressing his special position on the affected market.[239] A similar reasoning has also been followed in *Codorniu*.[240] As is well known, the registration of the trademark 'Gran Cremant de Codorniou', obtained back in 1924, has been

[232] A Arnull, 'Private Applicants and the Action for Annulment since Codorniou' (2000) *CML Rev* 51 and L Malferrari, 'The Functional Representation of the Individual's Interest Before the EC Courts: the Evolution of the Remedies System and the Pluralistic Deficit in the EC' (2005) 12 *Indiana Journal of Global Legal Studies* 2, 678.

[233] Case C-97/85 R, *Union Deutsche Lebensmittelwerke GmbH v Commission* [1985] 1331; Case T-398/94, *Kahn Scheepvaart* [1996] ECR II-477; Case 321/95 P *Stichting Greenpeace Council (Greenpeace International) v Commission* [1998] ECR 1651, paras 27–34.

[234] L Malferrari, above note 232, at 679. The same *Les Verts* judgment may be read under this perspective.

[235] Case 191/92, *Fediol* [1983] ECR 2913.

[236] See, eg, Case 26/76, *Metro* [1977] ECR 1901.

[237] See, eg, Case 169/84, *Cofaz* [1986] ECR 414.

[238] Case C-358/89, *Extramet* [1991] ECR 2501.

[239] The Court considered that the contested measure affected seriously its competitive situation by imposing an anti-dumping duty on a major product used by Extramet in its production process.

[240] Case C-309/89 *Codorniu* [1994] ECR 1853.

considered to correspond to 'a situation which, from the point of view of the contested provision, differentiates it from all other traders' and justified the admissibility of the action brought by the Spanish wine-maker.

Rhetoric or Logic of Completeness?

While this case law had already shown most of the limits of the remedies system of the Community, two successive cases, *Union de Pequeños Agricultores* (UPA)[241] and *Jégó-Quéré*,[242] by bringing momentum for a possible judicial reform of the system, have directly put into question the adequateness of the paradigm which had been elaborated in *Les Verts* (Article 234 may compensate for the limits of Article 230). In substance, the questions facing the Court were the following:

First, how a system of legal remedies which has been defined 'complete' may admit that there exist situations in which an individual may neither rely on Article 230 nor Article 234 in order to challenge the validity of an EC act?

Second, would the principle of effective judicial protection be secured when the sole available course of action for challenging the validity of a given Community act would consist in infringing EC law in order to trigger an administrative or judicial proceeding challengeable before national courts?

Third, in view of the 'completeness' of the system, shouldn't standing be granted where the application of Article 230(4) as interpreted in the case law would entail a denial of effective judicial protection?

As these questions show, the logic underpinning 30 years of diligent application of *Les Verts* was at stake. In particular, the specific circumstances of these cases were directly questioning the assumption developed in *Les Verts* according to which the preliminary ruling procedure, by providing effective judicial protection against general measures, would 'complete' the remedies system.

Would the rhetoric of completeness of the system stemming from *Les Verts* turn into a logic of completeness thus leading the Court to widen the conditions of admissibility under Article 230(4)?

This was the hot question entertaining the EC legal milieu during summer 2004.

Owing to the inconsistency of the prior case law examined above, a clear answer to the questions raised by these judgments could not be derived from any previous judgment. If, on the one hand, the *Greenpeace* judgment did not seem to exclude the possibility that standing might be granted where the application of the fourth paragraph of Article 230 EC as interpreted in the case law would entail a denial of effective judicial protection,[243] *Asocarne* appeared to strongly deny such a possibility insofar as it stated that 'In no case

[241] Case T-173/98 [1999] ECR II-3357 and Case C-50/00 P *Unión de Pequeños Agricultores v Council* [2002] ECR I-6677.

[242] Case T-177/01, *Jégo-Quéré v Commission* [2002] ECR II-2365 and Case C-263/02 P *Commission v Jégo-Quéré* [2004] ECR I-3425.

[243] Case 321/95 P *Greenpeace International* [1998] ECR 1651.

can such a circumstance allow an action for annulment brought by a natural or legal person which does not satisfy the conditions laid down by the fourth paragraph of Article 230 EC to be declared admissible'.[244]

In *UPA*, while AG Jacobs in his powerful Opinion had unmistakably recognised that 'proceedings before national courts are not ... capable of guaranteeing that individuals seeking to challenge the validity of Community measures are granted fully effective judicial protection',[245] the Court, after reiterating the existence of 'a complete system of legal remedies', clearly held that the absence of domestic remedies did not allow it to modify the system of remedies set up by the Treaty.[246] According to the ECJ, deciding otherwise, by requiring the EC Courts, in each individual case, to examine and interpret national procedural law, would inevitably go beyond their jurisdiction.

Nonetheless, while refusing to expressly recognise the limits of the proceedings before national courts, the Court tried to revive the assumption made in *Les Verts*, by adding that 'in accordance with the principle of sincere co-operation laid down in Article 5 of the Treaty, national courts are required, so far as possible, to interpret and apply national procedural rules governing the exercise of rights of action in a way that enables natural and legal persons to challenge before the courts the legality of any decision or other national measure relative to the application to them of a Community act of general application, by pleading the invalidity of such an act'. In the Court's logic, if—as stated in *Les Verts*—the system is 'complete' because of Article 234, it is on the Member States to adapt their national remedies and procedures in accordance with Article 10 EC, rather than for itself to revise its interpretation of Article 230(4), in order to ensure judicial protection.

In the following *Jego-Quéré* case, the CFI, by taking on the AG's opinion in UPA, went as far as to sanction the judicial death of *Les Verts* by holding that the system of legal remedies 'can no longer be regarded, in the light of Articles 6 and 13 of the ECHR and of Article 47 of the Charter of Fundamental Rights, as guaranteeing persons the right to an effective remedy enabling them to contest the legality of Community measures of general application which directly affect their legal situation'.[247] In appeal against this judgment, the ECJ restated its *UPA* reasoning building upon *Les Verts*[248] by clearly stating that an 'action for annulment before the Community Court should not on any view be available, even where it is apparent that the national procedural rules do not allow the individual to contest the validity of the Community measure at issue unless he has first contravened it'.[249] However, in a last effort to save what it was left of *Les Verts*, the Court made further suggestion aimed at ensuring that Article 234 preliminary procedure may still 'complete' the system: 'It is possible for domestic law to permit an individual directly concerned by a general legislative measure of national law which cannot be directly contested before the courts to seek from the national authorities under that legislation a measure which may itself be contested before the national courts, so that the individual may challenge the legislation indirectly.'[250]

[244] Order in Case C-10/95 P *Asocarne v Council* [1995] ECR I-4149, para 26.
[245] Opinion of AG Jacobs delivered on 21 March 2002 [ECR] 6677, para 40.
[246] Case C-50/00 P *Unión de Pequeños Agricultores v Council* [2002] ECR I-6677, para 43.
[247] Case T-177/01: *Jégo-Quéré* [2002] ECR 2365.
[248] Case C-263/02 P *Commission v Jégo-Quéré* [2004] ECR I-3425, para 30.
[249] *Ibid*, para 34.
[250] *Ibid*, para 35.

These judgments show how the rhetoric of completeness generated by *Les Verts* has lost through time part of its argumentative force by failing to persuade the Court itself to expand its established interpretation of 'direct and individual concern'. The attempt to revive *Les Verts* by relying on the principle of loyal co-operation to ensure that Article 234 may—once again—offer the solution to all problems seems problematic and short-sighted. Indeed, this solution, by making the access to justice dependent on the Member States' ability to provide for an appropriate legal remedy, does not ensure a uniform degree of judicial protection throughout Europe.[251]

It is predicted that the only way to revitalise the heritage of *Les Verts* is to rely upon its original logic (since individuals cannot always rely on Article 234, Article 230 must be judicially updated) in order to justify a generalised opening of the conditions of admissibility of Article 230(4). Although agonising, *Les Verts* still has enough evocative strength to make possible the shift from the actual *ubi remedium ibi jus* to the badly needed *ubi jus ibi remedium* within the Community legal order.[252]

[251] For a formulation of this principle see, eg, Case C-228/96 *Aprile* [1998] ECR I-7141 and Case C-255/00, *Grundig Italiana Spa v Ministero delle Finanze* [2002] ECR 8003, para 33. On the possible consequences stemming from reliance on Article 10 EC, see A Alemanno, 'British American Tobacco: nuovo capitolo della saga "Union de pequeños agricultores – Jégo Quéré"?' (2003) *Il diritto dell'Unione Europea* 3.

[252] Encouraging signs towards this direction can be found in Case C-432/05 *Unibet (London) Ltd and Unibet (International) Ltd* ('*Unibet*'), ECR 2271, para 37.

4

Opening or Closure? The Constitutional Intimations of the ECJ

NEIL WALKER

Constitutional Symbolism

Perhaps more so than any other decision of the Court of Justice, *Parti Ecologiste ('Les Verts') v European Parliament*[253] was and remains important for its symbolic rather than its doctrinal message. Not that the history of the Court is lacking in salient symbolic moments. As many of the essays in this collection testify, there is simply no precedent or analogy in the annals of national constitution-building for the key role the ECJ has played in the construction of Europe as an integrated polity.[254] And for each block put in place—direct effect, primacy, pre-emption, fundamental rights protection, implied powers etc—there is a handful of key cases which have come to symbolise its polity-building relevance. Yet in all these examples symbolic effect clearly reflects doctrinal significance. The cases are an important part of the story of the Court as told to external audiences precisely because, by any objective standard, they also transform the internal structure and content of the supranational legal order in some decisive manner. *Les Verts* is different. Its doctrinal message, in the name of a broad principle of judicial supervision extending the scope of reviewable acts beyond the institutions (that is, Commission and Council) specified in the plain words of the then Article 173 EC[255] to embrace those of the Parliament, was neither trivial nor uncontroversial. But it was palpably not of the same order of immediate or long-term transformative *significance* as many other headline cases. However, in terms of its *signification*—of what it connotes rather than denotes, and how this message fits into a broader public narrative of supranational polity-building, the path-breaking reference in *Les Verts* to the Treaty framework as the 'constitutional charter' of the EC is enough to secure its place in the pantheon.

In what follows, I will try to explain why this is so, but also why the legacy of *Les Verts* is an ambivalent one. The performative meaning in the wider political drama of constitutionalisation of the key EU judicial organ's adopting the language of constitutionalism cannot be overestimated. Yet there was a certain partiality in the 'c' word's invocation in *Les Verts* and in the subsequent line of cases. While this partial approach endorsed a

[253] Case 294/83 [1986] ECR 1339; [1987] 2 CMLR 343.

[254] For a recent insightful overview, see A Stone Sweet, *The Judicial Construction of Europe* (Oxford, Oxford University Press, 2004).

[255] See now Art 230 EC.

world-view which helped make the recent 'Big C'[256] constitutional process possible, in so doing it may also have contributed, however modestly and distantly, to the difficulties and divisions that arose in this latest documentary chapter of the constitutional drama. For in finding and pursuing the constitutional opening that it did, the Court foreshadowed an attitude of constitutional closure which has characterised the present impasse.

In pursuing the argument on such a broad symbolic canvas we will proceed from the top down, beginning with an examination of the range of things we might mean, and—even more importantly—signify, by talking about constitutionalism in general and the EU in particular. Only then will we be in a position to locate what the Court meant, and also what it signified, in the *Les Verts* line of cases.

The Orders of Constitutionalism

Constitutionalism is a famously protean concept. It means many things to many people, but we should not on that basis conclude that the search for some kind of conceptual common ground is either unimportant or impossible. It is clearly not unimportant, since, for reasons that will become clear, the very intensity of argument over the meaning of constitutionalism signals the gravity of what is at stake in the claim that something is or is not 'constitutional'. It is not impossible, since much disagreement over the precise meaning and import of constitutionalism in any particular context actually implies at least some element of agreement over what kinds of contexts count as 'constitutionally relevant' or 'constitutionally generative' in the first place. The most visible and sharply contested debates about the meaning of constitutionalism typically sound at the doctrinal level, concerning what in the courts, or in some other decisive or persuasive political forum, counts as a 'good' constitutional argument in treatment and resolution of a particular practical dispute or issue—call this the first-order question. Yet most such particular debate and disagreement take place against a backdrop of more or less shared understandings of the kinds of framing conditions, or contexts, be they juridical, institutional, authoritative or social, that count as constitutionally relevant or generative to begin with—call this the second-order question.[257] These framing conditions bear in an exclusionary sense on what is properly constitutional. They purport to tell us what can and cannot be constitutional—what lies within and what lies outside the boundaries of constitutional contemplation—prior to consideration of the right constitutional answer in any particular situation. It is this second-order question, as we shall see, that takes on a distinctive hue in the supranational context, one that notoriously attracts 'less' rather than 'more' by way of shared understandings.

To appreciate this, we must return to the etymological roots of the idea of constitution as it was adapted from its original context of reference—the human body—to the 'body politic'. In the pre-modern age, 'constitution' in its primitive adapted sense retained from its original context a purely empirical and descriptive reference, indicating simply the state or condition of a country. Gradually, however, in a process of double abstraction, it

256 N Walker, ' Big "C" or small "c"?' (2006) 12 *ELJ* 12–14.

257 See, eg, M Maduro, 'Where to Look for Legitimacy?' in EO Eriksen, JE Fossum and AJ Menendez (eds), *Constitution Making and Democracy* Arena Report No 5 (Oslo, Arena, 2002) 81.

acquired two extended references. In the first place, it gained a legal-normative edge, now referring to the state or condition of a country as established by and grounded in legal norms. Later it also gained a prescriptive edge, referring no longer just to the country's present condition but to its preferred and projected condition, albeit still understood not as a utopian ideal unrelated to its present condition but as a practical exercise in normative modelling taking the present condition as its baseline and starting point.[258] This intimate mix of fact and value and of description and prescription has left a powerful legacy—a historical layering of cumulative meaning that characterises and animates each of the second-order constitutional frames. Each speaks in its own register to the idea of the 'body politic' being constructed and maintained as a self-standing organism in 'good working order', with the 'good' referring both to its viability and effective functioning as a self-standing organism, and, through that effective functioning, to its possession or its potential to acquire certain beneficent qualities. Moreover, the sheer scale and complexity of what is involved in establishing and keeping a human association in 'good' working order in both of these aspects means that all the available frames, and all the distinctive registers in which they speak, are required for us to appreciate what a constitutional settlement in the fullest sense would amount to.

So what typically counts as constitutional in terms of the juridical frame, as we shall develop below, is the idea of a mature rule-based or legal order—one that reaches or aspires to a certain standard both of independent efficacy and of virtue that we associate with legal 'orderliness'. What typically counts as constitutional in institutional terms is the presence of a set of organs of government that provide an effective instrument of rule as well as promising a just form of internal balance. What typically counts as constitutional in authoritative terms is that the legal and institutional complex may plausibly be attributed to some *pouvoir constituant* that both is original to and distinctive of that polity and is qualified to claim a legitimate pedigree or authorial title. And, finally, what typically counts as constitutional in social terms is an idea of a community sufficiently integrated—call it a 'society' or a 'demos'—to be the subject of legal regulation and institutional action that is both plausibly effective in terms of collective implementation and compliance and capable of tracking some meaningful sense of that community's common good.

In summary, then, we can say that in its broader second-order sense the discourse of constitutionalism—the debate over what is properly within the constitutional frame—is inherently Janus-faced, involving in each of its registers both a status claim and a value judgment. It is concerned, as noted, with the two closely related but distinct sides of 'good working order'—with whether a certain complex of juridical, institutional, authoritative and social arrangements is sufficiently well developed to qualify as body-politic-constitutive, and also with whether these arrangements respect certain principles or standards or facilitate certain ends that are or may be regarded as valuable to those individuals and groups with whom they are concerned.

In the traditional state context, these second-order frames are typically so settled—and often so venerable—in their insistence that the status threshold has been crossed, and, in addition, they tend to fit together so closely and in such a familiar pattern, that we often take for granted just these two features. That is to say, both the factity and the co-articulation of the second-order frames are simply assumed—treated as always or

[258] See, eg D Grimm, 'The Constitution in the process of Denationalization' (2005) 12 *Constellations* 447–63, 448.

already in place. It follows, first, that discussion of the constitutional quality of each of the second-order frames tends to concentrate on the outstanding question of value; indeed, the constitutional framing question is often in practice *reduced* to its value-aspirational dimension. Whether, to take the registers separately, the legal system indeed possesses certain virtuous 'rule of law' qualities, or the institutional design of the polity does justice to the complex of interests it is supposed to represent, or constituent power is traceable to a legitimate source, or the defining values and operative goals of the polity speak to goods held in common by the members of that polity. Or, indeed, to view the value question holistically, whether the country has the constitution it 'needs' or 'deserves' (as opposed to the one it taken-for-grantedly *has*). It follows, secondly, that the various second-order registers tend to be collapsed together. Just because the juridical, institutional, authoritative and social registers typically are co-present in the state context, it is treated as natural and unproblematic that they should be co-present.

In the supranational context, neither of these assumptions holds. In the first place, the very status-claiming proposition that the EU has been 'constituted' as a 'body politic' in any way analogous to that of a state in the different and various registers with which we are concerned is itself far from uncontroversial, quite apart from—and prior to—the question of what it would take for the EU constitutional frame to qualify as 'good' in the evaluative sense.[259] In the second place, and related, nothing can be assumed about the co-articulation of the various framing contexts. As we shall see, it is particularly contentious whether the EU has been duly independently constituted *qua* polity or is capable of being duly constituted *qua* polity in an authoritative or in a social sense (that is, whether it possesses its own *pouvoir constituant* or its own demos) and, in turn, whether the absence or weakness of these framing registers is fatal to the supranational constitutional enterprise. Patently, these are not trivial semantic disputes. Separately and cumulatively the various framing questions go to the issue of what kind and quality of political organisation it is possible and legitimate for the EU to imagine and construct itself as and persuasively to project itself as to its key audiences—both its 'dual' citizens[260] and its state interlocutors. Questions of constitutional definition, then, remain just as important to answer at the supranational as at the state level. Whether it is or will ever be possible to answer them in a manner that commands general agreement—even at this second-order framing level—is much less clear.

The Court and the Legal Constitution

In invoking constitutionalism for the first time, the Court assumed and postulated as its second-order framing context or register in *Les Verts* the legal or juridical constitution. But what, more specifically, did this choice signify? To answer this, we have to dig a little more deeply into the distinctive socio-historical situation and trajectory of European supranationalism

That the ECJ should be primarily interested in the legal framework of the polity or putative polity within which it operates is unremarkable. From time to time all higher

[259] See, eg, Maduro, above note 256.
[260] Art 17 EC.

courts may be required to take note of and reflect upon the broad institutional, and, more rarely, the authoritative and social dimensions of the polity within which they operate, and may occasionally be able to make a difference in each of these registers by interpreting or re-interpreting its framework 'constitutional' meaning.[261] However, for a court the immediate frame, and the one to which by the very nature of its structural role as final guardian and arbiter of the law it may stand in an internal, constitutive relationship, is the juridical frame. And of all the constitutionally generative frames that tend to be treated as always or already in place at the state level, the possession of a self-standing legal order is without doubt *the* most taken for granted. This is partly because the legal order often predates the other orders in the evolution of the polity. What is more, its presence is presupposed in and by the presence of the other three constitutional registers—institutional, authoritative and social. So the legal order is both framework and object of the institutional design, it provides the full and more detailed regulatory reference point of the authorised or 'constituted' text, and it offers a normative model of and for its host 'society'. In short, it supplies a framing register without which it is impossible to situate and articulate any of the other framing registers.

Manifestly, however, the legal frame has not been taken for granted in the short history of the EU. Here, the combination of two indisputable absences—the absence of the evolution of any legal tradition indigenous to the supranational level prior to the founding Treaties of the 1950s, and the absence of any strong early-post-Treaty sense of the simultaneous emergence of a European polity in the deeper authoritative and social frames of constitutionalism—entailed that the legal frame lay exposed *above* the watermark of active and visible constitutional construction. Operating in a dynamic of mutual development with the new institutional frame, the legal order provided the basic ground on which a putative post-state polity sought to generate its first polity-constitutive elaborations and engagements.

Indeed, the widely recognised vital importance of the ECJ's early labelling of the community juridical system as 'a new legal order'[262] lies precisely in its self-anchoring of the basic legal frame. And even the most basic sketch of what is involved in the very idea of the identity or integrity or 'self-containment'[263] of a legal order shows up many elements where the ECJ has consolidated or built upon the foundations of the Treaty text. These include: the *self-ordering* properties of the putative legal order—its capacity through the development of doctrines such as supremacy and direct effect to embed and give priority to certain 'secondary' norms and to generate its own comprehensive body of 'primary' norms in accordance with the relevant secondary norms; its *self-defining* properties—its control, through the Court's insistence on having the final word, of its own jurisdiction or ambit of competence and also of the interpretation of its own normative meaning and

[261] In the EU context, a classic (and suitably rare) example is the *Maastricht* judgment of the German Constitutional Court, in which 'framing' questions of the security of the democratic 'constituent' pedigree of the German polity and the weakness of the social conditions required to ground the European polity were both to the fore. See *Brunner v European Union Treaty* 89 BVerfGE 155 [1994] 1 CMLR 57.

[262] *Van Gend en Loos v Nederlandse Administratie der Belastingen* [1963] ECR 1; *Costa v ENEL* [1964] ECR 585.

[263] To borrow the language of international law. See, eg B Simma and D Pulkowski, 'Of Planets and the Universe: Self-Contained Regimes in International Law' (2006) 17 *European Journal of International Law* 483–529.

purpose more generally; and its *self-enforcing* qualities—its capacity through the development of a body of adjectival or procedural law and associated sanctions to ensure the effective application of its own norms.[264]

But why, given the absence or weakness of the usual second-order constitutional accompaniments in the authoritative and social registers, should these labours of legal order self-construction and self-affirmation have come in due course to implicate the 'c' word? The answer is twofold, reflecting again the combination of status and value at the heart of constitutionalism.

First, there is the question of status. Just as it is not surprising that the Court has been deeply implicated in asserting and refining the integrity of the legal order *qua* legal order, so we should not be surprised that—even in this baseline juridical register— constitutionalisation has proved to be a protracted, complex and in some respects controversial affair. As the supranational legal order is not just another state legal order, it cannot simply be allocated to its own discrete box within the Westphalian system of state legal orders. Rather in the new 'relational'[265] global structure ushered in by European supranationalism and other transnational regimes, there is inevitably significant overlap between the EU's legal concerns and capacities and those of its Member States. In this changing configuration, self-ordering, self-definition and self-enforcement can never be complete. Legal 'autonomy without territorial exclusivity',[266] however, with autonomy understood as the external face of integrity—as the absence, at least in terms of a legal order's dominant self-understanding, of an overall relationship of dependence upon and subservience to any other legal order(s)—*is* still possible. And in the complex, part-competitive and part co-operative play of plural but interlocking legal orders, the invocation of the status-conferring, polity-implying language of constitutionalism can amplify and help bolster the claims to integrity and autonomy made on behalf of the EU legal order.

Second, there is the question of value, which, as always in the constitutional dynamic, depends upon the factual baseline of 'good working order'. For what the self-ordering, self-definition self-enforcement and overall (relative) autonomy of the legal order also make possible is a project of normative *self-discipline*; the aspiration that the legal order be sufficiently expansive in the coverage of its primary norms (self-ordering) and in its rules of standing, justiciability and liability (self-enforcement) and have acquired sufficient interpretive autonomy and flexibility (self-definition) to ensure that no actors implicated in the legal order, especially the institutional or governmental actors of that order, escape the discipline of legal restraint in accordance with that order. This idea of government limited by law, indeed, is a key part of all Western European legal traditions, whether couched in the language of 'rule of law', or *état de droit* or *Rechtstaat*, and in each case is a cornerstone of constitutionalism understood as a value-based discourse.

It might seem perfectly natural and unobjectionable, then, that the ECJ in *Les Verts* should choose the moment of consecration of the value-based 'rule of law' dimension of 'its' legal order to invoke the language of constitutionalism—indeed to insist, as the Court did, that the application of the label 'constitutional charter' to the Treaty framework and

[264] See, eg, N Walker, 'EU Constitutionalism in the State Constitutional Tradition' (2006) *Current Legal Problems* 51–90.

[265] *Ibid*, 70.

[266] See, eg, N Walker, 'Late Sovereignty in the European Union' in N Walker (ed), *Sovereignty in Transition* (Oxford, Hart Publishing, 2003) 3–32 at 23.

the descriptor 'community based on the rule of law' go hand in hand. What is more, although it might be argued that, as a matter of form and process, the Court was presumptuous or premature in extending its supervisory authority on its own initiative rather than leaving this to the legislative branch,[267] few if any would complain that, as a matter of principle, it was anything other than an improvement in 'rule of law' terms to subject the Parliament, as the supranational organ whose competence and capacity was expanding most rapidly during the relevant period, to a closer system of legal monitoring. Indeed, the fact that in subsequent and successive Treaty amendments at Maastricht and Amsterdam the Member States gave the highest legislative imprimatur, first, to the idea that the acts of Parliament be judicially reviewable,[268] and secondly, to the foundational status of the principle of 'rule of law'[269] in the jurisprudence of the Union, speaks to just such an accord. Yet if we keep in mind the wider symbolic picture painted above, a number of related doubts emerge about the wider consequences of the Court's choice of constitutional opening.

To begin with, by leading with constitutionalism's more attractive value-based face, the Court arguably drew attention away from the other and more contentious status claim associated with constitutionalism as an integrated and autonomous legal order. A short response to this charge would be that the Court was simply not concerned with that other dimension of constitutionalism in *Les Verts*. Yet if we recall that the 'de facto' claim of independent efficacy—the Janus-face of constitutionalism—is already presupposed by any broader value claim made on behalf of that independently efficacious order, then the status dimension cannot be so readily denied. This becomes apparent when we look to the only other case that it is well known for its recitation of the idea of the Treaty framework as a constitutional charter—namely the Court's first Opinion on the EEA Agreement handed down in 1991.[270] Here, the Court was 'strikingly assertive'[271] in its efforts to protect the integrity of the European legal order. The self-standing 'constitutional' status of the EC framework was explicitly contrasted with the merely 'international treaty basis' of the EEA. Diminished by that comparison, the proposed EEA Court, which would have had jurisdiction to interpret in a manner binding on its quite distinct Contracting Parties a corpus of trade and commercial law identical in wording to that found within the EC legal framework, was duly struck down as claiming a remit supposedly incompatible with the exclusive jurisdiction of the ECJ in the resolution of disputes over the interpretation or application of the EC Treaty—and so with the self-defining capacity of the EU legal order more generally.

Recalling the caveat with which the article began, we should not, however, be tempted to make too much of all this in doctrinal terms. On the few other occasions where the ECJ or its advocates-general or the Court of First Instance have referred to the idea of a constitutional charter[272] this has not been in pursuit of a protective or expansive agenda in

[267] See, eg, T Hartley, *The Foundations of European Community Law* 5th edn (Oxford, Oxford University Press, 2003), 80–1. But see S Douglas-Scott, *Constitutional law of the European Union* (Harlow, Longman, 2002) 351.

[268] See now Art 230 EC.

[269] See now Art 6 TEU.

[270] *Opinion 1/91(Draft Opinion on the EEA)* [1991] ECR I-6079.

[271] S Weatherill and P Beaumont, *EU Law* 3rd edn (London, Penguin, 1999) 7.

[272] The ECJ has been particularly reticent about using the constitutional charter language in the post-Maastricht years. For a rare exception, see Case C-15/00 *Commission v European Investment Bank* 2003/C 213/01.

terms of the 'legal order' status dimension of legal constitutionalism, as in the first EEA reference, but has instead reverted to the 'rule of law' dimension that dominated in *Les Verts*—to the Court's role as guardian and 'conscience' of the legal order rather than simply as its champion. More generally, moreover, while the constitutional rhetoric may have added some incidental ballast to both the 'rule of law' dimension and the 'legal order' dimension of the ECJ's reasoning in the relevant cases, it is simply not plausible to argue that in any particular instance it has made a decisive contribution in allowing the Court to advance into jurisprudential terrain that it could not otherwise have claimed.[273] That is to say, for all its rhetorical charge, the constitutional symbolism has not made *any* apparent internal doctrinal difference to the *acquis*.

What, then, of the contribution of the Court's symbolic language to the wider political debate on European constitutionalism? In leading with the value rather than the status dimension, the Court may have contributed marginally to the dissemination of a more 'virtuous' impression of legal constitutionalism, but this begs a deeper question. Should the Court have spoken in the register of legal *constitutionalism* at all, and what were the implications of its so doing? On the one hand, as already noted, of all the second-order constitutional frames, the legal frame is the most immediately and naturally within the Court's contemplation, and its explicit endorsement of that frame is to that extent predictable and unexceptionable. On the other hand, to suggest that this is an entirely innocent usage is to ignore the power of a certain type of narrative in the European constitutional debate.

As we have seen, it is precisely the second order question in its broadest variant—whether it is *ever* appropriate to invoke the discourse of constitutionalism for a non-state entity—that focuses the key 'polity identity' question for the EU. Crudely, the choice of answers opens up two fault lines.[274] One concerns those who believe the statist template of constitutionalism to be the only template meaningfully and legitimately available, and who on that basis sharply divide between traditional state-centred sceptics who believe the invocation of the idea of constitutionalism at the supranational level either to be concerned at root only with the limitation of supranational power in the name of state interests or, more categorically, to be a simple 'category error',[275] and those whose endorsement of the constitutional idea struggles not to sound like, and indeed function like, a bid for 'superstate' status. The other fault line is between the 'statist' mindset, with this sharp internal division, and an alternative cluster of mindsets which view the EU, and EU constitutionalism, as being *sui generic*—as possessing a meaning and a legitimacy independent of the statist template. Arguably, an important source of the current tribulations of European constitutionalism lies in the historical dominance of the *sui generic* approach. For, while that approach has been increasingly comfortable in entertaining the language of constitutionalism, in so doing it has failed properly to come to terms

[273] This, of course, is a double-edged conclusion. It may suggest a prudent avoidance of constitutional overreach. But on another, more negative, view, it suggests a lack of constitutional ambition. So it has frequently been remarked that the Court's constitutional rhetoric has failed to cure the palpable 'rule of law' defect of absence of effective judicial supervision of the Second (CFSP) Pillar. See, eg, B de Witte, 'The Nice Declaration: Time for a Constitutional Treaty of the European Union?' (2001) 36 *International Spectator* 21–30 at 22.

[274] For a less crudely reductive analysis of these positions, see N Walker, 'Europe's Constitutional Momentum and the Search for Polity Legitimacy' (2005) 4 *International Journal of Constitutional Law* 211–38.

[275] See A Moravcsik, 'A Category Error' (July 2006) *Prospect* 22–26 at 25.

with the statist tradition either, sociologically, as an resilient influence on the trajectory of constitutional debate at any site or, normatively, as a still relevant (if not decisive) evaluative measure of polity-building.

It is this *sui generic* approach that the Court has contributed to—a narrative of constitutional self-understanding focused upon incrementalism and the patient building of the legal and institutional infrastructure of the polity, but with little reference to its authoritative and social registers. It is a story, then, of disaggregated and 'low-intensity constitutionalism'[276] in which the absence of the co-articulate registers of constitutionalism familiar from the state constitutional *whole* is seen as no bar to the use of constitutional discourse for its discrete and modest *parts.* It is a story in which the Court's early implicit system-building legal constitutionalism plays a key role, but one which is given added definition by the later supply of a top layer of explicit constitutional discourse starting with *Les Verts.*[277] Crucially, it is a story that, in its reassuring 'low politics' modesty, helped make the recent documentary debate possible and one that, in turn, entered that debate in pole position, in search of 'vindication'[278] and homologation of its half century of accumulated wisdom—and so of final closure. Yet it is also a story which, given the very procedural and symbolic framework of that debate, not to mention its deeper if more attenuated origins in the increasingly controversial post-Maastricht 'high politics' of the EU, was unlikely ever to succeed in these narrow terms. For, notwithstanding the conservative ambitions of the vindicationalists with their default commitment to *droit constant*,[279] the very introduction of an element of popular political engagement to the constitutional debate through the explicitly documentary project of the Convention followed by national ratification imitated the procedures and invoked the 'Philadelphian' rituals of state documentary constitutionalism. And in so doing, it both created a window of opportunity and provided a symbolic cue for those of statist mindset—whether the nation state or an incipient European state—to air their constructive or critical voices.

To revert to the narrative metaphor, the incremental constitutional story now ran into other and, for some, more resonant constitutional stories based upon state-coded fears or hopes about European integration. According to these narratives and the visions of Europe's future that accompanied them, the time of documentary constitutional reckoning was not to be understood and seen as a celebration of the past 50 years and as a triumph of continuity, but as something discontinuous; as an occasion either to place definitive state-protecting limits on the development of the EU, or to push forward towards a more federalist institutional design and political culture. In so doing, these other

[276] M Maduro, 'The Importance of Being Called a Constitution' (2005) 4 *International Journal of Constitutional Law* 332–56 at 340.

[277] The narrative element cannot be overstated. I have lost count of the number of accounts of EU constitutionalisation I have read which have invoked *Les Verts* as a standard reference in the roll-call of key events. Indeed the relevant narrative has become so stylised, so formulaic, that it reads (and functions) like a mantra.

[278] Walker, above note 273, 228–30.

[279] In the protracted politics of the documentary constitutional debate, it is easy to lose sight of how much the initial ambitions of the landmark European Council meeting in Laeken in 2001 setting up the (Constitution-pioneering) Convention on the Future of Europe were linked to the consolidating virtues of simplification and reorganisation, and so to the vindicationalist agenda. Indeed it is only in the context of these modest goals that the 'C' word was used *at all* in the Laeken Declaration, and even then only as a long-term aspiration; Laeken Declaration on the Future of the European Union, Annex I to the Conclusions of the Laeken European Council, 14–15 December 2001, SN 300/101 Rev 1.

approaches asked tough evaluative questions of the existing 'thin' European constitutionalism from a 'thick' state-based register. In particular, they challenged the plausibility in principle and adequacy in practice of the EU's constitutional framing credentials in political and social registers—whether and on what basis we might talk of a self-standing and broadly inclusive constituent power and a distinctive European society as the respective subject and object of a European Constitution.

The unsurprising failure to find an early common answer to these questions has left the European constitutional debate in a hard place. The two fault lines remain, contributing to the ultimate failure of the first Constitutional Treaty and, as shown by the subsequent tribulations of the Lisbon Treaty,[280] frustrating attempts to find a way ahead at the level of broad polity development and definition even when, in reaction to the earlier failure, an explicitly constitutional language is once again eschewed. In the last analysis, there can be no closed and predefined right direction dictated by any of these distinctive polity visions—*sui generic*, statist or federalist—only the way, if any, that is found through the ongoing constitutional process; for there is in fact an internal and constructive relationship between any constitutional process that is capable of being the subject of both initial agreement and successful resolution on the one hand, and, on the other, the emergence of a polity vision that may plausibly claim and may further mobilise the overlapping consensus of the European people(s). In other words, the constitutional future of the EU is not fated to be the modest affair intimated by the Court, or indeed to correspond to *any* predetermined template, but is an open question that can only be resolved, if at all, through the constitutional (or some functionally equivalent) process itself.

The irony of the Court's modest contribution to constitutional modesty, then, is acute. Without the incremental understanding of polity development to which it contributed, an explicit political discourse and process of constitutionalism may not have emerged at all. But that truncated polity vision, in tending to close itself off from the thicker and more politically contentious questions of Europe's polity identity that a fully fledged constitutional debate inevitably raised, may also have contributed to the subsequent inability to find the minimal common terms which would allow such a debate to proceed in a fruitful manner. Only time will tell whether these paradoxical conditions of origin have merely accelerated the necessary growing pains of European constitutionalism, or whether instead they will prevent it from ever reaching maturity.

[280] See eg, N Walker 'Not the European Constitution' (2008) 15 *Maastricht Journal of European and Comparative Law* 135–41.

IX

Case C-85/96, *María Martínez Sala v Freistaat Bayern* and Case C-413/99, *Baumbast and R v Secretary of State for the Home Department*

1

Martínez Sala and *Baumbast* revisited

CHRISTIAAN TIMMERMANS*

In revisiting these two decisions of the Court of Justice[1] I propose to discuss essentially three questions: what has been the added value of these decisions? Is there any specific rationale that could explain this evolution in the case law? And, finally, has this new line of jurisprudence been confirmed and is there still potential for further evolution?

The Added Value of *Martínez Sala* and *Baumbast*

Citizenship of the Union, as a new status granted to the nationals of the Member States, was introduced by the Treaty of Maastricht of 1992 with the obvious aim of bringing the Union closer to its citizens. Many commentators at the time expected these new provisions of the EC Treaty, and particularly the articles which are now Articles 17 and 18 EC, to add little to the already existing Community law rights on free movement provided by the EC Treaty and secondary legislation.[2] The main message sent by the Court's decisions in *Martínez Sala* and *Baumbast* has been to contradict these expectations. They demonstrate that these provisions do not contain empty phrases and that they can have important legal consequences.

In that respect, both decisions are of course remarkably different. Baumbast has much further reaching consequences than Martínez Sala. The latter decision is still rather classic in its approach—it is daring, however, in the application of that approach. Mrs Sala, a Spanish national lawfully residing in Germany, was refused a child-caring allowance because she was not able to produce a residence permit, a formal condition which did not apply to German nationals wishing to obtain that allowance. The Court approaches the question under the heading of the prohibition of discrimination based on nationality laid down in Article 12 EC. The existence of such discrimination was in itself easily established, but could Mrs Sala benefit from this rule under the Treaty? She could, so the Court said, because as a citizen of the Union, according to Article 17, paragraph 2, she enjoyed the rights conferred by the Treaty. As a citizen of the Union, lawfully residing in a Member

* Judge of the Court of Justice of the European Communities. This contribution was concluded in February 2007.

[1] Case C-85/96 *Martínez Sala* [1998] ECR I-2691 and Case C-413/99 *Baumbast* [2002] ECR I-7091.

[2] Joseph Weiler, for instance, favoured the hypothesis 'that the citizenship clause … is little more than a cynical exercise in public relations on the part of the High Contracting Parties noteworthy more by what it does not do than what it does and which probably has backfired even as an exercise in public relations'. JHH Weiler, 'European Citizenship and Human Rights', in Jan A Winter *et al* (eds), *Reforming the Treaty on European Union—The Legal Debate* (The Hague, TMC Asser Instituut, 1996), 57 at 65 and 68.

State other than that of her origin, she could invoke the principle of non-discrimination under Article 12 EC in view of the fact that the child-caring allowance, *ratione materiae*, fell within the scope of application of the Treaty. The latter conclusion is perhaps the most daring step in the Court's reasoning. It justifies this conclusion by referring to the answers already given in the judgment as to the possible applicability of Article 7, paragraph 2 of Regulation 1612/68 and Regulation 1408/71 with regard to the child-caring allowance. This justification has been criticised because the possible application of these regulations does not explain why the allowance would also fall within the scope of application of the Treaty in a situation where neither of these Regulations applies.[3]

This, indeed, reveals the difficulty of the in itself attractive, because *prima facie* simple, approach of applying the prohibition of discrimination based on nationality: in each case it must be demonstrated that the substantive issue to which the discrimination relates falls within the scope of the Treaty. Subsequent case law, preceding the Court's decision in Baumbast, however, has followed a more sophisticated approach in this respect.[4] In the cases of *Bickel and Franz*,[5] *Grzelczyk*[6] and *D'Hoop*,[7] the Court accepted the situation of the Union citizen as coming, *ratione materiae*, within the scope of the Treaty because of the link between the personal situation of the persons concerned and the fact that they had exercised the right of free movement under Article 18 EC.[8] In *D'Hoop*, for instance, a Belgian national was refused the so-called tide-over allowance, an unemployment benefit granted under Belgian legislation to young people having completed their studies and seeking their first employment. The reason for that refusal was that Ms D'Hoop had obtained her secondary school diploma in France and not in Belgium. Consequently, it was because Ms D'Hoop had exercised her right of free movement under Article 18 EC that she was refused the allowance. As the exercise of the right of free movement was involved, her situation was considered to come within the scope of the Treaty, which allowed her to invoke the principle of non-discrimination under Article 12 EC. It is interesting to note that in applying this principle the Court does not pay particular attention to a condition of nationality, but seems to apply a principle of equal treatment according to which Union citizens having exercised their right of free movement must be treated equally in comparison with Union citizens who did not.[9] This approach—and that is its advantage—makes a separate analysis of whether the *sedes materiae* itself, in the case of Ms D'Hoop an allowance such as the tide-over allowance, falls within the scope of the Treaty, superfluous. That such an analysis may be delicate was already demonstrated by the decision in *Martínez Sala. Bickel and Franz* provides another example. Both persons, respectively an Austrian and a German national, involved in criminal proceedings in the city of Bolzano, invoked the language regime applying in the Province of Bolzano allowing German-speaking citizens to use the German language in court proceedings. Could they have recourse to the principle of non-discrimination under Article 12 EC in order to be

[3] See Christian Tomuschat, 'Radical Equality under Article 12 of the EC Treaty? The case of *Martínez Sala*' (2000) *CML Rev* 449.

[4] For a more detailed analysis see my contribution, 'Lifting the Veil of Union Citizens' Rights, to the Festschrift for Gil Carlos Rodríguez Iglesias, Une Communauté de droit' (Berlin, 2003) 95.

[5] Case C-274/96 [1998] ECR I-7637.

[6] Case C-184/99 [2001] ECR I-6193.

[7] Case C-224/98 [2002] ECR I-6191.

[8] See the in this respect more particular situation in Case C-403/03 *Schempp* [2005] ECR I-6421; see moreover Joined Cases C-502/01 and C-31/02 *Gaumain-Cerri* and *Barth* [2004] ECR I-6483.

[9] A further example is given by Case C-224/02 *Pusa* [2004] ECR I-5774.

able to benefit from this regime? The Court decided that persons in a situation like that of Bickel and Franz should be able to benefit from that principle because, having exercised their right of free movement under Article 18 EC, their situation should be considered as being governed by Community law. This conclusion dispensed the Court from considering the difficult question of whether the language regime in itself, *ratione materiae*, fell within the scope of the Treaty.

Whereas the decision in *Martínez Sala*, as further developed by subsequent case law, eased access for the Union citizen by virtue of Article 17 EC to the benefits of the principle of non-discrimination under Article 12 EC, the decision in *Baumbast*, taken four years later, still goes an important step further in accepting possible legal consequences flowing from the status of Union citizenship.[10] Mr Baumbast, a German national living in the United Kingdom but working for German companies in third countries, could not derive a right of residence in the UK from one of the economic freedoms under the EC Treaty, nor could he obtain such a right under the general Directive 90/364 on the right of residence because he did not satisfy the condition of a complete sickness insurance. The Court accepted, however, that he could directly invoke the right to move and reside under Article 18 EC. The Court accepts that right as a directly enforceable Community law right contrary to the position taken by the Member States intervening in the case and the Commission, but following the Opinion of Advocate General Geelhoed and Opinions already earlier expressed by Advocate Generals La Pergola[11] and Cosmas.[12] The Court rejected the main counter-argument based on the wording of Article 18 EC which makes the exercise of the right of free movement 'subject to the limitations and conditions laid down in this Treaty and by the measures adopted to give it effect', by considering that the application of such limitations and conditions is subject to judicial review. Baumbast itself confirms the reality of such judicial review. The Court, first of all, probes the justification of the financial conditions on which the exercise of the right of residence granted by Directive 90/364 is made dependent.[13] It implicitly accepts the legitimate interest of Member States, as referred to by the preamble of the Directive, to prevent that beneficiaries of the right of residence become an unreasonable burden on the public finances of the host Member State. However, the important proviso is added that the limitations and conditions referred to by Article 18 EC must be applied in compliance with the limits imposed by Community law and in accordance with the general principles of that law, in particular the principle of proportionality. As to a situation like Mr Baumbast's, the Court concludes, referring to the specific circumstances of the case, that refusing a right of residence under Article 18 EC would amount to a disproportionate interference with the exercise of that right.

The main innovation achieved by Baumbast is the acceptance of the right of free movement of the Union citizens conferred by Article 18 EC as a directly enforceable Community law right allowing that right to be upheld in Member States' courts against

[10] In fact there exists already an earlier, albeit less explicit, example: Case C-135/99 *Ursula Elsen* [2000] ECR I-10409.

[11] See Case C-85/96 *Martínez Sala* [1998] ECR I-2694.

[12] See Case C-378/97 *Wijsenbeek* [1999] ECR I-6209.

[13] Council Directive 90/364/EEC on the right of residence [1990] OJ L 180.

national measures unduly restricting that right. Subsequent case law has confirmed the possible impact of the right of free movement and the reality of judicial control as to restrictions of this right.

How to Explain this Evolution in the Case Law?

I shall consider this question more particularly with regard to the decision in *Baumbast*, *Martínez Sala* being, as I have said, much more traditional in its approach.

Is Baumbast another example of judicial activism for which the European Court of Justice is sometimes criticised? In my view it is not, but I might not be the best placed to answer that question. Let me just mention the following four elements which, I think, should be taken into account when discussing the rationale of this case law:

(1) There is, first of all, the wording itself of Article 18, which is the normal starting point for the interpretation process. Article 18 states unambiguously: 'Every citizen of the Union shall have the right to move and reside freely within the territory of the member States [...]'. Apart from the 'subject to the limitations and conditions [...]' clause to which I shall return, this text is clear and precise as the Court underlines in para 84 of its decision in *Baumbast*. It is moreover drafted in the strong terms of a 'right' which is being conferred on the citizens of the Union. It is true that Article 18 as amended by the Treaty of Nice, which entered into force after the Court's decision in *Baumbast*, now, refers in its second paragraph to the right of free movement conferred by the first paragraph in terms of an 'objective'. I do not think, however, that any significance should be attached to this change in wording because that same paragraph, subsequently maintains the 'rights' terminology.

(2) Secondly, this right is recognised at the level of the Treaty, that is, by primary law. The Court does not mention this, but having such a right which was already recognised by secondary legislation in the three directives previously mentioned, solemnly proclaimed by the EC Treaty itself in a New Part Two of that Treaty, immediately after the First Part on Principles, must carry some weight when considering the scope and status of this right. The Treaty on European Union reinforces this argument where in Article 2 of that Treaty it states as an objective of the Union: 'to strengthen the protection of the rights and interests of the nationals of its Member States through the introduction of a citizenship of the Union'. This might have been all the more reason for the Court to take the rights defined by Articles 17 and 18 EC seriously.

(3) The main objection to the acceptance of a directly effective Community law right of free movement under Article 18, as put forward in *Baumbast* by the intervening Member States and the Commission, relates to 'the limitations and restrictions' clause to which the right of free movement is being made subject. The Court dismisses that argument by simply stating that the application of that clause is subject to judicial review. For those who are familiar with the Court's case law on direct effect of Community law, this statement cannot have come as a surprise. As long ago as 1974 the Court ruled in the *Van Duyn* case that the explicit exception clauses to the fundamental freedoms such as the public policy exception under what is now Article 39, paragraph 3 EC, cannot be invoked as an argument to deny the direct effect of the fundamental Treaty rules on free movement of workers, the application of such an

exception being subject to judicial review.[14] Numerous examples can be found in the case law demonstrating that vague notions used by a Community law provision, the application of which may entail some margin of appreciation, or even provisions granting discretionary powers by allowing a choice between various options, do not necessarily exclude direct effect to be given to such provisions.[15]

(4) Fourthly, and finally, there is an element which is often forgotten when wondering why the Court has arrived at a certain interpretation which is considered to be important and innovative. That element is the referral decision of the national court, its motivation and more particularly the content of the preliminary questions themselves. Quite often, a new interpretation given by the Court builds upon the interpretative elements already discussed in the national reference and the arguments submitted by the parties in the main proceedings. It is not rare that it is the question as put forward by the national court and the way in which that question is drafted, which invites the Court to explore new avenues of interpretation and in a way unlocks the door to a new development in the interpretation of Community law. I regard this as one of the more substantive consequences of the dialogue between national courts and the European Court of Justice within the framework of the preliminary procedure. The *Baumbast* case itself gives a good example. The UK Immigration Appeal Tribunal explicitly raised the question about the direct effect of the right of residence pursuant to Article 18 EC and its decision touched upon the question of whether Article 18 grants any additional right of residence not found anywhere else in the Treaty. More generally, it can be said that all the early preliminary decisions on Union citizenship concerned situations where the persons concerned suffered from disadvantages linked to cross-border movement, difficulties which could not be resolved under the existing secondary legislation on free movement. Apparently, the referring national courts, by raising in most of these cases explicit questions as to the possible impact of Union citizens' rights, considered that the negative effects of cross-border movement fitted uneasily with the new language of the Treaty on Union citizens' rights, particularly that of free movement.

Has this New Line of Jurisprudence Been Confirmed? Is there still Potential for Further Evolution?

My answer to both questions would be an unqualified yes.

Obviously, the in itself cautiously phrased interpretation given in *Baumbast*, the results of which were closely linked to the circumstances of the case, has important potential for further development. The recognition of a directly effective right of the Union citizen to move and reside freely in the territory of another Member State could imply that this right can be invoked to oppose national measures restricting this right. If so, such restrictions, including their possible justification, would become justiciable under Article 18 EC. As to the justification, the existence of Community legislation allowing for specific conditions or limitations is, of course, relevant but not necessarily conclusive as Baumbast itself has

[14] Case 41/74 [1974] ECR-1337. In para 86 of its Decision in *Baumbast* the Court refers to this case.
[15] See, eg, Case 51/76 *VNO* [1977] ECR 113 and Case C-72/95 *Kraaijeveld* [1996] ECR I-5403.

shown. All this would mean that the fundamental right of free movement of the Union citizen under Article 18 EC could obtain a status similar to the fundamental economic freedoms of the Treaty (free movement of goods, services and capital, free movement of workers, right of establishment), in so far as this right of free movement would imply a prohibition of unjustified restrictions of this right. Another consequence could be that, just like the economic freedoms,[16] this right of free movement may restrict the discretion of the Community legislature when regulating the conditions for the exercise of this right. Also the Community legislature would have to respect the essence of this right and be barred from arbitrary or disproportionate intrusions of this right. Baumbast itself already demonstrated that the conditions imposed by the Directives on the right of residence (Directives 90/364, 90/365 and 93/94),[17] or at least the application of those conditions in an individual case, are not immune from judicial review.

Subsequent case law appears to have largely exploited this potential of the *Baumbast* decision. There has indeed been an evolution confirming the directly enforceable right of free movement under Article 18 EC to imply a prohibition of unjustified restrictions of the exercise of that right.

The decision of 29 April 2004 in Pusa[18] already goes a long way in accepting this. Mr Pusa, a Finish national who had moved to Spain, received a pension paid out in Finland on which an attachment had been authorised for the purpose of recovering a debt. In calculating the attachable part of the pension, the income tax paid by Mr Pusa in Spain was not deducted whereas, if he had resided in Finland, the tax which he would have then paid in Finland would have been so deducted. The referring Finnish Court asked whether Article 18 EC or any other rule of Community law precludes such legislation. The Court in giving an (in principle) affirmative answer to this question, does not refer explicitly to Article 18 EC. Indeed, the motivation of its answer is at first set in the key of the principle of non-discrimination based on nationality just as in previous cases like *Grzelczyk*, *D'Hoop* and *Garcia Avello* to which the Court refers. However, in developing its reasoning, the Court uses language which puts the emphasis on Article 18 EC and the right of free movement which the Member States must respect when exercising their competence with regard to enforcement for the recovery of debts (see paragraphs 22 and 31 particularly).[19]

The Decision of 19 October 2004 in *Chen* further confirms the autonomous nature of the right of free movement as a self-standing right, the restriction of which can under certain circumstances be directly opposed under Article 18 EC.[20] Mrs Chen had given birth to her child Catherine in Belfast so as to let her acquire Irish nationality. Under the then existing Irish legislation on nationality, each person born in Ireland, including Northern Ireland, was regarded as being an Irish national. The Court accepted that a child like Catherine had acquired the status of a citizen of the Union and could invoke the right of residence under Article 18 EC, in view of the fact that the financial conditions laid down in Directive 90/364 were also satisfied. The Court, moreover, accepted that Mrs

[16] See, eg, Cases 80 and 81/77 *Henri Ramel* [1978] ECR 927, 37/83 *Rewe* [1984] ECR 1229 and C-114/96 *Kieffer* [1997] ECR I-3629.

[17] Council Directive 90/364/EEC on the right of residence [1990] OJ L180; Council Directive 90/365/EC on the right of residence for employees and self-employed persons who have ceased their occupational activity [1990] OJ L 180; Council Directive 93/96/EEC on the right of residence of students [1993] OJ L 317.

[18] Case C-224/02 [2004] ECR I-5774.

[19] See also Case C-520/04 *Turpeinen* [2006] ECR I-10685.

[20] Case C-200/02 [2004] ECR I-9951.

Chen, who was of Chinese nationality, could also derive a right of residence from Article 18 EC because refusing her to reside with her child in the host Member State would deprive the child's right of residence of any useful effect. Article 18 EC was thus construed as prohibiting a restriction of the right of free movement.

The first case in which the Court explicitly interprets the right of free movement pursuant to Article 18 EC as including a general prohibition of unjustified restrictions of that right, quite similar to the approach followed for the economic fundamental freedoms, is that of De Cuyper, in a judgment of 18 July 2006, decided by the Grand Chamber.[21] Mr De Cuyper, a Belgian national, enjoyed an unemployment allowance in Belgium. After a certain period he was dispensed of the obligations to submit to the local control procedures imposed on unemployed persons and to register as a job seeker. However, under the applicable rules, he was still required to actually reside in Belgium. When an inquiry by the competent Belgian authority revealed that he was resident in France, his allowance was discontinued. Moreover, he was asked to reimburse the amount of the allowances received as from the date of his residence in France. The Brussels Labour Court submitted carefully phrased questions, essentially asking the Court whether Articles 17 and 18 EC preclude a residence requirement in a situation like that of Mr De Cuyper.

The Court gives a general, principled interpretation of the scope of the right of free movement pursuant to Article 18 EC, phrased in terms well-known from the case law on the economic fundamental freedoms:

> 39. It is established that national legislation such as that in this case which places at a disadvantage certain of its nationals simply because they have exercised their freedom to move and to reside in another Member State is a restriction on the freedoms conferred by Article 18 EC on every citizen of the Union.
>
> 40. Such a restriction can be justified, with regard to Community law, only if it is based on objective considerations of public interest independent of the nationality of the persons concerned and proportionate to the legitimate objective of the national provisions.

In the end, the residence requirement was deemed justified by the Court.

This precedent has been followed by the Decision of 28 October 2006 in *Tas-Hagen*.[22] The case concerns a Dutch regime on benefits for civilian victims of the Second World War, the benefit of which was refused to Mrs Tas-Hagen and Mr Tas because although their status as civilian war victims was recognised, at the moment they introduced their demand they had moved their residence from the Netherlands to Spain. The judgment, first of all, well illustrates the difference between an approach based on Article 17 and 12 EC—the *Martínez Sala* approach—and a direct application of Article 18 EC alone. Once again—and I refer to what I said earlier on the important role of the referring court in phrasing the preliminary questions—the national court, as in *De Cuyper*, focused its question on the interpretation of Article 18 EC. Some of the Member States intervening in the *Tas-Hagen* case argued that Article 18 EC could not be relied upon because the regime at issue in this case did not fall, *ratione materiae*, within the scope of Community law. Such a condition, which indeed needs to be satisfied to allow the non-discrimination principle of Article 12 EC to be invoked, was rejected by the Court with regard to Article 18 EC. It admitted that the matter at issue fell within the competence of the Member States but

[21] Case C-406/04 [2006] ECR I-6971.

[22] Case C-192/05 [2006] ECR I-10451.

Member States must exercise that competence in accordance with Community law, in particular the Treaty provisions on free movement of Union citizens. This wording closely resembles that used in the case law on the other fundamental freedoms, for instance regarding the relationship between those freedoms and national rules on direct taxation. The Court then considers that the right of free movement pursuant to Article 18 EC is involved in the case at hand for it was because of having exercised that right, that the applicants were refused the benefit in question. The Court, therefore, had no difficulty in establishing in a situation like this the existence of a restriction of the right of free movement. The notion of restriction is rather widely construed in terms which echo the definition of restriction ('entrave') in the context of the economic fundamental freedoms (the national legislation 'is liable to dissuade Netherlands nationals ... from exercising their freedom to move and reside outside the Netherlands').[23] The Court then examines the justification of the measure on the basis of a Rule of Reason (public interest test) defined in the same terms as in *De Cuyper*, to finally conclude that a condition of residence such as that used in the main proceedings fails to comply with the principle of proportionality.

This important evolution of the case law since *Baumbast* as to the acceptance of the directly applicable right of free movement pursuant to Article 18 EC as a prohibition of unjustified restrictions of that right has not replaced the *Martínez Sala* approach based on Articles 17 and 12 EC, nor made that approach superfluous. Also following *Baumbast*, cases have been decided by the Court on the basis of the latter approach. Again, that might be explained in the first place, by the fact that the referring national court had phrased its questions according to that approach. However, there are indeed cases in which a direct application of Article 18 EC can be of no avail to the Union citizen who suffers disadvantages because of or during his residence in another Member State whereas an application of Article 17 together with Article 12 can be of such avail. A good example is given by the case of Mr Trojani, a French national living in Belgium where he stayed in a Salvation Army hostel and followed a reintegration programme.[24] Mr Trojani's application to obtain the minimex, a minimum subsistance allowance, was refused because he was not a Belgian national and could not benefit from Regulation 1612/68. The Court considered that a person in a situation such as Mr Trojani's could not derive a right of free movement from Article 18 EC because he lacked sufficient financial resources. However, as a citizen of the Union lawfully residing in another Member State he could invoke the principle of non-discrimination under Article 12 EC, a social benefit such as the minimex, falling, *ratione materiae*, within the scope of the Treaty.

Another example demonstrating the possible added value of the approach based on Articles 17 and 12 EC is given by the case of Danny Bidar, a French national who, after having pursued and completed his secondary school education in the United Kingdom, had started university studies in that Member State.[25] His application for financial assistance to cover his maintenance costs was refused on the ground that he was not settled in the UK. Obviously, it would have been difficult for Mr Bidar to invoke Article 18 EC so as to qualify that refusal as an unjustified restriction of his right of free movement, Directive 93/96 on the right of residence for students explicitly excluding a right to

[23] Para 32 of the judgment.
[24] Case C-456/02 [2004] ECR I-7595.
[25] Case C-209/03 [2005] ECR I-2151.

payment of maintenance grants on the part of students benefiting from the right of residence. The Court accepted, however, that Mr Bidar as a Union citizen lawfully residing in another Member State could invoke Article 12 EC. His situation was considered to come *ratione materiae* within the scope of the Treaty because in pursuing his secondary education in the United Kingdom, Mr Bidar had exercised his right of free movement on the basis of Article 18 EC and the general Directive 90/364 on the right of residence. The objection that earlier case law had excluded assistance for maintenance costs for students from the scope of the Treaty was rejected in view of the evolution of Community law since the amendments of the EEC Treaty by the Treaty on European Union introducing citizenship of the Union and the new Chapter 3 of Part Three of the EC Treaty devoted *inter alia* to education and vocational training.

It follows from this case law that the *Martínez Sala* approach remains valid even after the case law in which the Court construed the right of free movement pursuant to Article 18 EC as a prohibition of unjustified restrictions of that right, in situations where the right of free movement cannot be invoked because of an, in itself legitimate, application of the limitations and conditions clause of Article 18 EC. If, however, a right of free movement can be invoked under Article 18 EC, that Article would seem to have to be applied and not the general provision of Article 12 together with Article 17 EC. In such cases Article 18 EC in prohibiting unjustified restrictions of that right also prohibits restrictions which constitute a discriminatory treatment of a Union citizen based on nationality. Then, Article 18 EC has to be considered as *lex specialis* with regard to the general prohibition of Article 12 EC, just as has been accepted in the case law in respect of the provisions of the Treaty embodying the economic fundamental freedoms.[26]

This continuing, but more residual scope of application of Article 12 EC to solve difficulties for Union citizens resulting from cross-border movement, resembles the interpretation given by the Court with regard to the relationship between the economic fundamental freedoms and the general non-discrimination principle of Article 12 EC, Cowan being a case in point.[27] In any event, the relationship between the restriction of free movement approach under Article 18 and a discrimination approach under the *Martínez Sala* test based on Articles 12 and 17 EC needs further clarification by the case law.

Yet another evolution in the case law could be mentioned which illustrates how the potential of the *Baumbast* judgment has fructified. A kind of spill-over effect can be detected in the case law, the newly created Union citizen rights appearing able to permeate the interpretation of the scope of the other, economic rights of free movement under the EC Treaty. A first, obvious example is the decision of 23 March 2004 in the case of Collins.[28] Mr Collins, an Irish national trying to find work in the United Kingdom, claimed a job seeker's allowance under UK law which was, however, refused on the ground that he was not habitually resident in the UK. Under Article 48 (now Article 39) EC and Regulation 1612/68 as interpreted in the case law a migrant job seeker can invoke the principle of equal treatment only as regards access to employment but not to claim the same social and tax advantages as national workers on the basis of Article 7(2) of that

[26] See, eg, Case C-55/98 *Vestergaard* [1999] ECR I-7641 para 16; Case C-251/98 *Baars* [2000] ECR I-2787 para 23.

[27] Case 186/887 [1989] ECR 195.

[28] Case C-138/02 [2004] ECR I-2733. See also Case C-258/04 *Ioannidis* [2005] ECR I-8293.

Regulation. That article only benefits migrant workers, not job seekers. However, referring to the interpretation in the case law of the scope of Article 12 EC taking into account the establishment of citizenship of the Union and Union citizens rights to equal treatment—the Court refers to its decisions in *Grzelczyk* and *Garcia Avello*—the Court holds that a financial benefit such as a job seeker's allowance can no longer be excluded from the scope of Article 39(2) EC. Consequently, it is the status of Mr Collins as a Union citizen lawfully residing in another Member State which motivates the Court to upgrade, so to speak, the scope of the principle of non-discrimination according to Article 39(2) EC. Even so, the Court accepted as a possible justification for a refusal of such an allowance, the possibility for a Member State to require the existence of a genuine link between the job seeker and the national employment market.

Another example of this spill-over effect can be found in the judgment of 29 April 2004 in joined cases *Orfanopoulos and others*.[29] It is standing case law that the public policy exception to the economic fundamental freedoms, as, for instance, laid down in Article 39(3) EC, must be strictly interpreted. The Court held in *Orfanopoulos*: 'It must be added that a particularly restrictive interpretation of the derogations from that freedom [of movement for workers] is required by virtue of a person's status as a citizen of the Union. As the Court has held, that status is destined to be the fundamental status of nationals of the Member States.'[30]

Is there still potential for further evolution? Undoubtedly so. First of all, the scope of Article 18 EC as a prohibition of unjustified restrictions of the right of free movement of the Union citizen needs to be clarified further, as must the relationship between a discrimination approach based upon Articles 12 and 17 EC and the right of free movement approach under Article 18 EC. Another issue, on which further evolution is possible if not probable, is what was previously called the spill-over effect. Further questions will certainly arise: what are the limits to be respected by the Community legislature under Article 18(1) EC? What is the scope of the Community competence by virtue of Article 18(2) EC in the light of the broad interpretation of the right of free movement pursuant to Article 18(1) EC? Can, for instance, Article 18(2) EC be used as a legal base for harmonisation initiatives in the field of private law which are not internal market related?

As to possible further evolution, I may conclude with a more specific remark concerning the interpretation of the limitations and conditions clause of Article 18(1) EC. *Baumbast* has already shown that this clause may not be interpreted as giving a *blanc seing*, an unrestricted authority to the Community legislature to lay down such limitations and conditions on the exercise by the Union citizen of his free movement right. Already in *Baumbast* the Court exercises some control, albeit with a light touch, as to the application by the Community legislature of this clause. The Court held that 'the limitations and conditions which are referred to in Article 18 EC and laid down by Directive 90/364 [on the right of residence] are based on the idea that the exercise of the right of residence of citizens of the Union can be subordinated to the legitimate interests of the Member States'. The Court then implicitly qualifies as such a legitimate interest of Member States, that beneficiaries of the right of residence do not become an unreasonable burden on the public finances of the host Member State, as the fourth recital in the preamble to Directive

[29] Joined Cases C-482/01 and C-493/01 [2004] ECR I-5295.
[30] Para 65 of the judgment.

90/364 explains. This statement was repeated in *Chen* (para 32). On the basis of this interpretation, the limitations and conditions clause could be construed as a codified rule of reason allowing the Community legislature to put restrictions on the exercise of the Union citizen's right of free movement provided a legitimate public interest to do so can be invoked and the restrictions are necessary and proportionate to the objective pursued.

Whatever further evolution will bring in this regard, we may already now conclude that the Treaty of Maastricht appears to have given birth to a new fundamental freedom next to the four classic fundamental freedoms of an economic nature existing under the EC Treaty.

2

A View of the Citizenship Classics: *Martínez Sala* and Subsequent Cases on Citizenship of the Union

JO SHAW[31]

Looking back at the judgment in *Martínez Sala*[32] with the benefit of more than 10 years' further experience with the judicial application of the EU citizenship provisions, what strikes one most is the extraordinary brevity of the reasoning of the Court of Justice. This is doubtless because 'citizenship' came late to the party in this particular case, which was originally posed as a set of questions to the Court of Justice couched solely in terms of the applicability of (what was then) Article 48, in conjunction with Regulations 1612/68 and 1408/71. Only at the oral hearing was the possibility of applying these provisions to a case concerning the entitlement of a Spanish citizen resident in Germany to a child-raising benefit actually raised, apparently by the Commission.[33] Consequently, more than two thirds of the judgment is couched in terms of the provisions on the free movement of workers and the co-ordination of social security entitlements, with the Court's consistent refrain in response to the national court's questions on these issues being that it had insufficient information definitively to answer the questions. These sections apparently left it to the national court finally to decide questions such as whether Martínez Sala could be defined as a worker, despite her marginal status in relation to the labour market, and/or whether she could be regarded as a person insured under national law in such a way as to benefit from the protection of Regulation 1408/71.[34]

Finally, at the very end of the judgment, the Court turns to citizenship of the Union. It referred back to its initial conclusion that the German child-raising benefit falls within the scope of Community law because of the applicability of Article 7(2) of Regulation 1612/68, ignoring the implication of previous case law that such a welfare benefit was only covered by Community law under Regulation 1612/68 precisely where it was claimed by a person entitled, as a migrant worker, to rely upon the protection of that regulation. It also concluded that the applicant was in a situation governed by Community law because of her lawful residence in Germany, even though the legal basis of that residence was not

[31] Salvesen Chair of European Institutions, University of Edinburgh. The author would like to acknowledge the benefit of conversations on EU citizenship in the Court of Justice with Dr. Síofra O'Leary of the European Court of Justice, and her colleague Dr Niamh Nic Shuibhne of Edinburgh Law School.

[32] Case C-85/96 *Martínez Sala v Freistadt Berlin* [1998] ECR-I 2691.

[33] I am grateful to Síofra O'Leary for reminding me of this important factual nugget.

[34] See the detailed analysis of S Fries and J Shaw, 'Citizenship of the Union: First Steps in the Court of Justice' (1998) 4 *European Public Law* 533.

clear.[35] Combining a situation in which it found the benefit and the applicant to be within the scope *ratione materiae* and *ratione personae* of the EC Treaty respectively, it found that the applicant in such a situation governed by Community law was entitled to rely upon the non-discrimination principle in Article 12 EC, which is 'attached' to the citizenship provisions by Article 17(2) EC. Since the German provisions discriminated against non-nationals by requiring them to produce residence documents not required by nationals, there was no space for the German Government to bring forward a justification for its rules and thus to save its policy of effectively restricting access to the benefit. In effect, this finally disposed of the case, leaving little leeway to the national court, despite the Court's earlier rulings on the worker-related aspects of the case.

It is difficult to argue convincingly that any of the subsequent cases on citizenship of the Union under the EC Treaty, including *Baumbast*,[36] are truly ground-breaking in the way that *Martínez Sala* undoubtedly was. On the contrary, I would see the succeeding cases, notably *Baumbast*, but also *Grzelczyk*,[37] *Bidar*,[38] *Collins*,[39] *D'Hoop*,[40] and *Garcia Avello*[41] amongst others, as exploiting in different ways the space opened upon in *Martínez Sala* for the interpretation of Articles 17–22 EC as conferring freestanding rights, which are arguably of constitutional status, upon the nationals of the Member States. The citizenship cases can perhaps best be seen, in that sense, as a package, although there is not a complete consistency of approach on the part of the Court to the different types of case. In particular there are differences discernible between those cases concerned directly with residence rights, those concerned with social benefits, and those concerned with other civil and political entitlements of citizens. However, in each of the cases cited, by invoking the citizenship provisions, the Court of Justice took the case law significantly further than it had done under the pre-Maastricht legal framework of the Treaty's free movement provisions, which it read in conjunction with the 1960s and 1970s framework of secondary legislation and the 1990/1993 directives on the free movement rights of retired persons, those of independent means and students. However, it is evident that the Court has made use not only of the constitutional gateway opened by *Martínez Sala* in order to develop its citizenship *acquis*, but also of other techniques of legal interpretation which it draws from elsewhere within the body of free movement law under the EC Treaty and—as I shall argue in conclusion—from the revolutionary approach to the application of the Article 12 non-discrimination principle taken in the much earlier cases of *Cowan*[42] and *Gravier*.[43] The signs of this latter approach are perhaps most clear in *Garcia Avello*, even though that earlier case law was not cited either by the Court or by the Advocate General (Jacobs[44]).

[35] It was, however, conceded by the German Government's legal representatives before the Court of Justice.

[36] Case C-413/99 *Baumbast and R* [2002] ECR I-7091.

[37] Case C-184/99 *Grzelczyk v Centre public d'aide sociale d'Ottignies-Louvain-La-Neuve* [2001] ECR-I 6193.

[38] Case C-209/03 *R v London Borough of Ealing, ex parte Bidar* [2005] ECR I-2119.

[39] Case C-138/02 *Collins v Secretary of State for Work and Pensions* [2004] ECR I-2703; see also along the same lines Case C-406/04 *De Cuyper*, judgment of 18 July 2006.

[40] Case C-224/98 *D'Hoop v Office National de l'Emploi* [2002] ECR I-6191; see also along the same lines Case C-224/02 *Pusa* [2004] ECR I-5763 and Case C-192/05 *Tas-Hagen*, judgment of 26 October 2006.

[41] Case C-148/02 *Garcia Avello v Belgian State* [2003] ECR I-11613.

[42] Case 186/87 *Cowan v Le Trésor public* [1989] ECR 195; what is notable about *Cowan* is that it has been very rarely cited by the Court of Justice, but none the less it is possible to see its clear influence on the case law since *Martínez Sala*, which concretises the constitutional status of EU citizenship.

[43] Case 293/83 *Gravier v City of Liège* [1985] ECR 593.

[44] This is particularly surprising, since Jacobs was also the AG in Case C-168/91 *Konstantinidis v Stadt Altensteig* [1993] ECR I-1191, where he failed in the attempt to persuade the Court to apply its approach to the

Baumbast is commonly regarded as establishing the direct effect of Article 18 EC;[45] this key ruling is to be found in that narrow portion of the judgment which relies upon the citizenship provisions in relation to the legal status in the UK of Baumbast *père*. He was neither a free-moving worker, nor a self-employed person working in another Member State, nor a service-provider, but a person employed in the Member State of which he was a national, providing services in third countries, but resident in a different Member State in which he used to be employed. This was an economic situation never envisaged explicitly by the Treaties or the secondary legislation. The conclusion that Article 18 had direct effect had in some respects been trailed by hints in earlier judgments and (especially) in the Opinions of various Advocates General,[46] but it was still striking to see the Court returning to something like the adventurous days of its *Defrenne* judgment in respect of its approach to direct effect,[47] in concluding that Article 18 EC contained a sufficiently precise and clear guarantee of the right of residence for nationals of the Member States in the host state for it to be capable of enforcement by a national court. It drew what has become a standard distinction between the *existence* and the *exercise* of the right of residence under Article 18 when it concluded that the reference to 'subject to limitations and conditions' did not render Article 18 any less effective; on the contrary, such limitations and conditions, whether contained in EU legislation such as the Citizens' Rights Directive or in national law, which go only to the *exercise* of the right of residence not its *existence*, are open to judicial review by the Court of Justice and by national courts, and must be proportionate in the light of the fundamental nature of the right of residence. This seems to be precisely the opposite of what the Member States intended when they negotiated the text of Article 18, but it can be said to follow logically from the interpretation given to the Students' Rights Directive of 1993[48] and from the right of residence of the applicant which the Court assumed in *Grzelczyk*.

The cases of *Grzelczyk* and *Bidar* significantly advanced the rights of migrant students to benefit from aspects of the general welfare system and the specific system of student support, by ignoring possible clashes between its reasoning and some of the relevant clauses of secondary legislation, now codified and consolidated in Directive 2004/38 on citizens' rights.[49] In *Bidar* it also reversed its earlier ruling in *Brown*[50] on the grounds of the value added provided by the introduction of the citizenship provisions. This is presaged by its treatment of the scope and effects of Article 7(2) of Regulation 1612/68 in *Martínez Sala*. However, it insisted in its generous ruling that a French school student residing with his grandmother in the UK who applied for a subsidised loan from the UK authorities even though he did not satisfy the habitual residence test, was discriminated

discrimination issue in *Cowan* to a case involving the transliteration of a Greek surname in Germany; the Court preferred to take a more narrow economistic view, focusing on the possibility of confusion in relation to surnames arising amongst Konstantinidis' customers.

[45] This was in any event explicitly confirmed by Case C-200/02 *Chen v Secretary of State for the Home Department* [2004] ECR I-9925.

[46] See below the discussion of Articles 17 and 18 by AG La Pergola in *Martínez Sala*, at note 52.

[47] Case 43/75 *Defrenne v Sabena* [1976] ECR 455.

[48] Council Directive 93/96, OJ 1993 L317/59.

[49] European Parliament and Council Directive 2004/38 on Citizens' Rights, OJ 2004 L158/77. See also more recently Case C-11/06 *Morgan v Bezirksregierung Köln* and Case C-12/06 *Bucher v Landrat des Kreises Düren* [2007] ECR I-9161 and, taking a somewhat different approach, Case C-158/07 *Förster v Hoofddirectie van de Informatie Beheer Groep*, judgment of 18 November 2008.

[50] Case 197/86 *Brown v Secretary of State for Scotland* [1988] ECR 3205.

against on grounds of nationality, that it was reasonable for the host Member State to 'require a genuine link between the student claiming assistance to cover his maintenance costs and the employment market of the host Member State'. This gives the lie to an assertion that the Court has *completely* abandoned market reasoning in its case law.

In *Grzelczyk*, contrary to the strict terms of the secondary legislation, it concluded that recourse to social assistance in the host Member State cannot in and of itself justify automatic expulsion, a position which relies upon its willingness in *Martínez Sala* to take a broad view of the lawfulness of the applicant's residence in Germany and also implicitly upon its earlier ruling in *Gravier* that the right of residence of a student pursuing a vocational training course is embedded in the system of the Treaty and results from the right to non-discrimination in relation to access to vocational training courses. Famously, the Court also opined that 'Union citizenship is destined to be the fundamental status of nationals of the Member States ...',[51] a phrase it has repeated on countless occasions since then. However, in *Grzelczyk* it amounted to a pure '*obiter dictum*'. The wording of this clause itself builds upon the Opinion of Advocate General La Pergola in *Martínez Sala*,[52] who suggested that citizenship of the Union 'is the fundamental legal status guaranteed to the citizen of every Member State by the legal order of the Community and now of the Union. This results from the unequivocal terms of [Article 17] of the Treaty'.[53] In the same paragraph La Pergola also anticipated the Court's subsequent conclusions in *Baumbast* on the direct effect of Article 18, by drawing a distinction between the *existence* and the *exercise* of the right of residence and of free movement. Crucially, however, the Court in *Grzelczyk* added a second clause to La Pergola's celebration of the fundamental status of citizenship, stating that citizenship enables 'those who find themselves in the same situation to enjoy the same treatment in law irrespective of their nationality, subject to such exceptions as are expressly provided for'. This, in truth, is the key phrase, rather than the more frequently repeated first section about 'fundamental status', as it opens the way for citizens to make a primary claim to equal treatment, without apparently having to establish first a connection to Community law. This is not the way in which citizenship is treated in all of the cases before the Court of Justice, as in some cases it continues to insist upon combining the scope *ratione materiae* and *ratione personae*, as it did in *Martínez Sala*, but the general principle of non-discrimination now underpins much of the Court's new approach.

In terms of the social context in which the cases on the benefits which students can claim arise,[54] one gains a general impression from the case law on students that a human capital mobility approach is being taken, with—in the spirit of Lisbon perhaps—students being treated as future economic actors who will make a contribution to human well-being and economic growth through their economic activities in the future. Perhaps the Court is also conscious of the significant successes of the ERASMUS programme, and

[51] At para 31.

[52] Opinion of 1 July 1997, at para 18.

[53] This was before the reference to the complementarity of Union citizenship by the Treaty of Amsterdam into Article 17 came into force in 1999. Indeed, an Opinion dated 1 July 1997 will have been finalised some time before the conclusion of the Treaty of Amsterdam at the end of June 1997. However, the Court's adoption of this statement in *Grzelczyk* (2001) came some time after this clause came into force.

[54] Changing social context has been an issue upon which Advocate General Geelhoed, who delivered many Opinions on citizenship, has frequently insisted, pointing to changes in both the employment market and in family formation patterns.

its successors, which reached its 20th anniversary in the same year as the Treaty of Rome reached its 50th anniversary (2007), as providing a robust framework for ongoing student mobility, and wants to place as few obstacles as possible in the way of such mobility. But as we shall see at the end, it was *Gravier* which launched ERASMUS, not citizenship of the Union.

In *Collins*, the Court required a Member State to justify the terms of its residence test as the basis for access to social benefits (in this case for workseekers), requiring objective justification for what amounts to an indirectly discriminatory test applied by national law. The proportionality of obstacles to free movement and limitations upon residence are the *leitmotiv* here, with the Court reading its approach across from the other free movement principles. In *D'Hoop* it went beyond discrimination altogether articulating the beginnings of a test which requires Member States not to place their own nationals, as well as the nationals of other Member States, at a *disadvantage* as a result of the exercise of free movement rights; this holistic approach to the right of residence as part of the free movement rules very much recalls the language of the Court of Justice in *Gebhard*.[55]

Garcia Avello is of a rather different ilk to the other cases, as it is concerned with civil rather than social entitlements. It draws directly upon the opening created in *Grzelczyk* in relation to the right to assert citizenship as the basis, in itself, of a claim to non-discrimination, subject only to exceptions and conditions imposed by law. The issue in *Garcia Avello* was the 'right to a name', in that case the right of a dual Belgian-Spanish national to use the Spanish version of his surname, incorporating elements of the mother's and the father's name, notwithstanding Belgian rules on the 'unity' of the surname. In approach, if not in outcome, *Garcia Avello* effectively reversed *Konstantinidis* so far as concerns the requirement of an economic link which the Court appeared to impose in that case, by opting for an approach based entirely on the risk of confusion in the marketplace faced by a person exercising their freedom of establishment under Article 43 EC, rather than choosing the broad-based citizenship and fundamental rights approaches advocated by AG Jacobs.[56] In *Standesamt Stadt Niebüll*, AG Jacobs referred to the significance of the post-Maastricht citizenship provisions in providing the answer to another case which was not dissimilar in nature to *Konstantinidis*, concluding that 'the combined effects of Articles 17 and 18(1) EC mean that it is now unnecessary to establish any economic link in order to demonstrate an infringement of the right to free movement.'[57] This position—without being explicitly confirmed—was upheld in substance by the Court of Justice, although not until 2008 when the same case came before it for a second time.[58]

Treating the case law since *Martínez Sala* as a package, albeit one which is not entirely uniform in approach, it is possible to summarise what we now know about the legal effects of citizenship of the Union:

- From *Martínez Sala* onwards, it has been possible to argue that Articles 17–22, in particular Articles 17 and 18, have a free-standing constitutional impact in relation to the legal position of nationals of the Member States, who are automatically citizens of the Union.

[55] Case C-55/94 *Gebhard v Consiglio dell'Ordine degli Avvocati e Procuratori di Milano* [1995] ECR I-4165.

[56] Case C-168/91 *Konstantinides v Stadt Altensteig* [1993] ECR I-1191.

[57] Case C-96/04 *Standesamt Stadt Niebüll* [2006] ECR I-3561; AG's Opinion of 30 June 2005, para 54.

[58] Case C-353/08 *Grunkin and Paul v Grunkin-Paul and Standesamt Stadt Niebüll*, judgment of 14 October 2008.

- The *dictum* in *Grzelczyk* has been elevated into a general proposition about the scope and effects of Union citizenship. It is frequently repeated (although sometimes without the second part on discrimination) by the Court. For example, according to the Court in the *Gibraltar* case,[59] 'citizenship of the Union is destined to be the fundamental status of nationals of the Member States, enabling those who find themselves in the same situation to receive the same treatment in law irrespective of their nationality, subject to such exceptions as are expressly provided for'. This phrasing omits any reference at the outset to the need to prove a link of any particular type to the material scope of Community law. There is consequently no longer an express need normally to identify an economic link in order to establish a breach of the free movement rules (including the right of residence in Article 18), although in some cases involving access to social benefits the Court has required evidence of a link to the employment market in the host state.
- Member States must exercise (effectively all) their national competences only in the light of the constraints imposed by EU citizenship, as they must also with respect to other free movement rights; there exists very little national margin of discretion or reserved area of sovereignty. One exception could be voting rights in those elections not covered explicitly by Article 19 EC (for example, national elections).[60] However, Member States do have to exercise their competences in relation to external voting rights in the light of the general principle of non-discrimination, which can affect groups of persons holding the same national citizenship, who are treated differently in relation to the right to vote in the European Parliament elections.[61]
- The *existence* of a directly effective right of residence under Article 18 is now uncontested and it may be relied upon by individuals in national courts, even if the right is not unlimited; limitations and conditions placed upon the *exercise* of the residence rights imposed by Member States are subject to a proportionality test, and the rules in the relevant secondary EU legislation (such as the 2004 Citizens' Rights Directive[62]) must also be interpreted in such a way that the restrictions they impose do not impede the fundamental nature of the right of residence under Article 18.
- The fact that an individual seeks to rely upon social assistance cannot in itself be grounds for expulsion from the national territory, even if he or she is not a migrant worker or an otherwise economically active migrant. This effectively extends to other categories of free moving citizens the protection given in the Citizens' Rights Directive to workers suffering involuntary unemployment, so far as they preserve their status as a worker, at least for a certain period of time.
- Article 17(2) attaches to citizens of the Union not only the right of non-discrimination on grounds of nationality under Article 12 EC, but also non-discrimination as a general principle protected under Community law.
- The type of treatment of EU citizens which is prohibited under the citizenship rules includes not only that which is directly or indirectly discriminatory, but also that

[59] Case C-145/04 *Spain v United Kingdom*, judgment of 12 September 2006, at para 74.

[60] See J Shaw, *The Transformation of Citizenship in the European Union. Electoral Rights and the Restructuring of Political Space* (Cambridge: Cambridge University Press, 2007), esp ch 6.

[61] Case C-300/04 *Eman and Sevinger v College van burgemeester en wethouders van Den Haag (Aruba)*, 12 September 2006.

[62] European Parliament and Council Directive 2004/38 on Citizens' Rights, OJ 2004 L158/77.

which tends to place an obstacle in the way of the exercise of free movement rights, by placing those who exercise free movement rights 'at a disadvantage'.

- Where Member States impose residence tests (such as a requirement of habitual residence) as access conditions for benefits and only accept certain forms of residence as 'habitual' (for example, not residence as a student), such measures are subject to a proportionality test.
- However, the interpretation of what is an 'unreasonable burden' on the host state and what is a reasonable level of solidarity between the Member States is central to the evaluation of whether the application of a residence test, for example, is justifiable. So far the nature of the evaluation is extremely unclear; for example, is it the status of the applicant (whether as an economically active person, as a schoolchild, a university student, a workseeker, a retired persons, etc), the quality of her residence (how integrated she is into the host state), or indeed the nature of the benefit which is decisive in the determination?
- Citizenship of the Union remains a residual category; generally speaking the Court only invokes the citizenship provisions when the other (economic-based) treaty free movement rules will not provide a satisfactory resolution of the problem before it. To that extent, the approach in *Martínez Sala* lives on in the current case law of the Court.

It is appropriate to conclude by returning to the question trailed earlier on, which concerns the continuing influence of some of the Court's case law dating from before the Treaty of Maastricht on the citizenship cases.[63] It is hard to envisage the Court making the leap in reasoning that it made in *Martínez Sala*, if it had not previously decided *Cowan* and *Gravier* in the way that it did. While *Cowan* is notable for putting Article 12 at the centre of the reasoning, with the issue of the applicant's status as a recipient of services (tourist) seemingly flowing from this, *Gravier* highlighted the Court's willingness to assert that just because a sector of the economy ostensibly fell outside the scope of Community competence (higher education), that did not mean that it could not take steps to restrict the freedom of the Member States to regulate that field in such a way as to discourage free movement by charging discriminatory fees, or by calling into question the residence rights of those involved. It is important to recall that *Gravier* established the residence rights of migrant students as flowing directly from the Treaty, not the later 1993 directive, which merely regulated the exercise of those rights. On the basis of the tenuous footing of what was then Article 128 EEC, the Court effectively launched what has become one of the EU's flagship programmes in respect of integration through action (student mobility, including—but not confined to—ERASMUS). It is arguable that these cases could be said to be the true foundational cases of the citizenship revolution, and it was they, and not the later cases of *Martínez Sala* and the rest, which fatally undermined the premise that any 'citizenship' flowing from Community law could only ever be a 'market citizenship'. However, in the era of uncertainty about the constitutional future of the European Union, it remains unclear what the next destination for Union citizenship might be. That may be for the next edition of *Classics*.

[63] If space permitted, it would be useful also to discuss the Court's approach to the interpretation of Article 7(2) of Regulation 1612/68 and the notion of social advantages, in particular cases such as Case 9/74 *Casagrande* [1974] ECR 773, which early on emphasised the human dimension of free movement rights.

3

European Citizenship after *Martínez Sala* and *Baumbast*: Has European Law Become More Human but Less Social?

AGUSTÍN JOSÉ MENÉNDEZ[64]

It is one thing to eliminate divisions and quite another to establish ties

Helen S Feldstein[65]

Introduction

The duo of rulings in the cases of *Martínez Sala* and *Baumbast* has become a milestone in the case law of the European Court of Justice. A good deal of the academic literature,[66] perhaps under the influence of the self-praising narrative of the Court of Justice and most especially of its Advocates General,[67] has hailed these judgments as path-breaking decisions which would have operated a 'civic turn' in Community law, putting flesh onto the bones of the citizenship provisions inserted by the Treaty of Maastricht.[68] In particular, it is not unusual to read that the Court would have redefined the value basis of Community law by expanding the personal scope of the freedom of personal movement

[64] Profesor Contratado Doctor Permanente, Universidad de Léon and RECON-fellow, Universitetet i Oslo. This chapter emanates from RECON (Reconstituting Democracy in Europe), an Integrated Project supported by the European Commission's Sixth Framework Programme (contract no CIT4-CT-2006-028698).

[65] 'A Study of Transaction and Political Integration: Transnational Labour Flow within the European Economic Community' (1967) 6 *Journal of Common Market Studies* 24–55 at 30.

[66] See, eg, Dora Kostakopolou, 'Ideas, Norms and European Citizenship: Explaining Institutional Change' (2005) 68 *MLR* 233–67.

[67] AG Jacobs already set the tone in his opinion in Opinion in Case C-168/91 *Konstantinidis* [1992] ECR I-1191, para 46: 'A Community national who goes to another Member State as a worker or self-employed person under Articles 48, 52 or 59 of the Treaty is entitled not just to pursue his trade or profession and to enjoy the same living and working conditions as nationals of the host State; he is in addition entitled to assume that, wherever he goes to earn his living in the European Community, he will be treated in accordance with a common code of fundamental values, in particular those laid down in the European Convention on Human Rights. In other words, he is entitled to say "civis europeus sum" and to invoke that status in order to oppose any violation of his fundamental rights.' Konstantinidis was decided after the signature of the Treaty of Maastricht, but before it entered into force. See also Francis Jacobs, 'Citizenship of the Union. A legal analysis' (2007) 13 *European Law Journal* 591–610.

[68] As is well known, one of the major amendments introduced by the Maastricht Treaty on the Rome Treaty was precisely the creation of the new status of European citizen. Although the Treaty was signed in 1992, it only entered into force in November 1993. Given that cases take quite some time to arrive at the Court, and to be decided by it, it is not surprising that *Martínez Sala*, decided in 1998, came more than four years after the entry into force of the Treaty.

from the economically defined category of worker to the general category of citizen (from *free movement of workers to free movement of persons*). The Court would have read into the newly enacted provisions a requirement to push the freedom protected by Community law beyond economically active individuals, to all European citizens without further qualifications.[69] Consequently, these cases would have proven again the emancipatory potential of European law, closely related to its redrawing the economic and political boundaries of the old continent. *Martínez Sala* and *Baumbast* would have given a new and more explicit turn to this old screw, by making the Community right-holder a civic and solidaristic political citizen and not a mere solitary and egotistic market actor.[70]

This chapter poses a moderate but straightforward challenge to this assessment and calls for a less triumphant evaluation of the jurisprudence of the Luxembourg Court. True, it is very probable that some citizens do now enjoy rights and freedoms which were denied to them before; it may also be accurate to say that some of the rulings in the trials of *Martínez Sala* and *Baumbast* might have laid the basis of a European we-feeling without which social integration through Community law may erode over time.[71] Still, it seems to me that the standard interpretation is not easy to sustain, either in purely legal or wider political terms. From a legal-dogmatic perspective, there is a bit of an exaggeration to characterise *Martínez Sala* and *Baumbast* as epochal judgments, given that most of the structural and substantive changes claimed to have been brought about by the two judgments here analysed were already under way in the pre-Maastricht case law. From a politico-normative standpoint, a proper assessment of the said rulings should combine attention on the implications for actual plaintiffs with an assessment of their systemic effects, and in particular, their institutional and (re)distributive implications. On such a basis, it is only fair to say that *Martínez Sala* and *Baumbast* have actually radicalised a trend that was already at work, and in doing so have exacerbated the processes of Europeanisation of what used to be exclusive national competences, and the judicialisation of decision-making processes where representative institutions used to have the exclusive word. But if there is more continuity than change, and if the process leads to outcomes which are far from obviously a blessing from a democratic standpoint, it cannot be that the story to be told is one of unstoppable emancipation of European citizens from their national and economic chains. On the contrary, it seems to me that the case law of the Court is deeply ambivalent. European law may have become more human, as Community law has forced national legal orders to partially dismantle some exclusion criteria from the enjoyment of rights, only at the expense of its being less social, to the extent it may import a non-solidaristic logic into provinces of the legal system previously protected from economic pressure, or may even force a social retrenchment.

To ground such claims, I proceed in three steps. First, I situate the case law on European citizenship within its legal-dogmatic context by means of reconstructing the legal and judicial definition of Community fundamental freedoms, and very specificially, free movement of actual persons prior to *Martínez Sala* and *Baumbast*. Second, I analyse the reasoning of the Court in the two leading cases, and offer a systematic reading of the

[69] See the excellent Álvaro Castro Oliveira, 'Workers and other persons: step-by-step from movement to citizenship' (2002) 39 *CML Rev* 77–127.

[70] Or perhaps one should say market citizen, following the apt term adapted from Ipsen by Michelle Everson in her 'The Legacy of the Market Citizen' in Jo Shaw and Gillian More (eds), *New Legal Dynamics of European Union* (Oxford, Clarendon, 1995), 73–89.

[71] Specifically, by means of putting into question the lines of exclusion built around nationality.

ensuing case law. Third, I assess the ambivalent implications of the two judgments for the evolution of European law and European integration in general.

Free Movement as a Fundamental Economic Freedom and as a Vehicle of Integration, from the Creation of the Communities to the Entry into Force of the Treaty on European Union

Both the 1951 Paris Treaty establishing the Coal and Steel Community and the 1957 Rome Treaty establishing the European Economic Community contained provisions which enshrined the principle of free movement of workers as a cornerstone of European Community law.[72] The key provision, Article 48 of the Treaty on the European Community, stated in its decisive second and third paragraphs that:

'2. Freedom of movement of workers] shall entail the abolition of any discrimination based on nationality between workers of the Member States as regards employment, remuneration and other conditions of work and employment.
3. It shall entail the right, subject to limitations justified on grounds of public policy, public security or public health:

a) to accept offers of employment actually made;
b) to move freely within the territory of the Member States for this purpose;
c) to stay in a Member State for the purpose of employment in accordance with the provisions governing the employment of nationals of that State laid down by law, regulation or administrative action;
d) to remain in the territory of a Member State having been employed in that State, subject to conditions which shall be embodied in implementing regulations to be drawn up by the Commission.'

The literal tenor of the provision enumerated a limited set of clear negative prescriptions, which would require abrogating a good many national laws regulating the access of foreigners to employment in each national 'labour market'. In the previous half century, European nation-states had perfected the institutional and normative instruments with the help of which they controlled the flow of people in and out of their borders.[73] The two world wars had dramatic military, economic and social consequences virtually leading to the creation of the state capacities which resulted in an intense and close monitoring of the movements of

[72] Cf Articles 68 and 69 of the Paris Treaty; Articles 48 to 51 of the Rome Treaty.

[73] Although the consolidation of the nation-state as the virtually exclusive form of political community at the end of the 18th century came hand in hand with the forging of legal criteria to distinguish nationals from foreigners, this did not result in the curbing or even the formal controlling of movement of people across European borders. On the evolution of the distinct set of civil rights assigned to foreigners (including limited rights to inherit or bequeath property, subjection to special taxes, commercial and financial restrictions and limits to their right to free movement within the state), see Peter Sahlins, *Unnaturally French: Foreign Citizens and the Old Regime and After* (Ithaca, Cornell University Press, 2004). Perhaps the explanation lies with the rather simple and straightforward fact that until the end of the First World War, European countries (with the only exception of France—see Patrick Weil, *La France et ses étrangères* (Paris, Gallimard, 2004) 21 *ff*) were not the destination of choice of most European immigrants, which rather headed almost exclusively to North and South America.

persons half a century later.[74] Indeed, the original drafting of Articles 48 to 51 of the EEC Treaty refers to all the key obstacles that those willing to migrate to other European countries were likely to find in their way. On the one hand, entry was made conditional on obtaining permits, issued at the complete discretion of the recipient state, for short periods of time (rarely longer than a year) and which could be rescinded at will (indeed, foreigners were regarded as 'buffer' labour, to be called and dismissed at 'national' convenience). On the other hand, foreign workers enjoyed not only a lesser protection of their political rights, but had their civic and social rights severely curtailed.[75] Thus, they were negatively discriminated against as to the terms of payment and the working conditions (with no guarantee that social security contributions would be aggregated at the time of calculating their pension either in their country of origin or destination; or for that matter, that they could enjoy their pension at all anywhere), they confronted draconian limits on several of their occupational rights, including the right to choose employment, especially if they had gained access to the country to work in a different job (they may have to apply for a new work permit, which may or may not be granted); their right to join trade unions; their right to be elected as workers' representatives, and their right to strike or engage in some other form of collective action; at the same time as housing, educational and welfare benefits in general were provided in less generous terms than those available to national workers. Free movement of workers was to put an end to this state of affairs, by means of transforming work permits from gratuitous concessions to regulated rights of workers if vacancies existed (as essentially foreseen in Article 49 TEC); and second, by means of ruling out discriminations based on nationality on what concerned access to the job, payment and working conditions (as required in Articles 48 and 51 TEC).

Thus, the core and uncontroversial content of Community free movement of workers resulted from *both* a normative vision of equal rights, not unrelated to the shattering of the European moral conscience by the atrocities committed by Nazi, Fascist and fellow travellers' governments, *and* from the economic needs of the founding six Member States in the post-war period (the prototypical Community right-holder being the economically active person moving across borders to undertake remunerated employment).[76] Five Member States were indeed in need of an influx of labour to render their economic recovery plans feasible, while the sixth, Italy, had a surplus labour force anxious to find work abroad.[77]

[74] First, pressing concerns of national security (or what were perceived as being so, ie the risk of a fifth column of enemy aliens undermining the war effort) led to the perfectioning of the state capacities to control population movements, from the creation and maintenance of a network of border outposts to the universalisation of identity cards (Klaus Bade, *Europa en Movimiento* (Barcelona, Crítica, 2003) 194; on identity cards, see among others, John Torpey, *The Invention of the Passport* (Cambridge, Cambridge University Press, 2000)). Secondly, the foreign population to be controlled increased dramatically. After the First World War, massive flows of outgoing population resulted from the fragmentation of the Austrian Empire, the revolution in Russia, and the redrawing of many national borders along the principle of national self-determination. Internal flows of populations after the Second World War had to do with the huge number of people which had been displaced and with the redrawing of borders (very especially in Central and Eastern Europe). Thirdly, the emergence of national welfare insurance requiring drawing a stronger distinction between nationals (or permanent foreign residents) and foreigners, if only to ensure that eligibility conditions were respected.

[75] A masterful recreation of the socio-economic circumstances of migrants in the 1920s and 1930s in B Traven, *The Death Ship*, 1926 (first translation into English 1934).

[76] Helen Feldstein, 'A Study of Transaction and Political Integration: Transnational Labour Flow within the European Economic Community' (1967) 6 *Journal of Common Market Studies* 24–55.

[77] See on the contemporary literature, among others, Attilio Oblath, 'The Problem of Surplus Manpower in Europe' (1954) 70 *International Labour Review* 301–22; Xavier Lannes, 'International Mobility of Manpower in

Still, it was far from obvious whether the legal substance of Treaty provisions was exhausted by the rules which were to be derived rather uncontroversially from the literal tenor of the provisions, or whether a far more ambitious legal and political programme was to be drawn through the systematic and teleological construction of the said sections. The answer to this question hinged very much on the conception of the European Communities according to which integration should proceed; indeed, different conceptions entailed different views on the purpose and rationale of free movement of workers. It goes without saying that such uncertainty was closely connected to the overall unclear legal and political status of European integration in its early days.[78]

A 'functional' characterisation of European integration would naturally support a literal and rather narrow interpretation of Articles 48 to 51, on the assumption that free movement of workers was one of the several pulleys and levers at the disposal of the supranational administrative structure created by the founding Treaties. From such a view, free movement of workers would indeed be a tool of problem-solving, the problem being insufficient productive efficiency, and the solution the opening of national labour markets so that labour could move where a higher salary was paid, on account of the better and more productive use to which labour could be put.[79] Both the end of the administrative management of the movement of people and the assignment of a fully equal status to foreign workers were operative requirements of a well-functioning (and rather self-regulating or at least self-correcting) market.

But free movement of workers could also be regarded as a vehicle of political integration. By making workers free to move within the European Communities, the gains would not be only economic, but also political, as workers would generate social ties binding across borders. But if that was so, the Treaty provisions, whose literal tenor was crowded by prohibitions to national legislatures, should be systematically and teleologically interpreted with a view to drawing the more general principle of freedom of action underlying it, from which more positive derivative norms could then be drawn,[80] with the help of which gaps were to be filled and concrete secondary Community and national norms were to be constructed, so as to to maximise the degree of realisation of the principle of free movement thus constructed. In the long run (perhaps in that long run in

Europe' (1957) 73 *International Labour Review* 1–24 and 135–51, especially 143. It was widely accepted that migration would alleaviate social tensions in Italy, while providing much-neeeded remittances with which to finance capital investments.

[78] A point worth insisting upon, given the anachronistic (but in legal-dogmatic terms rather unavoidable) tendency to read an inevitability in the development of integration which was far from obvious at the time. It may suffice to keep in mind the recent failure of the Defence and Political Communities, the decision of the United Kingdom not to join either the ECSC or the EC, and the soul-searching of French governments under De Gaulle. Indeed, it may be fair to say that the main importance of the ECSC—and one may adventurously add of the EC—was pshychological, not economic (as Tony Judt points in *Postwar* (London, Allen Lane, 2005) 158).

[79] It is pertinent to keep in mind that Part II of the EEC Treaty keeps to this day a division in Titles which reveals the central role assigned to free movement of goods, and the ancillary roles assigned to free movement of workers, services and capital. Thus, Title I deals with free movement of goods, and free movement of goods only, while the other three fundamental economic freedoms are spelt out in Title III; the second Title is devoted to Agriculture. This formal organisation was perfectly coherent with the contemporary understanding that the free flow of goods actually required the adequate regulation of the other factors of production. Thus, the other economic freedoms were so to the extent that they were a necessary precondition for the realisation of free movement of goods.

[80] The slow work of the Court of Justice led later to consolidation by the Commission. See, eg, Action Programme in favour of migrant workers and their families, COM (74) 2250, 7. Available at www.aei.pitt.edu.

which we all will be dead, following the famous Keynes' dictum), the process would result in the affirmation of a status of European citizen fully dissociated from engagement in economic activity.[81]

The tension between these two alternative conceptions of free movement of workers was never explicitly resolved (or even addressed), but secondary law (particularly Regulation 1612/68 on free movement and 1408/71 on social security) and the jurisprudence of the Court came be to informed by the second conception, which percolated into the legal and general public conceptions of European integration in general, and of free movement of workers in particular. Indeed, by 1975, the Court could claim that 'the migrant worker [was] not regarded by Community law (...) as a mere source of labour but [was to be] viewed as a human being'.[82] The case law of the European Court of Justice enlarged the breadth and scope of the provisions on free movement of workers by expanding the understanding of who was entitled to the right to free movement, and by means of recharacterising the value basis of free movement of workers.

First, a long series of cases expanded the numbers of those qualifying as workers, and thus entitled to Community rights when moving across borders, or when legally staying in a Member State other than that of which they were citizens. The opening move of the Court was to affirm the autonomous and differentiated interpretation of the concept of worker in Community law.[83] This quite obviously did not entail neglecting national definitions,[84] but merely reconstructing the rights and duties which characterised and distinguished an employment relationship in national legal orders in a critical fashion, with a view to realising the objectives of the founding Treaties of the Communities.[85] At the same time, the Court preserved the opportunity for the exercise of its own discretion by underlining that different provisions of the third Title of the second Part of the Treaty had different purposes, and drawing the conclusion that there was no need for a univocal definition of worker in Community law.[86] This first move created the structural conditions under which the concept of worker could be stretched beyond its characterisation as

[81] See, eg, the speech delivered by Jean Monnet on the delivery of the first passports entitling the holders to free movement within the Community to public servants of the ECSC, available at www.ena.lu?lang=1&doc=5114, in which such passports are regarded as the forerunners of a generalised European passport; thus implying that free movement was a political goal.

[82] Case 7/75, *Epoux F* [1975] 2 CMLR 442, at 450.

[83] A strategy that, as is well known, has been typically followed by the Court when suiting pro-integration objectives. Cf Case 75/63, *Hoekstra (née Unger)* [1964] ECR 177, para 1: 'If the definition of this term were a matter within the competence of national law, it would therefore be possible for each Member State to modify the meaning of the concept of "migrant worker" and to eliminate at will the protection afforded by the Treaty to certain categories of person . . . Articles 48 to 51 would therefore be deprived of all effect and the above-mentioned objectives of the Treaty would be frustrated if the meaning of such a term could be unilaterally fixed and modified by national law.'

[84] Thus, whether co-habitants should be assimilated to workers for the purpose of determining who has a right to reside in each Member State was decided negatively in Case 59/85, *Reed* [1986] ECR 1283, paras 13 and 15: 'In the absence of a general social development which could justify a broad construction, and in the absence of any indication to the contrary in the regulation, it must be held that the term "spouse" in Article 10 of the Regulation refers to a marital relationship only.'

[85] Case 66/85, *Lawrie-Blum* [1986] ECR 2121, para 17. The extensive interpretation moved the Court to reject the implicit differentiation of the status of the Community official, favoured by AG Rozès in Case 152/82 *Forcheri* [1983] ECR 2323. I have consulted the Opinion of the AG in [1984] 1 CMLR 334. Page 340 is the key one: 'It is necessary to exclude any consideration of the similar situation of migrant workers which requires the interpretation of provisions without relevance to the present case.'

[86] The Court has clearly distinguished the concept of worker for the purposes of free movement of workers and the concept of worker for the purpose of securing the co-ordination of national social security systems. Cf

a factor of production.[87] This led to both a) the expansion of the rank and file of workers by analogically extending the characterisation to family members, prospective workers and former workers; and b) the systemic reconstruction of free movement of workers (together with freedom of establishment and the freedom to receive services, derived from the right to provide them across borders) as part of a more general personal freedom of action.

a) Secondary legislation and jurisprudence assimilated the status of several persons who were not necessarily economically active to the status of 'worker' on the basis of the existence of a personal relationship linking them with a 'worker' or on the basis that they might become or had been workers themselves. This was particularly the case of family members, prospective workers and persons who had been employed in the national labour market but were no longer working. Let us consider each category in some detail.

Family members: Article 48 did not make reference to spouses of family members as ancillary or derivative beneficiaries of the right to free movement of workers. But Regulation 15[88] already granted Community rights to family members, although limiting them to the spouse and some children. Regulation 38/64/EC[89] and Regulation 1612/68[90] extended the rights to all children and also to elderly dependants (parents and grandparents dependent on the worker).[91] Directive 68/360 affirmed that such rights were independent of the nationality of the family members, thus turning eligible also citizens of third countries.[92] Regulation 1251/70 extended the rights beyond the death of the worker.[93] The Court of Justice pushed this assimilation further, by means of affirming (1) that the legal separation of spouses did not put an end to the rights deriving from marriage;[94] (2) that even unmarried companions could be granted rights, by means of regarding as a 'social advantage' the granting in national law of a leave of residence to non-married partners of nationals;[95] (3) that even spouses or partners without a valid

Case 66/85, *Lawrie-Blum* [1986] ECR 2121, para 17: 'The essential feature of an employment relationship, however, is that for a certain period of time a person performs services for and under the direction of another person in return for which he receives remuneration' with Case 182/78 *Pierik II* [1979] ECR 1977, para 4: 'Article 4(1) of Regulation No 1408/71 defines the concept of "worker" as any person who is compulsorily or voluntarily insured under one of the social security schemes referred to in subparagraphs (I) (II) or (III) of that provision . . . such a definition has a general scope, and in the light of that consideration, covers any person who has the capacity of a person insured under the social security legislation of one or more Member States, whether or not he pursues a professional or trade activity'.

87 Case C-53/81, *Levin* [1982] ECR 1035, paras 9 and 13: 'Although the rights deriving from the principle of freedom of movement for workers and more particularly the right to enter and stay in the territory of a Member State are thus linked to the status of a worker or of a person pursuing an activity as employed person or desirous of so doing, the terms "worker" and "activity as employed persons" are not expressly defined in any of the provisions on the subject ... In this respect, it must be stressed that these concepts define the field of application of one of the fundamental freedoms guaranteed by the Treaty and, as such, may not be interpreted restrictively.'

88 OJ No 57, 26.8.1961, p 1073.

89 OJ No 62, 17.4.1964, p 965.

90 OJ L 257, 19.10.1968, p 2.

91 Cf Kenneth A Dahlberg, 'The EEC Commission and the Politics of the Free Movement of Labour' (1968) 6 *Journal of Common Market Studies* 310–23.

92 Article 4.4, OJ L 257, 19.10.1968, p 13.

93 OJ 142 30.6.1970, p 24.

94 Case C-267/83, *Diatta* [1985] ECR 567, paras 17–20.

95 Case 58/95 *Reed* [1986] ECR 1283. While in paras 15–16 the Court denies that a right of residence could be derived from Article 10 of Regulation 1612/68, it considers in paras 29–30 that it can be regarded as a 'social advantage' ex Article 7 of the referred Regulation, regarding which nationals of other Member States should not be discriminated against.

national identity card or passport could gain access to the Member State, provided that they could both identify themselves and offer evidence of the link to the Community national.[96]

Prospective workers: Entry into the territory of another Member State was originally assumed to be conditional upon a previously and definitively offered position of employment. Community law transformed the obtaining of a work permit under such circumstances from a discretionary prerogative of the receiving Member State into a right of the prospective worker. This explains the relevance of the institutional and substantive provisions concerning the co-ordination of national employment services contained in Regulation 15, 38/64 and 1612/68. But it was only thanks to a Declaration attached to Regulation 1612/68 that the right to enter the territory of another Member State to seek employment without a previous offer was established. The Declaration required all Member States to acknowledge a right of abode of at least three months (which could be shortened only if the job seeker became dependent on welfare assistance before that time, in which case he or she would be invited to leave without further ado). The Court interpreted such a right even more extensively, by affirming that it would be opposable by the job seeker as long as he could offer evidence of genuine chances of being engaged.[97]

Those who *had been employed but were no longer working*: Both Regulation 3 and its replacement 1408/71 contributed to the assimilation to workers of all those who were insured against one of the risks covered by the Regulations when they would enjoy the benefits, something which in most cases entailed the beneficiaries no longer working, temporarily or definitively. This was the case with sickness, invalidity, old-age, work accidents and occupational diseases and unemployment benefits, all of them governed by Regulation 1408/71. In particular, retired persons have been the object of a specific directive regulating the right of residence in 1990.[98]

b) Free movement of workers was defined, together as freedom of provisions and receipt of services and freedom of establishment as concrete manifestations of a larger personal freedom of action, and in concrete a freedom of movement of persons,[99] which resulted in drawing, both in the legislation and in the case law, manifold connections between the rights and duties assigned to nationals of Member States as workers, providers and recipients of services or entrepreneurs.[100] In particular, the right of entry into any Member State on the mere production of an identity card as part of the right to

[96] Case C-459/99, *MRAX* [2002] ECR 6591, para 62: 'The answer to the first question referred for a preliminary ruling must therefore be that, on a proper construction of Article 3 of Directive 68/360, Article 3 of Directive 73/148 and Regulation No 2317/95, read in the light of the principle of proportionality, a Member State may not send back at the border a third country national who is married to a national of a Member State and attempts to enter its territory without being in possession of a valid identity card or passport or, if necessary, a visa, where he is able to prove his identity and the conjugal ties and there is no evidence to establish that he represents a risk to the requirements of public policy, public security or public health within the meaning of Article 10 of Directive 68/360 and Article 8 of Directive 73/148'.

[97] C-282/89, *Antonissen* [1991] ECR 745, paras 21–2.

[98] Directive 90/365 [1990] OJ L180, of 13.7.1990, p 28.

[99] See Preamble of Regulation 38/64/EC, OJ No 62, 17.4.1964, p 965.

[100] On right of entry and residence, see Directives 68/360 and 73/148; and the interpretation offered of them in Case 48/75 *Royer* [1976] ECR 497, paras 12 and 15: 'Nevetherless comparison of these different provisions shows that they are based on the same principles both in so far as they concern the entry into and residence in the territory of Member Status of persons covered by Community law and the prohibition of all discrimination between them on grounds of nationality.' On the substantive implications of the right to equal treatment, see Case 118/75, *Watson and Belmann*, [1976] ECR 1185, para 9 and see C-106/91 *Ramrath* [1992] ECR I-3351, para 17, and C-107/94, *Asscher* [1996] ECR I-3089, para 29.

provide and receive services.[101] A further step was taken when the condition of mere recipient of services was regarded as making anybody entitled to the protection afforded by the principle of non-discrimination on the basis of nationality (given the obvious fact that it is hard not to become a recipient of services on moving to another state, as modern societies are based on the division of labour and the use of the money medium).[102] The mutual influence of the personal freedoms explains the promulgation of two directives regulating the right of non-economically active citizens to reside in other Member States, the so-called general Directive of 1990,[103] and the directive applicable to students, of 1993.[104] In both instances the right of residence is subject to the double condition of full medical insurance and possession of sufficient means so as not to become a burden on the welfare system of the host state.

Secondly, the objective scope of free movement of workers was progressively widened by reconceptualising its grounding principle (from non-discrimination on the basis of nationality to the idea of personal freedom of action as just described)[105] and by the consequent refashioning of the substantive yardstick against which the European constitutionality of national laws was to be determined (from national constitutional standards to transcendental and self-standing Community standards). The Court operated that change by what apparently was a further expansion of the subjective scope of free movement of workers, namely by progressively relativising the assumption that freedom of movement was a liberty enjoyed by foreign workers who happened to be nationals of a Member State and who took remunerated employment in another Member State; the Court broke with such an assumption and brought free movement of workers to bear in relationships between Member States and their own nationals, provided that such citizens had been economically active (or had prepared for economic activity) in some other Member State. The first line of cases concerned the refusal of a home Member State to recognise trade qualifications acquired in another Member State.[106] Secondly, the Court ruled that it was also contrary to Community law to refuse computation of periods of work in another Member State when calculating pension rights,[107] or to impose greater social security contributions when the worker had been posted to another Member State by his or her employer, while being insured in the home state and regarded as non-resident for tax purposes.[108] Thirdly, it moved to apply the same rationale to *actual job seekers*, by considering contrary to Community law the refusal to acknowledge periods of employment in other Member States,[109] and then to *potential job seekers*, by means of

[101] Cf Joined Cases 286/82 and 26/83 *Luisi and Carbone* [1984] ECR 377, para 16: 'It follows that the freedom to provide services includes the freedom, for the recipients of services, to go to another Member State in order to receive a service there, without being obstructed by restrictions, even in relation to payments and that tourists, persons receiving medical treatment and persons travelling for the purpose of education or business are to be regarded as recipients of services.'

[102] Case 186/87, *Cowan* [1989] ECR 195; [1990] 2 CMLR 613 AG Lenz, 619: 'Delimitation of its substantive scope must be oriented towards the model of a common market in which all economic activities within the Community are freed from all restrictions on grounds of nationality or residence.'

[103] Directive 90/364 [1990] OJ L180, of 13.7.1990, p 26.

[104] Directive 93/96 [1993] OJ L 317, of 18.12.1993, p 59.

[105] A process closely related to the systemic interpretation of economic freedoms to which we have just referred.

[106] Case 115/78, *Knoors* [1979] ECR 399, paras 20 and 24.

[107] Case C-443/93, *Vougioukos* [1995] 4033, paras 39–41.

[108] Case C-18/95, *Terhoeve* [1999] 345, para 28.

[109] Case C-419/92, *Scholz* [1994] ECR I-505, para 9.

affirming explicitly that the question of whether a post-graduate academic title obtained in another Member State was to be recognised by the country of which a citizen is a national is governed by Community law, even if there was no secondary legislation on the matter.[110] Fourthly, it extended the protection of Community law to third country spouses with a right of residence when the citizen was resident in another Member State, but not automatically having it when returning home (in the case at hand, on account of suspicions concerning the genuineness of the marriage).[111] And finally, the Court ruled that Community law also applied when a German citizen acquires French nationality by marriage (while not renouncing her previous nationality) and sets her residence in France but works in Germany.[112] But what was at stake here was not a further overstretching of the term 'worker' so as to include the national worker, but the narrowing down of the scope of *internal situations* to which Community law did not apply. To the extent that discrimination *against own nationals of a Member State* (paradoxically enough, usually labelled as 'reverse discrimination')[113] continued to be considered unobjectionable according to European constitutional law,[114] the Court could only pretend that free movement of workers governed the relationships between a Member State and its own nationals by shifting the value basis of free movement from the principle of non-discrimination on the basis of nationality to the principle of freedom (essentially economic freedom) said to underlie the four economic freedoms enshrined in the Treaties, and by the consequent recharacterisation of what used to be internal situations as Community-relevant situations on account of the *obstacles* to the exercise of free movement of workers resulting from national legislation, even if exclusively applicable to nationals. Such a change pointed to a major shift in the source and content of the yardstick of European constitutionality, to which I return below.[115]

To conclude this section, both the case law of the European Court of Justice and the secondary legislation spelling out the implications of free movement of workers were underpinned by the view that free movement of workers was to be properly constructed as a vehicle of not only economic but also political integration. This goes a long away to account for the expansionary construction of the 'worker' in 'free movement of workers',

[110] Case C-19/92, *Dieter Kraus* [1993] ECR 1633, paras 16–22.

[111] Case C-370/90, *Singh* [1992] ECR I-4265, para 23: 'Accordingly, when a Community national who has availed himself or herself of those rights returns to his or her country of origin, his or her spouse must enjoy at least the same rights of entry and residence as would be granted to him or her under Community law if his or her spouse chose to enter and reside in another Member State.'

[112] Case C-336/96, *Gilly* [1998] ECR 2793, para 21.

[113] The scent of paradox comes from the fact that the term was coined in US schooling law in the aftermath of *Brown* to refer to what is now generally known as 'affirmative action' or 'positive discrimination'.

[114] The soundness of reverse discrimination is grounded on a logical and a normative basis. In logical terms, the assumption that there is a clear-cut division of legislative competences between the European Union and its Member States entails that certain situations may be defined as purely internal ones, where a standard different from the Community one would necessarily be applicable. In normative terms, reverse discrimination need not be tackled through the judicial review of the European constitutionality of national norms, as the national political process, in which the discriminated national citizens are represented, can sooner or later rectify the discrimination if that is perceived as adequate and/or necessary. On reverse discrimination on the free movement of goods, see Miguel Maduro, *We the Court* (Oxford, Hart, 1997) 154–9.

[115] As we will see in below in more detail, whereas economic freedoms as operationalisations of the principle of non-discrimination on the basis of nationality necessarily refer back to national constitutional standards (non-discrimination being a purely formal standard to be filled in with national substantive principles), (economic) freedom was bound to be linked to self-standing, transcendental standards directly derived from the Treaties (as the very idea of obstacles to the economic freedoms of nationals pointed beyond national constitutional standards).

which well before *Martínez Sala* and *Baumbast* had led to what could only be characterised as overstretching from a narrow literal point of view, and to a change in the understanding of which national norms and according to which standard could be subject to a constitutional review to determine their compliance with the requirements of free movement of workers. This had anticipated the change in the characterisation of this fundamental freedom as a concretisation of the principle of non-discrimination on the basis of nationality to a self-standing (and mainly economic) freedom.

The Two-headed Leading Case: What it Means and What it Has Implied

The leading character of *Martínez Sala* and *Baumbast* derives from the fact that the former case set, and the latter confirmed, the course which the ECJ has followed in the construction of the legal consequences of the insertion of the citizenship provisions in the Treaty establishing the European Community (ex Article G of the Treaty of Maastricht) upon the breadth and scope of the Community right to personal free movement.[116]

Before engaging with the analysis of the question covered in this section, it may be pertinent to refresh the reader on the content of the citizenship provisions as inserted by the Treaty of Maastricht. The literal tenor remains the same, although the numbering has changed: The two key sections for our present purposes (Articles 8 and 8a) read as follows:

> Article 8
>
> 1. Citizenship of the Union is hereby established.
>   Every person holding the nationality of a Member State shall be a citizen of the Union.
> 2. Citizens of the Union shall enjoy the rights conferred by this Treaty and shall be subject to the duties imposed thereby.
>
> Article 8a
>
> 1. Every citizen of the Union shall have the right to move and reside freely within the territory of the Member States, subject to the limitations and conditions laid down in this Treaty and by the measures adopted to give it effect.
> 2. The Council may adopt provisions with a view to facilitating the exercise of the rights referred to in paragraph 1; save as otherwise provided in this Treaty, the Council shall act unanimously on a proposal from the Commission and after obtaining the assent of the European Parliament.

This section is structured in three parts. First, I offer a summary presentation of the facts and the main elements of the rulings in *Martínez Sala* and *Baumbast.* Secondly, I consider the extent to which the case law of the ECJ refers to *Martínez Sala* and *Baumbast* to justify departures from the pre-Maastricht case law. Thirdly, I analyse the ensuing case law to determine the extent to which *Martínez Sala* and *Baumbast* have come to be regarded as

[116] On European citizenship, see Carlos Closa, 'The concept of citizenship in the Treaty on European Union' (1992) 29 *CML Rev* 1137–70; Massimo La Torre (ed), *European Citizenship. An institutional challenge* (Dordrecht, Kluwer, 1998) and Pietro Costa, 'From National to European Citizenship. A Historical Comparison' in Richard Bellamy, Dario Castiglione and Emilio Santoro (ed), *Lineages of Citizenship* (London, Palgrave, 2004) 207–26.

an authority on elements of the freedom of movement of workers which had been established in the pre-Maastricht jurisprudence, to test the extent to which the symbolic importance of *Martínez Sala* is reflected in its replacing the previous leading cases as *the* authoritative reference on free movement of persons (quite obviously, including workers).

Facts and Main Arguments of the Rulings in *Martínez Sala* and *Baumbast*

Martínez Sala

The plaintiff was a Spanish national who had been resident in Germany since childhood, except for a short spell of two years which she spent in her native country. From 1976 to 1986 she had had different jobs, although she also spent some occasional time on unemployment benefit. From 1986 to 1989 she was mostly unemployed and received welfare assistance from local and regional authorities. The plaintiff seems to have always complied with the requirement of applying for residence permits in accordance with German law. They were issued to her without question until 1984. From that year until 1994 she only managed to obtain the receipt for her application, presumably due to delays in the bureaucratic machinery. In January 1993, still waiting for a residence permit to be issued, her second child was born. Given the fact that she was not in any full-time employment, and for that purpose, any employment, she was in principle eligible for the payment of the child-raising allowance, a non-contributory benefit which is part of family policy in Germany. However, her application was rejected on the grounds that although she was resident in Germany, German law made the granting of the allowance to non-nationals conditional upon their being in possession of a valid residence permit.

Given that all parties agreed that the German decision was sound from a purely national perspective, but would be void when considered from a Community perspective, the key question was whether the case was governed by domestic German law or by Community law.[117] Before Maastricht, this may have been a clear-cut case. Martínez Sala was not a worker, or for that purpose, an economically active person, and under such circumstances, Community law simply did not apply.[118]

Accepting the suggestion of counsel for the plaintiff, the ECJ was ready to explore whether a European citizen, if legally resident in another Member State, could invoke rights granted by Community law against the Member State where she resided, and particularly, the right not to be discriminated on nationality grounds ex Article 8a (now 17). The Court affirmed that this was the case:

[117] All parties to the case, including the German government, acknowledged that denying Martínez Sala the allowance resulted in a discrimination exclusively based on her nationality. However, the German government further argued that the case did not fall within the scope of Community law, because Martínez Sala could not be regarded as a worker, either for the purposes of Article 48 TEC and Regulation 1612/68 or for the purposes of Article 51 and Regulation 1408/71. In straight opposition to such a claim, the counsel to the plaintiff argued that the very fact that Martínez Sala was a European citizen brought the facts under the scope of European law, independently of whether she was or was not a worker in a Community law sense. Thus the plaintiff was claiming that the insertion of citizenship provisions should require the Court to review its previous case law in depth, and further extend the subjective scope of Community law, transcending the idea that it only applied to persons engaged in cross-border economic activity.

[118] Paragraphs 34 and 45 of the Judgment. Similarly the AG in his Conclusions, although in para 12 he claimed that if it was the case that she was receiving social assistance at the time the child was born, she was to be regarded as covered against one of the risks described in Regulation 1408/71, and consequently, would fall within the scope of application of the Treaty.

> As a national of a Member State lawfully residing in the territory of another Member State, the appellant in the main proceedings comes within the scope *ratione personae* of the provisions of the Treaty on European citizenship.[119]

On this basis, the ECJ concluded that the denial of the child allowance by German authorities breached Community law; in a concrete sense, it led to discrimination based on nationality against somebody who was entitled to equal treatment. After Maastricht (and in particular, after European citizenship), the relations between a Member State and legally resident nationals of another Member State were governed by Community law, even if the European citizen was economically inactive. Still, the ruling of the Court left unanswered several key legal questions,[120] including the following three: a) whether Article 17 could be said to have direct effect, b) whether a right to enter into the territory of another Member State would stem from it, and c) whether nationals could invoke the new right against their own states.[121]

Indeed it was only when the Court gave its judgment on *Baumbast* and *R* that the core of the implications of *Martínez Sala* became clearer; and that is why it is proper to talk of a two-headed leading case.

Baumbast and R

The joined cases concerned two different but related states of affairs. In both proceedings we find mixed couples, one of whose members was a non-Community citizen. In *Baumbast*, she was a Colombian citizen, he a German national; in *R*, she was a US citizen, he a French national. Both couples established at some point their residence in the United Kingdom, and were later denied leave to reside there.

[119] Paragraph 61 of the Judgment.

[120] There were several reasons why *Martínez Sala* left some many questions open, but perhaps two were the most important ones. First, the facts of the case were very peculiar. It is not far-fetched to say that, was it not for the very restrictive character of German law as regards the acquisition of citizenship, Martínez Sala would have become a citizen many years before the facts of the case took place. In any other Member State of the Union at the time, she could have been naturalised and would have in all likehood opted for such an option if only to avoid further bureaucratic hassles. Because she was for all purposes and according to all possible criteria a 'de facto' member of German society, even if not in poseession of a German passport, the teutonic authorities were in a very weak position when it came to justifying their decision. Indeed, AG La Pergola affirmed explicitly that were the conditions required from Germans to be applied to Community nationals legally resident in Germany, such as Martínez Sala was, abuse was improbable (cf para 22 of his conclusions). Secondly, the Court limited the triggering effect of Article 17 to previous 'legal residence' in the host Member State, and intentionally set aside the question of what are the concrete implications of European citizenship in terms of gaining entry into another Member State. As can be read in para 60 of the judgment: 'It should, however, be pointed out that, in a case such as the present, it is not necessary to examine whether the person concerned can rely on Article 8a of the Treaty in order to obtain recognition of a new right to reside in the territory of the Member State concerned, since it is common ground that she has already been authorised to reside there, although she has been refused issue of a residence permit.' The decision to muddle through may also have been favoured in order to avoid the question of when the right of Martínez Sala not to be discriminated against was created. This was specially relevant in the case given that the child was born in early 1993, while the Treaty of Maastricht entered into force on 1 November 1993. The Advocate General stated the obvious when he explicitly excluded that it could be invoked vith a view to gain access to political rights reserved to nationals precisely because they are so; cf para 21 of his Conclusions: 'A claim by a resident who is a national of another Member State in relation to nationals of the host State will therefore be unfounded if it relates to rights which are to be understood as being reserved for the latter precisely on the ground that they are nationals of that State.'

[121] As acknowledged by AG La Pergola in his conclusions, para 23: 'This case is therefore a test case for a range of problems which could be referred to the Court in future.'

In *Baumbast*, the couple had a common child (who held both the nationality of his mother and that of his father), and also took care of one daughter from the previous marriage of the wife. When all of them arrived in the United Kingdom, Mr Baumbast worked for a British company. It was then that all members of the family were issued a residence permit valid until 1995. Before that, the husband put an end to the labour relationship with his employer, and started working as a self-employed person. Since 1993 he was on and off the dole, undertaking temporary contracts with German companies in third countries. When Mrs Baumbast asked in 1995 for indefinite leave of residence, she was denied it. The Baumbasts lived in the United Kingdom, where they owned a mortgaged home, and where their children attended school. Notwithstanding that, the British authorities claimed that none of them was a worker according to Community law, and thus they were not entitled to a residence permit according to the secondary law then in force. The key point of fact was that Mr Baumbast no longer worked in the British Isles, nor was insured against any social risk in Great Britain (all the family was covered by the German social insurance system, which did not extend to emergency treatment in the United Kingdom), something which the authorities considered was proof Mr Baumbast was not entitled to reside in Britain according to Directive 90/364, which then established the general regulation of the right of abode of nationals of Member States.[122]

The facts of *R* were somewhat different. The couple had two common children with dual US-French nationality. The husband had a right of residence on account of being a worker, and when his wife entered the UK she was granted a residence permit as a spouse of a Community national, valid until 1995. The couple divorced in 1992, following which the mother took primary care of the children (although it was explicitly stated that the children had to have contact with the father). She established herself as an interior decorator. When in 1995 she asked for a new residence permit, this was denied to her (although granted to the children) on account of her being a non-Community citizen who no longer was married to a Community national. Before the Court decided the case, she married a UK national and was granted leave of residence. The Court was consequently presented with three different sets of legal problems: (1) whether the children of the two couples had a right of residence; (2) whether the spouses, even if non-Community nationals, had a right of residence; (3) and whether Mr Baumbast himself, a Community national who no longer qualified as a worker either under Article 48 or 51 TEC, had a right of residence. In all three cases, the Court concluded that the plaintiffs concerned had a right of residence. But while the first two problems posed legal questions which were far from concerning the interplay between the case law of the Court and the citizenship provisions (and indeed were decided without major innovation upon the pre-Maastricht case law),[123] the third problem, the right of residence of Mr Baumbast himself, replayed

[122] For the sake of completeness, it must be added that before the preliminary question was actually solved, the children were acknowledged the right to reside in the United Kingdom on the basis of Article 12 of Regulation 1408/71, and so was Mrs Baumbast as prime carer; but Mr Baumbast kept on being denied leave of residence at the time the case was brought before the ECJ.

[123] The Court affirmed in each case the existence of a right of residence. On the first problem, the Court applied pretty straightforwardly the previous case law, affirming that the prospect of the children being denied the right to pursue their education in the host Member State on account of changes in the working or personal circumstances of the parents would create an obstacle to the effective exercise of the freedom of movement of workers (paras 51–2 of the judgment). The Court only went slightly beyond its previous case law when claiming that the effectiveness of free movement of workers required granting leave of residence to all children living with the spouses, even if some of them were descendants of only the non-Community national (para 57 of the

the legal questions underpinning *Martínez Sala*, precisely because what Mr Baumbast asked for amounted to the acknowledgment of his right to reside in the United Kingdom *even if no longer a worker*, not even according to the overstretched definition which the ECJ had come to sustain in its pre-Maastricht case law.

The Court, in contradiction with the submissions of the British and German governments and the Commission, claimed that European citizenship affirmed that Article 18(1) did have direct effect,[124] and thus conferred on all nationals of Member States[125] the right to move and reside freely in the territory of all other Member States even if economically inactive.[126] Such rights, as most rights, were not unlimited, but had to be weighed and balanced with the legitimate interests of the Member States if in conflict.[127] However, limitations had to respect the core content of the right[128] (the Court speaks of being in line with the limits imposed by EC law) and be proportional.[129] This obviously implies that any differentiated treatment of nationals and non-nationals becomes suspect, and could be the object of review by national courts. In the case at hand, it was out of any proportion to deny the right of residence to a self-sustaining citizen, who was not a burden on the British public finances, on account of his German insurance not covering emergency treatment in the United Kingdom.[130]

Martínez Sala and *Baumbast* as Leading Cases: The Subjective and Objective Scope of Free Movement in a European Citizenship Perspective

In this section, I consider the main doctrines on the meaning of Community free movement brought about by the case law developed following the lead of *Martínez Sala* and *Baumbast.* My core claim is that the Court has established that the establishment of a bond uniting all nationals of Member States as citizens of the European polity has produced a transformation in the value basis of Community law in general, and in particular of the four economic freedoms (and very particularly, personal freedom of movement). The Court has found that the establishment of European citizenships requires reconstructing the fundamental economic freedoms as aiming not only at the realisation of the principle of non-discrimination on the basis of nationality, but more widely and generally, the achievement of equal treatment of all nationals of Member States qua European citizens. Such a shift would require a reading of the provisions of free movement of workers resulting in the broadening of both their subjective and objective scopes. Regarding the former, the Community right of personal freedom of movement should be reputed to be held not only by 'workers' (that is, economically active citizens

judgment). As regards the second problem, the Court affirmed that the right of the children to reside would be rendered ineffective if it would not imply the right of residence of the partner who is in actual charge of them, in case she or he did not have another title of residence (as said in para 71 of the judgment; paragraph 72 affirms that this result is also required by the right to family life as enshrined in the European Convention of Human Rights).

124 Para 84 of the judgment.

125 Para 84.

126 Para 81 of the judgment.

127 Para 90 of the judgment.

128 Geelhoed, Conclusions, 110.

129 Para 91 of the judgment.

130 Paragraph 93 of the judgment.

and those assimilated to them in the pre-Maastricht case law of the ECJ); but 'supranational citizens', the term with which we could refer (and do refer hereafter) to the larger category of persons who are either workers or economically inactive legal residents in another Member State, where they have already developed a network of social relations. As regards the objective scope of personal freedom of movement, the 'citizenship turn' has led to an expansionary construction of the horizontal constitutional bite of the freedom, thus 'Europeanising' policy areas where Member States retain exclusive powers and which were regarded as fully excluded from the scope of Community law in the previous case law of the ECJ; and meddling to a larger extent than before in the relationships between the state and its own nationals.

Expanding the Subjective Scope of Community Law: From Market Citizen to Supranational Citizen as Subject of Community Law

The rulings in favour of both Martínez Sala and Baumbast necessarily led to the final abandonment of the concept of 'worker' as drawing the personal scope of Community law. The Court found that the insertion of citizenship provisions, and most especially, of section 1 of Article 8a, required enlarging the rank and file of those holding Community rights. Consequently, the concept of worker remains of importance to determine the scope of application of the bundle of rights assigned on account of taking employment in another Member State, but failure to qualify as a worker does not immediately entail not being granted rights by Community law.

A systematic reconstruction of the cases following on the trail of *Martínez Sala* and *Baumbast* shows that the Court has not proceeded to replace 'worker' by 'European citizen' *simpliciter* as the category drawing the sphere of application of Community law, but instead has favoured that of the 'supranational citizen'. Working remains an avenue of choice to develop such ties, but is not the exclusive one. Provided that entry and residence were legally enjoyed,[131] the mere fact of residence would trigger that status, even if the person has not become economically active all through the months or years thus spent.

The legal status of the supranational citizen has been defined positively in *Martínez Sala, Grzekzyck, Baumbast, Ninni-Orasche* (only in the Opinion of the AG),[132] *Trojani, Bidar* and *Ioannidis*, as that of somebody who is legally resident in another Member State even if she has never been or is no longer a worker. Martínez Sala had spent most of her life in Germany; Grzekzyck had already spent three years in Belgium; Baumbast had been living for a long period in the United Kingdom, and even owned a home there; Ninni-Orasche had been resident for two years and her residence permit was valid for another three; Trojani had been living in Belgium for two years, and had become engaged

[131] Although European citizens do indeed have a right to enter any other Member State, it could be the case that entry took place when the state of the nationality of the relevant individual was not yet a Member State (this hypothesis is far from artificial considering the fact that membership of the Union has almost doubled since 2004). Moreover, it continues to be the case that residence is conditional on not becoming a burden on national health and welfare systems, as restated in Article 7(1)(b) of the 2004 Directive on free movement and residence of European citizens (Directive 2004/38/EC of the European Parliament and the Council, of 29 April 2004, OJ L 158, of 30.4.2004, p 77). Thus, although nationals of any Member State have the right to enter any other Member State to seek employment, and they can persist in their search for a rather long time, they do not have a right to indefinite residence.

[132] Although the Court limited itself to answering the questions posed by the referring Court, and avoided the question of what implications Article 18 TEC had in the case at hand, the Opinion of AG Geelhoed in C-413/01, *Ninni-Orasche* [2003] ECR I-13187 constitutes the most clear effort to determine what concept of rightholder underlies the Martínez Sala jurisprudence; cf especially para 91 of the Opinion.

in a socio-occupational reintegration programme of the Salvation Army; Bidar had been living for two years in the United Kingdom; and Ioannidis had spent close to 10 years in Belgium. In Collins, the concept of 'supranational citizen' was negatively defined by means of excluding from its breadth those European citizens who had not developed consistent ties to the host state of their residence. In concrete, the ECJ found it problematic that eligibility for a job seeker's allowance would be conditioned to long-term residence, but considered very proper to require a 'connection between persons who claim entitlement to such an allowance and' the employment market.[133]

The contours of the right of residence of supranational citizens have also been considered in the case law. In *Baumbast* the ECJ declared it unjustified to deny a new leave of residence to a self-sustaining citizen on account of his insurance not covering emergency treatment. *Grezekczyk* also did incidentally touch on the issue, by redefining the resuming condition of becoming an 'unreasonable burden' on the public finances of the host state. The assignment of a permanent right of residence after five years of continued legal residence in the host state by Article 16 of the Residence Directive of 2004 constitutes a partial 'codification' of the rights stemming from this line of jurisprudence.[134]

Particularly important is the affirmation of the rights of non-Community spouses of national citizens to residence (in terms affirmed from *Akrich*[135] onwards). While Advocate General Geelhoed was extremely cautious in its conclusion, arguing that there were very good reasons to restrict the free entry and establishment of non-nationals when their only title to such entry and residence was marriage to a Community national, the Court ruled that limitations were virtually confined to Member States having good evidence of the faked character of the marriage (the right to family life in EC law would rule out the automatic denial of the right of residence even if the spouse was not legally resident in the EU country where established before entering the State of which her husband or his wife are nationals).

The 'supranational citizen' is a creature of the social, political and economic dynamics unleashed by integration.[136] Still, she was only partially within[137] (when not totally outside) the scope of application of Community law, and enjoyment of the ensuing rights, until the Treaty of Maastricht and its 'operationalisation' in *Martínez Sala* and *Baumbast.* By giving the supranational citizen a full 'droit de cité', the ECJ could not but redefine the objective scope of Community law, and in particular, of the personal freedom of movement.

[133] C-138/02, *Collins*, para 71. The Court hinted at the requirement that the person had genuinely sought work in the Member State. This fell short of the most strict standard suggested by the Advocate General, who considered that residence was a perfectly adequate condition of eligibility (para 75 of his Opinion) as it will disencourage 'benefit tourism'.

[134] Directive 2004/38/EC.

[135] C-109/01 Akrich [2003] ECR I-9607.

[136] Quite obviously, there were workers migrating to other states well before the Treaty of Rome entered into force. But the high numbers of Europeans spending part of their lives in another Member State to which we now have grown so accustomed as not to realise its novelty is the twin result of the technologies which make travelling easy and affordable and the legal framework established by Community law.

[137] Partially within because some of the supranational citizens had been absorbed as 'workers' in the overstretched definition of the term (very especially, as was indicated, in the parallel line of jurisprudence starting in *Cowan*) or were brought within the scope of application of Community law by means of other interpretative techniques, such as subjecting the definition of residence for tax purposes to a review of European constitutionality. See C-275/93 *Schumacker* [1995] ECR I-225.

The 'Objective' Breadth and Scope of Personal Free Movement: Constitutional 'Horizontal' Framing and the Communitarisation of the Relationships Between Member States and their Own Nationals

The 'citizenship' turn of personal freedom of movement has not only justified expanding the subjective scope of the freedom (from worker to supranational citizen), but has led to a reconsideration of the objective scope of the freedom. In particular, the ECJ has broadened the horizontal constitutional bite of free movement, or, to put it another way, the ECJ has reviewed the European constitutionality of a greater number of national laws using freedom of movement as a yardstick. In particular, the Court has opened up to review European constitutionality laws in exercise of exclusive national competences (and very significantly, on non-contributory welfare provisions) and has increased the teeth of the principle of freedom of movement in relations between a state and its own nationals. As a result, the province of 'purely internal situations' in free movement of persons has got dramatically reduced.[138]

New Areas of National Law to Be Constitutionally Reviewed against European Standards

The characterisation of the supranational citizen as a holder of rights and obligations under Community law implies *de facto* an enlargement of the scope of application of Community law which corresponds to the social and economic problems of supranational citizens which were not previously governed by Union law. But the new breadth of Community law did not come hand-in-hand with the assignment of positive or vertical competence to the Union, but with the affirmation that the validity of all national laws, even those promulgated in exercise of exclusive national competences, was dependent on its compliance with the requirements deriving from the right to free movement in the citizenship phase of Community law.

The 'horizontal constitutional effect of freedom of movement'[139] has had a major impact on the design of national welfare systems, and most especially, on the design of non-contributory benefits. The main concrete implication of *Martínez Sala* and *Baumbast* for the supranational citizen has been access to non-contributory social benefits, precisely the kind of benefits which basically fell outside the scope of application of Community law until Maastricht.[140] Not only had the Union virtually no competence in the matter, but it was barely affected by the horizontal effect of the economic freedoms given that they

[138] Indeed, the redefinition of the value basis of free movement is closely connected to the redefinition of the subjective scope of the right. If economically inactive citizens of another Member States are to be regarded as Community right-holders (as indeed *Martínez Sala* and *Baumbast* explicitly do), then the bonds uniting Europeans cannot be regarded to be based on mere economic interest, but must have transcended that stage and reached one of trust based on solidarity.

[139] Indeed AG Kokott in C-192/05, *Tas Hagen* [2006] ECR I-10451, paras 34 and 36 talk of a horizontal effect of the citizenship provision, echoed by the Court in para 23 of its judgment. AG Geelhoed in C-209/03, *Bidar* [2005] ECR I-2119, paras 29 and 52 constructs in such a way the judgment in *Collins*. And he follows such line of reasoning in the case at hand. The Court assumed in para 40 of its judgment that the Communities already had acquired competences on education.

[140] Explicitly, AG Geelhoed in C-209/03, *Bidar* [2005] ECR I-2119, 28: 'By placing emphasis on the fundamental character of EU citizenship, the Court makes clear that this is not merely a hollow or symbolic concept, but that it constitutes the basic status of all nationals of EU Member States, giving rise to certain rights and privileges in other Member States where they are resident . . . various social benefits which Member States previously granted to its nationals and to economically active persons under Regulations Nos 1612/68 or 1408/71 now have been extended to EU citizens who are lawfully resident in the host Member State.'

were granted on 'citizen' not 'market' grounds (that is, eligibility did not depend on holding the condition of worker or economically active person characteristically subject to Community law) and presupposed a 'long-term' relationship between the political community and the beneficiary (and consequently were clearly beyond the reach of the *Cowan* line of jurisprudence). By granting the supranational citizen the condition of holder of Community rights, *Martínez Sala* and *Baumbast* have turned suspicious any criteria of eligibility of non-contributory benefits which excludes them from the scope of eligibility, placing the argumentative burden on the side of the Member States. In *Collins*, the Court made it clear that the application of any limitation 'must rest on clear criteria known in advance and provision must be made for the possibility of a means of redress of a judicial nature'.[141] Thus, in *Martínez Sala* it was impossible to justify making the enjoyment of a child-rearing allowance conditional upon a merely declaratory residence permit; in *Grzejzczyk* it was unreasonable to assume that a student's right to residence came to an end because he applied for the *minimex* (a non-contributory benefit ensuring a minimum income); in *Trojani* the same argument was extended to a case in which the claimant was neither a worker not a student; in *Ninni-Orasche*, the Advocate General (although not the Court) found it was not justified to deny a study grant on account of nationality, given that the plaintif had genuine ties with Austria and there were clear indications that she did not change her residence in order to become eligible for such a benefit; in *Bidar* it was unreasonable to require a period of four years residence to be eligible for a maintenance grant while completing university studies; in *Ioannidis*, it was unreasonable to deny a tide-over allowance because the applicant had followed a training programme in another Member State.

The EU Law Government of Relationships between Citizens and their own State and the Shrinking Internal Situation

The expansion of the objective breadth of Community law has not only resulted in the constitutional framing of policy areas which were traditionally considered out of the reach of Community law, but also in an increased bite of Community law in the discipline of relationships between Member States and their own nationals, which has led to a dramatic reduction in the scope of purely internal situations to which Community law would not apply. Indeed, some Advocates General have maintained that Community law should also apply to cases of 'residual' reverse discrimination, something which would almost dispense with the pretence of drawing a line between purely internal and Community situations.

The Persistence of the Rights Acquired as a Mover and the Relationship between Citizens and States

As was argued above, relations between a Member State and its own nationals were brought within the scope of application of Community law even before the Maastricht Treaty, to the extent that nationals had already exercised their right to free movement taking up employment (or preparing for doing so) in another Member State.

The ECJ has expanded the constitutional role of free movement after *Martínez Sala* and *Baumbast* by claiming that relationships between a state and its nationals are governed by

[141] C-138/02, *Collins*, para 72.

Community law when nationals have previously exercised the right to personal free movement to another Member State, *whether for economic or non-economic purposes.* Thus, not only workers, but also students or pensioners enjoyed rights against their own Member States in cases where they were treated less favourably than another national who had not spent part of their life in another Member State on account of not having been there all the time.[142] If we make use of the same metaphor we employed when considering the expansion of the personal scope of application of Community law, what we are dealing with here is the acknowledgment that supranational citizens do not stop being so when they return to their home country.

In this particular relation, the strengthening of the right to free movement of nationals resulted in access to benefits and tax deductions being available both to nationals (and European citizens) who had had continuous residence, or to nationals who had exerted their right of free movements as workers. The easiest cases concerned citizens who had already returned to their home state or else were still resident in another Member State. *D'Hoop* was based on the lack of justification for the denial of a tide-over allowance on the ground that the applicant had not completed all her studies in Belgium, but followed part of them in France. In *Tas Hagen*, making the entitlement of a compensatory pension for war victims subject to residence in the country lacked any good reason. In *Turpeinen*, a Finnish norm applying a higher tax rate to the pension paid by Finnish authorities on account of residence in Spain was found groundless.[143] In *Pusa*, benefiting from a rule which limits the attachment order on a pension so that the debtor still receives an amount equal to the minimum income was rendered ineffective when not considering the income tax payable in the country of residence.[144] Rather more complicated were the cases of frontier workers discriminated against by their own state on account of being resident in a second Member State. In a handful of cases, the ECJ seemed to have no major difficulty in figuring out the sense of its ruling. In *Elsen*, the fact that residence (or actual payment of contributions) was required by German law to assimilate child-rearing periods during which the mother does not work to working periods for the purpose of calculating pension benefits was found utterly unjustified.[145] In *Ritter Colais*, the differential treatment of negative income losses stemming from the family home depending on the location of the home in Germany or in another Member State was regarded as lacking any good reason. In *Schwarz*, German tax law prevented school expenses incurred in another Member State being deductible, on account of these not being incurred in Germany, which was found contrary to the free movement exercised by the students themselves.[146] In *Van Pommeren*, the decision to deny benefits associated with her invalidity pension on account of residence in Belgium was quashed, despite the plaintiff not qualifying as a 'market citizen' because the only 'Community' factor was her residence in Belgium. However, some later cases have revealed the complexities involved here, and have rendered if not the Court, then the Advocates General less certain about the proper line of development of the case law. In *Hartmann*, AG Geelhoed put forward the claim that the rights under which citizens could oppose their Member States should only be those which

[142] Cf C-540/99, *Reisch*, AG Geelhoed, para 58, where he claimed that citizenship resulted in bringing within the scope of Community law the owner of a second residence in another Member State.

[143] Case C-520/04, *Turpeinen* [2006] ECR I-10685, paras 63–66.

[144] Case C-224/02, *Pusa* [2004] ECR I-5763, paras 34 and 35.

[145] Case C-135/99, *Elsen* [2000] ECR I-10409, para 35.

[146] Case C-76/05, *Schwarz*, not yet reported, para 90; AG Stix Hackl, para 91.

they could have acquired as a result of moving to another state. He doubted that the Hartmanns would have acquired such a right if they had both moved to Austria or Germany. And in *Hendrix*, AG Geelhoed had to consider whether the nature of the benefit supplementing the earnings of disabled people was 'more closely connected with the social environment of the claimant' and thus that it was justified to subject it to residence criteria' (paragraph 77).[147] Moreover, in *Schempp*, the Court refused to consider as discriminatory a higher tax burden resulting from the denial of a tax deduction on account of maintenance payments because the recipient was an Austrian national, and no evidence was produced of her income being subject to tax in Austria. If the spouse had been resident in Germany, Schempp would have been entitled to the deduction. However, the Court claimed that the outcome was due to the disparity in tax laws, which was the result of the allocation of powers between the Union and the Member States.[148]

What is Left of the 'Purely Internal Situation' in Personal Movement?

Perhaps the most radical implication of the citizenship turn of the ECJ is the dramatic reduction of the breadth and scope of 'purely internal situations'.

The drawing of a clear and meaningful line between 'internal' and 'Community' situations was predicated on a conception of the Community subject and of the project of European integration which has been progressively eroded in the case law of the ECJ, not only concerning the understanding of economic freedoms, but also concerning the legal basis of Community acts. At any rate, the legal doctrines that the ECJ built after *Martínez Sala* and *Baumbast* do necessarily imply a reduction of the breadth of purely internal situations.

The so-called doctrine of 'residual discrimination', proposed to the Court by Advocate General Maduro in a case concerning free movement of goods,[149] and applied to free movement of persons by AG Sharpston,[150] may accelerate the progress towards constitutional oblivion of the category of purely internal situations. The doctrine claims that Community law should govern purely internal situations when the review of European constitutionality results in invalidating a national norm which mainly applies to non-nationals, but still governs a residual number of nationals. The very use of the term 'residual' and the ensuing normative arguments (which seem to revolve around the need for Community law to protect victims of a discriminatory normative standard only

[147] But the ECJ limited this conclusion claiming that such restriction had to be justified and proportionate to the objective pursued (para 54 of the judgment).

[148] Case C-403/03, *Schempp* [2005] ECR I-6421, paras 17–18.

[149] Opinion of AG Maduro in Case C-72/03, *Carbonati Apuani* [2004] ECR I-8027, especially paras 68 and 69. The case involved an Italian law which imposed a tax calculated by reference to weight on all marble excavated in Carrara, with the exception of that transformed within the same municipality. Although this was a case of free movement of goods *par excellence*, Maduro invoked *Martínez Sala* and *Baumbast* to ground that also residents in Italy should benefit from the declaration of European inconstitutionality of the national law; otherwise Union law would tolerate a 'residual' discrimination of the minority of those who were neither from the municipality or the whole of the Union except Italy.

[150] Opinion of AG Sharpston in C-212/06 *Gouvernement de la Communauté française and Gouvernement wallon*, not yet reported, paras 154 and 157, where she concludes that subjecting to a condition of residence a social benefit aimed at those who have at their charge disabled persons is not only constitutive of a breach of the Community right not to be discriminated of non-Belgian European citizens who work in Flanders but do not have their residence there, but that Belgians have a similar Community right if they are in the same situation. This cannot be regarded as a purely internal situation because it is another case of residual discrimination. Quite cunningly, the AG predicts that the Court was unlikely to follow her train of reasoning, which it actually did not.

applicable to a very diminished minority once constitutional European law leads to its being set aside and rendered inapplicable to most of its original addressees; that is, Community law should apply because victims only became a tiny minority, unlikely to be heard in national political process, *after* the application of the Community standards of constitutionality apply) suggest that the expansion of the scope of Union law in these cases may indeed be a rather modest enterprise. Still, the symbolic, political and systemic implications cannot but be described as radical.

Martínez Sala as the Fundamental Leading Case on Free Movement of Persons: How it Became an Authority for all Case Law

The symbolic importance of *Martínez Sala* is proven by the fact that it has become a jurisprudential authority even on aspects of free movement of persons which had been settled parts of the case law of the Court before it (and of which it was not a leading case, but a mere application of such leading cases). Up to January 2008, *Martínez Sala* was put to such use in the following cases:

- in five Opinions of AGs and in one judgment of the Court the claim that there is no single definition of worker in Community law was based on paragraph 31 of the judgment in Martínez Sala;[151]
- in eight Opinions of AGs and in two judgments of the Court there was a reference to paragraph 32 of the judgment of *Martínez Sala*, which restated the broad interpretation of worker for the purpose of Article 48 TEC and Regulation 1612/68;[152]
- in six Opinions of AGs and in five judgments of the Court paragraph 36 of the judgment in *Martínez Sala* was referred to, given that it restated the broad interpretation of what a worker is for the purpose of Article 51 TEC and Regulation 1408/71;[153]

[151] Opinion of AG Cosmas in C-411/98, *Ferliri* [2000] ECR I-8081, para 50; Opinion of AG Jacobs in C-95/99, *Khalil* [2001] ECR I-7413, para 46; Opinion of AG Geelhoed in C-256/01, *Allonby* [2004] ECR I-873, para 63; Opinion of AG Kokott, in C-313/02, *Wippel* [2004] ECR I-9483, para 43; Opinion of AG Kokott, in C-302/02, *Laurin Effing* [2005] ECR I-553, para 26; Judgment of the Court in C-543/03, *Dodl* [2005], I-5049, para 27.

[152] Judgment in Case C-337/97, *Meussen* [1999] ECR I-3289, para 13; Opinion of AG Geelhoed, C-109/01 *Akrich* [2003] ECR I-9607, para 75; Opinion of AG Mischo, C-369/01, *Abatay* [2003] ECR I-12301, para 159; Judgment in C-138/02, *Collins* [2004] ECR I-2703, para 26; Opinion of AG Geelhoed in C-256/01, Allonby [2004] ECR I-873, para 67; Opinion of AG Kokott, in C-302/02, *Laurin Effing* [2005] ECR I-553, para 47; Opinion of AG Léger, in C-152/03, *Ritter Coulais* [2006] ECR I-1711, para 32; Opinion of AG Léger, in C-20/03, *Burmanjer* [2005] ECR I-4133, para 19; Opinion of AG Ruiz Jarabo, in C-258/04, *Ioannidis* [2005] ECR I-8275, para 39; Opinion of AG Léger in C-520/04, *Turpeinen* [2006] ECR I-10685, para 56.

[153] Judgment in Case C-275/96, *Kuusijärvi* [1998] ECR I-3419, para 21; Judgment in Case C-262/96 [1999] ECR I-2685, para 86; Opinion of AG Cosmas in Case C-411/98, *Ferliri* [2000] ECR I-8081, para 44; Opinion of AG Saggio in Case C-135/99, *Essen* [2000] ECR I-10409, para 16; Opinion of AG Tizzano in Case C-212/00, *Stallone* [2001] ECR I-7625, para 14; Opinion of AG Jacobs in C-28/00, *Kauer* [2002] ECR I-1343, para 43; Judgment Court in C-302/02, *Laurin Effing* [2005] ECR I-553, para 32; Judgment Court in C-372/02, *Adanez Vega* [2004] ECR I-10761, para 46; Opinion of AG Jarabo Colomer in C-138/02, *Collins* [2004] ECR I-2703, para 54 (reference was to para 44 of *Martínez Sala*); Opinion of AG Geelhoed, in C-543/03, *Dodl* [2005] ECR I-5049, para 11; Judgment Court in C-543/03, *Dodl* [2005] ECR I-5049, para 30.

- on two occasions Advocates General and on one the Court affirmed that the right to residence stemming from 1408/71 and 1612/68 could overlap on the basis of paragraph 27 of *Martínez Sala*;[154]
- four Opinions of Advocates General and one judgment of the Court invoked paragraph 25 of *Martínez Sala* to determine how social advantages should be defined in Community law;[155]
- five Opinions of Advocates General and three judgments of the Court made use of paragraph 32 of *Martínez Sala* to substantiate the premise that the end of the employment relationship did not result in all rights stemming from the status of worker ceasing immediately;[156]
- one Advocate General invoked paragraph 53 of *Martínez Sala* to affirm the declaratory, not constitutive nature, of the residence permit;[157]
- one Advocate General invoked *Martínez Sala* to ground the characterisation of the child-raising allowance as a benefit for the purpose of Regulation 1408/71; and one Advocate General did the same with regard to the definition of family benefit for the purpose of the said Regulation.[158]

This practice may suggest that *Martínez Sala* has become so much the reference ruling on free movement of persons, that indeed Advocates General and even the Court have come to see the legal force of elements of the case law predating *Martínez Sala* and *Baumbast* dependent on the previously mentioned causes confirming them. This fundamental role assigned to *Martínez Sala* may be best illustrated by the use made of the precedent by AG Tizzano in *Stallone*. In paragraph 14 of his Conclusions, Tizzano supports his claim that the situation at hand is not a purely internal one on the basis that the fifth recital of Regulation 1408/71 refers not only to workers, but also to the members of his or her family; such argument is then supported by a reference to paragraph 44 of the judgment in *Martínez Sala*, which actually concerns a very different matter (indeed, whether the plaintiff could be regarded as a worker if insured in respect of one single risk in Germany). Even if merely an editing mistake, it may reveal the significance accorded to *Martínez Sala*, which European judges feel is necessary to quote as a leading authority in the field.

[154] Judgment in C-185/96, *Commission v Greece* [1998] ECR 6601, para 19; Conclusions of AG Alber in Case C-85/99, *Offermanns* [2001] ECR I-3337, para 68; Conclusions of AG Alber in C-184/99, *Grzelczyk* [2001] ECR I-6193, paras 92–93.

[155] Judgment in C-185/96, *Commission v Greece* [1998] ECR 6601, para 20; Conclusions of AG Jarabo Colomer in C-138/02, *Collins* [2004] ECR I-2703, para 19; Conclusions of AG Geelhoed in C-413/01, *Ninni-Orasche* [2003] ECR I-13187, para 43; Conclusions of AG Tizzano in Joined Cases C-502/01 and 31/02, *Gaumain-Cerri* [2004] ECR I-6483, para 134; Conclusions of AG Kokott, in C-302/02, *Laurin Effing* [2005] ECR I-553, para 60.

[156] Conclusions of AG Alber in C-33/99, *Fahmi* [2001] ECR I-2415, para 66; in the same case, judgment of the Court, para 42; Conclusions of AG Jacobs in C-43/99, *Leclere and Deaconescu* [2001], ECR I-4265, para 94; in the same case, judgment of the Court, para 55; Judgment of the Court in Case C-388/99, *Rundgren* [2001] ECR I-3731, para 32; Conclusions of AG Jarabo Colomer in C-138/02, Collins [2004] ECR I-2703, paras 29–33; Conclusions of AG Geelhoed in C-413/01, *Ninni-Orasche* [2003] ECR I-13187, para 42; Conclusions of AG Kokott, in C-302/02, *Laurin Effing* [2005] ECR I-553, para 50.

[157] Conclusions of AG Alber in C-184/99, *Grzelczyk* [2001] ECR I-6193, para 87.

[158] Conclusions of AG Kokott, in C-302/02, *Laurin Effing* [2005] ECR I-553, para 61; Conclusions of AG Jacobs in C-333/00, *Maaheimo* [2002] ECR I-10087, para 27.

Legal and Normative Assessment of *Martínez Sala* and *Baumbast*

After having reconstructed the pre-Maastricht case law on free movement of workers, and analysed the changes brought about by the rulings of the ECJ led by *Martínez Sala* and *Baumbast*, it is time to assess the implications of the 'citizenship' turn of Community law in legal-dogmatic and in wider political terms. In particular, it is pertinent to consider (1) whether it is appropriate to characterise the two-headed leading case as a major turning point in the evolution of Community law, which would have exerted a major influence on the nature of Community law as a legal order and resulted in the transformation of free movement of workers into free movement of citizens; (2) whether *Martínez Sala* and *Baumbast* would have actually renewed the emancipatory promise of Community law by making the political and no longer the market citizen the central reference point of Community law. As we will see below, both questions are different, and should remain differentiated, but the answers to them are strongly connected.

A Legal Revolution?

As has already been said, the key innovations in the rulings in *Martínez Sala* and *Baumbast* consist in the broadening of the subjective and objective scope of personal freedom of movement under Community law. The insertion of citizenship provisions in the TEC has been taken to mean that free movement of persons is not to be considered as mainly a specification or concretisation of the principle of non-discrimination on the basis of nationality, but is to be more widely constructed as one of the key faculties attached to European citizenship as the fundamental status of all Europeans (one but not the only one among such rights being non-discrimination on the basis of nationality). This has led to to the acknowledgement of a Community right to personal freedom of movement to citizens who were not economically active, and thus could not qualify as workers. This, however, does not immediately mean that European citizens have the same rights of residence as nationals in all Member States. As we saw above, the case law of the Court following *Martínez Sala* and *Baumbast* has made it clear that the expansion of the personal scope of freedom of movements falls shorter than that, and indeed only extends to 'supranational citizens', who may be economically inactive but do have at least stable social links and bonds with the Member State on account of previous legal residence. Similarly, it has brought into the scope of Community law national laws and policies which were before regarded as fully outside the breadth of the review of European constitutionality, as well as increasing the bite of free movement in relationships between a state and its own nationals.

It suffices to consider briefly the case law of the Court as it developed before the Treaty of Maastricht to realise that *Martínez Sala* and *Baumbast* are not so much revolutionary judgments, as important cases which render explicit and push forward the main elements of jurisprudence of the Court. Or to put it differently, their importance does not reside so much in their revolutionary character (their structural and substantive implications are rather congenial to the previous case law of the Court, to the point that one may argue that the ECJ could have decided in similar terms even without the explicit insertion of citizenship provisions in the primary law of the Union)[159] as in the fact that they push quite far the process of 'abstraction' and 'humanisation' of the definition of right-holders of the Community freedom of movement; at the time that they increase the regulative salience of Community law in the legal relationships between a state and its own nationals.

Indeed, *Martínez Sala* and *Baumbast* can be said to contribute to the further realisation of the 'political' understanding of free movement of persons which has animated the case law of the Court of Justice since its first rulings on the matter; thus further disproving the soundness of the conception of free movement of persons as mere means of problem-solving and efficiency enhancement. The only major difference is perhaps the fact that the pre-Maastricht jurisprudence seemed to anchor its understanding of free movement in the implicit general freedom of action which necessarily underpinned the four fundamental economic freedoms; while since *Martínez Sala*, the new principled grounding of free movement of persons is European citizenship as a supranational political bond. But besides the general discussion concerning the relationship between citizenship and general freedom, especially when specified by reference to economic powers, it must be stressed that continuity is proven by the fact that citizenship, like general freedom before, plays the same structural role in justifying the declaration of unconstitutionality of national laws on account of their being non-discriminatory but placing obstacles in the way of enjoying any of the fundamental economic freedoms.

The logical and substantive connections between the traditional jurisprudence on freedom of movement of workers and *Martínez Sala* and *Baumbast* may be obscured by the laconic style of some of the judgments of the Court,[160] but they are easier to identify in the opinions of some Advocates General, and very especially of AG La Pergola in *Martínez Sala*. Indeed, the argument of AG La Pergola was built around the premise that European citizenship constituted an autonomous ground on which to claim the bundle of rights and protections offered by Community law:

> Citizenship of the Union ... is the fundamental legal status guaranteed to the citizen of every Member State by the legal order of the Community and now of the Union. This results from the unequivocal terms of the two paragraphs of Article 8 of the Treaty ... [It] comes through the fiat of the primary norm, being conferred directly on the individual, who is henceforth formally recognised as a subject of law who acquires and loses it together with citizenship of the national state to which he belongs and in no other way.[161]

However, he was very explicit in claiming that this new ground was the result of elucidating the more abstract legal principle underlying the pre-existing rights to freedom of movement of workers, to freedom of establishment and to freedom to provide and receive services, thus stressing the logical continuity in the evolution of the jurisprudence on freedom of movement:[162]

[159] An equivalent judgment in the absence of the citizenship provisions may have come later rather than sooner. But the successive 'stretching' of the meaning of 'market citizen', which reached its peak in *Cowan*, led logically to the acknowledgment of the status and problematique of the supranational citizen.

[160] But see C-274/96 *Bickel and Franz* [1998] ECR I-07637, paras 15–16, where the Court makes a revealing reference to *Cowan*.

[161] Conclusions of AG La Pergola, para 18.

[162] AG Geelhoed in *Baumbast* explicitly refers to the evolution of the scope of application of freedom of movement, at the same time that he tries to relate such changes to socio-economic transformations, some of which had not been duly thought through by the Community legislator. See his Conclusions, paras 22–33.

> Article 8a extracted the kernel from the other freedoms of movement—the freedom which we now find characterised as the right, not only to move, but also to reside in every Member State: a primary right, in the sense that it appears as the first of the rights ascribed to citizenship of the Union. That is how freedom of residence is conceived and systematised in the Treaty. It is not simply a derived right, but a right inseparable from citizenship of the Union in the same way as the other rights expressly crafted as necessary corollaries of such status (see Article 8b, c and d)—a new right, common to all citizens of the Member States without distinction.[163]

and

> In other words, the Union, as conceived in the Maastricht Treaty, requires that the principle of prohibiting discrimination should embrace the domain of the new legal status of common citizenship . . . I would, however, point out that the solution I propose represents a logical development of the case-law, which has already interpreted the prohibition of discrimination broadly and progressively ... I wonder, however, whether once the right of a recipient of services—of the abstract indiscriminate range of services which may be provided to him in any host State—not to suffer discrimination has been recognised [in the judgment given in the *Cowan* case], the Court ought not, in the interests of consistency, to take the further step which, I believe, the solution of the present problem requires and rule that this potential recipient of every kind of service may now also rely on his or her status of citizen of the Union in order to assert the principle of non-discrimination, throughout the entire area in which the case-law applies.[164]

To summarise, *Martínez Sala* and *Baumbast* are two very important judgments definitely to be regarded as leading cases on free movement of persons, not because they broke radically new ground, but because they pushed to their logical conclusion and rendered explicit the premises which were implicitly at work in the previous case law of the European Court of Justice.

More Human, but Less Social?

If we must conclude that there is more continuity than change in the case law of the Court, then it becomes rather obvious that we should ponder the soundness of the unqualified normative assessment of the two-headed leading case, as a major driving force

[163] Conclusions of AG La Pergola, para 18.

[164] Para 23 of the Opinion. Similary AG Geelhoed in *Baumbast*, para 105: 'Article 18 EC adds to these two sets of rules a general right of residence in favour of citizens of the European Union. In the words of Advocate General La Pergola, that right is inseparable from citizenship. Article 18 EC—and these are my words—establishes a fundamental right in favour of citizens of the European Union to move and reside freely within it. It subsumes the rights to move and to reside in favour of both economically active and economically non-active citizens under a single denominator. For the economically non-active Article 18 EC has additional significance. Since the introduction of Article 18 EC—in the Maastricht Treaty—the right to move and reside in favour of economically non-active persons stems directly from the Treaty and is no longer fully subject to the assessment of those entrusted with the enactment of secondary legislation.' See also Opinion of AG Geelhoed in Case C-109/01, *Akrich* [2003] ECR I-9607, paras 82–90. Indeed, many cases could be argued the same way without *Martínez Sala* and *Baumbast*. Take, for example, *Grzelczyk*. It could be claimed that by means of establishing a right to reside of students, the Community law maker was rendering effective the conditions for the enjoyment of educational opportunities across the Union. This will require interpreting the phrase 'unreasonable burden on public finances' in Directive 93/96 in a restrictive way because the very purpose of allowing entry in a Member State to pursue studies could be frustrated if students were to lose such a right if and when their financial situation were to change for the worse; thus, 'unreasonable burden' cannot be equal to 'temporary burden'. This interpretation is supported by the way in which AG Geelhoed distinguished *Grzelczyk* and *Ninni-Oresche*, see Case C-413/01 [2003] ECR I-13187, para 86 of the Opinion; see also Opinion of AG Jarabo Colomer in C-138/02, *Collins* [2004] ECR I-2703, para 67.

in the process of the 'politicisation' of the European Union.[165] After all, how can a major break be brought about by case law which operates according to a conception of European integration shared with those cases from which it is said to depart, and which pushes to its logical conclusion the premises implicit in the previous case law?

Indeed, it is my claim in the remainder of this sub-section that *Martínez Sala* and *Baumbast* also push to its logical conclusion the normative shortcomings of the case law of the European Court of Justice on free movement of persons. The attempt to advance a political conception of the process of European integration through what is a fundamental *economic* freedom has been paradoxical throughout. The limits of the approach have become increasingly clear. In particular, the line of jurisprudence led by *Martínez Sala* and *Baumbast* renders very clear the ensuing set of (three) main problems. First, the 'citizenship' turn has resulted in a structural process of Europeanisation and judicialisation of major areas of national law and policy, a development highly problematic according to a political and democratic characterisation of integration. Second, it has aggravated the bias in favour of 'individualistic' outcomes and 'commutative' distributive logics and against 'collective' outcomes and 'solidaristic' distributive logics, at the same time as it has promoted the emancipation of Community standards of constitutional review from the common constitutional traditions of the Member States, thus severing a key democratic connection ensuring the legitimacy of Community constitutional law. Third, it has actually resulted in very problematic distributive outcomes, strengthening the structural power of mobile (and better off) workers to the detriment of immobile (and generally worse off) ones; and thus quite likely undermining the effective power of democratic decision-making processes.

Furthering the Europeanisation and Judicialisation of National Law and Policy

The explicit affirmation of a larger subjective and objective scope of the right of individual free movement in Community law has propelled the twin processes of Europeanisation and judicialisation of national law and policy; in particular, it has extended them to sensitive areas until then regarded as of exclusive national competence and excluded altogether from the scope of Community law (as already said, that is the paradigmatic case of non-contributory welfare benefits).

The rulings result in the *Europeanisation* of policies to the extent that the greater breadth and scope of freedom of movement necessarily entails its constitutional horizontal framing of all national laws and policies, including those regarding which the European Union has no substantive competence, and which were supposed previously to be fully excluded from the scope of Community law.[166] Because Europeanisation proceeds exclusively through the subjection of ever-increasing areas of national law to the review of European constitutionality, without affirming any law-making or decision-making powers

[165] After all, if it is usually claimed that the narrow economic conceptualisation of the process of European integration, the focus on economic issues and means to the detriment of political matters and solutions, is the very jurisprudence of the Court of Justice, it is hard to understand how a major political break could have been operated by two very important wagons of the very train of legal reasoning of the Court of Justice.

[166] This was rather obvious in the way in which the facts and the law of the case were presented by the parties to *Martínez Sala*. There was wide agreement on what would be the proper solution to the case according to German law, and according to German law disciplined by the Community freedom of movement. Disagreement revolved on whether there was a genuine Community link which will bring the case into the normative space of European Union law.

at the supranational level,[167] it comes hand in hand with the transfer of decision-making powers from political and representative processes to judicial ones. Or, to put it another way, it is a process of Europeanisation through *judicialisation.*

Unless one assumes that the cause of integration is always best served by adding new powers to the supranational level of government, and that this is true regardless of the powers that are transferred, and how they are exercised, it is far from obvious that Europeanisation *per se* is to be regarded as a positive development in normative terms. This is especially the case when Europeanisation brings about a shift of power from representative political institutions to courts. Not only the democratic credentials of any court are by definition problematic besides the syllogistic application of law, but those of the ECJ on welfare matters are especially problematic. All courts have institutional limitations when dealing with distributive and solidaristic legal institutions, because they lack the knowledge and normative competence to review the key political decisions underlying them. It must be added here that the dramatic reduction of the scope of 'purely internal situations', and most especially, the increasing interference by the Court in situations of reverse discrimination, adds to the argument that the ECJ has entered terrain where it can only erode the legitimacy of European Union law. Indeed, the classical scope of the principle of non-discrimination on the basis of nationality was grounded on the assumption that national political processes may result in pathological discrimination against non-nationals because they were not *represented* politically; while the discriminatory treatment of nationals will, sooner or later, be properly taken into account by national political processes. That is why reverse discrimination was taken to be not justiciable.

In particular, it is important to notice that the redefinition of the value basis of free movement (from non-discrimination to European citizenship) furthers a process of *'emancipation' of the yardstick of European constitutionality from national constitutional traditions.*[168] As long as free movement of persons was considered as the working of the principle of non-discrimination on the basis of nationality, the constitutional standards being applied were still national ones, an outcome in full accordance with the key legal role played by the collective of national constitutions as the deep constitution of the European Union, and consequently as the key source of democratic legitimacy of the synthetic constitutional order.[169] This is so because non-discrimination calls for the review of equal treatment between nationals and non-nationals, and as is well known, equality is a purely formal criterion, which needs to be filled in by reference to specific substantive standards. As stated earlier, such standards were not imposed by Community law, but were directly taken from national constitutional law. But once we affirm that

[167] It could be further added that even if such powers were created, the present division of labour between law-making procedures generates a structural bias in favour of market-making and against market-correcting norms that will also lead to Europeanisation through judicialisation or accretion of power to judges, not political decision-making processes.

[168] Indeed, the Court followed here a path very similar to that trailed by the case law on all other fundamental economic freedoms, the main difference concerning the timing and the rationale for the shifts in the jurisprudence. In legal-dogmatic terms, the ratio decidendi of the first leading cases revolved around the characterisation of free movement of persons as the operationalisation of the interdiction of direct discrimination on the basis of nationality; that was later expanded to comprise indirect discrimination; finally, a national law could be considered unconstitutional from the standpoint of European Community law even if not discriminatory, as long as it posed obstacles to the exercise of free movement.

[169] On the synthetic character of European constitutional law, see Agustín José Menéndez, 'The European Democratic Challenge', (2009) 15 *European Law Journal* 277–308.

freedom of movement may be infringed by non-discriminatory national measures, we are necessarily emancipating the Community standard of constitutional review from the substantive standards of national constitutional law, and implicitly making reference to a supranational and transcendental standard to be drawn by the Court of Justice (who else?) from the rather abstract and general provisions of the Treaties. The democratic legitimacy of the latter is highly problematic, to say the least, given the peculiar supranational blend of the non-existent discipline of constitutional debates on the fundamental law of the Union, the inchoate character of the European political process, and the structural disconnection of European constitutional adjudication from national political processes.

The Structural Substantive Bias Against Distributive and Solidaristic Legal Norms: The Negative Framing of Socio-economic Rights

Martínez Sala and *Baumbast* have also exacerbated the substantive bias in Community law against distributive and solidaristic legal norms. The reason is relatively simple. The key standards of European constitutional review are the fundamental economic freedoms. Although recognition of the principle of protection of fundamental rights as an unwritten principle of Community law, and the progressive development of the case law up to the solemn proclamation of the Charter of Fundamental Rights, have fleshed out a second key component of the European yardstick of constitutionality,[170] it is still the case that the Court structurally favours in its review of national laws fundamental economic freedoms (as the judges first consider compliance with economic freedoms, and only afterwards consider whether the furthering of a 'non-economic' fundamental right justifies the breach of the economic freedom).[171] It is perhaps even more important that the absorption of a given policy area within the scope of Community law tends to lead judges to reframe the relevant issues in the mould characteristic of economic freedoms, namely by means of identifying the subjective, individualistic rights at stake, and policing the observance of principles of commutative justice. However, the nature of many of the underlying questions is thus simply distorted, resulting in what could be labelled a 'subreptitious economisation'. The formal logic of economic rights hides from plain sight the substantive logic of solidaristic obligations, which are founded on collective goods, not individual rights; and which are characterised by complex multilateral relations to be governed according to principles of distributive, not commutative justice. This can indeed be observed in the judgments of the European Court of Justice on the implications of *Martínez Sala* and *Baumbast* for the granting of non-contributory welfare benefits to supranational citizens. Whereas the extension of economic freedoms to non-nationals may result in a positive sum game, that is not necessarily the case when we are dealing with welfare benefits, which institutionalise what some citizens owe others, and thus necessarily entail a redistribution of resources. It is surely the case that a common citizenship should entail a modicum of solidarity towards the nationals of other Member States, whilst not obscuring the million-euro question of any welfare policy, which is to

[170] Agustín J Menéndez, 'Chartering Europe', (2002) 40 *Journal of Common Market Studies* 471–90.

[171] Indeed, two recent and much debated judgments of the ECJ concerned the unconstitutionality of European norms on account of its breach of fundamental rights. See C-402/05, *Kadi*, not yet reported and C-345/06, *Heinrich*, not yet reported.

determine who is and who is not eligible. Pretending that the extension of welfare rights does always lead to better protection of the welfare objective is simply illusionary, because the key point of any redistributive programme is to use the tax collected from some to comply with the obligations of distributive justice towards others.[172]

Indeed, it could be argued that the rhetoric of European citizenship has provided a nicer value ground to the process of transformation of economic freedoms, from concretisation of the principle of non-discrimination to transcendental freedoms which require setting aside all national laws which may be an obstacle to the operation of the single market (no matter what aim they pursued). Although that is not the place to do so, it would be worth exploring the relationship between *Martínez Sala* and *Baumbast*, the redefinition of the importance of free movement of capital in the *Golden Shares* judgments, the recharacterisation of market-making as a competence basis in *Tobacco Advertising* and the upper hand given to freedom of establishment to the detriment of collective socio-economic rights in *Viking* and *Laval*.[173]

The Substantive Distributive Implications of the Case Law

But beyond the structural process of transformation of the standards of review of European constitutionality, is it possible to ask the perhaps simpler question of who benefits from *Martínez Sala* and *Baumbast*? Or, to put it another way, can we observe any pattern in the socio-economic profile of the new right-holders?

At first sight, it may seem that the beneficiaries, as in *Martínez Sala* or *Grzekzyck*, are not necessarily the better-off in society. After all, Martínez Sala was an unemployed mother asking for a child allowance, and Grzekzyck was a student applying for a grant to be able to stop working part-time and concentrate on finishing his studies. But is this first impression correct? Not in my view, for the three following reasons. First, the right-holders added by *Martínez Sala* and *Baumbast* to the subjective scope of Community law would by definition be those capable of assuming the costs of establishing themselves in another Member State without the benefit of remunerated employment.[174] That is likely to be a mixed lot, which may include a far from negligible number of citizens who it would be hard to describe as the worst off in society. Still, a good deal of non-nationals now given the shelter of Community law may indeed deserve protection from a distributive, welfare perspective. Second, and more to the point, the key distributive implications revolve around the expansion of the objective scope of freedom of movement, and very especially, in the expansion of the breadth of the review of European constitutionality through the assignment of rights to citizens against their own states. These rights are not only bound to be enjoyed by the most mobile nationals (which in many cases tend to be among the best-off in society, as indeed reflected in a good number of the recent cases of the

[172] Which does not mean that overall a well-funded and generous welfare system may not increase the overall wealth of a society. There is wide and ample proof of that being the case. For a recent restatement, see Robert E Goodin, Bruce Headey and Ruud Muffels, *The Real Worlds of Welfare Capitalism* (Cambridge, Cambridge University Press, 1999).

[173] See Cases C-376/98, *Germany v Parliament and Council (Tobacco Advertising)* [2000] ECR I-8419; C-367/98, *Commission v Portugal (Golden Shares)* [2002] ECR I-4731; C-438/05, *Viking*, not yet reported; C-341/05, *Laval*, not yet reported; and C-346/06, *Rüffert*, not yet reported. The most persuasive theoretical account of European integration in recent years, Alexander Somek, *Individualism* (Oxford, Oxford University Press, 2008), starts connecting the dots in this regard.

[174] And, in addition, capable of mobilising Community law in their favour through the hiring of the adequate legal services.

Court[175]); but it also empowers nationals who can empower themselves by rather artificially bringing the case into the scope of Community law, or by simply rendering the negative consequences (generally economic) of their leaving the country even more forceful and credible. Third, the horizontal expansion of the potential right-holders of non-contributory benefits may be a disincentive to Member States willing to establish more generous welfare benefits than most other Member States. The deterring effect might well derive not so much from the actual costs incurred on account of *Martínez Sala* and *Baumbast*, but from the impossibility of keeping under control the actual cost of the programme once entitlement is no longer governed by national law, but partially determined by Community law.

Conclusion

Martínez Sala and *Baumbast* reveal the ambivalent nature of the unqualified expansion of rights in what may look like a 'cosmopolitan' direction. Because all fundamental rights, and most especially socio-economic fundamental rights, are institutionalisations of complex relationships of mutual obligation, it is far from obvious that the granting of new rights does not come at the price of denying or at least weakening other pre-existing rights. It is rarely the case that the key question is whether we should expand the breadth of one right, but rather how we should rebalance the relationship between several conflicting rights. Similarly, the key question is not whether Europeans should be solidaristic, but through which concrete institutional means and on the basis of which obligations. Thus, it is not only important that there is European solidarity, but also *whose* European solidarity Community law enforces. From this perspective, *Martínez Sala* and *Baumbast* are very ambiguous rulings, as they may have rendered the criteria of allocation of solidaristic contributions more encompassing at the price of actually reducing the substantive content of the entitlements. So perhaps the market citizen is not dead, but only has been dressed up as a political citizen.

175 *Schwarz* is as symbolic in that regard as *Martímez Sala*is (in a very different sense). The Schwarzes sent their children to a Scottish school, with fees at the time in excess of 33,000 euros per pupil per year. The ECJ came to the pious conclusion that the right of the Schwarzes to reduced income tax in Germany on account of such an expense was part and parcel of the right to European citizenship of the children (moving to Scotland to receive education). Note that the German authorities were more than happy to let the children go to Scotland, only denied a tax benefit. In a jocular mood, it must be added that the school was closed by the time the ECJ rendered its judgment, dragged down by a very negative assessment by Her Majesty Inspectors of Education. The Court seemed impervious to this fact (or perhaps had been kept in the dark about this by plaintiffs).

4

Martínez Sala and *Baumbast*: an institutionalist analysis

CARLOS CLOSA MONTERO

To Antonio La Pergola, in memoriam[176]

The explicit creation of the status of citizenship fuelled expectations that, despite its limited innovation and contents, it could provide solid grounds for the ECJ to strengthen its not so impressive foundation. Much of this faithful attitude derives from the traditional approach and position of the Court in furthering a line of interpretation that completes the incomplete designs of primary legislation. The Court came timely to its historical task even though it was a progressive and slow path: it took five years from 1993 to 1998 for the Court to deliver its first judgment referring to the interpretation of EU citizenship, and this was *Martínez Sala*. It took another four years, to 2002, for the Court to declare EU citizenship destined to be the fundamental status of nationals of Member States.[177] Once there, the Court delivered its judgment in *Baumbast*, which can be considered the first decisive, authoritative ECJ judgment on provisions on EU citizenship regarding free movement and residence. Both cases mark perfectly the evolution of the Court: after *Martínez Sala*, commentators argued that the decision simply paved the way for further difficult references on the content and scope of the residence rights enjoyed by Union citizens (O'Leary, 1999: 68). Other commentators, more interested in the substantive side of the judgment, declared that it represented the beginning of a new phase of EU incursion into national welfare sovereignty (Shaw and Fries, 1998: 533). *Baumbast*, in turn, was heralded as a ruling of constitutional significance as well as the emergence of a new model of social solidarity, whose terms of reference are partly domestic and partly *communautaire* (Dougan and Spaventa, 2003).

Read together, one may think that the Court acted as a single, unified actor pursuing an evolutional and teleological line of reasoning. When some reputable authors portrayed its behaviour using the term 'We, the Court', they attempted precisely to convey simultaneously its actorhood as well as its unified (at least on the surface) behaviour. Yet, one of the striking features of the Court's behaviour is precisely its institutional nature; rather than a finished and complete coherent interpretation of the Court's role through its case law, the emerging picture reveals threats of a complex interaction between several actors. This chapter will revise three aspects: first, the different attitudes of different Court actors and

[176] Antonio La Pergola, Judge and Advocate General of the ECJ passed away in Rome on 18 July 2007 while I was preparing this manuscript. I had the pleasure to meet him during his last years as Chairman of the Venice Commission for Democracy through Law.

[177] Case C-184/99 *Grzelcyk* [2001] ECR I-6193 at 81.

specifically, the Advocates General, in furthering the cause of EU citizenship. Second, it examines the influence that the interaction with other institutions may have in the Court's reasoning. And third, it reviews the influence of the Court's judgments as an engine for secondary legislation.

The Pathbreaking Role of Advocates General

Whilst it took almost nine years for a Court to state conclusively the value of EU citizenship, Advocates General had anticipated this in a number of opinions. This happened even before the Maastricht Treaty; thus, in 1991, Advocate General Jacobs had already anticipated the spirit of EU citizenship when he argued in *Konstantinidis*[178] that 'Member State nationals are entitled to claim *civis europeum sum* in order to oppose any violation of their fundamental rights'. The entry into force of the Treaty provided more solid foundations for these arguments: in 1994, Advocate General Lenz argued in *Faccini Dori*[179] that the 'introduction of citizenship of the Union raises expectations that citizens of the Union will enjoy equality, at least before Community law'. In 1996, Advocate General Léger in case *Boukhalfa*[180] stated that:

> All the conclusions inherent in that concept are drawn, every citizen of the Union must, whatever his nationality, enjoy exactly the same rights and be subject to the same obligations.

Then, in the joined cases *Stöiber and Pereira*,[181] Advocate General La Pergola argued that the EC provisions on citizenship represent progress of major significance in the construction of Europe, their ultimate purpose being to bring about increasing equality between citizens of the Union, irrespective of their nationality. At almost the same time as *Martínez Sala*, Advocate General Jacobs pushed these arguments a step further in *Bickel*:[182] in his view, the notion of citizenship of the Union 'implies a commonality of rights and obligations uniting Union citizens by a common bond transcending Member States' nationality'. Then, he constructed his argument linking citizenship and non-discrimination: against that background, it would be difficult to explain to a citizen

> how despite the language of Articles 6, 8 and 8a EC, a Member State other than his own could be permitted to discriminate against him on grounds of his nationality. Freedom from discrimination on grounds of nationality is the most fundamental right conferred by the Treaty and must be seen as a basic ingredient of Union citizenship.

And, finally, he moved the argument to the right of freedom of movement and residence deriving this from Article 8a:

> Where a citizen exercises his right to move and reside within the territory of the Member States, his situation falls within the scope of Treaty for the prohibition of discrimination on grounds of nationality.

178 Case -168/91 *Konstantinidis v Stadt Altensteig* [1993] ECR I-1191 at 1211–12.
179 Case C-91/92 *Faccini Dori* [1994] ECR 3225 at 53.
180 Case C-214/94 *Boukhalfa v Bundesrepublik Deutschland* [1996] ECR I-2253.
181 Joined Cases C-4/95 and C-5/95 *Stöiber and Pereira.*
182 Opinion 19 March 1998, Case C-274/96 *Bickel and Franz* 21 at 24.

Finally, Advocate General Cosmas argued in *Wijsenbeek*[183] that the drafters used a constitutional vocabulary with terms such as 'rights' and 'citizen of the Union' (81). This implied a fundamental change in relation to the classical principle of free movement of persons, which amounts to a change in the nature of rights and the intensity in their guarantee.

These opinions paved the way for the forceful argument of Advocate General La Pergola in *Martínez Sala.* He stated clearly EU citizenship as the source of the right of movement: since the entry into force of Article 8a EC, the right of residence can no longer be considered to have been created by the Directive. Moreover, in his opinion, his or her right of residence derives directly and autonomously from the primary rule in Article 8 EC 'regardless of whether a Union citizen complies with the conditions laid down in the Directive ... the appellant is entitled to equal treatment in her capacity as a citizen of the Union'(71). Against this background, one would expect an ambitious opinion from Advocate General Geelhold in *Baumbast.* But he did not avail himself of the opportunity to use the rich heritage available.

In summary, opinions of Advocates General were of a path-breaking character in contrast with the more cautious and occasionally aloof attitude that the Court adopted in its case law. Until *Baumbast* and *Grzelcyk*, the Court ignored encouragement to apply these provisions and preferred instead to use *lex specialis.* In several cases, the Court made clear that Articles 39 and 43 EC act as *lex specialis* whose beneficiaries need not rely upon citizenship provisions, and then refused to analyse preliminary references under Article 18(1) EC when the traditional free movement provisions can provide adequate guidance to national courts.[184]

Institutional Interaction

Then, the second institutional dimension to ponder the performance of the Court refers to the interaction between national courts and other parties in the cases. The composition of the Court remained relatively stable between the two cases at hand: in both cases, the Court assembled in plenary (a Grand Chamber); that is, 13 judges comprising the President (Gil Carlos Rodríguez Iglesias) and the presidents of the chambers of five judges. Six judges out of 13 appeared in both cases and Antonio La Pergola, who was Advocate General in *Martinez Sala*, was judge in *Baumbast.* It could also be assumed that the judges maintained a relatively stable set of preferences in their interpretation. This being so, it appears that the interaction with other actors' interpretations played a key role in shaping the Court's view.

Martínez Sala was the second preliminary reference in which the Court referred expressly to the citizenship provisions of the EC Treaty. In the first case, *Skavani,*[185] the Court interpreted the facts as falling within the scope of Article 52 EC, rendering unnecessary an interpretation of the provisions on citizenship and, specifically, Article 8a

[183] Case C-378/97 *Wijsenbeek* [1999] ECR I-6207.

[184] Examples of this are: Case C-100/01, *Olazabal* [2002] ECR I-10981; Case C-193/94 *Skavani* [1996] and Case C-92/01 *Stylianakis.* But, in different sense, Case C-274/96 *Bickel and Franz*; Case C-135/99 *Elsen* [2000] ECR I-10409.

[185] Case C-193/94 *Amstsanwalfshaft Berlin v Sofia Skavani* [1996] ECR I-929.

of the EC Treaty. Truly, the questions submitted to preliminary ruling were worded very differently in both cases; in *Skavani*, the *Amtsgericht Tiergarten*, Berlin, asked generally about the compatibility of Article 8a (*inter alia*) with a provision of national law. The Court managed to restrict its interpretation to the other provisions (that is, Articles 6 and 52 EC) hence it avoided interpreting Article 8a EC. In *Martínez Sala*, however, the *Bayerisches Ladessozialgericht* specificially targeted the interpretation of citizenship provisions and pointed out that

> Delays in granting (residence permits) for purely technical administrative reasons can materially affect the substantive rights enjoyed by citizens of the European Union [51].

The attitude of the two German courts in these cases confirms something that commentators had emphasized in relation to UK Courts: Article 8a EC attracted considerable attention in cases before UK courts, although it was given a narrow interpretation (Fries and Shaw, 1998: 537).

In the face of this interest from national courts, the ECJ confirmed its more cautious position from *Skavani*: in *Martínez Sala*, it relied on the instruments that it's case law had consolidated in relation to the free movement of persons concerning economic activity. In point 60 of the judgment, the Court spells out its case very clearly:

> It is not necessary to examine whether the person concerned can rely on Article 8a of the Treaty in order to obtain recognition of a new right to reside in the territory of the Member State concerned, since it is common ground that she has been authorised to reside there, although she has been refused issue of a residence permit.

Significantly, it is not only a question of substance but also of language: all through the judgment, the Court uses the more classical language and terminology, solidly established in the *acquis* of EU law: person, worker and national of a Member State and only in the last three paragraphs of the judgment, does the Court explicitly use the expression 'citizen of the Union'. In contrast, other parties use these concepts throughout the proceedings. In summary, in *Martínez Sala*, the Court has not yet fully internalised the language and meaning of EU citizenship.

However, *Martínez Sala* innovated in relation to *Skavani* and, what made a difference, in the opinion – which this author shares – of some commentators (O'Leary, 1999: 75), were the arguments of the Commission at the oral hearing. The Commission submitted that, in any event, since 1 November 1993 when the Treaty on European Union came into force, the appellant in the main proceedings had a right of residence under Article 8a of the EC Treaty. The Court, however, argued that in a case such as this, it was not necessary to examine whether the person concerned can rely on Article 8a of the Treaty in order to obtain recognition of a new right to reside in the territory of the Member State concerned, since it is common ground that she has already been authorised to reside there (notice that the authorisation—that is, an administrative measure—seems to take precedence over the existence of a right of residence). By doing so, the Court leans heavily towards the interpretation of the position of individuals *vis-à-vis* administration: the administrative authorisation renders unnecessary an assesment of the right of residence of citizens (which does not need authorisation even though it may be restricted in specific cases and situations).

However, the Court limited the impact of its previous argument combining the right of residence with the scope of *ratione materiae* for making available the principle of non-discrimination: a citizen of the European Union, such as the appellant in the main proceedings, lawfully resident in the territory of the host Member State, can rely on Article 6 of the Treaty in all situations which fall within the scope of *ratione materiae* of Community law. Thus, as a result of the arguments of the Commission a part of the ruling in *Martínez Sala* derives from the interpretation of Article 8.

Four years after *Martínez Sala*, *Baumbast* showed again the interplay between parties and, taking into account how the ECJ had avoided tackling the central issues relating to EU citizenship in the former case, it could be said that national courts provided the concepts and terms and 'pushed' the ECJ to the 'unavoidable' conclusion: the direct effect of Article 8a EC Treaty. There was, first, a primary positioning of the UK courts. Whilst the UK Immigration Adjudicator decided that *Baumbast* was not a worker or a person having a general right of residence under Directive 90/364 and the children did not have an independent right of residence under Article 12 of Regulation No 1612/68, the UK *Immigration Appeal Tribunal* changed the basis of the issue and, instead of relying exclusively on these pre-Maastricht norms, it took the view that the cases (*Baumbast* and *R*) relied on the interpretation of Article 18 EC (ex Article 8a). The same tribunal consistently used the concept of EU citizenship in formulating its questions and this probably framed and set the boundaries for the ECJ. Question 3 read: 'Does he, as an EU citizen, enjoy a directly effective right of residence in another EU Member State?' On this occasion, the Court did not shy away from the challenge raised by national courts.

The Contribution of the Court in Shaping Legislation

The central issue underlying both cases (*Martínez Sala* and *Baumbast* and, to a large extent, all the other cases referred to here) is the extent to which the provisions on EU citizenship are innovatary vis-à-vis the existing EU *acquis*. Innovation firstly referred to the direct effect of the new provisions, secondly the eventual enlargement of the category of persons protected, and thirdly the eventual limits placed on the right.

By and large, interpretations on the significance of Article 18 EC (ex Article 8a) were initially restrictive. Thus, some stated categorically that Member States, in their capacity as Treaty drafters, seem to have assumed that Article 18(1) EC was merely a codification of the *acquis communautaire* extant at the time of the Maastricht Treaty. The approach in Article 18(1) EC becomes novel only once we accept that this provision is capable of producing additional legal effects (Dougan and Spaventa, 2003: 702). Following this line of reasoning, others suggested that some considerable doubts have always remained as to whether Article 8a EC does indeed establish a universal right of residence—even one capable of being restricted by legislation—or rather, on the contrary, simply apes the limited nature of earlier Directives (Fries and Shaw, 1998: 537). The summary of the academic debate was presented as having largely concluded that, given the present state of EC law, the final proviso of Article 8a EC subjects the right of free movement and residence to the 'limits and conditions' laid down by the Treaties in secondary legislation and nullifies any possible addition to the existing regulation of the free movement of persons (Albors-Llorens, 1998: 463).

However, the need to recast the legislation in the light of citizenship of the Union was recognised by the Commission,[186] and confirmed by the Brussels European Council in December 1993.[187] Despite this initial position, the Commission's approach was very cautious: in the Report on the operation of the TEU in 1995,[188] the Commission opined that Article 8a is merely declaratory:

> Citizens of the Union have not been given general rights of freedom of movement and residence; rather, the exercise of these rights is subject to the 'limits and conditions' laid down by Community law.

The Commission followed a somewhat erratic line; in its first report on EU citizenship it announced a proposal for adapting the rules to the new Treaty provisions for 1995 but this was never advanced. In its second report,[189] the Commission argued instead for a Treaty change: in its view, the right of residence was still subject to different provisions which applied to different categories of citizens, since the secondary Community legislation consisted of two Regulations and nine Directives, excluding the provisions on social security. The Commission argued further that, as the EC Treaty did not provide for a common legal basis, it was not possible to adopt a single set of rules. Therefore, the Commission recommended 'revising Article 8A (present Article 18), upgrading it from a supplementary legal basis to a specific legal basis for free movement and right of residence'.

Martínez Sala impinged upon this landscape. As is known, the Court avoided tackling the thorny issues which the discussion of Article 8a EC would inevitably have provoked (that is, the compatibility of conditions imposed by the Directive with the right of free movement and residence and the right not to suffer discrimination on the grounds of nationality enjoyed by all citizens of the Union) (O'Leary; 1999: 77). It thus left open the issue of whether Article 8a EC gives the right of residence a wider content than the previously existing measures. Siofra O'Leary had premonitory words after *Martínez Sala*: it remains to be seen whether this relationship between a provision of primary Community law and the conditions imposed thereon by a piece of secondary legislation (that is, the 1990s Directives plus the 1968 Regulation) is a tenable one (O'Leary, 1999: 79).

Again, Advocates General have an important role. More specifically, Advocate General Cosmas suggested in *Wijsenbeek*[190] that the introduction of Union citizenship might ineluctably lead to a revised, updated reading of Community secondary legislation. This time, though, the Court reacted progressively and several judgments implicitly assumed that Article 18(1) EC is capable of producing legal effects within national legal orders.[191]

Then, in 2001, the Commission announced (in its Third Report on EU citizenship[192]) a proposal for a Directive on the right of movement and residence for EU citizens. According to the Commission, the proposal was a product of the legal and political environment created by the introduction of citizenship of the Union and it took into

[186] Report on the on the adaptation of community legislation to the subsidiarity principle, COM(93) 545 final of 24 November 1993.

[187] *Bull EC* 12–1993 p 14 point I.14.

[188] Report on the operation of the Treaty on European Union, SEC(95) 731 final of 10 May 1995.

[189] Second report on Citizenship of the Union, COM(97) 230 final of 27 May 1997.

[190] Case C-378/97, *Wijsenbeek* [1999] ECR I-6207.

[191] Case C-357/98, *Yiadam* [2000] ECR I-9265; Case C-135/99, *Elsen* [2000] ECR I-10409; Case C-184/99, *Grzelyck* [2001] ECR I-6193; Case C-98/00, *Kauer* [2002] ECR I-1343.

[192] Third Report on Citizenship of the Union, COM(2001) 506 final of 7 September 2001.

account, 'inter alia, the past rulings of the Court of Justice'. As is known, one of the cornerstones of the Directive was the full equalisation of long-term resident EU citizens with nationals of host states. And, to some extent, it was anticipating and clearing the way for *Baumbast.*

In 2002 in *Baumbast*, the Court first revised its former position to assert that the previous dependence of the right of residence on the condition of exercising economic activity has been superseded by the introduction of Union citizenship [81]. Then, it established firmly the principle of direct effect of Article 18 EC (against the interpretation of both the UK and German governments, who claimed that a right of residence cannot be derived directly from Article 18(1) EC) [78]. Finally, the Court determined the eventual limitations to the right. The Commission argued that pre-existing rules condition this right and establish who is eligible [79]. The Court did not call into question the legality of the conditions contained in the three Residence Directives. Indeed, the Court carefully avoided suggesting that the Community legislation had imposed conditions upon free movement which were in themselves capable of constituting a disproportionate restriction upon the citizens' rights under the Treaty (704). The Court established that limitations and conditions were permissible but they are subject to judicial review [86] and they must fulfil the principle of proportionality [91].

The Commission interpreted that the Directive on Citizens' Rights took stock of these legal developments and it codified in a single instrument the complex legislative corpus and the rich case law on free movement and residence.[193] The combination of ECJ case law with the new norm has substantive effects which advance towards full equality within the boundaries of a given Member State in terms of social benefits. The ECJ did not construct the right of free movement as fully unconditional. It may be subjected to limitations and conditions that serve to balance this right with the legitimate interest of Member States. But the limitations are quite thin: the right of residence must not become an unreasonable burden on the finances of the host Member State. Truly, a large number of EU citizens depending on social benefits of the host Member State may become an 'unreasonable burden' but this construction will be difficult to sustain in any given individual case: it will be difficult to argue that a single person becomes a 'burden' on the finances of the host state (even though its reasonability may be called into question).

Some interpreted *Martínez Sala* as providing roots for something close to a universal non-discrimination right including access to all manner of welfare benefits in Community law as a consequence of Union citizenship (Fries and Shaw, 1998: 536). But this being a precedent, it was *Baumbast* where the Court made an express link between residence, integration and solidarity: the longer migrants are resident, the more integrated they are in the society of the host state and thus, the more support they can expect from the host state in terms of benefits. The same philosophy underpins the new Citizens' Rights Directive 2004/38 (Barnard, 2005: 563).

Since *Baumbast*, the Court has used Union citizenship to expand the traditional moulds for crafting freedom of movement and residence. In *Chen*,[194] the Court argued that a third country national derived rights from a child who was a Union citizen in order to enjoy a right of residence in the UK. And in *Bidar*,[195] the Court consolidated its initial view on the

[193] Fourth Report on Citizenship of the Union, COM(2004) 695 final of 26 October 2004.
[194] Case C-200/02 *Chen v Secretary of State of the Home Department* [2004] ECR I-0000.
[195] Case C-204/03 *R (on the application of Danny Bidar) v London Borough of Ealing* [2005] ECR I-08389.

solidarity bonds underpinning the notion of EU citizen: non-economically active migrants, as Union citizens, can now enjoy benefits on the same terms as nationals, owing to a 'certain degree of financial solidarity' which host states have to show with nationals of other member states (Barnard, 2005: 563).

References

Albors-Llorens, A (1999), 'A Broader Construction of the EC Treaty Provisions on Citizenship?' 57 *CLJ* 461 at 463.

European Parliament and Council Directive 2004/38/EC of 29 April 2004 on the right of citizens of the Union and their family members to move and reside freely within the territory of the Member States amending Regulation (EEC) No 1612/68 and repealing Directives 64/221/EEC, 68/360/EEC, 72/194/EEC, 73/148/EEC, 75/34/EEC, 75/35/EEC, 90/364/EEC, 90/365/EEC and 93/96/EEC OJ L/158.

Barnard, C (2005), 'Of Students and Babies' 64 *CLJ* 560 at 563.

Dougan, M and Spaventa, E (2003) 'Educating Rudy and the (non-) English Patient: A Double-bill on Residency Rights under Article 18 EC' 28 *EL Rev* 699 at 712.

Fries, S and Shaw, J (1998), 'Citizenship of the Union: First Steps in the European Court of Justice' 1 *European Public Law* 533 at 536.

O'Leary, S (1999), 'Putting Flesh on the Bones of European Union Citizenship' 24 *EL Rev* 68 at 79.

X

Joint Cases C-6/90 and C-9/90, *Andrea Francovich and Danila Bonifaci and others v Italian Republic*

1

Once Upon a Time—*Francovich*: From Fairy Tale to Cruel Reality?

DAMASO RUIZ-JARABO COLOMER[1]

Introduction

Once upon a time there was a Union of Kingdoms in Europe within which no principle of state liability for the infringement of the law in its legal order existed; thus, citizens suffering a loss due to the illegal behaviour of their own countries, known as Member States, were left with no remedy or compensation for damages arising from the poor behaviour of their Member State. Then one day, a wonderful and magic day, a man called Mr Francovich, who had only received sporadic payments in lieu of his wages before his employer had become insolvent, had a brave idea: together with 33 other people, including Mrs Bonifaci, who had not only lost their jobs due to the insolvency of their employer but had been waiting in vain for more than five years for their overdue salaries to be paid, decided to consult a clever lawyer. This man, resourceful as only lawyers can be, found out that many years ago the wise and venerable King, called Council, had adopted a Directive according to which the Member State in question, let us call it Italy for argument's sake, a nice southern European country, had committed itself to create a guarantee system for the payment of outstanding claims from employment contracts. Sadly, the Member State had failed to implement this obligation, an oversight which had led Mr Francovich and Mrs Bonifaci into such an unsatisfactory predicament. The lawyer pleaded the case before the national court, but the national court, not knowing whether it could make the Member State responsible for failing to establish the guarantee system for the payment of the overdue salaries, stayed the proceedings and asked the augurs in Luxembourg, those governing the rules in the Union of Kingdoms. After pondering the matter thoroughly, the wise augurs delivered their judgment: the Member State should be held liable for not implementing the Directive and had to compensate the plaintiffs for all the damage suffered. Oh what incredible joy! Once again David had beaten Goliath! The doors of heaven seemed open on that glorious day. A man was not only a mere subject but had also rights which could even be claimed and enforced against Member States. And then, from that wonderful 11 November 1991, thanks to the wise men of Luxembourg, all the citizens of the Union of Kingdoms lived in peace and harmony until the end of time …

Although it may have been a useful exercise in order to recall the facts and legal questions in that particular judgment, it is really amazing how little legal disputes suit the

[1] Advocate General at the European Court of Justice.

fairy tale format. I wonder whether the attempt to transform a judgment into a fairy tale is worthwhile, or whether it has ever been previously attempted, since the outcome seems rather prosaic. However, the more important issue is not the *form* of telling, but the *message*: in that respect, I believe that *Francovich*[2] created far too many expectations regarding state liability, expectations which may well be considered to have been subsequently frustrated by further developments, especially considering that the Court of Justice has built the state liability doctrine under Community law on nearly the same principles governing the liability of the European institutions pursuant to Article 288(2) EC Treaty. I imagine Mr Francovich and Mrs Bonifaci certainly thought they were in heaven, exactly as Hansel and Gretel when they laid themselves down in the small beds after having had a good meal of milk and pancakes, with sugar, apples and nuts at the witch's cottage in the forest; but then, after the subsequent judgments, they must have felt like Hansel in the cage in which he was imprisoned by the old witch.[3]

When revisiting *Francovich* more than 15 years after the judgment was first handed down, three thoughts come to my mind: first, despite the undeniable value of the decision at the time, there is a need to read it in the light of previous case law, in order to ascertain its real place in terms of the development of Community law. Secondly, certain elements of the judgment may be criticised even if the whole solution appears to be right. Thirdly, the case law subsequently delivered by the Court of Justice has pushed the *Francovich* judgment into the background, dramatically limiting the scope it seemed to have had in the beginning.

Francovich in the Light of Previous Case Law: The Logical Next Step

The arguments upon which the reasoning of the Court relies in that judgment were certainly not taken without due consideration. Indeed, in paragraph 30 and beyond, the Court made a certain link, though perhaps not the most accurate one, with its previous case law, especially as regards two fundamental principles which it had previously established: the liability of Member States when an infringement had been declared by the Court following Article 226 EC procedure, and the principle of effectiveness of Community law.

In its judgment of 16 December 1960, *Humblet vs Belgium*,[4] the Court indicated that within the framework of the obligations for Member States arising from Article 228 EC to take all appropriate measures to ensure the fulfilment of their obligations under Community law, they had to nullify and make good the unlawful consequences of a breach of Community law. The recognition of the right to obtain compensation from Member States after an infringement procedure underlies the statement of the Court in its judgment of 7 February 1973,[5] declaring the admissibility of an action for infringement

[2] Joined Cases C-6/90 and C-9/90 *Francovich and Bonifaci and others v Italy* [1991] ECR I-5357.
[3] *Fairy Tales of the Brothers Grimm*, illustrated by Kay Nielsen with an introduction by Bryan Holme (New York, The Viking Press, 1979), 23 and 24.
[4] Case C-6/60 [1961] ECR 1128.
[5] Case 39/72 *Commission v Italy* [1973] ECR 101.

brought by the Commission even after the Member State had put an end to the infringement;[6] the declaration of the infringement by the Court could still be of interest for individuals as regards the responsibility of Member States for the time in which it was breaching Community law, since 'even if the breach was remedied after the expiry of the time-limit laid down by the Commission ... there is still an interest in continuing the proceedings ..., interest which may consist in establishing a basis for the liability which a Member State may incur, in particular ... towards individuals', as was explained in a later judgment of 20 February 1986.[7]

But in *Waterkeyn*, 14 December 1982,[8] the Court considered it necessary to deal in greater detail with the question of the rights conferred to individuals by a judgment declaring an infringement by a Member State. It stated that the right to compensation of the person who had suffered loss or damage did not arise from that declaration of infringement, but from the direct effect of the breached community law provisions. Properly understood, *Waterkeyn* does not set aside the importance of infringement judgments before national courts. This means that the rights invoked take their origin in the EC piece of legislation in question and not from the judicial declaration of the infringement.[9] In any event, this argument leads to the principle of effectiveness of Community law.

The Court has indeed established the link between the direct effect of the rights granted to individuals under Community law and the task of the national judiciary to protect adequately those rights by ensuring the direct effect of the conferring provisions.[10] Hence, it is for national law to establish the procedures and to designate the bodies entrusted with the task of protecting the rights of individuals under provisions of Community law which have direct effect, taking into account the principle of equivalence, according to which the procedural requirements to enforce rights deriving from Community law shall not be less favourable than those applicable to similar actions of a domestic nature.[11] Moreover, the consequences for national judges of the non-conformity of a national provision with direct applicable Community law were already well known long before *Francovich*, since in *Simmenthal*, 9 March 1978,[12] the Court had imposed the duty on national courts not to apply domestic provisions which infringe Community law.

But still the right to obtain compensation for damages caused in such circumstances had not yet been suggested. In that context, a judgment of 12 January 1976, *Russo v Aima*,[13] deserves some attention, as the Court said that where an individual had suffered a loss due to the intervention of a Member State which had to be regarded as being incompatible with EC agricultural market organisation, it was for that Member State to take responsibility for the consequences according to the provisions governing the liability of the state under national law. While relying on the national legal orders in order to make good the damage, the Court indirectly acknowledged the existence of a common principle

[6] D Simon and A Barav, 'La responsabilité de l'administration nationale en cas de violation du droit communautaire' (1987) 305 *Revue du Marché Commun* 166.

[7] Case 309/84, *Commission v Italy* [1986] ECR 599.

[8] Joined Cases 314/81, 316/81 and 38/82, *Procureur de la République v Waterkeyn* [1982] ECR 4337.

[9] Simon and Barav, p 167.

[10] Cases 33/76 *Rewe* and 45/76 *Comet* [1975] ECR 1989 and 2043.

[11] Case C-78/98 *Shirley Preston and others v Wolverhampton Healthcare NHS Trust and others* [2000] ECR 3201.

[12] Case 106/77 [1978] ECR 629. See also case 34/67 *Lück* [1968] ECR 360.

[13] Case 69/75 [1976] ECR 45.

of state liability in all Member States. In later cases, however, the Court did not carry out a comparative study of state liability in the different legal orders of Member States and even Advocate General Léger acknowledged the lack of common principles in that field.[14]

The fact that it took more than 15 years until that principle was declared inherent in the system of the Treaty (*Francovich*, paragraph 35) was probably due to the very limited number of cases submitted to the Court where this issue was at stake. But the delay in officially declaring the inherence of that principle in the Community legal order cannot hide the presence of all necessary elements to reach such a declaration in the development of the case law mentioned above, thus showing how *Francovich* constituted the inexorable next step towards the recognition of the state liability principle under Community law.

Some Critical Remarks Concerning the Judgment

As we know, before considering the existence and scope of Member States' liability for damages resulting from breach of their obligations under Community law, the Court first examined the direct effect of the provisions of Directive 80/897.[15] In order to ascertain whether the provisions of that piece of Community legislation were unconditional and sufficiently precise, the Court analysed the identity of the person entitled to the guarantee, the content of the latter and the identity of those under obligation to provide it. Having considered the first and the second requirements, the Court held that with regard to the third condition, there was not sufficient clarity to identify the person liable to provide the guarantee, a circumstance which did not allow finding the state liable on the sole ground that it had failed to take transposition measures within the prescribed period.[16]

Having said that, it is still worth recalling the argument put forward by the Commission according to which the possibility provided for in the Directive that the guarantee institutions might be entirely financed by the public authorities, made unacceptable the thwarting of the effects of the Directive by the Member States by merely asserting that they could have required other persons to bear partially or completely the financial burden resting upon it. Although the Court rejected that submission, I am not alone in upholding its correctness.[17] This could have led the Court to find the Directive provisions directly effective, thus making the state directly liable. Certainly, Member States enjoy discretion under Article 5 of the Directive, but it can be easily deduced from the same provision, subsection (b), that public authorities have to be involved in the financing of the guarantee institutions, since employers only have to 'contribute to the financing . . . unless it is fully covered by the public authorities'. It is clear from the wording of this provision that whatever the margin of appreciation regarding the establishment of the guarantee institution might be, public authorities had to provide, in any event, a substantial part of the financing. It may appear as if the Court desperately wanted to deny the direct effect of

[14] Opinion given in Case C-5/94 *The Queen v Ministry of Agriculture, Fisheries and Food ex p Hedley Lomas (Ireland) Ltd* [1996] ECR I-2553, paras 96–100.

[15] Directive 80/987/EEC of 20 October 1980 on the approximation of the laws of the Member States relating to the protection of employees in the event of the insolvency of the employer (OJ 1980 L 283, p 23).

[16] *Francovich*, paras 23–26.

[17] R Alonso García, 'La responsabilidad de los Estados miembros por infracción del Derecho comunitario' (Madrid, Civitas, 1997), 19.

the provision in question, in order to be free to settle the principle of state liability for infringement of Community law for the very first time.

A second issue I would like to address again[18] is the requirement in *Francovich* that the directives capable of giving rise to state liability have to grant rights to individuals. In my view, there is no justification for limiting state liability to these kinds of directives and it would therefore be more accurate to extend that fundamental principle to all kind of directives, thus placing the burden of proof on the individual that the breach of whichever directive by a Member State has affected his legitimate interests and caused him damage or loss. The reduction of the scope of the state liability principle to the directives conferring directly applicable rights to individuals seems to lack any justification and creates an artificial distinction between various kinds of Community legislation, since the breach of a directive not granting rights can nevertheless affect other rights conferred by domestic law.

Francovich in the Light of Subsequent Case Law

The subsequent judgments developing *Francovich* are well known and do not need an extensive explanation in this short Chapter. It is commonly accepted now that in *Brasserie du Pêcheur*,[19] with the nuances introduced not much later, especially by *British Telecommunications*,[20] *Lomas*,[21] *Dillenkofer*,[22] *Norbrook Laboratories*,[23] *Haim*[24] and *Köbler*,[25] the Court has toned down the *Francovich* doctrine in the cases where the breach of Community law arises from an action of Member States, whether of a legislative, administrative or judicial nature. In those cases, the conditions governing state liability are threefold: the rule infringed must be intended to confer rights on individuals; the breach must be sufficiently serious; and there must be a direct causal link between the breach of the obligation incumbent on the state and the damage or loss sustained by the injured parties.[26]

Especially the second condition, the seriousness of the breach of Community law, distinguishes itself from *Francovich*, though one can infer from *Brasserie du Pêcheur* that the Court considered this condition as being implicitly fulfilled in the former judgment.[27] The introduction, or the explicit mention, of that requirement was justified by the Court with the need to give the same treatment to state liability as to the liability of the Community institutions under Article 288(2) EC Treaty.

Soon after the *Francovich* judgment, but before the *Brasserie du Pêcheur* judgment, I warned of the risks Community law could incur by aligning state liability to the same

[18] D Ruiz-Jarabo Colomer, 'El juez nacional como juez comunitario' (Madrid, Civitas, 1993), 181.
[19] Joined Cases C-46/93 and C-48/93 *Brasserie du Pêcheur* and *Factortame* [1996] ECR I-1029.
[20] C-392/93 [1996] ECR I-1631.
[21] Case 69/75 [1976] ECR 45.
[22] Joined Cases C-178/94, C-179/94, C-188/94, C-189/94 and C-190/94 *Dillenkofer et al* [1996] ECR I-4845.
[23] C-127/95 [1998] ECR I-1531.
[24] C-424/97 [2000] ECR I-5123.
[25] C-224/01 [2003] ECR I-10239.
[26] *Haim*, para 36, and *Köbler*, para 51.
[27] *Brasserie du Pêcheur*, para 45; see also Alonso García, p 36.

principles as liability of Community institutions, due to the rigidity and the narrowness of the interpretation given to the conditions to which the liability of the Community institutions is bound.[28]

First of all, as Advocate General Léger pointed out in his opinion in *Hedley Lomas*, there is a fundamental difference between both kinds of liability: within the scope of Community law, the institutions act as a primary legislator while Member States are confined by the norms of Community law taking also into account the principle of primacy.[29] Therefore, the discretion enjoyed by Member States does not seem comparable to that of the Community institutions. Hence, the way in which Member States make use of their margin of discretion and the degree of this margin should be taken into account when assessing the seriousness of the breach of Community law, and attention should also be paid to the hierarchy of norms in the national legal orders. Thus, a breach committed by an administrative decision or by regulatory measures should not be treated in the same manner as a breach arising from an act of the national parliament; in the first two hypotheses, a simple transgression could be considered sufficient to trigger the liability of the public body, but not in the case of the infringement by a national law (meaning an act of national Parliament), due to its nature and historical significance.[30]

Secondly, it has been accurately pointed out[31] that the overlap between the conditions of state liability and those defined by the case law concerning the liability of the Community institutions does not seem to be complete. Thus, under Article 288(2) EC Treaty, the damage alleged by the applicants must go beyond the bounds of the economic risks of the activity in the sector concerned,[32] a requirement which was not included in *Brasserie du Pêcheur* as a prerequisite for establishing state liability. Even if I do believe that a distinction should be maintained, this one reveals the Court's incapacity, or unwillingness, to completely unify the criteria of liability for breach of Community law as regards Member States and the Community institutions, probably for reasons related to the limited cross-fertilisation between Article 288(2) and state liability.[33]

By using the same approach towards liability of Community institutions, and especially with regard to the condition of the serious breach of a community rule, the Court has increased the difficulties for individuals seeking to obtain damages, since the interpretation of that condition, but also of the third one (the causal link),[34] seems so uncertain that one can wonder whether it has provided a real remedy for those who have suffered loss and damage as a result of the incorrect application of community law.[35]

It is clear from the preceding ideas, that in the way the case law after *Francovich* has shaped the system, the role of national courts has been enhanced, due to the fact that

[28] Ruiz-Jarabo Colomer, p 180.

[29] Opinion of Advocate General Léger in *Hedley Lomas*, paras 101 *ff.*

[30] A Barav, 'Responsabilité et irresponsabilité de l'État en cas de méconnaissance du droit communautaire', in *Gouverner, administrer, juger—Liber amicorum Jean Waline* (Paris Dalloz, 2002), 441.

[31] T Tridimas, *Principles of EU law* (Oxford, EC Law Library, 2006), 512.

[32] Case C-5/88 *Wachauf v Bundesamt für Ernährung und Forstwirtschaft* [1989] ECR 2609.

[33] W van Gerven, 'Taking Article 215(2) EC seriously', in J Beatson and T Tridimas (eds), *New Directions in European Public Law* (Oxford, Hart Publishing, 1998), 35.

[34] See Cases C-319/96 *Brinkmann Tabakfabriken* [1998] ECR I-5255 and C-140/97 *Rechberger* [1999] ECR I-3499.

[35] P Aalto, 'Twelve years of Francovich in the European court of Justice: A survey of the case-law on the interpretation of the three conditions of liability' in S Moreira de Sousa and W Heusel (eds), *Enforcing Community law from Francovich to Köbler: Twelve years of the State liability principle* (Trier, Academy of European Law, vol 37, 2004), p 76.

national judges are responsible for the final decision making the necessary assessments of the damage, the seriousness of the breach of Community law and the causal link. Apart from the inherent difficulties of each case, it is questionable whether the judgments of the Court provide national courts with sufficient guidance in order to accomplish their task. Look at, for instance, the summary of the Court's decision in *Norbrook Laboratories*, according to which 'a breach is sufficiently serious where a Member State, in the exercise of its legislative powers, has manifestly and gravely disregarded the limits on its powers ... and, second, that where, at the time when it committed the infringement, the Member State in question was not called upon to make any legislative choices and had only considerably reduced or sometimes no discretion, the mere infringement of Community law being sufficient to establish the existence of a sufficiently serious breach'.[36] Thus, in the absence, first, of the recognition by the Court of horizontal direct effect on directives, which, as you may remember, is actually the latent conflict in this debate, and, second, in the absence of more accurate guidelines in Community case law, it inevitably will be for national courts to decide using their own criteria; certain divergences between the Member States seem then unavoidable when examining the conditions of the seriousness of the breach of Community law and the causal link between the latter and the damage caused, according to the law and tradition in the judiciary systems of Member States. If national courts have often proved to be reluctant to accept basic principles of Community law such as primacy, one can hardly expect a different attitude towards the application of state liability.[37] But this slight fragmentation has to be accepted as a consequence of the moving from a system of rather objective liability of Member States, as *Francovich* seemed to create, to a model based on more subjective elements. One can only hope that further questions for preliminary rulings will smooth the path for national courts.

Conclusion

No one can deny, and it is certainly not the intention of this article, the importance of *Francovich* as a key element in the case law of the Court of Justice, and especially how it has advanced one of the most relevant principles deriving from the rule of law (in the sense of *État de droit*), the liability of Member States for breach of Community law as a systemic principle of its legal order. Probably the success of the judgment lies in the clever way it strengthens the effectiveness of Community law, most certainly the principal objective, while sanctioning a Member State for its behaviour and, at the same time, granting more rights to individuals.

However, reducing *Francovich* to a matter of effectiveness would seem too short-sighted. Its consequences could have been more far-reaching in terms of guaranteeing individual rights, if the Court had not undertaken subsequently the attempt to align state liability to the same criteria as the liability of the Community institutions. By doing so, the Court has clearly limited the scope of the Member States' liability, introducing a set of

[36] Case C-127/95, *Norbrook Laboratories Ltd v Ministry of Agriculture, Fisheries and Food* [1998] ECR I-1531, para 109.

[37] For instance, as regards France, L Bernardeau, 'Le principe consacré par l'arrêt *Francovich* et le droit administratif français ou "les avancées dans une possible impasse"', in Moreira de Sousa and Heusel (eds), pp 145 *ff*. See, however, the recent developments in the Décision du Conseil d'État of 8 February 2007 (*Arcelor*).

conditions which are difficult to apply, and relegated *Francovich* to the realm of cruel reality: its scope amounts only to its narrowest meaning, that is, the case of complete failure of Member States to implement directives into national law.[38] Thus, in light of the preceding thoughts, one can only agree with Advocate General Mischo, who delivered the opinion on the *Francovich* case, and who, looking back at the judgment, wrote '... *cette jurisprudence n'est pas allée trop loin*'.[39]

But, rather than feeling sad because of the final destiny of the *Francovich* judgment, I would suggest taking the same attitude as Oscar Wilde did when he used to tell fairy tails to his sons Vyvyan and Cyril Holland. The former explains in a delightful book called *Son of Oscar Wilde*, how his father, when he was tired of playing with him and his brother, kept them quiet by telling them fairy stories. Cyril once asked his father why he had tears in his eyes when he told them the story of the Selfish Giant, and he replied that 'really beautiful things always made me cry'.[40]

[38] So also A Barav, 'The effectiveness of judicial protection and the role of the national courts' in *Judicial protection of rights in the Community legal order* (Brussels, Bruylant, 1997), 285.

[39] J Mischo, 'L'émergence du principe de la responsabilité de l'État' in Moreira de Sousa and Heusel (eds), p 58.

[40] M Mac Liammóir 'An introduction to the author', in Oscar Wilde, *The Happy Prince and other stories* 28th edn (London, Puffin Classics, 2003), p ix.

2

In Praise of *Francovich*

ANDREA BIONDI[41]

In dual-sovereign federal systems, the relationship between the individual, the Member State, and the central sovereign is perpetually problematic. Outside the area of fundamental human rights, for which modern supra-national legal systems guarantee protection to individual citizens, any other intervention by the central sovereign to protect individual legal interests even against encroachment by a Member State produces controversy. Something of a lovers' triangle is at work here. To be a bit anthropomorphic, the Member States generally want to maintain the relationship between themselves and their citizens. Citizens who cannot get satisfaction from their home state, however, turn to the federal sovereign for relief. The federal sovereign is therefore squeezed by competing loyalties, each of which is important for the federal sovereign's legitimacy and success. It does not want to offend its partner Member States by getting too involved, but at the same time, it does not want to abandon the individual citizen either. To continue the metaphor, as with all intimate fights, the most contentious issues often relate to money and who gets to decide who must spend it on whom. Just as in more personal settings, there is rarely a perfect solution. If a citizen has suffered personal injury at the hands of a private party, the state provides an unbiased forum in which the citizen may seek relief. But what if the injurer is the state itself? And the injury suffered is one that arises out of the Member State's refusal to abide by the law of the central sovereign? The citizen has no other choice but to turn to the federal sovereign. It is at this point that the problems start. The Member State is presented with the clearest example of what it really means to lose its full sovereignty, as it might end up paying money to one of its citizens because he has been smart enough to circumvent the Member State and appeal to the central sovereign. It is also difficult for the Member State to accept that it is just another potential tortfeasor from whom an individual can claim money damages.

Different dual sovereign federal systems treat these situations differently. In the US, for example, it is generally very difficult for individuals to get monetary damages even when state action has violated a legal right created by Congressional legislation under the auspices of the Constitution.[42] In the EU, the love triangle between Mr Francovich, Italy and the European Court of Justice opened up an entirely new state of affairs. The relationship between Mr Francovich and his own state had been notoriously tempestuous. In the words of Advocate General Mischo, 'rarely has the Court been called upon to decide a case in which the adverse consequences for the individuals concerned of a failure to

[41] Professor of European Union Law, King's College London.

[42] See, inter alia, C Vasquez, 'What is Eleventh Amendment Immunity?' in (1996–97) 106 *Yale Law Journal* 1683.

implement a directive were as shocking as in the case now before us'.[43] The Court of Justice sided with Mr Francovich and held that the Italian State failed to honour the guarantees provided for in Directive 80/987 relating to the protection of employees in the event of the insolvency of their employer and had therefore to pay him compensation. Further it warned all the other Member States that the 'principle whereby a State must be liable for loss and damage caused to individuals as a result of breaches of Community law for which the State can be held responsible is inherent in the system of the Treaty'.[44]

As is well known, in *Francovich* the Court cited the 'fantastic four' to support its findings: *Van Gend en Loos*; *Costa*; *Simmenthal*; *Factortame*—which make an otherwise very rare, collective appearance.[45] In those days when the Court had to establish the doctrine of supremacy of European law, it had to distance itself from the classic model of supremacy in international law, traditionally expressed in terms of state liability, so as to affirm the novelty of the European legal order by characterising it in terms of individual protection.[46] *Francovich* provides an elegantly performed variation, whereby the liability of the state and the individual right to claim compensation are an *unicum* which reaffirms the distinctiveness of the EU constitution. The notion that effective compliance with constitutional principles might take the form of deterrence is not, after all, a new phenomenon. Further, as has been noted with respect to constitutional norms, because of their countermajoritan character, the remedial scheme will be effective only if the power to obtain it is vested in private individuals.

This is all true; after 15 years of copious Community and national case law, and endless academic debate, the *Francovich* judgment is still resplendent because of the simplicity of its main achievement. Although some regard talk of money as rather vulgar, vindicating an injury to an individual requires monetary damages to be paid.[47] *Francovich* is thus a clear acknowledgment that—despite more sophisticated and elaborate possible alternatives—no given legal order is capable of 'doing away with tort law'.[48] It is interesting, therefore, that such a straightforward introduction of the right to reparation has attracted criticisms from the whole 'political' spectrum. From the 'right', not surprisingly the judgment has provoked many more hostile reactions within national establishments than even the doctrines of supremacy and direct effect. As recently as 2003 the Italian Court of Cassation resorted to a 17th-century idea of *pouvoir public* by ruling that an action for compensation bestowed upon individuals would breach the principle that the parliament and the government have unlimited freedom to legislate.[49] However, it is also true that just a month later, the same court took the opposite view and granted compensation to the individual concerned, faithfully applying the Court of Justice's case law.[50] At least they got there in the end …

[43] Opinion of AG Mischo in Joined Cases C-6 and C-9/90, *Francovich and others* [1991] ECR I-5357, para 1.

[44] *Francovich*, para 35.

[45] Case 26/62 *Van Gend en Loos* [1963] ECR 1; Case 6/64 *Costa v ENEL* [1964] ECR 585; Case 106/77 *Amministrazione delle Finanze dello Stato v Simmenthal* [1978] ECR 629 and Case C-213/89 *Factortame* [1990] ECR I-2433.

[46] B De Witte, 'Retour à Costa. La primauté du droit communautaire a la lumière du droit international' (1984) *Revue Trimestrielle de Droit Européen* 425.

[47] For discussion of the historical recognition and the significance of this point in both law and in economics, see HL Feldman, 'Loss' in (2006) 35 *New Mexico Law Review* 375.

[48] SD Sugarman, 'Doing Away with Tort Law' in (1985) 73 *California Law Review* 558.

[49] Corte di Cassazione, Sez III Civile, case no 4915 of 1 April 2003 reported in *Foro Italiano*, I, 2003, 2016.

[50] Corte di Cassazione, Case no 7630 of 16 May 2003, reported in *Foro Italiano*, I, 2003, 2016.

Much more surprising is the reaction from the 'left'. Apart from trite charges of judicial interventionism, *Francovich* is subject to several accusations. First, it has been said that the Court had not been 'modern' enough. Other, more sophisticated forms of redress should have been favoured. In particular, injunctive measures or equitable relief are supposedly more effective at ensuring the general welfare of society. In reality, the Court has always refrained from taking dogmatic positions on the merits of different forms of redress, avoiding any hierarchy between compensation, injunctive measures or equitable reliefs. It might be useful to remind ourselves that only eight months before *Francovich* the Court handed down its *Zuckerfabrik* judgment,[51] spelling out the condition for an EU interim relief action—a judgment that incidentally was used by Advocate General Mischo to support the introduction of a liability claim. Although the Court did not address the point, it seems to us implicit that injunctive relief and compensation were, at least in the Court's eyes, performing different functions, both of which were equally fundamental in ensuring a complete system of remedies in the EU legal order. The same approach is taken by the Court on the question of specific performance/compensation, a dualism that is solved not in the alternative but by 'co-operative' and flexible solutions.[52] This non-dogmatic and practical approach avoids overcharging the individual with tasks which he or she is not supposed to perform. Certainly injunctive reliefs, specific performances or equitable reliefs from the perspective of guaranteeing an effective implementation are probably more significant. However, the injured person does not bring suit as a policy-maker or a political theorist. He brings suit in order to be restored to his pre-injury status, as far as is feasible under the law.

Another accusation is that *Francovich* lacks a true theoretical foundation as it does not clarify what the real purpose of the compensation action really is. Thus it is routinely observed that while *Francovich* seemed to promise a regime of strict liability, whereby reparation of the losses sustained by the individual is the ultimate goal; the subsequent introduction of subjective criteria, such as the notion of serious breach, mitigation of losses and so on, have, however, created a pure sanction model, which concentrates on how badly Member States have behaved. In this vein, when the State has behaved really badly, such as, for instance, in *Factortame*,[53] the Court has even gone so far as to suggest the award of exemplary damages. In other more lenient instances, however, such as judicial responsibility in *Köbler*, the Court took the step to reserve for itself the decision to 'pardon' the national court in question.[54] Such a reconstruction might be correct but it is also perhaps somewhat unfair. It is unfair mainly because through *Francovich* the Court has lent its judicial support to allowing compensation for a variety of 'contemporary' subjective rights. It is easy to forget, for instance, that the *Francovich* action has become a powerful instrument in guaranteeing the right of consumers to a fair regulated market.[55]

[51] Joined Cases C-143/88 and C-92/89 *Zuckerfabrik* [1991] ECR I-415.

[52] For a pre-*Francovich* judgment see Case 14/83 *Von Colson and Kamann* [1984] ECR 1891. See also Case C-180/95 *Draehmpaehl* [1997] ECR I-2195. Case C-131/97 *Carbonari and Others v Università degli Studi di Bologna and Others* [1999] ECR I-1103 and Case C-201/02 *Wells* [2004] ECR I-723.

[53] Joined Cases C-46/93 and C-48/93 *Brasserie du Pêcheur* and *Factortame* [1996] ECR I-1029.

[54] Case C-224/01 *Köbler* [2003] ECR I-10239.

[55] Case C-91/92 *Faccini Dori* [1994] ECR I-3325, C-179/94, C-188/94, C-189/94 and C-190/94 *Dillenkofer and Others* [1996] ECR I-4845 and Case C-140/97 *Rechberger and Others v Austria* [1999] ECR I-3499.

The Court was also ready to accept an award of compensation for non-material damage.[56] Even in the much-criticised cases of *Maso* and *Bonifaci*, although the Court admitted that retroactive application in full of national implementing measures of a directive can, in principle, ensure that the harmful consequences of the breach of Community law are remedied, it specified that it would still be possible for the individual concerned to establish the existence of complementary loss sustained on account of the fact that they were unable to benefit, at the appropriate time, from the rights guaranteed by EC law.[57] Finally, a dogmatic dichotomy of rationales for permitting recovery and either/or insistence upon arguing from rights or arguing from deterrence, does not really exist in practice where the two components are often indistinguishable from each other. For instance deterrence is particularly relevant in cases where the tortfeasor is very wealthy and the non-punitive damages, therefore, comparatively small, but the tort is really serious from a public policy standpoint. At the same time, such a case reinforces corrective justice due to an individual who has suffered wrongful injury to be 'made whole' by the injurer.

Another *Francovich* 'regret' is that the minimum procedural conditions laid down by the Court in this judgment, and later elaborated on in *Factortame/Brasserie du Pêcheur*, create uncertainty and incoherence. This is first so because the Court in its *acquis* keeps on swinging from leaving the assessment of those conditions entirely to national courts to occasionally reserving it for itself; and secondly, the fact that the Court only laid down broad and minimum conditions for compensation makes the award of damages excessively dependent on the national system of remedies. In the traditional 'hard' areas of national competence, such as procedural law, leaving the actual application of a compensation action to domestic courts inevitably leads to divergent standards, different solutions, different time limits, different rules on interest calculations, different forms of compensatable damages and so on and so forth. Once again however, although undeniably true, those accusations are misplaced. As it has been vividly expressed the 'great genius of the European Court [in *Francovich*] has been to lure national courts into doing its bidding'.[58] Thus the Court made the most of the Italian court's preliminary reference, whereby the right to claim reparation of loss and damage sustained was intertwined with the question of the direct effect of the Directive in question. The three conditions—namely, that the result prescribed by a directive should entail the grant of rights to individuals; the identification of the content of those rights on the basis of the provisions of the directive; and the existence of a causal link between the breach of the state's obligation and the loss and damage suffered by the injured parties—might not be amazingly accurate, or particularly refined, but they are already a remarkable attempt to put some flesh on the bones of the law of state liability actions and they serve as a reminder that its application is taken away—albeit not entirely—from the vagaries of national law. Of course there is a lot to say about specific problems and the limits of the Court's approach on specific issues. Our main point of contention with many of the criticisms made against *Francovich*, however, is that those arguments are predominantly

[56] Case C-168/00 *Leitner* [2002] ECR I-2631. In the words of AG Tizzano, 'even in Community law, enjoyment of a holiday is treated as an asset worth protecting and damage arising out of the failure to enjoy it amounts to, in the context of a package contract, a specific loss which justifies compensation', at para 44.

[57] Case C-373/95 *Maso and Others* [1997] ECR I-4051 para 41 and Joined Cases C-94/95 and C-95/95 *Bonifaci and Others* and *Berto and Others* [1997] ECR I-3969, para 44.

[58] S Weatherill, 'Addressing problems of Imbalanced Implementation in EC law' in C Kilpatrick et al (eds), *The Future of Remedies in Europe* (Oxford, Hart, 2000) 87.

ideologically biased. There is a certain tendency—partially justified by the sometimes emphatic tone of some of the Court's judgments—to consider the law on judicial protection as merely functional to the regulatory model of the European Union of harmonisation and uniform application. Thus, the law on state liability is considered as a good case study for the uncertainty regarding the very soul of the European integration process. Depending on different 'political' views, state liability is criticised as failing to promote uniformity, or it is criticised for not acknowledging the necessity of regulatory differentiation. In this fashion, the posts of the debate are constantly being moved. First and foremost, these reconstructions do not do justice to the sophistication and peculiarities of a European model essentially based on the coexistence of different regulatory levels, consisting of a balancing exercise between uniformity and differentiation, with a call for all the different political and economic actors to be fully involved. The *Francovich* judgment is a perfect example of this method, as, on the one hand, it does introduce a new and far-reaching principle, and on the other, it reaffirms the centrality of the role of national courts and the value of the national systems of procedural law according to which they will have to apply the new principle. After all, the question of the relationship between EC liability and national liability procedural rules should not be considered in terms of conflict but rather of 'co-ordination'. Both sets of rules have the same aims of guaranteeing an efficient composition of conflicting interests, access to justice, and the protection of the rights of the parties. This is especially true if one considers the many transformations that national civil procedure systems have been recently going through. Labels such as 'adversarial'; 'inquisitorial'; 'liberal'; 'authoritarian'; or 'private/public' are dated. The focus has instead shifted on to how to guarantee effectively the rights of the individual in a reasonable time and at a reasonable cost whilst, at the same time, introducing measures to make sure that there is not a proliferation of unfounded suits or unending litigation.[59] To sum up, taking for granted the fact that any kind of remedy would have to go through some kind of procedural hoops, why not going through the ones that already exist? Community law works best not when it is imposed, but rather 'relocated' into national law. As once candidly observed by Advocate General Jacobs, a certain degree of non-uniformity in the application of EC law may be the price which has to be paid, but this phenomenon is somehow unavoidable in all legal systems, including that of the Community.[60]

In conclusion, it is clear that we like the *Francovich* judgment. We like it as it reaffirms the distinctiveness of the European legal system based on the special dignity of all its citizens; we like it as it requires a wrongful injurer to compensate the person harmed by the wrongful conduct. Making such a principle operational in a multi-layered system such as the European Union is certainly controversial. Mr Francovich knows that all too well. After more than six years from the time he brought his first action, he was told by the Italian courts that he had started his action too late and that he was not going to get any lira.[61] Still, his pleas for protection did not go unheard and his rights as a European citizen were fully recognised. The action for compensation for breach of EU law is now available to others and those citizens are also likely to get compensation in euros. Not bad for a single judgment …

[59] See in general N Trocker and V Varano, *The Reforms of Civil Procedure in Comparative Perspective* (Turin, Giappichelli, 2005).

[60] See AG Jacobs' Opinion in Case C-431/93, *Van Schijndel and others* [1995] ECR I-4705 at 4721.

[61] See C-479/93 *Francovich v Italy* [1995] ECR I-3843.

3

Francovich and Imperfect Law

JULIO BAQUERO CRUZ[62]

European Union law has a problematic, uncertain and ambivalent mode of being. Torn between the domestic, the federal and the international, it seems to be much more effective than most international law and yet less effective than most domestic and federal law. Its nature and authority do not seem to be as solid as those of other more established legal systems. They can never be taken for granted. They are always changing, never stable, sometimes improving, sometimes decaying. Union law itself and its doctrinal elaboration is impressive on paper, but social reality does not always follow sufficiently. The more Union law develops in words and structure, the more the social and legal reality of many Member States seems to resist that development, and the wider becomes the gap between the ideal order of things expressed in that law and things as they are. The resistance may be rebellious but most of the time it is unconscious, due to ignorance and habit. And even if the law of European integration is a clear success in terms of penetration and effectiveness, especially when compared to other international and regional systems of law, Union law still has many problems and shortcomings. It is indeed its very success and the rich jurisprudential elaboration of its norms that tend to magnify those very problems and shortcomings. These difficulties are mainly cultural. National legal cultures are deeply engrained. Many national legal actors and scholars still see the law of the European Union as something essentially foreign that does not concern them, that is not theirs. In many cases, Union law is not applied when and as it should. This problem may be more grave in peripheral countries or in countries that have a short experience as Member States of the European Union. To a variety of extents, however, it is a common trait in all of them. Hence if one reads a handbook on Union law one will not have a realistic view of that system of law. One will generally have an abstract and highly idealised view of the legal system that is only half of the story. To have the complete picture one needs to examine carefully its practical reception in the legal orders of the Member States. And there the picture is more blurred.

These ideas need to be nuanced even more, to be sure. Perhaps all systems of law share that problematic mode of being. The most effective national legal system is never realised to its full extent. There are always grey areas and a gap between norms and facts. The very notion of 'existence' of a legal system is difficult to understand and use. It is a misleading metaphor. For the notion of 'existence' is never a matter of degree, and presupposes autonomy from other beings, while the norms of legal systems can be realised to a variety of extents, more or less perfectly, and can never 'live' autonomously, independently of

[62] Member of the Legal Service of the European Commission. The opinions contained in this chapter are purely personal.

human agency and will. Their obligatory character is also a matter of degree, never black or white. But even if these difficulties are shared by all legal systems, one cannot deny that the mode of being of Union law is more or otherwise problematic than that of the laws of more conventional political communities. The difference is essential, for the 'existence' of Union law depends on its constant acceptance by the legal systems of the Member States, the very 'existence' of which as closed and self-contained systems is constantly put into question by Union law itself. This tension is characteristic of federal systems in their initial, critical or final phases. In the Union, however, that tension seems to be consubstantial to the general practice of the system, and no durable equilibrium may be available. From a legal and also from a political point of view, the European Union seems to be condemned to be a crisis system, never attaining a lasting balance.

The problematic mode of being of Union law manifests itself with great clarity in the *Francovich* line of case law, which includes other leading judgments such as *Brasserie du Pêcheur* and *Köbler*, and which can be seen as a particular dimension of the theme of the penetration of that law in the legal orders of the Member States. This is paradoxical. *Francovich*'s declaration that state liability is inherent in the system of the Treaty and the gradual development of the legal contours of that liability actually seem to transmit the opposite message: that the system has resources to cope with non-compliance; that Union law is 'normal' and effective law. Yet *Francovich*, more than any other judgment, speaks to us today about the uncertainty of Union law, about its fragile and difficult mode of existence, about the imperfect and unfinished character of the rule of law in the Union.

Francovich was decided in November 1991, a month before Opinion 1/91, in a period that can be seen as the high-water mark of constitutional development through case law in what then was the European Economic Community. It was also a good period for integration in general. The single market programme approached its completion and on 9–10 December 1991 the Maastricht summit reached a political agreement on the Treaty on European Union, which was signed in February the next year and included a system of fines that could be imposed on the Member States that do not comply with a judgment of the Court. It was this legal and political enthusiasm that led to the moments of crisis of the first Danish referendum, the near-crisis of the French referendum and the juridical *Götterdammerung* of the Maastricht-Urteil. But in December 1991 few expected this dramatic *dénouement*. I am not arguing that *Francovich* is a consequence of the legal and political climates. I am only suggesting that it has to be understood in this wider context. The decision might well have been the same in a context of political crisis, since the main force behind the ruling was precedent and legal argument. At most the Court could have avoided the issue of state liability with a minimalistic ruling. I do not think it would ever have negated squarely the principle of state liability for breaches of Community law.

It is curious how time acts upon the case law, how different it is to read it in different periods of time. In the early 1990s some commentators contested the legitimacy and soundness of *Francovich*, particularly in Germany. They argued that it had no basis whatsoever in the Treaty, that the reasoning was insufficient, that the Court was overstepping its competences, encroaching into the competences of the Community legislator and implicitly revising the Treaty. The leading English handbook continues to describe this judgment as 'the most dramatic and distinctive of the Court's interventionist rulings'. But this language may be a remnant of previous editions in want of a revision. It is hard indeed to see *Francovich* today as dramatic and interventionist, for it has become an established part of the legal landscape, at least of that abstract part of the landscape that

Union lawyers are more willing and used to seeing. And it would take little effort to argue that it was a natural consequence of the structure, spirit and text of that Treaty, and also of general principles common to the Member States, and that it followed quite logically and naturally from *Van Gend en Loos* and *Costa v ENEL*, completing and complementing them. Conversely, it is clear that a judgment denying that the Member States may be liable as a matter of Union law for breaches of that law would sit rather uncomfortably with the seminal cases of the 1960s. In any event, nobody seems to question the principles and legal arguments that stand behind *Francovich* any more. But *leading* cases need to lead, and if those supposed to be led do not follow them their authority is gradually eroded. What can and should be explored today, from this perspective, is to what extent the image or representation we have of the legal landscape coincides with the real world of practice in the Member States.

Now, *Francovich* was supposed to lead both national courts and the political institutions of the Union and the Member States. One could have expected the organs of the States (legislator, executive, administration and judiciary) to become more careful in their respect of Community law in order to avoid liability. Directives would have been implemented in time and more strictly. National judges would have respected their obligation to refer, applying European law when and as they had to. The myriad of administrative practices which are doubtful from the point of view of the Treaty would have been reviewed and eliminated. Individuals would have asserted their rights and state liability would have become widespread, even massive in some Member States. We should have seen many cases on state liability before the Court, and many more before national courts. The issue of state liability due to judicial decisions would have been raised shortly after *Francovich*. National legislators would have adapted their liability regimes to adapt to the rulings of the Court. The Union legislator would have intervened to harmonise the conditions of liability within the scope of Community law. The Commission would have been more active, issuing an interpretative communication and promoting the application of *Francovich*.

On almost all these counts, expectations have been deceived, and *Francovich* looks like a monument kept in bad repair. With regard to national courts we should bear in mind that, in spite of the formal recognition of direct effect, supremacy and state liability by national supreme courts—with limited exceptions by some constitutional courts—daily practice is not always fully respectful of Union law, due to the insufficient penetration of this legal culture in the legal cultures of the Member States. In some of them the penetration is stronger. In other states it is clearly insufficient. Whenever a national court of last resort does not refer a question to the Court when it should, and this happens often enough, the law of European integration is put at risk. If one scratches a little bit the surface of the case law of national courts of last resort in any Member State, it is not hard to find examples of this sort of disregard. And the available statistical studies on potential questions of Union law, questions raised by the parties, and questions actually referred to Luxembourg do not allow us to be very optimistic. This problem affects Union law as a whole, but it is particularly grave for the *Francovich* line of case law, which depends upon the good functioning of the preliminary rulings procedure. Caught in this circle, *Francovich* may have been rendered inefficient or insufficiently efficient by the problems of the preliminary rulings procedure, exposing even more the imperfections of the legal system instead of reducing them.

There is perhaps another sense in which the reception of *Francovich* has been deficient: it has not been recognised by the powers in charge of revising the Treaty, by the Community legislator, and by national legislators. It has not been overruled either, but in contrast to other important constitutional lines of case law (like that on the locus standi of the European Parliament or that on fundamental rights), state liability is still only 'inherent' in the system of the Treaty as interpreted by the Court, but not expressly recognised in the text of that Treaty. The European Union legislator has not acted either in a field in which its action might well be indispensable. With some exceptions, national legislators and administrations have not adapted their liability systems to Union law. The message sent by the Court does not seem to have been heard by the political organs.

Thus, in spite of *Francovich*, in many cases everything seems to go on much as before. Directives are not always implemented properly and in time. Dubious administrative practices are widespread in the Member States. Judgments of the Court are not always respected by state institutions. Not much has changed either from the point of view of individuals, if we except those litigants whose lawyers knew *Francovich* and were fortunate enough to find a sympathetic national court. From the date of *Francovich*, the cases dealing with state liability decided by the Court have not been many. In the Member States, the cases on state liability for breaches of Community law decided by national courts without a reference are not as many as one would expect. It took more than a decade for the important and flagrant issue of state liability due to judicial decisions of national courts of last resort to reach the Court. In the years following *Köbler*, only one other case has reached the Court on that issue. And many other potential consequences of *Francovich* concerning both substance and procedure are still unexplored. The relative paucity of cases on this issue could also be explained as a consequence of the stringent conditions of liability, to be sure, but I have the impression that the main reason is the insufficient penetration of Union law in the legal cultures of the Member States.

The problematic reception of *Francovich* can be linked to an old theme of legal theory. There is an old tradition of thought according to which a law without sanctions is not law in the proper sense of the word. It would be imperfect law, a kind of positive morality. According to a now also classical critique, legal obligations cannot depend only on the existence of sanctions, and not all law needs sanctions to be law proper. The old tradition is still meaningful, however, for extreme cases. A legal system that lacks any sanction whatsoever, in which no consequence at all derives from the eventual breaches of its rules, can hardly be seen as a successful or 'binding' legal system. Much international law would belong to the category of imperfect law. Community law has also been plagued for many decades by non-compliance and by the lack of effective sanctions. It has been an imperfect law, like international law, and the narrative of its development has been one of its drift from international into constitutional law, that is, from ineffectiveness and partial non-existence into effectiveness and full existence.

Together with the system of fines created in Maastricht a few weeks after *Francovich*, state liability for breaches of Union law could be seen as the ultimate sanction that the system wanted, as the closure of a system that could now be seen as a more perfect system of law. But that view may be deceptive, for at least two reasons. First, the sanction itself needs to be enforced, and the defects of the legal system will only be remedied if and to the extent that it actually is enforced. Now, we know that the extent to which *Francovich* is enforced is limited. With the non-enforcement of the sanctions that should be imposed for not enforcing the law we reach the limits of the legal system. An infinite regress of further sanctions for not enforcing the law and the sanctions themselves, which are also part of the legal order, is like sticking the finger deeper and deeper in the wound. In some extreme cases liability can be helpful, but it cannot resolve the wider structural problems of the system. As I argued above, in many cases state liability only makes more visible the fragility of Union law, as it happened with *Köbler.*

Second, sanctions are clearly not enough for a legal system to be 'perfect'. The law cannot survive if those obliged to respect it only do so because they fear the sanctions attached to violations of its norms. It can only survive if many of them respect those norms because they see themselves as members of the group in which those norms apply, if they see those norms as obligatory and good, if they take, in Hart's terms, 'an internal point of view'. In the European Union that habit does not seem to be general and widespread. Its degree varies from country to country, from the regular to the anecdotal. In some countries there seems to be, instead, a widespread habit of ignorance. Union law matters very little. Like that character of Molière who spoke prose without noticing it and was surprised when he realised it, even professional legal actors such as national judges only do Union law without knowing it when they apply national laws transposing directives (if transposed). But that's not enough, for Union law requires much more than that unconscious act, and presupposes that they take 'an internal point of view'. That point of view is the main thing that is lacking: most national legal actors still take an external point of view to Union law. The most powerful sanctions and liability rules will always be impotent against that simple fact.

These reflections suggest that in the European Union the rule of law is only respected to a limited extent, that Union law has not overcome completely the resistance of national legal cultures, that it is in part condemned to remain a fiction. All law is in part a fiction, some will argue, all law is in part an illusion. Indeed, but Union law may be even more of a fiction, more of an illusion, than other systems of law. Perhaps it is all that it can be for now, another will add. Perhaps we should rejoice in the mere fact that it exists, trying to improve it or at least to preserve it against the various forces of fragmentation and decay at work within the system, until we arrive at a stage in which the conditions that may allow for a more perfect European rule of law finally exist.

4

Francovich and its Aftermath: Member State Liability for Breaches of European Law from an Economic Perspective

ROGER VAN DEN BERGH*

Introduction

According to settled case law of the European Court of Justice (ECJ), Member States can be held liable for damage caused to individuals as a result of breaches of European law. In the landmark *Francovich* case,[63], the ECJ stated that individuals must be able to obtain compensation to guarantee the full effectiveness of Community law and the protection of the rights which it grants. This judgment established the basic conditions for deciding a liability claim in the case of non-implementation of a directive, but no guidance was given in relation to other breaches of European law. The conditions for state liability were further clarified in the joined cases *Brasserie du Pêcheur* and *Factortame III*.[64] The ECJ ruled that the state will be liable whichever organ of the state is responsible for the breach (the legislature, the executive or the judiciary) and regardless of the internal division of powers between constitutional authorities. Moreover, the conditions for state liability were spelled out with respect to other breaches of Community law, in particular an infringement by a Member State of the Treaty rules relating to free movement of goods. More recently, in the *Köbler* case[65] the ECJ explicitly confirmed that Member Sates must compensate the damage caused to individuals by infringements of Community law stemming from a decision of a court adjudicating at last instance. The ECJ clarified that the duty to compensate is subject to the same conditions as in the case of an infringement by a Member State of the fundamental economic freedoms protected by the Treaty.

It follows from the ECJ's case law that Member States are bound to compensate harm to individuals if they infringe a rule of European law which confers rights on individuals and there is a causal link between the breach and the damage suffered by the injured parties. In the case of non-implementation of a directive it must be possible to identify the content of those rights on the basis of its provisions. In the case of an infringement of the fundamental economic freedoms or a misinterpretation of a rule of European law by a

* Professor of Law and Economics, Erasmus University Rotterdam and Co-ordinator of the Erasmus Mundus European Master in Law and Economics (EMLE).

[63] Cases C-6 and 9/90 *Francovich and Bonifaci v Italy* [1991] ECR I-5357.

[64] Cases C-46/93 and C-48/93 *Brasserie du Pêcheur SA v Germany and R v Secretary of State for Transport, ex parte Factortame Ltd and others* [1996] ECR I-1029.

[65] Case C-224/01 *Gerhard Köbler v Republik Österreich* [2003] I-10239.

national court adjudicating at last instance, the infringement must be 'sufficiently serious'. This last condition has received the greatest attention in the literature. Some authors have argued that the requirement of a 'sufficiently serious' breach may be too restrictive and does not guarantee full compensation of the loss suffered by individuals.[66] However, from an economic perspective there are strong arguments to support the requirement set by the ECJ. After this introduction, the second section of this commentary will confront the concept of 'sufficiently serious breach' with the main insights from the literature on economic analysis of liability law. It will be shown that there are strong economic arguments to limit the scope of liability (in particular by not adopting a rule of strict liability and requiring a form of gross negligence) to avoid an inefficient outcome. In the third section, three leading cases of the ECJ will be analysed from an economic perspective. Finally, the most important conclusions will be summarised.

Economic Analysis of the Concept of a 'Sufficiently Serious Breach'

Pure Financial Losses and Imprecise Standards of Care

The facts of the cases decided by the ECJ make clear that individuals mainly seek compensation for financial losses: workers or employees complain not to be entitled to financial benefits because of the non-implementation of a directive or due to indirectly discriminatory rules of national law, or companies argue to have suffered financial losses because of a legal rule impeding their access to a national market for goods or services. From an economic perspective, there is an important difference between the violation of a property right which leads to the damage or destruction of an economic resource and a pure financial loss. If a house burns down, the value of the capital stock of society is diminished by the value of the destroyed house. The damage of the victim is equal to the damage of society. Conversely, in the case of a pure financial loss the social loss may be less than the personal loss. For example: if a company cannot import products into a national territory, it may claim compensation equal to the entire value of the lost sales. However, those sales will be diverted to domestic producers who will gain from the enforcement of the national rule which indirectly discriminates against foreign would-be exporters. The social loss consists of the difference between the gains of the domestic firms and the losses of the foreign firms (and potentially the losses of consumers in the import country). If foreign firms are entitled to full compensation, they will claim an amount of compensation which is several times higher than the social loss.

If the private loss is less than the social loss full compensation will be in excess of the social damage. It is a crucial insight of the economic analysis of law that a liability rule may provide incentives to individuals to change their behaviour in order to escape from

[66] See, eg, J Steiner, 'From Direct Effect to *Francovich*: Shifting Means of Enforcement of Community Law' (1993) 22 *EL Rev* 3; W van Gerven, 'Bridging the Unbridgeable: Community and National Tort Laws after *Francovich* and *Brasserie*' (1996) *ICLQ* 507; P Craig, 'Once More unto the Breach: the Community, the State and Damages Liability' (1997) 113 *LQR* 67.

the payment of damages.[67] In economic terms, individuals should be given incentives to adopt efficient preventative measures or, in other words, to choose an economically optimal level of care. Thereto the amount of the damage compensation must equal the social loss; in this way the negative externalities caused by the tort will be fully internalised in the decision-making process of the potential tortfeasor. A rational individual will choose the level of care which minimizes the sum of the costs of care and the harm caused (efficient care). However, if the amount of the compensation exceeds the social loss this may lead to over-deterrence and the choice of an excessively high level of care.

Whether or not over-deterrence will occur is dependent upon the degree of precision and clarity of the standard of care.[68] If the legal system (legislature or courts) fixes an efficient and precise standard of care, overcompensation cannot lead to over-deterrence. If the standard of care is observed, there will be no liability irrespective of whether the compensation payment is equal to or higher than the real social damage. This result is no longer valid if the legal standard of care is not exactly defined ex ante. If there is a wide gamut of possible precautions to avoid harm, it is unlikely that the law can exactly define ex ante which level of care is sufficiently high to avoid liability. Consequently, the negligence standard becomes somewhat fuzzy in the eyes of the tortfeasor. If the latter faces the risk of having to pay damage compensation which is several times higher than the social damage he or she may choose an inefficiently high level of care. The important insight is that overcompensation coupled with an imprecise standard of due care leads to over-deterrence. How can this be avoided?

To enhance optimal deterrence, the legal system may restrict compensation to cases in which the level of due care has been obviously violated. Whether this is termed obvious negligence, evident liability (*Evidenzhaftung*), gross negligence, or otherwise, the message will be the same. If the standard of care is imprecisely defined ex ante, the limitation of liability to cases of obvious negligence will act as a signal that very costly damage prevention projects are excluded from being candidates for the legally required level of care. The requirement of obvious negligence mitigates the imprecision of the required standard of care and thus reduces the risk of over-deterrence. For torts in the market place, which often result in high individual but small social losses,[69] a rule of obvious negligence is preferable to reach optimal deterrence.

Lessons for European Law

The above insights will now be applied to the requirement formulated by the ECJ that there must be a 'sufficiently serious breach' of Community law to trigger off liability of a Member State for harm caused to individuals. The cases in which this requirement has been formulated (in particular *Brasserie du Pêcheur* and *Köbler*) concerned liability claims where the individual loss exceeded the social loss and the standard of care was unclear, so that there were powerful economic reasons in favour of a rule of obvious negligence. The ECJ's requirement of a 'sufficiently serious breach' can be seen as a way to prevent

[67] See generally S Shavell, *Economic Analysis of Accident Law* (Cambridge, Harvard University Press, 1987).

[68] See generally H-B Schäfer and C Ott, *The Economic Analysis of Civil Law* (Cheltenham, Edward Elgar, 2004) 253–9.

[69] One may think of incorrect information about the financial situation of a firm, which benefits some shareholders but harms others. For a discussion of this example, see Schaefer and Ott, *ibid.*

over-investment in preventative measures and to avoid over-deterrence. In this respect it is efficient to increase the burden of proof. Conversely, expanding the domain of state liability by softening the proof of a fault committed by the state or accepting a rule of strict liability (implying that no breach of a duty of care is required to establish state liability) will lead to over-deterrence. Obviously, it must be added that the goal of optimal deterrence will be reached only if the concept of 'sufficiently serious breach' is interpreted in conformity with the economic concept of efficient care. In this respect, a critical look must be given at the factors which, according to the ECJ, are relevant for deciding whether a breach of European law is sufficiently serious.

In *Brasserie du Pêcheur*, the ECJ mentioned a number of criteria to be taken into consideration in assessing the seriousness of the breach: the clarity and precision of the rule breached, the measure of discretion left by that rule to the national authorities, whether the infringement was intentional or involuntary, whether any error of law was excusable or inexcusable, the fact that the position taken by a Community institution may have contributed towards the omission, and the adoption or retention of national measures or practices contrary to Community law. The ECJ concluded that a breach of Community law will clearly be sufficiently serious if it has persisted despite a judgment establishing the infringement, or a preliminary ruling or settled case law from which it is clear that the conduct constituted an infringement.[70] In *Köbler*, the ECJ repeated the same factors and added the non-compliance by the court in question with its obligation to make a reference for a preliminary ruling under Article 234(3) EC Treaty. The ECJ concluded that courts adjudicating at last instance commit a serious beach of Community law when the decision is made in manifest breach of settled case law.[71]

Many of the factors mentioned by the ECJ fit in an economic analysis of whether a rule of obvious negligence is efficient. If the rule breached is unclear or imprecise, a normal negligence rule causes a risk of over-deterrence if the claimed compensation for individual losses exceeds the social damage. If national authorities enjoy a great degree of discretion they should not too easily be held liable for exercising those discretionary powers in cases of damage claims for pure financial losses. An excusable error of law again may indicate that the rule of Community law breached was not sufficiently precise. Conversely, if the decision taken by a national legislative authority or a national court adjudicating at last instance violates a clear rule of Community law or is a manifest breach of the case law of the ECJ in the matter, liability of the state can be supported also on economic grounds. However, there is no full harmony between economic analysis and the case law of the ECJ on state liability for infringements of Community law. The term 'sufficiently serious breach' incorporates not only the clarity and precision of the rule breached but also other factors, such as the intention of the Member State to infringe Community law. The latter criterion may be relevant from a legal perspective but does not fit in an economic approach. To achieve optimal deterrence, the liability rule should provide incentives to take optimal care. Efficient care is reached where the marginal cost of additional care equals the marginal benefit in terms of reduction of the expected damage. Intention is irrelevant in an efficiency-based assessment. Also the criterion that the state was acting in an area where it had little discretionary power should not be used in a too formalistic way.

[70] Cases C-46/93 and C-48/93 *Brasserie du Pêcheur SA v Germany and R v Secretary of State for Transport, ex parte Factortame Ltd and others* [1996] ECR I-1029, at paras 56–57.

[71] Case C-224/01 *Gerhard Köbler v Republik Österreich* [2003] I-10239, at paras 55–56.

The crucial requirement is that the state must have acted in breach of a sufficiently precise rule; liability should be made dependent upon the showing of an obvious breach of a rule of Community law.[72]

Economic Analysis of Three Leading Cases

The *Francovich* Case: Non-implementation of a Directive

The landmark *Francovich* case established the principle of an action for compensation against a Member State for breach of Community law. The Italian government had failed to implement Directive 80/987 on the protection of employees in the event of their employer's insolvency. To guarantee payment of wages Italian employees could not invoke the direct effectiveness of the Directive, since its provisions lacked sufficient precision. However, the ECJ created an additional instrument to enhance the effectiveness of unimplemented directives by establishing the principle of state liability in damages as a general requirement of Community law.[73] The ECJ formulated three basic conditions for state liability in the case of non-implementation of a directive: i) the result prescribed by the directive must entail the grant of rights to individuals; ii) it must be possible to identify the content of those rights on the basis of the provisions of the directive, and iii) there must be a causal link between the breach of the state's obligation and the harm suffered by the injured parties.[74]

Most legal commentators have welcomed the *Francovich* decision, since the duty to compensate losses suffered by individuals may constitute an effective remedy for the enforcement of Community obligations imposed upon Member States. The economic analysis of law supports the basic tenet of this assessment. The economic function of liability is forcing actors to internalise the negative consequences of their actions imposed on third parties (in the economic jargon: negative externalities). The prospect of liability gives incentives to change the behaviour and take efficient measures to reduce the damage. In spite of this general positive assessment, an economic analysis also warns against potential negative consequences. There is a risk of over-deterrence, implying that actors take too much (inefficient) care if the compensation due is higher than the social damage and the duty of care is not sufficiently precise. However, in the case of non-implementation of a directive the latter concern is not directly relevant. The duty of care is very precisely formulated: Member States have to implement a Community directive within the time limits set by the directive. If they fail to do so, they commit an obvious

[72] R Van den Bergh and H-B Schäfer, 'State Liability for Infringement of the EC Treaty: Economic Arguments in Support of a Rule of "Obvious Negligence"' (1998) 23 *EL Rev* 552; for a technical elaboration, see R Van den Bergh and H-B Schäfer, 'Member States Liability for Infringement of the Free Movement of Goods in the EC: An Economic Analysis' (2000) 156 *Journal of Institutional and Theoretical Economics* 382–403.

[73] P Craig and G de Burca, *EU Law. Text, Cases and Materials* 3rd edn (Oxford, Oxford University Press, 2003) 259.

[74] Cases C-6 and 9/90 *Francovich and Bonifaci v Italy* [1991] ECR I-5357, at para 41.

infringement of Community law. In the case of non-implementation of a directive, there is no need for an explicit requirement of a 'sufficiently serious breach' of Community law. This is different in the following cases.

The *Brasserie du Pêcheur* Case: Potential Infringement of the Principle of Free Movement of Goods

In its *Brasserie du Pêcheur* judgment, the ECJ explicitly formulated the requirement of a 'sufficiently serious breach' of a provision of Community law protecting individuals' rights. The ECJ did not exclude the possibility of claiming compensation of financial losses but added that the decisive test for finding liability is 'whether the Member State manifestly and gravely disregarded the limits on its discretion'.[75] Important factors for deciding whether the latter behaviour occurred are the clarity and precision of the rule breached, the margin of discretion left to national authorities and the question whether an excusable error of law was made. Consequently, the German provisions concerning the purity of beer which prohibited the marketing under the German designation 'Bier' of beers imported from other Member States was seen as a sufficiently serious breach, whereas an excusable error of law was found to condone the prohibitions on the import of beers containing additives, in which field Community law was held to be significantly less conclusive.[76]

This judgment shows that the ECJ is able to reach conclusions, which are also defensible from an efficiency viewpoint. The outcome of this case is indeed not different from what the economic analysis of liability for pure financial losses would suggest. Economic analysis makes it clear that, if an efficient allocation of resources is to be achieved, automatic compensation of pure financial losses may lead to over-deterrence. In the *Brasserie du Pêcheur* case, the size of the social losses depends both on the extent to which alternative sales are made and the utility derived by German consumers from these alternative sales, as well as on the extent to which French firms may use resources devoted to the production of beer for the production of other goods. Consumer surplus may be reduced as a consequence of higher beer prices on the German market and less product diversity. In the absence of any relevant gains from the German purity law for the health or safety of consumers, the net result on consumer welfare may be negative. Additionally, there may be some losses of producer surplus if French firms shift their resources to second best alternatives. These effects are, however, counterbalanced by the increasing producer surplus of the German breweries. The important point is that the economic losses of the French beer producers are higher than the total social losses.

If private losses exceed social losses and standards of care are uncertain, economic analysis teaches that liability should be limited to obvious infringements of the duty of care. The ECJ reaches this result by requiring a 'sufficiently serious breach' which is to be assessed taking into account the clarity and precision of the relevant provision of

[75] Cases C-46/93 and C-48/93 *Brasserie du Pêcheur SA v Germany and R v Secretary of State for Transport, ex parte Factortame Ltd and others* [1996] ECR I-1029, at paras 86–87.

[76] It may be added that the German Bundesgerichtshof, which had to decide the compensation claim brought by French breweries, found that the prohibition on the use of additives was the predominant cause of the damage and, therefore, denied a right to compensation (BGH, 24 October 1996 (1997) *Neue Juristische Wochenschrift* 123).

Community law. Most other factors mentioned by the ECJ, such as the degree of discretion and the existence of an excusable error of law, may be subsumed under the crucial criterion of the clarity and precision of the rule breached. It seems that the ECJ has implicitly accepted the economic arguments against a too broad scope of state liability. In the absence of a the requirement of a 'sufficiently serious breach', the legislators of the Member States may be unduly deterred from taking legislative action to protect the interests of their citizens in fields such as consumer protection and environmental legislation. The explicit requirement of a sufficiently serious breach of Community law prevents this type of over-deterrence and contributes to an efficient outcome.

The *Köbler* Case: Alleged Infringement of European Law by a National Court

The *Köbler* case concerns the conformity with Community law on freedom of movement for workers of an Austrian provision excluding periods spent abroad for assessing the eligibility for receiving a special length-of-service increment on top of the regular salary. The answer to the question whether this Austrian rule infringes Community law is not obvious, since the issue is not expressly covered in secondary legislation and no clear answer can be found in the ECJ's case law. Consequently, the ECJ decided that the Austrian court adjudicating at last instance did not commit a manifest breach of Community law in reaching its decision on the matter. In the absence of a 'sufficiently serious breach' of Community law a Member State is not liable in damages.

The judgment in *Köbler* largely reconfirms earlier case law on state liability for breaches of Community law. It explicitly states that the principle of liability also applies to court decisions. Also this case concerned purely financial losses, so that the above economic arguments in favour of a rule of obvious negligence fully apply. Hence, the ECJ's decision can again be economically rationalised. The interesting point in *Köbler* is that the ECJ confirms the principle of state liability for judicial decisions, whereas the law in this respect varies quite considerably across Member States. Not surprisingly, national governments intervened in the case and formulated several objections to state liability for breach of Community law owing to a fault made by a court. These objections included: the principle of *res judicata* (that is, that the legal decision is held to be true between the parties), the principle of legal certainty, the independence of the judiciary and its authority and reputation. The ECJ rejected these arguments, arguing that an action in damages does not necessarily invalidate the judicial decision which was responsible for the damage, and stressing that the principle of liability does not concern the personal liability of the judge but that of the state.

Liability rules provide incentives for careful behaviour, and this is not different if judicial decisions are at stake. However, as it is the case with legislative action, over-deterrence must be avoided. In addition, the risk of frivolous suits must be reduced.[77] For these reasons, a standard of obvious negligence ('sufficiently serious breach' of Community law) again seems appropriate. Under the threat of a simple negligence rule, judges might spend too much time on their decisions or not feel free to make use of their

[77] See especially H Kerkmeester, 'State Liability for Judicial Decisions: An Economic Analysis' in H-B Schäfer and H-J Lwowski (eds), *Konsequenzen wirtschaftsrechtlicher Normen* (Wiesbaden, Gabler, 2002) 391.

experience and intuition. To remain on the safe side, a judge may be hesitant to deviate from precedents and look for new and potentially better rules. Next to the risk of an inefficiently high level of care, an unqualified negligence rule may also lead to frivolous suits. Parties who have lost a case and cannot appeal the decision because the court has judged at last instance may decide to claim damages to vent their anger. The vast majority of such suits would be frivolous. It must be acknowledged that the risks of both over-deterrence and frivolous suits are higher when individual judges are sued, rather than the state. However, also under a principle of state liability for judicial errors it may not be excluded that judges become too cautious to avoid that their decisions are labelled erroneous and damaging and that losing parties initiate frivolous suits. It should be recalled that the main argument of this Chapter is that a rule of obvious negligence is required to avoid over-deterrence in cases where private losses are higher than social losses and standards of care are uncertain. On top of this argument, the risk of frivolous suits supports a standard of gross negligence. In sum, there are powerful economic reasons to support the ECJ's ruling in *Köbler*, according to which state liability should be limited to 'sufficiently serious' infringements of Community law.

Conclusions

According to settled case law of the ECJ, Member States can be held liable for breaches of European law. Injured parties may claim damage compensation in the case of non-implementation of a directive, an infringement by a Member State of the principle of free movement of goods or a misinterpretation of a rule of European law by a national court adjudicating at last instance. Legal commentators have generally acclaimed this case law since the duty to compensate contributes to the full effectiveness of Community law and may constitute an effective sanction for the enforcement of obligations imposed upon Member States. However, they have also criticised the requirement that the infringement of European law must be 'sufficiently serious', since it puts a clear limitation on the compensation of losses.

This commentary has shown that there are powerful economic reasons to justify the requirement of a 'sufficiently serious breach'. It is crucial to avoid over-deterrence if purely financial losses must be compensated and the standards of care are imprecise. This is the case when it must be assessed whether a Member State has violated the rules on free movement of goods or a national court of last instance has misinterpreted a rule of European law. The losses suffered by harmed parties will often be purely financial and the damage to society will be smaller than the harm suffered by individuals. The law and economics literature has emphasised that the duty to compensate pure economic losses may cause over-deterrence in cases where the standard of care is imprecise. By requiring a 'sufficiently serious breach' the ECJ has reduced the risk of over-deterrence. In this way it is avoided that the legislature or the judiciary of Member States will be excessively hindered in performing their functions by the prospect of actions for damages.

XI

Case 8/74, *Procureur du Roi v Benoît and Gustave Dassonville* and Case 120/78, *Rewe-Zentral AG v Bundesmonopolverwaltung für Branntwein* (*Cassis de Dijon*)

1

Life after *Dassonville* and *Cassis:* Evolution but No Revolution

ALLAN ROSAS

Introduction

According to Article 28 EC, '[q]uantitative restrictions on imports and all measures having equivalent effect shall be prohibited between Member States'. Article 29 contains a similar provision relating to restrictions on exports. Article 30 lists a number of grounds such as public morality and the protection of health and life of humans, animals or plants which may justify prohibitions or restrictions on imports, exports or goods in transit.

The wording of these provisions, as compared with the other provisions of the EC Treaty relating to the fundamental economic freedoms, including Article 25 prohibiting customs duties on imports and exports and charges having equivalent effects, makes it clear that they concern the elimination of *non-fiscal barriers* to the *trade in goods*. But their rather sweeping formulations do not specify what is meant by 'quantitative restrictions', 'all measures having equivalent effect' or 'prohibited between Member States'. And how are the grounds for justifying restrictions listed in Article 30 to be applied and interpreted and is the list of derogations exhaustive?

Article XI of the General Agreement on Tariffs and Trade of 1947 (GATT)[1] also contains a prohibition of quantitative import and export restrictions. An indication that this provision today of almost universal application does not go as far as Articles 28 and 29 EC may be seen already in its wording, which does not contain a reference to 'all measures having equivalent effect' and gives examples of quantitative restrictions (quotas and import or export licences) which suggest that only rules which specifically bar the entry (or departure) of products across national borders are caught by the prohibition. Moreover, Article XI GATT has to be read in conjunction with Article III GATT, which does apply to internal rules on the sale, use, transportation, etc. of products independently of whether they are imported or domestic but is limited to a requirement of national treatment (non-discrimination of imported products).[2]

[1] The EC, together with the EU Member States, is a Contracting Party to GATT 1947 as well as the other multilateral trade agreements concluded under the umbrella of the World Trade Organization (WTO), Council Decision 94/800/EC of 22 December 1994 concerning the conclusion on behalf of the European Community, as regards matters within its competence, of the agreements reached in the Uruguay Round multilateral negotiations (1986–1994), [1994] OJ L/336/1.

[2] Measures which are applicable to both domestic and foreign products, even if applicable at the border, are covered by Article III, PC Mavroidis, *The General Agreement on Tariffs and Trade: A Commentary* (Oxford,

However, more important for the understanding of the differences between the EC rules on free movement of goods and the GATT regime are their respective context as well as object and purpose. While the GATT and the other WTO agreements establish a world-wide multilateral trade system falling short of a free-trade area,[3] the EU and its component the EC constitute not only a customs union but an *internal market* forming part of an economic and political Union of States and resembling in this respect the internal market of the United States of America.[4]

This is so particularly after a string of measures to break down gradually the barriers between Member States have taken effect, starting with a transitional period concerning the free movement of goods which ended in 1969[5] and followed notably by the Single European Act of 1987 and the abolishment of all remaining frontier controls on goods on 31 December 1992.[6]

The latter deadline today appears in Article 14(1) EC. According to Article 14(2) EC the internal market shall comprise an area 'without internal frontiers' in which the 'free movement of goods, persons, services and capital' is ensured in accordance with the provisions of the EC Treaty. Article 23(2) EC makes it clear that the principle of free movement of goods shall apply not only to products originating in EU Member States but also to products coming from third countries which are in free circulation in the internal market area.

The earlier texts of the EC Treaty spoke of a 'common market', a formulation still to be found, for instance, in Article 2 EC setting out the general purposes of the Community. In *Gaston Schul* (1982), the European Court of Justice (ECJ) observed that the common market involved the elimination of all obstacles to intra-Community trade in order to merge the national markets into a 'single market bringing about conditions as close as possible to those of a genuine internal market'.[7] Whatever are the differences, if any, between a 'common market', 'single market', 'genuine internal market' or the 'internal market' mentioned in Article 14,[8] the quotation from the ECJ's case law points to the role of the Court in the development of the concept of the internal market and the principle of free movement of goods within it.

Oxford University Press, 2005) 46. Also Article XX GATT, which provides for some general and rather far-reaching exceptions to the GATT rules, has to be taken into account.

[3] See also Article XXIV GATT which concerns free-trade areas and customs unions.

[4] See, eg, the comparison between 1) the WTO model, 2) the free-trade agreement model, 3) the EC model and 4) the federal state system which is made in the appeal submission of 6 October 1997 presented by the European Communities before the WTO Appellate Body in *European Communities—Measures Concerning Meat and Meat Products (Hormones)*, WT/DS26 and WT/DS48; Appellate Body Report adopted 13 February 1998. See also C Barnard, *The Substantive Law of the EU: The Four Freedoms* (Oxford, Oxford University Press, 2004) 9, who distinguishes between seven stages of integration.

[5] The transitional period was set out in Articles 31 to 35 of the then EEC Treaty and were later repealed by the Treaty of Amsterdam of 1997. See also Commission Directive 70/50/EEC of 22 December 1969 based on the provisions of Article 33(7), on the abolition of measures which have an effect equivalent to quantitative restrictions on imports and are not covered by other provisions adopted in pursuance of the EEC Treaty, [1970] OJ L/13/29.

[6] Article 8A of the EEC Treaty inserted by the Single European Act and later to become Article 14(1) of the EC Treaty. See, eg, V Constantinescu *et al* (eds), *Traité instituant la CEE. Commentaire article par article* (Paris, Economica, 1992) 73.

[7] Case 15/81 *Gaston Schul v Inspecteur der Invoerrechten* [1982] ECR 1409, para 33.

[8] See P Oliver assisted by M Jarvis, *Free Movement of Goods in the European Community under Article 28 to 30 of the EC Treaty* 4th edn (London, Sweet and Maxwell, 2003) 8, with references.

In fact, it is once again the case law of the Court which provides the flesh on the bones of the Treaty provisions in question. In this respect, the early cases of *Dassonville* (1974) and *Cassis de Dijon* (1979), in particular, are celebrated candidates for an ECJ Hall of Fame. It is to a brief description and analysis of these two cases that I shall now turn.

Dassonville

Some of the commentaries on the ECJ's case law with respect to the free movement of goods (as well as to some other areas of EU law) suffer from a lack of consideration of the particular circumstances of each case. Let us not make the same mistake here but instead provide a brief summary of the facts and national litigation which gave rise to the preliminary ruling in Case 8/74 *Procureur du Roi v Benoît and Gustave Dassonville.*[9]

The request for a preliminary ruling was made by a Belgian court of first instance (Tribunal de Première Instance de Bruxelles), thus attesting to the fact that many of the important preliminary rulings given by the ECJ have been at the instigation of lower national courts rather than supreme courts. The national court was faced with criminal proceedings brought against father and son Dassonville for having imported into and sold in Belgium a consignment of Scotch whisky, without being in possession of a certificate of authenticity ('Scotch whisky') issued by the British customs authorities, as required by Belgian law. The whisky had first been lawfully imported from the United Kingdom into France, which did not require such a certificate. The Dassonvilles, who had duly acquired the consignment in France while it was in free circulation, considered that it would be impossible or at least excessively difficult to obtain, at the later stage of the importation of the consignment into Belgium, a British certificate, taking into account that no such certificate had been issued nor required when the whisky was exported to France.[10]

The Court considered it as established that a trader, wishing to import into Belgium Scotch whisky which is already in free circulation in France, can obtain a certificate issued by the British customs authorities 'only with great difficulty, unlike the importer who imports directly from the producer country'. According to the answer given to the national judge, the requirement of a certificate of authenticity 'which is less easily obtainable by importers of an authentic product which has been put into free circulation in a regular manner in another Member State than by importers of the same product coming directly from the country of origin' constitutes a measure having an effect equivalent to a quantitative restriction as prohibited by the Treaty.

This emphasis on the unequal treatment of two categories of *importers* may or may not relate to the reserve made in the derogation clause of Article 30 for prohibitions or restrictions which constitute a means of 'arbitrary discrimination'. The question arises as the Court did go into Article 30, stating, it is true, that it was not necessary to rule

[9] [1974] ECR 837.

[10] To enable the sale of the bottles in Belgium, they themselves fixed a label on them with the printed text 'British Customs Certificate of Origin'. The facts of the case are summarised at the beginning of the judgment of 11 July 1974 in [1974] ECR 839–840.

definitively on the applicability of the provision but adding that, 'in any case', its last sentence rules out measures which constitute a means of 'arbitrary discrimination' or a 'disguised restriction' on trade.

But it may also be that the Court used the comparison with importers who import directly from the country of origin more as an illustration of the fact that the Dassonvilles were faced with a 'hindrance to trade between Member States' which was unreasonable, as they could not obtain the certificate required 'without facing serious difficulties'.[11] As the Court did not go into the unequal treatment that this could entail as compared to national (Belgian) producers (which is understandable as there were no national producers of whisky) the judgment can be seen as focusing on the existence of restrictions or barriers to inter-state trade rather than discriminatory or distinctly applicable measures.[12]

Such an assessment is, of course, buttressed by the famous *Dassonville* formula, which I have omitted to mention so far:

> All trading rules enacted by Member States which are capable of hindering, directly or indirectly, actually or potentially, intra-Community trade are to be considered as measures having an effect equivalent to quantitative restrictions.

One wonders on the other hand to what extent this formula, cited *ad nauseam* in subsequent case law and legal literature, was really meant to cover fully 'all' measures which may have an effect on trade but are indistinctly applicable to foreign and imported goods including domestic consumer legislation restricting certain selling techniques or domestic traffic regulation limiting the use of cars or certain cars. It is interesting to note that in some instant commentaries to the judgment, its paragraph 5 cited above was not particularly highlighted.[13]

In interpreting the *Dassonville* formula, account should be taken of the fact that the specific circumstances of the case concerned national requirements affecting imports only, that the judgment is somehow fuzzy on the distinction between Articles 28 and 30 and that the formula quoted above was immediately followed by a passage stating that a Member State, in the absence of Community measures guaranteeing for consumers the authenticity of a product's designation of origin, could take measures to prevent unfair practices but subject to the condition that the measures should be 'reasonable' and that the proof of authenticity required 'should not act as a hindrance to trade between Member States and should, in consequence, be accessible to all Community nationals'. The last-mentioned part of the judgment (which refers to consumer protection, which does not figure in Article 30) could, on the other hand, be seen as an antecedent to the 'rule of reason' and 'mandatory requirements' spelled out in *Cassis de Dijon.*[14]

[11] See paras 6 and 8 of the judgment.

[12] Barnard, 92.

[13] R Joliet, later to become judge at the Court, noted two elements of the formula, namely 1) that it covered potential barriers to trade, without there being a need to show that there was an actual reduction in the movement of goods, and 2) that the Court seemed to have implicitly recognised that the formula covered all existing national measures, including measures adopted before 1958 (the Belgian legislation had been adopted in the 1930s), 'EEC Law and Appellations of Origin: The Scotch Whisky Case' (1975) 38 *MLR* 200 at 202–3. See also L De Montblanc, Note de jurisprudence (1975) *Revue de jurisprudence commerciale* 195; A De Caluwe, Note de jurisprudence (1975) 8 *Jurisprudence commerciale de Belgique* 94; W Wellinghausen, Rechtsprechung (1975) 10 *Europarecht* 322.

[14] E White, ' In Search of the Limits to Article 30 of the EEC Treaty' (1989) 26 *CML Rev* 235 at 237; Barnard, 105 (footnote 129).

It should be noted in this context that the Advocate-General cited, apparently with approval, Commission Directive 70/50/EEC on the abolition of measures which have an effect equivalent to quantitative restrictions on imports[15] and its Articles 2 and 3. While Article 2 applies to distinctly applicable measures, Article 3 covers measures which are equally applicable to domestic and imported measures. However, Article 3 only mentions measures which affect the product itself (such as its shape or size) and moreover limits its effect to measures whose restrictive effect on the free movement of goods 'exceeds the effects intrinsic to trade rules' including in particular where the restrictive effects 'are out of proportion to their purpose'. The Advocate-General himself characterised a trade rule caught by Article 28 as a rule which 'considered in the context in which it applies, is capable of seriously hindering intra-Community trade in certain categories of goods',[16] thus using a formula more restrictive than the all-embracing formula subsequently associated with *Dassonville.*

Whatever was the precise intention behind the famous formula, it is a fact that it has assumed a life of its own, covering in principle a broad range of domestic regulatory measures, including measures not affecting directly the characteristics of products and including also such measures even if they apply indistinctly to domestic and imported products. While the Court's case law immediately following *Dassonville* suggested a more restrictive reading based on a non-discrimination approach,[17] and while the case law of the 1980s produced some judgments which did not insist on the application of Article 28 to certain non-product-related and indistinctly applicable measures,[18] a prevailing trend in case law and legal commentaries has been to understand the formula as a more or less all-encompassing principle.[19] It may be telling that the ECJ has in a number of judgments omitted the word 'trading', which in the original *Dassonville* formula qualifies the national rules in question.[20]

A broad understanding of the formula is also expressed in the ECJ's by now also famous effort in *Keck and Mithouard* (1993) to 're-examine and clarify' its case law on Article 28. As there had been an increasing tendency of traders to invoke this provision as a means of challenging rules whose effect was to limit their commercial freedom in general, using the effects on imports as a pretext, the Court stated that, 'contrary to what has been previously decided', the application of national provisions 'restricting or prohibiting certain selling arrangements' was not such as to hinder trade between Member States within the meaning of the *Dassonville* judgment.[21] While, as was noted above, the case law preceding *Keck and Mithouard* had been far from consistent on this point, it is the broad conception of

[15] See above, note 5.

[16] Opinion of Trabucchi AG of 20 June 1974 [1974] ECR 855 at 859.

[17] M Poiares Maduro, *We, The Court. The European Court of Justice and the European Economic Constitution: A Critical Reading of Article 30 of the EC Treaty* (Oxford, Hart Publishing, 1998) 50.

[18] White, 249–58. See also Oliver, 117–22; Barnard, 130–34; R Kovar, '*Dassonville, Keck* et les autres: de la mesure avant toute chose' (2006) 42 *Revue trimestrielle de droit européen* 213 at 215–22.

[19] Poiares Maduro, 35–58. See also J Weiler, 'The Constitution of the Common Market Place: Text and Context in the Evolution of the Free Movement of Goods' in P Craig and G de Búrca (eds), *The Evolution of EU Law* (Oxford, Oxford University Press, 1999) 349 at 351–64, who, it is submitted, exaggerates in stating that 'in *Dassonville*, the Court made its most famous pronouncement ever' (at 353).

[20] See, eg, Oliver, 102.

[21] Joined cases C-267/91 and C-268/91 *Criminal Proceedings against Bernard Keck and Daniel Mithouard* [1993] ECR I-6097, paras 14 and 16.

Dassonville, expressed in pre-Keck judgments such as *Cinéthèque* (1985) and *Torfaen* (1989)[22] that has left its mark on the development of Community law.

'Broad' has not meant the absence of any limits, however. This can be seen, inter alia, not only from the pre-*Keck* case law referred to above which applied a discrimination-based or otherwise more restrictive approach but also from a series of cases ruling out the application of Article 28 to measures where the possibility of their effecting imports has been considered too 'uncertain or indirect'.[23] More generally, the *Dassonville* formula and its application have not completely lost sight of the fact that Article 28 is about free movement of goods across Member States' borders, not economic liberalism in itself.[24]

The limits of the *Dassonville* formula are reflected in a judgment given shortly before this book went to print.[25] By this judgment, the Court dismissed an action by the Commission against Italy requesting the Court to find that a national prohibition to use a product in a certain way (motorcycles from towing a trailer) violated Article 28 EC. The Court here mentions three situations caught by this provision: 1) measures the object or effect of which is to treat products coming from other Member States *less favourably*; 2) measures which, in the absence of harmonisation of national legislation, imply obstacles to the free movement of goods which are the consequence of applying, to goods coming from other Member States *where they are lawfully manufactured and marketed*, rules that lay down *requirements to be met by such goods*, even if the rules in question apply to all products alike and 3) any other measure which *hinders access* of products originating in other Member States *to the market* of a Member State.[26]

The first and third category are relevant for all national measures, including measures which do not lay down requirements to be met by the products themselves (such as measures regulating their use or sale). The second category is limited to product-related requirements (such as their composition, shape, size or packaging) and brings into the spotlight the *Cassis de Dijon* line of the ECJ's case law. It is to this heritage that we shall now turn.

Cassis de Dijon

The factual circumstances of Case 120/78 *Rewe-Zentral AG v Bundesmonopolverwaltung für Branntwein*, better know as '*Cassis de Dijon*', are better known than those of *Dassonville* and I shall be very brief on this point.[27] Rewe-Zentral sought to import from France, for the purposes of marketing in the Federal Republic of Germany, certain potable spirits, including the liqueur 'Cassis de Dijon'. It was informed by the Federal Monopoly Administration for Spirits that, while no authorisation of import was required, the alcohol content of 'Cassis de Dijon' (from 15 to 20 per cent by volume) was too low to allow it to

[22] Joined cases 60/84 and 61/84 *Cinéthèque SA and Others v Fédération Nationale des Cinémas Français* [1985] ECR 2605; 145/88 *Torfaen Borough Council v B & Q* [1989] ECR 3851.

[23] The latter strand of case law, which, it is true, generally succeeds *Keck and Mithouard*, is not to be confused with a *de minimis* test, Oliver, 99–101, 103–4, 206–7.

[24] See also Poiares Maduro, 58–60, 78.

[25] Case C-110/05 *Commission v Italy*, judgment of 10 February 2009, nyr.

[26] *Ibid*, para 37.

[27] [1979] ECR 649. The facts and issues of the case are summarised at 651–60.

be sold in Germany, since German law required that spirits to be marketed had to have a higher alcohol content.[28] Rewe-Zentral brought an action against this decision before a German administrative court. Another court (the Hessisches Finanzgericht) to which the case was referred asked whether the concept of measures having an equivalent effect covered national rules fixing a minimum alcohol content for potable spirits 'the result of which is that traditional products of other Member States whose wine-spirit content is below the fixed limit cannot be put into free circulation' in the Federal Republic.

It will be noted that the ECJ was here faced squarely with an indistinctly applicable rule (applying equally to domestic and imported products) which on the other hand rendered imports of the product in question useless, or to cite the ECJ, had as its principal effect to promote alcoholic beverages having a high alcohol content 'by excluding from the national market' products of other Member States which did not answer that description.[29] The answer of the Court was that such a rule was caught by Article 28 ('falls within the prohibition laid down in that provision') provided that the alcoholic beverages in question had been 'lawfully produced and marketed in another Member State'.[30]

To arrive at this conclusion, the Court first, in a somewhat unusual order of reasoning, looked at possible justifications for the German rule (thus apparently assuming that Article 28 did apply[31]). This part of the judgment[32] introduced the famous 'mandatory requirements'[33] which a Member State should be allowed to satisfy. Among such requirements were mentioned, inter alia, 'the protection of public health' and 'the fairness of commercial transactions and the defence of the consumer'. While Article 30 mentions 'the protection of health and life of humans, animals and plants', consumer protection does not appear in its list of grounds for derogation. The dominant tendency in the Court's subsequent case law has been to treat the additional grounds of justification provided by the 'mandatory requirements' as a 'rule of reason' read into Article 28 rather than as a simple extension of the list contained in Article 30. This has also implied that, while Article 30 can allow a derogation with respect to distinctly applicable (discriminatory) measures, application of the justification on the basis of 'mandatory requirements' has generally been limited to measures which apply indistinctly to domestic and imported products (such as was the case in *Cassis*).[34]

Apart from the novelty introduced by the 'mandatory requirements' doctrine, the important contribution of *Cassis de Dijon* lies, of course, in the fact that, following the Opinion of its Advocate General,[35] the Court confirmed and clarified that national

[28] The Administration referred to a minimum content of 32 per cent (ECR at 651) whereas the ECJ's judgment speaks about a minimum content of 25 per cent applying to fruit liqueurs (at 660).

[29] Para 14.

[30] Para 15. See also para 14, last sentence, where it is stated that there is 'no valid reason why, provided that they have been lawfully produced and marketed in one of the Member States, alcoholic beverages should not be introduced into any other Member State'.

[31] White, 236.

[32] Paras 8–14.

[33] Also called in English 'imperative requirements' or 'overriding requirements in the public interest', Barnard, 108, or yet 'overriding requirements of of general public importance' or 'overriding requirements justifying a restriction on the free movement of goods', Oliver, 216.

[34] Oliver, 216–20 (who, however, detects an increasing tendency to apply the 'mandatory requirements' justification to situations of distinctly applicable measures as well); Barnard, 88, 108 (for references to case law immediately following *Cassis*, see her footnote 139); A Arnull *et al*, *Wyatt and Dashwood's European Union Law*, 5th edn (London, Sweet & Maxwell, 2006) 625. See further below, 'Perspectives and Challenges'.

[35] Opinion of Capotorti AG of 16 January 1979 [1979] ECR 666.

measures which are *indistinctly* applicable to domestic and imported goods may still constitute 'an obstacle to trade' which is incompatible with Article 28.[36] The reason but at the same time condition given was that the products to be imported and marketed are 'lawfully produced and marketed in another Member State'. This 'presumption of equivalence'[37] concerning such products implies that the exporter can in principle rely on a single regulation by the home state instead of having to cope with the dual regulation of both the home and host state.[38] The home state regulation is, as it were, extended to the entire internal market (but exceptions may be justified under Article 30 or one of the 'mandatory requirements').

Cassis de Dijon thus implies a clear departure from the approach of Commission Directive 70/50 on the abolition of measures which have an effect equivalent to quantitative restrictions on imports[39] which limited its effect to measures whose restrictive effect on the free movement of goods 'exceeds the effects intrinsic to trade rules' including in particular where the restrictive effects 'are out of proportion to their purpose'. One can say that the presumption has been reversed. It should be noted, on the other hand, that *Cassis* dealt with a measure which was head-on product-related. In order to have access to the German market, the French fruit liqueur would, in fact, have had to be substantially modified.[40]

The judgment attracted much more attention than *Dassonville* had done. Most commentators considered that it constituted, if not necessarily a 'revolutionary' judgment, an important clarification of both the notion of measures having equivalent effect and the means of justifying restrictions.[41] The Commission issued a Communication concerning the consequences of the judgment, in which it, after having noted and interpreted the principle of presumption of equivalence, stated that it could from now on direct its efforts at the harmonization of national laws which create barriers to trade.[42]

[36] See para 14, third subparagraph, of the judgment. Para 8, second subparagraph, refers to 'obstacles to movement within the Community resulting from disparities between the national laws relating to the marketing of products'.

[37] This expression is in my view to be preferred to 'mutual recognition' or 'functional parallelism'. Weiler, 365 prefers 'functional parallelism' while Barnard, 105, refers to 'presumption of equivalence' and 'mutual recognition'.

[38] Barnard, 106.

[39] Notes 5 and 15 above.

[40] In the Opinion of Capotorti AG it is, in fact, noted that because of the German legislation, a version of 'Cassis de Dijon' with an alcoholic strength of 25 per cent had been specially produced for the German market, [1979] ECR 673.

[41] See, eg, E Millarg, Rechtsprechung (1979) 14 *Europarecht* 420; D Mattera, 'L'arrêt "Cassis de Dijon": Une nouvelle approche pour la réalisation et le bon fonctionnement du marché intérieur' (1980) 23 *Revue du Marché Commun* 505; JC Masclet, 'Les articles 30, 36 et 100 du traité CEE à la lumière de l'arrêt "Cassis de Dijon"' (1980) 16 *Revue trimestrielle de droit européen* 611; D Wyatt, 'Article 30 and Non-Discriminatory Trade Restrictions' (1981) 6 *EL Rev* 185; L Gormley, '*Cassis de Dijon* and the Communication from the Commission' (1981) 6 *EL Rev* 454. But see Weiler, 367 who, while emphasising the importance of *Dassonville*, states that 'mutual recognition' or as he prefers to call it 'functional parallelism', 'is not a radical hermeneutic departure, but in fact a very conservative and fully justified application of the principle of proportionality'.

[42] Communication from the Commission concerning the consequences of the judgment given by the Court of Justice on 20 February 1979 in Case 120/78 ('*Cassis de Dijon*'), [1980] OJ C/256/2.

Subsequent Developments

It is not possible within the confines of this short contribution to analyse in depth and give full credit to the jurisprudential and other developments following *Dassonville* and *Cassis de Dijon.* I shall limit myself to a few comments on the ECJ's *Keck and Mithouard* judgment, which has already been alluded to above, and the main trends in case law following *Keck,* including the recent judgment in *Commission v Italy* also mentioned above.*Keck and Mithouard* was a reaction to concerns that the Court's case law could force Member States to justify before the Court a wide range of national legislation applying without distinction to all goods marketed on its territory and thus moving from regulating trade between the Member States towards market regulation in general. An important scholarly contribution of 1989[43] and the Opinion of an Advocate General in *Hünermund* (1993) can be singled out as examples of voices suggesting limits to the broad application of *Dassonville.*[44]

In its *Keck and Mithouard* judgment, the Court spoke of an 'increasing tendency to traders to invoke Article [28] of the Treaty as a means of challenging any rules whose effect is to limit their commercial freedom even where such rules are not aimed at products from other Member States'.[45] This last part of this formulation should probably not be taken literally, to imply that complaints about national restrictions which do not intentionally target imports would somehow be frivolous. In the following passage, in fact, the Court confirms its *Cassis de Dijon* case law but links it to 'rules that lay down requirements to be met by such goods (such as those relating to designation, form, size, weight, composition, presentation, labelling, packaging)' and thus to *product-related* requirements.[46] Such requirements accordingly continue to be caught by Article 28 even if they apply without distinction to domestic and imported products (unless they can be justified under Article 30 or the 'mandatory requirements').

In the national litigation before a French lower court (Tribunal de Grande Instance, Strasbourg), Keck and Mithouard were prosecuted for reselling products at a loss, contrary to French law. To the national judge's question whether the prohibition of resale at a loss was compatible with, inter alia, the principle of the free movement of goods, the ECJ answered that 'Article [28] of the EEC Treaty is to be interpreted as not applying to legislation of a Member State imposing a general prohibition on resale at a loss'. Such a prohibition was characterised by the Court as a 'selling arrangement' and in a passage following the above-mentioned reaffirmation of *Cassis de Dijon* as far as product-related requirements are concerned, it held that 'contrary to what has previously been decided', the application of national provisions restricting or prohibiting 'certain selling arrangements' is not such as to hinder trade within the meaning of the *Dassonville* judgment.

This benediction was made subject to two conditions: 1) that the national restrictions 'apply to all relevant traders operating within the national territory' and 2) that they 'affect in the same manner, in law and in fact, the marketing of domestic products and of those

[43] White. For an overview of relevant legal doctrine, see, eg, Poiares Maduro, 35–60.

[44] Opinion of Tesauro AG of 27 October 1993 (thus delivered around one month before the judgment in *Keck and Mithouard*) in Case C-292 *Ruth Hünermund and Others v Landesapothekerkammer Baden-Württemberg* [1993] ECR I-6787.

[45] See n 21 above, para 14 of the judgment.

[46] Para 15.

from other Member States'. The first condition thus relates to formal applicability of the rules to traders and the second to the effects, including factual effects, of the rules in question on the marketing of products. The Court finally explained why the selling arrangements were not caught by Article 28, provided that the two conditions were met. In that case, the application of the rules 'is not by nature such as to prevent their access to the market or impede access any more than it impedes access of domestic products'.[47] This market access language is thus presented not as a condition of its own, but rather as a consequence of the fact that we are dealing with selling arrangements which apply equally to all traders and affect in the same manner the marketing of domestic and imported products.

Despite the criticism expressed against *Keck and Mithouard* in legal literature[48] and by some Advocates General,[49] the subsequent case law of the ECJ has by and large applied a combination of *Dassonville*, *Cassis de Dijon* and *Keck* to assess alleged restrictions to the free movement of goods. As to national measures which have been found to be caught by the prohibition in Article 28, the case law has obviously furnished a number of indications on what national requirements can be justified as 'mandatory requirements' or under Article 30 as well as on the conditions of justification, notably the application of the principle of proportionality.[50] The Court has also had occasion to assess the balance to be struck between the principle of the free transit of goods, on the one hand, and the protection of the fundamental right to protest and demonstrate,[51] and the protection of the environment,[52] on the other.

As far as selling arrangements are concerned, the most notable development is probably the fact that, while in an early post-*Keck* case law, the Court did not pay much attention to the *conditions* for applying the *Keck* formula, a stricter approach can be seen in some later judgments such as *De Agostini* (1997), *TK Heimdienst* (2000), *Gourmet* (2001) and *DocMorris* (2003).[53] The fact that a national measure concerns a selling arrangements is not a magic formula bringing automatically the measure outside the prohibition of Article 28 EC. In its recent judgment in *Commission v Italy*, the Court seems to say that all measures, including those concerning selling arrangements, which hinder the market access of imported products are covered by the concept of measures having equivalent effect to quantitative restrictions of imports.[54]

[47] Para 17.

[48] See, eg, Oliver, 124, who (footnote 157) provides a list of articles and commentaries on *Keck*.

[49] See notably the Opinion of Jacobs AG in Case Case C-412/93 *Leclerc-Siplec v TF1 Publicité SA* [1995] ECR I-179; Opinion of Lenz AG in C-391/92 *Commission v Greece* [1995] ECR I-1621.

[50] See, eg, Oliver, 215–384.

[51] Case C-112/00 *Eugen Schmidberger, Internationale Transporte und Planzüge v Republik Österreich* [2003] ECR I-5659.

[52] Case C-320/03 *Commission v Austria* [2005] ECR I-9871.

[53] Barnard, 137–144. Joined Cases C-34–36/95 *Konsumentombudsmannen (KO) v De Agostini (Svenska) Förlag AB (C34/95)* and *TV-Shop i Sverige AB (C-35/95 and C-36/95)* [1997] ECR I-3843; Case C-254/98 *Schutzverband gegen unlauteren Wettbewerb v TK-Heimdienst Sass GmbH* [2000] ECR I-151; Case C-405/98 *Konsumentombudsmannen (KO) v Gourmet International Products* [2001] ECR I-1795; Case C-322/01 *Deutscher Apothekerverband eV v 0800 DocMorris NV and Jacques Waterval* [2003] ECR I-14887; Case C-441/04 *A-Punkt Schmuckhandels GmbH v Claudia Schmidt* [2006] ECR I-2093.

[54] See n 25 above, paras 36 and 37, and the discussion in 'Perspectives and Challenges' below. The market access notion is, in fact, to be found in the original Keck formula as well, but it is true that it is not expressly formulated as a condition but rather as an explanation or consequence.

The Court has also confirmed that the assessment of whether a national measure is caught by the prohibition in Article 28 'falls within the field of application' of Community law so as to make the fundamental rights case law relevant.[55] The post-1993 case law has given the Court occasion to give more indications as to what measures may constitute selling arrangements rather than product requirements.[56] In case of doubt as to whether the national rule is product-related or constitutes a selling arrangement, the Court seems to incline towards the former.[57]

Finally, it should be noted that the scope of direct application of Articles 28 to 30 EC may be reduced by Community legislation harmonising national laws. Especially recourse to Article 30 is ruled out if the matter is fully covered by harmonising Community measures.[58] The scope left for Article 28 depends on the harmonisation level chosen.[59] The ECJ has confirmed that the Community legislator enjoys discretion in choosing the appropriate harmonisation technique and that this can include so-called total harmonisation comprising several stages including a Community procedure to draw up positive lists of substances authorised throughout the Community, to the exclusion of all other products.[60] The development of Community harmonisation legislation may partly explain why the number of Article 28 cases brought before the ECJ is nowadays fairly limited.[61] The European Commission has estimated that approximately half of the trade in goods within the EU is covered by harmonised legislation, while the other half consists of the non-harmonised sector and is thus fully caught by the EC Treaty provisions.[62] For the latter case, there are some horizontal Community acts providing for notifications or other forms of transparency relating to national measures which may pose a threat to the free movement of goods.[63]

[55] Case C-71/02 *Herbert Karner Industrie-Auktionen GmbH v Troostwijk GmbH* [2004] ECR I-3025, paras 48–52.

[56] See, eg, Oliver, 125.

[57] Oliver, 125 cites Case C-470/93 *Verein gegen Unwesen im Handel v Mars* [1995] ECR I-1923 and Case C-368/95 *Vereinigte Familiapress v Heinrich Bauer Verlag* [1997] ECR I-3689.

[58] See, eg, Case 470/03 *AGM COS.MET Srl v Suomen valtio and Tarmo Lehtinen* [2007] ECR I-2749, para 50.

[59] Oliver, 478, 499–501.

[60] Case C-66/04 *United Kingdom v Parliament and Council* [2005] ECR I-10553.

[61] In 2006, out of more than 400 judgments or orders, only eight concerned the 'free movement of goods', while the corresponding figure for 2007 was 14, Annual Report of the Court of Justice of the European Communities 2006 (Luxembourg, 2007) 84; *ibid* 2007 (Luxembourg, 2008) 90.

[62] 'A Single Market for Goods', http://ec.europa.eu/internal_market/top_layer /index_18_en.htm.

[63] The most important of these is Directive 98/34/EC of the European Parliament and of the Council of 22 June 1998 laying down a procedure for the provision of information in the field of technical standards and regulations, [1998] OJ L/204/37, which concerns the obligatory pre-notification of planned product requirements. See also Decision No 3052/95/EC of the European Parliament and of the Council of 13 December 1995 establishing a procedure for the exchange of information on national measures derogating from the principle of the free movement of goods within the Community [1995] OJ L/321/1 (which is subsidiary in comparison with Directive 98/34/EC) and Council Regulation (EC) No 2679/98 of 7 December 1998 on the functioning of the internal market in relation to the free movement of goods among the Member States [1998] OJ L/337/8 (which purports to specify the obligations of Member States in case of action taken by private parties in particular to disrupt the free movement of goods).

Perspectives and Challenges

As was noted above, the ECJ's case law of today continues to be based on *Dassonville* and *Cassis de Dijon*, mitigated by *Keck and Mithouard* and clarified by the recent *Commission v Italy*. An abundant case law provides further clarification and refinement. While the ECJ's reasoning and rulings have not always been fully consistent, especially on a longer time-span, the case law has undoubtedly made an important contribution to the realisation of the internal market. Some conceptual and other question marks remain, however, and I shall, without a pretence to be exhaustive, mention a few of them.

It should be underlined at the outset that one should not exaggerate the importance of the conceptual structure of legal argument in the field of free movement of goods. According to a somewhat cynical view, the circumstances of each case led to a certain solution 'by instinct', which implies that the Court would by and large have arrived at the same results regardless of the conceptual tools chosen. The complex edifice involving distinctions such as between 'quantitative restrictions' and 'all measures having equivalent effect', between 'distinctly' and 'indistinctly' applicable measures, between 'product requirements' and 'selling arrangements' and between 'mandatory requirements' and exceptions based on Article 30 EC, undoubtedly has a ring of scholasticism to it.

This having been said, these distinctions may sometimes matter and have a bearing on the result of a given case.[64] In any case, conceptual clarity and consistency can do no harm in this rather complex field of Community law. Let me mention some of the questions that seem to merit special attention in this respect. The first question concerns the relation between the free movement of goods and the other economic freedoms. Should the approach to all the four freedoms be harmonised?[65] While acknowledging that they should be approached in a co-ordinated way, I tend to believe that there are limits to a harmonised approach, given the legal and factual differences which after all exist between, say, free movement of goods and free movement of capital, or free movement of goods and free movement of persons. There is a tendency in very recent case law to avoid applying two or more freedoms to the same factual situation, following a '*centre de gravité*' reasoning.[66] This does not necessarily require nor enhance a completely harmonised approach to the economic freedoms.

Another question relating more specifically to Article 28 is whether the 'mandatory requirements' formula introduced by *Cassis de Dijon* should continue to be limited to measures which are indistinctly applicable to domestic and imported goods. There are in

[64] See also Barnard, 142–3.

[65] See, eg, Barnard, 146–8. See also the Opinion of 30 March 2006 of Poiares Maduro AG in Joined Cases C-158/04 and C-159/04 *Alfa Vita Vassilopoulos AE and Carrefour Marinopoulos AE v Elliniko Dimosio and Nomarkhiaki Aftodiikisi Ioanninon* [2006] ECR I-8135.

[66] Concerning the relation between the free movements of goods and freedom to provide services, see, eg, Case C-71/02 *Herbert Karner-Industrie-Auktionen GmbH v Troostwijk GmbH* [2004] ECR I-3025, paras 45–7 (the free movement of goods aspect prevailed over the freedom to provide services aspect); Case C-36/02 *Omega Spielhallen- und Automatenaufstellungs-GmbH v Oberbürgermeisterin der Bundesstadt Bonn* [2004] ECR I-9609, paras 24–27 (freedom to provide services prevailed); Case C-20/03 *Marcel Burmanjer, René Alexander Van Der Linden and Anthony De Jong* [2005] ECR I-4133, para 35 (freedom of movement of goods prevailed). Concerning the relation between the free movement of capital, on the one hand, and the right to establishment and free movement of services, on the other hand, see Case C-196/04 *Cadbury Schweppes plc, Cadbury Schweppes Overseas Ltd v Commissioners of Inland Revenue* [2006] ECR I-7995, para 33; Case C-452/04 *Fidium Finanz AG v Bundesanstalt für Finanzdienstleistungsaufsicht* [2006] ECR I-9521, paras 28–34.

fact some cases in which the Court seems to have accepted such a justification in a situation where a distinction could be discerned between imported and domestic products. A recent example is offered by a case concerning the immatriculation of imported used cars, where the Court examined a mandatory requirement not mentioned in Article 30 (the protection of the environment) as a possible justification even if domestic cars and imported cars were treated differently.[67] There seem to be good reasons for not ruling out the use of environmental requirements as a possible justification for national measures which do imply a distinction between domestic and imported goods, taking into account that the protection of the environment has become a central Community objective only long after the drafting of Article 30 EC.[68]

As to the application and interpretation of the *Dassonville* formula, a fairly recent Opinion of an Advocate General has raised the question why the *Keck and Mithouard* exception should be limited to 'selling arrangements' and not cover domestic restrictions notably on the *use* of products.[69] Should the rules restricting the use of vehicles (for instance, the restriction, for environmental or road security reasons, of the use of cars in certain areas) which can be shown to affect the overall number of vehicles sold always be, under the broad *Dassonville* formula, regarded as measures having an equivalent effect? It will be noted that the seminal article by *Eric White* of 1989, which has often been seen as a source of inspiration for *Keck and Mithouard*, envisaged a certain limitation of *Dassonville* not only for selling arrangements but also for rules regulating the use of products, whether imported or domestically produced.[70]

Another fairly recent Opinion of an Advocate General proposes a dynamic interpretation of *Keck and Mithouard*, so as to focus on barriers to trade caused by discrimination, supplementary costs or measures which impede to a greater extent market access rather than the formal distinction between product requirements and selling arrangements.[71] In the case in question, the Court did not follow this approach but stated that the existence of a measure having equivalent effect followed from the fact that there was a product requirement, not a selling arrangement.[72]

The recent judgment in *Commission v Italy* mentioned above seems to be inspired by these two Opinions. In addition to national measures which treat imported products 'less favourably' than domestic products, and product-related measures covered by the *Cassis de Dijon* formula, the judgment speaks of 'any other measure' which 'hinders access' of imported products to the market of a Member State.[73] National rules regulating the use of

[67] Case C-524/07 *Commission v Austria*, judgment of 11 December 2008, not published in the ECR.

[68] C Timmermans, 'Creative Homogeneity' in M Johansson *et al* (eds), *Liber Amicorum in Honour of Sven Norberg: A European for All Seasons* (Brussels, Bruylant, 2006) 471 favours this approach and notes that the EFTA Court in two judgments of 1 July 2005 may have 'gone a step further than the ECJ by accepting without more ado the explicit Treaty provisions to the fundamental freedoms and the rule of reason as fully alternative sources of justification, irrespective of the nature of the national measure as being of distinct or indistinct application' (at 483–4).

[69] Opinion of Kokott AG of 14 December 2006 in Case C-142/05 *Åklagaren v Percy Michelsson v Joakim Roos.* At the time of writing (March 2009), the case is still pending before the ECJ.

[70] White, 253–5.

[71] Opinion of Poiares Maduro AG of 30 March 2006 in Joined Cases C-158/04 and C-159/04 *Alfa Vita Vassilopoulos AE and Carrefour Marinopoulos AE v Elliniko Dimosio and Nomarkhiaki Aftodiikisi Ioanninon.* See also the reference in note 49 above to earlier Opinions proposing alternatives to *Keck.*

[72] Case mentioned in the preceding note [2006] ECR I-8135.

[73] Judgment cited in note 25 above, para 37. See also Case C-442/04 *Caixa-Bank France v Ministère de l'Économie, des Finances et de l'Industrie* [2004] ECR I-8961, which in the context of freedom of establishment

products (the Commission action against Italy concerned precisely such rules) will thus not fall under the Dassonville formula unless they either treat imported products 'less favourably' or hinder their access to the national market. The judgment does cite *Keck* as well but as it, after references to the principle of non-discrimination, *Cassis* and *Keck*, concludes ('consequently') by mentioning the three categories mentioned above, that is, 'less favourable' treatment (in other words direct or indirect discrimination), product-related measures covered by *Cassis*, and for 'any other measure', the market access test, it would appear that all measures which are not product-related are treated in the same way, whether they are selling arrangements, rules on the use of products, or other non-product-related measures.[74]

If this is so, the judgment has preserved the baby, in other words the essence of *Dassonville* and *Cassis de Dijon*, while throwing out some cloudy bathwater. But how should the market access test be applied, *in concreto*? That will have to be further clarified in forthcoming case law. Those who have hoped that the ECJ has already said everything that can be said on Article 28 will be disappointed.

speaks of 'a serious obstacle to the pursuit of their activities ..., affecting their access to the market' (para 12) and establishes that 'access to the market by those establishments is thus made more difficult by such a prohibition' (para 14).

[74] See paras 33–37 of the judgment. In this context, it may be mentioned that the ECJ has recently adjusted its earlier case law also on Article 29 EC relating to exports (an issue not otherwise considered in this contribution), see Case C-205/07 *Lodewijk Gysbrechts and Santurel Inter BVBA*, judgment of 16 December 2008, nyr. Compare paras 40 and 43 of the judgment.

2

Kir Forever?

The Journey of a Political Scientist in the Landscape of Mutual Recognition

KALYPSO NICOLAÏDIS*

As this volume aspires to bring the Court's jurisprudence into interdisciplinary perspective, let me start with teaching anthropology. On the day I teach *Cassis* in my international political economy course, students usually find a bottle in the middle of the classroom table. 'Who has ever tasted *Cassis De Dijon*,' I ask the jittery group. A few hands go up. 'How about Kir?' 'Ah!' says the class. This is meant to be the first 'ah moment' in an exploration of the dialectics of economic integration, indeed more broadly of the transnational nature of integration. 'Can you believe that until 1979, not a soul had experienced the joys of Kir on German soil?' Ah! These are the micro-foundations to the macro-story of spillovers and inter-state bargains. 'This was because *Cassis* fell between two stools ... too strong for a wine ... but too weak for a spirit.' Ah! Discrimination veiled in the absurdities of state regulation. 'Still, the Germans could have won the day as they called the goddesses of "fairness" and "health" to their side.' Ah! Redemption through the rule of reason. And the conversation follows its course through its ultimate conclusion: Euro-Kir comes in many bottles.

Indeed, after almost three decades, it would seem far fetched to believe that the expectations created by the groundbreaking judgment have been fulfilled. At the EU summit in June 2007, the newly elected French president, Nicolas Sarkozy successfully lobbied to have the principle of 'undistorted competition' taken out of the formal objectives of the treaties. He might not have meant much by this except as a PR gesture, but the quick acquiescence of his peers is a sign of our times and one more echo of the protracted saga around the services directive, which culminated in the simple elimination of mutual recognition by the European Parliament. To a highly disgruntled EU legal community, this appeared as a public pillorying of *Cassis*. In the last few years, simply to utter support for the principle '*du pays d'origine*' in Paris's street or highbrow intellectual circles alike was enough to have one excommunicated to the burning hell of heartless neo-liberalism. Trust me. And yet, and at least, by issuing a clear political endorsement of the Court's *Cassis* jurisprudence, the directive succeeded in bringing EU services consumers closer than ever to the Kir fans of yesteryear.

Not only does Euro-Kir come in differently shaped bottles (Court decisions, Council-EP decisions, single country regulations), but it also comes in shades of red. Political scientists tend to see the bottles, legal scholars the subtle variation in shades.

* Kalypso Nicolaïdis is Professor of International Relations at Oxford University (Kalypso.Nicolaidis@sant.ox.ac.uk). More information can be found on her website: www.sant.ox.ac.uk/esc/knicolaidis/.

Indeed, when it comes to jurisprudential analysis, the dance between Articles 30 and 36, market integration and regulation, the European economic constitution and state autonomy, we must defer *inter alia* to our editor (Maduro 1998). Political science only asks about the before and after, the role of politics in legal judgments and vice versa—the why and the so what? Of course, the 'so what' feeds back into the 'why' as the Court considers the plausible institutional alternatives to its own decisions in its further jurisprudence. Nevertheless, it is fit for a contribution to an anniversary volume from the 'outside view' to ask about the legacy of *Cassis* (and its forbearer *Dassonville*) through an impressionist account of its ripple effects or echoes in the political sphere. As a heuristic, let me use three personal venture points, one decade at a time, which reflect my own journey in the landscape of mutual recognition: 1989, 1999, and our EU at 50.

Cassis in Action: Founding Myth, Conspiracy and Revolution

1989. When I recently asked Lord Cockfield, Commissioner for the internal market, what he considered the greatest achievement of his career, he answered without a beat: to have exported *Cassis* from the European Court of Justice and goods to the single market Europe 1992 programme. Indeed, there are many like him in the Commission who seem to believe that without *Cassis* and the aura of legitimacy it lent to their 'new approach' they would not have been able to pull through the legal coup spelled out in Cockfield's White Paper endorsed by Member States through Delors' Single Act only three years ago. An EU without *Cassis* would have borne 'the cost of non-Europe', the several points of GDP growth famously uncovered by Padoa Schioppa. Well, that might be true, but we still need to address a few nagging questions.

To start with, why the gap between this pan-*Cassis* rhetoric and the actual court jurisprudence of the last 10 years when reviewing national measures with an effect on trade under Article 30 and then Article 57 for services? Take one of my favourites, the *machine tool* decision. French workers will not have the privilege of using those German machines built for their better-trained counterparts across the Rhine. This is wise if the judges do not relish the prospect of receiving a finger in the mail! As for services, not a modicum of liberalisation has survived the tests of mandatory requirements and the rule of reason. Even in the *insurance* decision three years ago, the judges felt that recognition could be applied to non-mass risk but shied away from doing it themselves. Of course, they know that even businesses cannot always read the fine print in their insurance contracts. Indeed, the Court has stepped back from the recognition abyss even in the beverage and foods department, as with cheese additives banned by the Dutch. No matter that most Europeans, indeed most human beings, while they delight in very different tastes, find the same poisons poisonous. Even then different publics, consumers, societies might accept different levels of risk. And when the Court did strike—it did often enough to ensure the free movement of beer, butter, oil and pasta—not everyone was happy. 'Ah, I cannot recognise as *pasta* anything which comes so gluey out of the pot,' a well-loved Italian ECJ judge confided in me the other day. Ultimate recognition lies in the eye of the beholder—or in this case his stomach.

Since 1986, the press coverage of the EC and the single market has increased by orders of magnitude, along with the mentions of *Cassis* in the popular press, but no-one seems to pay attention to this paradox. To be sure, the Court's cautious jurisprudence, even after *Cassis*, is not surprising. *Cassis* was not only about casting the net of Article 30 more widely (after all, this was what *Dassonville* was about), but most importantly about widening the Article 36 gaps in the net through which fishy state regulations would be able to escape the rigours of liberalisation.

The question then is not why the Court has shied away from extending 'recognition of equivalence' to a wide array of cases beyond *Cassis*, but how come Cockfield and his friends were able to use *Cassis* in spite of the subsequent record, as if this was a matter of choosing a new bottle not of exploring shades of red. The reason is simple. Like all enterprises calling for individual sacrifice in the name of a collective, the new single market programme required its galvanising founding myth. Cassis happily obliged. The court provided EU worriers with a single formula, a motto easy to understand—'all … products lawfully produced and marketed … must be recognised as equivalent.' Freedom has always been a good rallying cry. No matter the full story—the decision's contingent and narrow applicability and the constraining nature of the list of 'mandatory requirements'. Founding myths are about agreeing on what to forget.

Indeed, the myth has several additional strands, outside the EC law profession of course. One is that Cassis 'introduced' mutual recognition in the EC legal landscape. Well of course lawyers know that the real radical breakthrough came with *Dassonville* in which, five earlier, the court struck down a Belgian provision requiring that imported goods bearing a designation of origin be accompanied by a certificate of origin. The formula may have been more sweeping—all measures with an 'equivalent effect' to quotas are to be struck down! But it was also less memorable and its timing less propitious. More to the point, mutual recognition can be found in the Treaty of Rome itself, referring to the mutual recognition of diploma, a task finally tackled seriously this year with the general system directive.

Another strand of the myth, popular these days among political scientists, is that recognition was one of several options available out there and that with *Cassis* the Court provided a new focal point for legislators. False. In fact, there are no other options. The question is not *which* but *whether*. In most instances of regulated goods or services, mutual recognition is the only game in town for effective free movement short of harmonisation. Even harmonisation is not an alternative to mutual recognition when it comes to the need to do away with host country certification—unless of course the EU was to be one regulatory jurisdiction, a goal neither desirable nor feasible.

One can legitimately ask, then, how did we get here? How did a judgment merely meant to popularise Kir beyond the French border end up changing the European constitutional order? A first part of the answer I believe is that it certainly was not 'merely meant' to do that. Indeed, as the story goes, the Commission fished around for a case of this sort and worked closely with the plaintiffs to bring it forward. No wonder, then, that as soon as the Court spoke, the Commission was ready to issue a detailed communication on its implications beyond alcoholic products, suggesting a detailed game plan to generalise the judgment to most regulated goods, including through an information and consultation procedure between national regulators and legislators. In the space of 10 years, this crucial

Commission communication seems to have been all but forgotten. We can legitimately infer that the initial conspiracy worked including as a conspiracy of silence—myths cannot afford to lose their innocence.

In short, taken together, the Commission's 1979 communication and 1986 White Paper (labelled as Cockfield's) simply took the decision to its ultimate logic in both *scope* and *depth*:

1) Generalising it in three steps: from alcoholic products to all products, from underlying standards to certification, and from goods to services.
2) Turning this judicial principle of 'recognition of equivalence' into a legislative-political principle of 'mutual recognition'. The latter does obviously imply an assessment of *equivalence* between home and host countries' rules, but the word, and thus the strictly legal constraint, is removed. Recognition becomes a political judgment, which does not necessarily need to be made on a careful case-by-case basis, but can be predicated on a host of other factors like trust, solidarity, proximity, political mood, linkage politics, paternalism . . .

Brilliant!

Why did Member States buy this? Apparently a majority of them did not even like *Cassis* in the first place, let alone its dual extension as engineered by the Commission. *Cassis* introduced (or uncovered depending on your legal school of thought), more visibly and strategically than *Dassonville*, Constitutional limits to state intervention beyond the bounds of intended discrimination. Europe 1992 then sets these limits into legislative stone through majority voting! Political scientists have it all wrong when they explain the turn to mutual recognition as a choice for the 'easy option', easier than harmonisation. To be sure, it might take longer to come up with a common standard on the height of lights in the back of trucks but once it is done, citizens live with a regulation to which their government of the day contributed. Under mutual recognition, they must live with regulations adopted in other polities, in which they have no say. In democratic terms such horizontal transfer of sovereignty is a much more radical option than a vertical one.

And of course if we move from static to a dynamic analysis, the picture is even starker. How will national regulators, their political master and their market clients react to this new state of affairs? Will such competition between rules significantly affect the ways rules are designed in the first place? How will regulators and legislators reconcile the contradictory pulls between competitiveness/cost effects of high standards and their reputational/benefits effects? Clearly, every mutual recognition deal seems to be predicated on opposite predictions on the part of politicians. The Thatchers of this world believe that it will help them export deregulation. The Mitterrands and Kohls tend to believe that it will induce reregulation. Analysts are starting to build models, which argue the usual: it depends.

Whatever the case may be, it seems as thought the myth has become a self-fulfilling prophecy. The hype seems warranted, as *Cassis* has truly proved to spell the start of a revolution in European affairs. Thanks to the supranational conspiracy uniting the Court, the Commission and big business, it has set off a revolution in decision makers' thinking about market integration that simply cannot be stopped. Yet, my prediction (the argument of my doctoral thesis), for what it is worth is that such radical horizontal transfer of sovereignty between states is highly conflictual and will not happen without serious resistance.

Kalypso Nicolaïdis

Cassis Fever: The Era of Managed Mutual Recognition

1999. In the last 10 years, old questions have been clarified while new ones have arisen. Clearly, the progress made towards a single market in services through the White Paper directives owes a lot to the adoption of mutual recognition as a guiding core principle. And there has been no blatant 'race to the bottom', rather 'to the top'.

But resistance there has been! Indeed, when I asked at the time: why did the Member States buy it, I had identified the wrong 'it'. What Member States have imported from the Court's jurisprudence has had little to do with the mere extension of the *Cassis* formula (as opposed to the entire judgment) to other products and sectors, an outcome which we can call 'pure recognition' (considering the labelling requirement as *de facto* not a costly adaptation). Instead, Member States have adopted a highly politicised version of recognition involving complex sets of rules and procedures that may serve precisely to reduce, if not eliminate, the open-endedness of mutual recognition. This I have called managed mutual recognition.

This is the conclusion I have drawn from analysing not only single market directives in services but also the attempts by the EU to export *Cassis* beyond its borders. As an outcome, managed mutual recognition can be contrasted with 'pure' mutual recognition in the same sense as managed trade can be contrasted with absolute free trade. Pure mutual recognition implies the granting of fully unconditional and open-ended rights (of action, access) to private market agents as a product of a free trade contract between states. In contrast, managed mutual recognition introduces conditionality in the contract. The four main dimensions along which mutual recognition can be managed or fine-tuned are: (a) prior conditions for equivalence, from convergence to inter-institutional agreements; (b) varying degrees of automaticity of access (for example, residual host country requirements; (c) scope of activities or features covered by recognition; and (d) *ex post* guarantees or safeguards, including mutual monitoring and ultimately provisions for reversibility. On this basis, managed mutual recognition can be viewed in a static or a dynamic manner. Statically, variation along each of these dimensions can be seen to indicate how far parties have travelled down the road to full recognition. Dynamically, the management of mutual recognition can be viewed as a process, involving trade-offs between these dimensions that may change over time. In short, the burden of co-operation is shifted in time from *ex ante* to *ex post* costs, so that liberalisation can appear to occur immediately, while it will need to be managed to be sustainable.

I have come to believe that a better understanding of these trade-offs and their dynamic adaptation over time is key to reaching agreements on mutual recognition in the first place.

Clearly then, 'managed' mutual recognition belongs to the political, not the judicial sphere. Nevertheless, it deeply bears the marks of the Court's footprints. First, it is the Court which traces the frontier, or the equivalence threshold, beyond which political decisions and political action will be necessary in order to ensure free movement on the basis of a home country rule. It also makes clear that such political action might not necessarily be harmonisation or centralised regulation. When deciding whether to replace a given state regulation with its own assessment of that regulation, the Court may or may not be weighing the institutional alternatives to its own approach, but it certainly shapes such alternatives.

Indeed, the Court is all the more relevant when we understand the legacy of *Cassis* as that of managed recognition. Take the debate that has dominated both the case law of the Court and the legal writing on the review of state measures under Article 30, namely whether the Court does/should apply a non-discrimination test or a balancing test in such cases. As Maduro argues in his recent book, even when apparently restricting decisions to an anti-discrimination test the Court always weighs costs and benefits and balances between the desirability of centralisation versus decentralisation, deregulation versus sustained regulation. Such balancing tests might lean towards a decentralised approach and yet determine that national treatment (or pure anti-discrimination) does not suffice to ensure free trade; they might point to the need for sustained regulation in a given sector but assess a home country approach to be sufficient, if the necessary safeguards are taken. In both cases, it may call for mutual recognition while stopping short of its judicial imposition.

When generalised through the legislative process most of the ECJ jurisprudence post-*Cassis* translates as managed, not pure recognition, whereby recognition is not an alternative to national treatment and harmonisation but an overarching principle, which retains residual host country control and harmonisation. In this sense, *Cassis* after all was not a continuation but a break from *Dassonville*. The latter's jurisprudence of generalising an *obstacles-based approach* to national regulation, whereby all national rules are potentially subject to an assessment of illegality, amounts to pure mutual recognition by judicial fiat. In contrast, the more circumscribed *Cassis* doctrine of *functional equivalence*, especially as further constrained in *Keck*, involves precisely the identification of the conditions and limits of recognition. But only by migrating from the judicial to the legislative arena is it possible to spell out the full panoply of instruments for the management of recognition.

While it is important to analyse the role of the rulings of the ECJ in the European story of mutual recognition, it is also true that all the Court could do when it came to designing this more sophisticated understanding of the principle was to provide a *roadmap* for politicians and technical experts later crafting legislation. For instance, the distinction made in the first, second and third generation insurance directives between types of consumers that could or could not withstand the logic of mutual recognition was an instance of political translation of the Court's jurisprudence. The Court had not imposed judicial recognition but pointed to the possibility of using this distinction to reduce the initial scope of recognition and introduce it in a progressive manner; or take the 1996 directive on the posting of workers—the line drawn between home and host country jurisdiction is a direct reading of the jurisprudence. If and when the political arena generates a demand for effective liberalisation, the Commission takes the politicians at their word in fact 'upping the ante' by proposing a radical generalisation of the Court's approach to complete the single market, which is after all what the political masters are asking for. But during the properly political process of bargaining, a winning coalition of Member States succeeds in watering down the extent of horizontal transfer of sovereignty in order to make liberalisation politically acceptable.

In this decade, managed mutual recognition has become the name of the game in the field of services, whether through residual host country control (professions), reduced scope (finance) or ex-post monitoring (media). In the field of goods, it has led not only to the new approach and agreement on minimal standards as prior condition, but also to the global approach whereby certification bodies throughout Europe can sustain recognition without undue fear of lowered standards thanks to an extensive process of mutual monitoring—mutual spying, as I like to say. In spite of these collaborative networks between certifiers, recognition has been far from automatic in many instances. It should come as no surprise, then, that when exported into the transatlantic realm, and even while restricting it to certification, rather than recognition of the underlying standards, mutual recognition has been highly managed. When covering highly sensitive sectors like pharmaceuticals, mutual recognition agreements (MRAs) have stopped short of denying the FDA (Federal Drugs Agency) its right of residual control even if at the last stages of the approval process. And MRAs have simply floundered when it comes to services. At the global (WTO) level, under TBT (technical barriers to trade) and GATS (the services agreement) recognition is optional and conditional, not subject to MFN, and has been cumbersome to apply. Non-discriminatory mutual recognition could appear as an oxymoron to the non-legally trained eye.

Perhaps in order to counter the natural inertia of regulators and their resistance to any trade-induced assault on their autonomy, the OECD trade directorate—which has appointed me as their 'mutual recognition expert'—has launched a multi-year programme on the promotion of trade-friendly regulatory reform around the world. Fascinating to see attempts at the liberalisation of professional services meet resistance to horizontal approaches, precisely because each believes their particularities require a specific approach to managing recognition, from fiddling with acceptable titles to the need for additional training, adaptation periods and the like. Yet, what is a 'trade-friendly' regulatory reform if not one where modes and avenues for recognising foreign standards and actors are embedded in the very process of drafting law?

Cassis on Trial: Polish Plumbers, Butchers and Models

2009. This time around *Cassis* has truly been invoked in vain. If the recourse to mutual recognition has long been considered as a path of least resistance, 'easier than harmonisation', we can no longer doubt its highly contentious character. Twenty years after Lord Cockfield, another liberal Commissioner, Fritz Bolkestein considered worthy of a personal crusade the export of mutual recognition to the realm of all services trade spared until then from legislative scrutiny. And yet, the analogy stops here. In contrast to 20 years ago, mutual recognition has not been hailed as the magic bullet but has been put on trial along with Polish plumbers and butchers seeking temporary work in France and Germany (who in fact are required to work under host state laws but actually work under home state of mind).

To be sure, the public hysteria and PR disaster spurred by the Commission's draft directive can be attributed to many factors, including the propensity of some trade unions to play up their members' fears of globalisation and unfair competition. Moreover, the radical enlargement of the EU may well have lowered the 'mutual recognition tolerance threshold' while at the same time increasing the social, economic and regulatory diversity of the Union.

But given these factors, the Commission made a crucial mistake: to depart from its experience with managed mutual recognition and to press for a radical form of recognition across the board. It should have been clear by now to Brussels law drafters that a blanket application of home country jurisdiction is not faithful to the *Cassis* spirit. Under the Court's jurisprudence, recognition was a conditional process and did not have the either-or character of the country-of-origin principle. A test must be applied to host state measures, and if found 'un-equivalent' with that of the home state they can be considered justified restriction to free trade. To adjudicate *a priori* between home and host state law is akin to setting a rule under a 'conflict of law' agreement, whereby mutual recognition becomes an unconditional obligation. In fact, the final draft to emerge from the European Parliament's negotiations amounts to endorsing the Court's jurisprudence, prescribing the usual proportionality and necessity tests for host country rules—a glass half full for advocates of a cautious and progressive approach to liberalisation, but half empty for those who believed that 20 years after the Treaty of Rome political actors could afford to take a bolder step than judges.

The Poles, thankfully, were undeterred. During the crisis, an ad from their Tourism Ministry featured the picture of a handsome plumber with the caption 'Come to see me, I am staying at home'. In the end, whether or not he leaves home, all will want to claim him. Maduro argues that Member States should be able to make different policy judgments. What we should not permit is that they ignore out-of-state interests in the making of those judgments. Others like Regan argue that the same result can be obtained from a fair representation of *all* domestic interests, as *proxies* for the under-represented interests from the outside. Whatever the benchmark, however, this normative view calls for a recognition managed by state regulators themselves but policed by the Commission, the Court, consumers and providers alike.

Cassis in Spirit: Europe as a Demoi-cratic Politics

What would EU law have been without *Cassis*? Indeed, what would the EU be without *Cassis*? Almost 30 years ago, at a time when the EC was ripe for a new approach that would deliver the completion of a market promised 20 years earlier, I believe there would have been another similar case, sooner or later. Perhaps the greatest irony today is that while questioned in the single market area, the spirit of *Cassis* thrives elsewhere. For one, we are witnessing a systematic extension of the principle of mutual recognition to the realm of justice and home affairs, in other words the acceptance by judges and police forces throughout Europe of each other's procedures and judgments. To be sure, 'wanted in one EU country, wanted everywhere in the EU' does not sound as liberal as its *Cassis* forbear and we do not yet have refugees 'admitted here, admitted everywhere'. But the time will come. In the meanwhile we must live with the 'rejected here, rejected everywhere'.

Indeed, an (idealised) European vision is becoming increasingly realistic which understands the enterprise as a one of intertwined polities, open to each other's soft influences and hard laws, and bound together not by some overarching sense of common identity or peoplehood but by the daily practice of mutual recognition of identities, histories and social contracts (Nicolaidis, 2007). To live in such a European 'demoi-cracy' means living with our differences and seeking to harmonise if and only if such differences are illegitimate in the eyes of either one of the parties involved. Recognition is a tough call on all sides of the political spectrum. The left fears social dumping when recognition means importing market rules; libertarians fear political dumping when recognition means importing, say, curbs on free speech. Even if these fears can be exploited, they must be assuaged through respecting the spirit of *Cassis*, that of managed recognition. Ultimately, however, they must be transcended if we are to live in Europe and in the world as a community of others, in Weiler's inspired formula.

References

Maduro, Miguel Poiares (1998), *We, the Court. The European Court of Justice and the European Economic Constitution* (Oxford, Hart Publishing).

Nicolaïdis, Kalypso (1989) 'Mutual Recognition: The Next Frontier of Multilateralism?' (July 1989) Project Promethee Perspectives, Paris.

——, 'Promising Approaches and Principal Obstacles to Mutual Recognition' in *International Trade in Professional Services: Advancing Liberalization through Regulatory Reform* (OECD Publications, 1997).

——, 'Non-Discriminatory Mutual Recognition: An Oxymoron in the New WTO Lexicon?' in Petros Mavroidis and Patrick Blatter, eds, *Non Discrimination in the WTO: Past and Present, Journal of World Trade* (University of Michigan Press, The World Trade Forum series, 2000).

——, 'Non-Discriminatory Mutual Recognition: An Oxymoron in the New WTO Lexicon?' in Petros Mavroidis and Patrick Blatter, eds, *Non Discrimination in the WTO: Past and Present, Journal of World Trade* (University of Michigan Press, The World Trade Forum series, 2000).

——, 'Harmonisation and Recognition: What Have we Learned?' in *Trade and Regulatory Reform: Insights from Country Experience* (Paris, OECD Publications, 2001)

——, 'Europe and beyond: struggles for recognition' (Feb 2006) *Open Democracy* available at *www.opendemocracy.net/faith-europe_islam/recognition_3288.jsp*

Nicolaïdis, Kalypso (2007), 'Trusting the Poles? Constructing Europe through Mutual Recognition' (May 2007) 13 *Journal of European Public Policy*.

Nicloaidis, K, and JP Trachtman, 'From Policed Regulation to Managed Recognition: Mapping the Boundary in GATS' in P Sauve and RM Stern, eds, Services 2000: *New Directions in Services Trade Liberalization* (Washington DC, Brookings Institution Press, 2000).

Nicolaidis, K and M Egan, 'Regional Policy Externality and Market Governance: Why Recognize Foreign Standards?' (Aug 2001) *Journal Of European Public Policy* (Reprinted in *The Political Economy of Standardization*, Walter Mattli, ed, Cambridge University Press, 2001).

Nicolaïdis, Kalypso and Gregory Shaffer (2005), 'Transnational Mutual Recognition Regimes: Governance without Global Government' (2005) 68 *Michigan Review of International Law* 267–322.

Nicolaidis, K and S Schmidt 'Mutual recognition "on trial": the long road to services liberalization' (2007)14 (5) *Journal of European Public Policy* 717–34.

Schioppa, Fiorella Kostoris Padoa (ed) (2005), *The principle of mutual recognition in the European integration process*, Houndmills, Palgrave Macmillan, 224–31.

Weiler, Joseph, 'Mutual Recognition, Functional Equivalence and Harmonization in the Evolution of the European Common Market and the WTO', in F Kostoris Padoa Schioppa (ed), *The principle of mutual recognition in the European Integration process*, Basingstoke, Palgrave Macmillan.

3

On the Art of Not Mixing One's Drinks: *Dassonville* and *Cassis de Dijon* Revisited

NICOLAS BERNARD

In classical legal narratives on the development of the law on the free movement of goods within the European internal market, the judgments of the Court in *Dassonville*[75] and *Cassis de Dijon*[76] are usually presented as fateful moments, in which the Court took a momentous decision destined to shape the future evolution of the law. In these accounts, however, the two cases do not stand on an equal footing. Conceptually, the more important one is *Dassonville*, in the sense that it is there that the Kuhnian[77] paradigm shift takes place, that the conceptual ground is moved and the legal revolution operated. In this perspective, *Cassis de Dijon* acts primarily as a clarification and tidying-up exercise, as well as a revealer for the heretofore undiscovered potential inherent in *Dassonville*.

An excellent example of this kind of narrative is provided by Joseph Weiler's account of the 'Constitution of the Common Market Place':[78] Weiler identifies five generations in the development of the internal market, with *Dassonville* and *Cassis de Dijon* playing a prominent role in the first two phases. *Dassonville* represents the first, foundational period in which free movement law is firmly based on a logic of removal of obstacles to free trade, as distinct from a mere anti-discrimination/anti-protectionist regime. *Cassis de Dijon* then represents the second generation in which key issues left unsolved by *Dassonville* are addressed, namely the need to provide a mechanism to safeguard legitimate measures that could not be foreseen in 1957 and therefore not included in the grounds of derogations of the ex Article 36 EEC and to address the problem of market fragmentation resulting from the adoption of differing standards by the Member States coupled with the *blocage* of decision making under ex Article 100 EEC. The 'mandatory requirements' doctrine and the so-called 'mutual recognition' or, as Weiler prefers, 'functional equivalence' principles in *Cassis* respectively address each of these two problems.

The beauty of Weiler's account, the reason why it resonates so much with us, is that it presents the development of the case law[79] as the product of conscious, deliberate choices by the Court of Justice at crucial moments. We progress from one generation to the next, if not seamlessly at least logically. The Court wanted to move away from a discrimination

[75] Case 8/74 *Procureur du Roi v Dassonville* [1974] ECR 837.

[76] Case 120/78 *Cassis de Dijon* [1979] ECR 649.

[77] T Kuhn, *The Structure of Scientific Revolutions* 3rd edn (Chicago, University Of Chicago Press, 1996).

[78] JHH Weiler, 'The Constitution of the Common Market Place: Text and Context in the Evolution of the Free Movement of Goods' in P Craig and G De Búrca (eds), *The Evolution of EU Law* (Oxford, Oxford University Press, 1999), 349–76.

[79] Weiler is far too sophisticated to confuse the development of the case law and the development of the law and acknowledges the limitations of an approach that focuses on cases, and especially on key cases.

approach in *Dassonville* and therefore adopted the '*Dassonville* formula'. *Dassonville* left some issues unsolved. The Court then set out to address some of these through the mandatory requirements doctrine and the mutual recognition principle in *Cassis*. This does not mean that the Court never gets it wrong, even within its own terms, or never changes its mind, as *Keck*[80] shows. Nonetheless, we remain within a narrative of deliberate, progressive and continuous case law development by the Court.

The downside of such narratives, however, is that they are written, necessarily, with the benefit of hindsight and may unconsciously read cases in the light of later developments and, in so doing, invest judgments with a meaning and significance that they did not necessarily possess, or were meant to possess, when they were first handed down. Weiler's account of *Dassonville* puts the emphasis on the *Dassonville* formula. Indeed, *Dassonville* becomes the *Dassonville* formula. *Cassis de Dijon* is read so as to provide continuity with *Dassonville*. In the following pages, I shall put forward an alternative reading of these cases, downplaying the significance of the *Dassonville* formula and emphasising a clash between the approaches adopted by the Court in *Dassonville* and in *Cassis de Dijon*. My purpose is not to argue that Weiler's reading of these cases is 'wrong'. Certainly, historically, Weiler's account is 'right' in the sense that this is the way in which we have come to understand those cases. Rather, my aim is to emphasise how our reading of the cases in a particular way has resulted in some pathological developments in the law that have bedevilled and continue to bedevil the development of the law of the internal market.

This Chapter consists of three main sections. In the first two sections, I will revisit *Dassonville* and *Cassis de Dijon* to highlight some profound differences between those two cases in they way they approach the problem of attributing meaning to the prohibition on measures having equivalent effect to quantitative restrictions in the context of the European internal market. In the third section, I will consider some problems created by the *Dassonville* and *Cassis de Dijon* case law, and how, in particular, a pathological reading of the relationship between these cases has promoted an unhealthy development of the law relating to free movement in the internal market. Finally, in conclusion, I will return to Weiler's classic account to assess the appropriateness, from a normative perspective, of convergence between the EC and international trade regimes.

The Dassonville Formula: Myth or Reality?

'All trading rules enacted by the Member States which are capable of hindering, directly or indirectly, actually or potentially, intra-Community trade are to be considered as measures having an effect equivalent to quantitative restrictions.'

Clearly, if read literally and free of all context, the *Dassonville* formula is capable of supporting the wide interpretation that has later been attributed to it, both in textbooks and in case law, an interpretation that underpins Weiler's claim of a deliberate move away from a logic of anti-protectionism and non-discrimination in the law relating to the free movement of goods. However, this is not how we normally read cases, or, for that matter, most texts. Meaning is usually regarded as determined by context and just about everything in the context of the *Dassonville* formula would suggest another reading. The

[80] Joined cases C-267 and 268/91 *Keck and Mithouard* [1993] ECR I-6097.

facts of the case, as construed by the Court, the overall language of the judgment as well as the wider context of European integration all push in a different direction.

As regards the facts of the case, for the Court, the problem with the Belgian legislation was that it created a barrier to parallel imports. If the Court's purpose was to put forward a wide obstacle theory of the kind it would later use in such cases as *Cinéthèque*[81] or the Sunday Trading cases,[82] this is a rather bizarre way to look at the issue. One would have expected it to note that any formality prior to placing goods on the market constitutes a *prima facie* obstacle to inter-state trade, in much the same way as import formalities constitute such obstacles.[83] The channelling effect seems largely irrelevant in an obstacle analysis. At most, it might be of secondary relevance at the level of justification. The Court, however, is very clear right at the beginning of the judgment that the issue in the case is that 'a trader, wishing to import into Belgium Scotch whisky which is already in free circulation in France, can obtain such a certificate only with great difficulty, unlike the importer who imports directly from the producer country'.[84] Put in the terminology currently in vogue, as read by the Court, the rule did not create a barrier to market access for the product as such, but favoured certain channels of distribution over others. This was clearly confirmed in *Dassonville II*,[85] where the Court found that there was no longer any breach of ex Article 30 EEC after Belgium amended its legislation and practices to facilitate parallel imports.[86]

As regards the language of the judgment as a whole, one cannot fail to notice that it is saturated with the language of discrimination. It is particularly noteworthy that the Court states that the power of Member States to adopt measures to prevent unfair practices in connection to guarantees of authenticity of product is, in the absence of Community legislation, subject to a requirement of reasonableness and that the means of proof required 'should not act as a hindrance to trade between Member States and *should, in consequence, be accessible to all Community nationals*'.[87]

With regard to the wider context of European integration, one might perhaps be tempted to draw a parallel with the Court's judgment in *Reyners*,[88] decided a mere three weeks earlier, in which the Court held that ex Article 52 EEC (now Article 43 EC) was capable of direct effect. The Court has often been credited for kick-starting the stalled engine of European integration in the face of stagnant political processes in that period of 'Eurosclerosis'. Yet, there is a problem in seeing the Court in *Dassonville* as making up for the deficiencies of the legislative process by strengthening negative integration, as it undoubtedly does in *Reyners*. The problem in *Dassonville* is not one of lack of harmonisation. Like *Keck* and unlike *Cassis de Dijon*, *Dassonville* was not concerned with an

[81] Joined cases 60–61/84 *Cinéthèque v FNCF* [1985] ECR 2605.

[82] Eg Case 145/88 *Torfaen BC v B & Q plc* [1989] ECR 385.

[83] On import formalities, see Joined cases 51–54/71 *International Fruit Company v Produktschap voor Groenten en Fruit* [1971] ECR 1107. The significance of *Dassonville* compared to this case law would have been that formalities at the marketing stage rather than the importation stage would also constitute measures having equivalent effect to a quantitative restriction.

[84] See paragraph 4 of the judgment.

[85] Case 2/78 *Commission v Belgium* [1979] ECR 1761.

[86] Some authors dismiss *Dassonville II* as anomalous (see P Oliver, *Free Movement of Goods in the European Community* (London, Sweet & Maxwell, 2003), 133–4). However, it is only anomalous if we accept that the *Dassonville* formula has to be taken at face value ignoring the context of the case. This might have been justified later on, as the Court's case law developed in that direction, but not at that point in time.

[87] See paragraph 6 of the judgment (emphasis added).

[88] Case 2/74 *Reyners v Belgian State* [1974] ECR 631.

obstacle resulting from disparities between the laws of the Member States. It would therefore seem singularly inappropriate to read it as a case of substitution of the Court for the weakness of political processes.

There is therefore little in the context of the case to suggest that it constituted a momentous decision to radically alter the conceptual basis of the free movement of goods. Indeed, later case law until *Cassis de Dijon* would seem to confirm this. In the period between *Dassonville* and *Cassis*, *Dassonville* appears to have been cited by either the Advocate-General or the Court itself in 23 cases. These cases fall in three broad categories: (i) cases concerning obstacles to parallel imports;[89] (ii) cases in which the Court conditions the applicability of ex Article 30 EEC to the existence of discrimination against imports[90] and (iii) cases in which ex Article 30 EEC is neither interpreted nor applied.[91] In none of these cases was the *Dassonville* formula used to strike down a non-discriminatory regulatory measure adopted by a Member State.

A final reason why it is rather strange that Dassonville should be regarded as constituting a deliberate move by the Court heralding a new era, opening wide the scope of ex Article 30 EEC, lies in its rather limited analytical approach. At no point is there any attempt in the judgment to explain how the building of an internal market differs from liberalisation of international trade. If the Court did intend to move away from the logic of anti-protectionism and non-discrimination then prevalent in international trade liberalisation instruments, such as GATT, one would have expected a greater degree of elaboration of the issues. Admittedly, at that time, the style of the Court was rather terser than it currently is. But even so, other cases in which the Court justifies a departure from traditional approaches, such as *Van Gend en Loos* and *Costa v ENEL*,[92] were rather more explicit on the need for a departure from ordinary international law in the EU context.

Cassis de Dijon: Actual or Potential Mutual Recognition?

It is precisely on this last point that *Cassis* differs markedly from *Dassonville*. *Dassonville* proceeds by way of a peremptory definition without any explanation as to why the context of the internal market necessitates such a definition. It is as if the notion of a measure having equivalent effect was so self-evident as not to require any explanation. By way of contrast, instead of starting from an *a priori* definition, the Court in *Cassis* begins by characterising the problem as one of disparities between the laws of the Member States. If we start from the Court's definition of the internal market in *Schul*[93] as entailing the

[89] These are primarily cases concerning intellectual property rights and the doctrine of exhaustion (see, eg, Case 119/75 *Terrapin v Terranova* [1976] ECR 1039).

[90] The majority of these cases concern either measures applying specifically to imports (eg phyto-sanitary inspections as the border as in Case 4/75 *Rewe v Landwirtschaftskammer* [1975] ECR 43) or price control measures (see, eg, Case 82/77 *Van Tiggele* [1978] ECR 25).

[91] See, eg, Case 31/74 *Galli* [1975] ECR 47 concerning the inability of Member States to take unilateral action in the context of the common organisation of agricultural markets when the matter is regulated at Community level.

[92] See also Case 270/80 *Polydor v Harlequin* [1982] ECR 329 for another example of the Court explaining the specificity of the internal market context to justify a different solution in intra-EC trade as compared to ordinary international treaties.

[93] Case 15/81 *Schul* [1982] ECR 1409, para 33.

elimination 'of all obstacles to intra-community trade in order to merge the national markets into a single market bringing about conditions as close as possible to those of a genuine internal market', it is clear that the issue of disparities between the laws of the Member States lies at the heart of the *problématique* of free movement in the internal market. Plurality of legal orders, and therefore potential disparities between those legal orders, are precisely what distinguishes a multi-state market compared with a domestic market within a single jurisdiction. In the context of classic international trade law, we are bound to proceed from the principle of state sovereignty and therefore recognise the competence of each state to regulate its own market. Regulatory competence therefore falls on the host state and, as a result, obstacles resulting from disparities between national laws are unavoidable. We can seek to minimise them but, ultimately, we have to accept that different polities will make different regulatory choices and that such differences will create insurmountable obstacles to trade. In an internal market, however, we cannot content ourselves with such an answer. The abolition of all obstacles to trade, including those resulting from disparities between the laws of the Member States, is precisely what distinguishes an internal market from a mere liberalised international trade regime. The only question is how we go about removing those obstacles. If, to use Poiares Maduro's tripartite classification,[94] the decentralised model of host state control does not solve the problem, we still have a choice between either the 'centralised model' of harmonisation or the 'competitive model' of mutual recognition. Thus, regulatory competence falls either in the hands of the Community under the centralised model or in the hands of the home state under the mutual recognition regime.

Cassis has been widely criticised for introducing the principle of mutual recognition in the legal landscape. However, this introduction was immediately neutralised by the mandatory requirements doctrine. The possibility for the host state to justify rules by reference to legitimate public interest objectives ensured that what was presented as the default principle, namely that products lawfully produced and marketed in one Member State should in principle be admitted in all other Member States, was confined to marginal situations, where no significant regulatory objectives were at stake. There is, therefore, something slightly disingenuous in stating that mutual recognition was a 'colossal market failure'[95] when the Court precisely rejected the mutual recognition route in anything but marginal cases.

There are, of course, good reasons why the Court refused to engage down the route of what we might call, by analogy with Tiebout's model of fiscal federalism,[96] 'regulatory federalism' and the risk of a race to the bottom attendant on it. Whether the economic situation among the then nine—soon to be 10—Member States made such a race a genuine and realistic threat rather than a purely theoretical prospect is a moot point, as there can in any event be no denying of the salience of the point from a political point of view. It is also probable that a system based on regulatory competition would have added a layer of difficulties in successive enlargement negotiations. The controversy surrounding the so-called 'Bolkenstein Directive' on services in the internal market[97] serves as an *a posteriori* vindication of the wisdom of a cautious approach on this issue.

[94] M Poiares Maduro, *We the Court—The European Court of Justice and the European Economic Constitution* (Oxford, Hart Publishing, 1997).

[95] Weiler, above note 78, at 368.

[96] C Tiebout, 'A Pure Theory of Local Expenditures' (1956) 64 *Journal of Political Economy* 416–24.

[97] Directive 2006/123/EC of the European Parliament and of the Council of 12 December 2006 on services in the internal market, [2006] OJ L376/36.

Even as a virtual rather than operative legal principle, mutual recognition is an important point of reference and *Cassis*, unlike previous case law—least of all *Dassonville*—provides us with a conceptual framework in which to think about the problem of regulation in the internal market and the role of harmonisation in it. This significance was not lost on the Commission[98] and opened the door to a programme of harmonisation based on essential requirements, which would later become one of the elements of the new approach to technical harmonisation.

Re-reading *Dassonville* post-*Cassis*: Why Whisky and Crème de Cassis Do not Mix

While *Cassis de Dijon* represented a major intellectual breakthrough, it nonetheless gave rise to two kinds of problems.

The first problem, which has already been alluded to, is one of disappointed expectations. If mutual recognition and home country control were supposed to single-handedly solve the problem of realising the internal market and obviate the need for harmonisation, then clearly this has not happened. However, this would have been an unrealistic expectation of mutual recognition. The problem stems from seeing mutual recognition and home country control as a replacement for harmonisation. A regulatory system based entirely on mutual recognition and home country control would place high demands in terms of homogeneity and mutual trust among the Member States, which is plainly unrealistic in the European internal market. The real potential of mutual recognition and home country control in the single market is in conjunction with, rather than instead of, harmonisation, so as to promote a more reflective and selective approach to harmonisation. To some extent, this has happened with the focus on essential requirements in the context of the new approach to technical harmonisation. Mutual recognition of diplomas outside the harmonised professions could also be cited as another example, as well as Directive 98/5 on freedom of establishment for lawyers.[99] However, the potential of a combination of harmonisation and mutual recognition has not been fully exploited. The preference given to total harmonisation, particularly in the context of the new approach—rather than minimal harmonisation coupled with a free movement clause for products complying with home country rules—has limited the potential for regulatory experimentation and innovation, even though the voluntary nature of compliance to standards has somewhat alleviated the danger of ossification and obsolescence inherent in total harmonisation.

The second problem is more directly concerned with the case law of the Court and its interpretation of Article 28 EC. The issue here concerns the relationship between *Cassis de Dijon* and *Dassonville*. While *Dassonville* had until then remained pretty much dormant, it was invested with a new vigour after *Cassis*. This involved re-reading *Dassonville* in the

[98] Communication from the Commission concerning the consequences of the judgment given by the Court of Justice on 20 February 1979 in Case 120/78 (*Cassis de Dijon*), [1980] OJ C256/2.

[99] Directive 98/5/EC of the European Parliament and of the Council of 16 February 1998 to facilitate the practice of the profession of lawyer on a permanent basis in a Member State other than that in which the qualification was obtained, [1998] OJ L77/36.

light of *Cassis* and, conversely, interpreting *Cassis* as a confirmation and clarification of *Dassonville. Dassonville* ceased being regarded as a case about parallel imports and, instead, as the basis for a general theory of measures having equivalent effect to quantitative restrictions based on the *Dassonville* formula. From this perspective, *Cassis* was to be seen as having first and foremost expanded on the 'rule of reason' in *Dassonville* through the development of the mandatory requirements and mutual recognition dismissed as mere rhetorical fluff, a nice formula which adds strictly nothing to the existing body of law, since the job of bringing a measure within the scope of Article 28 EC was done by the *Dassonville* formula.

This return to *Dassonville* constituted a major impoverishment of the intellectual debate. To the conceptual richness of *Cassis*, stimulating reflection on tools and techniques of market integration, was substituted the vacuity of the *Dassonville* formula. The limitations of that formula as a conceptual basis on which to found the internal market are patent: the formula has little to tell us beyond the assertion that regulation is bad for the internal market: 'all trading rules' are prima facie suspect although they may have to be, reluctantly, tolerated under the rule of reason. The only way to endow the formula with any intellectual content and respectability is to adopt a neo-liberal reading of the Treaty designed to minimise public intervention in the market and maximise private commercial freedom. Some authors, notably in the German ordo-liberal school, have defended such a reading of the Treaty.[100] The problem for those authors is that neither the historical context nor the structure and wording of the Treaty, whether in its original form or following the amendments introduced by the Single European Act and the Maastricht Treaty, offer convincing support for a neo-liberal reading.

As some authors have observed,[101] the Court has, rightfully, not gone down that route and has, through the mandatory requirements doctrine, been quite tolerant of state regulation in the internal market. However, it has, unfortunately, listened to the sirens calling for a reading of *Cassis de Dijon* as an extension of the *Dassonville* formula. The problem with interpreting Article 28 EC on the basis of a formula whose sole underlying message is that regulation is inimical to the internal market is that it invites litigants to use Article 28 EC whenever they object to constraints on their commercial freedom inherent in any regulation, even in situations which do not raise any genuine issue of market integration.

The Court in *Keck*[102] attempted to redress the excesses to which excessive reliance on the *Dassonville* formula had led. Unfortunately, it did so by following a number of authors in addressing the symptoms rather than the root cause. The source of the problem is that *Cassis* was designed to deal with the core issue of free movement in a multi-state market, namely the problem of disparities between the laws of the Member States. The reason why *Keck* should have remained outside the scope of Article 28 EC is not so much that it concerned 'selling arrangements' *per se* but rather that it—like for that matter the Sunday Trading cases[103] or, in the context of the other freedoms, *Alpine Investments* [104]—did not raise any issue of disparities between the laws of the Member States. In all these cases, we

[100] Cf, eg, ME Streit and W Mussler, 'The Economic Constitution of the European Community: From "Rome" to "Maastricht"', (1995) 1 *European Law Journal* 5.

[101] See, eg, M Poiares Maduro, above note 74.

[102] Joined cases C-267 and 268/91 *Keck and Mithouard* [1993] ECR I-6097.

[103] Eg Case 145/88 *Torfaen BC v B & Q plc* [1989] ECR 385.

[104] Case C-384/93 *Alpine Investments v Minister van Financiën* [1995] ECR I-1141.

were dealing with home state regulation,[105] which, in the absence of discrimination, should remain outside the scope of free movement law, as established by the Court in its case law on Article 29 EC.[106]

The Court's decision in *Keck* attracted strong criticisms for its opportunistic but rather unprincipled distinction between rules relating to the product itself and rules concerning selling arrangements. While those criticisms are justified, the alternatives put forward, such as those centred on the notion of a restriction or hindrance to 'market access' are also problematic. If we take restriction on market access as meaning impossibility to sell in the host state market, then clearly the test is too narrow. If, on the other hand, we take it as meaning making sales more difficult in the host market, the test looks as vacuous as the *Dassonville* formula as it is capable of covering virtually any kind of regulation. The conceptual emptiness of the market access test is implicitly recognised by the more sophisticated of its advocates, such as Weatherill[107] or Advocate-General Jacobs,[108] who feel compelled to qualify it by requiring a *substantial* hindrance or barrier to market access, where the job of delineating the scope of Article 28 EC rests entirely on the test of intensity or remoteness implied in the notion of a substantial hindrance, rather than in the notion of a hindrance to market access itself. There is, of course, nothing objectionable in using the language of market access *per se*. It is a rather nice form of words, like the *Dassonville* formula in its day. However, we should accept it for what it is, viz. a discursive technique or rhetorical device whose conceptual content verges on nil and which is incapable of providing any meaningful guidance on the problem of legitimate regulation in the internal market or the scope of free movement law.

Tempting though it may be, the search for yet another set of words to act as the perfect definition of a measure having an equivalent effect or the ultimate test for the scope of Article 28 EC or the other internal market freedoms, is unlikely to prove very fruitful. The strength of *Cassis* lay precisely in putting the emphasis on the structure of regulation in the internal market rather than searching for a dogmatic definition of a measure having equivalent effect. *Keck* and the post-Keck case law show that the full potential of *Cassis* in this respect has still not yet been fully explored. Such exploration could provide rather more useful pointers for the interpretation of the treaty provisions on internal market freedoms than the search for that elusive formula to define the scope of Article 28 EC.

Conclusion: Beyond the Internal Market: *Cassis* and International Trade

In conclusion, I would like to return to Weiler's classic paper on the Constitution of the Common Market Place.[109] For Weiler, the next phase in the evolution of this Constitution, the 'fifth generation', would be one of convergence between the international trade regime

[105] It is beyond the scope of this contribution to discuss why *Keck* should be seen as a home country control case. On this issue, see N Bernard, *Multilevel Governance in the European Union* (London and The Hague, Kluwer Law International, 2002), 24 *ff.*

[106] See Case 15/79 *Groenveld* [1979] ECR 3409.

[107] S Weatherill, 'After *Keck*: Some thoughts on how to clarify the clarification' (1996) 33 *CML Rev* 885.

[108] See, in particular, his Opinion in Case 412/93 *Leclerc-Siplec* [1995] ECR I-179.

[109] Above note 78.

of GATT and that of the European internal market. That such a convergence can be identified, as an empirical matter, is plain. How far that convergence should be taken, as a normative matter, is a different question. Weiler makes much of a number of similarities between the WTO regime and the EC Treaty, notably the parallel that can be established between Article XI of GATT and Article 28 EC or the development in the WTO context of various tools providing a partial functional equivalent to the harmonisation provisions of Articles 94 and 95 EC.

In this Chapter, I have insisted on the importance of the context in which provisions are situated for their interpretation and contrasted, in this respect, the judgment of the Court in *Cassis de Dijon*, which focused on the issues raised by the process of constructing an internal market from problematic interpretations based on a decontextualised *Dassonville* formula. The same is, of course, true of the WTO regime. From this perspective, there is a world of difference between, on the one hand, establishing a worldwide fair trade regime between sovereign nations with vastly different social, economic and political conditions and, on the other, developing a single market among a relatively homogenous group of countries as part of a project of political integration for which the Member States have, 'albeit within limited fields', agreed to limit their sovereign rights. Despite a fairly dense institutional network for the communication of economic, social and political preferences, the EU is constantly confronted with legitimation difficulties. We should proceed with caution lest we overload an international system with demands that far outstrip its legitimation capabilities.

4

An Outsider's View of *Dassonville* and *Cassis de Dijon*: On Interpretation and Policy

DONALD H REGAN*

My interest in the EC law on free movement of goods is long-standing and more than casual, but much less than scholarly. So I am delighted to contribute some remarks without pretending to expertise.

On Interpretation

Dassonville purports to interpret the Treaty of Rome. As interpretation, it has always seemed to me obtuse, or tendentious—or both—whether the Treaty is viewed as a treaty or as a constitution. The Court could have saved itself a lot of grief, and the volte-face of *Keck and Mithouard*, with a more thoughtful analysis at the start.

In *Dassonville*, the Court simply announces that all measures that have any tendency to reduce imports are 'measures having equivalent effect' to quantitative restrictions.[110] The implicit argument seems to be: 'Quantitative restrictions reduce imports. Therefore any sort of measure that reduces imports has "equivalent effect".' This is a bad argument. There are many ways to describe the effects of traditional quantitative restrictions (embargoes and quotas). They do reduce imports. More particularly, they reduce imports without reducing domestic production or sales. More particularly still, they reduce imports, without reducing domestic production or sales, and their form is such as to ground a (rebuttable) presumption that they are not justified by any positive effects they may have on domestic non-economic values. We now have three descriptions of quantitative restrictions in terms of their effects. Which should the Court choose? The third, the most complete. The Court is going to condemn (presumptively) any measure whose effects fall within its chosen description of quantitative restrictions. So the description it chooses should be complete enough to explain why quantitative restrictions *themselves* are condemned (presumptively). The description the Court chooses in *Dassonville* fails this test. Only the third description passes this test. And even though it covers many fewer

[110] *Procureur du Roi v Dassonville* (Case 8/74) [1974] ECR 837, para 5. I ignore para 6, as many others have, including the Court. Even if para 6 tempers the rule of para 5 by saying that 'reasonable' measures will be allowed, that does nothing to limit the extraordinary range of measures that para 5 says courts will review for reasonableness.

measures than *Dassonville*, the third description still encompasses not only border measures other than core quantitative restrictions (which Articles 31 and 32 of the Treaty of Rome, now repealed, suggest were probably the main thing the drafters were thinking about), but also facially discriminatory internal measures (which they may have been thinking about, with GATT Article III in mind), and arguably even the sort of facially neutral measures on products/packaging/labeling covered by *Cassis de Dijon*.

In defence of *Dassonville*, one might argue that *Dassonville* and *Keck* were both right when they were decided, at least as policy, since the Single European Act intervened, creating a more effective legislator. But my argument below suggests that *Dassonville* was bad policy as well as bad interpretation, even when it was decided.[111] Alternatively, one might argue that it was necessary for the Court to state an extreme view in *Dassonville*, even if it would prove untenable in the long run, in order to get the attention of national regulators and also of private enterprises, who needed encouragement to challenge trade-reducing regulation (they certainly took the bait!).[112] But just announcing the narrower rule of *Cassis de Dijon* in 1974 would have got regulators' attention and encouraged private challenges, and it would have been much more defensible as interpretation, as well as maintainable over time.[113]

In the next paragraph I shall explain why the result in *Cassis* is more defensible than *Dassonville* as a reading of Article 28(30). But even if the result in *Cassis* is more defensible, the opinion is still very disappointing. The crucial paragraph 8 begins by saying that in the absence of harmonisation, 'it is for the Member States to regulate all matters relating to' alcohol, and 'obstacles to movement within the Community resulting from disparities between the national laws [on marketing alcohol] must be accepted,' . . . and then it takes it back, saying regulations are acceptable only if the Court approves their goal and confirms their necessity.[114] The Court offers no explanation of how such broad powers of review flow from Article 28(30). It offers only an *ipse dixit* cloaked in rhetorical prevarication.

How might one argue that the regulations covered by *Cassis*, when they exclude foreign goods, should be presumed on the basis of their form to be unjustified (thus making them 'equivalent' to quantitative restrictions)? The argument has to be cobbled together from claims that are partly explicit and partly only implicit in the Court's discussion after paragraph 8. The argument is that if goods are allowed to be marketed in one Member State, then they are unlikely to present any serious problems with health, or safety, or the like, and any other problems about consumer awareness that arise if the goods are marketed in another Member State can be dealt with by labelling. So we can presume that

[111] See especially note 131 below.

[112] The point about the need to encourage private parties to challenge regulation was suggested to me by Miguel Maduro.

[113] Just a few years before *Dassonville*, the United States Supreme Court announced an equally broad constitutional rule without the backing of any constitutional provision that explicitly limits state powers of economic regulation: *Pike v Bruce Church, Inc*, 397 US 137 (1970). But the *Pike* test was offered as a summary of more than a century of cases, and the old cases that established the 'dormant commerce clause' were arguably better grounded in the interpretive tradition of their day than *Dassonville* in 1974. In any event, by 1970 the Supreme Court's practice was much narrower than what *Pike* described, and it had been for decades, and it continued so after *Pike*. D Regan, 'The Supreme Court and State Protectionism: Making Sense of the Dormant Commerce Clause' (1986) 84 *Michigan Law Review* 1091–1287.

[114] *Rewe-Zentrale AG v Bundesmonopolverwaltung für Branntwein (Cassis de Dijon)* (Case 120/78) [1979] ECR 649, para 8.

a flat exclusion from the other Member State is not justified; it is unnecessarily restrictive. I do not find this wholly convincing. I wonder whether the Member States are sufficiently homogeneous in their risk-preferences about health, safety, and the environment so that a presumption of equivalence is justified. In addition, I think the Court may be too cavalier in its argument about labelling. The Court ignores the fact that consumers often do not read labels, and the equally important fact that if they did study the labels of everything they buy, this could become a serious inconvenience.[115] The Court favours German consumers who want more choice, at the expense of others who want less choice and easier shopping. Normally, it is the province of the German government to say which group should prevail.[116]

Commentators often defend *Cassis* by arguments about 'double burdens' or discriminatory effect. The Court does not make these arguments, and rightly not. The Court recognises that low-alcohol cassis and high-alcohol cassis are genuinely different products (although it thinks any problem caused by the difference can be dealt with by labelling), and it appears to recognise implicitly that when the products are different, then the mere fact that some regulation affects them differently does not make that regulation discriminatory in any objectionable sense. To ground the claim that different treatment amounts to discrimination, we must argue that the products are in relevant respects the same. One way to do this is by finding protectionist purpose, which reveals that the regulating country itself sees no genuine regulatory distinction.[117] Alternatively, it can be done directly by establishing (or asserting empirical grounds for presuming) that the foreign product is equivalent to the local product in respect of the regulatory concern. But notice that if the foreign product is equivalent, then a regulation that excludes it is more restrictive than necessary, and this is a completely sufficient objection to the regulation, without regard to whether the regulation has discriminatory effect. So in the end, discriminatory effect plays no role (as the *Cassis* Court seems to have recognised), except as evidence that would be relevant to an inquiry into regulatory purpose.[118]

One final point. To this outsider, it seems the Community institutions have made a fetish of the idea that a product marketed anywhere in the Community ought to be marketable everywhere. In its Communication concerning *Cassis*, the Commission appears to say that it will proceed against national regulations that are illegal under *Cassis*,

[115] For an excellent discussion, see H-C von Heydebrand u.d. Lasa, 'Free Movement of Foodstuffs, Consumer Protection and Food Standards in the European Community: Has the Court of Justice Got It Wrong?' (1991) 16 *EL Rev* 391–415.

[116] But don't we need the Court to protect French producer interests, the reader may ask. I shall explain why, counterintuitively, only German interests need be considered—but why the Court *might* still be right to intervene.

[117] Many people dislike purpose review. Some would say 'equivalent effect' in Article 28(30) was designed to exclude purpose review, although I doubt that. But the text makes it clear that considering purpose is an essential aspect of an 'effects' review that extends to discriminatory effect from facially neutral measures. See also note 122 below.

[118] Under the *Cassis* approach, it may seem that discriminatory effect does play a role; it may seem that we are inferring unnecessary restrictiveness from discriminatory effect, since we are inferring unnecessary restrictiveness from the fact that goods that are allowed to be sold abroad (which our suggested justification for *Cassis* presumes on empirical grounds to be equivalent) are being excluded, and that sounds like discrimination. But there is not necessarily any discrimination, even in effect; it might be that other foreign goods are still admitted, and that local producers who would like to produce to the foreign standard are being prevented, and that there is no net effect on foreign versus domestic market shares. All that matters is the presumption of equivalence (that is, the presumption that the foreign good satisfies the domestic regulatory concern) based on the fact that the goods are allowed abroad. No proposition about comparative treatment plays any essential role.

and that where national regulations are legal under *Cassis* but still exclude goods from another Member State, this problem must be dealt with by harmonisation.[119] But what is the problem harmonisation solves, unless it is assumed that the totally unimpeded circulation of every product marketed anywhere in the Community is more important than allowing different Members to have *justifiably* different standards? If the 'single market' requires such totally unimpeded circulation, we should not want a fully perfected single market.[120]

On Policy

In his famous opinion in *Leclerc-Siplec*, Advocate General Jacobs says 'the central concern of the Treaty provisions on the free movement of goods is to prevent unjustified obstacles to trade between Member States'.[121] Taking this as a starting point for analysis, the next question is, what does 'justification' mean here, and what should it mean? I shall develop a thesis about what it should mean, but let me start with a specific question about what it does mean that has long puzzled me: what is the role of 'proportionality' in EC free movement doctrine?

Abstract discussions of 'proportionality' in EU law always describe a three-part test: (1) Does the regulation contribute to the achievement of some legitimate purpose?[122] (2) Is there is any alternative way to achieve the purpose to the same degree with less damage to whatever Community value(s) the regulation threatens? (3) Even if the regulation is the least-damaging way to achieve whatever it achieves, is it worth it? Does the national benefit outweigh the damage to the relevant Community value(s)?[123] Now, it is clear that in some areas of EU law, all three questions get considered. What is not clear to me is the role of the third question, sometimes referred to as 'proportionality in the strict sense', in the law of free movement of goods. In many free movement cases, a 'proportionality' test is stated explicitly, but only the first two questions are mentioned; and yet there are some cases that seem hard to explain except by reference to the third question.[124] Many sources seem thoroughly ambivalent. Consider the following paragraph from *Stoke-on-Trent*:

[119] *Commission Communication*, 3 October 1980 [1980] OJ C256/2; and see Craig and De Búrca, *EU Law: Text, Cases, and Materials* (Oxford, Oxford University Press, 1998) 639.

[120] The United States, often mentioned as a model, is not a single market in this sense. Incidentally, on economies of scale, see note 141 below.

[121] *Société d'Importation Edouard Leclerc-Siplec v TFI Publicité & M6 Publicité* (Case C-412/93) [1995] ECR I-179 at I-194.

[122] Note that this question requires ascertaining the regulator's actual purpose, unless we are prepared to justify a regulation by reference to a purpose that is asserted hypocritically. I should also mention *Cassis*'s second major innovation, 'mandatory requirements'. Some such tinkering with the Treaty text is unavoidable once we expand Article 28(30) beyond border measures and facially discriminatory internal measures, but it follows from the argument in the rest of this essay that the Court should have offered a negative list of illegitimate purposes rather than embarking on a positive listing of approved purposes. In practice, it may not have made any difference.

[123] Eg G de Búrca, 'The Principle of Proportionality and Its Application in EC Law' (1994) *Yearbook of European Law 1993*, 105–50, 113; F Jacobs, 'Recent Developments in the Principle of Proportionality in European Community Law' in E Ellis (ed), *The Principle of Proportionality in the Laws of Europe* (Oxford, Hart Publishing, 1999), 1–21 at 1.

[124] Eg, the holding on non-approved bottles in *Commission v Denmark* (Case 302/86) [1988] ECR 4607.

> Appraising the proportionality of national rules which pursue a legitimate aim under Community law involves weighing the national interest in attaining that aim against the Community interest in ensuring the free movement of goods. In that regard, in order to verify that the restrictive effects on intra-Community trade of the rules at issue do not exceed what is necessary to achieve the aim in view, it must be considered whether those effects are direct, indirect or purely speculative and whether those effects do not impede the marketing of imported products more than the marketing of national products.[125]

The metaphor of 'weighing' in the first sentence suggests a comparison of the value or importance of the national benefit with the value or importance of the Community cost, a comparison required only in connection with proportionality in the strict sense.[126] And yet, the second sentence of the quoted paragraph, with its focus on what is 'necessary' to achieve the aim, seems to contemplate only the second question and its less-restrictive-alternative inquiry.

If it is unclear whether courts actually ask the third question in movement-of-goods cases, *should* they ask it? Here the answer is clear. There is no need to worry about proportionality in the strict sense, no need to balance national interests against foreign interests. (So those movement of goods cases that do not ask the third question have got the theory right.) The reason is that, in the present context, regulation that optimises over all affected domestic interests (regulation that is 'domestically rational', as I shall say) also optimises over the interests of the Community as a whole (it is 'globally efficient'). In a nutshell: *domestically rational regulation is globally efficient.*[127]

I shall explain in a moment why the thesis just stated is true. Let me first explain why it is important, including why it makes the test of proportionality in the strict sense unnecessary.[128] First, the thesis entails that even if the goal of Article 28(30) is to eliminate national regulation that is economically inefficient from the *Community* perspective, it suffices to eliminate regulation that is *irrational from the point of view of the enacting country.*[129] Since foreign interests as such do not figure into the definition of the national interest, or of domestic rationality, there is simply no need for courts to attend to foreign interests. In particular, there is no need to balance foreign harms against local benefits under 'proportionality in the strict sense'. Notice that this argument does *not* undercut the 'less restrictive alternative' test. We often speak as if the point of that test is to prevent unnecessary harm to foreign interests, but in fact unnecessarily trade-restrictive measures

[125] *Stoke-on-Trent CC v B & Q plc* (Case C-169/91) [1992] ECR I-6635, para 15.

[126] A less-restrictive-alternative inquiry involves no comparison between benefit and cost, but only a comparison of the costs of different measures that would achieve the benefit. See D Regan, 'The Meaning of "Necessary" in GATT Article XX and GATS Article XIV: The Myth of Cost-Benefit Balancing' (2007) 6 *World Trade Review*, 3, 347–69.

[127] I am employing here the standard notion of economic efficiency (but remember that efficiency is about satisfying preferences, not just maximising production). The EU has always had non-economic goals as well as economic. But I assume that what the provisions on *free movement of goods* are currently thought to aim at *directly* is economic efficiency. Note that even to the extent we might want to entangle the Members' economies for non-economic reasons, we will achieve most, if not all, of the desirable entanglement if we just eliminate economically inefficient regulation.

[128] For a much fuller discussion of why the thesis is true and important, and of all the topics discussed in the remainder of this essay, see D Regan, 'What Are Trade Agreements For? – Two Conflicting Stories Told by Economists, With a Lesson for Lawyers', (2006) 9 *Journal of International Economic Law* 4, 951–88.

[129] This is true regardless of our definition of the national interest (national welfare), provided we define the national interest the same way when we are thinking about global efficiency as when we are thinking about domestic rationality.

also damage unnecessarily the interests of *locals* who would like to engage in trade but are prevented; such measures are *domestically* irrational.[130]

Second, if the real question about a measure is whether it is domestically rational, we should generally presume that the local political/regulatory process is more likely to make right choices than transnational courts. That is not to say the national institutions are always right. Producer interests tend to have exaggerated political influence, leading to purposeful protectionism, which is normally domestically irrational. The regulatory process may sometimes rely on inadequate science. And so on. The crucial question for the Court then becomes: what kinds of political/regulatory failure (remember, failure with regard to *domestic* interests) can it and the rest of the judicial system recognise sufficiently reliably so that they should intervene? And how should the intervention be structured so as to interfere as little as possible with desirable national regulation?[131]

I have no space to discuss further what rules are best, except to note that the answer will presumably be specific to the European Communities in some respects. Here are two possible examples. First, Miguel Maduro has argued in defence of *Cassis* that national regulation of products and packaging, even if not motivated by protectionism either historically or in the present maintenance of old laws, has often 'frozen' the market so that consumers are unaware of the potential benefits of access to foreign products. This can be viewed as a sort of malfunction of the political process; consumers are systematically unaware of how laws affect their own interests.[132] This is the best argument I know of for the approach of *Cassis*, and it has special plausibility in the EC context.

Second, I have been told that these days the ECJ often finds a national regulation in violation of Article 28(30) and then leaves it to the referring national court to decide whether there is an exception under Article 30(36) (and that the national courts do not consider proportionality in the strict sense). This is an option that is not available in all systems, and it makes excellent institutional sense once we understand that the real issue is domestic rationality, at least if we trust the national courts. National courts are much better positioned than the ECJ to review national regulation for domestic rationality, perhaps even with a smaller margin of appreciation for the regulator than a transnational court should allow. In effect, the contribution of European law is to identify cases in which the national courts must undertake serious review, whether or not they would do so under national law, and with the Community watching.

So finally, why is it true that domestically rational regulation is globally efficient? The short answer is that if we make a number of reasonable assumptions, this thesis is a mathematical theorem. I cannot offer a formal proof here.[133] I shall offer two quick

[130] There is a mild paradox in my view. I acknowledge that the only reason we have trade agreements is to protect foreign interests, *in the following sense*: there would be no trade agreements if national regulation did not affect foreign interests. But there is no inconsistency between that and my claim that when it comes to ascertaining precisely what national regulations have unjustified (inefficient) foreign effects and should be suppressed, it turns out that it is only regulations that are domestically irrational. So the *test* for justification can ignore foreign interests.

[131] Incidentally, since there is no need to balance or reconcile foreign interests with domestic, the existence or non-existence of an effective transnational legislature makes less difference than one might initially assume to what the Court should do.

[132] Personal conversation, and see M Maduro, 'Market Integration Through Law—The Law of Free Movement in the EU and the US' in D Halberstam and M Maduro (eds), *People, Power, and Politics: Comparing Constitutionalism in the EU and US* (Cambridge, Cambridge University Press, forthcoming).

[133] The basic theorem, in the tariff context, and stated in different terms, is proved in Kyle Bagwell and Robert W Staiger, 'An Economic Theory of GATT' (1999) 89 *American Economic Review* 1, 215–48 at 222–3.

intuitive explanations. But first I need to introduce the two assumptions that are most critical to an intuitive understanding. First, it must be true (as it is in the movement of goods context) that the foreign effects of any challenged regulation are all mediated by the grant or denial of market opportunities.[134] My thesis has no application to environmental law, for example, where our concern is with *physical* cross-border effects of national regulation or non-regulation.[135] Nor does it apply when a regulation is challenged on individual rights principles, where the issue is not efficiency or cross-border effects at all.

Second, I assume countries do not purposefully exploit their market power vis-à-vis other countries. What do I mean by 'exploiting market power'? Roughly speaking, I mean adopting a regulation in part *for the reason* that some of the cost of achieving the regulation's domestic benefits will be borne by foreign interests. I emphasise that whether there is market power exploitation in this sense depends on the *motivation* for the regulation. Almost anything a large country does will have effects abroad; often it will impose costs abroad. But the mere fact of harmful *effects* abroad gives us no reason at all to think the regulation is inefficient (even globally, from the point of view of the world as a whole), if it is not *motivated* to any extent by the fact that some of the costs are borne by foreigners. In the absence of exploitive motivation (which can be formally modelled by various assumptions about the regulator's objective function), regulation that is rational from the point of view of domestic national welfare is also globally efficient. That is what our theorem tells us.[136] Many readers may find it counterintuitive that motivation is so central for determining whether a measure is or is not globally efficient. But it is.[137]

Let us have some examples. The *locus classicus* for thinking about exploitation of market power is the tariff. A traditional 'optimum tariff' is exploitive in our sense. It uses market power to drive down the price foreign producers can charge for their exports. It is a tax on imports that is imposed *precisely because* part of the revenue raised by the tax comes ultimately from foreign producers. In contrast, a tariff motivated solely by protectionism (that is, by the desire to improve the lot of domestic import-competing producers), is not exploitive in our sense. It may be natural to think of the protectionist tariff as an attempt to help domestic producers at the expense of foreign producers, but in fact, the harm to foreign producers is no part of what is aimed at, neither as the ultimate goal nor even as a necessary means. That becomes clear if we remember that even a country with no market power can pursue a policy of protectionism. Since a tariff adopted by a country with no market power has no effect outside that country, the goal of protectionism must be understandable in purely domestic terms (most naturally as securing some target price for domestic producers). Hence even when there *is* market power and harm to foreign

[134] With regard to the other three of the 'four freedoms', the thesis does not apply to cases on the movement of persons; it will apply to some services cases and capital cases and not to others. The issue is always the nature of the cross-border effects.

[135] But notice that cases like the Danish bottle cases, which are 'environmental' cases in some general sense, *are* covered by the thesis: Denmark's regulation, which was the subject of the challenge, affected other countries only by the grant or denial of market access.

[136] As noted above (note 129), the theorem is true on any definition of national welfare, so long as we define national welfare the same way when we ask about domestic rationality and about global efficiency: if the regulation is domestically rational, it is globally efficient. Of course, how we define national welfare will matter greatly to whether the antecedent in the conditional statement just presented is true (and thus to whether the consequent is true as well); but that is another matter.

[137] The reader may think that motivation cannot matter ultimately, because efficiency is about effects. Well, yes and no. Efficiency is about satisfying preferences; so it is about effects *as they are valued*. Motivation is central because (rational) regulatory purpose reflects social valuation.

producers, the foreign harm from a protectionist tariff is merely incidental to the protectionist project. And what our theorem tells us is that while an exploitive 'optimum tariff' is both domestically rational and globally inefficient, a tariff motivated solely by protectionism cannot be both domestically rational and globally inefficient (even if the country has market power). The protectionist tariff can be domestically rational or not;[138] it can be globally efficient or not; but the two dimensions are logically linked. If it is domestically rational, it is also globally efficient.

So much for market power exploitation in the tariff context. What is market power exploitation in the context of setting facially neutral product standards, which is our main concern in this Chapter? In this context, a country exploits market power when it sets an inefficiently high standard *precisely because* some of the cost of securing the domestic benefit from the standard will be borne by foreign producers.[139] Such a policy will be domestically rational but globally inefficient. But if the regulator does not think about whether producers are local or foreign – if it just tries to set an efficient standard – then there is no market power exploitation. Even though the standard imposes costs on foreign producers, regulation that is domestically rational will be globally efficient. It is an empirical question, of course, whether countries engage in market power exploitation in general, and whether they engage in it in the specific context of setting product standards. My own view is that there is very little empirical evidence of market power exploitation in any context, even tariff-setting, and even less in the context of setting product standards.[140] This much we can say with certainty: a regulation that has the effect of excluding foreign producers from the domestic market entirely, which is the situation in many or most cases in the *Cassis* line, *cannot* be market power exploitation. No domestic benefit from the higher standard is being secured at foreign producers' expense if foreign producers do not bother to meet the standard at all.[141]

Now finally, the two intuitive explanations for the thesis (not competing explanations, just different approaches): (1) If countries do not purposefully exploit market power as importers, then domestically rational regulation will be designed to correct market failures

[138] The reader may remember from some introduction to international economics that protectionism is domestically irrational. This claim depends on taking a particular perspective on national welfare. In some trade models, protectionism is viewed as domestically rational (hence globally efficient, hence not something a trade agreement should try to suppress). Lest the reader doubt, my own view is that protectionism is generally domestically irrational (and globally inefficient), and that suppressing protectionism is the principal task of judicial review in this area.

[139] An inefficiently high standard is a standard whose cost to producers (wherever located) is greater than the benefit to the consumers or the victims of an externality. Notice incidentally that an 'inefficiently high standard' is *not* the same thing as 'a higher standard than would be set if all producers were domestic'. If all producers are domestic, the excessive political influence of producer groups is likely to lead to an inefficiently *low* standard. Ironically, some of the producers' being foreign, and having less political influence, may be just what is needed to achieve an *efficient* standard. But that is not market power exploitation.

[140] My view contradicts a central assumption of the standard formal theory of trade agreements; but I have argued elsewhere that the standard assumption is based more on the needs of the standard model than on empirical evidence. See Regan, 'What Are Trade Agreements For?', note 128 above, at 969–82.

[141] The other assumptions that make my thesis a theorem (aside from purely technical mathematical assumptions) are competitive domestic markets and constant returns to scale. These assumptions are idealisations, but they are standard in much of trade theory. More importantly, it seems particularly undesirable for courts to try to decide case-by-case how the results in movement-of-goods cases should reflect imperfect competition or possible economies of scale. Economies of scale are mentioned so often as a reason for wanting a single market that I should point out that substantial economies of scale will be made possible (probably all or almost all of what is desirable), if we merely eliminate national regulation that is inefficient even without regard to scale economies. We do not need courts to think about scale economies in order to achieve them.

in the domestic economy (including consumers' ignoring domestic externalities imposed by goods they buy from abroad). Such regulation guarantees that the national demand curve for imports correctly reflects all affected domestic interests. If the exporting country's (non-exploitive) supply curve similarly reflects all interests in that country, then, given that there are no physical cross-border externalities, the international price mechanism will generate an efficient result, just as it does in a competitive domestic market. (2) Alternatively: foreign producers are not harmed by a regulation unless there are domestic consumers who would deal with them but are prevented from doing so. But if there are such consumers, they are also harmed by the regulation. So domestic consumers will end up representing the foreign producers in the domestic political process (effectively or not, according to how well they represent themselves). I am not saying the interests of the consumers and the producers are identical. The interests are distinct, and if there is inefficient regulation, the total loss is the sum of the losses to consumers and producers. Still, absent market power exploitation, there can be no inefficiency-based loss to foreign producers without corresponding inefficiency-based loss to domestic consumers. Hence, if we eliminate the inefficiency-based loss to domestic consumers, we necessarily eliminate the inefficiency-based loss to foreign producers as well (not *all* the loss from regulation, but the inefficiency-based loss). In other words, domestically rational regulation is globally efficient.

In formulating movement-of-goods doctrine, the Court should be asking how courts can best restrain national regulation that is domestically irrational, while allowing regulation that is domestically rational. How well the Court is doing I leave it to EU scholars to say.

XII

Case C-415/93, *Union Royale Belge des Sociétés de Football Association ASBL v Jean-Marc Bosman, Royal Club Liégeois SA v Jean-Marc Bosman and Others* and *Union des Associations Européennes de Football (UEFA) v Jean-Marc Bosman*

1

The Development of the Law and the Practice in the post-*Bosman* Era

MARKO ILEŠIČ [1]

It was more than 10 years ago when my late brother published a legal analysis of the famous *Bosman* judgment[2] of the Court of Justice of the European Communities (ECJ). He stated that hardly any of the thousands of decisions taken by the judges of the ECJ in Luxembourg had achieved such broad popularity.[3]

The reasons for his conclusions were mainly two:

(1) it interfered with the well-established rules of the sports organisations concerning indemnities by the transfers of professional athletes and nationality quotas;
(2) it terminated the discussion on the thesis that autonomous sports rules escape from the scope of the general principles of law.[4]

The ECJ obviously entered into a highly sensitive area and we should not underestimate the decision's influence—not only on the sport's regulations. We should be aware, namely, that the *Bosman* ruling did not affect only sporting matters, as is usually understood. It dealt also with several other legal issues, from human rights to social questions, tax problems, etc.

After a decade had passed, it may be of some interest to rethink—from a certain historical distance—the importance of this courageous decision and to try to establish the contribution it brought—if any—for the development of the Community law and for legal relations in the field of sport.

I must stress that it is not my intention to enter deep into all possible consequences and impacts of the judgment. I would primarily like to verify whether the repercussions of ' the case' really met the expectations. This brief contribution is not intended, naturally, to

[1] Judge at the Court of Justice of the European Communities, Luxembourg, former Professor and Dean of the Faculty of law, University of Ljubljana, Slovenia, former member of different bodies of the Football Associations of Yugoslavia and Slovenia, of UEFA (Union of European Football Association) and of FIFA (Fédération Internationale de Football Association), as well as the Olympic Committee of Slovenia and EOC (European Olympic Committees). The statements in this contribution do not, of course, necessarily reflect the opinion of any of the above-mentioned institutions.

[2] Case C-415/93, 15.12.1995, *Union Royale Belge des Sociétés de Football Association and others v Bosman* (1995) ECR I-4291.

[3] There should be at least 5,000 references to be found on the website (see R Strunz: *Der Fall Bosman: Bilanz und neue Fragen* (Munich) ZEuP, 2005) 341). And we can take it for sure that there are more commentaries on it, in less expanded languages and lesser known publications.

[4] Ilešič, Mirko, Pravo Evropske skupnosti in položaj poklicnih športnikov—analiza primera 'Bosman' (The Law of the European Community and the status of Professional Athletes—an Analysis of the *Bosman* case). The article was published in Slovenian in the Ljubljana review (1997) 379 *Pravna praksa* (*Legal Practice*) 15 *ff.*

present any global view on the legal issues contained in the judgment, but mainly to try to respond to the questions of what would the EU law have been without it and whether the forecasts of its message have been fulfilled.

The abundant doctrine predicted, sometimes, very dramatic follow-ups of the Court's decision, especially in the field of football, but also in other sporting activities. There had, for example, existed a fear ... 'that many professional clubs will no longer exist in 20 years' time'—what was even called a 'Doomsday scenario'.[5] It looks now as if it did not happen, at least not in that tragic way.

Bosman itself was not a complete revolution. The doubts of the legal correctness of professional sporting contracts were expressed well before and also treated in case law in the United Kingdom[6] and, as well known, in the European Community.[7]

Bosman case law was followed, *mutatis mutandis*, in the subsequent decisions of the ECJ, namely in *Deliège*,[8] *Lehtonen*,[9] *Kolpak*,[10] and *Simutenkov*.[11] In the last two, the Court expanded the *Bosman* nationality quota rule to the citizens of non-Member States, that is, of Slovakia (not yet a member at the time, but associated and thus 'on the way' to the EC) and Russia (linked to the EC by a partnership agreement). This broadening of the idea of *Bosman* has not been accepted with enthusiasm by everybody.[12] The fear also appeared that the same rule could apply also to the citizens of some 77 countries from Africa, the Caribbean and the Pacific, on the basis of the ACP agreement from 2000 (the so-called Cotonou agreement).[13] This is not excluded, but it would be necessary to examine whether the Cotonou agreement finds itself in the same context (not only wording) as the ECJ found in the case of the Russian one where it did not apply automatically the same approach as in the Kolpak case, but looked (and not found, eventually) for possible distinguishing elements.

It seems, however, that the epected development in the direction of full implementation of the Community law in the field of sports has reached its highest point—which is, probably, not the summit, which will hardly ever be conquered. *Bosman* showed clearly that Community rules prevail over sporting ones as to situations of an economic nature, but that they (including the rules on the free movement of persons and services) are not in conflict with practices related to cases of non-economic interest, but of a purely sporting nature, with purely competitive content.[14]

[5] McArdle D, *From Boot Money to Bosman: Football, Society and the Law* (London, Sydney, Cavendish Publishing, 2000) 13.

[6] See cases quoted by McArdle, 19 *ff*: the oldest one seems to be *Kingaby-Aston Villa* from 1912.

[7] Cases *Walrave and Koch* (1975) and *Dona v Mantero* (1976) are somehow precedents of *Bosman*.

[8] C-51/96 and C-191/97.

[9] C-176/96.

[10] C-438/00.

[11] C-265/03.

[12] Cf, eg, Hamernik P, Rozsudek Europského soudního dvora Simutenkov—definitivní konec cizineckých kvót ve sportu v EU? (The Judgment of the European Court of Justice Simutenkov—the Final End of the Foreigners' Quotas in the Sport in the EU?), published in Czech in the review (2005) 21 *Pravni rozhledy*. See especially the quotations at 798.

[13] Fritzweiler *et al*, *Praxishandbuch Sportrecht* (Munich, Beck, 2007) 622.

[14] Panagiotopulos D, *Sports Law, A European Dimension* (Athens, Komotini, 2003), 67.

Yet it is possible to conclude that the ECJ made further steps from *Bosman* onwards. In the recent cases of *Piau*[15] and *Meca-Medina*[16] it expanded the applicability of the Community competition law to sporting activities. It held, however, that sporting[17] exceptions were justified.

In spite of the fact that several football and sports bodies did not, at the time, really like *Bosman*, and even did not hesitate to express their non-satisfaction publicly, they however respected the judgment and modified their rules. There has also been a fruitful co-operation between them and the EU institutions in the following years and new transfer regulations of FIFA have been implemented recently.[18]

The last development in looking for an appropriate way to conciliate the remaining different opinions (finally) happened in the last two years. In 2006, a publication called 'Independent European Sport Review 2006' appeared. As its main author, José Luis Arnaut, emphasised in his foreword, this text is taking into account the thoughts and feedback received from the Sports Ministers who met in Brussels on 19 September 2006 to consider the finding contained in the analysis. And he continues with the last remark, namely that the ECJ ruling in the *Meca-Medina* case has only added to the urgency of the task.[19] The book includes different aspects of the 'European Sports Model', it comments on the case law of the ECJ and the European Commission's opinions, as well as the UEFA and FIFA views. The *Bosman* message remains the leading authority as to the international transfer system, but it (the system) 'was re-modelled in accordance with a set of principles agreed between the European Commission and FIFA in 2001'.[20]

The logical continuation of this movement was the presentation by the Commission of the White Paper on Sports in June 2007 and the new rule on the role of sports in the EU in the Lisbon Treaty from December 2007.

This short survey of the direct and indirect implication of the *Bosman* judgment clearly shows that it had a major impact on the sports regulations, especially those concerning the legal status of athletes, including their contractual relations with clubs and their freedom to move. On the other hand, the feeling that the case should mean the end of the endeavours to achieve the goal of absolute legal autonomy of sports or its absolute surrender in relationship to European law, has not been realised. The long discussion, including some negotiations, too, and a relatively coherent interpretation of the affected questions by the ECJ, succeeded in a compromise which respects both fundamental principles of the European law and the inherent values of sports activities. Fair play, indeed!

[15] C-171/05P.

[16] C-519/04P.

[17] It is under discussion whether the exception was really a sporting one, because the ECJ based it on the (non-sporting) jurisprudence *Wouters*. See comments of Wathelet M (former judge at the ECJ!) in (2006) 41 *Jurisprudence de Liège, Mons et Bruxelles* 1808–09.

[18] It would take too much space to present the whole story of negotiations and its happy ending (hopefully). See, eg, Fritzweiler, 625 *ff*; Gardiner *et al*, *Sports Law* 3rd edn, (London, Cavendish Publishing, 2006), 511 *ff*.

[19] At 14.

[20] At 38.

2

Bosman Changed Everything: The Rise of EC Sports Law

STEPHEN WEATHERILL

Before *Bosman*

When, in *Walrave and Koch v Union Cycliste Internationale*, the first case involving sport to reach the European Court,[21] the Court stated that the practice of sport is subject to Community law 'in so far as it constitutes an economic activity within the meaning of Article 2 of the Treaty' it was impossible to avoid a *frisson* of intellectual excitement. Sport was not—is not—an explicit legislative competence of the EC, yet the functionally broad ambit of the Treaty's economic law provisions wash over jurisdictionally distant shores—including those of sports federations. Enticing questions loom. How does one determine whether a particular sporting practice falls within the scope of the Treaty? And if it does, how does its compatibility with the Treaty fall to be assessed, given the absence of any explicit articulation of the intended relationship between EC trade law and sport? What innovative thinking is being demanded of the institutions of the EU?

Two years later the Court confirmed its approach in *Donà v Mantero*.[22] But could there be any practical consequences? Would dispute-settlement in the governance of sport really shift appreciably from its traditional Swiss homes to Luxembourg? *Walrave and Koch* suggested not. True, the European Court decided that sport is not immune from EC law. But sports federations confronted by the threat of litigation have advantages unavailable in many sectors of the economy. It is a major deterrent that a career will probably be over even if the sports federation defeated in the courtroom is willing to welcome its adversary back on to the playing field. In fact it probably won't be. Walrave and Koch themselves declined to press for judgment, apparently in the face of a threat by the defendant sporting body, the UCI, to withdraw their event from the world cycling championship schedule.[23] Even the ban on the participation of all English football clubs in profitable European club competition imposed in the wake of the Heysel Stadium disaster in 1985 stimulated no challenge based on EC law, even though it was probably a disproportionate interference with economic freedoms guaranteed under Community law.[24]

[21] Case 36/74 [1974] ECR 1405.

[22] Case 13/76 [1976] ECR 1333.

[23] H Van Staveren, 18th Colloquy on European Law, *Sport and the Law* (Proceedings published by the Council of Europe, Strasbourg, 1989) 67.

[24] Cf A Evans, 'Freedom of Trade under the Common Law and EC Law: the Case of the Football Bans' (1986) 102 *LQR* 510.

Bosman changed everything.[25]

Since *Bosman*, sports federations have (of course) continued to argue that the law should not intrude on their autonomy. And it is still daunting in practice to choose the path of litigation when the opponent is a sports federation. But *Bosman* set a trend. *Bosman* provided litigants with a legal vocabulary that is apt to put sporting rule makers on the defensive. And the ruling propelled the institutions of the EU onto a course that obliged them to make sense of the intersection between EC law and sport against a forbiddingly barren background in the Treaty. The story of how a 'policy' can be concocted in the EC out of constitutionally unpromising material represents the enduring lesson of *Bosman*. That narrative, which transcends sport alone, infuses this contribution.

Bosman

The essence of the system of which Jean-Marc Bosman fell foul is simply described. Players were unable to exercise contractual freedom to move between clubs. A club was—and is—able to field a player in an official match only once it has secured the player's registration, held by the previous employer. That registration will be released only when the previous club is satisfied with the terms offered by the new club, which has typically involved payment of a fee.

The European Court concluded that the system violated (what is now) Article 39 EC. And the same fate met rules requiring discrimination on the basis of nationality in European club football competition.

The vital point, however, is that the Court did not deny that football possesses unusual characteristics that distinguish it from 'normal' commercial activity. In paragraph 106 of the ruling it declared that:

> In view of the considerable social importance of sporting activities and in particular football in the Community, the aims of maintaining a balance between clubs by preserving a certain degree of equality and uncertainty as to results and of encouraging the recruitment and training of young players must be accepted as legitimate.

Sport *is* special! Most of all, there is an interdependence between teams in a sports league which is not present in the relationship between rivals in a typical marketplace. A monopoly supplier of goods or services is in a position of immense economic power. By contrast there is literally no point to a single football club, deprived of an opponent. Sport assumes rivalry, a degree of balance between the participants and uncertainty as to result.[26]

In *Bosman* the Court's objection was in short that the transfer system did not achieve what was claimed. The rules neither precluded richer clubs buying the best players nor prevented the 'availability of financial resources from being a decisive factor in competitive sport thus considerably altering the balance between clubs'. Moreover, the system was

[25] Case C-415/93 [1995] ECR I-4921.

[26] For economic analysis, see, eg, S Dobson and J Goddard, *The Economics of Football* (Cambridge, Cambridge University Press, 2001); L Buzzacchi, S Szymanski and T Valletti, 'Equality of opportunity and equality of outcome: open leagues, closed leagues and competitive balance' (2003) 3 *Journal of Industry, Competition and Trade* 167.

hit-and-miss, rather than a carefully constructed distributive mechanism. The Court concluded that 'the same aims can be achieved at least as efficiently by other means which do not impede freedom of movement for workers'.[27]

Famously, the consequences of the ruling were that nationality-discrimination in club football had to be eliminated and the transfer system had to be radically amended. EC law did not stipulate what replacement transfer system should be introduced, if any—that would overstep its mandate—but it did require the elimination of existing unlawful practices.[28] Sport was accordingly forced to undergo significant adjustment as a result of the demands of EC law. But this was not because EC law is blind to sport's special concerns, but rather because the Court was unpersuaded that the impugned rules advanced those concerns. Paragraph 106 of the *Bosman* ruling is central to understanding that EC trade law can be and has been converted into a regime which is open to the particular sensitivities of the sector subject to its supervision.

Bosman and the Rise of 'EC Sports Law'

This is the challenge of 'EC sports law'. The Treaty does not help. It does not mention sport. But *ab initio* in *Walrave and Koch*[29] the Court rejected a line of reasoning that would have rigidly separated sports governance from EC law. That would have sheltered a huge range of practices with economic impact from the assumptions of EC law, damaging the achievement of the objectives of the Treaty. But nor did the Court apply EC law to sport as if it were merely a normal industry. Instead a more ambitious, creative and yet realistic approach has been adopted, requiring a significant investment of resources in making sense of the intersection between the demands of EC law and the aspirations of sport. The EU institutions necessarily proceed in an incremental manner. The opportunities to shape a 'policy' are constrained by the constitutional limitations on the matters to which they may pay attention. Article 5(1) stipulates that the EC possesses only the competences attributed to it, and sport is not one. The EC's authority to supervise sporting practices derives from the broad functional reach of the relevant rules of EC trade law (free movement and competition law, most conspicuously), but it is denied any specific legislative competence in the field of sport. Incrementalism is also ensured by the patterns of litigation, which may cause practice to develop according to unexpected, eccentric rhythms. These observations concern most prominently the Court and the Commission, both of whom are responsible for individual decisions applying the law, though the broader policy direction periodically offered by the Council, the European Council and the Parliament may also serve to embroider the tapestry.

This is not a challenge unique to sport. In fact, across a great many areas of EC law, policy and practice, one is confronted by the need to make some sort of sense of a set of laws and practices which are not constitutionally dedicated to dealing with the particular subject matter of concern and which frequently lack detail and sophistication. The Court's

[27] Para 110 of the judgment; and see more fully the Opinion of AG Lenz.

[28] Cf B Dabscheck, 'The Globe at their Feet: FIFA's New Employment Rules' (2004) 7 *Culture, Sport and Society* 69; J-C Drolet, 'Extra Time: Are the New FIFA Transfer Rules Doomed?' [2006] 1–2 *International Sports Law Journal* 66.

[29] Case 36/74 [1974] ECR 1405.

ruling in *ex parte Watts* deals with cross-border provision of medical care, but it encapsulates the Court's approach in a number of fields where EC trade law sweeps far beyond the limits of EC legislative competence:

> ... although Community law does not detract from the power of the Member States to organise their social security systems and decide the level of resources to be allocated to their operation, the achievement of the fundamental freedoms guaranteed by the Treaty nevertheless inevitably requires Member States to make adjustments to those systems. It does not follow that this undermines their sovereign powers in the field.[30]

This has become a standard formula in cases where the achievement of economic integration collides with Member States' powers to act in realms where the Community is not competent to act as a substitute *legislator*. Social security is a common example[31]; taxation is another[32]; and even the maintenance of public order and the safeguarding of internal security have been revealed as matters of national competence that are nevertheless reviewable in so far as their pursuit impedes cross-border trade.[33] Free movement law stops states acting in the absence of justification for chosen practices that impede cross-border trade. The Community cannot go further than this: it cannot set the ground rules for the organisation of social security systems or taxation or for preserving public order, any more than it could in *Bosman* dictate how football should shape its transfer system. Naturally one may argue that the Court is disingenuous when it declares that the achievement of the fundamental freedoms requires an adjustment by the Member States which does not undermine 'their sovereign powers in the field'. EC law radically circumscribes the scope of sovereign state choices. True enough, yet it is submitted that the Court is simply following the logic of the Treaty itself. The Treaty does not place particular sectors of economic activity beyond the reach of its basic rules. To interpret it in a way that manufactured such exclusions would subvert its aim. Accordingly the Court, charged with the mission of ensuring the law established by the Treaty is observed, is correct to interpret the free movement and competition rules in an expansive manner. But those provisions do not automatically outlaw practices. Instead they put them to the test of justification. And it is in that process of justification that the Court is called on to recognise the particular features of each industry.

For sport generally, the story of its subjection to EC law follows this narrative closely, albeit that powers formally in *private* hands are normally under scrutiny. The reach of EC trade law goes beyond the limitations on the EC's *legislative* competence under the Treaty, and this generates a need to develop a 'policy' that is driven by the dictates of trade integration yet is also appropriately sensitive to the particular needs of sport. This approach is embedded in the ruling in *Bosman*.[34] Sport, like other sectors such as environmental policy,[35] labour market regulation,[36] culture,[37] health care,[38] family

[30] Case C-372/04 [2006] ECR I-4325, para 121.

[31] Cf, eg, Case C-512/03 *JEJ Blankaert* [2005] ECR I-7685.

[32] Cf, eg, Case C-446/03 *Marks and Spencer v Halsey* [2005] ECR I-10837.

[33] Case C-265/95 *Commission v France* [1997] ECR I-6959.

[34] Case C-415/93 [1995] ECR I-4921.

[35] See, eg, J Jans and H Vedder, *European Environmental Law* 3rd edn (Groningen, Europa Law Publishing, 2007).

[36] See, eg, J Kenner, *EU Employment Law: From Rome to Amsterdam and Beyond* (Oxford, Hart, 2003), C Barnard, *EC Employment Law* 3rd edn (Oxford, Oxford University Press, 2006).

[37] See R Craufurd Smith (ed), *Culture in European Union Law* (Oxford, Oxford University Press, 2004).

[38] See, eg, T Hervey and J McHale, *Health Law and the European Union* (Cambridge, Cambridge University Press, 2004).

law,[39] consumer protection,[40] private law more generally[41] and even property law,[42] demonstrates how the law of the EC may exercise a wider influence than a formal inspection of the text of the Treaty may lead one to expect, primarily because of the extended reach of the rules governing the building of an integrated, competitive market.

Is there an 'EC policy' to be discerned in such circumstances? Might this suggest a degree of order and systematisation that the EC is constitutionally incapable of delivering? Such questions are common in many areas. EC law and practice 'spills over' to provoke new academic sub-disciplines such as EC environmental law and EC consumer law and so on, as the 'Europeanisation' of many policy sectors that are in explicit terms subject to only a limited interventionist EC competence gathers pace. The EC Treaty does not lend itself to the shaping of a comprehensive policy of the type that one might expect to find in a national setting, but this does not entail that it is flawed, only that it is different. There is every reason to attempt to bring a degree of order and understanding to this complex background of overlapping sources of legal authority, drawing on limited incremental legislative incursion combined with the concrete application of the free movement and competition rules in the Treaty.

Put another way, EC trade law is porous. The EU's institutions have to shape a policy of sorts on all manner of things, even if they suffer under a constitutional disability to claim a general mandate to shape policy in the way that one might expect in a purely national context. Such is the *practice* of attributed competence, guaranteed as a *principle* of EC law by Article 5(1) of the Treaty.

Since *Bosman*

Let us return to paragraph 106 of its *Bosman* ruling, already mentioned above. The Court remarked that:

> In view of the considerable social importance of sporting activities and in particular football in the Community, the aims of maintaining a balance between clubs by preserving a certain degree of equality and uncertainty as to results and of encouraging the recruitment and training of young players must be accepted as legitimate.

The Court, while finding that the particular practices impugned in *Bosman* fell foul of EC law because they did not adequately contribute to these legitimate aims, showed itself receptive to embrace of the special features of sport. One might, of course, dispute the particular choices made by the EC's institutions. But *Bosman* shows that the case law of the Court accommodates a certain vision of the nature and functioning of sport within EC (trade) law.

[39] See, eg, E Caracciolo di Torella and A Masselot, 'Under construction: EU family law' (2004) 29 *EL Rev* 32.

[40] See, eg, S Weatherill, *EU Consumer Law and Policy* (Cheltenham, Elgar, 2005); N Reich and H-W Micklitz, *Europäisches Verbraucherrecht* (Baden-Baden, Nomos, 2003); H Rösler, *Europäisches Konsumentenvertragsrecht* (Munich, CH Beck, 2004).

[41] See, eg, S Grundmann, 'European Contract Law(s) of What Colour?' (2005) 1 ERCL 184; K Riesenhuber, *Europäisches Vertragsrecht* (Gruyter, Berlin, 2003).

[42] See, eg, U Drobnig, HJ Snijders and E-J Zippro (eds), *Divergences of Property Law, an obstacle to the internal market?* (Munich, Sellier European Law Publishers [2006]).

Both the European Court and the Commission have been challenged to refine the contours of the acceptance that 'sport is—to some extent—special', and to elaborate the implications of this nuanced legal test in its application to particular sporting practices.

Deliège concerned selection of individual athletes (*in casu*, judokas) for international competition.[43] Participation was not open. One had to be chosen by the national federation. If one was not chosen, one's economic interests would be damaged. Could EC law be used to attack the selection decision? This was a classic case which brought the basic organisational structure of sport into contact with the economic interests of participants. The Court stated that selection rules 'inevitably have the effect of limiting the number of participants in a tournament' but that 'such a limitation is inherent in the conduct of an international high-level sports event, which necessarily involves certain selection rules or criteria being adopted'.[44] Accordingly the rules did not in themselves constitute a restriction on the freedom to provide services prohibited by Article 49. So a detrimental effect felt by an individual sportsman does not mean that rules are *incompatible* with EC law. The *Deliège* judgment is respectful of sporting autonomy, but according to reasoning which treats EC law and 'internal' sports law as potentially overlapping.

The application of the Treaty competition rules to sport was a matter carefully avoided by the Court in *Bosman* itself. But the Commission has adopted a functionally comparable approach in its application of Article 81 to sport. In *Champions League* it accepted that agreeing fixtures in a league would not be a 'restriction' on competition, but rather a process essential to its effective organisation. However, by contrast, an agreement to sell rights to broadcast matches in common is not essential to the league's functioning, because individual selling by clubs is perfectly possible (though doubtless less convenient and lucrative). So collective selling *is* a restriction on competition within the meaning of Article 81(1) and it damages the economic interests of, in particular, broadcasters denied a market populated by competing individual sellers. So an agreement to sell rights in common can stand only if exempted according to the orthodox criteria set out in Article 81(3).[45] The Commission also took account of sport's peculiar economics in its *ENIC/UEFA* decision,[46] in which it concluded that rules forbidding multiple ownership of football clubs suppressed demand but were indispensable to the maintenance of a credible competition marked by uncertainty as to the outcome of all matches. A competition's basic appeal would be shattered were consumers to suspect the clubs were not true rivals. The principal message here is that sporting practices typically have an economic effect and that accordingly they cannot be sealed off from the expectations of EC law—but within the area of overlap between EC law and 'internal' sports law there is room for recognition of the features of sport which may differ from 'normal' industries.

Meca-Medina and Majcen v Commission, a decision of July 2006,[47] maintains the thematic receptivity to sport's special concerns in the application of EC law. The applicants, professional swimmers who had failed a drug test and been banned for two years, had complained unsuccessfully to the Commission of a violation of the Treaty

[43] Cases C-51/96 and C-191/97 *Deliège v Ligue de Judo* [2000] ECR I-2549.

[44] Para 64 of the judgment.

[45] Dec 2003/778 *Champions League* [2003] OJ L291/25, paras 125–131. Exemption pursuant to Art 81(3) *was* granted on the facts. See S Weatherill, 'The sale of rights to broadcast sporting events under EC law' [2006] 3/4 *The International Sports Law Journal* 3.

[46] COMP 37.806 ENIC/ UEFA, IP/02/942, 27 June 2002.

[47] Case C-519/04 P judgment of 18 July 2006.

competition rules. The CFI rejected an application for annulment.[48] So did the ECJ. But whereas the CFI attempted to insist that anti-doping rules concern exclusively non-economic aspects of sport, designed to preserve 'noble competition',[49] the ECJ instead stated that 'the mere fact that a rule is purely sporting in nature does not have the effect of removing from the scope of the Treaty the person engaging in the activity governed by that rule or the body which has laid it down'.[50] And if the sporting activity in question falls within the scope of the Treaty, the rules which govern that activity must satisfy the requirements of the Treaty 'which, in particular, seek to ensure freedom of movement for workers, freedom of establishment, freedom to provide services, or competition'.[51] A practice may be of a sporting nature—and perhaps even 'purely sporting' in *intent*—but it falls to be tested against the demands of EC trade law where it exerts economic *effects*. But the Court did not abandon its thematically consistent readiness to ensure that sport's special concerns should be carefully and sensitively fed into the analysis. It took the view that the general objective of the rules was to combat doping in order for competitive sport to be conducted on a fair basis; and the adverse effect of penalties on athletes' freedom of action must be considered to be inherent in the anti-doping rules. On the facts the swimmers failed, for they had not shown that the rules concerning the definition of an offence or the severity of the penalties imposed went beyond what was necessary for the organisation of the sport.

In *Meca-Medina* the Court took a broad view of the scope of Community trade law, but having brought sporting rules within the scope of the Treaty it shows itself readily prepared to draw on the importance of matters not explicitly described as 'justifications' in the Treaty in order to permit the continued application of challenged practices which are shown to be necessary to achieve legitimate sporting objectives and/or are inherent in the organisation of sport. That, then, becomes the core of the argument when EC law overlaps with sports governance: can a sport show why prejudicial economic effects must be tolerated in a particular case?[52] As the Court put it in *Meca-Medina*, restrictions imposed by rules adopted by sports federations 'must be limited to what is necessary to ensure the proper conduct of competitive sport'.[53] This is a statement of the *conditional autonomy* of sports federations under EC law. An overlap between EC law and 'internal' sports law is recognised but within that area of overlap, as foreshadowed in *Bosman*, sporting bodies have room to show how and why their rules, even if apparently antagonistic to the free movement and/or competition provisions in the Treaty, are necessary to accommodate their particular concerns—fair play, credible competition, national representative teams, and so on.

[48] Case T-313/02 [2004] ECR II-3291.

[49] Para 49 CFI.

[50] Para 27 ECJ.

[51] Para 28 ECJ.

[52] See S Weatherill, 'Anti-doping revisited—the demise of the rule of "purely sporting interest"?' [2006] *European Competition Law Review* 645; M Wathelet, 'L'arrêt Meca-Medina et Majcen: plus qu'un coup dans l'eau' (2006) 41 *Revue de Jurisprudence de Liège, Mons et Bruxelles* 1799.

[53] Para 47 ECJ.

Stephen Weatherill

Without *Bosman*?

A rich literature explores the concept of EC sports law and policy.[54] It explores *inter alia* how the institutions of the EU seek to piece together a coherent approach to the regulation of sport against a Treaty background which does not elucidate the peculiarities of sport; how diverse public and private actors, at national, European and international level, seek to exploit EC law to achieve their objectives or to keep it at bay in order to protect their privileges; and generally how EC law erodes the self-regulatory paradigm which has for so long been dominant in sports governance.

I believe that the practice of the European Court and Commission reveals a painstaking concern to piece together a sports policy at EU level which combines respect for the special needs of sport with an appreciation for the difficult balance to be struck between the need for a broad interpretation of the scope of EC trade law and the absence of clear guidance in the Treaty about the EC's stance on sport. Without *Bosman*'s bold acceptance that 'sport is special' but also of economic significance the evolution of this policy would have been less successful and less illuminating.

[54] Eg R Parrish, Sports law and policy in the European Union (Manchester University Press, 2003); S Greenfield and G Osborn (eds), *Law and Sport in Contemporary Society* (Frank Cass Publishing, London, 2000); S Van den Bogaert and A Vermeersch, 'Sport and the EC Treaty: a Tale of Uneasy Bedfellows' (2006) 31 *EL Rev* 821.

3

Bosman: The Genesis of European Sports Law

STEFAAN VAN DEN BOGAERT*

On 15 December 1995, the undivided attention of the sporting world was focused for once on Luxembourg. That day, the European Court of Justice rendered its judgment in the *Bosman* case, outlawing certain aspects of the traditional transfer system as well as the so-called '3+2' nationality clauses in professional football in Europe for infringing the EC Treaty rules on free movement for workers.[55] In almost no time, this ruling acquired a place in the Court's Hall of Fame of legendary judgments.[56] In the first place, this is due to the fact that it called for drastic changes to be put in place in the football industry. As an immediate consequence, clubs can no longer ask for a transfer sum when one of their EU/EEA football players at the end of his contract intends to move to a club in another EU/EEA country. Sporting associations are also no longer authorised to impose limitations on the number of EU/EEA sportsmen to be fielded during official matches. But the actual impact of the decision goes far beyond the sphere of football, or sport in general. It perfectly illustrates how European law, albeit indirectly via the free movement and/or competition law provisions, applies to economic aspects in sectors of society for which the EU may not have been given any—or only complementary—express competence to act. Furthermore, several of the statements of principle established or reaffirmed by the Court in this case have become of great relevance for the development of Community law. Finally, the case is also important for all the media attention it received, allowing ordinary European citizens to get acquainted with the existence, role and functioning of Europe's supreme court. It is fair to state that *Bosman* constitutes to date the most well-known

* Professor in European law, Leiden University. I would like to thank Anne-Pieter van der Mei, An Vermeersch, Katja Lubina and Floris de Witte for their comments on an earlier version of this article. The usual disclaimer applies.

[55] Case C-415/93 *URBSFA v Bosman* [1995] ECR I-4921.

[56] From the wealth of analysis, see, eg, R Blanpain, *Het Statuut van de Sportbeoefenaar naar Internationaal, Europees, Belgisch en Gemeenschapsrecht* (Brussels, Larcier, 2002); J.-P. Dubey, *La libre circulation des sportifs en Europe* (Brussels, Bruylant, 2000); D O'Keeffe and P Osborne, 'L'affaire Bosman: un arrêt important pour le bon fonctionnement du Marché Unique Européen' (1996) 1 *Revue du Marché Unique Européen* 17; M Thill, 'L'arrêt "Bosman" et ses implications pour la libre circulation des sportifs à l'intérieur de l'Union européenne dans des contextes factuels différents de ceux de l'affaire "Bosman"' (1996) 1 *Revue du Marché Unique Européen*, 89; S Van den Bogaert, *Practical Regulation of the Mobility of Sportsmen in the EU Post Bosman* (European Monographs 48, The Hague, Kluwer Law International, 2005); S Weatherill, 'European Football Law' in *Collected Courses of the Academy of European Law, European University Institute, Florence,Vol VII, Book I,* (Kluwer Law International, 1999), 350.

judgment in the history of the European Court of Justice. More than a decade has passed since it was first delivered. Even though the dust has not really settled in yet, it is time for an appraisal.

General Remarks

As a preliminary, it must be observed that the legal setting of the case was not unequivocally clear. Sport had not been included in the original Treaty of Rome. It was the Court of Justice which established in *Walrave* and reiterated in *Donà* that sport nonetheless formed part of Community law insofar it constituted an economic activity in the meaning of Article 2 EEC.[57] The Court subsequently addressed the conformity with EC free movement law of the contested rules of, respectively, the International Cycling Union and the Italian Football Federation. In both cases, the sporting federations heavily disputed the Court's jurisdiction to tackle the issues referred to it by the national courts. Sporting associations are often formidably powerful and influential private organisations. At the time, they used to sort out their affairs autonomously and regarded legal interferences from outside the sporting world as unwarranted. Rather than accepting the applicability of Community law, the federations tried to ignore the Court's dicta or complied with them only reluctantly and to the minimum extent possible. Afterwards, it was business as usual again. These two decisions thus did not really produce the desired wider or long-term effects.

The build-up towards *Bosman* could therefore hardly be termed gradual. Since the *Walrave* and *Donà* rulings in the 1970s, no substantial legal or judicial developments had occurred in the field of sport. The *Bosman* decision came thus as quite a surprise. Not so much the actual outcome of the case was sensational; after all, the opinion of Advocate General Lenz delivered three months prior to it already did not bode well for the incriminated rules. Rather, the fact that the dispute was ultimately settled by the Court of Justice was unexpected, in several ways. When Belgian footballer Jean-Marc Bosman in 1990 commenced legal proceedings to challenge the rules that prevented him from freely contracting with the club of his choice, even though he was no longer contractually bound to his previous club, he exposed himself to heavy pressure from the football establishment to drop the case or at least come to a settlement out of court. He had to resist various kinds of cunning legal manoeuvres to slow down the process of the case before the various courts. Had it not been for his perseverance, stubbornness and dogged determination to defy the football system, there would simply not have been a *Bosman* case at all. It is by no means unconceivable that without Bosman, the transfer rules and nationality clauses would still exist today. Ultimately, one player thus managed to defeat the whole football establishment, a story reminiscent of David's mythical victory over Goliath. The Court's ruling in Bosman's favour clearly conveys the message that citizens' rights are taken seriously under EC law. But then again, there is also a darker side to this coin: to vindicate his rights, Bosman basically had to sacrifice his career. One career for all players' freedom at the expiry of contracts: that was the high price to be paid.

[57] Case 36/74 *Walrave and Koch v UCI* [1974] ECR 1405, para 4; Case 13/76 *Donà v Mantero* [1976] ECR 1333, para 12.

Moreover, for *Bosman* to become such an important judgment, at least some credit must go to Advocate General Lenz. His contribution was particularly instrumental with regard to the issue of the Court's jurisdiction. Some of the football federations and several intervening governments had forcefully observed that the contested nationality clauses had no connection with the concrete dispute, which concerned only the application of the transfer rules. They asserted the alleged impediments to Bosman's career arising out of the nationality clauses were purely hypothetical and did not justify a preliminary ruling by the Court on the interpretation of the Treaty in this regard.[58] Advocate General Lenz acknowledged that the Court was 'at most entitled, but by no means obliged, to dismiss the question … as inadmissible'.[59] He emphatically recommended the Court not to make use of that possibility. In his opinion, the Court 'would be assisting in the administration of justice in the Member States by answering this question; otherwise regulation of this field would continue to be left to the whim of the sporting associations'.[60] The Court, anxious not to let such an opportunity slip away, followed suit. Arguments of strict legal orthodoxy thus succumbed to the judicial consciousness that a similar occasion to clarify the law and denounce discriminatory practices based on nationality in sport would not easily present itself again. *Bosman* constitutes more than an accidental *démarche* of the Court in this respect. The Court's case law with regard to the admissibility of preliminary references appears somewhat inconsistent. Barnard and Sharpston commented that 'if the Court wants to answer a reference because it raises an interesting or important point of law, it will find a way to do so'.[61] Or as Lenaerts put it mildly, 'the Court is not systematically adopting a narrow view of its jurisdiction'.[62] This sometimes sensible and goal-oriented attitude of the Court towards Article 234 EC references, inspired by the particular circumstances of the case, is perfectly legitimate.

Freedom of Movement

Once the Court had accepted jurisdiction to tackle the transfer rules and nationality clauses, the federations were basically fighting a lost cause. Admittedly, the Court had to adopt a wide conception of the free movement provisions to denounce the contested rules as incompatible with Community law.[63] But the Court's case law with regard to the fundamental freedoms had already moved gradually but undeniably in this direction.[64] The principles established or reaffirmed by the Court in *Bosman*, important as they may be, appear thus predominantly as logical and natural steps in the evolution of the law on free movement for workers.

[58] *Bosman*, para 57.

[59] O Lenz AG in *Bosman*, para 111.

[60] O Lenz AG in *Bosman*, para 117.

[61] C Barnard and E Sharpston, 'The Changing Face of Article 177 References' (1997) 34 *CML Rev* 1113 at 1144.

[62] K Lenaerts, 'Form and Substance of the Preliminary Rulings Procedure' in D Curtin and T Heukels (eds), *Institutional Dynamics of European Integration: Essays in Honour of Henry G. Schermers, Vol II* (Dordrecht, Martinus Nijhoff Publishers, 1994), 355.

[63] O'Keeffe and Osborne, above note 56.

[64] C Barnard, 'Fitting the remaining pieces into the goods and persons jigsaw' (2001) 26 *EL Rev* 58.

First and foremost, the transfer rules at issue in *Bosman* were held to constitute an obstacle to the free movement of players who wish to pursue their activity in another Member State by preventing or deterring them from leaving the clubs to which they belong even after the expiry of their contracts of employment, even though they applied irrespective of the nationality of the players.[65] It was the first time that genuinely non-discriminatory measures were covered under the scope of Article 39 EC. Previously, in *Kraus*[66] and *Ramrath*,[67] the Court had merely alluded to this. A similar evolution from a discrimination-based examination to a wider analysis centred on the notion of restriction to freedom of movement had already occurred in the fields of goods (*Dassonville*[68] and *Cassis de Dijon*[69]), services (*Säger*[70]) and establishment (*Gebhard*[71]). This development thus fits squarely in the general trend towards convergence of the fundamental freedoms.[72]

With the introduction of the formal distinction between selling arrangements and product characteristics in *Keck*, the principle of discrimination was prominently brought to the forefront again in the field of goods.[73] Until now, *Keck* has never actually been transposed to the other freedoms.[74] However, in *Bosman* the notion of market access in para 17 of *Keck* was borrowed to delimit the concept of restrictions. The transfer rules were held to directly affect players' access to the employment market in other Member States and were thus capable of restricting free movement for workers.[75] This link between the concepts of restriction and market access has since been consolidated in further case law.[76] Nowadays, there seems to be a common agreement that when access to the market is prohibited, impeded or rendered less advantageous, freedom of movement is restricted; conversely, when market access is not hindered, for example when it is too uncertain and indirect a possibility for legislation to be regarded as liable to hamper free movement,[77] the principle of non-discrimination should offer adequate protection.[78] This corresponds with Advocate General Tesauro's view that the purpose of the free movement provisions is to establish a single integrated market, eliminating those national measures which hinder intra-Community trade; their purpose is not to strike down the most widely differing

[65] *Bosman*, paras 92–104.

[66] Case C-19/72 *Kraus v Land Baden-Württemberg* [1993] ECR I-1663.

[67] Case C-106/91 *Ramrath v Ministre de la Justice* [1992] ECR I-3351.

[68] Case 8/74 *Procureur du Roi v Dassonville* [1974] ECR 837.

[69] Case 120/78 *Rewe-Zentrale AG v Bundesmonopolverwaltung für Branntwein ('Cassis de Dijon')* [1979] ECR 649.

[70] Case C-76/90 *Säger v Dennemeyer* [1991] ECR I-4221.

[71] Case C-55/94 *Gebhard v Consiglio dell'Ordine degli Avvocati e Procuratori di Milano* [1995] ECR I-4165.

[72] See, eg, P Behrens, 'Die Konvergenz der wirtschaftlichen Freiheiten im europäischen Gemeinschaftsrecht' (1992) 27 *Europarecht* 145; D Martin, '"Discriminations", "entraves" et "raisons impérieuses" dans le Traité CE: trois concepts en quête d'identité', première partie (1998) *Cahiers de Droit Européen* 261 ; K Mortelmans, 'Excepties bij non-tarifaire intracommunautaire belemmeringen: assimilatie in het nieuwe EG-Verdrag?' (1997) 5 *Sociaal-Economische Wetgeving* 182.

[73] Cases C-267 and 268/91 *Criminal Proceedings against Keck and Mithouard* [1993] ECR I-6097.

[74] See also, for services, Case C-384/93 *Alpine Investments v Minister van Financiën* [1995] ECR-1141. D O'Keeffe and A Bavasso, 'Four Freedoms, One Market and National Competence. In Search of a Dividing Line', in D O'Keeffe and A Bavasso (eds), *Judicial Review in EU Law* (The Hague, Kluwer Law International, 2000).

[75] *Bosman*, para 103.

[76] Eg Case C-18/95 *Terhoeve v Inspecteur van de Belastingsdienst Particulieren* [1999] ECR I-345.

[77] Case C-190/98 *Graf v Filzmoser Maschinenbau GmBH* [2000] ECR I-493.

[78] D Chalmers, C Hadjiemmanuil, G Monti and A Tomkins, *European Union Law* (Cambridge, Cambridge University Press, 2006) ch 16.

measures in order to ensure the greatest possible expansion of trade.[79] Be that as it may, it is still not always unequivocally clear when market access is impeded. Future case law is needed to offer further guidance in this respect.

In applying Article 39 EC to the non-discriminatory transfer rules of the sporting federations in *Bosman*, the Court also broadened the scope of the issue of horizontal direct effect of the free movement provisions.[80] Previously in *Walrave*, the Court had established that Articles 39 and 49 EC not only apply to the action of public authorities, but also extend to rules of any other nature aimed at regulating gainful employment in a collective manner.[81] In that case, a discriminatory rule was contested. The rules of these sporting federations are considered to have a quasi-legislative character. Later, the Court confirmed the step taken in *Bosman* to scrutinise equally non-discriminatory collective private rules in *Lehtonen*[82] and in *Wouters*,[83] relating to establishment and services. Recently, the Court established in *Viking*[84] and *Laval*[85] that Articles 43 and 49 EC also apply to collective action organised by trade unions. In *Angonese*, the Court took matters even further, applying Article 39 EC to a purely private dispute between an individual and a private bank concerning a particular language requirement in a competition for a vacancy which was held to be indirectly discriminatory.[86] The issue of horizontal direct effect currently thus divides the fundamental freedoms: from the outset, the Court has made it clear that Article 28 EC only applies to state measures, and not to measures taken by private parties[87]; whereas Articles 39, 43 and 49 EC can be applied to merely restrictive private rules adopted in a collective manner, and Article 39 EC even to discriminatory private rules where no collective action was involved.[88]

Finally, the way in which the Court dealt with the issue of justification of the '3+2' nationality clauses was remarkable and caused some controversy. In spite of the overtly discriminatory character of nationality clauses according to which football clubs may field only a limited number of football players who are nationals of other Member States in official matches, the Court merely established the existence of an obstacle to the freedom of movement for workers.[89] As such, that was not objectionable. It became problematic, however, when the Court subsequently proceeded with the issue of justification. Ultimately, the Court stipulated that the nationality clauses could not be deemed to be in

[79] G Tesauro AG in Case C-292/92 *Hünermund v Landesapothekerkammer Baden-Württemberg* [1993] ECR-6800, para 28.

[80] See, eg, J Baquero Cruz, *Between Competition and Free Movement: The Economic Constitutional Law of the European Community* (Oxford, Hart Publishing, 2002) 105–25; J Snell, 'Private Parties and the Free Movement of Goods and Services' in M Andenas and W-H Roth, *Services and Free Movement in EU Law* (Oxford, Oxford University Press, 2002) 211; S Van den Bogaert, 'Horizontality' in C Barnard and J Scott (eds), *The Law of the Single European Market: Unpacking the Premises* (Oxford, Hart Publishing, 2002) 123.

[81] *Walrave*, para 17.

[82] Case C-176/96 *Lehtonen and Castors Namur-Braine v FRBSB* [2000] ECR I-2681.

[83] Case C-309/99 *Wouters v Algemene Raad van de Nederlandse Orde van Advocaten* [2002] ECR I-1653.

[84] Case C-438/05 *International Transport Workers' Federation and Finnish Seamen's Union v Viking* [2007] ECR I-10779.

[85] Case C-341/05 *Laval un Partneri* [2007] ECR I-11767.

[86] Case C-281/98 *Angonese v Cassa di Risparmio di Bolzano* [2000] ECR I-4139.

[87] The only dissonant in this context is Case 58/80 *Dansk Supermarket v Imerco* [1981] ECR 181, a case to which the Court of Justice has never referred in later case law. Conversely, see, eg, Joined Cases 177 and 178/82 *Criminal proceedings against Van de Haar and Kaveka de Meern* [1984] ECR 1797.

[88] For more detail, see also P Oliver and W-H Roth, 'The Internal Market and the Four Freedoms' (2004) 41 *CML Rev* 407 at 421–9.

[89] *Bosman*, paras 116–121.

accordance with Article 39 EC, but only after having carefully considered the various justification arguments, namely the maintenance of the traditional link between each club and its country, the creation of a pool of players for the national team and the maintenance of a competitive balance between clubs.[90] These must all be qualified as judicially created overriding requirements in the general interest. Essentially the same scenario had already unfolded itself in *Commission v Belgium*, a case concerning the disposal of waste in the region of Wallonia.[91] Also in this case, the Court did not explicitly concede that it looked at mandatory requirements to justify a discriminatory measure. According to the prevailing doctrine,[92] however, a distinction must be made between directly discriminatory measures, which can only be upheld by means of express Treaty derogations, and indirectly discriminatory or non-discriminatory measures, for which also justifications other than those set out in the Treaty can be invoked. In principle, the Court should thus have simply dismissed the arguments on the ground that directly discriminatory measures such as the nationality clauses cannot be objectively justified. The fact that it couched its ruling in terms of a mere obstacle to Article 39 EC does not detract from this conclusion. Until today, the Court still holds on to this traditional dichotomy. This is unfortunate. There seems to be no valid reason why in given circumstances a mandatory requirement could not be invoked to justify a directly discriminatory measure. All that should matter really is that the aim pursued in the general interest is legitimate and that the restriction complies with the principle of proportionality.[93] Besides, in this respect, Advocate General Jacobs forcefully stated that 'in any event, the more discriminatory the measure, the more unlikely it is that the measure complies with the principle of proportionality'.[94]

EC Law and Sport

Bosman may be an important but perhaps not ground-breaking case for the development of some Community law principles, but with regard to the relationship between EC law and sport it absolutely constitutes the landmark case. Its influence is first and foremost apparent judicially. After *Bosman*, the sporting associations were suddenly and definitively stripped of their aura of inviolability. Even if they remain the primary regulatory authority within their respective disciplines and undoubtedly still have a wide margin of discretion to organise their affairs, they can no longer simply ignore the reality of Community law. *Bosman* raised players' awareness that they possess rights and that they can assert them. Conflicts between the main actors in sport—athletes, clubs and federations—are nowadays still predominantly settled out of court, but the mere fact that the possibility to start legal proceedings does exist has led to a reassessment of the balance of power in sports.

[90] *Bosman*, paras 123–125.

[91] Case C-2/90 *Commission v Belgium* [1992] ECR I-4431.

[92] For an extensive analysis, see G Tesauro AG in Case C-120/95 *Decker v Caisse de maladie des employés privés* [1998] ECR I-1831. He favours a more uniform approach, though.

[93] Concurring, eg F Jacobs AG in Case C-379/98 *PreussenElektra AG v Schlesweg AG* [2001] ECR I-2099; S O'Leary and JM Fernandez Martin, Judicially Created Exceptions to the Free Provision of Services' in M Andenas and W-H Roth, above note 80, 163.

[94] F Jacobs AG in Case C-136/00 *Danner* [2002] ECR I-8147.

The Court has often been criticised for abolishing the whole transfer system in *Bosman*. It did, however, only invalidate the one specifically targeted rule concerning out-of-contract transfer payments. What is more, the Court did generously recognise the aims of maintaining a financial and competitive balance between clubs and of supporting the search for talent and the training of young players as legitimate objectives, 'in view of the considerable social importance of sporting activities and in particular football in the Community'.[95] It thus left the door ajar for the football authorities to independently elaborate acceptable alternatives. Only when the federations seemed unwilling to make any substantial changes to the remaining transfer rules did the European Commission launch an official infringement procedure against several of their aspects. This time, the federations managed to escape another condemnation. A profoundly revised transfer system saw the light in 2001, putting heavy reliance on contractual stability and compensation for the training of young players.[96] It is uncertain whether the current FIFA Regulations on the status and transfer of players are fully in conformity with Community law, but for now, they remain unchallenged.[97]

Conversely, the Court was less clement for the nationality clauses in *Bosman*. It did leave nationality restrictions in national teams off the hook as a restriction on the scope of the Treaty, earmarking matches between national teams as being of 'purely sporting interest'.[98] However, it turned down all arguments submitted to preserve nationality clauses at club level.[99] These were meant to ensure the participation of local players in domestic leagues. The EU sports employment market was thus fully liberalised for athletes from EU/EEA countries. Despite the clear rejection in *Bosman*, many sporting associations held on to quota with regard to third-country nationals. In *Kolpak*[100] and *Simutenkov*,[101] the Court unequivocally ruled that these nationality restrictions cannot be applied to certain privileged third-country national sportsmen. It suffices that they are legally employed in a host Member State and that they can rely upon a directly effective provision relating to equal treatment as regards working conditions in relation to the host state's nationals of an international agreement establishing a partnership between the European Communities and their country of origin, regardless of whether accession to the EU is envisaged or not. Be that as it may, abandoning nationality restrictions still does not seem to be a viable option in several sporting disciplines.[102] Currently, some new rules favouring domestic players do even find support from the European Parliament and the European Commission.[103] Clearly, the last word on nationality clauses has not yet been spoken.

[95] *Bosman*, para 106.

[96] For a detailed analysis, see S Van den Bogaert, above note 56, ch 5.

[97] Interestingly, in the pending case C-325/08 *Olympique Lyon v Bernard and Newcastle United*, the Court is asked to rule on the conformity with Article 39 EC of a provision of national law pursuant to which an *espoir* player who at the end of his training period signs a professional player's contract with a club of another Member State of the EU may be ordered to pay damages. The outcome of this case may have consequences for the FIFA rules on training compensation as well.

[98] *Bosman*, para 127.

[99] *Bosman*, paras 121–137.

[100] Case C-438/00 *Deutscher Handballbund eV v Kolpak* [2003] ECR I-4135.

[101] Case C-265/03 *Simutenkov v Ministerio de Educación y Cultura and RFEF* [2005] I-2579.

[102] S Van den Bogaert and A Vermeersch, 'Sport and the EC Treaty: a tale of uneasy bedfellows?' (2006) 31 *EL Rev* 821 at 828–30.

[103] (A6 0036/2007) Motion for a European Parliament Resolution on the future of professional football in Europe, 13 February 2007; European Commission, UEFA rule on 'home-grown players': compatibility with the

In the aftermath of *Bosman*, the Court also decided a number of other sports-related disputes on the basis of the free movement provisions. On each occasion, it clearly showed receptiveness towards the specific sporting cause. In *Deliège*, the Court acknowledged that selection rules inevitably had the effect of limiting the number of participants in tournament, but it nonetheless regarded such a limitation as being 'inherent in the conduct of an international high-level sports event, which necessarily involves certain selection rules or criteria being adopted'.[104] Hence, the contested rules did not constitute a restriction to freedom of movement. In *Lehtonen*, the Court accepted that the setting of transfer deadlines, although liable to restrict the freedom of movement of players, could meet the legitimate objective of ensuring the regularity of competitions.[105]

Initially, the Court invariably solved sports issues on the basis of the free movement provisions, despite the clear guidelines on how to apply the competition law rules provided by Advocate General Lenz and some of his colleagues in their opinions.[106] Arguably, *Bosman* could and perhaps even should have been decided on the basis of the competition law provisions.[107] Even though the transfer rules clearly restricted the mobility of players, the cross-border element was purely incidental. The problem was simply that the transfer rules existed. A plausible explanation for the Court's initial reticence in this respect lies in the fact that a pronunciation on the applicability of the competition rules to sports rules and practices would potentially have a much wider impact on the sporting world—given their broader scope—than a ruling on Articles 39–49 EC. This way, the Court implicitly offered the associations the opportunity to autonomously implement some modifications to their rules without legal interference. Conversely, the European Commission didn't eschew from using Articles 81 and 82 EC to solve disputes relating to, inter alia, the independence of sport clubs,[108] the venue of sporting events,[109] ticket sales arrangements[110] or the central marketing of commercial rights of sporting events.[111] Ultimately, the Courts in Luxembourg also brought competition law into the sports arena.[112] *Meca-Medina* especially has the credentials to become a new paradigm judgment.[113] First, the Court stipulated that 'the mere fact that a rule is purely sporting in nature does not have the effect of removing from the scope of the Treaty the person engaging in the activity governed by that rule', thereby marginalising the vague concept of 'rule of purely sporting interest'.[114] Subsequently, the Court seems to have established a new general framework for reference in sports cases: to assess the

principle of free movement of persons, IP/08/807, Brussels, 28 May 2008. Conversely, the Parliament and the Commission regard the '6+5' plan proposed by FIFA, which is reminiscent of the '3+2' rules in *Bosman*, as incompatible with EC law.

[104] Joined Cases C-51/96 and C-191/97 *Deliège v LFJ et Disciplines ASBL and others* [2000] ECR I-2549, para 64

[105] *Lehtonen*, paras 53–54.

[106] O Lenz AG in *Bosman*; G Cosmas AG in *Deliège*; S Alber AG in *Lehtonen.*

[107] See also S Weatherill, above note 56, 364.

[108] Case COMP 37.806 ENIC/UEFA.

[109] IP 99/965, *UEFA/Mouscron*, 9 December 1999.

[110] Commission Decision of 20 July 1999 relating to a proceeding under Art 82 EC and Art 54 EEA (Case IV/36.888 – 1998 Football World Cup) [2000] OJ L 5/55.

[111] Commission Decision of 23 July 2003 on the joint selling of the commercial rights of the UEFA Champions League (COMP/C 2–37.398) [2003] OJ L 291/25.

[112] Case T-193/02 *Piau v Commission* [2005] ECR II-209; Case C-49/07 *MOTOE*, judgment of 1 July 2008, nyr.

[113] Case C-519/04P *Meca-Medina and Majcen v Commission* [2006] ECR I-6991.

[114] *Meca Medina*, para 27.

compatibility of a sporting rule with the EC competition rules, first of all, the overall context in which this rule was taken or produces its effects and, more specifically, the objectives it pursues must be taken into account; secondly, it must be considered whether the consequential effects restrictive of competition are inherent in the pursuit of those objectives and are proportionate to them.[115] It is too soon to measure the precise impact of these crucial statements, but a significant consequence already appears to be that even anti-doping rules no longer receive automatic shelter from competition law scrutiny.[116] Evidently, a wide array of sporting rules potentially comes under EC competition law scrutiny.

The *Bosman* decision also triggered political initiatives to enact legislation on the subject. So far, these haven't been very successful and effective yet. Despite extensive lobbying from the sporting world, no general consensus could be found to exempt sport from the scope of application of the Treaty. Merely two Declarations, emphasising the specific characteristics of sport and its social, educational and cultural importance, have been adopted during the Intergovernmental Conferences of Amsterdam and Nice.[117] The European Convention managed to include an express reference to sport in the Constitutional Treaty.[118] The Article was preserved in the Reform Treaty.[119] Despite being by no means sensational in content, it would have the advantage of clarifying the legal environment of sport and would turn sport into an official Union policy.[120] However, its faith hinges upon that of the entire Treaty of Lisbon. The current situation is thus characterised by a status quo, implying that the Community institutions simply continue with their activities in the field of sport. This is by no means problematic, but maybe not ideal, mainly for reasons of legal certainty. In 2007, the European Commission issued a White Paper on sport, addressing sport-related issues in a comprehensive manner. This initiative seeks, in particular, to give strategic orientation on the role of sport in Europe, to provide guidelines on the application of EU law to sport and to set out further sports-related action at EU level.[121]

The Greater Good of *Bosman*

The *Bosman* case has led to an intensification and a deepening of Community interventions in sport matters which, taken together, form EC sports law and policy. The Court of Justice has subjected sporting rules and practices to Community law because they have economic effects, even though the EC Treaty attributes no direct competence in sport to

[115] *Meca Medina*, para 42.

[116] E Szyszczak, 'Competition and sport' (2007) 32 *EL Rev* 95; S Weatherill, 'Anti-doping revisited—the demise of the rule of "purely sporting interest"?' (2006) 27 *European Competition Law Review* 645.

[117] Declaration (No. 29) on Sport, annexed to the final act of the Treaty of Amsterdam [1997] OJ C340/136; Declaration on the specific characteristics of sport and its social function in Europe, of which account should be taken in implementing common policies, annexed to the Conclusions of the Nice European Council, Bulletin EU, 12–2000.

[118] Article III-282 Treaty establishing a Constitution for Europe [2004] OJ L310.

[119] Article 165 Consolidated version of the Treaty on the Functioning of the EU [2008] OJ C115/47

[120] Van den Bogaert and Vermeersch, above note 102 at 837–9.

[121] European Commission, *The White Paper on Sport* (COM 2007) 391 final, 11 July 2007, available at http://ec.europa.eu/sport/white-paper/index_en.htm.

the Community. When scrutinising sporting rules, the European Commission and the Court must carefully perform a balancing act, which involves adequate protection of the exigencies of Community trade law and also respect for and sensitivity towards the specific characteristics of sport. This challenge to reconcile the demands of Community law with sector-specific needs presents itself also in other fields in which the Community has no or only limited direct competence to act, such as culture or social security. This is the main reason why the importance of the *Bosman* ruling exceeds sport. *Bosman* is a perfect illustration of this search for the golden mean.

4

Inherit the Wind: A Comment on the *Bosman* Jurisprudence

GIANNI INFANTINO[122] & PETROS C MAVROIDIS[123]

Abstract

The *Bosman* jurisprudence has marked a sea-change in the organisation of professional football in Europe: the Court opened the door to free movement of players, liberating them from constraints such as nationality clauses and the transfer fees that had to be agreed across clubs even for players at the end of their contract. Importantly, by confirming prior case law, it established the Court's attitude to subject aspects of professional football to the authority of EC law. *Bosman* was not part and parcel of a wider EC strategy on this score: it is not the role of the Court to do that, and the Commission, on its own admission, was not after a common football market. *Bosman* does not discuss the application of EC competition law on football, it limits itself to a discussion of the free movement of labour. What followed it, nevertheless, has been an ongoing attempt to subject an ever-increasing part of football-related activities to a body of law (EC law) which was simply not designed to deal in extensor with such issues. The culmination point is last year's *Meca-Medina* judgment. This Chapter aims at addressing *Bosman* in this context. We raise two issues: first, to what extent one can legitimately trace back to *Bosman* the ever-changing ratio between sporting and economic aspects of football (the latter, only, being accountable under EC law); second, to what extent the Court, in the absence of clarification of the ratio described above by the law-making EC organs, is well positioned to take the lead on such issues. Our response is, unsurprisingly maybe, that clarification of the ratio through a law-making exercise becomes all the more important, if not urgent, in today's post-*Bosman* world.

[122] Secretary General, UEFA.
[123] Edwin B Parker Professor of Law at Columbia Law School, New York, Professor of Law at the University of Neuchâtel, and Research Fellow at CEPR.

The Facts and the Court's Decision

The Facts

Had Jean-Marc Bosman requested a transfer to another Belgian club, this remarkable jurisprudence would not have seen the light of the day, at least, not at that time. As things stand, Bosman was seeking transfer from a Belgian to a French club, which was not finalized because of the disagreement between the two clubs on the amount of the transfer fee. Bosman, it should be noted, was at the end of his contract.

Bosman was challenging the legality of two non-discriminatory barriers to freedom of movement of workers, assuming of course, that football players could be regarded as workers:

(a) the request for transfer fees for players at the end of their contract;

(b)the nationality clauses limiting the number of foreign players in professional teams.

Bosman's lawyers were arguing the consistency of these two measures with Article 48 (now, 39) of the ECT[124] (free movement of workers), as well as Articles 85 and 86 (now, 81 and 82) of the ECT.

The Court's Decision

The Court found that both measures were in violation of Article 48 ECT. In light of this finding, the Court found it unnecessary to pronounce on the applicability of EC competition law on the disputed issues. The Advocate General, nevertheless, did make some comments on this score, and we will return to this issue below.

Causes of Concern

Distinguishing between Economic and Sporting Aspects of Football

The question was raised during the proceedings, to what extent the application of Article 48 ECT was precluded in this case. The *Bosman* Court dismissed this argument. It referred to its prior case law (14/76 *Donà Marteno*), where it held that

> the provisions of Community law concerning freedom of movement of persons and of provision of services do not preclude rules or practices justified on non-economic grounds which relate to the particular nature and context of certain matches (para 76).

The *Donà Marteno* Court had held that matches among national teams are of non-economic nature; Member States could thus legitimately preclude the participation of foreign players in their national team. The *Bosman* Court recognises the 'difficulty of

[124] ECT stands for the European Community Treaty.

severing the economic aspects from the sporting aspects of football' (para 76), but it does not sever its ties with the distinction. Instead, it goes on to state that a restriction on the scope of the provisions in question must remain limited and cannot justify the exclusion of the whole of the sporting activity from the scope of the ECT (para 76). The question is, where do we draw the line?

The line had not been drawn ex ante. The Commission had no strategy to which the Court should react, the Court had no theory to back its judgment. It reacted to an argument made, repeated verbatim its prior case law, and did not spend any time thinking about the repercussions of its judgment. *Bosman*, and its heirs, epitomise the risks of haphazard judgments. We should not, nevertheless over-dramatise the Court's judgment in this respect. It is hard to argue with the *in principle* application of Article 48 ECT on this case. What is more problematic is the manner in which the Court dealt with public order exceptions (Article 48(3) ECT), for it is there whether the distinction between sporting and economic aspects should come into place.

When we reach this discussion (existence of justifications), there is nothing on the distinction between sporting and economic aspects. The Court dismisses summarily the two grounds advanced by the defendant (paras 107 *ff*):

(a)transfer fees are necessary in order to maintain financial and competitive balance across clubs: the Court rejected this argument since, in its view, transfer fees do not prevent rich clubs from buying out available talent[125];

(b)receiving a transfer fee provides the incentive for training clubs to continue investing in new talent: the Court rejected this argument as well since, in its view, the fees received are unrelated to the cost of training.

It is difficult to accept these points. The counter-factual to the first point is that, in the absence of fees, small clubs lose their best players *and* receive no compensation either (which means, they are in a worse position than when losing players but being compensated: if at all, receiving some money means that the distance between rich and poor clubs will be narrower). The second point is equally counter-intuitive. Training players has a parallel with intellectual property protection. In light of the uncertainty as to the eventual outcome, the legislator allows the successful inventor to charge a monopolistic price; such price, by backwards induction, will provide the inventor with the necessary incentive to invest in the first place. The same is true in the world of football: unless clubs are allowed to charge a market price for their best talents (a price which will compensate them for the amounts spent on players who did not make the grade), they will have little incentive in investing in football. As a result, professional football will suffer, since it will have to draw from a smaller pond.

This is not to say that clubs should charge fees for professional players at the end of the contract, as was the case for Jean-Marc Bosman, who had no contractual obligation to their old club. The Court could, and probably should, have dismissed the arguments by the defendants on grounds other than those invoked. Unfortunately, however, the follow-up to *Bosman* led to a system of regulated fees for various footballers (including those who start their career).

[125] The Court, nevertheless, accepted that maintaining competitive balance across clubs is a lawful objective that could be legitimately pursued. The Court outlawed only the means to pursue it, and not the end itself.

The *Bosman* Court, based on these grounds, held in favour of the applicability of Article 48 ECT. In an informal document,[126] years after the *Bosman* judgment, the Commission tried to draw the line between economic and sporting aspects. It provided a (exhaustive) list of practices[127] that would escape the reach of EC antitrust laws. This list included items such as the sporting rules of the game, but also rules for the organisation of sport on a geographical basis (national, regional, or local). Although it stopped short of confirming that it would not touch on the current organisation of football in Europe, the Commission made it almost explicit that this was its intention:

> One of the most significant aspects of the existing production of sports events in Europe is the fact that the clubs or players can be selected to take part in national and international competitions on the basis of their sporting performance. An organisation that undermined this possibility notably for reasons of an essentially economic nature could impair the chances of small clubs entering national and international competitions.[128]

This opinion was further cemented in the Commission's response to an oral question by a member of the European Parliament: with respect to the request by Wimbledon FC (an English football club) to play its home matches in Dublin, Ireland, the Commission responded:

> It seems at first sight that the organisation of national football leagues on a territorial basis is not related to the economic issues of sport but to the very nature of the sport in question.[129]

The Commission followed a similar attitude in the dispute between Mouscron FC (a Belgian football club) which was challenging the UEFA rules requesting it to play its home games within the football association where it had been enlisted, and not in France as Mouscron FC wished. The Commission expressed the wish that the UEFA rules should control for attendant circumstances for frontier regions, without, nevertheless, putting into question the UEFA rules in this respect.[130]

In the meantime, a series of Court decisions, culminating in the recent *Meca-Medina* judgment, have rendered the distinction between economic and sporting aspects almost futile.[131] And yet, as much as this distinction rests on arguably inaccurate terms,[132] it is useful in the sense that it signals the division of competences across the EC on the one hand, and national (and international) football authorities on the other. Subjecting, even in principle, all rules originating in football authorities to the purview of EC law might lead to an untenable situation: EC law was not meant, as the Commission itself has admitted, to create a common market of football. Consequently, the application of EC law on (many) football issues is a pure matter of interpretation, the outcome of an exercise of discretion by EC organs which is difficult to discern ex ante. This sounds like legal insecurity, an outcome that surely neither the EC nor the football authorities would like to

[126] European Commission, Preliminary Guidelines on the application of the competition rules to sport, Brussels, 15 February 1999, hereinafter 'Preliminary Guidelines'.

[127] See Preliminary Guidelines, 30–1.

[128] See Preliminary Guidelines, 13.

[129] See Preliminary Guidelines, 13.

[130] Case IV/36.851.

[131] The *Meca-Medina* Court held that the applicability of EC law on sporting issues has to be evaluated on a case-by-case basis; it thus did not *a priori* exclude the applicability of EC law on *any* sporting issue.

[132] Indeed, even the purest of sporting rules have an economic repercussion.

encourage. To avoid any misunderstandings on this score: it is not *Bosman* that created legal insecurity; it is its heirs: *Bosman* did not close a door that its heirs subsequently removed altogether.

The reach of Antitrust

In para 138 the *Bosman* Court held that, in light of its findings under Article 48 ECT, it was unnecessary to pronounce on Articles 85 and 86 ECT. The Advocate-General, nevertheless, held that institutions such as the UEFA and the FIFA come under the purview of EC competition law, since they are undertakings of associations. We know where the Advocate General stands, but not where the Court stands on this issue. On the Commission's own admission,

> following the *Bosman* judgment, the application of the competition rules to sport is without doubt the aspect which is causing the greatest uncertainty in the world of sport.[133]

Subsequently, the EC Commissioner for Competition and the sporting authorities signed an 'agreement' on transfer fees, which is neither a *formal* agreement[134] (the Commission, as the Court has held, has no such competence), nor about competition. Even a brief perusal of the EC webpage suggests that there is no doubt that, in the Commission's eyes, competition law is applicable to at least some sporting transactions. The question is, yet again, where do we draw the line?

The Advocate General in *Bosman* did not draw it anywhere. Yet the very function of antitrust law suggests that a line must be drawn: antitrust law is a means to ensure that rivalry will be preserved in a given (relevant product) market. By using proxies such as the incidence of practices on consumer welfare, antitrust authorities will intervene and outlaw practices detrimental to the desirable function of a market. Rivalry, on the other hand, is the *sine qua non* for football: Microsoft will be happier without competition; Arsenal FC cannot operate without Tottenham Hotspur FC. Indeed, the very product (a football game) cannot be produced unless two rivals compete on a football pitch. The economics of sports organisation are thus diametrically opposed to those of the typical markets that the antitrust legislator (and practitioner) has in mind. This is one idiosyncratic element. There are more. It is difficult, if not impossible altogether, to assign market shares to football clubs. First of all, some of them participate in national competitions, whereas others participate in both national and European competitions (and there is uncertainty as to who participates in the latter). Second, football for (some) fans is but a sport and (some) fans might switch to other sports (or to amateur football) if clubs raise, for example, the price for tickets beyond what they can afford. This means that it will be difficult (but not unthinkable) to subject individual clubs to the disciplines of EC antitrust. This is probably what led the Advocate General in *Bosman* to contemplate the application of EC antitrust to UEFA and FIFA. UEFA and FIFA, nevertheless, are non-profit organisations, and should be subjected to the disciplines of EC antitrust law only when they behave as economic agents (for example, when they regulate TV rights). They do not, however, *always* behave as economic agents. Where should we draw the line?

133 See Preliminary Guidelines, 1.

134 Its consistency with EC rules has never been challenged so far.

Bosman did not discuss it, nor did its heirs. Once again, the absence of ex ante clarification has not helped. The words of the Commission cited early on in this sub-section continue, unfortunately, to be of relevance even today.

Non-discriminatory Market Access

In paragraphs 97–99, the Court gives its own understanding of the ambit of Article 48 ECT. Citing prior case law (from the area of free movement of services), the Court held that the transfer laws in question were in breach of Article 48 ECT, even though they applied on nationals and foreigners alike. Take a two country-scenario: A prohibits one economic activity (on a non-discriminatory basis) and B does not. According to this case law (as extended in *Bosman*), A can lawfully continue to prohibit the activity at hand, only if A can come up with a justification that, in the Court's eyes, is acceptable. The extreme case would be that 1 out of 27 members of the modern-day European Union allows for an activity and 26 do not. All 26 would have to come up with a justification were they to lawfully block entry to their national market of nationals from the country allowing for that activity and seeking employment abroad. Moreover, recall that *Bosman* was not dealing with a case of absolute embargo: assuming an agreement as to the transfer fee between the old and the new club, nothing could stop Jean-Marc Bosman from playing for his new club.

The Court here enters into dangerous waters. Why should there be a presumption that the state with the permissive regulation is doing things right?[135] And what if the opinions of the Court and the regulating state as to the legitimacy of a regulatory intervention are at variance? In such a case, the non discrimination imperative embedded in Article 48 ECT becomes tantamount to deregulation. Is it for the Court, an agent entrusted with the application of the law as agreed by the principals, to decide such issues?[136]

The Court, at about the same time, did make a remarkable turnaround on this score in the field of free movement of goods: the *Keck* jurisprudence marks the re-emergence of the discrimination-test.[137] The *Keck* test is not crystal clear, as has already been acknowledged[138]; it removes, nevertheless, the presumption that legislation impsoing restrictions on free movement of goods is, in principle at the very least, suspect. Such presumption is not only at odds with the umambiguous letter of the Treaty, but unwarranted indeed. Countries regulate for a variety of reasons. The ECT takes issue with a subset of the total regulation that aimed at protecting domestic producers' welfare. Recourse to an *intent*-test seems a necessity; alas, the Court has never *decisively* moved in this direction. True, in an asymmetry of information-context, where parties have an incentive to behave in an opportunistic manner (cheat), detection of intent is far from a day in the park. This does not mean, nevertheless, that the difficulty of the exercise should lead us to abandon the exercise altogether. Courts could have recourse to appropriate proxies (who bears the cost of the legislation? Is the measure the least restrictive measure to reach the unilaterally

[135] See on this score, the thoughts of Weiler (1999).

[136] Cf Maduro (1998).

[137] There are dozens of articles on this score. Joliet (1994) provides in a very succinct manner the essence of the Court's judgment. Reich (1994) compares the *Keck* jursirpudence to the prior case law. For a detailed account, see Oliver (2004). Contextual interpretations of *Keck* are offered in Maduro (1998) and Weiler (1999).

[138] See Weatherill (1996).

stated objective?, etc.) in order to form an idea of the intent of the challenged legislation. *Keck* goes some considerable way towards establishing the proper test, without being explicit on its *modalities. Bosman* does not follow *Keck* on this score.

Concluding Remarks: A Look into Today's Issues

In this Chapter, we addressed three criticisms of the *Bosman* jurisprudence. The last point indirectly, and the first two directly so, address the question of how EC law affects the organisation of football in Europe? The answer is disappointing: we do not know. There is a lot of uncertainty surrounding the application of EC law, and especially competition law, on the organisation of football, and it is high time a clarification is officially sought. Clarification in turn cannot come through case law. Courts, by their very mandate, which is transaction-specific, are ill-equipped to deal with such issues. We would add, rightly so, since it is not their institutional role to act as legislator. Clarification has to come from the law-making bodies of the EC system.

Bosman as such is prone to different readings: until 1993, the EC integration process could happily co-exist with the previous football régime. Article 48 ECT was not invented in 1993. The Court, through its interpretation, accelerated a process of co-ordinated action between the EC and the football authorities already under way, to achieve a better organisation of football. Lured by the Court's quick and fast solutions, a number of interested parties privileged recourse to adjudication, rather than to legislation. *Bosman*, thus, beyond compensating a football player who should have been compensated anyway, unfortunately signalled the end of co-ordinated legislative efforts as well.

As such *Bosman* is not shocking: indeed, from a purely contractual perspective, it is rather shocking that a football player, after his contract with his previous employer has expired, cannot freely choose his new employer. This was an agreed deviation from national contract laws and is indeed unprecedented. The problem is that there is (still) nothing like a common contract law across EC Member States, and the end to this régime, on a Europe-wide basis, had to come through the extension of Article 48 ECT to cover (probably unintended by the EC legislator) transactions. It is highly surprising that until Jean-Marc Bosman challenged this rule before a national court no-one, irrespective of the pace of the European integration process, thought of challenging it before a national court. The rest is now history.

There are many *Bosmanesque* challenges around: the regulation of transfer fees, the issue of home grown-players are those that have made the headlines in recent times. The list is growing by the day, as a result of the ever-growing importance of football, which is also one of the biggest markets on a worldwide basis. The shortcomings of *Bosman* should provide the *ratione materiae* competent authorities with the incentive to return to the negotiating table and seek legislative solutions.

References

Joliet, Réné (1994), La libre circulation des marchandises: l'arrêt Keck et Mithouard et les nouvelles orientations de la jurisprudence, *Journal des Tribunaux* 12, 249–55.

Maduro, Miguel Poiares (1998), *We the Court: the European Court of Justice and the European Economic Constitution*, Oxford, Hart Publishing.

Oliver, Peter (2004), *Free movement of goods in the European Community*, London, Sweet & Maxwell.

Reich, Norbert (1994), 'The November Revolution of the Court of Justice' (1994) *CML Rev* 31, 407–41.

Weatherill, Stephen (1996), 'After *Keck*: thoughts on how to clarify the clarifications' (1996) *CML Rev* 33, 885–906.

Weiler, Joseph HH (1999), 'The constitution of the common market place: text and context in the evolution of free movement of goods' in Paul Craig and Grainne de Búrca (eds), *The Evolution of EU Law*, Oxford, Oxford University Press, 349 *ff*.

Index

Introductory Note
References such as '138–9' indicate (not necessarily continuous) discussion of a topic across a range of pages. Wherever possible in the case of topics with many references, these have either been divided into sub-topics or only the most significant discussions of the topic are listed. Because the entire volume is about 'EU law', the use of this term (and certain others occurring throughout the work) as an entry point has been minimized. Information will be found under the corresponding detailed topics.